THE LIFE OF
HUGH PRICE HUGHES

H. Price Hughes.

THE LIFE OF
HUGH PRICE HUGHES

By HIS DAUGHTER

WITH PHOTOGRAVURE PORTRAIT

SECOND EDITION

LONDON

HODDER AND STOUGHTON

27 PATERNOSTER ROW

1904

NOTE

THE writer takes this opportunity of again warmly thanking those kind friends who, by information of various kinds, and by reading the chapters, have rendered her invaluable assistance in the writing of this book.

" NOT SELF-ASSERTION, BUT LIMITLESS SELF-
SUPPRESSION IS THE SECRET OF LIFE."

*(Sermon preached by Hugh Price Hughes on
the death of Father Damien)*

The tale will be continued by fellow-students, the observers and critics of his character and powers. Their story will be taken up by those who, feeling the stagnation and low ebb of their life, look upon him as their leader, and under his banner sweep all before them till they attain a return to the age of chivalry. This age is viewed by many classes of persons and understood by two — those living in it, and those whose imagination can transport them to such an epoch. These perceive that the exploits of chivalry are dear, and that personal considerations, like silver in the age of Solomon, are nothing accounted of.

In the latter portion of the Life, that specially concerned with ecclesiastical affairs, a voice which has been the undertone of all the others, the voice of spiritual intimacy, will take the lead, and will seek to reveal his ideals and motives.

Party and denomination have their claims; but the Church, as he conceived her, is best served in such an undertaking as the present by unswerving loyalty to an aim higher than party or denomination — by the fearless showing forth of what in all ages she has declared to be the miracle of Nature, a human character.

DOROTHEA PRICE HUGHES.

November 1904.

out life, as he constantly testified, he felt Christ nearer to him than anything mortal, and on the stone above his grave he enjoined that the following words and none other should be engraved as expressive of his faith and experience, " Thou, O Christ, art all I want."

In that mystery of the Church, the one body of Christ, he was a most devout, nay, an impassioned participator, doing all that in him lay towards undoing her dismemberment and establishing within her that godly concord which, while permitting all those divergences essential to diverse humanity and to many orders of mind, yet laid reiterated stress on that which was held in common by all.

In the mystery of the Resurrection he was a participator in that he assumed it. Faith does not pry into the unseen, seeking to remove the veil which God has placed, but busies herself with that eternal life which manifests itself in the present rather than in speculation as to how it will manifest itself in the future.

Lovers of their kind who do not find in the Christian mysteries all that he did will nevertheless find, it is hoped, in this delineation of him that sympathy with their aspirations which he always accorded them in the days of his flesh. One of them wrote at his death, " He made the Church human to me," and as that was so his tale is fittingly told by the following interpreters.

In the character of his ancestors something will be shown of that life, religious and personal, from which he sprang. There are seasons when societies and Churches seem to be falling into decline, but these may be periods of great recuperative power. Of societies as of individuals, it is true that they fall to rise, sleep to wake.

b

the social reformer or saint, is devoid of humanity, not pulsating as they to a full and varied existence. Some defect in his organisation, they pretend, conduces to his self-sacrifice or his sainthood. Were he more human he would enjoy or tolerate the planet as others do. Now a private opinion concerning a saint is as the very wine of life. Yet it may be salutary to forego the exhilarating draught, and in this case at any rate the reader must be denied its solace.

Few men have ever enjoyed terrestrial life more than did this prophet, and, though his years were years of terrible toil, he managed to find a good deal more pleasure on this planet than many who spend their time in seeking it. Still neither his joys nor his sorrows were planetary, despite the fact that his feet trod firmly and familiarly that earth on which he found himself. For close on the joyous associations of the Incarnation lowers the shadow of the Passion. The world knows prophets by their fruits, but they know themselves by their own straitening, by hourly conformity to a will that is not theirs. To enter at all into the inner life of a prophet is therefore to gain some insight into what must have been part of Christ's Passion.

The mystery of the Atonement also broods over his whole life, since he had a sense of sin, and became reconciled to God, not only finding reconciliation himself but becoming the instrument of the same reconciliation to thousands of others.

The underlying meaning of the mystery of the sacraments also haunted him, making of him a devout sacramentarian who held that the essence of the Christian life lies in constant mystical feeding upon Christ in the heart by faith. Through-

PREFACE

THIS is the story of a prophet wrestling with human nature, first in himself and afterwards in others. The reader will sympathise first with the prophet in that he was human, and secondly with those with whom he wrestled in that they also were human. The struggle was spiritual, manifesting itself in particular measures and forces, but not contained within them. He fought principalities and powers as they hold sway over the inner life of men and women.

So that his memory be honoured, it will be shown that he was in very truth a prophet, criticised, misunderstood, yet fortunate beyond most of his kind in that he had even in his lifetime a great following and rare rewards and consolations. His life was a continuous strife, and to make it appear otherwise would be not to write it; and perhaps prophets would not be so scarce in the Church if their lives were more frankly written!

Of all that he was, of all that he advocated or sought, the root is always to be found in one of the mysteries of the Christian faith. The mystery of the Incarnation teaches the Church that humanity is to be worshipped, and his humanity has received full oblation. It is sacred, and must be regarded as such. At his death one said of him, " He was the most human saint that ever lived," and that was true.

It is the private consolation of many that the pioneer,

CONTENTS

ERRATA

Page 8, line 23, read "*Tad*" for "Fad."
Page 14, line 29, read "*seven*" for "nine."
Page 423, line 14, read "*Sandro*" for "Sandra."

CHAPTER I

ANCESTRY AND CHILDHOOD. ÆTAT 1–13. 1847–1860

"Immense have been the preparations for me,
Faithful and friendly the arms that have help'd me."
Song of Myself, WHITMAN.

HUGH PRICE HUGHES was born in the ancient town of Carmarthen in the year 1847. The little house, the quaint old street,[1] where his eyes first saw the light, wore a drowsy aspect which vanished on market days, when the countrywomen with their high hats and baskets came clattering into town. For all its dreamy appearance, the city had seen stirring times.

Seventy years after the birth of our Lord, it was an outlying encampment of the Romans when they invaded this island, and in later years the Princes of South Wales built a castle within it, and defied invaders with no mean resistance. In the twelfth century the town fell into the hands of the English, and was the scene of the last desperate struggles for national freedom. Even when the old racial animosity had subsided, the town must needs play battledore and shuttlecock between the Royalists and the Parliamentarians, as if it was fated to give birth to battle. But if it were thus fierce in spirit, it was gentle at heart, fostering the institutions of holy religion within its walls, and paying due court to the monks and nuns who lived pious, and I should imagine perturbed, lives within them.

To this day, for all its gentleness of aspect, it seems to sleep beneath the shadow of mighty warriors. The gaol, perched high up above the River Towy, is built on the ruins of the old castle and looks such another. Nursemaids take their charges for an airing in the old parade, and in the western and high quarter of the town stands the monument of General Picton,

---

[1] Number 10 King Street, near to the Post Office.

I

who died at Waterloo on the 18th of June 1815, "gloriously
fighting for his country and the liberties of Europe," as the
inscription runs.   On the walls of the old church is a
tablet inscribed to the memory of another general who died
fighting for the same liberties, a bishop of St. David's, who was
burnt to death in the reign of Mary, on the 13th of March
1555.   Men are uncertain as to the exact site of the martyr-
dom, some pointing to the south side of the market cross, and
others to a cross in Priory Street, half-way between the priory
and St. Peter's Church, but all know how and why he died.
I think the memory of him was sweeter to the child who grew
up in that little house of which I have spoken than any other
of the gallant warriors whose names have been associated with
the town.   The thought and the memory of him crept somehow into the blood after the manner of early impressions,
showing how good men never die in vain.

In the loftiest and most wooded of the hills surrounding
the town lies the dust, not of a warrior, so the old women in
the high hats have handed it down, but of the enchanter
Merlin, who cast his spell over Carmarthen as early as the fifth
century, a spell which lies heavy upon the place to this day.
For a time the Princes of Wales and the warriors who came
after dispelled it, but during the last two hundred years or so
it has reasserted its ancient force.   From time to time, however, a son or daughter of the town arises who breaks it, and,
scorning inglorious ease, follows in their train.   The most
intrepid enter the apostolic succession upheld by Bishop
Ferrar, and fight the battles of the spirit either known or
unknown to fame.

In the year 1847 there was no sign of any abatement
in the wizard's art.   It lurked as ever in the ripple of that
winding river over which the fisherman in his coracle glided
silently as of yore.   It whispered sweetly along Llangunner,
where lovers wandered, telling of the coming spring-time and
of the swift, mad joys of youth, but changed to sighing in
the churchyard over the old riddle that no enchanter can
fathom.   Down in the narrow streets the spell had crept
into the voices of the people, so clear, musical, and sing-song,
and in the market-place it was quite rampant, where the
women in the high hats spoke the language which the Princes

of Wales had spoken. Not a sound could a passer-by have detected to denote that Europe was on the eve of a series of convulsions out of which the latter half of the century was to emerge in new and fuller life.

Kossuth in Austria, Mazzini and Garibaldi in Italy, were preparing insurrection which came to a head in 1848, in which all failed, only to rouse themselves for fresh and successful effort in the sixties. On the other side of the Channel the Bonapartists were meditating the deposition of Louis Philippe, which actually occurred in the eventful year of 1848, and in the final coup a few years later, which resulted in the establishment of their dynasty till the outbreak of the Franco-German War. In soberer England itself, where Queen Victoria had been ten years on the throne, the Chartists were contemplating a united rising, which took place a year after my father's birth, creating little disturbance save in the terrified breasts of good citizens.

A year or two back Carmarthen itself had been agitated by rumours of the Rebecca riots in different parts of the Principality, and though the excitement had been great at the time, it had quickly subsided with the riots. The churches also in which this child was to play a memorable part, partook of the revolutionary character of the epoch, forces bursting to the surface which had long been smouldering beneath. Of all the eras for his birth, my father would have chosen what Englishmen know as the Victorian. Indeed, I have often heard him praise God that he was born in no other. He also praised Him for being born a Welshman, though of his native town and country he was destined to see comparatively little. Yet he loved to refer to them, and would often remind listeners, as if in extenuation of his peculiarities, that he had not a drop of English blood in his veins. This was true.

The Welshman is as superior a person to the Englishman as a Scotchman or Irishman. He knows, as my father was never tired of pouring into the English ear, that it is only through the Celtic intermixture that they have ever risen above the national inertia in all those matters where the divine fire is an essential ingredient. If it be true, as Saxon travellers remark, that the land becomes poorer as you get into Wales, so does the heart become richer and more expansive. The air has the same vivifying qualities as that immediately north of the Cheviots. You breathe at once an alien and more elastic tradition. Class distinction ceases to be vital. Education is regarded as a serious matter, and, strangest of all, people positively enjoy going to chapel. Above all, you are conscious of an all-pervading geniality (so forgiving is the race), and Carmarthen overflowed with the national characteristic. The most diverse persons lived cheek by jowl in the street where my father lived as a boy, and had an intimate knowledge of each other. At one end was the parish church, at the other the county gaol, and houses of all sizes and degrees connected the two.

When my grandfather, Dr. John Hughes, walked down the street, he saluted all who met him after the manner of a general, raising his stick, or his hand, to his head at almost every step he took. He was only known to take his hat off to one person, the bishop of the diocese, Bishop Thirlwall, for whose learning and character he had a profound respect. He was a doctor by profession, and was known in that capacity for miles around. To skill in his profession he united rare administrative ability, and there was scarcely any public or municipal office that he did not fill at one time in his career. He was Coroner, Chairman of the Board of Guardians, Chairman of the School Board, Borough Magistrate, County Magistrate, Income Tax Commissioner, Member of the Board of Conservators, Member of the Burial Board, Certifying Factory Surgeon, Police Surgeon, Governor of the Grammar School, Surgeon of the Railway Provident Societies, and President of the Literary and Scientific Institute. In the discharge of these offices he was feared as well as beloved, for he did not share the Welsh laxity. In certain slack quarters of the town, indeed, he was known as Bismarck, a title which caused amusement among those who knew him and saw into that deep and tender heart, the workings of which he did not often show, but which a chance word or scene would sometimes summon to the surface. Tears always came into his eyes at the mention of his son, and he obstinately refused to hear him preach. " I should be dragged to the penitent form," he would remark, with something between a wry face and a twinkle.

He was especially efficient as Chairman of Committee, insisting on a punctuality and standard of behaviour that surprised its members; yet for all his great capability he dreaded publicity, and so disliked the noise and commotion of a great city that he could seldom be persuaded to visit London, where his white head and magnificent stature rendered him almost as conspicuous as in his own town. His study, which was separated from the rest of the house by the surgery and a long passage, was a very peaceful, primitive kind of place. A jug of cold tea was always sent to him after meals, and he would sit at his desk smoking in a crownless straw hat and an old coat that he would not have parted with for three times its original value. For furniture there were huge medical volumes and two deep rocking-chairs, in which his granddaughters used to ensconce themselves. Here they related to him their experiences, or endeavoured to assuage the thirst of their minds. An old drawer in the desk contained medals and curios which he occasionally displayed to them. To walk with him, one on either side, in the streets amid the general salute, was an inexpressible delight to the three concerned.

"Why does everybody here know you so well, grandpapa?"

"Because I see most of them into the world and out of it, my dear."

"We are going home to-morrow, grandpapa. Shall you be sorry?"

"No, my dear, I shall not."

"Why, grandpapa (in chorus)?"

"Because you are two such rascals. I shall be able to walk out in peace. Right turn!"

"Grandpapa, who lives in that house?"

"Mr. John Jones, my dear, a very disreputable fellow."

"What is disreputable, grandpapa?"

"Somebody, my dear, who gets drunk on Sunday instead of going to chapel."

At times the conversation took a literary turn.

"The Welsh have no literature, have they, grandpapa?"

The deep-set eyes might have been wrathful, so alive were they with lightnings. "No literature! You don't know what you are talking about, child. We can trace the date of the first Olympiad, but no one knows the date of the first Eisteddfod. The beginnings of our race are lost in the mists of time."

In private life he was retiring and unassertive to a fault. The religion of my grandfather, like his emotion, lay on most occasions too deep for words. He was constant in attendance at the Methodist Chapel, and his love for Methodism grew with the years. On the plain cross that marks his grave his children have written two lines of an old hymn,

> "Nothing in my hand I bring,
> Simply to Thy cross I cling"

—the only inscription he could have tolerated. He was the son of a saint better known to fame than he, for the name of Hugh Hughes is one to conjure with in the Principality. Early Methodism in Wales is associated and hallowed by his name, much as that of St. Francis is connected with the revival of religion in mediæval Italy. When he finished his wanderings as a Methodist preacher in the year 1843, and settled in Carmarthen as a supernumerary, there was not a man in Wales more beloved than he. His portrait, painted by Jackson, reveals a face in which keenness and kindliness are strangely blended. In Welsh somewhere there is an account of his life and his doings ; but his spirit has been embodied for his descendants in those kindly, tender, humorous blue eyes— the type of man who is so intensely unworldly that he hasn't a care worth thinking about, and whose temperament and work in life are such that he is for ever brimming over with a certain joyousness from on high that temporal affairs cannot quench. Yet his life had not been spent on cushions, by any means.

Though dating back his descent to Llewellyn, Prince of Wales, and past him again to the clan from which Arthur sprang (he took much delight in tracing out the family tree, when he had time for such light matters, in his old age at Carmarthen), in youth he had espoused the original calling of mankind, that of gardener. Princes and their descendants appear ill-starred in Wales, partly of course from the unceremonious treatment which they have received from the sister peninsula, and partly because it is not easy to keep up the princely state in so democratic a country. Vicissitude in fortune does not strike the anguish into the breast that it does into that of less aristocratic races—races that cannot point to national festivals lost in the mists of time. "If you are a good man, now, it doesn't much matter whether you are a prince or gardener—if you are a good man," the true Welsh-man will tell you, for however great a sinner he is his sentiments always do credit to the national piety.

But though Hugh Price Hughes' grandfather was a gardener, he was not, strange to say, a good man—at least in the full sense of that term. He used to tell his own gardener, as they sat side by side resting themselves after the exercise of their common art, that those fists of his had done strange things in the days gone by when he had been the gardener in that great house over at Bristol. At which David, reverently quaffing his mug of beer by his side, would exclaim, "Indeed, now!" partly as a tribute to the great house, and partly as an expression of surprise that so gentle and friendly a master should ever have used his fists in unseemly ways. The story of how his master was turned from these ways to holier things is one that never ceased to scintillate in David's memory. He told me it quite recently. It was on a Sunday, of course, at the chapel in Bristol, when the master of the great house was away and the gardener and the butler were free to roam the town and follow their own devices. The butler, who couldn't have been a Welshman, scorned the idea of chapel, and left his young companion to go there alone, preferring the world and the vanity thereof. Who should be preaching now but Hugh Hughes's own brother, though he never knew it till he had got up from the penitent form and was a new man. "Ay, he was a mon," burst out David. Do you think the butler was allowed to proceed with his evil ways and false view of things when there was his dear friend the gardener close by ready to lend him a hand and to show him something of the mind of God? Or that the under-gardener, or the footman, or the cook, or the housemaid, were not "tur-r-r-ned" every one of them, and so filled with love and joy unspeakable that the master did not know what to think of it all when he came back from abroad? So the gardener had to explain it to him, and he did it in so simple and enticing a manner that his master had nothing for it but to "tur-r-r-n" too. What a house it must have been! No wonder that that gardener had that perennial twinkle in his eye. But after two years, the spirit having moved within him the while, he addressed his master as follows:—"I am very sorry indeed to leave, but I must preach the gospel." And his master was very sorry, as indeed he might be, losing such a gardener and with so large a garden, but he wished him God-speed, for he was a new "mon" now too, and knew something of the exigencies of the kingdom of heaven.

And the young Methodist minister had need of his master's benediction. For he went to Wales to tell the good news to his people, the Welsh, who were sinners, many of them, and used to fling rotten eggs in his face, and anything else they could lay their hands on. They were in the habit also of using such language that it was horrible to hear them. One day he bought a white mare, and the white mare took him to all manner of unpronounceable places throughout the Principality, and everywhere the people were falling on their knees and kissing the footprints of the mare, in an agony of repentance that they should ever have reviled or ill-treated its rider. Smiles greeted him wherever he rode, the children running and crying out "Fad," which is being interpreted "Papa,"—for this minister of the gospel carried sweets and apples in his pocket, and when he began to preach the sky used to stop raining and give out sunshine instead. The animals loved him too as well as the children, for he "had a way" with them, turning their fierceness and timidity into confidence and love.

One day in Breconshire a very handsome young lady came to hear him preach, with a complexion and a spirit that made three counties her slave. Her handsomeness was of the order that reveals strength of character and decision, and whose features in their open play of force and feeling have nothing to conceal. She was a true daughter of the Prices, who had held their heads high and kept open house for more generations than men cared to count, and she remembered with shame how she had revelled in the good things of this life, in dancing, and in chattering, as if there wasn't such a thing as God's life in the soul and its attendant responsibilities. The greatest

honour that ever came into her life was when the Rev. Hugh
Hughes asked her to be his wife—at least so she thought,
though many a disconsolate swain must have looked on and
wondered, for her future husband was considerably her senior.
The grandmother of Hugh Price Hughes was of the kind that
know no half-measures, and her " tur-r-r-ning " was of the right-
about description.   Like the prophet Daniel, she was in the
habit of praying three times a day, and, unlike him, for his
apparently were solitary prayers, she insisted on her household
joining in them.   She would rather have died than miss
attending service at the little Welsh Methodist Chapel, and
she would equally rather have died than have been found
intimately chatting with gardeners and suchlike, as her
husband was in the habit of doing.   A Price could never
be as others, nor could her children, and there were scarcely
any in Carmarthen whom she deemed fit to associate with
these.   The lack of manners and the art of living generally,
on the part of the easy-going townspeople, never ceased to
astonish her.   On meeting a little girl who did not curtsey
to her, she took her by the hand and conducted her homewards as much in grief as in wrath.   " Let me beg of you,"
she said to the amazed mother, " to bring your child up to
better manners in future."   On Sunday her eagle eye spotted
a young girl in colours who should have been attired in
mourning.   She accosted her at once: " Don't you know
that your uncle So-and-so of L——y is dead?   Mind that you
come fittingly attired next Sunday."   Acts of charity, in
which she was assiduous, had to be performed like all else
with due ceremony and in suitable crockery.   When she was
an old lady, bereft of her " king," as she used to call her husband,
and there were no children to sit at the table, her maids
had to undergo no little training before they could serve the
solitary meal in a becoming manner.   She loved her son
John so much that she contradicted nearly everything he said
to her.   " Good-morning, mother," he would say, as he paid
a dutiful call in the midst of his rounds; " a beautiful day,
isn't it? "   " Very cold and disagreeable, John.   It will be
snowing before the evening."

Her " king " was the only living being whom she was
not known to contradict, for she could no more help her

contradictoriness than she could help breathing. She found her match at last in her daughter-in-law, the wife of her adored John and the mother of Hugh Price Hughes. Not enough has been said of this lithe, graceful Jewish mother, of the part that her Semitic blood and tense vitality was to play in the life of her son. The wonder of her cast even her mother-in-law into the shade. She was unique in Carmarthen society, as much an alien to it as if she had dropped from the clouds. Beyond the fact that her grandfather had been a rich Jew at Haverfordwest and a banker, nothing was known of her. This grandfather originally bore the name of Levi, but he changed it to Phillips on becoming a Christian. One of his sons was the father of Mrs. John Hughes. She was still a tiny child and an orphan when this grandfather died, when her uncle sent her to a superior school at Brighton, where her dress and accessories generally won even the admiration of her superior schoolfellows. In other ways the child fended for herself, and she was the last person to support the ordeal of a loveless upbringing. In highly charged natures such a youth often sows a bitterness which the years and happier circumstances cannot eliminate. On a visit to Carmarthen she met young Mr. Hughes, just returned from the hospitals in London, and the beau of the town. She was so beautiful and vivacious that he fell in love with her at first sight; and though Miss Phillips was on her mettle at first, she succumbed in due course after the manner of women, for the simple reason that none of her other lovers approached this one, laugh at him as she might. Carmarthen, with all its experience in such matters, had never seen a more striking couple. No one had ever walked or dressed or entertained in the town quite as she did.

Old Mrs. Hughes was taught pretty plainly that her domain, wherever it was, was not in her son's establishment. The armed truce which these ladies finally adopted must have been the easier on account of certain points of vital agreement between them, to wit, social exclusiveness. Moreover, the heart of the daughter of the Prices must have thrilled at that mien, those accessories, that astonishing vivacity of speech and brain. Young Mrs. Hughes' babies and her over-anxiety concerning them, as well as her delicate health, prevented her from entering the lists of such county society as the neighbourhood had to offer, though the leading families paid civilities to the wife of Dr. Hughes, who had been appointed doctor to the militia. This Jewish mother longed for sons, and nearly broke her heart when first her eldest and then her third boy were taken from her. Only little Hugh remained, the most delicate of the three. "She simply wore herself out for her babies," writes one of the daughters, "and much of her latter invalidism was due to this cause." "If it were not for her tender, unceasing care, Hugh would never have lived . . . when a few weeks old the doctor told my mother not to set her heart on the boy, as he wouldn't live beyond his seventh year. He was so tiny that he had to be carried on a pillow." It was scarcely surprising that she never felt easy about him a moment, and that she spoiled him in consequence. All that she hoped for and thought about this boy was never known to most people, and certainly not to him. She ceased to spoil her children as they grew up, for there was generally a younger child who demanded all her powers in that direction. She was a creature of whims and moods, and of a great brilliance, energy, and vitality, for which her life in that little town, especially as her children became men and women, could find no scope or outlet. The same daughter writes, "Many competent critics have avowed that dear mother's brains and capacities generally were much more exceptional than father's"; yet these capacities had received no further training than that afforded by a superior boarding school in the early portion of the last century.

"When you told her a piece of news," one related, "she saw in a flash exactly how it would affect the whole of Carmarthen, and what you yourself thought about it before you knew that you had formed an opinion." Whether it was a question in a book or in the life around her, she saw through it and round it in an instant. Her brain was like lightning, and her conclusions were arrived at by a series of scintillations. In this as in other things Hugh Price Hughes was the son of his mother. He saw the bearings of a point with astonishing rapidity, and his power of speech, which will be remembered as long as his name is remembered, came straight from her. She never hesitated for a word. Expression and epigram rolled from her at white heat as if from a book. Something pent up conveyed itself into that wonderful pictorial speech, which could be so amusing or so scathing when she chose. Her satire was something never to be forgotten. The wonder was that you could hear it and yet live. She saw and noted everything around her, in the town and her own family (of which she was a very impartial critic), and her conversation was a comment on these. Her power of entertainment in this way never flagged, even when she lay ill on her sofa at the end of her life reading the newspapers, alert, scintillating to the last. In her son this great gift found transmutation, and a wider and worthier channel. Often when he crushed an unworthy or presumptuous opponent, it was a flash of that mother. Best of all, she gave him that Jewish strain which more than anything else made his personality so potent. Opposition, persecution, misunderstanding have pierced the heart of Israel through all time; but it can neither eliminate or abate the predominance of the chosen people. To endeavour to crush them is only to strain their strength, that strength which was given to their father Abraham in ages past, when he gat him from Ur of the Chaldees, and wandered a stranger through the land.

Their faculty for successfully conducting their life in this world, and appropriating the good things of it whenever the Gentile gives them an opportunity, has always been a source of wonder to the latter, and has prevented him from recognising the profound religious instinct which is so woven into the heart of the race that no Ghetto can deprive them of it. "I am a Jew," he would often exclaim, and his references to the race were always kindly and sympathetic. In particular, he appreciated their exaltation of family life, and the ties associated with it. He had not much public intercommunion with them, but there was a tacit sympathy between him and their most refined and philanthropic representatives. A nursing sister related that Polish Jews in Soho were reading paragraphs about him in the halfpenny papers the day after his death with no little interest. Jews in London of all degrees, representing all parts of Europe, mourned with the Christian at his passing away. Knowing nothing of many sides of him, diverging from him in much, they yet exclaimed with the pride and piety of the best of their race, " He was a good man, he did good work, he was of us." [1]   The heart of many a despised exile felt warmer because the heart of this servant of Jehovah was so large towards his brethren.   One who was in constant attendance on his mother during the last years of her life told the writer that she evinced much interest in Zangwill's novels, and was fond of saying, " Our people will return to Jerusalem one day, I know they will, I am sure of it."   This was all the more striking as she was singularly reserved about her ancestry. She also told this same attendant something that impressed her.   " Every day of my life," she said, " since Hugh was born, I have prayed that he might do a good and great work, and be aided in the doing of it."   That Mrs. Hughes should pray the Almighty that her son should undertake a great work was not surprising to this attendant.   It was the insistence on its being good as well as great that haunted her memory.   Tears were in her eyes as she added, " She was an aristocrat, your father's mother, every bit of her.   She didn't like travelling anything but first class, and always the best of everything.   I never saw any woman like her, so clever she was."   If she had paid the tragic price for aristocracy, she might have trembled somewhat, for part of her strange nature was very frail and clinging in its frailty, but she would have had the spirit and the tongue to dumfound any Madame Defarge who might presume to bring her knitting into the vicinity, and she would have dumfounded her with a sentence.   But history is remarkable for the people to whom it does not afford its coveted footlight.

The greatest scope ever afforded my father's mother was the market-place on Saturdays, where the whole town and country-side were in the habit of congregating.   David walked behind her with a large basket on his arm, and woe to him if he overstepped the prescribed number of paces between him and his mistress.   Then in the market square, where the carriages were rolling, a smile, an inclination, perhaps a few words to one or two acquaintances, and then Israel for ever at the stalls.   Israel met Celt, and as at Babel there was a confusion of tongues.   There must be something peculiarly vital about the poultry and cheese sold in the

[1] Actually said to a friend of the family by a Hungarian Jew.

Carmarthen market. The fate of nations appeared to be bound up with them. The excitement of David's mistress was of the white-heat order, though she could fall to coaxing like a Celt. "Why, my good woman, four shillings and sixpence for a bird with no skin on it. Serve it up for your old man this evening, and see what he thinks of your rearing. But you must cook up a bit of meat for your daughter, for she has a good appetite, I know, and wants something more than dry bones for supper. Here, David, show her that plump fowl we got at three shillings from that good woman over there. Poor thing, she knows how to keep her fowls fat, though she's got so thin herself that I hardly know her. She does not eat heartily, I expect, like David here. Where's the man? No, no, my good woman, no fowls to-day; they are too skinny. Give me that knife now, and let me taste a bit of your cheese. You are not going to give it me without wiping it; you should keep a cloth handy. Ah, here's one in the basket. But supposing my man had not brought it, what would you have done? On market days you should be prepared for ladies and gentlemen, not for common people of the town. Now give me a bit of that other cheese, and David too, for he looks very much as if he'd like a bit, poor fellow. He didn't breakfast very early, either, so you needn't give him a large piece." And so on without intermission, while the good people scarcely knew whether to laugh or to be annoyed.

It was the opinion of Mrs. Hughes' contemporaries that she was over-anxious about her eldest son. When he was put to the dame's school with the other little boys of the town, he was carried across the road to the school, though he was nine years of age. Yet he was fond of active pursuits, and eager to take part in them when permitted. On Christmas Day, Noes Cyn Nadolig, as the Welsh call it, it was the immemorial custom for the young men and boys of the town to take part in a torchlight procession and a general masquerade, joined by sailors from the quay and other gallant spirits. On this occasion young Hugh Price and his friend were very conspicuous. Among the vivacious, they were the most vivacious, waving their torches, jumping and shouting till the old streets rang again. His friend remembers to this day how impatiently he waited for the hour of lighting up to arrive, and how he entered heart and soul into the festivities of the evening. David, who was in constant attendance on Hugh and his little sister, was struck with the boy's obedience. Through life this was a natural instinct with my father. By temperament he was very sensitive and easily moved to tears. When his mother cried, he cried too. Once when his little sister was very ill, they found him praying for her in the rain and darkness in the garden.

At nine years of age he was moved to the grammar school where he had fine times in the playground. A little girl cousin remembers to this day the wonderful stories he used to tell her of these doings. His mind must have been saturated with the *Arabian Nights*, which always attracted him, as he used to describe how they had dug a deep, deep hole, and discovered a long winding passage which led to a palace stored with treasure, the description of which exceeded her wildest imaginings. " When you come next time, I will tell you more," he used to say ; and she used to come, wondering.

After he had been here two years his father thought it better to send him to a boarding school, and over his choice he spent no little care. His wife was anxious that it should be as near Carmarthen as possible, and a school where delicate boys received especial care. A Mr. Colston, a Methodist, had such an establishment at Swansea, of which some friends spoke highly, and his wife was known to take a motherly interest in her pupils. She certainly sat up with Hugh Price one or two nights during his first terms, at which period a master describes him as very short for his age and conspicuously agile and lively. He was never still, and from the first a leader among the other boys, both in studies and in games. " Whatever he undertook, he was first in," says this same master. The only accomplishment which did not appear natural to him was that of spelling, of which defect he appears conscious in brief letters to his friend. These letters are interesting as showing that, though arrived at his twelfth year, he was backward rather than precocious in his general development. They consist, for the most part, of affectionate inquiries after his friends ; but he never was a letter-writer.

When he came home for the holidays he was manlier than when he went away, and freer, apparently, to join in the sports

that he loved. When it freezes at Christmas-time at Carmarthen, all who can, resort to the Bishop's pond at Abergwili,
where they spend many happy hours. Hugh Price (it is not
fashionable to have one name in the Principality) was very eager
on those occasions, and once stole a march on his faithful
Fidus Achates, who was sharing his struggles to master the
intricacies of the figure eight. " I can do it now," he exclaimed
to him one morning. " I was practising up here ever so late
after you had gone last night." Another occupation in these
days was riding through the streets on an old blind white pony
belonging to a farm where he was in the habit of visiting.
Amid these activities he did not omit to pay a call on his
grandmother, who was living in very solitary state in those
days, bereft of her " king," the one being whom she had loved
too much ever to contradict. Particularly was he assiduous
when he was just returning to school. On such occasions she
was not only in the habit of greeting her grandson with a kiss,
but of dismissing him with half a crown.

The solitariness of her state had been foreseen by her
husband, who wrote about this and other matters to his
son John, on signing his last will and testament. After
exhorting his son and referring to the fact that he had much
for which to thank God, both as regards his good understanding (the writer appreciated that commodity, and was
remarkable among Welsh Methodist ministers for his literary
interests) and the success of his practice, he thus concludes
with painful effort, judging by the writing and composition: "I must beg of you to be very tender and kind to
your dear mother, who strove very hard to bring up . . .[1]
Much was her care and anxiety for you and the rest of her
family. I feel much in thinking to leave her in this very
trying and tempting world. We have lived together very
comfortably, upward of forty-two years, without hardly a cross
word. No doubt but what she had much to try her in my
conduct, but part we must for a little while, but in sure hope
to meet soon in a place where parting will never be any more,
soon shall our dear son John and his family meet us there."
Though, adds the grandfather of Hugh Price Hughes, " I wish
you and dear family to live long to glorify our loving God

[1] From feeling or weakness the sentence is left unfinished.

in this world! Now, dear John, I shall conclude my fervent wish and desire in the word of God," which he proceeds to do, though he closes with his own unmistakable words, "Now I finish my long letter. May God grant you His help. Amen, amen. So saith your father. H. Hughes, Nov. 19, 1855."

No cloud rested on that departing spirit save the leaving of those he loved. The triumph, which had been the dominant note of his life, broke forth in the inscription over his dust:

"Here lies all that was mortal of the Rev. Hugh Hughes, Wesleyan Minister, who, having spent forty-eight years of his life in proclaiming the gospel of Christ through the whole of the Principality, finished his course with joy. December 17th, 1855. Aged 78 years."

CHAPTER II

CONVERSION. ÆTAT 13–18. 1860–1865

"In quella parte del libro della mia memoria dinanzi alla quella poco
si potrebbe leggere si trova una rubrica, la quala dice : *Incipit Vita Nuova.*"

(In that part of the book of my memory before which little can be
read, a motto is found which says : Here begins the New Life.—Dante,
The New Life.)

THE people called Methodists were removed from their early
fervours when my father was a boy—the fervour that had
animated his grandfather. Nor were the congregations at
Carmarthen and Swansea, where he worshipped as a boy,
exceptional in this respect. Yet what he would have termed
the "deadly respectability" of the Carmarthen congregation,
sprang, like much else in the town, from the native geniality.
Wesleyanism had scarcely severed itself from the Anglican
Church, of which it was originally an offshoot, and Anglicanism was strong because liberal in Carmarthen. Around the
old Parish Church of St. Peter's, the associations of generations
clustered. So it was quite customary for the first worshippers
at the little Welsh chapel to retain a pew in St. Peter's, and
to communicate there. Their own service on Sunday evenings was a kind of spiritual privilege, something limited and
sacred to what were called "the Wesleyan families," but in
no ways shutting them off from the good graces of the Parish
Church. The old church, consecrated by the great life events
of the townspeople, and sheltering within itself the shattered
flags of great British wars, must have made a lifelong impression on their children, to which my father was the last to
be insensible.

Once, at assize time, when the judge and corporation
came in state to the old church and streamed up the aisle

with the sunlight glancing on the scarlet and ermine from the high narrow windows, he whispered smilingly to the friend of his youth, a staunch Anglican, "You beat us in this, Tom." Then—for it was after he had begun to take an interest in religious matters—"I can quite understand your reverence for this old church, and am rather envious that we have not a Methodist chapel of the same age and association." His eye flashing over the scene sufficiently indicated what the "this" signified. It was that tradition, that veneration for the past, which he was to appear to combat and to which, in the imagination of some, he seemed to be insensible. There was never a greater error.

The chapel at Swansea must have seemed cold indeed after the warmth and geniality of St. Peter's, or the little chapel which was as friendly as it was simple, where his family and their friends loved to meet. The high pews, of which he used to complain later, were then in their sombre glory, and behind them he used to sit with a row of his schoolfellows as children used to sit in those days, neither seen nor heard.

The town itself, with the narrow, plain streets, was as unpicturesque as the chapel, and as different as possible from Carmarthen, where every street had a certain dreamy enchantment, and where he could never get away from a view of the everlasting hills. But two years after his arrival the school moved to the Mumbles close by, into an ivy-covered old house overlooking the most glorious bay of the coast. It must be the modesty of the Principality that has not given this spot a wider repute. Travellers from Italy compare it to the Bay of Naples, which indeed it much resembles. It has the same extent, the same vista of mountain tiers melting into space and cloud, and on a fine summer day, something of the deep blue which dyes the sea and sky of the southern bay. In this air, amid these scenes, my father's health greatly improved, and he was fortunate enough to spend five healthy, happy years amid conditions which must have done not a little to build up that strength on which he was afterwards to make such severe demands. In a few weeks, far from the great world and its ways, he saw in one flashing vision what others take many years to learn, and often painfully.

I am not intimating that my father did not immensely

develop after that first boyish vision, for till the day of his leaving us his growth in spirit and outlook was the most interesting characteristic to a thoughtful observer. But the nature of that development was decided once and for all by the remarkable depth and fervour of what Methodists call conversion. The Greek equivalent is perhaps the more expressive, "illumination"; and my father, the bent of whose later theology was mystic and Greek rather than Latin and legal, was fond of substituting this word in discourses on conversion in later years. To the ordinary mind it is certainly more expressive, as the surrender of the will to Christ, which conversion implies, cannot take place without some enlargement of the natural vision.

Doubtless with a heritage such as his, lofty tendencies asserted themselves from the first, though the many-sided nature suffers from its own exuberance of inclination. His powers slept as yet, but had he felt them stirring, as he walked or ran (walking was not habitual to him) beside the Welsh coast? Already his father, listening quietly, as was his wont, to his talkative family, had been struck by the boy's argumentative powers, and had decided to make a barrister of him, and in this his son had apparently acquiesced. But his dreams for the future, whatever they were, were quickly transformed and taken out of his keeping. Christ dreamt for him. The cry that conversion sent up rose like that of the prophet in the wilderness,—"He must increase, but I must decrease,"—and it came to pass on this wise.

A boat of Cornish fishermen sailed into the Mumbles Bay one bright summer morning. Being of a godly disposition, they dragged up their boat on the shingle, heartening each other the while, as was their wont, and made their way to the chapel on the cliff to join in the service at which good Mr. Colston had his scholars duly assembled. How these men of God contained themselves during the service history does not relate, but in the prayer-meeting that followed they poured out their soul before their Maker. And He, the Lord not only of their mortal frame, but of the sea, the firmament, and the wonder of them, was yet strangely kind to His children, speaking to a man of low degree as to a friend, as He had done to the psalmist of old. Their voices welling up from their deep chests had something of the thunder and swell of the waves with which old Ulysses himself could scarcely have been more familiar; and those lined faces — how majestic, mysterious! What epitomes of wind and storm and rain and all the might and adventure of the universe! Yet the eyes, when they opened upon you, were soft and kind like the eyes of that Eternal to whom they prayed. My father's whole being was electrified. He had never heard or imagined anything like it. It was a reality in prayer such as he had never witnessed before. Hitherto a prayer-meeting was part of the Sunday or week-night discipline, something to be sat through and to be risen from with joyous alacrity when terminated. The first of these fishermen could not have prayed long, or my father would not have approved of it. One must have quickly succeeded another in prayer while the others heartened him, just as they had heartened one another when they drew up their boat on the shingle down below. The whole chapel must have caught up their heartening, even the most decorous present stifling an Amen. For there was something in those men and their manner of calling upon the Almighty which set the blood tingling. Children of the deep, they seemed to have flung off the appurtenances that beset and cramped their brethren on land, and to have come face to face with great Nature, and the God who spoke to their hearts from behind. No Welshman certainly could listen to them unmoved. Their prayers over, Mr. Colston invited the men to supper at his house, and my father was able to study and question them to his heart's delight. The visit was repeated, and the first impression intensified.

Child as he was (he was but thirteen), he was thrown into what he afterwards described as a "great perplexity and distress of soul." He could not claim that harmony and intimacy with the heart of the Eternal that the fishermen did. Something was between him and God. What was it? His sin. An idea coloured, the reader may say, by the theology in which he had been brought up. Yes, to a certain extent, when the matter is regarded superficially; but no, when examined from its deeps. A sense of sin is only possible where there is a deep aspiration after holiness—it is its necessary complement. Where there is little or no desire for holiness, there is little or no sense of sin. A later generation does not sufficiently aspire perhaps to the morning constellation of holiness to understand that sense of personal unworthiness which has wrung groans and tears from men and women of strong and deep natures. Ethically, it might be described as a consciousness of the Divine idea of human existence and its infinite falling short of that idea. It was Isaiah, the gifted and blameless youth of his day, who cried out, " Woe is me, for I am undone, because I am a man of unclean lips, and I dwell in the midst of a people of unclean lips. For mine eyes have seen the King, the Lord of Hosts." My father always loved this story, and he was an Isaiah in point. In addition, doubtless, to this revelation of the self, which might well startle and disturb even a boy of thirteen, there was mixed up a fear of God which was heathenish, and which was far more common, mercifully, than it is to-day. Sayings of his nurse showed that from a young child he was imbued with that stern Calvinistic conception of the Almighty which was so characteristic of the humbler Welsh.

Never accustomed to hide a feeling, he betrayed his state to his elders. Though he volunteered no confidence, they quickly divined and rejoiced. They had noted his eager attention at the prayer-meeting, his questionings afterwards, and the solemnity so new to a lively and mischievous boy. The master of the junior scholars,[1] now a white-haired old man, in particular observed him. He was a man of delicacy and tact and of a rare humility. He was of the first order of Methodists, and could talk, like the fishermen, both familiarly and reverently of the things pertaining to God. One day my father and this master wandered away over the cliff and stood facing, as they had often done before, the glorious vista of the Swansea coast. But there was a solemnity in my father's eyes that was new to them. The fight of opposing forces within him, whatever they were, had ceased. He was listening to his master's persuasion to yield to Christ. Unconsciously resting his foot on a large stone, he repeated, " I submit myself to Christ," though the peace which he felt in later years should attend such a declaration was not yet his. He could still hardly bear to look on the face of the Eternal. Christ the

[1] Mr. Leaker.

loving and gracious had died for his sins, and Scripture had spoken of Him as the propitiator of those who put their trust in Him. But how was he to keep himself clean from sin? His nature was ardent, and often not easy to curb. It was of the mettlesome order, easily irritated, and quicksilver throughout, swift to act and to speak.

His elders were by no means perturbed at his continued uneasiness. Too swift a spiritual deliverance in one "travailing for salvation" was not in keeping with tradition. His "assurance" would come in good time, and when it did come it was of a quality and of fibre that would have startled them could they have gauged it.

Some weeks later an American minister came to preach at the chapel, who was quite unknown in the neighbourhood. The love of God must have entered into him not a little, for as he spoke concerning God's love in Christ the scales of fear and doubt fell from my father's eyes, and he felt the love of God like a great wave of sunlight flooding his soul. "I saw," as he described it afterwards, "that I had nothing more to do, only to receive the light and joy of Christ which was waiting for me all the time, only I was such a fool that I couldn't see it."

The joyous shock of this discovery never left him. Whenever he spoke of it he seemed to be living through that early moment, seeing something which he could tell in words, but which he could not describe. "My heart danced within me, and I scarcely knew how to contain myself as I sat shoulder to shoulder with my fellows."

From that day forward my father always saw God in the face of Christ and man too. He refused to admit any conception of God that could not be applied to Christ. Over and over again as a child I have heard him impressing his congregation to correct any notion they might have formed of God in the Old Testament by the only infallible standard who is the centre of the New. If a later generation is able to think of God as Love, and not as an avenging Judge, it is partly owing to the spiritual travail and life of such men. There began also that long curbing and controlling of himself at which few guessed, and from which only death relieved him. A superior quickness to his companions—for he excelled them in whatsoever he undertook, either in games or studies—made him impatient and dictatorial, and there were sometimes slight disagreements between him and the other boys. But after his conversion such disagreements ceased.

Hugh Price set the fashion of being religious and going to prayer-meetings, and talking of religious matters with his masters, so his companions regarded it as a dispensation of Providence, and followed unquestioning in its wake. A boy who was captain of the cricket team, who could get the best of any argument, and pass the Senior Oxford while he was yet a junior, and who assumed in addition to all this to lead his companions in all their undertakings, fascinated their youthful intelligence. The new gentleness and fervour about their souls, of which they had heard much, but of which they were scarcely conscious, affected some of them. He did not suffer any serious persecution, nor did it occur to him to anticipate it. The happy humanity of his religion commended itself to his schoolfellows, much as it did to the outside world in later years. Too much cannot be said of the men who were the masters of that school, and who throughout accorded a sympathy to my father, as affectionate evidently as it was tactful. One scarcely likes to think of the misery and jangling of that nature, if those masters had been anything but humble Christian men able to understand the first ecstasy of a passionate soul. One night Mr. Colston was attracted by a light in my father's dormitory at an hour when lights were forbidden, and when the boys were supposed to be sleeping. Somewhat wondering, for Hugh Price was not a breaker of rules, he ran upstairs and walked straight into the room. The boys were holding a prayer-meeting. After a few quiet words of reproof, he advanced to the light, turned it out, and left the room without a word. Nor did he ever refer to the incident, which was not repeated.

In due course my father was encouraged to become a lay preacher. The gift of preaching among Methodists, especially among the Welsh, has always been regarded very much as the gift of song or painting, a natural endowment which needs cultivation certainly, but which is born in a man or woman, and which can show itself at a very early age. That Hugh Price should preach at fourteen was no stranger than the singing of the birds, and his youth and slightness of stature only added to its effectiveness. Such a gift was really from above, straight from the source of all things.

The old women to whom he preached his first sermon in the little cottage on the cliff talked of him for many a day after that evening when he stood on the table and repeated by heart a sermon on the text, " This is a faithful saying, and worthy of all acceptation, that Christ Jesus came into the world to save sinners." As he quietly got up from his seat in the Swansea chapel and advanced to the pulpit to preach the sermon, his schoolfellows were filled with something approaching awe. Already the prophecy was taking root in their breasts that Hugh Price would be President of the Methodist Conference. The old women in the village said it, so did the fishermen, and the masters believed it too, they were certain. Yes, Hugh Price, out and out the best bowler at cricket, who was top of the school, and who knew all things, was to be President of the Methodist Conference, that dread assembly.

At last he left them altogether, because he was tired of being top so long, and there was nothing more that he could learn. All that remained for him was to go right away to college somewhere, and when he was a little bit older and taller—he would have to be taller—he could become President. First, though, and preparatory to becoming President, he was to become a Wesleyan minister, for so Hugh Price had decided to the astonishment of some of his contemporaries. " What do you think," wrote one of them to his home people, " Hughes is to become a Methodist minister." Nothing is more striking about his conversion than the decision as to the future which it accompanied. One cannot help thinking that as he laid his foot upon the stone upon the Mumbles cliff and said simply, " I submit to Christ," he was thinking " Robert John and Benjamin David " (for his schoolfellows must have had some such names amongst them), " they will have to submit too. How shall I induce them to do so, I wonder." Forceful characters are in the habit of realising that a new step is not a purely personal concern. To wield a wide influence often means deprivation to a person at all conscientious in its use. Every action, every power, becomes unconsciously moulded by the ever-present thought of those whose weal it is bound to affect. This became increasingly the case with my father, who realised unusually early in life, despite the training that spoiling had given him, that he came not to be ministered unto, but to minister. He must do something special for Christ——what? The implied, half-uttered suggestion of those around him, above all the gift of preaching, seemed to point in the one direction, that he should be a Methodist minister like his grandfather.

When he preached in the cottages he did not preach alone. Robert John and Benjamin David, and one or two others whose company he had desired, were with him. He must communicate to others what he had seen and felt what was in him. He had seen the light and love of Christ, and so must others.

He never in his after-life gave the impression that any struggle or sacrifice had been involved. People said to him, You should have been this or that, and he would smile with pleasure that they should think well enough of his capabilities to suggest that he would have been an ornament to a profession that was not his. But anything like regret at the choice he had made never entered his mind. It was the very opposite of that feeling. Men of the world, particularly those who were young in it, said, "What a pity that Hughes is a parson," the only approved form of complimenting the cloth in certain gilded circles. A little over forty years after this choice of a profession, as he was riding on the top of an omnibus with a relative past Westminster and the Houses of Parliament, the thoughts of the two gravitated by common consent to the scene that they knew was being enacted within the lighted House.

"You should have been there," said the relative.

"What, what, dear? Where should I be?"

"In Parliament."

"Ah, Parliament, why?"

"Well, because you would have been a leader there."

"You really think so?" very gravely. "A leader, I should have been a leader, should I? Now what makes you think that?" The attitude was suggestive of the keenest and most throbbing interest. "What induced you to make that state-ment? . . . Ah, you really think so?" Attention resolved itself into transparent delight, but a certain tender gravity succeeded.

" There is nothing that I would rather be than a minister of the gospel of Christ." The thought that one near him should think him capable of leading a great party was more perturbing than the possibility of his ever having been such a leader. His mind had been made up on that score long, long ago.

His departure from Thistleboon did not put a stop to the rumours and predictions concerning him. A well-known Methodist minister, preaching in Swansea, was reported to have pointed to the gallery in which a group of boys were standing, and to have said something as follows : " We do not know what the future may have in store for those boys. One of them may be a great preacher." Hugh Price was among the group. Persons of authority who heard his trial sermon as local preacher uttered the same prediction, which was re-echoed in the neighbourhood of his native town. For, in holiday times, he made excursions into the country and tried his 'prentice hand in the country chapels. The chapel-keepers were not a little amazed at his appearance, and one of them could scarcely be restrained from sending him about his business. He had lived to see strange sights in his day, but that a boy in an Eton jacket, turned down collar, and a high voice, should be the preacher appointed for that evening, was more than he could swallow. That chapel-keeper must have had a Saxon intermixture. A pure Welshman is always more ready for the marvellous.

The news of his decision to become a Wesleyan preacher had set the grey house in Spilman Street a-tingling. Nothing could have been terser than the method of its communication.

" MY DEAR FATHER,—I believe it is the will of God that I should be a Methodist preacher.—Your affectionate son, HUGH."

Margaret, the gardener's wife, was sweeping, and sweeping well, too, for Mrs. Hughes had a lynx eye for dusty corners. Thus placidly engaged, she was startled by the apparition of her mistress, white as a sheet, and in tears. " Oh, Margaret bach, such news ! " She was trembling from head to foot. Margaret, being a true Celt, was prepared for a death at least, and let her broom drop and her hands go up in consequence. "Indeed, now." No one can quite describe the mournful exaltation experienced by a Celt on hearing that a soul has burst its mortal bounds. A birth or a marriage is not comparable with it. The vision seen is the illimitable, that which only the chastened imagination can pierce, hence the exaltation. But the sad world is the sadder for a ghostly embarkation, hence the mournfulness. "Hugh is going to be a minister," came out amid the sobs. "He wrote to the doctor this morning." If the news had been anything but this Margaret would have been bitterly disappointed, but to be a minister, that also was illimitable. How many souls might he not bring to clearer vision amid the mistiness of the Vale of Tears! How many sinners to a knowledge of their sins and to repentance before the Almighty! Thinking such thoughts, she had reproved her mistress before she knew what she was about.

"Don't weep, now, laugh; it is not for weeping, Mrs. Hughes bach, we must laugh; there is nothing to weep about." She did not know that Mrs. Hughes was at that moment Celtic as she, weeping because the joyous emotion was too deep, too complicated for answer. God had answered her prayer, but like a bolt from the blue. Would he ever live and be strong enough to be a great preacher? So little and frail he was. She had done her best to make him hale and hearty ever since he was the baby at her side, when they all said he would die. God must do the rest. Now he would have to go right away. These reflections must have suddenly come to a halt at the sight of Margaret gaping, with her broom on the floor. "Take up your broom, my good woman, and don't stand staring at me. What's that on the floor there? Don't tell me you've cleaned out that corner. What's the good of your coming here if you can't brush? Go on, my woman; you're not deaf, surely." For Margaret was bewildered as usual by her mistress's sudden shiftings, and was still lost in speculation on the illimitable.

As likely as not she continued her occupation to the story of her delinquencies, ending in a solemnly extracted promise that she would keep what Mrs. Hughes had said to herself, and not go babbling it about the town. Oaths of secrecy were not unduly binding in Carmarthen. The atmosphere was altogether too genial. Meanwhile that father, in the distant study, was writing in the hand that none could read :

" MY DEAR SON,—I would rather you were a Wesleyan preacher than Lord Chancellor of England."

It was David who remembered my father's first essays in preaching. The holidays after his decision to become a preacher were memorable for an increased gravity and self-possession on his part. He hastened to communicate his determination and its consequences to the friend of his boyhood, who was not a little impressed. He was led to understand that skatings, ridings, etc., were no longer the object of his ambition. As he was anxious to postpone preaching in the town till he felt surer of himself, David was employed to drive him to country appointments. " Twice he preached at Llanstephan," said David, " and twice at Laugharne ; and at Llanstephan he was preaching to all the gentry and to Lady Hamilton, for she would come to hear him like the rest."

" And what did my father preach about to Lady Hamilton and the gentry when they came to hear him, David ? " I asked.

David's family and friends intimated by their smiles that when a man is over fourscore he can scarcely be expected to remember a sermon preached over forty years ago, when he has heard so many thousands of them since. " And I was taking him by the hand up to Llanstephan, up to the castle, as it was very steep, for I was often at Llanstephan with him and Miss Bessie, both of them, one on either side of me." David fell into a reverie, and into Welsh. The time when he had taken little Hugh Price and his sister to clamber about the sands and cliffs of Llanstephan was very near to that when he had driven him to preach at the Methodist chapel. The two were so near that his mind refused to separate them. About my father's efforts at Laugharne there is more explicit information. A lady who was in the congregation describes the service as follows :

" The text was the first chapter of St. John's Gospel, fourth verse—' *In Him* was life ; and the life was the light of men.' And to me the chapel seemed to be full of life and light. It was a blessed time to us all."

On this particular occasion the youthful preacher got

locked into the bedroom, where he had retired for meditation. But, with his usual resource, he managed to descend from the window.

The chapel-keeper of the Welsh Wesleyan chapel at Carmarthen had an interesting story to tell. Young Mr. Hughes was always coming and worrying her for the key of the building. One day she and the doctor, wondering what the boy was about, went and looked through one of the windows and found him rehearsing a sermon to an imaginary congregation. He was not a little anxious concerning the sermon which he was to preach in his native town before his kinsfolk and acquaintance, and which was eventually preached on December 21, 1863, when the preacher was sixteen years of age. His mother and sisters were present, though his father, as usual, could not face the ordeal and make a fool of himself, so he thought, before the town. The friend of his boyhood was also one of the souls packed into that crowded chapel, and he wonders to this day at my father's self-possession on that occasion, at the flow of words that fell so easily and glibly apparently from his lips. The text was taken from the words, " I am not ashamed of the gospel of Christ," which might also be considered the text of all his other sermons. One listener I have not mentioned, erect for all her trembling, Mrs. Hugh Hughes, the preacher's grandmother. When the service was over, she gripped a friend by the shoulder, " Oh, that Hugh had been here to hear him." She could not stifle that plaint of the heart, so constant ever since the day when she had heard from her John that Hugh was to take after his grandfather in more things than in name. The following year he preached his first sermon in the English Wesleyan chapel (July 31, 1864). Both these sermons in his native town were preached after he had left school, as already intimated, for when my father was nearing sixteen my grandfather removed him from Mr. Colston's care, where he was top boy and idling his time because he had already outstripped the resources of the staff.

My father had much improved in health, and his physical development had set in apace. He was no longer frail-looking and undersized. He delighted, as he had always done, in cricket, to the horror of his grandmother. " I cannot think," she said, " that such a pastime is fitting for a future

Wesleyan preacher." Her daughter-in-law was more sensible, and, as usual, disagreed with her. "Whatever builds up the health of my son will build him up as a preacher." His conversion had been the prelude of a singular bursting forth of his mental powers. Quick as he had been at his studies hitherto, it had been the mere surface quickness of an unreflecting child which may or may not develop into genuine mental vitality. The opening of the doors of the spirit was also that of the mind.[1] His interests soared from the playground to the doings of the great work which stretched beyond. He astonished his elders in Carmarthen by frequenting the reading-room during holiday time, and when he came home to live at Spilman Street he had a daily fight with his father for the *Times*. To read the papers and know what was going on in the world was instinctive with him. He could no more have set out on a day's work without feeling the pulse of affairs, than he could have neglected to wind his watch. He had thus become noted at school for his constant discussions on European matters with the French master, a Hungarian refugee, and he did not accord with the revolutionary sentiments of one who had risen under Kossuth against Austria. His schoolfellows clustered around the disputants, and there were occasions when it was widely felt that Hugh Price had the best of it. He afterwards mentioned this master as the first person who aroused his interest in European countries, especially in the direction of sympathy to oppressed peoples. All the while that he was standing up to the old tutor and endeavouring to pull his argument to pieces, he must, boy as he was, have been noting, grasping, and imbibing what he said—a habit of his. No man ever learnt more from his opponents. The gift of debate was quite inborn, and needed no learning on his part. As soon as he began to think or care about a subject, he could defend it, and, if necessary, against odds. My grandfather was evidently anxious to have his son at home with him for a couple of years, where he could prepare himself to enter the Wesleyan Theological College, and have the opportunity of preaching in the neighbourhood. In after years he knew that opportunities

[1] That this was always the case was a great contention of my father's in after-life. He knew many humble, uneducated men whose spiritual life had quickened their mental.

for seeing him would be few and far between. Oxford and Cambridge were not open in these days to Nonconformists, and Wales had not yet attained to a national university.

Thus the advantages that he would have delighted to procure for his son were not in his power to give. His son, however, must have received intellectual encouragement from him, for he ventured, according to his own account, into deep waters, studying *Butler's Analogy, Pearson on the Creed*, and *Watson's Institutes*.

About this time also, in addition to his theological reading, he read Carlyle's *French Revolution* with such a vivid intensity that the spell of it never left him. The period of the Revolution he found peculiarly fascinating, both for the outburst of great writers which it followed, and the tropical richness of its drama and vicissitude. Dramatic to the core, and loving drama for its own sake, he lived again past periods, re-enacting in his own emotions the hopes and fears and agonies of those who had participated in them. He was not the less tense in the reading of fiction: gloomy and abstracted while the hero and heroine were in the toils of an adverse fate, and only regaining serenity when they became unentangled and united at the close. This was the more surprising, as he never read a novel without first glancing at the end. With the same vivid emotions he read Motley's *Rise of the Dutch Republic*, which, together with the *French Revolution*, must have watered the seeds of political sympathy that the Hungarian master had sown in his breast.

My grandfather was essentially an enlightened Conservative, by no means of the hard-headed order, and he brought up his son to regard things from this standpoint. It was the Conservatism that is allied to temperament and to modes of thinking, rather than to prejudice, which was not strong in him as a political factor at any rate. His sympathies were so free from the ordinary Tory bias that he took the more liberal view against his son's ultra-Toryism; thus my father's account of this period was that my grandfather was a Liberal, while he was Conservative, and that in after years they both reversed their positions. But I imagine that it was he who did the reversing, not my grandfather. Almost inevitably also a boy of sixteen and his father would take opposite sides, from the contrariety that springs out of affectionate intercourse. It would be a mental instinct to both to maintain the opposite sides of a question. There was a strong contradictory element in my father, as there was in his grandmother and the family generally.

The great events in the public mind while my father was a child at school were the war in the Crimea and the Indian Mutiny. In 1863, when he was at home, that mind was again turned, not to the sight of English soldiers in the battlefield, but to their kinsmen on the other side of the Atlantic engaged in the life-and-death struggle of civil war. This war had a lasting effect on him. It made it impossible for him ever to adopt the Quaker attitude. He had felt the enthusiasm of a righteous war, of men laying down their lives for a noble cause. He much resented the idea that death was to be avoided at all costs. There were occasions when a true man must court it. Yet at the commencement of the war his sympathies were with the Southerners, believing that they were fighting for State rights, and he had combats with the Hungarian master in consequence. It was not till he read the account of Beecher's Abolitionist speeches in Liverpool that he " tur-r-r-ned " in the right-about manner of the family. The Quaker stories in *Uncle Tom's Cabin* were often cited by him with relish. It is easy to imagine him reading the book with tears in his eyes, and in after-life he would often exclaim, " Harriet Beecher Stowe abolished slavery! " He could never recall also, without a pang, that ministers of Christ had advocated the retention of slavery. It was a startling instance of how earnest Christian men could sincerely oppose a great reform, which their successors point to with pride as the work of His Spirit. It taught him a lesson which his reading and observation constantly repeated, that official representatives of the Church of Christ are too often found, not only indifferent to the work of Christ's Spirit in the life and thought of nations, but actually in opposition to it. As mental growth enabled him to see Jesus of Nazareth in history, and to view more clearly the nature of the ideals and principles that He had inculcated, he became increasingly anxious to be found on their side, and to fervently pray God that he might have the spiritual insight to discern the cloud in the horizon which foretells the course of the blowing of His Spirit.

3

He greatly loved prayer-meetings, especially early prayer-meetings when other people were abed. So listeners were scarcely surprised when his master told how he used to come and rouse him for the early Sunday morning prayer-meetings when he was at the Mumbles. An early prayer-meeting seemed to occupy something of the same place in his religious life as early celebration does to High Anglicans. He loved to commune with his Lord in the first freshness of the day, when the sun was still low in the heavens and the day all hallowed as yet and a meet offering to Christ. Perhaps the peculiar sanctity that he attached to the prayer-meeting lay in the fact that it was during the prayers of a Cornish fisherman at a prayer-meeting that he first felt the life of the soul rising strongly within him.

My father's eldest sister tells the story of how her brother insisted on her attendance at his prayer-meetings when he came home for the holidays. When she demurred, he would exclaim, " Very well, Bessie, I shall put my head in the fire " —a threat which never failed to reduce her to submission. He seemed to have felt from the first that he was required not only to pray, but to induce others to pray with him. Christ needed many more prayers than his. He was always a great advocate of fellowship in the religious life, and would quote Aristotle's saying that man is a social being. But this act of coercion is the only one that I know of him, and that is on hearsay. He was thrown a good deal with this elder sister, who was destined to become distinguished, but who was so backward as a child in her studies that she could scarcely read at the age of ten; but having once made a start a year or two later, she left the rest of her generation behind her, much as her brother had done. My father always prided himself on the aid that he had been permitted to give his learned sister in the chrysalis state of her intelligence. " Poor Bessie," he would remark, " how unhappy she was—and how mercifully I was enabled to shed light into her dark mind. She understood nothing, positively nothing, but I toiled and perspired and made it all clear to her. I should have been a coach. I have a great faculty for making people see the gist of a thing."

His position in matters spiritual at this period is indicated by a letter that he wrote to his master, Mr. Leaker, when he was seventeen years of age:

"CARMARTHEN, 1st *July* 1864.

"DEAR SIR,—I have to thank you for the rudiments of my education, and for your great kindness, but above all for your spiritual advice and encouragement. I owe you a debt I do not, and never can, estimate—a debt that will be due through all eternity. I cannot express myself. You understand me, though the worldly cannot. The field seems opened to me. I trust I shall be a minister; but I shall never forget that it all springs from your and Mr. Watson's religious instructions and example. I won't wish you temporal prosperity—that is but a gilded bauble. May your reward, sir, be an inheritance, 'incorruptible, undefiled, and which fadeth not away.' May we meet in heaven.—I remain, dear Sir, yours affectionately, HUGH P. HUGHES."

A remarkable letter, and still more so when it is read in the light of the life that followed. Very significant from those lips is the admission at the beginning—" I cannot express myself. You understand me, though the worldly cannot." One to whom power of speech was involuntary and easy as breathing was yet almost tortured through life by something in him that he could not communicate, that was in the nature of it incommunicable. It was always with him, especially at the end. He seemed to feel his own helplessness. Though he revealed spiritual things to multitudes of his fellow-men and women, he was not designed to be this instrument to all, and he knew it.

He was a child of the Spirit, never speaking except as He gave him utterance. He never talked to a man or woman who did not want to talk to him. He had far too fine a spiritual and mental perception to converse with persons on high themes when their mood or wish forbade it. It has been forgotten how much that tongue and pen served Christ by its silences.

A somewhat different letter was written by him the year previous on behalf of the cricket team at Thistleboon House, which he was just leaving:

"THISTLEBOON HOUSE, *August* 1863.

"DEAR SIR,—On behalf of the members of the Club I beg to acknowledge the receipt of your letter, and to return our warmest thanks for its contents. Remembering that, 'A friend in need is a friend indeed,' we feel doubly indebted to you, especially as there exists no circumstance that does at all oblige you to support us. Yours is a perfectly free and uncalled-for gift, and as such we receive it. In conclusion, we hope that by unremitted endeavours to excel in the game of cricket, and by frequent victories, we may show ourselves worthy of your kindness.—I remain, dear Sir, yours truly,

"HUGH P. HUGHES, *Secretary*.

"Mr. Knapp."

At the time when my father wrote these letters, and confessed to something in him which the world could not comprehend, he was nearing the end of the first stage of the long probation through which a Methodist preacher must pass before he is eligible for ordination.

His grandmother took great interest in the way that he acquitted himself during this first probationary period, and her John must have kept her posted up in the latest particulars. In order to facilitate his studies, she prepared her best room for his habitation, the house in Spilman Street, I imagine, being too electric in its atmosphere to comfortably house a student. The wind had a habit of blowing from all quarters, and it was impossible to foretell the manner of its blowing. General Booth of the Salvation Army, who dined with the family on a visit to the town some years later, said he had never witnessed so much diversity of opinion and personality at one table. The mother, wrapped up at this period in her youngest and very delicate child, left her mother-in-law all the freer to watch over the promise of her eldest grandson. But the joy that it gave her poor soul must have been curiously barbed; an incessant longing for a presence of the past pierced and chastened the proud spirit of the daughter of the Prices in her old age.

Too little, rather than too much, has been said of my father's ancestors. He manifested to Methodism and the world, not only their physical vitality and mental vigour, but their spiritual power, which was too large, too rich in its quality to be contained within any but the widest bounds.   By the magnificent unworldliness of sober, God-fearing men, with whom duty was a habit, and the administration of affairs a delight, he found it easier to be pure and unworldly, as other men have found it far from easy.

He was pre-eminently the child of the women of his race. What draughts he drank of their vitality and audacity!   Their hearts are still and the light in their eyes has faded, but assuredly the triumph of their faith was not in vain.   Somewhere in this universe they are satisfied, seeing the meaning and outcome of that fraction of life in which they were visible to us, sharing in the joy of its steady fulfilment.

CHAPTER III

" What's in the scroll," quoth he, " thou keepest furled ?
    Show me their shaping,
Theirs who most studied man, the bard and sage,—
    Give ! "—So, he gowned him.
        A Grammarian's Funeral, BROWNING.

MY father entered Richmond College under favourable
auspices. Though only eighteen years of age (and looking
even younger than his years), he had acquitted himself with
distinction in the final examination. The youngest save one,
he ranked second out of a hundred and forty-six candidates.
He had impressed his fellow-candidates even more than the
examiners at Westminster. The singular lightness of his
attire and demeanour impressed men who were dejected by
an ordeal which apparently occasioned him scarcely a qualm.
He wore a straw hat and a blue coat, and expressed himself
with much freedom and vivacity, chaffing his companions, and
incessantly informing them, as was his habit, of much that they
might be interested to know. One of them, after the *mauvais
quart d'heure* with the examiners, remarked to my father, " If
it is the will of God, I shall enter College this autumn." My
father could not repress a smile. " If you have passed your
examination, my dear fellow," he corrected. If a fellow had
not the brains to pass his examination it was not likely that
God Almighty or any one else could help him. But years
afterwards he confessed to this young man, who was a true
and esteemed friend [1] of his in later life, that his views of Divine
Providence had strangely altered since then, and that God was
as much to be consulted in the passing of an examination as
anything else.

[1] Rev. W. D. Walters.

38

He was fortunate, moreover, in entering the College when the staff was very able. The Rev. Alfred Barrett, the governor, was a man of true culture and saintliness. He was a strong advocate of the necessity of learning on the part of the ministry, by no means according with the old idea that the business of a Wesleyan preacher is to save souls and neglect the tending of every gift that might aid him in his task. Indeed, he held that ministers of religion could not faithfully discharge their duty without cultivating to the highest the various phases of inner life—thought, imagination, sympathy, and the insight that springs from these. In one of his pastoral addresses he remarks:

"It is a great mistake to suppose that educated and tasteful hearers alone require a well-trained and qualified ministry. Who needs a soul thoroughly conversant with the whole region of truth, so alive to the importance of putting it in its various aspects, so able to strip away from it all perplexing encumbrances, so ready to seize on its more salient and spirit-stirring bearings as the preacher to the unlearned? The unlearned, who are not necessarily the torpid, the unconcerned, or the incapable."

I have quoted this selection from his writing as the best method of showing the manner of man he was, and the spirit of exquisite tact, sympathy, and urbanity that characterised the rule under which my father lived. Sternness with him, in which he did not fail when the necessity arose, was thus more to be avoided than it was in a less gentle man. He was an exact theologian, and he started a course of lectures on mental and moral philosophy, in addition to the ordinary course on Church polity and theology; but his special subject, and that in which he was widely read, were the writings of the early Fathers, in whom naturally he created a keen interest, both among the staff and the more intelligent students. In temperament he was deeply poetic, tinged with melancholy. He must have found a contrast to himself in the brilliant combative young Welshman, but he was quick to understand that devotion of the same intense quality as his own which burnt beneath the outer characteristics, somewhat obtrusive at times, of his pupil. He knew infallibly by intuition the intensity of his love for Christ. Nor had my father any need to tell him of it or prove it to him. In the class-meeting that the Governor conducted weekly in the " good old style " (as it has been described), my father seems to have been silent rather than communicative of his spiritual experience. When others spoke of young Hughes as didactic and conceited, Mr. Barrett would say quietly, " He has great abilities, and he will become famous one day." He listened to his conversation with interest and pleasure, and perhaps secretly admired the gifts which he did not possess. Such is the sweet humility of the saints! He would bring honour to Methodism, and, what was more, to Christ and Christianity at large. For the Governor was, above all things, catholic, two of the most impressive of his pastoral addresses bearing upon this point.

" We are too apt to regard our own little enclosure as our world : but if we actually make it such, it is a poor condition of religious life. It is, I think, a mere religious childhood if we can be content to cherish solely in our affections the worn-out sayings, especial doings, or neglects of doing, and the unvarying external forms of some single congregation or church to which we belong."

He recognised, probably, the germs of the same catholicity in my father's breast; a germ which was to bear such fruit in after years, not as a poetic ideal merely, but as an actual fact in church organisation and outlook. Much of what my father did in after-life was to put into practice and disseminate among the masses of the people what the choice spirits of Methodism had repeated from the days of John Wesley downwards. Mr. Barrett must have delighted in my father's intellectual zest and ability. The eager mental life which he had begun as a boy at Carmarthen widened and deepened under the Governor's sympathetic régime. Indeed, it became a species of torrent, bearing him unresisting on its wave. Its incitement and guidance was mainly due to Dr. Moulton—the ablest all-round scholar that Methodism has produced. The classical tutor, Mr. Hellier,—a man whose sterling qualities made him much beloved,—had been fortunate enough to obtain his assistance as classical tutor the year before. Dr. Moulton was about thirty years of age at this time, and already versed in many branches of human learning, particularly in mathematics, classics, Hebrew, the various branches of natural science, and the principal modern languages. He was an adept also in the theory of music, and took much delight throughout life in playing and hearing the organ. " Nothing," writes his son, " seemed to lie altogether outside his acquaintance." While my father's quality of mind was essentially of the brilliant order, quick to grasp facts and to arrive at conclusions, Dr. Moulton's was that of the scholar, the man of great grasp and power of mind, who, for all his mental voracity, is carefully slow at first, rather than swift in mental processes, and invariably cautious before generalising.

Despite their differences, mental and temperamental, tutor and pupil formed a mutual affection and an admiration for each other's qualities that lasted through life. The doctor, while he was struck by my father's fleetness of mind, yet, scholar-like, considered this same fleetness something of an impediment to its profounder workings. But this swiftness was to stand him in good stead in the years to come, when in debate or committee, or action generally, his nimble wits had the same advantage over slower contemporaries, as the little English ships were said to have had over the heavy Spanish galleons. My father, on his part, had a veneration amounting to awe for the doctor. There seemed no end to that vista of learning, and the Celtic mind delights in the vista that is illimitable.

One day when he had been " toiling and perspiring," to quote his own phrase, over mathematics (trigonometry, I believe) for many months, the doctor re-adjusted his spectacles and made the inevitable remark of mathematical tutors to deserving pupils, " Now, Hughes, we are at last in a position to commence mathematics." That was a severe shock to my father, and his veneration for the doctor increased tenfold.

Here was one to whose learning he could never hope to attain. Meanwhile, he must derive all possible benefit from intercourse with so extraordinary a man—and he did. He decided to graduate at London University, at the suggestion of his tutor, who had himself attained great distinction there. His mind, as it had done when he was in the playground at Thistleboon, soared beyond the confines of the old College, which was not without its spell, though it was not that of Merlin. The smooth lawn was suggestive of the best traditions of academicism, and on Sundays the Governor and the members of his staff would meditatively pace its velvet surface. On week-days the shrubberies were resonant with children's

voices and laughter, the families of the Governor and the classical
tutor living halcyon days under the shadow of the grey walls.
In their early youth they were intent on the manufacture of
mud-pies, and, as the years advanced, on adventures which,
from their own standpoint, were of the true heroic character.
Roofs were scaled in order to pour water down offending
students' chimneys, and feats performed on land and water
which were greeted with smiles from the elder members of the
Governor's family, scarcely stepped from childhood themselves,
but as distinct from their juniors in the general conception as
if they had dropped from the clouds, where such aërial elegance
might be supposed to reside.   Outside the gates, despite the
serene aspect of the old town, were vibrations from the great
world.   The carriages of the Comte de Paris and the Duc
de Chartres and other adherents of the exiled royal house of
France bowled along the terrace or beneath the gnarled oaks
in the park.   The Prince and Princess of Wales also and some
of the royal children would often drive over on a summer afternoon to take tea at the White Lodge and enjoy the cool
privacy of the garden.

My father must have often looked with interest at the
French aristocrats driving leisurely past him, for he was profoundly fascinated by the race, and the various drama of their
history, though in after years he attacked them as a factor in
European politics without stint.   He would often refer with
pleasure to the triumph of Germany in 1870, which he never
anticipated.   Zola's description in *La Débâcle* of the splendid
efficiency of the German preparations against the miserable
counter inefficiency of the foe, stirred him to mingled enthusiasm.
For he never gave to Germany a quarter of the love he gave
to France.   It was never surprising to find him attacking that
with which a corner of himself sympathised—hence the merci-
lessness of the attack.

At this period he was, to quote the words of his principal
friend at College, " the most ultra of Conservatives."   A debating
society was formed by him in his third year in the form of a
parliament, and he led the Conservative side of the House,
fighting the Liberals right valiantly amid scenes of much
excitement.   The questions which principally agitated the
country during these College years were the conduct of General

Eyre in Jamaica, the Reform Bill, and the Disestablishment of the Anglican Church in Ireland. In company with many of the determined defenders of law and order, my father should have joined the General's supporters, as did some distinguished contemporaries; but from all I heard him say, he must have burnt with shame at the reports which filtered home, first discredited, but afterwards authenticated by Royal Commission. He never forgave Kingsley for going to welcome General Eyre on his return : others he might have forgiven; not Kingsley. The charm and humanitarianism of such a man made his conduct unforgivable—he was too valuable to be spared to the foe.

My father, as Sir Laird Clowes once told him, would have made a splendid general. He had all the necessary instincts. As regards the Reform Bill, it is related that he wrote an article against Mr. Gladstone's measure of 1866 in the students' newspaper, *The Anchorite*, which has since disappeared.[1] My father was fascinated by the picturesque personality of Beaconsfield; nor was he without his full quota of class prejudice. The College was aware of this latter. The ministry has no social or professional prestige, and is proud of the fact. Men, when they receive " the call," as it is termed, come, whoever they may be or wherever they are, like Matthew from the receipt of custom, or like Peter from the boat. In the brotherhood which the ministry forms, the only birth it professes to take into account is that of which Christ spoke to the Jewish lawyer many centuries ago.

None the less a social entourage that means refinement, and the other advantages accruing therefrom, is a great advantage to a minister, and his brethren are swift to recognise it and to pay him honour if he will use it in the service of the brotherhood and the aim for which it exists.

My father, with one or two exceptions, did not make friends as the other students did, though he had a singular faculty for making acquaintanceships when he wished to do so. From the first he was a recognised leader, and popular by dint of his brilliance and his good spirits, though he had not, as a rule, sufficient *bonhomie* to make him popular in the sense in

[1] Tradition relates that Dr. Osborn, one of the tutors, confiscated it, my father protesting.

which young men usually apply that term. He was essentially the student; even the outburst in *The Anchorite* giving way to the pressure of his studies, and his unflagging industry in their pursuit. Late reading by gaslight marred his eyesight, necessitating the wearing of glasses, and to his "folly" in this respect he would repeatedly refer in after years. But the sport of his boyhood—cricket—was still his delight. He was captain of the College cricket team, and without an equal, so it is said. Athletics were quite a venture at the College; the general idea among the older ministers being that young men qualifying for the ministry were best employed in prayer and the Greek Testament, and that any diversion, however innocent, was to be at most winked at as an inevitable folly of youth, but not to be encouraged. The Rev. Alfred Barrett was blamed by a section for his leniency to athletics, though like most who are blamed for innovation, he has set the fashion to posterity. Boating was also started in my father's day, but he never took much part in it. When football was being played, for innovation had so far advanced, he contented himself with shouting "Go ahead!" in the Welsh tongue.

In his management of the cricket team he had ideas of his own, as he had about other things. In the yearly match at the end of the first year, he wished to have a barrel of beer on the field so that his men might quench their thirst and obtain refreshment. When this intention leaked out, great indignation was felt by the group of abstainers among the students, and they worked up a College meeting of protest. My father's supporters urged that he had *carte blanche* in his position to do whatever was not absolutely wrong; but the opponents carried the day, insisting on the ties attending his representative character. The scruples of his temperance associates were amusing to one of my father's temperament. He overwhelmed them with chaff, crisp and keen as himself, and out of sheer kindheartedness restrained the smile which crept to his lips at the slightly virtuous air with which a member of the group would pass the beer at supper, served as a matter of course at that time at all educational establishments. In his third year, a regular temperance society was formed, which the majority of the students were induced to join, only my father and one or two others standing obstinately aloof. In his humorous contempt, he termed this company the "Insane Society," and derived much innocent amusement from a criticism of its ways and airs. This criticism was part of the sunshine that emanated from his presence at this period, more calculated to provoke an answering smile than to hurt. But on certain occasions his speech had a power of stinging, and deeply too; the men who were keen on what was known as direct evangelical work did not find a sympathiser in him. One of them organised bands for daily prayer and renewal of consecration with a view to inducing fervour in soul-saving, and could get scarcely any men in my father's year to fall in with his scheme. He was not so much opposed to it as indifferent; energies and thoughts were absorbed in different matters. He regarded his time at Richmond as pre-eminently to be given up to study, and too short for all that should be got into it. Yet for what he would term the "namby-pambyism" of certain characters laying claim to evangelical fervour, he had no toleration and much crushing satire. Like the unthinking world, he was too apt to regard the ardent evangelical as a sham without further inquiry.

He was able to get so much into his life because, particularly in its earlier stages, he took one thing at a time. The one thing that was occupying him, engaged him heart and soul for the time being, and would often leave but scant room for other vital interests. He had boundless faith in the Divine ordering of his life, and was willing to wait for the next course on the table that Providence prepares.

The young students who were ardent to save souls must have worried over my father not a little. The ambitious among them were eager to capture the best students, so as to prove that evangelical and scholastic propensities were not antagonistic; and though he consented to join them in distributing tracts in various districts, he was not specially interested in the task, reserving his vital heat for intellectual studies. They must have been the more puzzled, as in the words of one of them, they could clearly discern in him "a genuine moral and spiritual undertone which was unusual." Mrs. Moulton relates how at their table he would speak with strong disapproval both of revivalistic methods and of teetotalism.

At this particular period he could not see any reason why he should desist from drinking a glass of beer every night as he had been accustomed to do at home with his father. He was not, he thought, in the habit of taking more than was good for him, and was in no danger of doing so. Excessive drinking would, of course, have been opposed both to taste and principle. It was perhaps the lack of utility in total abstinence' that made him dub them the "Insane Society," though their insanity, like most else that he encountered in his fellows, was fuel to his mirth. Perhaps there never was a gayer seeker after learning; for the seriousness of his tastes appeared to cast no shadow over his spirit. A candidate for the ministry came up during vacation when my father was about to enter for matriculation, and he remembers to this day the July afternoon when Hughes joined him and six others at tea in the College hall. He was feeling depressed himself at the thought of the trial sermon he was to preach before Dr. Moulton in the College chapel the following day, and a similar depression seemed to hang over his companions, who were in the last stages of preparation for examination. But with my father's entry there was an instant transformation. Each became irradiated, on his mettle. The new arrival was attired in a straw hat attached to his person with a string, and a light jacket, and as usual he carried a book in his hand. He lost no time in addressing the downcast probationer and in inquiring into his business, which having learned, he proceeded to chaff him with much goodwill, giving him much erroneous advice as to how to comport himself on the following day; and the young candidate laughed in spite of himself as everybody else was laughing, and as they continued to laugh and to question and to contradict till Hughes betook himself and his book to the garden from whence he had come. The College grounds were a favourite resort of his, and it was a familiar sight to see him pacing to and fro intent on his book. Often his companions eyed him, not without comment, from the windows; his brilliance was felt to be distinctly uncanny, especially as it manifested itself in all its omnipotence in debate. One wiseacre in particular shook his head with the gloom that pertains to fulness of wisdom, and muttered to the effect that such a fire must be built upon an insufficiency of fuel, and that in middle life Hughes would burn himself down to mediocrity.

It was the wideness of reading and interest that astonished his contemporaries. Other students were capable of reading for examination as well or better than he, for some were men of real ability, but as to his conversation—there never was such a leaping, dancing, bewildering, tearing torrent since the world began. It was difficult to know when he was serious or when he was only in fun. He ransacked heaven and earth and the waters under the earth to prove a proposition, and then not only withdrew it, but disclaimed it. He quoted Shakespeare by the yard, and seemed to have the history of the Greeks and Romans at his finger-tips. There was always a book or a question with which he was bursting, and the books absorbed him more and more. Having denounced Mr. Gladstone's Reform Bill and chaffed at Dizzy's ultra-democratic fabrication in 1867, he left Mr. Gladstone to deal with the Anglican Church in Ireland without much comment other than in the course of ordinary conversation. One of the books that fascinated him at this period was Lecky's *History of European Morals.*

His sermons were distinctly intellectual, and it was predicted that in a riper future he would win the hearing of a cultured and critical congregation. Mr. Hellier, a keen critic, wrote down in his notebook after hearing him preach one day—" Sermon full of thought—in choice language—gives promise of an able preacher."

The students sometimes resented what they termed Hughes' " masterfulness," and it was the common opinion that he was conceited. One of them charged him with this one day when he had appeared unusually infallible. " I admit to you," answered my father, with the gentleness and reasonableness with which he always accepted criticism when gently and reasonably given, " that I have a just appreciation of my own abilities; I am not conceited, I only know what I can do." That a man should justly and soberly estimate his own capacities was always a great point with him. He said it jarred upon him to hear Mr. Gladstone speaking of his humble services, and poor powers, and kindred phrases, as if he could really mean it, or obtain credence in saying it. St. Paul had said that a man should not "think of himself more highly than he ought," but "soberly."

In the opinion of those who knew him, this estimation of his powers erred on the side of modesty. People often confused a championship of a course or a principle with a championing of himself, as if the two were not distinct. As regards his own personal character, he had deep misgivings; in a sense he was always conscious of sin, *i.e.* of shortcoming, though he was equally conscious that the life of Christ was in him and that it was weakness, not will, on his part that suffered that life from having its full play in him. Often unknown to the majority of his companions, he suffered from fits of deep depression, dark valleys alternating with the uplands which he usually trod. The cause of this seems to have lain in struggles with his own nature, some unforeseen spark from the fomenting life within him leaping up into day. Most of his fellow-students imagined that Hughes lived for ever in the full glare of the sunshine which he shed about him. In a sense he did, and more than most men, but he was not spared the valleys, and they seemed deeply shadowed sometimes, in contrast with the higher ground from which he apparently so suddenly descended. He felt himself to be less attractive and more faulty than others; that men should follow his lead and pay tribute to his powers did not surprise him, but that they should love him was very startling to him. He did not think there was much in him to call for love; how could there be? From his youth up he was increasingly impelled to fight against men's prejudice, and he supposed that he did not fight in a very agreeable way.

To his friend at this period he would often with characteristic impetuosity pour out a confession of his misgivings, his folly, his stupidity, his irritability, and much else that troubled him. "His standard was very high," this friend adds, "and he was harder on himself than on others where he fell short of it." Then, as after, he was deeply sensitive both to kindliness and to the reverse of it; for years he remembered, and was grateful, to the student who came to meet him on his first arrival at the College and insisted on carrying his bag. A personal slight or unkindliness he would receive in silence, and perhaps because he was so silent, few knew how he suffered.

Another student of those days writes very beautifully about him: "I do not think he made many intimate friends at this time. He won perhaps more admiration than affection, for 'his soul was like a star, and dwelt apart,' and the light he shed might be described by a phrase he was fond of using, 'the dry light of the intellect,' yet there were other elements in his nature not often revealed to his fellows; in one of these rare moments of self-revelation he came to my bedroom towards the close of the third year and began to talk about himself and others as I had never heard him talk before. He discussed his own career in a disparaging way, stoutly maintaining that others, myself in particular, had done better than he, during our three years' course. In that hour he unveiled his inner life, spoke of his hopes and ambitions, and the prospects of the work that lay before us in the most frank and unreserved manner, and predicted for others a more brilliant future than his own would be."

He never forgot old friends or changed in his behaviour to them. In his second year at College he wrote a characteristic letter to the friend of his boyhood at Carmarthen, Mr. Tom Brigstocke:—

"COLLEGE, RICHMOND, SURREY, S.W.,
"*April* 3, 1866.

"MY DEAR TOM,—Grief, sorrow, remorse, indignation, pity, wretchedness, suffering, pain, woe, misery, anguish, crowd into my breast at the perusal of your pathetic and heart-stirring epistle—the keen irony, the elaborate sarcasm, the touching allusions, the plaintive bleatings, combine to rack and ulcerate my every feeling—and when you reach in your splendid peroration that point where reference is made to your 'baby-hood,' my emotions get too many for me—my brain reels—air! air! breath! where—am-m-m—I, I, I?—chaos. My apparent neglect has arisen from a concatenation of circumstances which really justify me. At least one dozen times have I grasped my quill and written 'My dear Tom' at the top of a sheet of paper, and at least a dozen times have events arisen to prevent any further progress. A great press of work, numerous ministerial duties, and the attention and anxiety which failing sight require account for it all. I suppose you know that I am obliged to perambulate in specs. Jem was

4

with me when I bought them.   I look such a guy.   All hopes
of matrimony are gone, old fellow. . . .   There are finer fish
here than ever swam in the Towy.   Do you understand a
figure? . . .   I went to see the University boat race last
Saturday week, stood about two hundred yards from the
winning post — a glorious sight — went to Crystal Palace
yesterday and saw that wonderful fellow Ethardo.   While I
think about it, don't direct your next letter Wesleyan Training
College.   It is no more a training college than Oxford.   Our
training college is at Westminster.   I don't care about it
myself, but the fellows refer to the writer of that envelope in a
way not pleasing to your friend.   It certainly is not agreeable
for my fellow-students to imagine that I correspond with an
'ignoramus' or an 'uneducated young man from the country,'
as they do now.   When are you coming to town?   Remember
me to your mother, etc.   I am glad a slight leisure during the
Easter recess has given me an opportunity of dropping a line.
What do you think of the Reform Bill?—A splendid thing in
Punch last week.   Do you see the *Contemporary*, a new Review
edited by Alford,—fine thing.   I hear you have been unwell.
How are you now?   Vale! Vale! *au revoir.*—Yours affec.
"HUGH P. HUGHES.
"T. E. Brigstocke, Esq."

This letter gives some idea of the high spirits which no
grief, sorrow, remorse, etc., was able to quell.   He had need of
them, for he was twice, despite industry and good conduct,
brought into collision with the authorities.   On both occasions
it was for what he was always getting into trouble about—a
Cause, which other persons could not regard in the detached
light that he did.

The world outside the College grounds, throbbing with that
transitionary era in which society is still struggling, sent an
arrow into their midst in the spring of the year 1868, though
to some as it turned out it appeared not so much an arrow as
a species of bomb.   In that same year, as previously noted, the
universities were still closed to Nonconformists, Roman as well
as Protestant.   From whence it arose that the Liberation
Society, in addition to other items on its programme, was
stoutly advocating their nationalisation and preparing a petition

to Parliament with that end in view. Naturally it sent round to the various Nonconformist colleges to ask for signatures—daring in its boldness to approach even so anti-Liberal an institution as a Wesleyan Theological College.

The Wesleyans were known as a body not only to repudiate the term Nonconformist—for they had never, they said, refused to conform—but to look with marked disfavour on anything that was opposed to the most conservative ideals in politics and out of it. This intense conservatism, political and ecclesiastical, had its roots in their history, and the struggle everywhere visible in the Churches since the French Revolution against what appeared to be the non-Christian ideals of a new and revolutionary era.[1]

Much of the impulse underlying Newman's conversion to Rome seems to have lain in the desire to escape from this contamination; and while the Methodist fathers were staunch and unbending in their adherence to the essential principles of Protestantism, they stifled any signs of Liberal sympathies within their own fold. The Revolution, accompanied as it had been in the first instance by excesses and by open hostility to religion, produced a class of Liberalism which the early Methodists of the century were undoubtedly justified in restraining. In after years my father always prided himself on the fact that the early Methodist Revival among the masses of the people in England had done much to prevent the excesses which occurred in other countries, and that it had infused a genuine religious element which was quite absent among other peoples.[2] But what the fathers failed to see as time wore on was the new character that Liberalism was assuming under the leavening influence of great religious characters like Cobden and Bright. That they should disagree with their views and those of their adherents was quite comprehensible. The dangerous element came in when they treated their political opponents as anathema. Naturally feeling ran incredibly high in those days on both sides, and it is not easy for the present generation to transport itself to the forties, but it was a great

[1] See Newman's *Apologia pro vita sua*, and the part that anti-Liberal instincts played in his conversion.

[2] Mr. Lecky, it will be remembered, expressed the same estimate of the Methodist Revival as did Frederick Denison Maurice.

pity, as the sequel proved that the fathers could not realise that Liberals, even Radicals, might be as devout Christians and Methodists as themselves. It was this intolerance on their part that helped to make the terrible disruption in 1849, which nearly succeeded in destroying Methodism altogether. The people left in their thousands, and those whom they left behind feared more than ever to raise so much as a finger that might displease the Establishment or savour in any way of Liberal flightiness. So decided indeed was the impression that they created on outsiders in this respect that one of the characters in Lord Beaconsfield's novels speaks of the Methodists as " a preserve of the Tory party." [1]

Their deference to the Establishment lay partly in their history and origin, which was quite different from that of other Nonconformists. Nor did the fact that the Establishment was undergoing modification and was further away from them than she was at the beginning of the century, make any difference to the traditional attitude of Methodism of the sixties, which held itself almost as much aloof from the other Nonconforming bodies as the Establishment held itself aloof from all Protestant bodies outside its pale.

Thus the arrow discharged into the midst of the academic repose of the Theological College was doubly barbed, not only with so novel a programme as that persons outside the Establishment should aggressively claim a share in the best national education, but also with the further proposal (up the Society's sleeve, so to speak) of dissevering the Church from the State. To approve the first might mean to approve the second. Thus, however plausible the actual suggestion, to what extremes and impieties might it not lead, proceeding as it did from so outrageous a Society. That was the keynote of the Methodism of the sixties. It had no objection, it urged, to novelty, only to what novelty might lead to. To desist from resisting the tide was to be borne along helpless on its current.

As if aware of the consternation its proposal might create, the Society seems to have appealed to the students. The whole matter fell into my father's hands, who is represented at this juncture as canvassing the College for signatures. As soon as anything seemed right and desirable in his eyes he

[1] *Coningsby.*

at once acted in accordance with that conviction. It followed as the night the day, and the usual hesitations did not occur to him. What was the course that would best enable Nonconformists to obtain a university education? — the most effective canvassing at his command. In due course he must have repaired to the Governor's sanctum, and the picture to the writer is a vivid one. Mr. Barrett, after a courteous reception, must have looked at Mr. Hughes once or twice and yet again as he drank in a forceful and lucid explanation of the aims of that particular portion of the Society's programme.

No predilection for the Conservative party deterred my father's eloquence. It was something so desirable on the face of it, so framed to advance the intellectual status of the ministry. He may even have implied a certain respectful surprise that the Governor did not dash his name off to the petition there and then. The Governor also may not have been without wonder as to what this young man was going to do in Methodism, and what would be the outcome of it all. A Methodist ministry drinking in the culture of the times, responding to the questionings of the most eager and imaginative souls, and betraying both in word and act those gracious and fair realms in which the student of literature is able to wander, made a very tempting picture. Never having been to a university, they doubtless idealised it, colouring centres of learning with their own conceptions rather than with those of contemporary youth who besieged its portals.

Yet the vision could not blot out the awful word Liberation. Had he, as Governor of the Wesleyan Theological College, any right to sign a document bearing the imprimatur of such a Society? Yet Mr. Hughes was a most astonishing young man. What a picture he drew, to be sure. So he hesitated long before finally refusing, and when he did so it was from the conscientious conviction that his official capacity as Governor of the Wesleyan Theological College did not permit him to sign a petition drawn up by the Liberation Society. No figure is more representative of what was best in bygone Methodism. He loved, they say, the poet Wordsworth—but regarded his early sympathy with the Revolution as something inexplicable—one of those dark abysses in personalities of which he tried not to think. The Methodism which was to become associated with the name of his leading student was to have a greater understanding of the feelings and motives that induced the great poet of Nature to welcome the advent of Democracy, before it denied its birthright and aroused the horror of the world. That leading student, moreover, used often to say that the great poet of Nature ought not to have deserted the banner of Democracy for all the horror that he naturally shared with the world at those early excesses. He should have gone on believing and hoping.[1]

Some of the tutors signed the petition, for they were in a more independent position than the Governor. Among these was my father's tutor, Dr. Moulton, whose sympathies, despite scholarly moderation and deliberation, were always markedly liberal. On his head and my father's the storm broke, when it was mooted abroad that a petition from the Liberation Society was to go to Parliament signed by tutors and students of the Wesleyan Theological College. A tutor who had not signed said this description was incorrect and a libel on the staff. My father replied that he had not written " the tutors " but " tutors," and had never intended to convey any but a correct impression. Finally, resentment seems to have settled upon Dr. Moulton's head, for at the governing committee of the College a well-known lay member moved a vote of censure upon Dr. Moulton for his audacity in signing the petition. But even a Methodist official assembly in the sixties was unable to produce a seconder in the case of a man whose scholarship and character were, even at that early period of life, increasingly venerated.

The second imbroglio in which my father was the only culprit was of a far more serious character, and was near having a serious effect upon his career. As it was, it created an enmity, against which he had to contend throughout the earlier portion of his ministry. Its springs lay in the ecclesiastical condition of Methodism at the time, and were the direct product of the ecclesiastical strife during the latter portion of the first half of the century. The history and fruits of this strife, embittered as we have noted, by political animus, does not belong to this volume. It is sufficient to state that the

---

[1] He would insist that Browning referred to Wordsworth when he wrote the " Lost Leader."

long contest between Conference—the absolutely clerical body in whom Wesley had vested his powers—and the local governing bodies (the district meetings now called Synods) in which the laity were represented, had led in 1849 to the great tragedy of modern Methodism which lay at the root of its strange one-sided state in the sixties, the spiritual crippling as it seemed to many. The more liberal section, after repeated efforts to make itself heard in Conference, was discredited by the action of its own " Left " in 1848 and 1849. The slanderous and anonymous publications with which certain were accredited were followed by such severe and retaliatory measures on the part of their opponents that a hundred thousand of the rank and file of the people left Methodism that year. By this the community was not only terribly impoverished, but the light cavalry of the body,—the so-called cranks and firebrands,— who are difficult to dispense with if the army is to move, left bag and baggage, and were never heard of more.[1] That a community should practically become that of one party, political or ecclesiastical, is never desirable, be the party reactionary or revolutionary—and it was least of all desirable in a period like the latter half of the last century, when great new forces and ideals were at work upon society.

Among the laity, as the following chapters will indicate, was a widespread if inaudible discontent at the state of affairs, and a disposition to respond to any wind which might waft the boat from stagnant waters, though a certain minority were well satisfied with their present harbourage. The unfortunate issue of the whole situation seems to have lain in a growing gulf between the official group who controlled affairs and the majority of the ministry and people. Decisions and orders were given that savoured of arbitrariness, and were at variance with what many thought to be the welfare of the " Connexion." Such an edict was suddenly imposed upon Wesleyan Methodism in the year 1868. Mr. Barrett had failed in health and was about to retire. Another Theological College was to be erected at Headingley, of which Mr. Benjamin Hellier, the classical

---

[1] Perhaps there is no parallel in modern ecclesiastical history to such an overwhelming disaffection. The people left by whole families and congregations all over the country. Many went to form the United Methodist Free Church. Thousands were lost to the Churches altogether.

tutor, had been appointed governor. With the consequent changes in staff there also took place what seemed an arbitrary change in the character of the College, which was from henceforward to be reserved for students preparing for the Foreign Mission field; all who were intended for Home work were to be drafted henceforward to the new College at Headingley. The new governor, the Rev. Daniel Sanderson, was a former missionary, and the new tutor, Dr. Osborn, came straight from an official position in the Mission House; these, it was urged, and their colleagues could better promote the missionary spirit and equipment among a community that consisted entirely of intending missionaries than in one distracted by Home students, whose problems and equipments were necessarily divergent.

Among the students in particular there was the keenest dissatisfaction at the new arrangement, which, it was seen, would further increase the isolation of the missionary. The success of foreign missions depended in great part on the co-operation of the ministers and congregations at home. To keep up interest and support from home is to this day the struggle of the missionary society, and anything that went to weaken the bonds between future ministers at home and abroad was bad policy. Moreover, apart from policy altogether, there was a keen personal aspect of the arrangement. When a missionary returned on leave to his native land after years of absence, he would not find many faces that knew him and brightened at his approach. To the majority he must necessarily be a stranger. Throughout the year 1868 in the rooms of students and their friends waves of criticism lashed themselves against the fiat of the authorities. Like the ocean, which knows it must recede from the barriers men have erected, malcontents of all classes like to dash themselves, however vainly, against such walls. The retreat seems easier after a burst of ineffectual spray. At least, it was felt, the standpoint of the students who were so much affected by the new arrangement might have been taken into account.

The lithe form of the omniscient debater passed, as it had done at the examination at Westminster, from group to group, drinking in all that was said, and giving out those crisp conclusions and items of information that bore upon the matter in hand. He was not a missionary student, despite the pressure that had been brought upon him, and the present crisis had no bearing whatsoever on his own prospects and career any more than the petition of the Liberation Society, which was framed to affect future students at the Wesleyan colleges.

At this junction therefore, despite the Liberation upset, he was in good odour with the authorities as a remarkably industrious and promising student. But the stars while they smiled upon him were imperious as to his path—they generally are when they smile. Just as the generality are fated to retire before the barrier set to oppose their strivings, so are others equally fated by the mighty energies stored within them to leap in defiance over its summit. On this particular instance there were any number of wavelets rippling at the base, but only one was fated to rear itself in actual defiance against the main structure, and it happened quite simply and inevitably. As he had championed the Liberation Society, so was it agreed that he should champion his fellow-students in their grievance. The students' missionary meeting held in the December of that year was felt to be the fitting opportunity for giving expression to the general view — to wit, that the decision ratified by Conference was not in accordance with the welfare of missionary work or with the feelings of many of its friends and well-wishers in Methodism. The speech was written out at length beforehand, and submitted to one or two youthful advisers, whose hearts beat high as the fatal day approached. Their champion would put the case both with succinctness and discretion, a conclusion which they did not keep to themselves. Men who had gone to their first circuits in the previous September, and who liked to see the spray leaping against the barriers of officialdom, came up for the day just to see the fun. Thus my father had scarcely begun the eagerly anticipated portion of his speech before he was drowned in applause, an occurrence which, according to one of his listeners, seemed to carry him off his feet somewhat, and to induce him to make statements which had certainly not appeared on the written forecast of his speech. Report has it that he uttered the awful dictum : " Even the decisions of the Conference are not infallible."

Such a saying, certain in the audience felt, was the purest

treason, not to say revolution, for it was a reappearance of the old sin that had shattered Methodism in 1849, and would shatter her further still if the wisdom of the fathers was again to be set at nought and called in question.

Fellow-students have hinted that the youthful speaker scarcely knew the magnitude of his own offence and all that was implied by his action. There was a good deal of mystery rife in the sixties, and it may have been possible that my father did not probe to the full the intricacies of the structure against which he dashed himself, and it is more than probable that he did not know the part taken in the new arrangement by Dr. Osborn, who was sitting in the front row, and altogether at a loss to epitomise the situation. At any rate, either before or after his speech, there is reason to conjecture that he held strong views on the " oligarchical structure " of the contemporary government of Methodism, comparing it, indeed, to that which had once held sway in Sparta. In any case, neither on this occasion nor on any other, did he contemplate anything approaching insubordination to the authorities, oligarchical or no. He merely expressed a criticism that was widespread respecting one of their decisions. His attitude to authority was not unlike that of the proverbial shield, looking, until closely approached, a species of contradiction.

Unfortunately, Dr. Osborn took my father's expression of the general criticism as a species of personal insult, though no such reflection was ever intended. He was deeply chagrined, and wished to punish the offender by putting him back two years, i.e. adding two years to his probation, full already in the ordinary course. With tears in his eyes—so the story runs— the Doctor brought his proposal forward in the District Synod (" Meeting," as it was then called), but was defeated by a large majority. Dr. Moulton rose as usual to champion his pupil, pleading that in view of Mr. Hughes' uniform good conduct, and on his acknowledgment of the impropriety of criticising Conference, no further action should be taken, a proposal which commended itself to those present. Previous to the sitting of the Synod there had naturally been not a little fluttering in Methodist circles ; the culprit being divided between amazement and depression that he was such a villain, yet unconscious why he was. In particular, at the house in

Spilman Street there was not a little anxiety respecting the boy for whose future they had hoped so much, and over whom a cloud seemed suddenly to have descended. The father, sitting in his study, took up his pen and indited, in hiero-glyphical characters, a letter to Dr. Moulton, showing his anxiety—an anxiety which, though dignified, is somewhat puzzled. The ruling powers in Methodism were acting in a way that it was not quite easy for a Methodist in Carmarthen to understand. Yet there is no mistaking the loyalty to authority which rings out at the close. The magistrate, in whose blood ran the keenest civic instincts, could not write otherwise. For this reason the epistle is all the more touching.

"CARMARTHEN, *January* 16, 1869.

" DEAR SIR,—I write to you because my son, H. P. Hughes, has always told me of your great kindness to him on all occasions, and therefore (a very poor non-sequitur) I am going to trench still more on your good nature.

" Hugh tells me that in consequence of some impolitic observations made in a speech of his at the missionary meeting at Richmond, the Committee has resolved to recom-mend the district meeting to advise the Conference to take from him one year of travelling which had been allowed him last Conference—a punishment which, from the necessary publicity that must be given to it, is certainly severe, though it may be deserved. The favour I have to ask of you is to let me know if you know what is the precise nature of his offence, of which I am quite ignorant. Hugh never said one word to me about it during the Christmas holiday, and *The Recorder* certainly does not contain the observations complained of, though I knew from his manner that there was something wrong about him, as he was not as cheerful as usual. I saw also, or fancied, that *The Recorder* did not contain all that he had said. To-day, for the first time, I received a letter from him, and even now he does not say what the precise obser-vations were which called for so severe a punishment. I do not expect any information from you which you ought not to give me, nor anything which you only know as an official, of course, but simply his offence, although I may at the same time say that anything you might inform me of I shall consider as given in confidence, and sacredly respect. If he has deserved this punishment, I have only to regret it, and to submit to what is to me, I confess, a great mortification.

"I hope, however, under any circumstances, that you will forgive my application to you; and if you should feel it to be either your duty or wish not to enter into any correspondence upon the subject—and I quite understand that such might be the case—in that case I shall not trouble you any further on the subject.

"With many thanks to you for your continued kindness to my son,—I am, dear Sir, yours very truly,

"JOHN HUGHES.

"Rev. W. F. Moulton, M.A., Richmond."

The manner in which my father's apology was greeted by the Synod did not tend to improve matters. The elder ministers listened quietly enough when it was read before them, but the younger burst forth into clapping of hands. The framer was quite able to construct an "apologia" which left the youthful fancy free play, and which, while it answered the purpose in hand, took care by delicate wording not entirely to surrender the position to the enemy. Dr. Osborn apparently was indignant, and rebuked the applauders. "Do not applaud," he exclaimed, "a penitent sinner."

The motives that actuated this apology, and the spirit in which it was written, seem shrouded in that impenetrable veil which hangs over the fifties and sixties, though the writer has heard vague rumours of a culprit being interviewed by one or more of the fathers and brought to some sense of his manifest impropriety of behaviour. Certainly he was meek enough for anything, and so conscious of shortcoming, that it is not to be doubted that an interview could have wrung from him an expression of humility. But that the position was altogether surrendered to the enemy does not seem likely, in that the young ministers broke into applause because they perceived that their champion had not failed them. Certainly the spectacle of the culprit and the fathers is strangely instructive, and suggests to the present generation very careful dealings with delinquents. So immense have been the changes in the last fifty years that the present generation is in danger of underestimating and misconstruing the fathers, with their widely different environment and problems. It is the duty of age surely, in the Church as elsewhere, to guard what has been committed to it, though in the sixties, unfortunately, youth, which must add to the inheritance if it is to continue among men, was simply being ruled out of court altogether. The hardest and most imaginative thing in life must be——first, to understand the new generation, and second, to gracefully yield to its just demands. Undoubtedly the culprit in question was something very new and foreign to their ways of thinking, and he became increasingly so when the College gates closed behind him. They beheld in him a new and, as it turned out, irrepressible order of youth, and it was not to be expected that they should at first understand him.

On the other hand, this speech of my father's has been spoken of as if it were a mere vagary or ebullition of himself— an early escapade for which he had his own impetuosity to thank. He himself was so unaware of his sublime unselfishness that other men were unaware of it too. Nor had he any of the airs and assumptions of sanctity—considering himself as a sinner at the best. Doubtless if he had risen with woeful face and crossed hands, and in a voice, soft as even, expressed his regret that august Conference had not in its wisdom contemplated a different course, etc., the public sentiment would have been more willing to canonise him. But when he charged, he did so right doughtily like any of the old warriors whose shadow broods over his native town. What conceivable advantage it was to him personally to plead that the missionary students should not be isolated as Conference had decreed, or indeed to plead any of the things that he pleaded, is difficult to understand. In the words of one who heard him on that occasion, " he was always expressing what others thought, and what they had not the courage to say." It seems the epitome of his life.

As it was, in a year or two Conference was obliged to endorse the advice contained in his speech, as in later years it was to endorse the advice of other speeches. Meanwhile in that same year, 1869, he took his B.A. at London with the Rev. G. England Sheers, his chief friend while at College. He always talked very freely to Mr. Sheers—so freely indeed that he confided to him something which leads to the next chapter.

CHAPTER IV

MARY KATHERINE

" Her's is a spirit deep and crystal-clear ;
  Calmly beneath her earnest face it lies,
Free without boldness, meek without a fear,
  Quicker to look than speak its sympathies.
   .   .   .   .
Most gentle is she ; her large charity
  (An all unwitting, child-like gift in her),
Not freer is to give than meek to bear ;
  And, though herself not unacquaint with care,
Hath in her heart wide room for all that be."

J. R. LOWELL.

THE students, as they watched my father pacing the College grounds, noted, about the year 1868, that he was not pacing them alone. One of the Governor's daughters was with him.

He was not so " drily intellectual " evidently as might have been anticipated. As she had lately arrived at the demure age of fifteen, her attire had already begun to speak young ladyhood ; but it did not sit quite comfortably upon her, for all the dignity that she could upon occasion assume. All the inculcations of her stately mother could not transform her into the young lady of the story-book. Her curls bunched in their close ringlets at the back ; the frilled skirt, almost too long for comfort, constituted the only resemblance. Her eyes danced with mischief, for her spirit was dauntless even in those days. The dolls to which her playfellows were devoted she regarded as so much cargo for driving. To harness the College donkey to the cart and drive this numerous and varied family round the grounds was a joy that only the intrepid can experience. Animals she loved, not dolls ; the latter could not breathe or feel or respond. An employé drowned a little green-eyed cat of hers under the impression that it was ill, and she took years to forgive her. Her mother, in language chosen almost as that of Portia, pleaded for mercy, but in vain. Afterwards Mary Katherine—for she was always known under the double epithet—relented, but she never forgot the struggle. Her occupations outside the schoolroom till this period are best described by something that she has written herself.

"Those happy childhood days at Richmond glided swiftly away. What glorious times I and my little companions had—the rows on the river, the rambles in the park and Petersham Wood, and the games and adventures that took place in the beautiful college grounds. The place lent itself to childish adventure ; for were there not towers and battlemented roofs, to which we crept when unseen by our elders and held high sport, storming imaginary fortresses, often with considerable peril to life and limb? Then, were there not dark and gruesome cellars beneath, to which, with the aid of candle-ends, we made excursions, thrilling with delicious ghostly terror and excitement, our timid spirits sustained by the manly courage of our small brothers? The chilly depths of the icehouse were also explored by us, the descent to which was perilous, difficult, and dark as night. Our curiosity was insatiable. The top of the hay-rick and the roofs of outhouses formed a delightful retreat from the world. Also, the depths of the thick shrubberies, where in summer time we made to ourselves cool and shady bowers, where we had dolls' feasts and gave tea-parties to our friends, whom we beguiled from theological study and meditation to join us in our play.

"We were decidedly dramatic in our tastes, and acting in any shape or form was our delight.

"Bunyan's *Pilgrim's Progress* formed part of our Sunday reading, but it also lent itself most felicitously to our week-day recreations, and we acted it through with entire satisfaction and enjoyment to ourselves."

Richmond and its surroundings sank deep into her heart, and gave her a special kind of love for all she had known there ; but she said, some years ago, that the place was sad to her now, full of shades and memories, for the quaint old town on the hill and much that was in it had changed its character since those days. Nothing seemed as it was, save that view from the terrace which had so enthralled her as a child.

She was twelve years old when she met my father, and of a by no means romantic turn of mind. She remembered him afterwards as a slip of a youth dressed in a grey suit and cricket-cap, who was walking across the College grounds with a bat in his hands. "I distinctly remember feeling," she writes, "that I had met someone who was going to influence my future life. I made friends by asking him to subscribe to my missionary collecting-book. At first he refused, because he had already promised my friend Lizzie Hellier, but finally he relented and agreed to give me a penny a week. I had to go to his rooms to collect this penny, and he used to tease me by pretending that he had a curious animal concealed in a big box. He was an awful tease, and one day, to avoid him, I took a flying leap through an open window on the ground, but he just managed to catch hold of my frock, which was my best one, and the skirt was rent in twain in his hands."

On this particular occasion, in 1868, she was walking with my father on the lawn, acutely conscious probably that she had put away childish things. So the students at the windows divined. It followed of course, as the night the day; they had almost begun to guess it—now they were certain of it. Well, well, well—there really was no knowing what Hughes was after or what he might be doing next!

He was a favourite with all the Governor's family. His smartness and wit were much appreciated, especially by the younger portion. Once when they had been making mud-pies for hours and hours, and had ranged them all out for the students to buy, Mr. Hughes came and, sad to say, would not stay after the first few minutes. But such a story he told them! It filled them with love for him, and remorse that he should leave them. He told them that he must go and see his grandmother, that his grandmother was waiting for him, that she had been waiting a long time, and that she always did wait, that the reason of her waiting was difficult to define, because her dwelling was . . . Then followed words, and description, and words; but the refrain was always, that she had been waiting for a long time. Afterwards it dawned upon them, that the waiting grandmother was Mary Katherine.

When he took the Bible-class his satire shrivelled their impish spirits to scorn, and they adored him for it. The elder young ladies were amused at him, and liked to take the opposite side in an argument when he came to tea or supper with the Governor's family. He took off his hat and clutched it in a species of desperation, when he first met them floating down the long passage. For all his talkativeness he was very shy at times, but he recovered himself surprisingly in argument.

So the family powers were not so enlightened as the students, and when the shock came it was quite unexpected. Again Mr. Hughes approached the Governor, and again the Governor regarded him. Probably Mr. Hughes found it far easier to plead for the Liberation Society. The Governor's scrutiny, though piercing, was gentle; the hesitancy that had been apparent in that earlier interview was not apparent in this. "She is very young," he remarked; "far too young for such thoughts. She has much to learn—you both have, I may say; but personally I would willingly trust her with you—if God so will it. . . ."

My father had many compliments paid him later on in life, but never a greater than this.

To the Governor's wife the shock was considerably greater. She talked long and seriously to her daughter, and very wisely, too, from what I have heard. She felt she was dealing with two children, and she wanted to impress upon them that they were children. Mr. Hughes had always alarmed her with his precocity, and here was precocity indeed. Mary Katherine listened with exemplary meekness, and had her own thoughts. As far as waiting went, she was willing to wait till doomsday. Even in those early days she was conscious of something in her that could hold on and endure against great odds. Assertive was the last word that could be applied to her. By nature she was always retiring; but what she concluded to be her duty—that she would cling to till death, if necessary.

The true nature of their relationship was more accurately divined by her father than her mother. Very naturally her mother regarded it as a youthful fancy, and blamed herself for not intervening earlier. All life was a species of worship to this devout soul, and every act momentous because performed in God's sight. Yet rumour had it that, in her early youth, she too had been something of a tom-boy; and every now and again the humour of events would take her with fits of silent laughter. It was to this humour that her future son-in-law always appealed. The monstrosity of his designs, backed by his ludicrous way of putting things when he chose, increasingly appealed to her. In her amusement she forgot to be scandalised. Her notions of right and wrong made her stern to her own children, but she was sternest of all to herself. The

5

poetry of religion and life, and therefore the insight into them, was more the possession of her husband. He saw that the bond between my mother and father from the first—even at its most youthful period—contained something of the highly serious, *i.e.*, the highly religious. It was not even then of the ordinary nature.

Yet my grandmother's conception of life was also my father's, for all their seeming divergence. If he had not so fully consecrated himself, he could never have done what he did for other men and women. His extraordinary strength and freedom in working, arose from the wife he had chosen. He was able to do and to effect many things, just because he was old-fashioned like his mother-in-law; and though his Celtic instincts made him keenly alive to the romantic side of life, he seemed to have regarded it in a far higher light than most people did at his age. Indeed, Arthur, his reputed ancestor, never had a more indomitable son. Idealist in all things, he was supremely so in his conception of marriage.

To quote the words of his friend, he recognised in my mother "the one who was to help him in his life-work." Other men think this also, but they do not proclaim it throughout their lives as he did. He was always quoting her, and referring to her share in his work. He could never do any of it without her, and he said that he could not. The publicity that he caused to play around her name shocked a good many, but the public acknowledgment that he insisted in giving to his wife was part of his contribution to the age. At this very early period she had little or no intellectual interest, so the strong sympathy which existed between them was all the more strange to outsiders. At school afterwards, under able teachers, these interests quickly ripened. Yet it was to her that my father confided his intense love for Tennyson, especially "In Memoriam." The brethren, I believe, found it difficult to couple my father and poetic rapture, until they heard a burst of it. Fighting and debating was Hughes' line; the young man devoted to the Muses must be dreamy, and above all peaceable, with a voice of honey and an incapacity to hold his own in the world at large. My father, for all his coat of mail, had as much devotion for poetry as the mediæval warrior who delighted to listen to the lyre in the days of peace. He was not guiltless, either, of striking upon it himself. He adored Tennyson, when he was a young man, hungrily devouring everything that he wrote; and the adoration began after the first perusal of " In Memoriam." Till then he had wondered "what the poet was after," to quote his own expression; but "In Memoriam" entered into his life blood. The opening stanzas addressed to Christ expressed his deepest feelings.

The lines

> "Our wills are ours, we know not how,
> Our wills are ours to make them Thine"

he was incessantly quoting, and he never seemed tired of doing so. The great fascination it exercised over him must have been due to one or two causes; partly, no doubt, to its pure poetic merit, for Tennyson's melody and care in writing always appealed to him. He loved beauty of diction, and had a fastidious ear. But the " In Memoriam," as he told my mother, helped him more than he could say. Yet he never knew a great bereavement. Its special appeal must have lain in the unique portrayal of the contest between the negative spirit of science and pure reason, and the affirmative spirit of Christ and love, ending in the triumph of the latter. But perhaps during the period that he was reading " In Memoriam " he was experiencing certain difficulties in his inner life which a rapid mental development had engendered, and which were both expressed and reassured by the poet. The whole poem breathed Christ to him—Christ triumphant over the shadow and darkness of life.

At this moment I have a copy of the poem with his markings. The section beginning

> "Love is and was my Lord and King"

is heavily bracketed, and particularly the last verse, where the poet speaks of hearing at times

> . . . . . . "a sentinel,
> Who moves about from place to place,
> And whispers to the worlds of space,
> In the deep night, that all is well."

The last three words are underlined. I could almost imagine that he had composed that verse, and not the poet Tennyson, so resonant is it of him, of that deep abiding calm beneath the tempestuous sea of his outer life.

The section

"Who loves not knowledge";

and especially

"I trust I have not wasted breath :
I think we are not wholly brain"

is much emphasised ; also the section commencing

"That which we dare invoke to bless ;
Our dearest faith ; our ghastliest doubt."

The whole soul, too, found vent in a verse such as—

"Perplext in faith but pure in deeds,
At last he beat his music out" ;

the " deeds " bearing a strong pencil emphasis.

In 1868, when the Governor and his family left Richmond, my mother was sent to school.   They promised not to correspond with one another, and to treat the whole affair as if it had not been until school days were over.   Apparently they had no doubt of each other, and bore the parting with that assurance, in some strange united future, which had been so present with them from the first.   A year later my father was appointed to Dover as his first circuit, and he contemplated this initial contact with the outer world with much hopefulness.

CHAPTER V

DOVER. ÆTAT 22–25. 1869–1872

"The Spirit of the Lord is upon me, because he hath anointed me to preach the gospel to the poor ; he hath sent me to heal the broken-hearted, to preach deliverance to the captives, and recovering of sight to the blind, to set at liberty them that are bruised."—ST. LUKE iv. 18.

WINDSWEPT Dover, sheltering beneath the beetling crag on which the castle stands, is more like a grey town in the canny north than a southern watering-place. Like Ithaca of old it was framed in its ruggedness to be an excellent nurse to the youthful soul, and the ruggedness lay not so much in the environment of nature as in those sharp problems of everyday life with which he found it to abound. He was able to mould some of his conceptions into Dover, because Dover first moulded conceptions into him. It did more than that, it transformed him ; as he learnt eagerly, assiduously, at College, so with equal assiduity he learnt at Dover. His whole life long he was always learning from any one whom he could get to teach him, and there was much to teach him in that seaport town. He had imbibed to the full not only the political sentiments of his previous environment but the dominant ideas in his own Church at that period. In addition, he thought that intellect was the great weapon in the hands of an able young preacher—to know and grapple with the thought of the time, those thoughts for ever fomenting within him, was his peculiar province. It was to be so in a sense, but not in the special academic sense that he had anticipated, and which had been his habit at College.

From this altitude also, he could not but despise preachers of the gospel pure and simple, who led men to what was called "decision" there and then. That it was necessary and admirable work he had not a doubt, but it was not to be his.　Any good fellow who had mastered the rudiments could be a revivalist, if he had the necessary gift of preaching.

Teetotalism also was a fit hobby for this class of person; harmless, perhaps even necessary in many cases, but not worth the attention of self-controlled and thoughtful persons.　In common with other Methodists, he distrusted what was called the "extreme tendency of the times"; reform was in the air; the masses of the people were showing a disposition to take things into their own hands, which was to be deprecated.　In all these things he was to "turn," as his grandmother had "turned" when she was a young girl in Cardiganshire; and his turning, as it always was in that family, was of the right-about description.

All the while he was living and learning so eagerly, he pined greatly because my mother was not with him, chafing at the unavoidable delay which her extreme youth necessitated, and pitying himself greatly in consequence.　He was as true to her as my mother in the schoolroom was true to him.　For this reason he was not much approved by the young ladyhood of the town, in whose presence he talked politics and high matters as vociferously as if God had not created male and female in the beginning of time.　The politics and high matters, it is not to be doubted, covered at times not a little shyness.　Woman, except for my mother, was an unknown quantity; afterwards he got to know her better, and even at that age he was her most impassioned champion.　Dover, in addition to other things, made him that.

The revolution commenced on a Sunday night at Snargate Street Methodist Chapel, on the occasion of his first sermon. Methodism, to use the expression of the Methodists living in the town, was "dead."　To the Methodist people, at any rate, Methodism has always been primarily the conversion of their fellow-men, and their instinct has always echoed the conclusion of the writer of *Ecce Homo*, when he says that "the article of conversion is the true 'articulus stantis aut cadentis ecclesiæ.' When the power of reclaiming the lost dies out of the Church, it ceases to be the Church.　It may remain a useful institution, though it is most likely to become an immoral and mischievous one.　Where the power remains, there, whatever is wanting, it may still be said that 'the tabernacle of God is with men.'"

From this one conception, all the peculiar institutions of Methodism have sprung; so it is small wonder that the people of Methodism have a continual hankering after a dramatic witnessing of a miracle, to guard which the Church may be said to exist. "I had been dissatisfied for many years," said one of the Dover Methodists, "at the lack of manifestation of Divine power in our services." They had been so far unused to its manifestation that, when eighteen penitents came to the front at the end of my father's first sermon, they did not quite understand what had happened. Like the people of Galilee, they had never seen it on this wise—but their fathers had. The pale, spectacled young minister—a mere boy in years, as they knew him to be—was to recall Methodism to its early fervour, with nothing of the tumultuous or emotional; but miraculous, lofty, sustained as it was that evening with something still and solemn in its nature, as they had pictured that evening long ago, when God came down to Eden and talked face to face with man. Persons who had been present dropped their voice when they spoke of it. God had spoken to them. How—whence—they knew not. The scene, especially in the minds of the younger people, became burnt into them like a picture, along with the last words of their dying mother.

Yet who could have anticipated such a scene? Certainly my father did not; the words came leaping out of their own accord; they were his, and not his. At the close he asked the congregation to follow him down to the schoolroom below, and hold a short prayer-meeting. They came, and a child who was present has since described it:—

"That memorable prayer-meeting! It was all so startling, new, and strange. It all comes back so vividly. The quaint old schoolroom beneath the chapel, to which he had adjourned after the evening service; the pale-faced, grave young minister; no noisy excitement, but an indescribable hush of expectancy which seemed to pervade the place. Then, as the meeting went on, one after another went forward to the front, until eighteen souls were bowed in penitence before the Lord."

The text of the sermon, related another, was: "What think

ye of Christ ? "   " He seemed to speak to each one of us, and
ask us what Christ was to us, and we to Him."

Again, as when my father listened to the fishermen, some
of those listening divined an intimacy in which they did not
share.   What was to prevent them ?   Their sin.   Who could
take it away ?   None but their Saviour.   Weeping, they came
forward to confess Him and seek Him.   My father did not
believe in the necessity for the Methodist " travailing "—the
quicker a man could see that God " had blotted out his
transgressions for His own sake," [1] the better it was surely
for him and everybody concerned.   In later years he found
out that the Parable of the Prodigal Son was not the Parable
of the Prodigal Son at all but that of the Loving Father, and
he never ceased to congratulate himself in particular and
humanity in general on the discovery.

So began my father's career as Evangelistic Preacher, for
that is the title accorded to men who preach heart to heart
to the people, and are not satisfied unless their preaching
results in changing the nature of their hearers.   There is
necessarily the danger of overestimating outward and visible
results, but there was not much danger when my father came
on the field.   Methodists talked much of seed-time and of the
slowness of God's working, but they seemed to have forgotten
that a period of sunshine is often necessary for the ripening of
the corn.   My father had the faculty, or the genius rather,
for ripening what was best in a man.   Like a burst of tropical
sunshine he appeared to force the frail growth into life and
vitality.   He could not help doing it ; it was pure genius ; and
because it was genius, his talents, and they were considerable,
had to be sacrificed to that which was not a talent.   He never
cultivated it or took any pains about it ; it came from on high,
as the old woman had thought in the cottage ; and its vehicle
was speech—the speech which had stirred the congregations
in Wales, the little children playing in the gardens, and the
Governor of the College.

While at Dover he occupied lodgings next door to the
Buckland Street Chapel, of which he was the minister, in
the centre of the poor quarter of the town.   His study was
scarcely large enough to swing a cat in, but it had a fair-sized

[1] That quotation from Isaiah was a great favourite of his.

window, out of which he looked eagerly, and from which he
imbibed what no book or history ever taught him. Even in
those days the dwellings of the labouring classes formed, in
that part of the town, a vista to the eye, and, as usual, their
life surged on the pavement rather than in the narrow confines
of their homes, if some of them could be called such. He
had not long been a spectator of the drama of that street
before he knew not only its tragedy but the prime actors in
that tragedy. His homely landlady and her husband became
objects of close cross-examination. He had the faculty of
putting men and women at their ease. " Now, my dear
brother," he would say, " sit down and speak the truth and
shame the devil."

At Richmond he had held himself more or less aloof,
but he had always been able to win the confidence of men,
if he desired to do so. His listening powers were on a par
with his gift of utterance. If a person had something to say,
he drank it in to the dregs, thirstily ; he prided himself on his
power of cross-examination, which was terrific, though he could
also listen spell-bound to the graphic narration of anything.
The dramatic spring in him lay very near the surface, and
responded to the slightest touch. So in the street, in the
houses, in his own study, at the window, he drank in matter
not only for his own learning, but for that of his Church and
other Churches in addition.

His was the strange lot to be a prophet ; men of his own
time, with their more limited vision, were not to read the skies
as he did, or to denote the cloud on the horizon, no bigger
seemingly than a man's hand, that should break in showers
over the land.

Another prophet of a different calibre was living at Dover
—to wit, an old sailor, also residing in that humble quarter of
the town, and ridiculed for his prophecy. Among his household
gods was a quaint two-faced image, representing a decent,
pleasant-faced working man on the one side, and a drunken
one on the other. Now both these representatives stood for
one and the same man ; hence the burden of his text, of which,
poor fellow, he never wearied. He had not only looked out
of the window, but had been bitten himself by the dragon—
fiercer than any of which the fables tell—which preys on

society. He knew what it can do and leave undone for a man and a woman and a child. The hell of theology must have had little terror for him; he knew what it was on earth, so he continued to preach his text and to treasure his image till he died.

In the room that he and a few disciples hired for this purpose, the respectable youth of the town would slink in at times out of sheer curiosity. What was this Teetotalism? Was it pure madness—a revival of antique Puritanism, or what was it? One young man—a Wesleyan by upbringing— stole in there one day. He was young and impressionable, and the image haunted him. He could not get it out of his head; he saw it everywhere, even in the faces of the dirty children whom he passed in the street. Some men have not to learn to love their fellow-men, they are born so. The Temperance crusade, though it had barely started in Dover, was fighting its first battle in other parts of the kingdom; and its most scathing opponents were found, strange to say, not among the publicans, but among the well-to-do and the more or less educated, who deprecated, as my father had done at College, a movement that appeared so fanatical in origin. The leaders, who had come face to face with life and its drunkenness, like the old sailor, had already with prophetic instinct seized upon the children, springing up every day like flowers in a great wilderness, only to wither and to be trodden under foot because there was no sun to shine upon them and no one to care for them. "Let us organise them," said these fanatics, "into bands, Bands of Hope." So they began organising them, and as some of them were strange, unlearned fellows, they organised strange bands. But they were Bands of "Hope" none the less, and it occurred to the young Wesleyan that he ought to organise one too at Snargate Street Chapel, which for all its cheerlessness was yet the centre of the family aspirations.

His mother and her mother before her had been Methodists, and with the life that they had given to him were the deep desires and aspirations which had coloured it. But their religion did not inspire him as it had them. It was essentially cheerless and in his childhood terrifying. Nor did manhood altogether dissipate the terrors. It was part of his life, yet strangely alien to it. The emotions and desires with which society at large was beginning to vibrate found no echo within it. Writers, poets, social reformers, politicians, lay outside its domain. Its one concern was the future and man's fate therein. Humanity and this present life lay outside the province of the Church.

I mention the inner life of this young man because it was the inner state of so many young men at the time that my father began his ministry; there were hundreds of them in the middle classes, the offspring of two or more generations of singularly upright life, who, owing to the lack of life in their own Church (which means the lack of spirituality), had inherited the form and the narrow confines of their fathers' religion without the great vital element that makes religion large, generous, and human. If they showed any signs of it in the Church, its officials suppressed them, so it was not without trepidation that this young man thought of approaching the young minister at Buckland Street.

True, he was a wonderful preacher. He had never heard any one talk in the pulpit as he did or behave as he did. But would he countenance temperance—a Band of Hope? Surely he was too clever, too religious (for he had been the means of saving sinners). He was not left long in doubt. My father grasped him by the hand and bade him be seated. "Certainly, the idea is excellent. I will speak to my superintendent and see what can be done in the matter." The superintendent—a saintly old gentleman with a hobby for old china—was Methodist enough to approve of his colleague's evangelistic gifts, and to encourage the use of them, but in common with all the elder ministry he could not see the point of teetotalism. Still, he could not well say nay, and he allowed the band to be formed though he never approved it, and there was a little friction in consequence. First of the band to sign the temperance pledge was Mr. Hughes himself. He, too, had become a member of the "Insane Society," and was to become a member of other such societies before his course was done, a course which could never rid itself of that study window at Dover and its lessons.

The humanitarian aspect of teetotalism was always strongly insisted on by him. In his eyes it was essentially an act of sacrifice performed for the sake of others, not at a normal period but at a highly diseased extraordinary period. A person desirous of helping his fellow-men, and particularly a minister of Christ, he thought, could best persuade men not to drink intoxicating liquors by abstaining from drinking them himself. He knew that with the masses of the people it must be total abstinence or nothing. Tendencies to intemperance were too much in the blood, and temptation too omnipresent to make it possible for those untrained in self-control to drink temperately. This is the plea put forward by those who do not know the homes of the people, but never by the people themselves, who know too well what they can and cannot do. At least he would have it said of him that, however much he had left undone, he had abstained from the wine which caused his brother and sister to stumble, and that by his abstaining and his example he had made the way a little easier for them.

He did think, incidentally, that in the present drunken state of England, where elections, so it is said, are often won by beer, and where scarcely a family is to be found that has not suffered in some way from the effects of intemperance, men and women are better for not using alcoholic drinks as beverages. He always admitted that alcohol was a valuable medicine, under certain circumstances, though he considered that doctors incurred grave responsibilities by ordering it unnecessarily. Yet he did not lay stress on the physical aspect of the case, or enter into the pros and cons of the effect of wine upon the system, as other teetotallers had done. It was the unselfish, the humanitarian, the Christ-like side of it which appealed to him, and on which he insisted. A man helped his brother-man by making himself one with him, and he thought it was the only way of helping him. On the other hand, to use his own phrase, he knew that there were many "excellent Christians" who did not feel about it as he did, and whose eyes had not been opened as his had been, and that it was no good hurling anathemas at them because they did not.

For ordinary men to give up drinking intoxicants for Christ-like or patriotic reasons was, he knew, an innovation. He might as well have expected some of them to give up eating beef. Though he believed that masses of his fellow-country-men would never attain to anything like sobriety till the best men and women became teetotallers for their sake, he saw that the movement must be a voluntary one, something born of sympathy and love for others. Though he flung himself heart and soul into the Temperance movement, and introduced it wherever he went, yet he never sided with the extreme section. As in other movements he restrained as well as inspired, despite the restlessness of followers. When a section of Temperance reformers, more ardent than wise, wanted to debar from office in the Wesleyan Methodist Church all who had any interest in the sale of alcoholic beverages, he was not a little distressed and much opposed to their proposal. He saw what havoc and disorder it would introduce into a Church not yet recovered from a terrible rupture, as well as the harm done to the cause they were advocating. By such extreme suggestions they were only alienating classes of persons who would be won over in due time, if only Temperance advocates would be a little wiser. So many failed to understand him, and were very angry in consequence—but that was many years later.

The idea he had brought with him from College, that ministers of his own communion should be more influential in public and municipal affairs, was the more striking as it was in opposition to the established tenets of Wesleyan Methodism at that date. So venturesome was he, that he engaged in a spirited controversy in the Dover papers with a High Anglican curate, who refused to address him as Reverend, and who had been trying to dissuade a member of his congregation from attending chapel.

At a meeting held for the purpose of upholding and explaining a Prohibitory Liquor Bill, just introduced into Parliament by Sir Wilfrid Lawson, the publicans came in a body and tried heckling my father when he got up to speak. But they soon stopped, because they got better than they gave ; to contradict or interrupt him in a speech was never tried by any one with success. Indeed, people sometimes believed that the interruptions were prepared beforehand. On this particular occasion he assured the astonished publicans, that he was delighted at their presence, which would give the meeting the opportunity of hearing all sides of the question. In particular, he pointed out that this movement was originated without any desire to injure them as a class, but for the purpose of remedying an evil with which it was their unfortunate lot to be more or less associated. He believed the liquor traffic was more injurious to them than any one else, and he sympathised with them as an overworked class. He was sorry that the meeting should appear antagonistic to them, still he took comfort from the fact that they had a strong hold upon the sympathies of the public, that they had not a few supporters in Parliament, but taking it all round they were well able to take care of themselves, etc. etc.

He then went on to prove that the Bill was not a party measure, but possessed supporters on both sides of the House. Statistics proved that excessive drunkenness was the root of crime and poverty, and that, with those statistics in view, the meeting must support the following resolution, which he proceeded to distinctly enunciate. His voice as a speaker was singularly clear and penetrating; however much persons disliked what he said, they had to listen to him. The publicans listened on this occasion like lambs. Their chosen orator was simply struck dumb. Those who were present, related that they had never seen anything like his management of that meeting. He was a master of men from his youth up, and he seemed at times to be able to play upon them exactly as he chose.

The platform at that meeting was very suggestive; sitting upon it were some of the leading men and ministers of the town, including my father's second superintendent, Dr. Kessen. The Temperance movement had now won the support of the churches of Dover, and my father and his sympathisers formed an energetic group, known as the Dover Temperance Reformers, the first of many similar companies whom he delighted to leave behind him.

Supporting the Dover Reformers on this occasion was a certain Alderman Rees, a Welshman as his named denoted, a Methodist and a red-hot Radical, a fusion which went to form a very striking personality. He was beloved by many of his townsmen, though he was in flat contradiction to the conservative ideas of the place. He was the type of man who arouses interest and a following wherever he may be. If Rees had been " at it," men read the paper to see what Rees had been " at." He was part of the Dover of the sixties and seventies, and my father may be said to have fallen into his arms at once. He was constantly at his house, drinking in what he said, and communicating his ideas and impressions.

His new sympathy and personal contact with the people was the dominant factor undoubtedly in his change of political opinion at this time; but Alderman Rees was the presiding genius of the crisis. He was Celtic to the core, and fiery as he, so it was as well that they happened to find themselves in agreement.

Thirty-three years afterwards, on hearing of the death of Alderman Rees, he wrote to his son (a brother minister), as follows :—

"My dear Rees,—I have often wished to write to you, since you informed me that your father had entered into his rest. Amid all the hurry of Conference I did manage to put one or two notes into the *Methodist Times*, to indicate how much I loved and reverenced your father. He was the first Methodist friend I ever had. He and your family showed me the greatest possible kindness when I went to my first appointment ; he influenced me in many ways, and I cannot possibly tell you how deeply indebted I feel to him. I have often wished that I could see him in his old age. Few persons have exerted so much influence over me as he did. I can also sympathise with you. The death of a father, even after we have ourselves reached to man's estate, creates a certain consciousness of loss that no one else can fill.

"When my father died a year or two ago, I felt that I had no one to fall back upon. I am very glad that your father and mine were spared to us for so many years."

.   .   .   .

My father began to look into the political fermentation of the time, and to see it in quite another light. The Liberal and Democratic movement which originated with the French Revolution, and which the religious had been taught to fear and to condemn, had now assumed quite another character. It was no longer lawless and anti-Christian. Cobden and Bright, in their humane campaign against the Corn Laws, had infused into it a new and religious spirit.

Nor was this all they did. Their triumph lay not only in the actual repeal of those laws. It lay in the conversion of a man so high principled and conservative as Mr. Gladstone, into an understanding of the causes underlying popular agitations and into the conviction that the only way to allay these was to throw aside every superficial and received diagnosis, and to go to the root of the social disease itself. The very last element was lawlessness. Cobden and Bright were Christian Englishmen of the middle classes, and law-abiding to the core; they taught the English people how to conduct an agitation. Their book was the Bible, their logic that of Manchester. Their object was to reason with rather than to incite a crowd, for they were the very opposite of the Continental agitators, being indeed the ideal of the sober middle classes, who are the backbone of Nonconformity.

The Wesleyan Methodist ministry was not sympathetic with the new enthusiasm that had fired the younger men who made up their congregations. The ministry, in the eyes of the latter, was necessary for the maintenance of religion, but scarcely for social amelioration. To such men everywhere, my father was an inspiration; and they would describe him afterwards by saying, " He began life to me." The young Wesleyan, struggling with his Band of Hope, drank in draughts of the new life. He had no idea that religion or the round world could be half so inspiring. He began to see Christ differently, because my father also began to see Him differently. That He would save them from their sins and from the wrath of God they believed mechanically, because they had been brought up to believe it—unless, indeed, the free-thinkers were right and the whole business was a species of delusion, fit for women and children but not for their husbands and fathers— but here was a parson who made them feel that Jesus Christ of Nazareth really cared for the temporal welfare of ordinary men and women. Did not He weep over Jerusalem—as Mr. Hughes pointed out—because they were as sheep without a shepherd? and was He not, when He was in the flesh, a carpenter?

My father, indeed, at Dover began to see his Saviour—as many outside the Church had begun to see Him—as a lover of *men*, and of men in starved, ungainly bodies. This conception of Christ as the lover of man, and the whole of him, underlay all his distinctive teaching. It was the lever of most that he said and did. But he knew Christ first as his own personal Saviour, and it was this aspect that he dealt with in the pulpit, though the two overlapped each other. They were so merged in him, that they became more and more

merged in his preaching and teaching. Man minus body
became increasingly unthinkable, both to him and to the
other seers of the period, and in like manner Christ became
unthinkable without his essential humanity, which the Church,
in order to preserve her doctrine of the Atonement, was in
danger of overlooking. Bit by bit, Christ was to dawn on
this disciple as the greatest social reformer the world had
yet known—in sympathy, not only with the classes who
shouted for order, but with the masses who rebelled against
that order because their interests had not been considered in it.
The present generation perhaps can scarcely realise the full
significance of this revolution in Christian thought. It was
familiar to thought, but not to so-called Christian thought; and
just because it was not so familiar, my father had to fight
battles in Methodism. With Beaconsfield in politics, he had
various picturesque sympathies, and, like many others in the
country, he was fascinated by the potency and mystery of his
personality. But henceforth he became an ardent Gladstonian,
rejoicing in the various democratic reforms which that statesman was introducing.

Thus my father's master in Democracy, as in all other
departments of his life, was his own personal Saviour—Jesus
Christ of Nazareth. He had also another teacher; he saw what
Cobden and Bright had done for the English middle classes
in purifying their politics and extending their sympathies. He
greatly admired them; but he was conscious of certain limits,
especially in their followers, and against those limits he
rebelled. It was too charged with the prosaic sense, the prejudices and the environment of the English middle classes,
to captivate his mind.

He had a great appreciation of the French and Italian
political writers. He was a Celt, and could worship the ideal,
and that the ordinary Englishman cannot. The creed of the
latter is to hang on to what he has until someone can show him
a concrete better. This is not so with the Celt. If any one can
show him a pattern in the heavens, he is willing to pull to pieces
his own received pattern and to construct it all afresh. Now,
my father fully understood this, though he could not always
act as the Celtic portion of him dictated. He often spoke as
it dictated, but his deeds were fitted to his environment, which,

6

especially in its ecclesiastical side, was English to the roots. Of all men who had ever lived, he most admired Mazzini. His sublime and highly religious conceptions of Democracy fired him with a passion unspeakable. Mazzini pleaded and felt for the peoples of Europe as no middle-class Englishman, well housed from his birth, could plead and feel for them. And how he pleaded! With all the colour and the fervour of the south, which was so attractive to my father. What sense and exaltation combined with what sensibility and tenderness! Mazzini's saying, that " every right presupposes a duty " became the interpretation of his political ideas much as " In Memoriam " had entered into the deepest interpretation of his own religious experience. Yet this sufferer and lover of mankind denied that Jesus Christ was his Saviour. His admirer could scarcely countenance the thought. Oh that he had been by, to have a few words with him! All the religion that Mazzini knew about was what the Italian priests were full of. The mass of men on the Continent were in a great darkness. The priests had made religion hateful, in that they had allowed no place in it for teaching based on the love of man. Christ's pure teaching, as shown in the New Testament and much of the workings of His Spirit, was a sealed book to them. Oh to save men everywhere and bring them to Christ! It was something to bring a few men to Him at Dover, but what a drop in the ocean!

The *Letters of Louis Blanc* were also a factor in his political development. This social side of my father's teaching sank into the mind of the young man I have mentioned, and later it was to sink into thousands of others, not only among the laity but among the younger ministry. Of the companies of young men who everywhere clustered round him, there was always one who was Fidus Achates, who knew him, and to whom he revealed himself with a singular simplicity and spontaneity. In later years when Fidus Achates was busy, not only in earning his daily bread, but in municipal and philanthropic endeavour, he could not understand when people told him Mr. Hughes was proud.

Somewhat dictatorial, perhaps, and assured that his own way was right (and it was, too), but proud—well! Let the speaker have a talk with some of the congregation—see some of the letters he had written to them—and he'd learn a thing or two. He was too great to be proud.

Fidus Achates being a man in humble circumstances and of some aspirations to live the life that God had breathed into him, not stifled portions of it, and sensitive withal, knew what it was—often—to

"bear the whips and scorns of time,"

and had his opinion as to whether a man or minister was humble or not. In the Society classes, when my father met with the young, the old days were revived, and men could tell each other of that which their Saviour had done for them. Did He not change the lives of many of them, speaking to them in that still small voice on Sunday evening and on all manner of occasions? Where faith was tottering, she grew bold. An ordinary man had not time to inquire into the origin of species or anything else, or to see what Mr. Huxley and Mr. Darwin were after, but they could see when a man turned right about in his acts and ways and thoughts. Talk about miracles—there were nothing but miracles at Dover in those days. The elder men were not so pleased with my father. When he first met them in class he looked at the scanty list of members with an air that was almost regal. "Do you want any more?" he inquired; "if so, you shall have them." When he was a boy at the Mumbles he used to run about with a lamp to beat up an evening congregation, and he did not see why a class could not be collected in a similar manner. But his hearers were offended. "Twenty-two," they thought, was taking too much upon itself. Here as elsewhere he took a keen interest in village work, and as usual he induced others to share in this interest.

In 1871 Dover was stirred to the core by an institution which it would never have suspected of causing any such com-motion, to wit, the Young Men's Christian Association, which, in my father's eyes at any rate, was too much given to the singing of hymns and too little to the good of this present world. He was one of its members none the less, and there he met several of the Evangelical churchmen of the town, and endeared himself to them. They could not see with him eye to eye about temperance and other subjects, but they delighted in his gift as an evangelist and admired his force as a debater. When he first began to speak there, people started and whispered, "Who is he?" and no one seemed to have a satisfactory answer. On one occasion he criticised the act of a veteran member and questioned its legitimacy. The old man drew himself to his full height. "Young man," he declaimed, eyeing the slight youth who had dared to intrude upon him; "young man, I was putting resolutions when you were in swaddling-clothes." Cool as a cucumber a voice replied, "I am aware that there is childhood at both ends of life," and the assembly was convulsed.

The debates became a good deal more animated than was their wont, so that sisters and sweethearts of the speakers were found with their ears to the door to catch what they could of what was going on within. One day a small house voted for the exclusion of *Punch* from the reading-room, as a publication "contemptuous of religious influences, if not absolutely hostile to them"—an instance of the extreme narrowness of the Evangelicism of the day and its lack of the saving salt of humour. The comments in the local press were taken up and repeated by the press of the whole country. The world generally, particularly the press, was full of scorn. My father and others lost no time in quickly signing a petition of protest, and summoned an extraordinary meeting to reconsider the question, when he made a speech that was very characteristic. In that speech he began one of the great patient works of his life—the education of the narrow-minded. He was for ever striving with them and being misunderstood by them. He understood, as other men of his outlook did not, the prejudices of a narrow Puritan tradition. Like most good Englishmen he had some Puritan prejudices himself, and those that he had not, he did not laugh at or get angry with, as is the general habit of the more enlightened. In that speech he laboured with the greatest courtesy and understanding, quoting Elijah and the other prophets to bring home to such minds that the prophets indulged in humour, and the Saviour Himself in satire. God, he explained, had given human beings faculties capable of appreciating humour and satire; and it was not His intention, he thought, that one particular faculty should be pushed to a morbid excess, but that the entire nature should have free development. The speaker carried the day by four votes, and *Punch* presented him with his " royal thanks " in the next number. He had not only defended humour but had made a spirited vindication of the private lives of Thackeray and Mark Lemon and others of its contributors.

Another time, at an anniversary meeting, he begged the association to extend its borders, to introduce a wider and more instructive course of lectures, and to make additions to their library, which should include masters of English literature, such as Shakespeare, Milton, and Bacon. " Only by a greater application of educational influences," he said, " would the members of the Association be enabled to battle against the errors which surrounded them, from the growing pretensions of the Roman Catholic hierarchy and the teachings of the Positivists."

While he made no secret of his sympathies for the programme of the Liberal party, he refused to be bound and tied by that party as such. He was not a party politician, and this he early declared. Sir Wilfrid Lawson, the Temperance advocate in the House, was a Liberal, and for many years that party was the only one to propose Temperance legislation. None the less, Liberal politicians saw the unpopularity of Temperance, and resented having their party mixed up in it. The president of the Liberal Association at Dover, with this thought in mind, called on the young Temperance advocate, so as to give him a word of warning. He was a man of not a little social distinction, and was much looked up to in the town. On being ushered into the room, scarcely large enough to swing a cat in, he delivered, with the weight of a man of position who has the interests of his party at heart, " You must not upset the party with your teetotalism, Hughes." " Your party," exclaimed my father, who was standing with his back to the fire-place (a favourite attitude of his), " what do I care for your party? I have to do with Temperance and the cause of God." His listener took his leave awed. He had met a young man who dared to say what was in him.

It was at Dover that he began a crusade, which was an agony to him, in connection with the Social Purity Movement inaugurated by Mrs. Josephine Butler. Of all women he honoured in his time, he honoured her the most. Alderman

Rees introduced him to her, and he attended meetings of hers
in the town.   While she was speaking he burst into tears and
hastily quitted the platform.   Those tears should be told of
him wherever his story is related to men ; they explained the
white heat of his feelings on the subject which consumed him,
as his fabled ancestor Arthur might have been consumed on
similar provocation.   " He is inhuman," men said, watching
that indignation, terrible because much of it was repressed
rather than enunciated.   Perhaps—so was Arthur.   Whether
he wept at the long story of human wrong and suffering, or at
the sufferings incalculable of the woman who dared to tell some
of it, it is difficult to know.   He wept for both, I think, but
especially for her.   " I knew I had met a young man who
could do good work in the cause," she said of this incident,
which did not escape her.

All who knew him, and who were struggling to uphold the
weak, felt the same thing.   " He had a passion for the weak,"
wrote one woman at the time of his passing.   It was the
summing up of his career.   Most of the fury of which men
accused him was lavished in the defence of them, in upholding
those causes and policies which he thought ministered to their
needs.

The Franco-German War was raging during his stay at
Dover, and this roused in him his great horror of unnecessary
war.   He would refer strongly to the subject as early as those
days.   He had closely followed French politics, and, like the
rest of the world, was totally unprepared for the result of the
struggle with Germany.   A former member of the French
Senate, an exile, attended my father's services at Snargate
Street with manifest pleasure.   He sat in the gallery, and his
distinguished appearance as he sat there made him a figure of
romance to the congregation.   After my father left Dover this
gentleman entered into correspondence with him, and it was
felt that he was responsible for many of my father's " radical
notions."

At the farewell services, Snargate Street was crowded with
all sorts and conditions, and the proceedings were reported at
some length in the local press, for many besides Methodists
were present and mourned his departure.   The poor in particular were inconsolable, lading him with pincushions and all

manner of queer presents. He loved the poor from the first, and was far from content with watching them from his study window. When he could help them he did. An old woman was one day carrying a heavy bundle up the steep path between the chapel and his lodgings—he carried it for her. A man fell ill of the smallpox—he visited him. "Do you know I have the smallpox, sir?" said the man, "you'll catch it."

"The wind will blow it away," was the answer.

In his farewell sermon he referred with sorrow to the fact that he had not been able to visit the poor more in their own homes. He had never the leisure to do much of this himself, though he inspired others to do it. Yet, by some instinct of the heart, they knew he was feeling for them.

Dover should stand out in the story of my father's life. It was there he blew the trumpet-note of defiance. Few who help their fellows begin otherwise. Men of action, as well as thinkers and artists who are remembered of men, have begun in that way, throwing aside received opinions and prejudice. As often as not these trumpet-notes are not so revolutionary as contemporaries imagine. They summon men and churches to traditions so timeworn, that the majority have quite forgotten them. It is interesting to note, among other incidents of this time, that he took a leading part in an effort to assist a struggling Congregational church, and to re-establish its work. It was a foreshadowing of that catholic conception of Christianity which dominated his later life.

My father was always old-fashioned, even in youth. He set great store by the virtue of obedience. He never refused obedience to those who had the right to claim it. Perhaps this was the virtue he admired most of all, because he knew that so little could be done without it. Everywhere there was the same story of his relation with the superintendent; the people were the more impressed because he came to be regarded as a revolutionist. His second superintendent at Dover, Dr. Kessen, was a man such as he always loved. He was a scholar to begin with, versed in many Oriental languages, and of great mildness and beauty of disposition. Such men, my father felt, possessed the virtues in which he was deficient, and he admired them greatly. They, he felt, were lovable, soothing men instead of irritating them as he did. One night this old minister set off to preach in one of the villages of the neighbourhood, and despite wind and rain he set out heroically as many another has done in similar circumstances. He had not gone far before my father caught him up. " Go back, sir ; this is a night for a young man like me." The elder man demurred. " Thank you, Mr. Hughes. No, no, I have started, and I will go on with it."

" I am sorry I was not in time, sir, but you must go back. I insist upon it." After some struggle, my father won the day.

An elder man who tried to suppress him unfairly, like his fellow-debater at the Institute, received short shrift at his hands. But to one who was kindly disposed towards him, he responded surprisingly, even vehemently. There was not enough that he could do for such. This office performed for the gentle and kindly old minister was one of several similar offices which the recipient often mentioned in after days.

This curious blend of defiance and obedience, of respect and disrespect, of veneration for the past and what appeared to be the opposite of such veneration, was the puzzle as it was the strength of his character.

The following letters to his friends at this period will prove interesting. The first deals with a projected visit to the Rhine with the friend of his boyhood, which he was finally prevented from undertaking, much to his disappointment.

The third reveals the very tender side of his nature ; it is written to his College friend on the death of his father.

"DOVER, *May* 9, 1870.

" MY DEAR TOM,—You have probably concluded, either that I am dead or that your letter was destroyed by the postman. Neither is the case. I received your missive with joy, but not being like yourself, a gentleman at large, able to make what arrangements I like for continental trips, the great difficulty in the way was the moral necessity to visit my parents in the summer and yet find time for the Rhine—in other words, how could I screw a *month's* holiday out of a Methodist circuit. Seeing that our ministerial fathers never had a single *day's* holiday, the operation was not an easy one.

At last the Gordian knot is cut. I think I may manipulate the matter as follows:—I propose to come to Carmarthen in *July* for a fortnight, and then get another preacher's week, *i.e.* a fortnight in *September*, and accompany you to the Rhine. I am told that September is the correct time for such a voyage, it being too hot in midsummer. If this suggestion is agreeable, we may arrange details when I have the joy of seeing you at Carmarthen. I think, however, that it would be *most* desirable to get Cook's excursion tickets if possible. I believe, if you write to his London offices, he will supply you with a sort of catalogue of all the journeys (expenses, etc.), he intends to take during the current month. My father offers no opposition—nay, he positively urges me to go with you. You will let me know how this suggestion suits your wishes.

I hope you are all well at home. Please to remember me to your mother, etc. How are Arthur, Jem, and Llewellyn getting on? Relieve my solitude by a letter, and tell me your history since I saw you. I have not observed your name yet in the *Times'* list of marriages. You will be deeply grieved to hear that I have now developed into a ferocious and revolutionary republican. This, added to my temperance vagaries, should lead you to put up your shutters when I come to Carmarthen and go into the deepest mourning.[1] You ought to be at Dover. The Establishment flourishes here like a green bay-tree—three or four gigantic churches are filled from week to week. This is a very old and aristocratic place, but I apprehend the ballot will upset the Tory member at the next election. Our chapels are much better attended than they were, and there is a considerable increase in the Society. I am very happy here, especially that God has given me power in the Holy Ghost to bring many to salvation. We have five or six thousand troops here—infantry, engineers, and artillery. The fortifications are very extensive. As Wesleyan minister I have a special pass to all the barracks. Do you still teach in St. Peter's Sunday school? We have 600 Sunday-school children in Dover.—Yours sincerely,

"HUGH P. HUGHES.

"T. E. Brigstocke, Esq."

[1] His friend was a wine merchant.

"DOVER, *July* 26, 1872.

"MY DEAR TOM,—I am very much obliged to you for your carte. I think it is very good. Your moustache is becoming visible at last, and assuming an overwhelmingly aristocratic shape. I am coming home on Tuesday week. Please to arrange to give us a day for a row down to Llanstephan, as last year. I shall be at home for nearly three weeks, so that if you would fix a day when the tide is favourable you would do me a great service. I am very much afraid you will get married before this time next year, when, if you are still in single (un)blessedness, I shall expect you to fulfil your ancient promise to assist me over the difficulty. Katie was very pleased when I told her that you had promised years ago to be my best man, provided you didn't get settled yourself before. It is so hot that I can't sleep at night. Your friend, So-and-so, is still, in literal fulfilment of Mr. Gladstone's phrase, 'alive and kicking.' Please to gather up and arrange all the local gossip, in order that I may receive it in as compact and concentrated a form as possible when I come home. I speak at a great Temperance demonstration at Spurgeon's Tabernacle next week—you had therefore better get into another line of business as soon as possible.—Yours very affectionately,

"HUGH P. HUGHES.

"Mr. T. Brigstocke."

"DOVER, *September* 25, 1871.

"MY DEAR SHEERS,—I was very much shocked and grieved to receive the card which announced your father's death. I had only just been making up my mind to write to you. Little did I think the main topic of my letter would be one so sad. Of course when one loses a father, so certainly a Christian, we know very well that he has gone to a world of unspeakable happiness. . . . Nevertheless our natural human affection refuses to be so comforted, at least for a time. When I think of the agonies I should endure if my dear father was taken from me, I feel utterly unable to console you. Yet I know that time and religion will reconcile you to this deed of Providence. I can only hope that our blissful hope of immortality may stanch the wound, and that you and I may be led more and more to fix our affections and thoughts upon the things which are unseen and eternal.

"Oh that we may be able to say—

> 'My hands are but engaged below,
> My heart is still with thee.'

"I suppose you are married. I rarely see the Methodist papers, so that I only conclude it is so from the probabilities of the case. I feel daily, with increasing force, the mysterious sanctity and the transcendental consequences of marriage. I can scarcely avoid envying your happiness. May the rich blessing of God rest upon you and your wife. It is a matter for gratitude that your father was spared for you until marriage had created for you a new home. How rapidly time passes. I hear almost daily of little girls who played with me in nurseries, who are now married, and mothers! . . .

"Well, let us 'do with our might,' for the time is short.

"We are getting along quietly here. I am not without a good deal of visible and tangible fruit of my ministry. The new super charms us all. To-night there is a great teetotal meeting. Katie visited my home after Conference. . . . I am longing to hear from you.—Your sincere and sympathising friend,

"HUGH P. HUGHES."

CHAPTER VI

MARRIAGE AND EARLY MINISTERIAL WORK

ÆTAT 25–34.   1872–1881

"Thou seemest human and divine,
    The highest, holiest manhood, Thou :
    Our wills are ours, we know not how ;
Our wills are ours, to make them Thine.
    .   .   .   .   .   .

I held it truth, with him who sings
    To one clear harp in divers tones,
    That men may rise on stepping-stones
Of their dead selves to higher things."

In Memoriam, TENNYSON.

AT the end of my father's second year at Dover, my mother left school, and correspondence between them was resumed— of a very despairing nature on my father's side. She had attained her eighteenth year, and was altogether a very different person from the child of fifteen who had paced the lawn with my father at Richmond. More than ever her future was my father's. Even then she was unconsciously setting herself to him, and she did this, not by suppressing her own opinions, so as to drink in his, but by forming opinions of her own which should be the necessary complement to his. It was not surprising that the mind of one so early awakened to womanhood as hers should have already responded to the religious unrest of the times, and asked itself some of the old, old questions, all the tenser in those reacting against the limits of Puritan tradition and environment.

She writes :

"Two books that I read when I was about seventeen greatly influenced me. The first was Stopford Brooke's *Life of Robertson,* and the second a volume of essays by Channing. The first absolutely captivated my imagination. I entered with pure sympathy into that heroic life, with its struggle for wider and fuller conceptions of God and the Christ life, its beauty and its pathos.

"The teaching of Robertson, which has comforted and helped so many troubled and bewildered souls, came to me like a new message of hope and peace, for, girl though I was, and brought up in carefully guarded surroundings, my mind had begun to be troubled with many questionings, and the religious ideas of my youth, never doubted before, seemed suddenly to shake and tremble. It was the spirit of the age, which it was impossible for me to escape.

"Channing's essays made me realise Christ as never before. Hitherto He had been a historical character, who, by His death, procured for me immortality, and in whom I trusted for salvation; but now He became a living reality, a great object, aim and hope of all Christian life and endeavour. My girlish doubts and questionings very largely receded before the image and reality of Christ, conveyed to my mind by the teaching of Channing.

"I have owed much to other writers in later years; but when I reach the shores of the other world I should like, if permitted me, to find Robertson and Channing, and thank them for what they did for me on the threshold of life."

My father had a boundless admiration for Channing, independently of my mother, and was greatly influenced by him. The essays on self-culture, on the elevation of the labouring classes, on temperance, on education, on the present age, on the inimitableness of Christ's character, he specially appreciated. How he differed from him is shown in the lines which he wrote on the fly-leaf of a copy of his works, which he gave to my mother:—

"Channing unhappily did not see the glory of God in the face of Jesus Christ, and we must guard against the peculiarities of his Unitarian creed; but he touches, in language choicer and sublimer than mine, what I should like to say to you concerning war, civil, intellectual, and spiritual liberty, the equality of all men, real greatness, the true purpose of life, and the boundless capacities of the spirit of man.

"HUGH."

Robertson was more my mother's hero; my father giving
her a copy of his life, because he knew her admiration for him;
that was always a quaint way of his. He might deprecate
the influence of a teacher whom he did not altogether approve,
but that would not prevent him from presenting a copy of his
works with a suitable warning. " Poor So-and-so," he would say
in explanation, " is so infatuated with such-and-such a person
that I have given him a copy of his latest book." Then, after a
pause, " I told So-and-so the error, and bade him beware of it."

Robertson, as the exponent of the Gospel of Suffering,
could scarcely be understood, perhaps, by one whose gospel
was essentially that of service. They had the same generous
sympathies, but trod totally different paths. My father had
a happy life, Robertson an unhappy one. While my father
possessed sensibility to a greater degree than was supposed, he
did not possess it to such a degree as did the essentially artist
nature of Robertson.

Yet he knew the power and the attractiveness of Robertson
as he knew that of Kingsley—how they had it in them to
captivate generation after generation of impressionable youth.
Churches and systems may rise and fall, but, as long as
humanity remains, Robertson will have a message to some
men and women. It was just this attractiveness for which he
could not quite forgive them. Robertson had revolted from a
narrow form of Evangelicism, and Kingsley had drawn Dissent,
he considered, in an unfair and biassed manner. When one of
his children spoke to him one day of Robertson, he burst out,
" He had no conception of the truths of Evangelicism." Such
an epitome was unfair to Robertson, and damping to the child,
but he could not help himself. If the speaker had not been so
nearly related to him, he might have restrained his feelings;
but it was more than he could bear that a child of his should
be led to form false conceptions of Evangelicism, the religion
of the poor, which the whole literary world united to revile and
to misrepresent.

To Kingsley my father was never just, which was strange,
as certain among his own ministry regarded him as Kingsley's
prototype in Methodism. The intense artist nature in Robertson and the unhappiness of his life appealed to deep and
tender veins in my father. That, he supposed, accounted for

a vein of morbidity—a certain lack of vigour. His regret was that he had not been happier, and that someone had not been at hand to put Evangelicism and its truths in a faithful light. My mother also helped to make the man intelligible to him. But for Kingsley he had no such compunctions. His support of that " act of insane and diabolical folly," the Crimean War, his daring to go and welcome " that scoundrel Eyre " after his return from Jamaica, and last but not least his presentations of Dissent in *Alton Locke* were unforgivable, coupled with the fact that he was such a saintly man in many ways, and that both as writer and preacher he had such a hold on his generation. He said once that he thought Kingsley ought to reappear in some visible form and apologise to humanity for his presentation of Nonconformity in *Alton Locke*, erase it if need be, so that generations of the refined might not grow up with those vulgar and untrue conceptions of Nonconformity. As in most cases there was much reason in my father's unreason. He knew the immense power of art and literature and works of imagination generally, especially in an era of peace like the latter decades of the last century. He knew also that artists of all kinds had thrown a glamour over that portion of Christ's Church which was High Anglican or Roman, and that the Evangelistic portion, representing for the most part the poor and the humble, had been very badly and unfairly treated at their hands.

His attitude to what is called the Broad Church school was interesting. He certainly immensely sympathised with the social side of their teaching, and with the humanity that they infused into many theological conceptions, but this latter was a cautious sympathy. With his strategic instinct he was ever looking at the army of Christendom, wondering how certain new conceptions about things would affect its united action in a world of sin and misery. He intensely deprecated theological strife, at any rate among amateurs, who should, he thought, be better employed, reserving their energies in that direction for the other world, when they would presumably have more leisure and certainly added illumination. Theology as a portion of science belonged to the careful manipulation of the expert as much as any other portion of the organised field of knowledge. It was the spiritual side of the Broad Churchman that he did not find easy to understand. The Roman Catholic, High Anglican, or intense Evangelical he understood better. He was probably conscious also, that while Broad Churchmen had built excellent tabernacles for the few, they had not built them for mankind.

My mother, while still at school, had awakened to the social ideas and needs of the time. She writes:

" It was during my school-days that I first thought seriously of life and its responsibilities, and that ideas came to me which influenced my future life. I was at Laleham, that famous school that was ruled over so many years by the unique personality and genius of Miss Pipe. To her Christian influence, lofty ideals, and noble and wide-minded teaching, many Englishwomen to-day owe a debt that nothing can ever repay.

" Miss Ellen Thorneycroft Fowler, in her well-known novel, *The Farringdons*, has drawn a picture of Laleham (Foxhowe); but not even her able pen can fully describe what the word ' Laleham ' means to many women in all parts of the country.

" While at Laleham I met Miss Octavia Hill. She came, at Miss Pipe's request, to talk to the girls about the condition of the poor in London. At that time very little was known of the misery of the poor in our great cities. The great wave of social sympathy and reform which passed over this country like a flood-tide some years later was just then beginning to gather.

" Miss Octavia Hill, in the simple account that she gave us of her own work among the poor in the East End, opened my eyes to the misery of human life, and to the responsibility of the privileged and strong to help the weak and degraded. Two courses of lectures, also, that I attended at Laleham greatly influenced my mind at that time, and led me to think for myself. The first was a course on Constitutional History by Miss Alice Malleson, and the second a course on English Law by the late Professor Sheldon Amos. I can scarcely remember a word of what those two lecturers said, but the impulse which they gave to my thoughts remains with me to-day."

My mother's letters to my father are remarkable for independence of judgment and for the freedom with which she gives both her own criticisms and those of others. " Dr. Moulton," she says in one place, " said a good many nice things about you which I shall not repeat, but he is anxious about your interest in politics, and fears it may lead you astray." Her letters are also remarkable for constant reference to an opposition to their engagement, in which many of her well-wishers seemed to have shared. These painted her future in gloomy colours, saying she little knew what she was undertaking in becoming the wife of a Wesleyan minister, and that her life would be one of such penury, drudgery, and general effacement, that she ought to be deterred from entering upon it. To Mr. Hughes, they said, they had no personal objection, but marriages were not made in heaven but on solid earth, where incomes and attendant questions were an important consideration. But her parents were not long in deciding in her favour. Her father had always been sympathetic, and her mother's counsels, while serious and prudent, were from the altitude that was to be expected from such a character. " Mama has been talking to me very kindly and gravely this morning," she writes ; " but, as I say to her, I do not feel dismayed. I have good health, and can work hard, and am not made of porcelain, as they seem to think I am." The perturbation, indeed, distressed my father a good deal more than my mother, particularly when one who was interested in her welfare wrote him a letter in which wisdom and kindliness were subtly blended. In reply he quotes Schiller in justification of their engagement, and concludes by claiming the promises of " The Book," which insure full provision for those who seek first the kingdom of God, and cast their care upon Him.

At last, in a letter to the friend of his boyhood, he is able to announce his engagement as follows :—

" *Confidential.*

"DOVER, *April* 10, 1871.

" I hereby publish the engagement between Hugh Price Hughes, bachelor, of Dover, and Mary Katherine Howard (fourth daughter of Rev. A. Barrett), of London, spinster. If

7

any of you know cause, or just impediment, why these two
persons should not be joined together in holy matrimony (at a
distant date), ye are to declare it.   This is the first time of
mentioning it (outside the circle of the family).

"Witness my hand this tenth day of April.

"HUGH PRICE HUGHES.

"T. Brigstocke, Esq."

My mother lived quietly at home, taking painting lessons
and teaching in her sister's school, a book or letter from my
father being the events of her existence.   In the summer they
went down to Carmarthen, and created a delirium almost equal
to that which had arisen on the news of their first boy and
girl betrothal three years ago.   My grandfather, in particular,
had been indignant.   What the two were about he could not
divine, and as for the girl she ought to be nursing her doll.
His wife disagreed.   She believed, she said, that such an
engagement would be the best possible thing for Hugh, if the
girl was good and tidy, and fitted to make him a good wife.
Her daughters regarded the interloper with resentment, as
somebody who had for ever ousted them from their brother's
affection.   Their radiant advent brought peace, and my
mother's future mother-in-law was delighted with the "tidy-
ness," while my grandfather was chaffed incessantly as to the
doll which he should have provided for so youthful a visitor.
Their youth and lightness struck every observer.   "Fancy,"
my mother's sisters used to say, when they watched their
airy departure for a walk, "just fancy Hugh and Katie in
Methodism!"

George Eliot was the great figure in the literary world at
this time, and my father was devouring her novels.   To his
children, in after years, he would speak moodily, almost
slightingly, concerning her.   "She lost," he said, "in her later
books, the simple faith which she portrays in *Adam Bede*."
Here was one who so little understood Christianity as to give
up believing in it after reading some volumes of German
philosophy.   But what power and genius the woman had!
Why did not the avowed followers of Christ bring more genius
and power into His service?   For *Middlemarch* he had a
great admiration, its study of character, in particular, interest-

ing him, as did the study of Tito Melema in *Romola*. He thought he saw traces of that gentleman in some of his contemporaries.

While all this reading and correspondence was in progress, my father had moved to Brighton, and was continuing the activities that he had begun at Dover. The main lines of his later career were found in the Dover ministry, though they did not all work together harmoniously until he went to Oxford. At Brighton, for instance, the purely intellectual side, as opposed to the simple and evangelistic, was again in the ascendant, and his ministry there was, strangely enough, not distinguished for its conversions. My mother's newly awakened interest in literature may doubtless have incited him towards intellectualism at this period, and perhaps it partly lay in the nature of his environment, which was not so sympathetic as that of Dover. The Methodism of the sixties was there in its most acute form, and did not take kindly either to youth or to quickening. There were no Methodists like Alderman Rees and his set, and the older men, in whose hands lay the ordering of affairs, were quite unable to gauge him or to understand what he was after.

His temperance vagaries in particular, which he continued with unabated zeal, were distasteful to them. One of these called upon my mother after their marriage, and solemnly entreated her to use her influence with her husband so as to prevent him from ruining his career in this manner. Needless to say, my mother refused. He and the Dover Reformers, as they were called, came in style to the Dome, and were present at a very forcible lecture of his called " The Black Bottle Delusion." An Evangelical clergyman was in the chair, and Alderman Rees was sitting behind him. Altogether my father had a fine time. Glancing through the contents of his speech, as fully reported in the local press, the reader is struck with the consciousness of an opposition, on the part of the religious, that does not exist to-day. Apathy is in danger of taking its place. The religious world quoted the Bible " as if," said my father, " it was intended to teach us domestic details instead of great principles." The following sentiment was wrung from him :—" It was never designed that we should imitate the accidents of Christ's human existence, but that we should imitate the great Divine spirit which animated that peerless life, whose highest characteristic was self-sacrifice for the good of man. Oh! with what holy indignation must the cheeks of my blessed Saviour burn, when He hears infatuated men pleading His example in defence of selfish appetites, cherished at the cost of so much wretchedness and so much sin!"

Two months after his meeting in June, he was married. The following letter written to his old friend at Carmarthen may prove instructive:—

"29 DEVONSHIRE PLACE, *July* 22, 1873.

"MY DEAR TOM,—The day has been once more changed from the 19th to the 20th of August, which falls on a Wednesday. Your special duty will be to keep me from fainting in the extremity of my terror, and from over-sleeping myself on the awful morning, if I sleep at all.

.   .   .   .

"I daresay you will laugh at this unscientific and awkward description, but I am not at all up in tailoring phraseography, although I understand what I mean to say, which I hope you do.

.   .   .   .

"To-morrow month! after waiting six years. Can you understand my emotions? I hope God may make me a good husband. I am quite convinced that nothing but His blessing can make my marriage truly happy. Is there anything else that I could tell you? If you are going to the Continent, Carter's in Oxford Street (patronised by the members of the Alpine Club, but not dear) is the man for our outfits. All sorts of ingenious conveniences to save weight and space. I could almost literally put all the things I am going to take with me into my top-coat pocket, and yet there'll be no deficiency. It is certain I shall never need a porter. My knapsack will carry all, with room to spare. Please to remember me to your mother and to all at home; and, hoping to get a letter from you soon, I am, my dear Tom, your affectionate friend,

"HUGH.

"Mr. T. E. Brigstocke."

The family from Carmarthen assembled in force the day before the ceremony, my grandfather towering conspicuously above the other men of the company. " Are you all giants in Wales ? " somebody asked at the evening meal that day. The Welsh and their women laughed merrily. There was no restraining their glee and vivacity that evening. Here was matter for seeing and living indeed, and my father's mother must have been quite pale with intensity of emotion and observation.

The best man was sleepless, as it was his lot to propose the health of the bridesmaids. The bridegroom, who was always self-possessed in a crisis, reassured him. " Endow them, my dear sir, with every imaginable charm and virtue, both human and divine."

The wedding carriages the next day got confused with those of a funeral procession, and my mother's old nurse wrung her hands at the spectacle. But nothing could damp, I am told, the joyous bearing of my mother and father. It was customary in those days for brides to shed tears in public, and the bridegroom greatly deprecated the custom. But, as he said afterwards, he need not have feared.

At the wedding breakfast, the best man wondered at his friend, as he had often done ; the same self-possession that had characterised his first sermon at Carmarthen was his when he rose to return thanks for the good wishes of the company. He began with a quotation from Shakespeare : " I were but little happy, if I could say how much," and concluded with a reference to the Book of Genesis, in which he compared himself to Jacob, who had worked seven years for Rachel, with the difference that Jacob had the good fortune to serve all his time in her father's house—he had not. All agreed that so brilliant and felicitous a speech had seldom fallen from the lips of a bridegroom.

The honeymoon was spent in Switzerland, on returning from which my father wrote to his friend as follows :

" 29 DEVONSHIRE PLACE, *Sept.* 19, 1873.

" MY DEAR TOM,—I find that, soon after we left, a letter for you was delivered here—and it has been lying on my desk with many others awaiting my return. I now send it to the rightful owner.

" I have heard from home that you have had an excellent tour, in which I rejoice, and that you just missed us at Thun, for which I am very sorry.   I should much like to know what parts of Switzerland you saw.   You know our route, I think. Paris, Basle, Lucerne, Fluelen, Hospenthal (St. Gothard Pass), Grimsel, Meiringen, Brienz, back over the Scheideck to Grindelwald.   Thence over Wengern Alp to Lauterbrunnen, Interlaken, Thun, and thence by Kandersteg over the Gemmi to Leukerbad, Rhone Valley, Martigny, Col de Balme, Chamounix, Geneva, Lausanne, back to Geneva and Paris, *via* Macon and Dijon. . . . We enjoyed ourselves thoroughly, and were in excellent health.   I should much like to know what you did after we left on the 20th.   I want very much to thank you for all the kindness you showed me before and during the wedding.   It was a great happiness to me that you were my man, and I often think of the kind way in which you helped me at Brighton and London with my preparations.   I hope you will come and see us some day.   Katie wishes to be remembered to you.   Be good enough to remember me to your mother, and write soon to—Your affectionate friend,

" HUGH PRICE HUGHES.

" What did you think of the wedding and the wedding-party?

" Mr. T. E. Brigstocke."

To a College friend, who had lost his young wife, he also wrote a week or two later :

" 29 DEVONSHIRE PLACE, *Oct.* 6, 1873.

" MY DEAR SHEERS,—I was deeply distressed to receive the memorial card which you so kindly and thoughtfully sent me.   I have been in Switzerland for a month, and since my return I haven't seen a Methodist paper, so that I don't know what was the cause of your dear wife's death, though I might form a conjecture.   Under any circumstances it is an unutterably distressing event, and, amid all the hope and happiness of my own recent marriage, I feel the contrast between your present and your past most keenly.   My dear friend, what shall I say to you ?   Without doubt, your wife is in heaven—

happy for ever.   But your grief is too fresh for you to find much comfort yet in that delightful fact.   I am sure that our loving Father will overrule this sad event to your spiritual profit. I feel daily more and more confident in His love.   Not a sparrow falls without Him, still less does the wife of one of His servants die, except in obedience to those inscrutable but all-wise spiritual laws by which His love is working out the salvation and happiness of us all.   Remember all His dealings with you ; and must we not believe that He who withheld not His own dear Son—in the greatness of His love to us—will make all things work together for our real eternal good ?   In the abounding love of God must we find the key to this mystery.   That love and the gentle hand of time will bring you peace, and, in the meanwhile, rest assured, my dear friend, that Katie (who shares my sorrow for you) and I will not fail to offer our daily prayers to the God of all comfort and consolation on your behalf.   In deepest sympathy, your affectionate friend,

"HUGH PRICE HUGHES.

"Rev. G. E. Sheers."

A young lady with whom my father had previously made friends, the daughter of one of the circuit stewards, expressed herself much satisfied with my mother, about whose character she had been anxious.   "Mrs. Hughes has her own opinions and can stick up for them.   I am so glad."

This lady was very different from most of the young ladies he had met at Brighton.   She was intellectual, highly capable, and lively—a union of qualities that he much admired in the sex.   She was engrossed in Matthew Arnold at the time, and had many discussions with my father on this and kindred subjects.   She did not feel, to use her own expression, that Methodism could "hold" him ; a young man so intellectual, so devoted to culture, and to liturgical services, must ultimately find a harbour in the Established Church, she thought. She was far from desiring it, as she felt he could never do there what he could do in Nonconformity.   His *penchant* for a dignified and choral liturgical service developed at this period, to the uneasiness of a good many Methodists.   From the commencement of his ministry at Dover he had stickled for reverence and order in all things pertaining to church worship. The moving of chairs or the shuffling of feet at an inauspicious moment would provoke a rebuke. When sinners were smitten at his words the silence was so intense you could hear a pin drop. His tastes at this period were felt to be Anglican in various directions. Some of his hearers complained of over-intellectualism in his sermons.

Of course, Fidus Achates was not missing; he was early selected, and others like unto him. A Band of Hope was started, and fresh life and energy thrown into the Sunday school. A " Mutual Improvement Society, for the Religious, Moral, and Intellectual Improvement of its Members," also had a flourishing existence under my father's auspices. In the year 1873 the town was stirred by the formation of the new School Board, in which the best and most philanthropic of the day were deeply interested. My father threw himself heart and soul into the election, and was largely instrumental in returning a Progressive majority.

Yet this, added to some of his temperance vagaries, was the last straw on the backs of some of the congregation. A deputation reasoned with him on the error of his ways. Was not he their pastor? Was it not incumbent upon him to devote more time to his charge? They had welcomed him, under the impression that he would convert souls, not address public meetings. To their surprise, he partly agreed; he saw, he said, their standpoint. They were moved by his humility, and the friction between them was much softened.

The birth of a daughter, as their correspondence reveals, was the event of this portion of my parents' life. My father's anxiety concerning the treatment and manipulation of the new arrival was far greater than my mother's. He invented certain patent methods of soothing a baby's cries, and never failed to rush to the window to watch the infant down the length of the street as it was carried out for its daily airing.

The publication of Green's *Short History of the English People* about that time made the greatest impression upon him, which was followed in due course by a careful reading of the complete work. It was one of the books that entered into his life, of which he continually spoke. " For the first time," he said, " a true English history has been written, of the people, their inspirations, and their aims; not about a group of kings and the wars that they fought with one another."

Yet Brighton, for all the intellectual interests that he crowded into it, was essentially a spiritual crisis in his life rather than an intellectual. A Holiness Convention was held in the town a few months before he left, in the summer of 1875, under the presidency of Mr. and Mrs. Pearsall Smith, whose sessions deeply interested him. The idea that sin is not a necessary condition of existence, but that a special outpouring of God's Spirit can lead to holiness in act and thought, was something of a revelation to many of the religious of the day, who had come to regard man's proneness to sin as inevitable. My father recognised in the addresses, of which he was a rapt listener, a repetition of Wesley's doctrine of "entire sanctification," which Methodism had largely forgotten. Deeper still sank the declaration that "entire sanctification" was based on "entire surrender." He had surrendered himself years ago at his conversion, and was continually repeating the act, but what of a surrender deeper than he had hitherto dreamed? Certain ambitions still lurked at the back of his mind, which he was silently determined to cherish, outside any consultation of God's will concerning him. They had so crept into the stream of his existence that, until that moment perhaps, he had scarcely differentiated them from other channels. He would never have done anything unworthy to gratify these—he loved Christ too much for that; but none the less there would have been a friction in his inner history, which was henceforward to disappear. For Christ and humanity's sake he would have resigned himself to the will of God, but often with a sense that that will was somewhat hard, crushing and damping a man instead of furthering his interests and happiness.

Despite the revelation of God's love in Christ, he had not until then entered into the idea which so possessed him later— that God's will concerning a man must be altogether for his ultimate and deepest self-expression and happiness. As at the Mumbles there was a vision of the love of God, and a deeper and fuller one than was possible to a boy of thirteen, how-ever spiritually quickened. He consecrated not so much life, as manhood. For his ambitions were never sordid, nor was he tempted by what besets the ordinary man. They were of an intellectual description—the desire to attain the highest culture and knowledge, and to appeal by these to that portion of society which rejected the message of Christianity in its simplicity and fulness, because it had no comprehension of its essence, and was repelled by the narrow-mindedness and the lack of wide social sympathies on the part of its adherents ; in a word, he aspired to be, what is called, a great preacher, feeling the power to be such, and yet mysteriously stayed from exercising that power.

Moreover, his present close association with unpopular causes, however successful he might be in their propagation, was not quite what he had imagined for himself at College, when he bought his B.A. gown, because he thought it might be serviceable to him in the future. Men and women, despite the assumption of humanity at large that they are following their own depraved instincts, are not generally found in unpopular causes without an inner history or disturbance of some sort. It is not natural to a gifted man to oppose a consensus of the educated, the influential, and the rich, as my father did, in openly espousing the causes with which he became associated, to wit, direct Evangelical preaching, temperance, and measures connected with social purity. He was willing to acquiesce in God's will concerning him, but he could not altogether acquiesce in thinking it the position for which he was best suited and which he would most happily fill. He spoke little of his inmost feelings, but I can remember his referring two or three times to a period of painful inner history, which preceded his attendance at this Convention. The new conception that it gave him, put an end to this. In the deepest sense, " His will" became " our peace," and a peace that was joy, which nothing ever ruffled, however agitated the surface of his life, however keen the momentary periods of disappointment and depression. The immediate effect was to recall him more than ever to the original inspiration which had come to him at the Mumbles, while the deepening of what is called the purely spiritual side of character enabled him to adjust more truly the difficult balance between the purely ministerial and those great public duties which it was part of that ministry to emphatically recognise.

The first of the following letters is an extract from one sent him by the headmistress of an establishment for young ladies, when it was feared that he would have to leave Brighton previous to his marriage, as it was uncertain whether the circuit would be able to house a married minister. Finally, two-roomed lodgings were procured and a minimum salary. I quote from this letter, as it not only shows that he was not altogether neglecting the souls of his congregation, as his critics said he was, but as representing his influence over the members of girls' schools which was very marked in the period included in this chapter. Nor were these establishments always Methodist. At Oxford such a school included a variety of denominations. My father's influence even at this period was not limited to Fidus Achates and School Board elections.

"We have heard a rumour that you are thinking of leaving Brighton, and I cannot tell you with what regret and pain we heard the hint of such a loss. I am sure your preaching has aroused deep religious feeling in many of my girls, and caused several to pray who did not think before. You have sown good seed in many hearts, and I hope you will remain with us long enough to see a glorious harvest in Brighton. You will not think me rude in thus trying to influence your decision —will you? If you should bring your young wife here I should greatly like to be useful to her, and if we can in any way add to her happiness we will do our utmost. Am I taking a liberty in thus writing? I pray that God may give you a right judgment, and bless you in whatever sphere you may labour.—Believe me, my dear Sir, yours faithfully,

"JANE HEBB."

"1 PEMBURY RD., TOTTENHAM, N.,
"*Nov.* 5, 1875.

"MY DEAR SIR,—Reading your letter hurriedly, I did not notice that the request was for so near a date. Hence, being engaged in the city the whole of this week, until to-day, from 9 a.m. to 10 p.m., I deferred my reply until I could make it the opportunity of writing a letter to you as well. I am very sorry that I did not realise the necessity of replying at once, especially as I cannot possibly come. Indeed, one reason why I did not send you a postcard at once, was because I wished to explain at length why I could not come, and how *very* sorry I was. I am already engaged to attend a great Good Templar Meeting at the Memorial Hall—the U. K. Alliance Annual at Exeter Hall—and a great gathering of the Sunday School Union in the same place. Now I must not devote more than a certain amount of time to these extra subjects, or my own pastoral duties will be neglected. I have also some literary and newspaper work to do—I have editorial work in connection with two papers!—so that I cannot conscientiously neglect my own engagements here. I have a Bible class and a Young Men's Mutual Improvement and a Children's class, and also a Bible class in a Ladies' School— and these things must be attended to. You cannot realise how very painful it is to me to say no to you—but I will try to silver the pill. I am coming to Dover in March or April (D.V.), to preach sermons on behalf of the new schoolroom at Tower Hamlets. I will, if possible, remain over the Monday on that occasion ; and let us get up a tea meeting and public meeting at Margate, when I will try to throw a little temperance life into them. I deeply sympathise with you in your comparative temperance loneliness, but *God* is with you. Please to give my kind regards to Mrs. Atkins, your father and mother, and all other kind friends whom I hope to see in the spring.—Yours very sincerely,

"H. P. HUGHES."

"29 DEVONSHIRE PLACE, *Feb.* 23, 1874.

"MY DEAR SIR,—I am very much obliged to you and to my friends at Dover for the kind invitation you have conveyed to me, but am sorry to say that my time is so fully occupied that I can't come. In addition to my ordinary circuit duties I have now a large Bible class and a Mutual Improvement Society, both of which meet every week, and as a result I am very much tied at home. I hope that you will be able to get someone else who will serve you better than I could. It is the quarterly meeting of our District Lodge to-morrow. The D. D. has been away in the Mediterranean, and in his absence I (as D. V. T.) have been performing the duties of the District Deputy, and disagreeable and wearisome enough I found them. I should be very glad to hear from you at any time about the Temperance work in Dover, and yet more about the affairs of our Church there. Do send me some interesting gossip occasionally. When I was over in Tunbridge Wells I saw two of your sisters-in-law, as I have no doubt you have heard. We are slowly growing here—adding numbers from time to time—our increase in the year is about fifty. The congregations are much better. We are building a new chapel for about £1000 at one of our two country places. Please to remember me to Mrs. Atkins, your father and mother [here comes a string of names], and all the other kind people, whose names would occupy more paper than I have left, but in all of whom I feel the greatest interest, and for whom, with yourself and Mrs. Atkins, I pray the richest blessings of God.—Yours very affectionately,

"HUGH P. HUGHES.

"Mr. Atkins."

To the friend of his boyhood concerning his approaching marriage, he writes:—

"29 DEVONSHIRE PLACE, *April* 27, 1874.

"MY DEAR TOM,—I deeply regret that absence from home, etc., have prevented me from replying to your letter before. I must confess that a vague rumour of its contents had reached me before, so that I was not altogether unpre- pared. From the bottom of my heart do I wish you complete happiness. I am very glad that you are thoroughly in love, because that is a most honourable and most delightful state in which to be found, and I congratulate you that your sweet- heart is not so far from you as mine was, so that, instead of being limited to letters and visits at distant intervals, you can continually seek, what I pray may prove, continually increasing happiness in one another's society. I have the most perfect confidence that you will prove an affectionate and faithful husband. I think the step you have taken is in every respect an appropriate one. You have reached that time of life and that position in business when it is right for you to claim the loftiest privileges of a man. I am sure you will take this with a due and religious sense of the great and solemn obligations and responsibilities, human and divine, which it involves. I most earnestly pray that the blessing of God, without which everything is vain, may rest upon you and your future wife.

"I have only one other wish to express, and that is a selfish one. I hope you will get married in the autumn, when I shall be in Carmarthen. *Long engagements are a mistake. Take the advice of an old husband.*

"I can quite understand your elation at recent events. Are you never afraid that it is a little *too* good to last? Already one gentleman has been obliged to decline the Solicitor-Generalship for fear of losing his seat, and Fawcett is returned for Hackney. However, if the present Government set their faces against the deadly policy of truckling to the Papists, I shall be half-inclined to vote for them. The great battle of the future is Liberty of Conscience against the despotism of Rome. Read the admirable article in the Tory Quarterly for this month on the war between Germany and the Pope. If the Archbishop fails to carry his bill against the Ritualists, the Church will be disestablished *in twelve years*, as a helpless anomaly. If he carries it, you will probably be able to tyrannise over me a little longer. How dreadfully bigoted and malignant the Welsh clergy seem to be. See report of Archdeacon North's visitation in the *Welshman*. I hope you will write to me soon. It gives me so much happiness to receive letters from you.

"Please to remember me to your mother and all at home. Yours very affectionately,

"HUGH P. HUGHES.

"Katie wishes to be remembered to you.

"T. E. Brigstocke, Esq."

So his ministry at Tottenham in 1875 began with a struggle more determined than ever against the rust of stagnation. Lord Beaconsfield was making the Queen Empress of India, and the attention of the nation was largely turned to foreign affairs. But since 1869, and contemporary with the war in France, the most extraordinary series of domestic reforms[1] had been perpetrated under Mr. Gladstone's Administration, whose number and variety had the effect of taking men's breath away. Not so my father's. To live was good in those days; men as lofty in aim as they were able sat in that dauntless Administration, and he breathed the better for it. The reforms were for the masses of the people whom he loved.

The Mutual Improvement Society, with a valiant Fidus Achates as the secretary, discussed heaven and earth and the waters under the earth. Mr. Gladstone was a very mild reformer compared to these gentlemen. Another characteristic institution was a large Bible class for young men and young women, where a young man and a young woman were free to ask questions and to stand up and speak their minds.

"Was it not strange," asked Fidus Achates of my father, "that the Saviour should call His mother 'Woman'?" "Woman," came the answer, "is a far finer title than 'Lady.'" Then sharp and crisp, "Any cobbler calls his wife a lady!"

When many of his more elaborate sayings had sunk into oblivion, such as these haunted the memory of his listeners. Another phrase of his was "spiritual audacity," and another, "many Christians to-day are really guilty of practical atheism, because of their want of aggressiveness."

Someone accused him of lack of moderation after a sermon on temperance. "Moderate men, my dear sir, have been the curse of manhood."

Tottenham in those days was more a small country town than a suburb of London, and was not without certain old-world elements. In Bruce Grove were mansions with leafy gardens, one of which sheltered, so the legend runs, a member of Parliament!

Little did residents basking beneath its shadow guess at the invasion that was at hand. Certainly the tiny homesteads, betokening the artisan, had begun to appear in the land, but they were not as yet in full possession. Tottenham was one of the first to fall before the invaders of the suburbs now advancing on all sides, and creating a new order and new needs. My father discerned the creeping houses of the working people,

[1] The Irish Land Bill, the Formation of School Boards, the Abolition of Purchase in the Army, the Introduction of the Ballot, the Abolition of Tests, and a Bill in favour of Trades Unions.

and trimmed his lamp in readiness; for the gift of seeing ahead is as instinctive as the perception of beauty. So he set to work to prepare his congregation for the invaders, speaking much of the masses of the people and the necessity of providing for their needs, so that some of them wondered whether " the masses " had turned his brain, or what it was. A mission hall was opened in consequence.

As usual he hankered after a full liturgical service, and started a musical society. Both at the meetings of this society and at the choir practices he made a point of being present. Together with his insistence on the needs of the masses he insisted on reverence and a good musical service. One day he actually preached a sermon on the liturgy. Fresh heads were shaken.

A great event at this time was the war between Russia and Turkey and the Eastern problem. Mr. Gladstone was for driving the Turks out at all costs; Lord Beaconsfield was for resisting the advance of Russia, equally at all costs. Their two parties surged throughout the land, and my father surged with them. Throughout his life he was no believer in the Russian " bogey." He hated the Crimean War, and sided with Russia in the contemporary war against Turkey. In a debate of the Mutual Improvement Society he contended that Russia was justified in going to war with Turkey, which was surprising, as he was known to have an abhorrence of war in general. Once when Fidus Achates came to visit him in his study (where he was already collecting the little library of which he was so proud) he commented on the pictures which were of a very peaceful character. Then my father began speaking to him about war, in the passionate way that he could speak on such a subject. " I will not," he said, " have any picture that might familiarise my children with the horrors of war."

A second daughter had been born to him, and he was already anxious that certain elements in the usual upbringing of young children should be absent in that of his own.

Yet he never adopted the Quaker attitude, as has been stated earlier in this volume, and he maintained his usual position in a discussion on this subject in the Friends' meeting-house in the neighbourhood.

In the autumn of 1877 a wave of horror spread over the country at the report of the Bulgarian atrocities.   Certain political circles evinced incredulity, only to vanish before their definite corroboration.   Mr. Gladstone came out of retirement to lead what my father regarded as one of the greatest of his campaigns—that of rousing the moral indignation of the country against the oppression of the weak.

Nothing, perhaps, appealed to his Arthurian instincts like that; the trumpet-call which aroused men not on behalf of their own interests and passions, but on behalf of the interests of those who were powerless to defend their own interests.

One autumn day the great statesman was to address a meeting on Blackheath.   Fidus Achates, like many thousands of others that morning, started betimes and met his chief, somewhat to his surprise, at Liverpool Street station.   With their usual joyousness when in company, they made their way to the heath right up to the railings of the enclosure reserved for ticket-holders.   The ticket-holders were late in arriving, which provoked my father's comments.   It was then close on the time when Mr. Gladstone was to appear, yet the space was still half-empty.   The temptation was too strong for them, and he and Achates had squeezed under the railings and were sitting side by side with an aspect that was altogether irreproachable.   If persons could not arrive in time to hear the gospel on Blackheath or elsewhere, they must take the consequences, my father said.   Scarcely had the proceedings commenced when it began to rain.   " The Tories will say it is a judgment on us," he smiled ; then the sun came out.   About 30,000 people were present, the whole scene resembling a vast sea of black coats.   No one present ever forgot it.   The striking feature of Mr. Gladstone's oratory was its deliberation, and my father commented on this afterwards to Fidus Achates in the train.   As usual, he was busy noting and drawing conclusions. Behind all the seeming wildness of his talk was something curiously cool and level.   " The fault of most young men," he continued, " is to speak too quickly.   You do now."

At Tottenham, more than at any other time, my parents felt the pinch of straitened means.   " It did not, however," says my mother, " interfere with our happiness, and in after years we were glad of the experience.   It taught us sympathy

8

with a side of life which we could not well otherwise have gained."

A young lady who was staying with my mother, and who, like many others, was devoted to her, and anxious to be of service, was quite terrified at my father. A more impulsive, untamed creature, she felt she had never met. He used to instruct her as to how to hold the baby, and although she profoundly disagreed, she was too frightened to say him nay. Yet the thought that she regarded him as anything but an amicable and anxious father never entered his head. He did not know how his Celtic intensity could alarm certain natures. When my mother pointed this out to him, his repentance partook of the vehemence that occasioned the offence. This trait is mentioned because it so entirely disappeared in after years, when both visitors and servants were struck with his gentleness and consideration. More than ever, at this period, he contributed to the amusement of his mother-in-law, who was living close by at Stamford Hill. They would breakfast there sometimes, with the result that my grandmother was severely perturbed before the resumption of the day's duties.

Dulwich, where he next " travelled," was considered a very superior appointment. There were two other ministers in residence, and my father was third minister in charge of a handsome new chapel that had lately been erected in the Barry Road, where a good deal of effective work had already been accomplished. His little house was only a few yards away from it, and he could thus exercise a constant surveillance. As usual, he struck everybody as extraordinarily energetic, though, to the biographer, Dulwich appears to have been a comparatively quiet circuit, with nothing stirring. The congregation consisted for the most part of city men and their families living more or less peacefully away from the great city. In the evenings especially and on Sundays, they thought it due to them to be left in peace, but my father did not see it in that light. In addition to the large Bible class, similar to the one taken at Tottenham, he started a literary society, and set them all reading and thinking and essay-writing. He insisted also on their attending the prayer-meeting. What help could they expect in this life or the next, if they could not take the trouble to go to church and ask for it?

"We want rest, Mr. Hughes," said one of the congregation to him one day. "Rest! rest!" he exclaimed; "rest, my dear sir, when you get to heaven." But with all these tart replies, which sometimes rebuffed a man at the start, it came to be felt that a kindlier and more buoyant soul never breathed. A perfect passion and tenderness of sympathy would overtake him at times, as, for instance, when a member of his congregation lost a child, or when some pathetic and stirring incident was repeated to him. At last he was successful in introducing the full choral liturgical service for which he pined. The congregation at Barry Road was already a very various one, and he added to its variety. Excessive ritualism in the neighbouring churches drove Anglican Churchmen to a service which resembled their own, and men of all creeds were attracted by his preaching, which became a special feature of his ministry at this time.

Fidus Achates thought his later preaching in London was not so careful or full of thought as his sermons at Barry Road. The explanation was simple. My father was studying for his M.A. degree at that time, and was entering more deeply into the intellectual life than his labours often permitted. A minister who had been a fellow-student at Richmond had just taken his M.A. degree while performing full pastoral duties, and my father thought he might do the same. For some time he had been meditating doing so, and this finally decided him.[1] But the secret was carefully kept till the superintendent gave out the new title with marked emphasis on the following Sunday. He took his degree in philosophy principally, and unless he had been such a constant and wide reader he could not have succeeded in his double rôle at this time. At Tottenham, he had been reading Sir William Hamilton, so it was not unlikely that underlying all his intellectual endeavours was the hope of putting them to some academic use at a later period. He had also been toiling at German, in order to read Goethe and Schiller, whose works he possessed, and with whom

---

[1] Thus he astonished his congregation on one occasion by delivering a sermon on money, so that the business men present began to think that he knew more about that commodity than they did. Hugely he must have chuckled, for he was straight from his books on economics. Once more a simple Methodist preacher was letting light into the "dark minds of the learned!"

he was very fairly familiar. Goethe, however, was no favourite of his. He would have agreed with Lord Tennyson that he lacked the "divine intensity." No greatness of his mind or art, no interpretation of Carlyle, could atone for what he considered his monstrous selfishness; but he quoted him with much impressiveness in the pulpit none the less.

In seeming antithesis to the student side of his nature was the mission that he held at Barry Road Chapel early during his residence. The neighbourhood was divided into between thirty and forty districts, each of which was entrusted to two helpers, who visited every house and asked the occupants to attend. Walls and public places were placarded with announcements of the same. The result was astonishing. In the general canvass not a person was omitted. Comfortable city gentlemen found themselves asking clergymen of the Anglican Church and proprietors of public-houses to attend a special mission. Their excuse, they felt, lay in the fact that the mission was special. As it had been at Dover, so it was at Dulwich and elsewhere—the silent depths of a man were stirred; there was no appeal to emotionalism. A speaker unrivalled in influencing others appealed to what was best and wisest in a man. It was another Mr. Gladstone appealing to the heroic in manhood and womanhood. The divine touch was its commonsense. Why not live the best life, the life of love for Christ and men, since it was there to live? The love of man that consumed the preacher gradually dawned upon them; his feeling for the poor, the weak, the oppressed, and his total abstinence for their sakes, which had at first offended some of them. His politics never appeared in the pulpit, but in those days of fervent Gladstonianism some were inclined to think the better of him and to rejoice in the sayings that were repeated from lip to lip.

He had a faculty of changing and enlarging the ideals of men and women; they could not be the same afterwards. Most notably was this the case in some who winced under what he said, and who strove not a little against his conclusions, which were generally at variance with what prudence and comfort dictated. His power as a revivalist, to use the old-fashioned Methodist term, made him in request during these early years as a special preacher. In Cornwall he stirred those outward demonstrations of religious feeling for which the Methodists in that county are famed; but this tendency he instantly restrained. In out-of-the-way mission halls in the suburbs his very presence, as a man lately related, helped to solve doubts and questionings. As another wrote at his passing, "He was so real." It was his purity of motive and his dead earnestness that laid hold of men. As other men pursued money and pleasure, he seemed intent on pursuing their best self, on making it live and breathe in spite of themselves. It was not that his arguments were always convincing, but he was. It was the unuttered element that was the great element in his sermons. He knew that it was, and for that reason he restrained his utterance when he preached to people. For this reason the effect he produced was often indescribable. "What was it that you heard?" a listener of his was once asked. "I cannot say exactly," was the answer; and then, after a pause, "The wind bloweth where it listeth, and no one knoweth whither it goeth and whence it cometh."

He had a strong conviction at this period, as later, that if underlying moral convictions are followed, doubts, intellectual or otherwise, will solve themselves. The world of thought in which he found himself was one of chaos, men and systems changing places and floating hither and thither, many of them, like the lost souls in one of those confused regions which Dante describes. Doubts and questionings about much that he considered non-essential could not, he knew, be settled in a day— even in many days. By all means let men follow the questionings of thinkers and men of science, for the mind and its hunger, as Shakespeare said, was the most Godlike of these faculties; but first of all let men follow Christ and then fall to wondering about themselves and Him. Otherwise their wonderings would be unprofitable, leading from darkness into darkness. With this thought in view, he preached a sermon on the words, "What has that to do with thou Me."

To do right, he considered, was half-way t Thus with persons whom he felt instinctively moral and spiritual ebb, he never engaged in c doubts of certain orders of mind, he did not

period of his life to understand; but he embraced a great deal
of humanity for one single lifetime, and the person who was
brought into direct personal contact with him, and who did not
live and think the deeper for it, was an altogether exceptional
person.   He was always affecting people in some way or
another, and they had no need to agree with him, or with what
he said, in order to be thus affected.

The incessant twinkling of his blue eyes was long
remembered by certain members of his congregation.   They
twinkled specially at a meeting held for some purpose or
other in the chapel, which was more than usually " various "
in character.   " Why," he exclaimed, " I believe the whole
Church of Christ is represented here this evening.   There is
So-and-so, and So-and-so, and So-and-so "—then in a burst of
joyousness—" there is even a Roman Catholic in our midst."
The *jeu d'esprit*, the word of banter, was always on his lip, and
for this youth loved him.   At a meeting held to raise money
for the new schools in connection with the church, he appealed
to men's purses as he did to their consciences.   A sure sign of
loving Christ was to give to His work, and city gentlemen of
moderate means opened their purses and gave, and were the
happier for giving.   Yet he was amusing them all the time
as if it was a species of entertainment, and he the principal
entertainer.   " Mr. Mason, I see, sends one guinea.   We shall
soon have the masonry up"; and so on, with sly allusions,
sometimes comic, often graceful, and always unrestrainedly
genial.

So his capacity to obtain money from audiences soon
began to be spread abroad in Methodism, together with his
evangelistic powers.

In the exposition of the organisation of Wesleyan
Methodism he took a peculiar delight, but not all shared
his feelings in the matter.   One man in particular of unusual
intellectual capacity was so annoyed with him on some such
point, that he found it difficult to see any good in him.   But
these were quite in the minority.   The rest, to quote their
own expression, " he drove into the kingdom of heaven," and
by their manner of referring to it, they seem to have enjoyed
the driving.   The strong driver of his flock was always a very
contradictory person.   To his daughters he was an inordinately

merry being, always slapping his legs, and exclaiming
" Jehoshaphat," an expression which seemed to epitomise his
wonder at the universe and the strange fellows who walked it.
He comforted them in grief, and recited to them a poem of his
own composing which never failed to dry their tears :

> There was a little man and his name was Uncle Ned,
> And he stood on his head,
> Till he was dead,
> Long, long ago, ho-ho—ago—ho-ho—long, long ago—ho-ho.

The triumph of that last long ago, ho-ho, was something quite
indescribable save to those who witnessed it.   It proclaimed the
essential sunshine of things, and the mists and terrors that for
some strange reason darkened its surface, fled at the sound.
In severe crises he would be at hand, shouting or beating a
tune with the fire-irons as their peculiar susceptibilities might
demand.   He was careful to teach them Queen's English, and
greatly distressed at an imperfect pronunciation of the letter
" r."   In solemn tones he abjured them to renounce the title
papa for that of father.   Papa was " horrible," " foolish," " fitted
for babies " ; father was beautiful, fitted for good and intelligent
children.   But always the old title slipped out ; they took a
long time to cure themselves.

Early and dimly their minds awakened to the importance
of two personages, the Government and Mr. Gladstone.
"Who is Mr. Gladstone, father?"   "A man who says his
prayers every morning," was the prompt reply.

About the Government they could not feel equally clear.
He sat at a desk, they imagined, and was a tall, grave
gentleman about whom there was a great deal of agitation.
Gradually things grew clearer ; to be a Conservative was not
desirable.   They insisted to their mother that they were
Liberals.   Their mother thought that it was not incumbent
upon them as yet to join that party, but her words fell on
idle ears.   When their brother was born, joy was mixed with
solemnity.   " Is he," they inquired, " a Liberal or a Conservative?" and they were assured that his sympathies were
undoubtedly Liberal.   Dr. Moulton, in accordance with a
long understanding, came to christen their eldest brother,
who was given the name of Arnold, after Dr. Arnold of Rugby,
for whom my father had a great veneration.   Jowett, he would

say, was the greatest master of a college that the century had produced, and Arnold the greatest schoolmaster.

The maids and others who from time to time stayed in the house had the same impression of inordinate merriment. When the master of the house came back with the news that he had taken his degree, the mistress set all the bells aringing. The daughters thought he had been running a race of some kind, and had come in second at the goal. Someone, he said, had been ahead of him. Still, it was a glorious victory, and the story of Uncle Ned and his unseemly end suggested depths of triumph hitherto unimagined. To the composer, as they understood afterwards, depths were also opened. The progress begun might be continued ; he would take a degree in science. He had ever a hankering after that magic realm then and afterwards. He would no longer be the outsider that he felt himself to be. Clear as day the pathway of the future stretched before him, with a vista of white light shed by the sciences. He sketched it both to himself and to those around him. His wife's brother shook his head. " Hugh, you are a preacher of the gospel. That is your first duty. You cannot do everything." With the meekness that he always displayed where he could be got to listen to any one, he debated within and appeared to be lost in prayer. The pathway of the future stretched before him once again, but this time there was no white light of the sciences, only his Saviour and those multitudes over whom He had wept. The old command first heard by the lake rang in his ears, " Feed My lambs." His mind was made up.

The year 1880 was famous for the General Election and Mr. Gladstone's return to power. Members of Parliament resought the suffrages of their electors. Mr. Hughes and his daughters, and other Gladstonians, entertained alternately high hopes and cold fears as to the result, so that the house throbbed with the fortunes of the country. The return of a Liberal meant the recital of the story of Uncle Ned, and fresh strains of exaltation at the prehistoric date of his demise. The return of a Conservative meant silence and gloom, and sometimes tears. One night the political daughters lay sleepless in their beds waiting for the Dulwich returns. At last the well-known voice was heard proclaiming the result, heroical-wise, but downcast. A minute had not elapsed before the house was filled with lamentation. The Conservative member was returned for Dulwich, and the political daughters could not be comforted.

Every summer the family went to Carmarthen by the special wish and provision of the thoughtful grandparents. As they neared the Welsh border my father would inform his daughters that he was able to breathe. They did not need any explanation of this statement. A good Liberal sat for every division. While the vehement nature of my father's politics commended him to many of the younger spirits, it did the very reverse with many of their elders. One old lady, to whom some sayings of his were repeated, said after deliberation, " It would have been good for that young man if he had never been born ! "

In the wider public life of Methodism his method of expressing his political sentiments did not stand him in good stead, and indeed formed erroneous impressions, which it took years to dissipate.

Even those who did not resent his politics, wondered at their intensity. Most men belong to a political party, because their father did before them, and because they think it the best. He favoured the Liberal party for neither of these reasons, but because its great objects at that time had come to be a portion of his religion. His vehemence came in great measure from his struggle with his own nature, so that it often reminded of a swimmer clinging to a lifebuoy.

The hero of his early youth was not Gladstone but Disraeli.

At Carmarthen the arguments with his father were resumed, who tried to temper what he considered his rashness. " My dear Hugh," he used to say, " there is one book you really must read, and that is the book called *Mind your own Business.*" His son thought, on the contrary, that everything was everybody's business.

At the close of his first year's ministry at Tottenham, my father suffered from symptoms of overwork. My ever-watchful grandfather insisted on providing him with another holiday in Switzerland, which he took in company with his brother-in-law, Dr. Howard Barrett.

The following extracts are from letters to my mother :—

"HOTEL DE MONT CERVIN, ZERMATT,
"*August* 20, 1876.

". . . Of course, the first notable event was the ascent of the Breithorn on Tuesday. The Greens, ourselves, and guides —eleven in all—started from the Riffel at four—reached the top at noon, and were back, not very exhausted—at 6.15. As far as the Theodule Pass it was comparatively level walking, but after that we had a series of steep slopes, and near the top a short ice slope, over which we had to cut steps. It was, however, both safe and easy. I often thought and spoke of you, and of my strong desire to take you to the top some day. You could do it quite well. A snowstorm broke over us on the way up, and we were all covered with white—in August. At the top a cold mist received us, and we saw nothing but one another. For all that it was a very pleasant and exhilarating excursion. The mountains which we ought to have seen I had other opportunities of beholding, I believe to equal advantage. Descending, we had some food in the Theodule Cabane, the highest building in Europe.

"Wednesday (16) we rested, and formed the acquaintance of several interesting clergymen. I was discovered by a Brighton clergyman—St. Mary's—where Mr. Beney goes, and he made me known to the rest. We had a kind of Church Congress in the Gorner Grat—an extreme Ritualist, a Broad Churchman, an Evangelical, and myself talked theology and became great friends. Howard smoked and watched the scene from afar. We became quite friendly with the vicar of Stanmoor, who exchanged cards with us, and asked us to call upon him when we returned. Stopford Brooke and Dr. Parker are here, a pleasant mixture, also Mr. Sulivan of Brighton. On Thursday (17) we walked along the Gorner Glacier (crossing chamois tracks), as far as the Cima de Gazi, and then down the Weissthor. If we had known the nature of that precipitous descent before, I do not think we should have attempted it. It goes almost sheer down for thousands of feet. At one particularly awkward corner, both Howard and I stuck fast."

Another is as follows :—

" I should add that Johann was close behind me, and that if I had slipped he would have pulled me up with the rope. However, it was not needed.   I must again impress upon you that these slopes are so situated that, whatever performance I had attempted, I could not possibly have come to any harm. You may be quite sure that nothing will ever induce me to run the slightest risk.

" We then crossed the pass ridge and descended over snow slopes for hours.   We were altogether nine hours on the snow. We ultimately reached Engelberg at 7.10.   The guide-books greatly understate the distance.   Notwithstanding puggaree (is that how you spell it ?), dark glasses and veil, I was a good deal burnt.

" The next day, as I have already informed you, we rested and went up to the Trübsee Châlet in the evening.   Yesterday morning we set out at 1.45 in a beautiful moonlight, which spared the necessity for lanterns.   We reached the halting-place—at the foot of the rocks, a snug little ledge—at 3.30. Here we took our second breakfast.   I should say that we had been fortunate to secure as our leading guide, Eugene Hess, the principal one at Engelberg, a famous guide.   At the glacier, having climbed the rocks, we were roped—first Hess, then Howard, then I, then Johann.   We reached the top easily at 5.45 ; the sun rising as we were crossing the glacier, we instantly began our third breakfast—cold chicken, hard-boiled eggs, bread, butter, and cheese, beer and wine.   The view was *perfect*.   Last year Howard had a cloudless day, but this year it was finer than that, similar to the day you and I had on Pilatus, but finer because so much nearer the great snow mountains and so much higher (I might say that Uri Roth-stock is 9800 feet and Titlis 10,400 feet high).   We shall not see, and we cannot see, a finer scene than presented itself to our astonished eyes yesterday morning at half-past five, when you were probably fast asleep.   The descent, the passage of the famous Joch Pass, and the lovely valley walk to Innhof was very pleasant.   To-day, of course, we are resting.   This is a Protestant canton, and I am going to attend the service in the parish church.   They have none in the morning.   Howard

and I are constantly regretting you are not with us. Three
ladies reached the top of Titlis while we were there, but not in
the style you would accomplish it. You will send this letter
on to Carmarthen. To-morrow we go to the Grimsel, and
then after a day's rest to the Eggischorn. . . ."

The following was written from Cornwall to my mother,
who was spending a few days with her sister at Bedford :—

"TRURO, *Tuesday*.

". . . You can have no idea how difficult I find it is to
get a quiet moment to write to you. People are invited
to meet me, and I have a journey every day and a meeting
every night, and then the necessity of correcting the proofs for
the next Protest now due, which took me four hours yesterday.
In ten minutes I start for St. Columb. We had a glorious
time here on Sunday night, marvellous prayer-meeting and
many penitents, so much so that we were obliged to hold a
prayer-meeting last night after the home missionary meeting,
when there were more penitents. We had a special prayer-
meeting at 7.30 a.m. this morning, and there is to be a service
every evening this week ; it seems as if a very genuine revival
had begun. A number of 'respectable' people have found
peace, those who do not usually take part in such meetings.
Last night I took supper with Mr. Lake (whose daughter is
at Clapton). To-morrow, Bodmin ; Thursday, St. Austell ;
Friday, Taunton ; and Saturday, home. The great success
of my Sunday evening service has encouraged me much. The
finest chapel I have yet seen in Cornwall. It *seats* sixteen
hundred. We have nothing to fear from the new 'Bishop of
Truro,' if God be with us thus.

"You will see the political news in the *Spectator*. I have
not seen a London newspaper since I left home ! . . ."

"1 PEMBURY ROAD, TOTTENHAM, N.,
"*Feb.* 18, 1877.

". . . I reached Tottenham at 4 p.m. yesterday. At 4.30
Mr. Riggall called. To explain his visit I must go back to
last Sunday. Then, as I have informed you, we had a very
good time—a revival began in Truro. Mr. Riggall called to
say that the President had received two telegrams and a letter

informing him that in connection with my visit a great revival had begun, and imploring him to send me, or some suitable person, to conduct the services. The President would undertake to have all my appointments supplied. I consulted with Mr. Mather, and felt with him that this was indeed the call of God, and I return by the Flying Dutchman to-morrow morning to Truro, and I expect to be home to-morrow week.

> "Address,
> c/o Rev. John Knowles,
> 4 Agar Road,
> Truro.

"This sudden and unexpected work has left me scarcely time to turn. I have been obliged to write many letters to-day, and I am now about to go to Clapham to tea, *en route* for Stoke Newington. Agnes came last night about six, and I could have cried when I saw her, I had felt so lonely. 'Flesh and blood' resist going to Cornwall again at once, especially as I shall not see you for a week—but the will of the Lord be done."

The three following letters were written to my mother, who was staying in the Isle of Wight with her old friends, Mr., Mrs., and Miss Gardner, after her recovery from an attack of typhoid fever:—

> "11 CLARENDON VILLAS, BARRY ROAD,
> "PECKHAM RYE, S.E., *Sept.* 18, 1878.

". . . Y——'s case came on at two yesterday. I helped to collect the witnesses, and got quite known by the policemen about the corridors. The barrister who examined me thought I was an Anglican divine—that was my hat, I guess. I am delighted to say that ——, instead of getting five or ten years, got only nine months ; everybody in court seemed amazed at the lightness of the verdict. I am so thankful, for his poor wife's sake. At the district meeting yesterday—according to rule—two laymen and the Chairman, Dr. Rigg, were deputed to visit my house and report if they had made proper provision for my comfort. Until that is done, the Connexional grant is not paid. I am going to write to know what time will suit them. Your letter of this morning is as delightful as its predecessors.

My letter yesterday was addressed to the Post Office, Ventnor, because I did not know your other address when it was written. What a delightful drive you had! Mind that you don't get wet with rain or spray. Certainly, if you are getting wicked, it must be *you*, and no longer the gentle invalid under my influence. Would it not be better for me to forward letters than for you to have the trouble of writing to Clapton? *I wish you would write to my mother at Carmarthen, if it is only once.* She inquires very anxiously about you. If you have not time to write to her and to me, write to her next time. . . ."

" 11 CLARENDON VILLAS, BARRY ROAD,
"PECKHAM RYE, S.E., *Sept.* 23, 1878.

". . . Your letter each morning fills the day with sunshine. I had almost said that it is a pleasant thing for you to be away, so refreshing and welcome are your letters. I am probably too fidgety about the bathing; however, Howard's post-card will settle the matter. I can scarcely believe that you walked six miles on Saturday. In the eye of my imagination you are still a drooping invalid. . . . Please now to lay up such a store of health as will last you until we change circuits. Such an opportunity won't come every year. . . .

". . . I made my first round of visits on Saturday, calling on the people in this road. . . . I believe there will be some nice people among them. I am going to see a lot of people this week. I call systematically from house to house like a postman. I have a list of their names and addresses. I had a good time yesterday. Last night, the largest prayer-meeting they have known—and at least twenty persons stood up during silent prayer, as a sign of their willingness to become true disciples of Christ. The quarterly meeting is this afternoon. All is well. . . ."

"*Sept.* 20, 1878.

". . . Let me know the day the Gardners return home, that I may have the joy of definite expectation. I scarcely expected you next week, but the time flies. Yesterday afternoon, I saw some more people, not in so respectable a quarter this time. To-day I am going to have another turn, and then to hear Gough to-night. . . . The two second circuit stewards have just been here by the direction of the District Meeting to inspect the house. The servants have put bedrooms and all in apple-pie order, so they went away duly impressed with our splendour. Our card plate is full; there will be lots of people for you to call on when you return. . . . You must especially encourage me to visit the people. We must, with God's help, make that a strong point in this circuit. . . ."

The August before quitting Dulwich, he paid his third visit to Switzerland. Mr. Horace Marshall, the publisher, was a leading member of the congregation, and always showed my father, both then and afterwards, the greatest courtesy and kindness. At this particular time, he wished his son (now Sir Horace Marshall) to have a holiday in Switzerland, and was further desirous that my father, who was showing signs of unusual fatigue after his labours, ministerial and scholastic, should be his travelling companion. Extracts from the following letters, written during his journey, will prove of interest:—

"HOTEL BEAU RIVAGE, OUCHY,
"*Tuesday, Aug. 9.*

". . . We started all right from Holborn Viaduct; had a pleasant run to Dover. The sea was very calm. I remained on deck all the time. . . . Found Mr. Gibson on board returning to Paris. Got good places in the Paris train, after a good rest and dinner at Calais. Got to Paris in a very slow coach to the Gare de Lyon, a long way off. Had a very hurried dinner, and then found every seat taken! However, some members of the Alpine Club had mercy on us and found us seats in their carriage. . . . We arrived at Lausanne punctually at 7.35. Horace is now writing home. At noon we take the late steamer to Bouveret, then to Vernayaz by train, where we spend the night. To-morrow we take train to Sion, then drive to Evolena, then walk to Arolla, where we hope to meet Howard. The Swiss air seems to be already doing me good. . . . Give much love to the children. I want already to be home. I cannot give you dates and places to write to until I see Howard. The weather has been very fine hitherto, but it is a little too hazy and cloudy now to see Mont Blanc. I well remember when you and I were here and saw your cousin. Mind to get

to-day's (Tuesday's) *Recorder*. It will contain a speech of mine.
Also get this week's *Watchman, Methodist,* and (Friday)
Recorder, and send them all to me with the *Spectator*—then I
shall know a little of what is going on. . . ."

"HOTEL ROYALE, COURMAYEUR,
"*Sunday, Aug.* 1, 1881.

". . . I was so very happy to receive a letter from you
yesterday. As you will have learned from my letters, I have
not received your first letter or the *Spectator*. They will be
forwarded from Chamonix. I was delighted to hear of your
prolonged stay at Stonard House. You will probably find
several of my letters when you go home. I have been addressing them to Barry Road, under the impression you were there.
I hope both you and the Colwyn Bay party are having finer
weather. I am very glad you thought of inviting Mrs. ——
for a day to Stonard House, and am very thankful to learn
that your house-cleaning difficulties have been overcome. I
think you have taken the right course with respect to Mr.
——'s letter. We cannot leave before the Wednesday. I
suppose it is all right about Dixon's van. Have you heard
from him? Perhaps I had better drop him a line when I
return. . . . Poor Gwendolen! I hope the doll is re-headed
successfully. . . . You do not seem to have received all my
letters. I have written nearly every day. I have written to
Carmarthen once, and will do so again, if I can find time; but
our movements henceforth will be rapid. Yesterday we
lounged about, and I read *The First Violin* through, not a bad
bit of work for one day. Unfortunately, it is very wet to-day,
and that endangers my plans. We had arranged to walk up
this evening to a little inn, high up the mountain-side, so as to
break the long journey to-morrow over the Col de Géant. It
is now 3 p.m., and still raining. If the rain does not stop
within two hours, we must abandon that plan and start at two
o'clock in the morning. If it should still be wet to-morrow
morning I scarcely know what to do, because I have already
telegraphed for rooms at Chamonix, and secured places in the
diligence from Chamonix to Geneva. Courmayeur is such an
out-of-the-way place that it is very difficult to get from here to
Chamonix, unless the weather permit us to take a glacier path.

I will keep this letter open until the state of the weather finally determines whether I can leave this evening or not.   I think you will like Oxford.   I have given your love to Howard and Miss Howard.   Tell [mentioning his children] that I am so very glad that they are very good.   It fills me with happiness. I am longing very much to have them on my knee again. Oh, I am so glad I shall be with you in less than a week. . . . We have finally decided to start to-night, the weather has improved a little.   Of course we shall return here if the weather is not fine to-morrow morning."

CHAPTER VII

OXFORD. ÆTAT 34–37. 1881–1884

"And these things I see suddenly, what mean they?
As if some miracle, some hand divine unseal'd my eyes,
Shadowy vast shapes smile through the air and sky,
And on the distant waves sail countless ships,
And anthems in new tongues I hear saluting me."

Prayer of Columbus, WHITMAN.

THE city with the dreaming spires was next to claim my
father's ministrations.   He was invited, moreover, as first
minister—superintendent, as the Methodists express it—and
for this office he was regarded as full young in a Church where
age is the principal certificate to merit.   It marked a distinct
stage in his life, much as Dover had done.   In particular, he
had been led to regard not only the state of society at large,
but the equipment and position of his own Church in that
society.   How far could Methodism, not Wesleyan Methodism
in particular, but the whole organisation that owed its birth to
the great religious revival at the close of the eighteenth century,
meet the new conditions of the democratic era into which the
English-speaking peoples were passing ?   More accurately than
any other member of his Church perhaps, he gauged that era,
the enormous changes in thought and life which it must bring.
The seething amid which he lived was not the end of all
things, but the birth of new.   Anxiously scanning the troubled
horizon, he knew for a certainty what the day must bring
forth.   So that to many he must have appeared a possessed
being, teaching as Socrates did to the youth, that the better
things were the worser, and *vice versâ*.   He and his works
generally suggested curiosity and ridicule to the sane person
who had not felt the magic of his influence.   " What was it

all about, to what end, to what purpose?" but he knew, and that was the main thing, just as Elijah knew, and Isaiah, and Mazzini, and all the rest of the prophets.

The mad should be judged by their peers; in my father's madness, moreover, there was an astonishing amount of method, and on that method he had already begun to meditate when at Oxford. Its exact nature and stages might be the subject of another volume, but it is due to an understanding of his personality to lay stress on the fact that his inner life of observation and thought, so full of swift shiftings, was to find much of its ultimate focus in an attempt to spiritually rejuvenate his own Church. For this his own influence and example was not sufficient, the battle had to be fought in headquarters, in select committees, in Conference itself, the supreme and final council in Wesleyan Methodism; and in Conference he was at that time of no account. Though his voice was first heard in it at that period, it was considered altogether astonishing, as if in the palmy days of the Roman Senate a young Patrician had risen to give his opinion in the presence of the Fathers. He must influence not only the people,—he did that easily enough, —but the pastorate, and that he did with difficulty, for various reasons. In the organisation of Wesleyan Methodism he was a great believer, but he considered it needed modification and greater elasticity in order to cope with the present and the future. The form of religion in England which had been contemporaneous with the French Revolution and the birth of modern democracy was, he believed, destined to survive as a religious form of that democracy, only it needed reanimating, and the original new wine pouring in at all points. The bottles had been made not for old wine but for new. "Be true to the spirit that animated your past" was his watchword, and you will meet the future. Already the hopelessness of a rigid three years' system in towns had come home to him as it had done to some others of the ministry gifted above their fellows. Some of these left it; he stayed. If he found the bed narrow, as a brother minister suggested in an article concerning him, he none the less clung to it, widening it wherever he could, in accordance with his own stature. Already he seems to have been regarded as a leader of the new party, for there is a letter at this period from a young minister respecting the rigidity of the itineracy and the sad state of English Methodism, to which my father sent a cheering reply.

"SELBORNE VILLA, BLACK HALL ROAD, OXFORD,
"*May* 29, 1883.

"DEAR SIR,—I think you have hit upon a very useful suggestion, which, with one or two modifications, ought to become law. It would probably be necessary to enact that the transfer shall in every case be *signed by the minister*, but the mechanical details might be proposed and carried out by lay officers. I shall be very glad to ventilate the idea and consult some of our leading ministers about it. I believe, however, there is another and deeper reason *why* we have so tremendous a leakage, and that is the necessary change after *so* short a pastorate as three years. I am heartily in favour of the principle of the itineracy, but I think three years is not always long enough in existing social circumstances. I hope you will always give your mind to questions of this kind, as you may be able, and not hesitate to make such suggestions as may occur to you. If Methodism is to flourish we must be continually adapting it to new circumstances. We lose more members than any other Church—that is our weakness. May God help us to remedy it.—Yours very sincerely,

"H. P. HUGHES.

"Rev. L. H. Hodson."

Amid such cogitations he did not fail to drink deep of life as usual. The city spoke to him of Wesley's student days, and still more audibly of Newman. Apart from their practical utility, he loved comparisons, and he found this comparison a fruitful one. He was for ever pondering it; to his mind the two giant figures were for ever wrestling over the people of this country. To understand them became his meat and drink, Newman as well as Wesley. He liked to understand an ecclesiastical opponent before he measured swords with him, and to sympathise with him if he could. He doubtless used the sympathy for an unforeseen purpose, but it was there all the same. The speech made to the Young Men's Christian Association at Dover and to the Licensed Victuallers, was characteristic of many of his speeches and habits of thought.

It was the note of sympathy with the other side that made them irresistible. As he watched a contradictory city, the elements within him were stirred to unusual contradiction. The trees bursting into spring greenness against the grey walls and towers of St. John's suggested the eternal contradiction of the place, the blossoming of new life, against the background of the old. As he eagerly watched the passers-by, with their gowns afloat in the breeze, and entered as the season dictated into the various features of university social life, the special lectures, the races, and festivities in spring, the schools in June, the gossip and personalities of the place, he scarcely knew whether he loved or hated it, so much was there that was venerable and human allied with so much that was petty and antiquated.

His younger sisters used often to visit him at this period, and enter into the gaieties of Eights Week and Commemoration, and he was as interested in their doings and observations as in everything else that came under his notice. The personalities in particular interested him, and there were great personalities in those days. Jowett held high court at Balliol, and my father must have often turned to look after him under beetling brows, wondering as to the secret of the man, and pondering as to the last story he had heard concerning him. At certain periods Ruskin was a familiar figure in the streets, and he must have regarded him with no small reverence. " Ruskin," he said, " awoke the English people to Art." For his books he had the highest regard, though he was sorry that they were not published at a more popular price. Later he possessed a complete edition of his works, presented to him by a friend. The only personal extravagance that he permitted himself was in books. The writings of Romanes, Nettleship, and others were known to him, then or later. But he did not know them to speak to any more than he knew Max Müller and Jowett. Years after, someone expressed his surprise that a man of his parts had known so few celebrities at the university. " I was surprised to find," said this gentleman, " that he did not even know Max Müller." He was so given up to causes that he had no time to make interesting acquaintances, though he did so by the way and accidentally. Yet he often regretted this deficiency. "The fact is," he would say sadly, "I have not time. I don't know how it is, but I have not time for anything."

Then he was inordinately modest if it came to pushing himself instead of pushing a cause. He felt "nobody," to quote his own expression, in the presence of the learned. They did not want to be bothered with a fellow like himself.

Yet on one occasion one of the great men of the place called upon him shortly after his arrival, Thomas Hill Green. This call led to further acquaintance, and he made the profoundest impression on my father. On hearing of his death a year or so later, he could scarcely restrain himself from tears. His letter, written to Mrs. Green on receipt of the news, was unusually ardent and sympathetic, even for him. "Green," he said, "was the most splendid Christian that I ever knew." He attended a course of his lectures, and one who was an undergraduate at the time writes that he well remembers the enthusiasm with which my father read out the notes taken from his discourses. "Fifteen years afterwards," the writer continues, "I heard him again refer to these lectures, and I imagine that they must have been with him throughout his life. 'You know,' he would say, 'how I loved the man, and how his words have sunk into my soul.' They were Green's remarks on the possibilities of perfecting the ego by a due union of altruism with an enlightened egoism. 'Here,' said Mr. Hughes, when he had finished, 'you have the philosophical expression of the good old Methodist doctrine of entire sanctification,' and instantly, as his manner was, he went on, his own mind actively transmuting the ideas given by another, to put the ideas of Green into another form." Unsuspected by many of his contemporaries lay a deep mystical element such as there was in Gordon, and like him he was a student of Bishop Horne's *Christ Mystical*, of which he had a copy with Gordon's own markings. The secret sources of strength of great men of action might surprise a sceptical world. With this vein in him it is not surprising that for the English school of philosophers (whom he read diligently for his M.A. degree) he had never a high regard, and that he preferred the transcendentalists and the Germans. He would recite Kant in particular with ecstasy, dwelling on his distinction between the Vernunft and the Verstand, "the higher Reason and the mere Understanding." [1]

On one occasion Green read a paper on Education before the Chapel Literary Society, which as usual was a pet society of my father's. At this time, also, as at Brighton, and through intercourse with Green and other university men, his interest in the principles that should underlie education must have been not a little stimulated. In a speech given at this time he repeated what he had advocated at Brighton and throughout his life, that each year only deepened the conviction that dogmatic theological teaching was not necessary in primary schools, though it was highly essential that the teaching should be animated by a truly religious spirit. The working classes, he continued, must know how to exercise the sacred functions entrusted to them. He often groaned mentally over Disraeli's Reform Bill in 1867, as he had groaned in his college days over Mr. Gladstone's more moderate measure of the previous year. The working classes had been admitted too quickly, he thought, into the franchise before they were fit to use it. Dizzy had indeed "dished the Whigs."

Education, he said in this same speech, would do much to break down the barriers between the gentry and the labouring classes. There were no reasons why the latter should not be as refined as the former. As in much else, he was studying and understanding the horizon. Already he beheld the breach in social barriers, which is perhaps the most characteristic product of the age.

Yet he was far from pinning his faith to education for the uplifting of the working classes; he went too deep for that. Fidus Achates and others who were not Fidus Achates, never forgot a saying of his at a great meeting in London.[2] Referring to contemporary maxims, such as "Educate, educate, educate," or "Legislate, legislate, legislate," he contradicted them by supplying another dictum with all the force and fire of which he was capable: "No! Regenerate, regenerate, regenerate!" What men and women wanted

[1] Yet he once remarked à propos of Mill that everybody could fall upon him, because the fellow made himself so intelligible and the others did not.

[2] He said this on many occasions, but the occasion which Fidus Achates remembered was an annual meeting of railway servants.

everywhere, he said, were new natures, new ways of looking at things.

For this reason he could not devote himself to the pursuits he loved. Years afterwards he said, *à propos* of the study of the natural sciences, for which he had always a hankering, " I often wish that I had made more use of my time at Oxford. What a fool I was! And there was a splendid laboratory at my disposal. But I had no time, you know. I never have for anything."

In amusing contradiction to this saying was that of one of the Oxford Methodists, in answer to an inquisitive member of his own Church, who whispered to him one day, " Well, what did you think of Hughes when he was here, and his goings-on? What was the impression created in Oxford Methodism? " " Think," was the reply, " he did not give us any time to think. We had not the breath, I tell you." The " thinking," as in Methodism generally, had to be done after he had left it, though certainly there was no breath lacking for criticism. A comet that has flashed across the dull heavens is explained after it has vanished into the ether.

His peculiar regard for Professor Green lay in his character, I imagine, more than in his ideas. First of distinguished university men, he spanned the gulf that separated the university from the town council. Hitherto the two had been at loggerheads, the university despising the town, so it was felt, and the town cordially detesting while fawning upon the university. The old town and gown rows lingered in a certain social animosity, which abides there to this day. Professor Green shared my father's love of humanity and all forms of it. He knew that the tradesman no more than the don is contained betwixt his hat and his boots, as the American poet puts it.

The deadness of Oxford Methodism[1] had almost become a proverb; as well might the dead rise from their graves as Methodism rise in Oxford. Wesleyans, if they thought about it at all, put it down to the all-pervading influence of Newman, and the old quarrel between Culture and Methodism. For though Methodism owed its origin to a gentleman of culture, it, no more than early Christianity, had been the religion of

[1] The word " Methodism " is here used in its original and aggressive sense.

the *beau monde.* Lady Huntingdon attempted to introduce Methodism among the aristocracy of this country, but it never got much beyond the attempt. The religious revival which had taken towns and villages of the three kingdoms by storm, and which had overspread America and the western colonies, and many other spots where Christian men had not yet penetrated, did not seem suited apparently to rear itself beneath the shadow of those grey walls. Providence had clearly ordained that it should not. Indeed, a well-known minister had said to my father, on hearing that he was appointed to Oxford: "Hughes, I pity you from the bottom of my heart! Methodism in Oxford is dead. You are throwing yourself away!" But my father did not interpret the designs of Providence in that light.

He knew, in the first place, that the passing of the University Test Act in 1871 was as momentous a social change in its way as the passing of the Reform Bill. Nonconformists must flock from henceforth to the ancient universities, and Methodists among the number. This would inevitably strengthen the hands of the Nonconformity of the town, only that Nonconformity must look alive, must be in a position to greet and grip its sons. In the town itself, as he was swift to detect, there was a vigorous young life which had shared, like the rest of undistinguished mankind, in the aspirations of the new era. Almost immediately after his arrival in November he turned his attention to the young Methodists of the university, and formed them into the Wesley Guild, a guild which has flourished since that day. For the impression that he made upon these and other young university men, I cannot do better than quote from some interesting reminiscences which I have received from Mr. Kellett of the Leys School, Cambridge:—

"Since Mr. Hughes left Oxford in 1884 I have seen him but three times, and spoken to him but twice. Strange to say, I never heard him at the West End Mission; I never saw him as President of the Conference; and all the great work by which he will be known was to me a matter of hearsay. I have often regretted this as a great loss to myself; but perhaps it will assist me to give a fair historic view of Mr. Hughes's three years at Oxford, undisturbed by the glamour of subsequent events.

"I first saw him on a November morning in 1881, when I came up to Oxford to compete for a scholarship. He had been so good as to promise to look out for lodgings for me during my week of examination; and I was struck then, as often afterwards, by the vigorous cordiality of his manner. He welcomed me with something far more energetic than even the ordinary kindness with which a Methodist minister usually receives a son of the manse ; there were even in so simple a matter, signs of that extraordinary activity of mind and body which characterised him from first to last, and which made him do everything with all his might. My landlady, I remember, was deaf ; but Mr. Hughes contrived without an effort to make her hear, and she assured me afterwards that he was the only minister whose preaching she had no difficulty in following. This clearness and decisiveness of utterance was, as everybody knows, a special mark of Mr. Hughes.

" He was then a young man of thirty-four ; young indeed to be superintendent of a circuit, but looking, with his bearded face and spectacled eyes, considerably older than he was, and already fully equal to any post in the Connexion. I heard him preach on a Sunday evening, and I must confess that the first impression was a little disappointing. Earlier in the year I had heard one of the last of Dr. Punshon's addresses, and superb rhetoric was not unnaturally the ideal of a schoolboy. Of rhetoric and fireworks there was not a trace in Mr. Hughes's business-like method of speech. It was not till the end of the sermon that I noticed its *effectiveness* ; I had not missed a single word. This quality of not only arresting, but keeping attention, was Mr. Hughes's most extraordinary mark as a speaker ; and the effect was attained by the simplest means. There were no outbursts, no purple 'patches'; everything was plain and unadorned ; but I do not believe that any speaker ever lived who had more thoroughly learned the secret of establishing a *rapport* with his hearers in his first sentence, and maintaining it unimpaired to the end. At night I took supper with him, and I noticed then, what I often noticed afterwards, the active and creative power of his mind. No subject was mentioned, but spontaneously and unconsciously he began to *work* upon it. Usually of course his mind took a practical rather than a speculative turn ; he always seemed to be devising, rejecting, renewing a scheme of action. For example, the conversation turned upon Kingswood School. His whole line was, ' Can something be done there ? ' ' Don't you think something might be effected here ? ' He had to the full the statesman's power of assimilating ideas ; but those ideas nearly always took a practical shape. . . ."

Here the writer speaks of his interest in Green's lectures. Then after describing the inauguration of the Guild :—

" On these occasions he was an undergraduate with undergraduates. I still remember his manner while talking. As he grew enthusiastic in defence of State interference or of ' Christian audacity,' he would rise from his chair and stand in front of the fireplace, his left hand holding his cup of coffee, and his right engaged in pointing his oratorical thrusts. I often trembled for the crockery ; and admired the way in which Mrs. Hughes, keeping an ear for her husband's eloquence, and an eye for the cup and saucer, would dexterously remove the latter without interrupting the flow of the former. Not that he was unable to listen. He was compelled to do so ; for undergraduates are no more inclined to suppress their opinions than a mother to be silent about her firstborn. But he always had a reply ready, and was quick in finding a second generalisation to qualify the sweeping nature of his first. Vehement and uncompromising as he was, I do not think I ever heard an unkind word from him. . . . For all his antagonists, and he had many, he never, I am sure, harboured the slightest ill-feeling, and his strongest expressions never went beyond a good-humoured joke.

"In these meetings with Mr. Hughes I was struck once again with the extraordinary power of assimilating ideas, to which I have already referred. One Saturday evening, I remember, he was in particularly 'fine form,' discoursing on some subject of the day. I do not think I ever saw him so vigorous. A few hours later, one of the guild members said to me, 'Have you seen the *Spectator*?' I replied in the negative. 'Well,' he said, 'you will see there a germ of Mr. Hughes's Saturday speech.' I looked at the article; and as a matter of fact, the subject *was* treated in the *Spectator*, and to some extent on Mr. Hughes's lines; but what struck me was the fact that throughout the evening Mr. Hughes had been so original. The *Spectator* had suggested the idea; it had passed in his mind through a transmuting process, and came out part of himself. What I thought was not 'This was borrowed,' but 'With what amazing rapidity does Mr. Hughes seize upon a new thought and make it part and parcel of his own personality!' He had read that article in the morning; all the afternoon he had been doing the work of ten men over the circuit; yet in the evening he was able to give us the finished product of his thoughts that must, only an hour or two ago, have been entirely new to him.

"He never assumed any superiority. The leading position he took was of course due largely to his age and standing, but far more to his natural gifts. His native modesty shone out through his dominance and uncompromising assertions of principle. Just as in later years, when planning the *Methodist Times,* he actually wrote and consulted some of his undergraduate friends as to their ideas of its main features, so now he never failed to show respect and deference to their opinions, and never manifested any impatience of their crudities of paradox or dogmatism.

"To address the Wesley Guild he would from time to time invite men of eminence with whom he was acquainted. . . . [Here the writer mentions the names of some well-known ministers.] But the figure of Mr. Hughes himself occupies the chief place in our memory. Much of what he said has of course passed into oblivion; but his remarks on some points I can never forget. He was the first from whom I heard public reference to the subject of social purity; and I still recall with admiration the mingled firmness and delicacy with which he spoke; the indignation with which he spoke of a certain member of Parliament who boasted that he was an immoral man himself, and could do nothing to prevent others being immoral if they chose; and the passionate enthusiasm of his eulogy on Mrs. Josephine Butler, whom he supported on her mission to Oxford. 'I have the honour'—he paused— 'I have the *high* honour of possessing an acquaintance with this eminent saint.' He spoke without any inflammatory tones; but no man could hear his words without being the better for them.

"In speaking of Mr. Hughes's general influence on the undergraduates with whom he came into contact, I am in a certain difficulty. Oxford was then, and possibly is now, possessed by a *nil admirari* fashion—that demon of which Shakespeare may have been thinking when he said 'The prince of darkness is a gentleman.' It was the mode to pretend a hatred of all enthusiasm. The university has always been, in a special sense, 'the home of lost causes'; at any rate it was the custom to talk as if all causes were lost, and as if no cause were worth the trouble of working for. 'Surtout, point de zèle,' was a favourite quotation; and men, in their ordinary talk, made a point of pretending to live up to it. If ever a man were caught in a momentary fit of enthusiasm, he invariably became ashamed of it in a few hours. Undergraduates, like those of the Wesley Guild, soon caught this bad manner, and often outdid their exemplars in expressing their haughty superiority to fanaticism. It was inevitable, then, that they should, *in talk*, pretend to think that Mr. Hughes's enthusiasm was 'bad form.' Anyone who did not understand the *lingua franca* in which Oxford men then habitually disguised their real sentiments, might have fancied, from their ordinary conversation, that they were ashamed of the influence Mr. Hughes exerted on them. Yet such an idea would be a great mistake. The manner, bad as it was, was never more than an affectation, and an affectation on all sides understood to be such. It was, indeed, almost a confession how deeply Mr. Hughes had really secured their confidence. No one, at any rate, could long resist his personal influence. I remember one man, in whom this habit was very strongly developed, and who in cold blood would rather have died than say plainly how highly he admired Mr. Hughes, turning to me in the midst of a strong and uncompromising display of 'temperance enthusiasm,' and saying, 'This is all true, and it is nonsense to pretend it isn't.'

"Over some men his influence was great and permanent, and even acknowledged. One in particular never made any show of disguising his captivity. Scarcely a day passed without his paying a visit to Mr. Hughes's house; and it was a matter of common observation how he hung upon his master's every word. He had been, till Mr. Hughes's advent, something of a free-thinker, and fully impregnated with Oxford's lackadaisical spirit—a not uncommon result of intercourse with Jowett. A few weeks of Mr. Hughes transformed him; the star of Jowett set almost immediately; and he became the most enthusiastic and energetic of evangelical workers.

"A safe test of influence is to get work out of one's adherents. At Oxford, as I have said, it was not the fashion to admire a man in words. No one was ever openly confessed to be a leader. Nevertheless, leaders of action were not wanting; and among these Mr. Hughes took his natural place. He had indeed an extraordinary power of extracting out of people the utmost exertion of which they are capable; and he did not fail with us. One of his achievements—and it was no mean one in a place like Oxford— was to get us to go to a ragged school mission about two miles from the centre of the town. Some of us found it hard work to speak to the children, and it was besides not easy for an undergraduate, with the high-flown notions of the undergraduate as to personal dignity, to face the little martyrdoms involved in visiting so barbarous a place. But Mr. Hughes held us to it. . . .

"The mission lasted until Mr. Hughes left ; after he had gone it flagged and died. What he did in the way of stirring up people to work could hardly be chronicled here. I remember his successor saying that it was a daily wonder to him to find out something new that Mr. Hughes had done ; and one of his colleagues half-humorously complained in my presence that he was always afraid to meet his 'super' for fear of learning of some new scheme of work. Mr. Hughes's vitality, indeed, was so immense that he could hardly conceive of his subordinates becoming weary. The circuit simply bristled with new organisations while he was in it. He never spared himself, and with his matchless energy he kept them going ; but his panting subordinates often toiled after him in vain ; and when he left, or when circumstances compelled his absence, things often ceased to move. His enthusiasm also was so contagious that it often gave him false ideas of the state of affairs. A cause was declining, and the workers were losing heart. He had but to appear, and the corpse was galvanised into momentary life ; the listless became animated, the weary active. Hence he would go away with the idea that the cause, really dying, was flourishing. Such had been the magic of his contagious energy that the moribund put on new vitality. But when he was not there, it sank down to nothing. I remember well how, after I had visited a place where a certain work was decaying, I heard Mr. Hughes declare that he had never seen his workers more enthusiastic. It was true ; his presence had compelled enthusiasm ; and in the nature of things he could not see the effect of his absence. Nevertheless, the sight of such stupendous energy often put a permanent and not a merely transitory life into a village that seemed as if Elijah himself could not move it ; and in many places the work he had started lasted with undiminished vigour for years after he had gone.

"I have heard that Mr. Hughes used to say that the happiest years of his life were those spent at Oxford ; and I can well believe it. Though his great powers demanded, and inevitably obtained, a wider sphere, yet in some respects I can imagine that he felt himself more in place at Oxford than anywhere else. Practical man as he was, he was a scholar and a university man ; and it was a matter of regret to him that his multitudinous affairs prevented him from keeping up his reading. I remember once when he was breakfasting with a Cambridge man, an Oxford man, and myself, how enthusiastically he proposed that there should be an annual meeting of Methodist members of the great universities, in order to keep up the spirit of unity among these scattered, and often lonely, lights of learning. It was an *obiter dictum* ; and as with so many of his *obiter dicta*, I do not know how far he would have felt himself bound by it in cooler moments ; but he spoke with an enthusiasm which showed how deeply ingrained in him was his love of culture and of cultivated men. As things turned out, he became the guide of uneducated thousands ; but I think he would have been equally successful as the guide and friend of the educated few."

The closing sentence opens an aspect, a vista of his life, of which some were peculiarly conscious. Behind the evangelist, the man of affairs, was the scholar, often an impassioned one. His meeting with persons of true cultivation was often quite pathetic, so eager was he to elucidate their thought and then at times to contradict it. Indeed, this absorption in such persons sometimes provoked comment from the less cultivated among whom he was a leader. " It was evident," some of them said, " that Mr. Hughes had no ears except for clever persons."

Another undergraduate of those days writes from America to my mother as follows:—

"There are some influences that cannot come into a man's life more than once, and the force of Mr. Hughes's teaching and spirit in my undergraduate days was of this nature. No later influence has meant, or can mean, quite the same thing to me. I have learnt many lessons from Mr. Hughes's more public career, but to-day it is more natural for me to think of his Oxford ministry, which left an indelible impression on my own ideals of Christian faith and service. I believe that, in innumerable instances besides, his work was done in such a way that the impulse he communicated will not in the least be interrupted by his death, however acute a sense of personal bereavement this may bring. Mr. Hughes's true memorial will not be so much in the visible results of his ministry, though these have been great, as in a quickening of the conscience which will reproduce itself from generation to generation.

" I have sent you a copy of last Saturday's *Boston Transcript*, in which I have tried to make American readers understand something of the character of Mr. Hughes's influence upon his followers, though I confess I find it difficult to represent the fascination of that personality to those who have only known him and his work by hearsay.

"Among my memories of New Inn Hall Street is one of a sermon on 'Death' which revolutionised my whole conception of the break which comes between this life and the next. My friend —— of Balliol, who had that day received the news of his mother's death, was also at the service ; and I remember how vividly the new light broke in upon him too, and how he was strengthened to bear his loss. People do not often think of Mr. Hughes as a comforting preacher, but the ministry of comfort was not lacking in his exposition of a complete gospel, and I hope that the great truths of the love of God which he made real to thousands of hearers, will now support his own wife and family in the time of their need."

In the second year of his residence he held a special mission, as he had done at Dulwich, which introduces Fidus Achates, a very doughty gentleman, who early responded to the call. He was the son of a woman of marked saintliness and ability, and went to chapel chiefly because she did. To enter into Church work of any kind had never entered into his wildest dreams. He had a flourishing business in the Oxford market, and was much to the fore in municipal and political elections. My father's interest in such matters, and his wide social outlook, attracted him from the first. That it was as much a good man's duty to vote for the right candidate at elections as to say his prayers, sounded pleasantly in his ears.

He was therefore quite amiable when the new superintendent called upon him and asked for his assistance in organising a special mission. " I want you to map out the town into districts, just as you do for canvassing purposes at elections." Achates complied, and made such a plan. Among the persons to be visited were the heads of houses, which caused not a little heart-sinking among the organising committee. Surely such a deed had never been performed since the world began—to call upon the head of a house and ask him to attend a special mission. The gentleman to whom this task was finally deputed lay awake more than one night nerving himself for his task. Methodism in the old days, as the superintendent always remembered, had claimed the whole world as its parish. It came into existence to quicken God's life in the soul, irrespective of Church, or creed, or station. The head of a house might be in as much need of a special mission as anybody else. He had indeed a theory that academics saw only the half of life. They would be less puzzled themselves, and puzzle others less, he thought, if they could see with their own eyes what the gospel can do for a man and a woman, how it can transform them and the whole tenor of their life. As he remarked once of Hegel, " He left the Church and its evidences out of his calculations like the rest of the philosophers." This omission of great thinkers was one that he often commented upon.

A friend of his has related an interesting anecdote of this period which touches on this subject. One day when my father was walking down a street of the city he noticed a member of the university—one of the dons—on the opposite pavement. A strong constraint possessed him to cross the road and ask that gentleman a question. The question was

an unconventional one, and its very unconventionality made
him hesitate.   He was not intimate with the graduate in
question, and he did not altogether relish the idea of intruding
upon him.   None the less he crossed the road with beetling
brows, battling, as he often did off the platform, against
shyness.   After a word or two he asked his question.   " Excuse me, but I am curiously constrained to come and ask you
a question.   What is your opinion of Jesus Christ of Nazareth?
How does it stand between you and Him ? "

The gentleman to whom he spoke looked at him with
a peculiar fixity.   " Mr. Hughes," he said, " I have been
waiting for twenty years for somebody to ask me that question.   Come to my rooms and talk to me."   Later on, as the
Methodists put it, he " found peace."

This incident, much as many others in my father's life,
might have happened to John Wesley, whom in many ways he
resembled, and not the least in the doing and advocating of
that to which by natural instinct he was opposed.   It reads
indeed like a bit of the Journals.

The pamphlet which he distributed among his congregation on the occasion of the special mission bears the same
impress.   " Numbers die in darkness every day.   By your
pity for unhappy souls, by your love for the Church of God,
by the rapid flight of your own day of labour and influence, by
your obligations to Him who has redeemed you by His blood,
and whose heart yearns over the wanderer, we implore you to
join heartily in this mission for bringing sinners to God."
Very characteristic also of the writer is the close.   " We have
no desire to proselytise from other Churches.   Converts will
be left to decide for themselves what Church they will join."

That is a most important feature of my father's aggressive
efforts, which distinguished them from most other efforts of
the same kind.   He was a marvellous combination of uncompromising zeal and an equally uncompromising tolerance, a
combination which is unusual, and of which the world stands
in great need.   Not the slightest constraint, either morally or
otherwise, was ever put upon a convert to join the Methodist
Church.   This was one of the chief points in which he trained
his followers ; first in the ordinary circuit work, and afterwards
in London.   It was just in this direction that the intolerant,

who belong to all Churches, could not understand his efforts, for the atmosphere of tolerance is simply incomprehensible to those who have never breathed it. The first convert at this particular mission was a young man who afterwards became an Anglican clergyman, and numbers of the men and women who came under my father's influence never joined Methodism, and knew nothing of it all their lives. On the other hand, a certain number who were unattached and outside the Churches altogether, naturally joined that Church to which my father belonged. In this tolerance, which was utter and absolute, like all that he sincerely believed, lay much of the success of his aggressive zeal, which was the puzzle and the envy of some of his contemporaries. It was the more remarkable, as it was united to a passionate predilection for his own Church.

A relative who had been brought up in Methodism, but who, for various reasons, felt that she could never happily enter into its fellowship, he urged to join the Anglican communion, seeing that she had for years longed to do so. This tolerance made him all the more resent the attitude of some of the Anglican clergy. He would have scorned to try and make Methodists of Anglicans; his appeal in this mission and on similar occasions was primarily to those who did not go to church at all, and his one aim was to deepen and quicken the spiritual life of men and women.

Of course a week of special prayer preceded the mission. Like Cromwell's Ironsides, he never went into action without this observance, and it was as passionate with him as with them. He might verily have been about to encounter the devil and all his angels. He talked a great deal of the spirit of darkness both then and afterwards, and scandalised people until they got accustomed to it. Darkness and sin were as real to him as Christ was. About this time, or a little after, Dr. Parker, speaking of the Christian ministers of his day, said, with the shakes of the head and the deep emphasised tones for which he was famous: "As for my friend Mr. Hughes, he positively lies in wait for the devil at every corner"—a saying which was much repeated.

But his devil was not the mediæval creature with horns, whose special privilege it is to frighten little children. Christ was wrestling with him, and must in the end conquer. His

10

spiritual existence was not to make good men tremble, but to brace them for the fight. Everybody knew what Mr. Hughes meant by the " devil "; it was the spirit against which all his crusades were directed. The saying of Wesley's that a man may be as orthodox as the devil and as wicked, was one in which he delighted, and which he often quoted.

Persons of all classes in Oxford, from undergraduates down to a chimney-sweeper, so it is related, responded to my father's invitation to submit themselves to Christ; a good many joined the Church in New Inn Hall Street, others went to other Churches. To say that all these persons were in after-life a credit to their religion, would be altogether too much to vouch for in a perplexing world, but he was undoubtedly the means in the majority of cases at missions of permanently affecting men and women. Life was not the same afterwards. The high-water mark of spiritual aspiration was altogether extended. Conscience became more exacting, religion and God more real.

After drawing up the plan as my father had directed, Fidus Achates wrote a letter to his superintendent, wishing him to rest under no misconceptions. His part was now done. He would have nothing to do with the " spiritual portion." " But he would come to hear him," said the superintendent; " surely he would do that?" " Well, he might do that."

When he got to the chapel, the superintendent beckoned him into the vestry. " You cannot imagine how lonely a mission preacher feels. Surely you will sit in the front where I can speak to you if I require anything."

Achates sat in the front, and in the course of the service he heard himself called upon to pray. When he got up to do so, he felt, to use his own expression, as if " all heaven were opened before his eyes." The difficulty was to keep back the thoughts that crowded into his mind, to refrain from uttering one-half of what he saw and felt. " I had a new tongue," he told me, " a new brain, a new heart "; and to the wonder of his friends he was the superintendent's right hand throughout the mission, and in many undertakings after it. My father would not have called upon him to pray unless he had known the dormant power and inclination of the man. As always, he knew with whom he was dealing.

One point of difference they had, since the beginning—the Temperance question. "You drink your water, and I'll drink my beer," said Achates. "Water pleases you, and beer pleases me." So the superintendent consented to leave the matter for the time. But preparatory to addressing the converts who were assembled at New Inn Hall Street, he drew Achates aside. "I am troubled," he said, "concerning some of them. If they fall back into old ways it will be through drink. I hesitate to break my promise, but I do feel very strongly about it. Could not you, for their sake, and for example's sake generally, take the pledge as I shall ask them to do this evening?" "No, I cannot," said Achates, "and I shall not come to the meeting this evening. What about promises, Mr. Hughes?" And he went his way ill at ease. At last he could bear it no longer, and went to the superintendent's house to inquire if he was in. Finding he was, he made his way to the study. "Ah, Mr. Nix, you here. What's up now?" "I have come to sign the pledge." "To sign the pledge, my dear sir!" "Yes, to sign the pledge. And as I am going to, I had better do it at once." "No, no, not now, but this evening, my dear fellow, this evening, before all those converts! What an opportunity for you!" So Achates signed it that evening. Many others have signed it since through his agency.

The importance of this special mission lay not only in its essence, which was an unconventional attempt to bring as many of the men and women of Oxford as might be under the direct sway of the personality of Christ, without reference to diversities of worship and creed, but in its strategic aspect. It was only another proof to my father that Methodism in England, for all its appearance to the contrary, had a future before her. The old special power of quickening men's hearts and consciences was still hers, and with greater resources than in the past, if she would only make use of these, instead of strangling them, as she was in danger of doing. Disunion, the result of her internal quarrels, was the curse of Methodism, and the cause of her present impotence in the nation's life. The Free Methodist Chapel in New Inn Hall Street greeted the strategic eye in the nature of an eyesore. There it stood, a forbidding emblem of the tragedy of 1848. The immediate problem was to bring about a union with that chapel and his own, and it was not long before he was making overtures. The fact that these were not successful only deepened the significance of two Methodist chapels in the same street. Not that the general's eye was by any means confined to this street. It swept, as usual, wider fields, and in this particular instance, the villages of Oxfordshire. Isolated chapels were scattered here and there, but they were lonely and in need of much—preachers who could stir a man, harmoniums to help the singing, and in some places a congregation to sing. Previous to holding the special mission a special muster of village Methodists was convened at New Inn Hall Street—a convention, my father and Fidus Achates called it. In they came for miles around, in carts and all manner of vehicles, speaking the Oxfordshire dialect, and greatly delighted to find themselves one of a large number. Indeed, from the superintendent's way of talking to them the Methodists in this world were like the stars in heaven, without number, and beyond a man's power of counting. And Achates came with the rest, as he always did.

Achates-of-the-fields was less interested in social problems than Achates-of-the-town, but being a child of the soil, and an intelligent child, he pondered the realities, to wit, the price of corn, the amount of annual rainfall, and underlying these and kindred topics, personal and otherwise, the meaning and import of religion. " What was this sin," he asked himself, " that the preacher talked about ? " " All men," they said, " both good and bad, had sinned, and salvation came from repentance for sin." Now he, for one, could not feel this repentance. He was decent on the whole, and would fain do right, but as for squeezing out groans and tears about himself, he could not rise to it. The protest of the age against an unnatural theology, brooded over the furrow and the silent soil. Perhaps it first sprang from these. But the new superintendent, so Achates felt, put matters right. " My dear sir," he said, " are you sorry for anything you have done that is contrary to God's will? Do you want now to live in accordance with it, and to trust in Christ your Saviour? Very well, you are saved now. All that you have to do is to rejoice in the thought that no mother ever loved her child as God loves you, and you will do this all the easier if you will come and help me in this village and become a local preacher, and help others to rejoice also."

So great was the joy of Achates-in-the-fields that it prevented him from sleeping. Religion had become part of the joy of the earth, not its terror, suitable for spring mornings. It pleased him too, that trick of speech of the superintendent's, " Come and help me," not " Get along, you idle sinner, and do some good work, for heaven's sake."

The superintendent in a village was not quite the same as he was in a town. Insensibly he became acclimatised. The writer never liked to hear him so well as on a Sabbath evening in an English village. It was always a story from the life of our Lord, some great miracle of His. The preacher leant over the pulpit in much the same way as they said his grandfather used to do in Wales—as if he were talking to the people rather than preaching to them. The intense stillness both without and within—that stillness which is never felt away from the fields—seemed to point to the presence of the great Healer. " He is here," the preacher used to say, " in our very midst, just as He was two thousand years ago in Galilee. He is the same yesterday, to-day, and for ever, and He can heal us all if we will come to Him." The old remember him as one who pleaded. The hostile influences of which he was often so conscious when preaching in London were not felt by him in country places. He knew less of the evil and apathy of villages than he did of the evil and quick wit of towns. Only once did the writer note him to fail in feeling the pulse of a country audience, and that was when he was Ex-President, distressed in mind at various things (what he feared to be the frivolity and worldliness of the children of rich Methodists), and anxious to impress ecclesiastical conceptions to which the soil was not habituated.

The villages of Oxfordshire, my father felt, were a splendid field for the young men and women who had joined New Inn Hall Street, and were anxious to lead holier and more useful lives. Soon he and Fidus Achates organised a corps of local preachers that remains to this day, with detached officials of great variety of gifts. Gifts, the superintendent said, must be consecrated and put on Christ's altar at once. In fact, the whole circuit hummed and his strategic eye gladdened at the sound.

Methodism, the superintendent thought, had shown its face in Oxford, and if it could show it there, it could show it anywhere. That distinguished minister of Methodism, the Rev. William Arthur, visited the circuit, and published what he saw in the *Methodist Recorder*, so that the superintendent's fame became bruited through the Connexion. On the strength of it he was invited to address the annual Missionary Breakfast Meeting of the Wesleyan Methodist Missionary Society, and to preach the Missionary sermon on the following Sunday, and he addressed it to some purpose. My father's oratory has been criticised, if not denied. He had not, they said,

> "that great voice which, rising, brought
> Red wrath to faces pale with thought,
> And falling, fell with showers of tears."

He had not, as a rule. Nor did he lay claim to such or aim at it. Men and women did not weep (though at times they have been seen to do so); they either sat very still or felt for their purses. Yet, whether the oratory is greater which draws forth the tears or the purse, is a debatable matter, and one which Socrates would have rejoiced to argue with the Sophists of his day. Mr. Holyoake, in commenting on this subject, remarked that my father said what he wanted to say, and in a very clear and pungent manner, which was what Demosthenes did.

Perhaps a man must speak to his own people to be an orator in the great sense, as Mark Antony did. It is then that he has complete command of his instrument, then that he is *en rapport* with all about him, so that the people listening seem not to hear him, but their own hearts.

A debt of £8000 was still hanging over the Missionary Society, for which reason further "retrenchment" was advocated. That word stuck in my father's throat; he could not swallow it; nor, he determined, should the meeting. Retrenchment! it made him feel sick, fresh from dreams for Methodism at Oxford. It was as if a member of the Athenian Assembly had risen in the presence of Demosthenes and proposed terms with Philip. "O God, that men and Missionary Societies should be so crushed and restricted in aims, with the continents before them to conquer!" And this people; he thought he knew their heart, and its greatness, despite the annual missionary meeting, where they sat in rows eating sandwiches, and forgetful of their fathers! When he was called upon to speak, the audience had the vision of a figure almost ascetic in its strenuous slimness which flashed to the front of the platform, and whose speech went through them like a sword.

"The martyrs, their fathers, who had first borne the Cross to the ends of the earth—what remained of their endeavours— what recked the Church of them? The weeds grew over their graves, their dust slept unhonoured, untended beneath. The pioneers flung away their lives to spread Christ's kingdom, and the people after them retrenched! Retrenched! when all creation was travailing, when Europe, in the act of flinging off the hated yoke of the priests, was white unto harvest for the gracious unfettered gospel of the Son of God. This cursed debt of £8000! Let them now—this day—wipe it out of their midst, so that it might never offend the eye of the Methodist people again! Let them bring joy to their brethren toiling over the seas, and wonder to the heart of London, the city of the golden calf, that Christians could actually contribute £8000 to the service of Christ and His Church!"

Like an ancient race recalled to the memory of days long ago, to the faces and deeds of those who were long since silent, the audience forgot the lapse of time, the incitement to prudence and moderation with which the present abounded. They gave each as they were able, and some, the poorest, more. The total of £4000 was collected, when the speaker suggested that the remaining half should be collected at the second meeting of the Society two days later. The gentlemen who sat with him on the platform, some with prepared speeches, did not appear over-pleased at this interruption. The inconvenience of prophets is that they upset programmes. Nothing took place as the authorities had arranged that it should take place; there is a certain lack of fine feeling in prophets. Mindful of this, they were careful to have a full programme of the meeting two days after, and to leave five minutes for the prophet at the close. Many feared that the other £4000 would not be forthcoming, and anxious looks had been cast

in my father's direction as he sat pale and contained, apparently unmoved by the impatient audience who persisted in
calling out his name.   But the heart of the people had been
too deeply stirred, and in half an hour the whole £8000 was
raised.   The Society never thanked the prophet for his services.[1]
No sooner was the meeting over than my father beckoned to
Fidus Achates, who was one of the audience.   " Let us get out
of this," he said ; "I have to preach in Oxfordshire this evening."
Achates being by no means loath, they had soon turned their
backs on the assembly.   When Achates-in-the-fields heard
how he had returned from his triumph to the plough, he was
glad at heart.   " That's him," he said.

Too often my father's brethren thought of him solely as
a prophet, which was a pity.   But the majority had not the
opportunity of knowing him as had many of the humble laity .
In my memory at this moment lurks a picture of the time
when the superintendent and his circuit took a holiday.   At
an appointed hour joyous brakes (I am obliged to apply that
adjective) started from the Martyr's Memorial and drove along
the dusty roads to one of the villages which my father's eye
had swept, and included in his operations.   On the green, in
the afternoon, the company played cricket, the superintendent
bowling full craftily sometimes.   As if it were yesterday, some
can hear him, " Some of those fellows at the wicket were
giving those poor girls a dreadful time ; there they were toiling
in vain, till I felt filled with pity for them.   So I offered to
help them, and at that all the fellows began to grin slightly,
and to wink, as much as to say, ' Here's a parson going to
make a fool of himself.'   So I did not say much, but in a few
moments I had surprised them a little.   Did you notice it,
Katie, did you notice it ? "—appealing to his wife as usual.
But when Fidus Achates came and batted, then the fun began.
And oh, when Achates had to run, for he was portly, and the
fielders were hallooing for the balls!   The superintendent
clapped his hands, and laughed aloud in his glee.   " Don't

[1] At another time he raised £1110 at a Foreign Missionary Meeting in bank notes.
At another, ladies put their jewellery into the plate.   Before the collection of the
Twentieth Century Fund someone asked him how much he had collected for his own
Church in various ways.   My father calculated, and thought it must be considerably
over a quarter of a million.

stop, my dear fellow, there is not a moment to lose, not the thousandth part of a moment."

To the spectator, the playing of cricket, and the desire to see Fidus Achates run, might have been the chief objects of his existence. He abandoned himself to the pursuit of the moment with an extraordinary intensity, which was the cause of much of the misconception concerning him. To hear him at the Foreign Missionary Meeting on "Retrenchment," you might have imagined that he thought all day and half the night on the subject of the extension of missions, home and foreign. He did not: he was always a good sleeper, and he lived from hour to hour not unlike a child, never examining into himself as is the more modern habit, and quite unaware that he presented any incongruous aspects. Life had gone well with him from the first, and he was always healthy and objective. No stone had impeded its first strong glad current, fretting and torturing its course as is often the case. Men do not weary in giving themselves and their energies; it is some folly of their own, some thrust of Providence, which consumes the strength that is in them.

Very literally he seemed to press on to what was before, forgetting what lay behind. He kept no diary, scarcely ever wrote such a thing as a really personal and intimate letter, and if he allowed himself regret for the past, it was but momentary. The future he hailed, and in and for it he increasingly lived. In the balance of his nature, for all its tense Hebraic Celtic elements, there was something Hellenic and eminently sound. He did not, when he was in health, consume himself for no purpose, nor did he, from acquaintance with evil and short-coming, suffer himself to see life and persons in a distorted and one-sided manner, the too common fault of those who preach crusades. Whatever might be his speech and passion at times, he was capable, particularly in his study, and from the tops of omnibuses, of seeing life steadily, and seeing it whole. His many-sided mind inclined him to a balanced view of things, however much his emotions might occasionally send down one side of the scale to cavernous depths. Often many minutes would not elapse before the opposite scale was similarly weighted. It was the balanced mind which made him a leader.

It was in the evening that the merriment of these festivities reached its height. A harmonium needed buying or a debt clearing; so the visitors from town as well as their hosts had an opportunity of contributing in the village chapel, and more than they intended. In that lay the peculiar charm. Hymns were sung, an address was given, and then—oh, joy of joys!—the collection. Then the time for wit to scintillate. (To Fidus Achates) " Now, So-and-so, have you got those forms filled in ? "—or, " you ought to have done by now. You seem to be talking enough about them. What is the matter, my dear sir ? You seem to be talking so volubly that I feel quite envious of you. Ah ! Mr. John Smith, Mr. John Smith, where are you ? Ah, here ! I like to see a generous man as well as to hear of him. Now, who will follow the example of my friend, Mr. John Smith ? Have not you done yet ? Well, really, what it is to see a really talkative man ! I wish you would communicate your powers to me, sir. I am such a silent brother ; my wife does all the talking.

" —— A Farm Labourer, 1d. God bless you, sir ; He knows how generous you are in His service more than we can ever do. (To Fidus Achates) At last, one full after all that commotion—let me see.

" Mr. X. of Oxford, 10s. What should we do without Mr. X. ? He's our right hand in every good work.

" Master X., 3s. 6d. ; Miss X., 2s. 6d. Following, you see, in the footsteps of their father. May they long do so. May they be better than their father. Unless our children are better than ourselves, what is to happen to the human race ?

" Mrs. Brown, 3s. 8d. ; Master Brown, 2s. 6d. ; Miss Polly Brown, 2s. Well, I never — Miss Susan Brown, 1s. 6d. Jehoshaphat ! This is a very remarkable family—and, as I live — Mr. Henry Brown, 10s. Mrs. Brown and her four children have set us and our children a good example. May we all follow it. We should be as willing to give 10s. in the service of the Church as well as any other service. I find that the more men give, the more they get. Mr. Henry Brown, I believe, is a case in point. Have not you a large store at the entrance of the village, Mr. Brown ? I thought I saw your name on it this morning, with all kinds of things in the window —tinned rhinoceros and—what—what ? . . . Oh, Mr. Henry

Brown is a cousin of Mrs. Brown, not a son. Perhaps some other cousin of Mrs. Brown will give us 10s. Now's the time, my dear sir, wherever you are. There, nothing like paying off old debts in the church or anywhere else. Ah (to Fidus Achates), don't hurry too much. You have run so much this afternoon that I would not unduly tire you!"

Fidus Achates. "I shan't tire, sir!"

"You won't tire yourself, you say. Well, I don't know. You can never prophesy what such a smart fellow will be adorning himself with next. Another name. (To Achates again, who is busy in a corner) Well, I declare! You did not think I saw you—you forget how visible you are to the naked eye!"

"Shall I come up, sir?"

"Certainly—come out from the corner now, sir. We'll let you out now."

The last was always the climax, the chaffing with Fidus Achates. Sometimes he thought he got the best of a bout, and then his delight was intensified. People held their sides at this point, and so did Achates.

Such a holiday might not have commended itself to all, but it did to the superintendent and his band, who were very simple-hearted people, with pleasures and sorrows that were peculiarly their own. They worked hard at their avocations, most of them, and found it easy to laugh and be merry, particularly when the superintendent was about.

At the suggestion of one of the band, the superintendent arranged for services on the village greens, which were a great delight to him, not only from the strategic but from the historic standpoint. So in days gone by had Wesley and his early followers preached to the people. Oh, what had happened to them all since those days! How conventional they had all become, how tied up with red tape and formalism! Though he nerved himself to bear the thought, he could not. Why was he so conventional? He felt appalled at himself and the New Inn Hall Street congregation as well. The early Christians—they had not succumbed in this way; and those strange devotees of Newman did not spare themselves in advocating their religion. What devotion they had, to be sure! Worthy of a better cause. Clear as noonday shone the idea;

he and the New Inn Hall Street congregation should worship God in the open air as Christ's followers had done from time immemorial. A field was procured near Holywell, the oldest and most picturesque street in Oxford, and arrangements were made for a day out, provided, of course, that the weather were propitious. The whole assembly was to march, four deep, from the gates of New Inn Hall Street, and make a good tour of the city previous to entering the camp prepared for it. In warning his army of the projected expedition, he was aware of a certain hostility in the atmosphere. Such an expedition was utter innovation, and, besides, that sort of thing could surely be left to the Salvationists! The choir at first refused point-blank to accompany him, but the superintendent evinced no dismay. As with much that was said in opposition to his ideas and feelings, he received the criticisms in silence, and continued his preparations. On the Sunday morning previous to the great day, he fixed his congregation with an eye half-humorous, half-menacing.

"The question is, my dear friends, not whether you are too respectable to join our procession, but whether you are respectable enough. We start this afternoon from this church at 2.30 precisely. The circuit stewards and choir will accompany me." They did.

The earth was at her fairest that memorable afternoon, and the city enhanced the fairness thereof; man's work and Nature's blending and according as they do not often elsewhere, so long and loving has been the intimacy between mellowed wall and clinging lichen, between the green of grass and tree, and the stateliness of quadrangle, between the richness of summer flowers and that of

> "Storied windows, richly dight,
> Casting a dim religious light."

How nimble was the superintendent that afternoon! How the sunshine and the birds and the trees responded to this inner mood, and became part of it. The children led the way, singing, four deep, and the rest followed, waxing bolder with every step. At the corner of Broad Street the dilapidated faces of the Roman Emperors grinned in a ghastly fashion, as they well might, from the precincts of the Ashmolean, and the impassive forms on the roof stood out against the overarching blue, like the goddesses of old time come to view the city and the procession. He knew they were not dead, that literature and society were full of their tenets; yes, universities too—full. No wonder our public men were often heathens. The days of impressionable youth were spent over the gospel of Horace and Plato and Aristotle; not that of Christ. Christ's was a dead letter to them.

"Onward, Christian soldiers,"

sang the little girls in front, with hymn-sheets fluttering. All along the pavement the figures with floating gowns were stopping and staring. One in particular, outside the garden of Trinity, a very antediluvian brother, was opening his mouth at them.

"Marching as to war,"

sang the children,

"With the cross of Jesus"—

Ah! it was always the weak in this world who carried that cross—little children might well sing of it—there was his own little daughter, too, among the number, strutting along in that Mother Hubbard bonnet as if the whole city belonged to her—

"Going on before,"

sang the children, turning down Holywell, and singing as lustily as Fra Angelico's angels; though the superintendent had not yet made his acquaintance with these latter. But that other daughter, he thought—what a queer fish she was, marching like a sentinel along the pavement, and waiting for the procession at the street corners. She had far better join them, and so render herself less noticeable. Poor thing, poor thing; how she had inherited his failings! Yet it was too comic for words! to see her on the beat just like a policeman. . . .

"Christ, the royal Master,
Leads against the foe,"

acclaimed the singers. The sun threw deep shadows over the narrow street, and heads were being thrust out of the casements. Thank God that he had lived to see this day! to see a congregation of Christians proclaim themselves before all

men! What had the Methodists been about to let the Salvationist movement get out of their hand? . . .

> " Forward into battle,
>   See His banners go."

Ah, what had they been about, indeed, what had they been
about? . . . He scarcely heard what the children were singing
till the words—

> " We are not divided,
>   All one body we,"

smote him as a species of mockery. " That's a lie," he
thought— . . .

> " One in hope, in doctrine,
>   One in charity."

Yes, and yet they were divided. What was he to do to
bring some of them together again? Still, he must look alive,
or his particular contingent would not get to the camp at the
appointed time. What were they waiting for? . . . Don't
wait—what? nonsense, nonsense—of course we must go on—
don't listen to their tomfoolery! (To his daughter) " Is not
this fine? Are you not enjoying it, dear? I am immensely!
I wish poor So-and-so would come and join us. She looks
very unhappy, marching by herself up and down there! "

> " Crowns and thrones may perish,"

sang the little daughter and her companions, and away they
all went again.

The singular light-heartedness of that superintendent was
not misplaced. Not a few were to rise from cushioned seats
in the Church of Christ and go forth into the streets and highways because he drove forth his congregation that day. That
act was an epitome of many of his acts. In after years he
would march along Piccadilly in like manner, but it was never
quite the same as when he first walked with his choir and
circuit stewards through the city of the dreaming spires.

The visit of Mr. Moody to the city had deepened the
impression that the Church was ruining herself with smugness.
The freshness and vigour of the American enchanted him, as
did his power in preaching Christ's gospel, and bringing it

home to the hearts and consciences of men and women.
Tennyson's saying that the Churches have killed their Christ
was one that was often sadly quoted by him. It was the
tragedy of history.

He wanted his daughters to hear and to remember Moody,
so they were taken to some of the meetings, and he himself
accompanied them to the house where Moody was staying.
Before parting, he asked Moody to offer up a prayer. " He is
a very good man," he said to the daughters, " and you will be
proud to remember one day that you saw him. I did not
want him to leave Oxford without your knowing each other."
They drank in the saying as they drank in all that he told
them. They were not yet old enough to know that much of
what he said was in contradiction with what other people
said. He was the one infallible law, the stay and strength
in affliction and crisis. Whenever these latter came in special
force, they turned to him as to a strong deliverer. There was
any amount of domestic crisis at this period, particularly when
the measles attacked them, during which period their second
and youngest brother was born ; so the house was upside
down. But the strong deliverer was in his element. In the
first place, the whole atmosphere reeked with carbolic. He
extended a sheet outside the patients' door, and incessantly
imbued it with a preparation of his own brewing. The nurse
was very irate about it, but as, to quote my father's own
expression, she was a " very godly woman," he bore her ire
with much 'meekness, and continued his lubrications. The
patients lay and tossed all day for his advent.

" Really," he said to his wife some weeks later, " I never
know what I shall find when I come home, Katie. I always
look anxiously at the windows to see if the blinds are down."

Another time the eldest boy drank poison, or tried to, but
the strong deliverer was off to the chemist in the thousandth
part of a second, and sustained the agony of the daughters on
his return. He appeared to them in a more serious light than
he had done formerly. Justice dwelt with him and righteousness.
Wrong-doing, moreover, was hateful in his sight. On Easter
morning, walking with them to chapel, he told them how
St. Peter on going to the sepulchre found that Christ had risen,
and how the grave-clothes had been left, neatly folded, each

article in a place by itself. That showed how tidy we should be—how we should never leave our things without folding them up. The details of life were always a great point with him.

During the upside-down period Mr. Percy Bunting came to visit the superintendent. To discourse with one who was a Liberal, a university man, and a Methodist, was an opportunity indeed. He dined with us, and as my mother was not present, my father officiated, a task which he generally left to her. He held the carving knife and fork in a perpendicular position, and talked with his guest about Oxford, and politics, and his ideas, without showing any disposition to attack the joint. At intervals, when besought by the maid in attendance, or one of the children, he carved a slice and let it lie, and then by degrees conveyed it on to the plate. It was only by a series of providential accidents, and by repeated requests, that anybody got any dinner that day. I do not remember any other occasion on which my father was so preoccupied. Unfortunately memory does not recall the gist of the conversation, only the perpendicular knife and fork and the smoking joint.

Thus the three years at Oxford swiftly glided away, the fullest and most decisive so far in his ministry. He left the city known to Methodism at large and to an increasing number outside. The influences of this epoch cannot be overestimated, the more subtle and unseen, as well as the more palpable. Oxford was far more to him than a circuit in which he had been enabled to revive a dying Methodism. The University impressed his mind and imagination. For all his duality of feeling concerning it, he had a profound respect for some of its "antediluvian" inhabitants. He and my mother were happier there than in any of their circuits previous to coming to London. He greatly enjoyed intercourse with university men, and learnt much from it.

It opened up a side of English life and feeling which he had not hitherto had the opportunity of studying. He saw more clearly the defects of contemporary Nonconformity, and its consequent needs. At a time when his own personal observations had led him to reflect on the unsatisfactory position of his own and kindred communions in the national life, he was stirred to deeper reflection by the social and educational centre in which he worked. Here, as my mother puts it, he first realised the strength of what is called the High Church position. Previous to that, she considers, he had been more of a Congregationalist, if one can use that term respecting a Methodist. An Anglican clergyman who used to visit at our house at Oxford said that my father was a good deal more of a High Churchman than he was. If Oxford taught him anything, it was the need of catholic ideas, of wide organisation, in Church and State. Indeed, much that startled his friends in later years was already in embryo.

My father was always haunted by the knowledge that the great majority of European and British manhood lies outside the Churches, and in more or less hostility to its ministry. Instincts which had been in him from the first—intuitive knowledge of classes and aspects of mankind—were rendered acuter by his stay at the university. To quote the expression of the Methodists in the city, " He gave Nonconformity altogether a lift up." Both in the villages and in the city itself he had a propensity for taking the largest available building. His gifts as a speaker were so much in demand that when a royal princess came to attend a function in the city, the wife of the Dean of Christchurch went to Fidus Achates at his stall in the market, and asked if there was any possibility of securing Mr. Hughes for the ceremony. Mr. Hughes, however, was unable to comply. At the mayor's annual banquet, he astonished those present by his allusions to political affairs. The aldermen and the company sat up generally. Was this fellow a parliamentary candidate or a Methodist parson, that he had the imbroglios of Europe and the Government Bills at his finger-ends? At a meeting where the Rev. Mark Pattison, Rector of Lincoln College, was in the chair, my father referred to the fact that no adequate memorial of John Wesley existed in a university, of whose sons he was one of the greatest.

The rector stirred, and audibly corrected, " Not one of the *greatest*."

Hearing which the speaker replied, " I repeat what I said, sir ; one of the *greatest*. Indeed," he continued, " nothing has caused me greater astonishment since I came to Oxford, than the ignorance of the University with regard to the world-wide work and influence of Wesley. The founder of a Church which numbers twenty-five millions "—

11

" No, no, Mr. Hughes," interrupted the rector ; " twenty-five thousand, you mean, not twenty-five millions."

Amid breathless silence the speaker dived into his coat pocket and produced a pocket-book, from which he proceeded to verify his statement. A correspondence ensued, in which the rector and the superintendent had a long discussion upon Wesley's claims to greatness. If a man with so world-wide an influence, and so palpable an effect on history, was not great, was the substance of his argument, who then was ?

The two following letters are characteristic. The second points to the progress of the Temperance cause in Methodism. Conference had appointed a Temperance Committee, of which my father was the secretary.

" SELBORNE VILLA, BLACK HALL ROAD, OXFORD,
"*June* 29, 1882.

" MY DEAR FRIEND,—Go on, go on, go on. I am much interested in your work. I would gladly do anything in my power to help you, but I am overwhelmed just now in anticipation of Conference.

" Let *cheerful audacity* be your motto. Keep your eyes and ears open. The *Salvation Army* may suggest methods of work to you, so may the *Ritualists*, so may the *devil.* Imitate anybody or anything in whatever is innocent and seemly. . . . . The great need of London Methodism, with all its splendid virtues just now, is direct aggressive work among the poor and the outcasts. Go on, then, and the Lord be with you. Let me hear how you are getting on.—Yours very sincerely,

" H. P.HUGHES.

" Mr. Hogben."

" SELBORNE VILLA, BLACK HALL ROAD, OXFORD,
"*July* 4, 1883.

" MY DEAR BROTHER,—I learn from the Conference circular that upon you rests the solemn responsibility of distributing the bodies of your brethren over Great Thornton Street Chapel. Will you kindly take note of the fact that it has pleased providence to furnish the Temperance Secretary with legs of unusual length and sensibility, and that, consequently, any undue compression of those legs in an inadequate pew would have a most distressing effect upon the temper of the Temperance Secretary and upon the Conference. It is also of great importance that the Temperance Secretary should have a full view of the platform, that he might drink in without distraction all the godly counsels which flow so freely from that watershed. The Temperance Secretary will be most happy to reward any Christian attention to his legs, in the usual English manner, by free gifts of his favourite beverage.

"Trusting that your duties may not give you much trouble, —Yours sincerely,

"H. P. HUGHES.

"Rev. R. Bentley."

During the winter of 1883–1884 he saw less of Oxford, as he was appointed to conduct special missions in various large towns throughout the country.

In the meantime he had accepted an invitation to become superintendent of the Brixton Hill Circuit at the ensuing Conference.

The following characteristic letter is written to my mother, while he was away on one of these special missions :—

"*Dec.* 4, 1882.

"I was greatly delighted to receive your welcome letter, and to learn that all was well. On Saturday night I met a large number of the workers, and we had a lively time. The Sunday morning congregation was nothing special, but on Sunday afternoon the first mission service—arranged for men only—was a glorious success. The huge chapel was crowded in every part by men. We had at least two thousand there! They say they never before had such a service there. God was with us, and a good many went into the inquiry rooms. At night, although it was raining, the chapel was packed, and many in the aisles. We took eighty names in the vestries yesterday. We have made a very hopeful beginning. I am very comfortable here. I like the —— very much. The girls are capital company, and we get on together well. They had the most extraordinary ideas of me before I came. They expected a short, fat, supercilious, æsthetic, very clever, terrible being, who scanned everybody through his glasses, talked most learnedly, made everybody feel small, who never associated except with the leading families of Methodism, had a great deal of aristocratic hauteur, etc. In fact, they were quite frightened, and thought I should never be able to put up with such homely and common people as themselves! Isn't it amusing? How is it I have this reputation for being so clever, so aristocratic, and so terrible? I, poor meek dog, that tremble in your presence.

"I hope you are quite well again. Go on praying for me.

"Give much love to the children, but most of all to yourself.

"Longing to be with you again.—Your devoted,

"HUGH.

"Mrs. Hughes."

CHAPTER VIII

A JOURNAL OF RELIGIOUS AND SOCIAL MOVEMENT

ÆTAT 37–40. 1884–1887

"With that deep insight which detects
    All great things in the small,
And knows how each man's life affects
    The spiritual life of all,
He walked by faith and not by sight,
    By love and not by law ;
The presence of the wrong or right
    He rather felt than saw.

He felt that wrong with wrong partakes,
    That nothing stands alone,
That whoso gives the motive, makes
    His brother's sin his own.
And, pausing not for doubtful choice
    Of evils great or small,
He listened to that inward voice
    Which called away from all."

                                        WHITTIER.

"An age burdened and distracted by innumerable publications has a
right to demand unimpeachable credentials from a new journal. We believe that the course of events will justify our existence ; but we hasten at
once to state the long-felt want which has so suddenly and so unexpectedly
taken shape. The younger generation of Methodists have hitherto had no
literary organ through which they could freely interchange thoughts, convictions, and aspirations. Thackeray said that a great need of English
society was a journal written by gentlemen for gentlemen. The great need
of that vast movement called Methodism is a journal written by young
Methodists for young Methodists. During the last quarter of a century
a silent educational revolution has been gradually effecting an immense
change. We do not believe that the younger generation has abandoned
any one of the essential doctrines of John Wesley. We, at any rate, are
prepared to argue in detail that the broad, catholic, tender-hearted theology
of early Methodism is the goal towards which the best modern thought, the
discoveries of science, and the generous humanitarianism of our day are

165

perpetually tending. Nevertheless, the intellectual environment of the younger generation is widely different from that in which their fathers lived. The standpoint is greatly changed. The horizon is indefinitely widened. New worlds of thought and fact have come into full view."— *Extract from first leader of " Methodist Times," January* 1, 1885.

MY father's removal to what was then one of the pleasantest of London suburbs, did not check the new phase in his career which Oxford had commenced. He had long ceased to be a separate individual in society at large—its hopes and fears and problems had for many years been his own, and now he ceased to be an individual in the life of the Churches. The two strains of Christian humanitarianism and Church statesmanship may be said to have run in parallel lines, so did the two provide answers for each other's necessities.

As already mentioned, he was a disciple of Maurice, and almost unconsciously, in common with the most thoughtful and unselfish minds, he had been led to study the problems and conditions of the great cities, more particularly of London, on the outskirts of which he was living. A lady who often stayed with my mother and father during the early portion of their married life, told me that she never found them where she had left them. Some book or contemporary incident had caused them to move on several paces to her one ; at one time it was the Larger Hope, at another the doings and ideas of a particular statesman, at another their own thoughts and comments. It was in their united life that much of the leadership of the so-called Forward Movement in Methodism took its rise.

Another factor in the movement was undoubtedly the observation of contemporary life, coupled with its fellow, experiment. He was swift in observing as in everything else, and noted the smallest details with unerring exactitude.[1]

Even more than observation, he delighted in the Socratic questioning, which he pursued even more mercilessly than Socrates. Omnibus drivers, navvies, shop assistants, railway

---

[1] Any small imperfection, whether in dress, household appointments, or in the arrangements for meetings and services, never escaped his eye, and gave him the greatest distress. He would often amuse his family by descriptions of his misery, because Mr. So-and-so's coat did not fit him properly, or at such-and-such a meeting the arrangements were all promiscuous and slovenly.

men, all manner of persons in railway carriages, were to him fields of endless inquiry. Friends and relatives in particular exercised a spacious field for his art. " I always feel," said a friend of one of his daughters, " that your father squeezes me like a sponge and then drops me." His children scarcely needed questioning, so trained were they to know what would interest him. If they had seen anything of interest, they must describe it; if they had read anything, they must tell him what they had read. That was the way of entertaining him. They knew at once whether this information was of any account. If it was, came the invariable " What—what? what was that, dear?" and a clutch at their arm; if it was not, he appeared abstracted, and murmured, " Very pretty," or " Just so," which was ignominy. Innocent persons whom he met in trains poured forth their souls, imagining, as the sons and daughters never imagined, that every item was equally precious.

One who was afterwards a member of the sisterhood that he and my mother inaugurated, remembers to this day how he plied a working man whom he met in the train near White-chapel. Afterwards, when the idea of a London mission was mooted, she remembered the incident; some of the method which underlay his madness became apparent to her.

Observation certainly did much to foster what contemporaries laughingly called the " Forward Movement."[1] He talked so much about going forward, and was such an embodiment of movement, that the epithet arose almost of necessity. Nor was the movement confined to Methodism, any more than the agitation produced by a strong wind is confined to one particular portion of the ocean. It much resembled, indeed, such an elemental disturbance. The silent deeps responded to the strong wind of his spirit, and became voiceful. In particular, the hearts of the people called Methodists, from east to west and back again from west to east, were swept like a lyre by that strong wind, and gave that deep reverberating response which only proceeds from the heart of a people. As he con-

---

[1] This title was first given to the new movement by Mrs. Alexander McArthur, at a dinner-party held at her house at Brixton Hill. Some one present was speaking slightingly of the work and aspirations of the superintendent, and his hostess at once interrupted him with: "Oh, Mr. ——, you must not say that here. *We* all belong to the 'Forward' party." It was fitting that the Forward Movement first received its title from the lips of a woman.

sidered that all Methodists should be Catholics in a sense that will be described later,[1] and lovers of mankind, he spoke for sections of the community who knew nothing whatsoever of Methodism, and lived quite outside it. Once in a debate in Conference a witty opponent remarked, " We have heard a great deal of the ' Forward Movement' lately, but I cannot see any movement, though " (looking at my father) " I can see a great deal of forwardness ! " The object of this witticism much appreciated it, and often quoted it against himself.

Where was the movement indeed ? Deeper than plummet ever sounded, where the eye of pure wit could not penetrate. If those who felt it could have sent representatives into the Conference that day, and said, " Please, Mr. President, we are the Forward Movement," what a very various collection they would have been—as surprising to the leader of the movement as to his opponents. Certainly the last named should have sent a representative, if only to bear testimony to the extent to which their opposition had made life interesting to them. All critics and disapprovers of the movement were profoundly indebted to it, as well as those persons who have nothing to talk about but Mr. So-and-so's new brougham, and what he said while he was getting out of it. Heaven only knows what Mr. Hughes and the movement did for some of these. For all the Semitic assertiveness of certain portions of his personality, he could never cease wondering that he should be regarded as the originator of the movement, so conscious was he, under all the subjectiveness of which some men accused him, that he was merely expressing, eliciting, what lay in others. " Is it not strange," he would say, " that they identify me with all this ? I don't know how it is, I am sure. Are not you surprised at it ? "

The first great wave that the disturbance sent rolling up on the shore of contemporary affairs was the *Methodist Times* —the expression in writing of what it thought and felt, and often very specially what Hugh Price Hughes thought and felt ; for he was its editor. The position had not been undertaken without some discussion and a good deal of diffidence on his part.

With a group of friends at Brixton he had been advocating

[1] *See* Chapter XVII. " The Catholic Idea of the Church."

such a newspaper. Even in those reactionary days there had been attempts to start a more liberal organ—both political and ecclesiastical—than those which already existed. But he could scarcely face the thought of being its editor — he doubted his competency. Post-haste he wrote to Dr. Moulton, his revered adviser, and to some of the undergraduates to whom he used to lay down the law in his own drawing-room at Oxford. They would advise, perhaps encourage him. They encouraged him, and he became editor. While there is no doubt that it added to his daily labour, it became a most congenial portion, and so much part of himself that it is impossible to picture his career without it. "A very Hughesful paper," his opponents called it.

The paper came to reflect not only the new life and aspiration which had come into Methodism, but the aspiration and thought of many persons of other communions and no communions, who were in sympathy with lovers of mankind, and who would have deemed it impossible a few months back that they should ever be contributors to a Methodist paper. The editor had a great knack of gathering such around him. A suggestion was made indeed among the little conclave who first hatched the new scheme, that the paper should be entitled the "British" instead of the *Methodist Times*, but it was quickly overruled. They were Methodists, and they wished the world to know that as Methodists they felt and thought in a particular manner. But as one closely associated with the paper related, "Our circulation would have been larger if we had. The word Methodist shut out ever so many." Now my father wanted the word so to bewitch men that they would fly to a journal bearing such a title. As it was, it had a larger circulation outside Methodism than any other Methodist paper. Persons at the ecclesiastical poles took it in, if only to see what that amazing editor was about. To this day it is the only Methodist paper taken in the reading-rooms of the Oxford University Union, and it is to be had in libraries and reading-rooms, the solitary representative of the religious journal.

In the days of its sharpest engagements—for with such an editor it was bound to go forth to battle—the circulation would go up surprisingly, and most unlooked-for persons would be found poring over its columns. Normally it had a circulation

of twenty-four thousand, but that was far from indicating the
radius of its influence. Not only was it read by men and
women who were more thoughtful and able than those around
them, and therefore leaders in their different capacities, but in
many districts where readers could not afford to take in an
additional paper, one copy would be passed round to as many
as six or ten people. Fidus Achates—and the number of
him increased in leaps and bounds in these later years—read
it wherever he was, and that was sometimes far over the seas,
where the reader had never seen the editor, or heard his
resonant voice. Its circulation in the colonies was its most
unique feature—perhaps the greatest contribution to the
Imperial Methodism which it propagated. It brought such
men into touch with the editor's personality. They heard his
voice crying to them to consecrate life and all its sides, social,
political, and domestic, to that Christ about whom he wrote so
vehemently. Some of them had hitherto held that man was
only bound to serve his Master in his own home, for by that
means he would save his soul from destruction. So it startled
men, as it had startled Achates in the suburbs, that he was no
more free to serve what he considered his own peculiar interests
outside the family circle, than he was within. Achates was
generally of Methodist descent, and had cause to know what
this religious revival had done for the elevation of family life,
but he never imagined it outstepping those proscribed grounds.
The extension, while it surprised, yet fascinated and stirred him.
The Forward Movement was really a very old movement, and
dated back its origin to the Crusades, and the figure appealed
to odd strains of mediæval chivalry within him.

A Welsh minister who wrote to us at the time of my
father's passing could not restrain a certain glee at this aspect
of his character, though, like all who speak his tongue, he finds
Anglo-Saxon rather a hindrance in the expression of the higher
emotions.

"Personally, I have viewed the steady rising of the Rev. Hugh Price
Hughes into public note for many years, and lawfully prided in the gallantry,
yea, the sanctified prowess of the Welshman, who fearlessly thrusted the
sword of truth to the very hilt into the very heart of the enemy of God, a
virtue irrespective of and regardless personal gain or loss. . . .

"The catholicity of his heart, which was large enough to embrace

Christianity, placed him on the very summit of the Christian Church of to-day. . . .

"Oh! what a loss Christendom has received! The loss of one whose faith in the possibilities of the Christian Church was unlimited. One who could make his plans broad enough for God to enter into them and to call forth His infinite power to carry them into effect. Mr. Hughes appeared to me always as a man to whom incessant labour and suffering carried to him great charm in their train."

Not the least striking adherents of the movement were those who never saw or heard its leader. In America there were bishops and professors who read the *Methodist Times* with nods of affirmation, as if they were reading the gospel; while the leaders of Wesleyan Methodism in England—as one old minister lately told me—thought it "a flash in the pan," so hardly is a prophet judged in his own country.

"The *Methodist Times*," wrote the President of an American university to a member of the family, "has just arrived, and is awaiting me on the breakfast table."

"You surprise me. I agree with it heart and soul," said an American bishop to some English critics, to whose prejudices it was a species of red rag. There was a saltness in those trenchant editorial utterances which reminded him of the breezes of his own Atlantic.

The editor would never write for any but strenuous souls. He demolished at once any effort to popularise the paper and make it pay by the usual concessions to human weakness. Certainly ceremonies and marriages and personalia had a place in it from time to time, but it was a studiously minor place. If men and women wanted such commodities they must buy another paper—he was not going to cater for them. The idea of making it a monetary concern was a species of horror to him. He would rather have given up the paper altogether.

The first leader was perhaps the most characteristic thing he ever wrote. It epitomised that urbanity and delight in the many-sidedness of life which the fierceness of his fights sometimes prevented men from seeing. He sees in it a new order of young Methodists imbibing to the full the privileges of the new and happier era—trained in those universities to which their fathers were denied access. He is very careful also in the use of his pronouns to show that there are women in the new order, side by side with the men, and that he is writing for them and to them quite as much as he is writing to the others. Not many of his contemporaries saw woman quite as he saw her. It was something unique. All through this early urbane period, full of Oxford reminiscences, he is most careful to include and address woman, not as a wearer of bonnets, but as the possessor of a soul as strenuous as his own. The reason why this urbanity so suddenly ceases is because all at once he becomes engaged in her defence, and continues to be so with scarcely a break till the end.

His eye rested lovingly on this order of privileged youth, and with equal love and a peculiar throb of compassion on what writers and speakers called "the masses," the myriads of souls who labour and are forgotten, and who in modern times are struggling towards articulation. He wanted the *Methodist Times* to help them towards this articulation.

In particular, he looked to, and was interested in, the intelligent artisan—a distinct and new feature in the social horizon, and the best representative of the classes from which he sprang. He was eminently representative of those classes in that he seldom or never went to church—so as early as the first number there was an article by Mr. Broadhurst entitled " Are the Working Classes indifferent to Religion ? "

He wanted questions to be fairly and squarely handled from all points, so that they could be grappled with, and that there might be no chance of the saints living in a vain delusion. In addition, he could never cease sorrowing that Methodism had lost hold of this class for whose ministrations she had largely, in the first instance, been created. Alack, alack, she had ceased to be the Church of the people, to express and to respond to their needs. One side of him, for all his joyousness, was a suppressed lamentation. Ground had been lost irretrievably ; but if he could manage it, the *Methodist Times* should help the toilers in their articulation, particularly, as was fitting, those who had been at all influenced by or connected with Methodism. In course of time a column was specially devoted to local preachers, that order which, perhaps more than any other, has kept her in touch with Democracy. The gratitude of the working man for the editor's regard was very touching. A companion remembers his reading a long letter from one of them, and this must have been one of many. They would suddenly accost him also in the streets with, " I should like to shake hands with the editor of the *Methodist Times* "; and, as one of them afterwards expressed it, " He said ' Here you are then,' and shook hands very heartily." The wearer of bonnets was not, it is to be feared, as grateful as she ought to have been. She preferred those journals which conceded to human weakness.

But in addition to representing sections of humanity and its aspirations which were not represented in Wesleyan Methodism, the *Methodist Times* did in a special sense articulate the editor, so that its early critics were half-justified in regarding the paper as "Hughes-ful." His shifting moods and impressions were revealed in it with mirror-like fidelity. If he saw or read anything that specially interested him—in short, if he admired or hated anything—if contemporary affairs or a special incident stirred him to reflections, lament, or prognostication, it was all there, straight from his pen, in a kind of red-hot condition that gave the paper its peculiar personality. He wrote his notes (for they, with the leader, were his peculiar preserves) at odd moments, immediately after reading or hearing anything that struck him. He did not wait to write them one after the other in decorous and reflective style, unless indeed he wrote a series so as to render some of his " charges " and reflections more effective. It became increasingly his habit to dictate the notes and often the leaders. As he dictated he would pace up and down his study with a fervour that would have astonished anyone but his secretary. The audience to whom he wrote was arrayed in spirit before him, and he addressed them with all that force and inward consuming of which he was capable. He dictated much as he spoke, only more deliberately, and he scarcely ever corrected himself. He was eminently the speaker, not the writer, and in that lay the charm of what he wrote to many. " We hear his voice," they said—and after he had passed away, and they took up the paper again—" It is very good, but his voice is not there."

When he wrote, it was with astonishing rapidity. As an instance of his facility in this respect, the following story is told at the office. A leading Methodist, Sir William McArthur, died suddenly on the day the paper went to press. My father had just left the printer's when he heard the news. "It is too late," they said; "we cannot possibly insert it this week." "No, no," was the reply, "we must have it." Whereupon he hurried back to the printer's, took out pencil and paper, sat down on the nearest available seat, and in about half an hour had produced a full obituary.

There was always something strong, definite, and clear that he wished to say, and he said it in the epigrammatic, forceful way that he put things to men—deliberately, one is tempted to think. The mass of mankind does not remember discourses and trains of argument, and, unfortunately, not as they might, deep poetic utterances, but they do pithy and startling sayings; perhaps that was why our Lord spoke in paradoxes. So men of pedantic and unimaginative minds were often much horrified at my father's way of putting things, but the majority of men who live altogether outside academicism, turned his sayings over in their hearts—to good account, many of them—while even the ultra-academics were so stirred to opposition by the apparent "one-sidedness" of what he said, that their vision and position was visibly enriched and fortified. In some cases the monstrous sayings came home to them afterwards, with an import that they would not in days past have deemed possible.

The press, in commenting upon his journalistic powers, which all sections agreed to be striking, gave as their secret that felicitous manner of turning into a phrase the thought that was in his mind. He "coined expressions," one said, and made them "current." A really wonderful expression at this period to designate the Methodism of the sixties was "our Chinese inflexibility." Another pregnant saying was "the devil loves melancholy saints," and another, "men are evangelised in sections."

The element of deliberation in his method came out in his proof-correcting. Persons who were connected with him in this respect were often almost annoyed because he was so particular. He did not like anything to go to press till he had revised it two or three times.

But revise it as he might, it was the paper of a Celt, and that was why so many English people did not understand it. A good test of pure Celtic origin was to read the *Methodist Times* without turning a hair. You might disagree, but if you were a pure Celt you did not regard the way of putting things as otherwise than normal. I knew an Irish lady who was quite surprised that people should be offended at my father's utterances, though she did not always agree with him herself by any means. "Why, of course, if he does not like what anybody's doing, he just writes as if he hates them—so should I"; and the writer was quite unconscious that he had ever suggested such an emotion, especially when he was opposing men with whom he had some divergence. Perhaps when he opposed the strong *versus* the weak, he did hate the enemy in a certain sense—not individually, but collectively as a force in society, and for that evil in man which they represented. They were of their father the devil. His wrath was elemental, like the rest of him, and it was pure as the elements are pure.

Men could not forget what he wrote any more than they could forget him. A member of the Liberal Government once said to a friend, "I can't sleep at night. Hughes is at me in the Notes."

"Don't read them," replied the wise friend.

"I must," was the answer.

But the *Methodist Times* was also his in a very special and intimate sense—it revealed what was unexpected in him. Once a relative said to him, "Hugh, you never write. We simply know nothing about you." "Read," he answered, "the *Methodist Times*. They are my letters." The advice was repeated as one of his most outrageous utterances; in reality it was one of his sanest. They were his letters to mankind, and his relatives included. They contained much of what he felt and thought from day to day, and if he had been able to write more private letters than he did, he would but have said the same things over again in shorter form.

In notes that the journalist's swift glance omitted, in leaders that Fidus Achates perhaps wondered why he wrote, he revealed those contradictory flashes of himself, those unsuspected regions of his personality, which a certain spiritual intimacy could only divine. It was the suggestions of development that made him specially dear to such. They honoured him, not for what he had actually accomplished, as others did, but for what he was still striving to do. Certain regions of him had to lie fallow here; he strove to plough and water them, but could not. A good many knew him only on the fallow side.

As George Eliot once remarked, " There is more unmapped territory in persons' natures than they imagine," and there was much that was unmapped in his. He was very surprised and piqued when someone mentioned this to him. " Unmapped territory," he kept repeating to himself. Then when friends came to see him he would accost them with, " I say, have you any unmapped territory ? "

In addition to facility of expression, he had an instinct for affairs and for picking out what was most salient in them. His wide newspaper reading from his youth up, and his powers of observation, sent him fully equipped to his task, for all his diffidence in its assumption. Last, and not least, he had the faculty, which his overcrowded life did not permit him to fully use, of gathering round him a variety of contributors, and in every gifted or representative person with whom he conversed he saw a possible article. A lady who afterwards became a friend of his, had an unusual insight into Browning, and gave my father the benefit of it when he was staying in Devonshire. " We must have some interpretations of yours in the *Methodist Times*," he said; and they had. The literary reviews were always one of its features. The first number came out on January 1, 1885, and the editor was in a fever of impatience the whole of the previous night. The printers were behind-hand, and he was obliged to leave the office without seeing the first printed number, in order to conduct the watchnight service at his church at Brixton Hill. But no sooner was the service over than he came bounding back, and took a long walk with one of the directors and two members of the staff round St. Paul's and Covent Garden and back again to the office. At four o'clock in the morning he was waving the first copy over his head. Well might his critics describe his paper as " The Boy's Own."

His humour and buoyancy in the office never flagged all the years that he was editor, except on rare occasions when he was physically overwrought. His staunchest adherents, and the most faithful among the ranks of Achates, were to be found in Fleet Street. The neighbourhood, for all its ceaseless rush and turmoil in a world that stands still for nobody, still speaks to them of him, and recalls his ever-remembered presence. At the French café at the bottom of Ludgate Hill, the first directors of the paper used to meet on Thursday mornings to see how things were getting on, and the editor sat with them, radiant "as a child over a new toy," so observers have expressed it. Even more voiceful is the A.B.C. in Fetter Lane, where the editor, arm in arm with the sub., used to resort in the afternoon to have a cup of his favourite beverage. As they crossed the road, the editor's arm gripped that of the sub. like a vice, for he knew the sub. to be impetuous, and he feared he would be run over. When they walked laughing and chatting into the shop and all the people turned to look at them, he would say, still with his arm in that of the sub., "They are wondering what I am doing in the company of such a villain as you." In that part of London the editor came to be a familiar figure, and in later years a brother minister noted how passers-by turned to look at him as he walked down the Strand.

His advent on Wednesday was ever the signal for a general rising of spirits and that bracing of activities, bodily and mental, that generally accompanies a transportation to the seaside. To the eldest member of the staff, a venerable man who adored him, he would say, "What wild deed are you at present contemplating? Jump from the window, my dear sir, or from the roof, and make a name for yourself, and the paper and all of us. It would be exquisite to see your agile leap, and if you only led the way I might summon up courage to follow." Then to the sub., "What new idea have you got? with what are you going to startle the world?"

The most delightful he seemed to them of all their companions; yet, what a leader! particularly when times were bad. "We have got to fight for great principles," he said, "and we shall win in the end." Like all who worked with him in whatever capacity, they laid stress on the fact that he was the reverse of exorbitant, and never autocratic in a position where the mildest men look upon autocracy as something quite justifiable. He got the best out of them, partly because his confidence in their capacity and trustworthiness was so boundless that it overwhelmed them, and partly because it was part

12

of his influence to scoop out all the grit there was in a person. But, while admitting this, they laid stress on his intense sympathy and appreciativeness, not only with the difficulties of their work, but with the difficulties and the joys of their lives. When they were in a difficult place they told him of it, and he did his best to help them out. When they were out, he experienced the greatest relief, and was readier than ever to light up at the next joy that befell them. He would take the youngest assistant into his confidence, asking his advice and listening to his suggestions, as if he were equally concerned as himself in giving the paper a " lift up."

Any special bit of painstaking or improvement in their work he was quick to note and to approve. The post-cards, which some of them carefully preserved, bear the same mark of genial intimacy. One such missive to the business editor bears the advice, " I have done everything you wanted. Oh, what a good boy am I ! "

" A nature that," to quote the business manager, " had a habit of retiring into its shell," blossomed in the society of kindly and genial souls.

For all his communicativeness and conversational powers, few men wanted more knowing, a fact to which the business manager gave his assent. Not a year passed but opened up something fresh in his chief, and went to increase the admiration in which he held his character. The weeks which had followed his death had been like so many Black Fridays one after the other. It was a veritable house of mourning, and how they kept the old boat going none of them knew.

In less than a year after a mellifluous beginning, the paper was in the thick of its first fight over the revelations that appeared in Mr. Stead's articles on " The Maiden Tribute of Modern Babylon " in the *Pall Mall Gazette*. Mr. Stead, who knew my father well as a fighter and in no other capacity, has told the tale of how he came to him on the morning of their publication, white and pale and quite terrible to look upon, so repressed was his wrath.

" Is it true ? " he asked simply. He found it so hard to believe that he wanted assurance, but having obtained it, he did not hesitate. Every trenchant word and adjective that his tongue could frame or his pen could write, every chord of his great heart, he brought with him into the field that day. Those qualities which made him make mountains out of molehills stood him in good stead on that and similar occasions. Not one whit did he care who came out to meet him, friend or foe, in the Church or out of it, they were all equally Apollyon to him—enemies to Christ and His little ones, rather than offend whom a man had better have a millstone cast about his neck and be cast to the depths of the sea. He neither gave quarter nor asked for it when he did battle for the weak. Yet some persons were too holy to read the revelations, to read of what was pitilessly going on. " My God," he thought, " and Thou didst suffer for the innocent ; for these Thy bloody sweat was shed in Gethsemane. How men smiled and smiled and were villains. And there, in the suburbs, men and women sang hymns in cushioned pews, and were inclined to disapprove of any person who told them of these facts and broke in upon their pharisaic calm. No, Lord, it was not for Thy little ones that Thou agonised—they have done no wrong—it was for these." Such must have been the nature of his thoughts.

Till Mr. Stead came out of prison and was grasped by his hand when he was yet a few minutes' walk from the door, he had one champion who never let him out of sight. Later, he joined Mr. Stead and Mr. Benjamin Waugh in their campaign through the country, which led to the passing of the Criminal Law Amendment Act.

It must have been about this time that he offended some of the inhabitants of the suburbs by his allusions, from the pulpit, to their manner of living. These allusions were often not untouched with humour, and the friends and admirers, of whom he had many, despite all his critics, smiled as they listened. To pray collectively about the saints and their cushioned seats was not quite the same as looking down upon them at sermon time, and remembering that they were but mortal. " Convert us all, Lord," he prayed once, " to the depths of our pockets ! " He knew that that was the rub, but the saints were scandalised. How irreverent ! " We don't want," they would say in the intervals of Sunday dinner, " to be inspired any more. We want to be built up."

But some of their sons and daughters were all agog, a

company of them joining the Mission Band under the leadership of Fidus Achates, *alias* Mr. Nix, who had accompanied
my father from Oxford as lay agent. When the season of
a special mission came round, which was frequent, they would
patrol the streets of the neighbourhood, and on one occasion
in the snow at six o'clock in the morning. "Everybody," said
a lady who was in this patrol, "came to the windows in their
night attire and stared at us. There was a good attendance
at the chapel, as I am sure many of the people thought we
were mad and were anxious to see what we were after."

The crowded building is one of the most vivid memories
of that period. The arithmetic teacher at the High School
used to come struggling up the aisle with the rest whenever
my father preached, and her mobile face and her shrugs at his
sallies, half-fearful to his children because she shrugged over
their arithmetic books, was a peculiarly fascinating study.
Did she approve, they wondered? Apparently, for she often
came again. She appeared to smile and shrug over what he
said, and then to let it sink into her mind, and to smile at the
remembrance. At recreation time at school she would come
and ask when he was to preach again, with the smile on her
face that his name always seemed to evoke. It was then
that they began dimly to realise that there was an exceptional
element in their father; this and other incidents, coupled with
the talk of the chapel-keeper and his wife, and the crowds that
were always expected at his services, made him appear in a new
aspect.

Sometimes his words aroused opposition. A massive-
looking man in front of their pew in chapel shook his head
violently several times during the sermon. The youngest,
with the keen political instinct of the family, solved the
enigma. "'Spects he's a 'servative,"—a solution which was
repeated to the preacher. He was as interested as they were.

Another time, a gentleman bowed his head in his hands
in the middle of a sermon and sobbed unrestrainedly—a very
unusual occurrence. People's faces were often expressive
enough, but they were not in the habit of giving outward
expression to their feelings.

That the tenets of the world were not necessarily in accordance with their father's was borne upon his children by the

comments that he made on the ideas of their English history mistress. The greatest divergence between them apparently lay in their conceptions of Charles I. She spoke very tenderly of the monarch, and said that, being what he was, he could not help feeling and acting as he did. My father was scornful. " Supposing," he said, " I was to go and give her a kick, do you think she would say I could not help it ? " The simile appealed to them, and they took to repeating all she and others said in the hope of eliciting similar similes.

But the greatest divergence between him and a large portion of mankind was brought home to them by two words that came to be writ larger and larger in their mental horizon, to wit, " Home Rule." Some of their relations began to perplex them at this point. They said that they wondered a man so clever as their father could advocate anything so unheard-of. Their listeners strove for Home Rule and for him. As they learnt later, he had been opposed to Home Rule in earlier years on account chiefly of the representations of the Irish Methodist ministry, but Mr. Gladstone's championship had finally caused him to change his mind. The scenes taking place in the House with regard to the admission of Mr. Bradlaugh provoked comment, and were painful to him.

On a very early morning in June 1887, there was an unusual roll of carriages down Brixton Hill, and the household throbbed with the fact that its master had gone to Westminster to see the Jubilee. The *Methodist Times* took him ; he went as an editor. Home Rule had temporarily given way to the most fervent expressions of loyalty, and the family waited agog till his return. He was first at the door——that was reiterated, but it was what they had anticipated——and he sat in a place where he had a good view of the members of the Houses of Parliament. The peers and peeresses were always getting up and bobbing, but the Commons, as became their innate superiority, leant backwards with folded arms, rarely rising, and that for the most illustrious. Suddenly they all sprang to their feet as did everybody else, and without exception,——generals, ambassadors, attachés, high chamberlains, noble dukes and earls, cabinet ministers, sticks-in-waiting, and all the rest. The Queen had come, and the organ was pealing " God Save Her." There was no more rank now : the cabinet minister

was the same as an editor, all equally subjects. Such a hush
there was then, such a lowering as of a cornfield before the
wind, the stillness of common reverence. There was no more
precedence and heart-burning, but a Queen who made all men
one. This transformation sank deep into the most observant of
editors. It was a transformation that inspired him, and he
often saw it again in vision, but with a difference in the central
figure, seeking as he always did, like his beloved St. John on
Patmos, to describe heavenly things in earthly imagery. For
he had a habit of according pageants, as he had accorded the
university at Oxford, a significance and a symbolism that other
men did not accord them, who saw men and things and nothing
more. The generals and the ambassadors and the attachés
and the dukes and the high chamberlains and the editors and
the labour candidates and the poets and the professors, all
stood up and were all one. And there was no more precedence
and heart-burning. Jesus Christ of Nazareth was in their
midst, the Son of God, who had not where to lay His head
when He came to this world, because He came to found a
kingdom that was not of it. The kingdom had come, as the
disciple whom He loved saw it, coming down out of heaven.
Ah, that was it—out of heaven—not safe shut up within—
while good men sang maudlin hymns about it below. That
coming down out of heaven was the meaning of all his madness and the transports of Fidus Achates. For the present,
though far from that day, he saluted it, and in evening services
at St. James's Hall afterwards the "salute" would become contagious as he repeated this incident—those sitting behind him
and scattered members of the congregations ready to jump
there and then from their seats because the King of Glory was
passing by, and the generals and ambassadors and dukes and
high chamberlains and editors and labour candidates and poets
and professors were going at last to own their King, to accept
the ethic and the politic and the ideals of His kingdom, and to
become His subjects.

When the Thanksgiving was over, the Queen kissed all her
children and grandchildren, and the editor of the *Methodist
Times* was much affected at that, wiping his eyes as his own
father might have done during one of his sermons. The tears
did not prevent him from noting whom she kissed twice over,

from which he deduced that some of her descendants were dearer to her than the others. In particular, she kissed the Crown Prince of Germany twice over, as she well might, and as he would have done in her place. Now there was a prince for you! He could not take his eyes off him, tall and kingly and beautiful to look upon, and so devout—his eyes tight shut through all the prayers. A man of peace, too, from all he had heard and could divine—not like his warlike father. If he had had a prepossession in favour of the Crown Prince, it increased tenfold from that day. The Crown Prince and his wife were the two royal figures in Europe that he loved best. He did not think they would find it difficult to stand up when the King of Glory went by.

And our Queen, she had been devout too; he saw her singing the hymns, and she shut her eyes just as her grandson did. She was the only good monarch we have ever had, with the exception of King Alfred and perhaps William III. They had all been a very disreputable lot. In addition to her domestic virtues, she had quietly made concessions to the people, and allowed them to govern themselves; that was why the people should pay her honour.

By this time the editor and his daughters were having tea with Fidus Achates at Norwood, preparatory to seeing the fireworks at the Crystal Palace. The conversation had shifted to the people, and John Bright's portrait was turned to the wall —the people were leaving him behind, and that was why his picture was thus reversed. Home Rule, of course, was the key to the puzzle—and they were back again waving the old banner while the enemy raged. The march of the people became strangely impressive, but they wished well to our Queen—that was certain and reassuring. When she died a Republican party might be formed, but not until then.[1]

My father shook his head at the suggestion; the country was not ripe, or indeed suited, for such a Government. Who was to keep the dukes and attachés in order; the bobbing, as

---

[1] A glance at the politics of the time showed that his prognostication was by no means unjustified. The Liberal and Progressive Government which was in power was at its zenith of popularity, and it had, like most powerful parties, an extreme left, the Radical party, as they were called, in which Mr. Chamberlain and Sir Charles Dilke were conspicuous.

he had witnessed it that morning, gave them something to do. Half-sadly he made what he was always making, concessions to Anglo-Saxon environment; the English race had to be taken as it was, not as it might be. But the people went on marching, and there were crowds of them soon at the Crystal Palace to witness the fireworks.

"Shall we see?" my father inquired of Fidus Achates. "How do you know our position is a good one?"

"Ah!" There was a hitch in the framework of the finale, and my father and his companion commanded the moving figures with their glasses. Not much was said of the people, as the moments were felt to be highly critical.

"What's that fellow doing? that one over there? Ah! Very annoying for them, isn't it? Now there's another meddling with something over there! What? What?"

When the finale did come off, there was no mistaking it. Her Majesty the Queen, the Prince and the Princess of Wales, all blazing in front of us—wonderful and more wonderful. "God Save the Queen," and then home for dear life.

Her Majesty's Jubilee seemed to close and sum up the father of their childhood. He was never quite the same after. The schemes which were already in his mind and heart were to eat into his life more than he or anybody else could foretell. The tide of life must have been pleasantly full to him at that time; he was finding increasingly new outlets for himself, yet amid them all he had opportunities of very agreeable social intercourse, great courtesy and kindness being shown to him by the members of the circuit, though Brixton was by no means exceptional in this respect. He made friends widely as he always did when he had time and opportunity, and in particular the loved friend of his life, Dr. Lunn.

Dr. Lunn was at that time at Dublin taking a medical course prior to becoming a medical missionary. The banner which agitated our household was flapping over the whole country in that year—1886—as Mr. Gladstone had appealed to the country over his Home Rule Bill, and both sides were agog. Dr. Lunn, who shared my father's keen interest in social and political issues, was a member of the Protestant Home Rule Association, and had come over to England to campaign on its behalf and that of the Bill. He had just started on his tour when he received a telegram from the Mission House, worded: " Stop political action. — Wesley, London," which left him in some perplexity as to how to act.

My parents had visited the Wesleyan Theological College at Headingley, while he was there a year or two previously, and he had been struck, like everyone else, with my father's personality. Along with his fellow-students he saw in him a new order of minister—one who was keenly interested evidently in scholarly pursuits and the thought of the day, and was yet an impassioned and popular evangelist. This was a combination that had not hitherto seemed possible in their eyes, and the surprise that it provoked in them was beginning to be shared by the whole of Methodism.

In addition, venturesome youth felt a certain aroma of romance about the man who was known to be at variance, in various ways, with the predilections of the authorities, and to have publicly criticised some of their decisions, while still a student at college. Such a champion, and one who was a Home Ruler to boot, would certainly befriend a young minister in his present difficulty, so he telegraphed to my father asking if he could see him, and arrived at Brixton shortly after my father's reply.

Resistance was felt to be the more legitimate, as it was undoubtedly believed at the time—though one does not know with what justification—that the authorities were themselves actively engaged in backing the Conservative and anti-Gladstonian party.

To Dr. Lunn's surprise, he said resistance was not legitimate. He owed obedience, he insisted, to the Church. There was a divine right of rebellion against authority in the Church and out of it, but it was rare—oh, very rare, and the occasion had to be full worth it, and the rebel the discreetest of persons. Freedom of speech and opinion, the ventilation of grievances, was one thing, which he had always advocated in Methodism, as his hearer knew; but to disobey a direct injunction of the authorities was quite another. Despite the listener's manifest astonishment, my father's advice was quite consistent with his own conduct at college and after it. He had never disobeyed a direct mandate of the authorities. This astonishment was Dr. Lunn's first insight into my father's character. For all the sound advice delivered at moments, as if he were one of the Fathers themselves, it was impossible for my father to resist a certain warming of the heart, at the aspect of so well-disposed an agitator.

"I will go down with you now to the Mission House and see what can be done," he volunteered; for he saw Dr. Lunn's difficulty in breaking engagements to which he was already committed, and which he had suddenly been commanded at the very last moment to throw over without explanation. The rest of the story which lay between Dr. Lunn and the authorities does not concern the present chapter, but it serves to indicate a very important side of my father's character.

"It was not in the least," said Dr. Lunn, "obedience to what he wished, but to the Church or the authority that could rightfully claim it." Such obedience was to him a vital quality in the Christian character.

In the spring of 1887 Dr. Lunn came to take a preaching appointment in the circuit, and had further intercourse with my father. They dropped into intimacy at once. "Here's this fellow Lunn," my father called out to my mother on the morning that he arrived. Their buoyancy and joy in each other's society was quite intoxicating. They would sit out on the balcony overlooking the strip of back garden until late into the night, talking of their plans and of the future, my mother joining with them. Dr. Lunn was considerably my father's junior, and his contact with him at an impressionable period, as well as the special interest and affection that my father in his turn at once conceived for him, was to lead to a friendship that was deep and unbroken. But for all his veneration he spoke freely to my father, and was quite capable of criticising him, as a letter written about this time clearly proves.

What this letter fails to see, and what the writer afterwards did see, was the devotion and spirituality that lay beneath the gifts, and the parts which had first awakened the interest of his eager youth. At present they only served to startle him— certain quaintnesses more in keeping with a stay-at-home saint than this militant, social, reforming "Pan-Methodist," as he described him.

As my father was accompanying him to the station, he said, half-wistfully, "Do you know of any circuit in the neighbourhood where the superintendent is in need of a young assistant like me? It would be good practice, and I could be of some service, I think—don't you?"

"I am such a superintendent," was the answer. "I have to be away constantly this winter, in order to conduct some special missions. Come for three months and take my work. I am sure it could be managed." He came.

Dr. Lunn's interest in the world at large and in politics was a quality that appealed to my father. He would go and listen to debates in the House, and describe them afterwards, to his listener's intense delight. Moreover, he would pull my father's arguments to pieces and take him by the horns on all occasions. These horns resembled those in a fable. You had only to make for them, and they vanished in your grasp; indeed, a lamb looked up at you.

Perhaps my father partly loved Dr. Lunn for this audacity. He did not have sufficient private intercourse with equipped minds—sufficient give and take. He evolved ideas in a certain isolation, and then laid them down to others. It was because he was so ready to modify these that this isolation was not the more divined. From humanity and its collective life he learnt immensely, but scarcely at all from reciprocal intercourse with a group of individuals as other leaders have done.

As a man, he was one of the most dependent that ever lived, but as an ecclesiastic—a leader—he was self-sufficing. Since he had made friends as a boy in his native town he had always fraternised with other men as their leader. It was instinctive, and an instinct which the circumstances of his life increasingly engendered. He led as naturally as others are led.

His young colleague was much impressed by a mission that my father held in his own circuit. He urged not only submission to Christ, but what he would term " full consecration," the yielding of the whole nature and all its powers and opportunities and secret desires to the will and purpose of God. As from the beginning of his ministry, he would ask for visible signs signifying such acts of surrender. A lady who attended one of his after-meetings on Sunday evenings, and who was unaccustomed to such displays, related that it was very impressive, but ghostly. " I dared not look," she said, " at the figures I knew to be silently rising round me. It was just as if souls were bursting forth from the body proclaiming themselves. My training had fostered a deep reserve on spiritual matters, and I had always regarded these as an intimate personal possession. It was a shock to me, but it was very fine."

At the prayer-meetings, on which he laid such insistence, he would fight, as he always had done, against long and melancholy prayers. "The devil," he would say, "loves long prayers." It was noteworthy that while the elder members of his congregation were at first scandalised by this method of expressing himself, it was not long before he endeared himself to them, either by some act of courtesy and kindness, or by the irresistible originality of his way of putting things, which caused them, after the first plunge, much secret chuckling.

The piety of the militant Pan-Methodist became more in keeping with Dr. Lunn's conception of him. He began dimly to divine its depth and breadth. So did a poor woman who dropped in to the chapel one Sunday morning—but that was not surprising. This woman, like many whose hearts he touched, never made herself known to the preacher, but she wrote to his family at the time of his death. The very handwriting, they noted, betrayed the weariness that is her lot in this life.

". . . And I had almost lost all hope. Times were very hard, but one Sunday I went in to the chapel where Mr. Hughes was preaching, and I shall never forget him. He said, 'Wake up, ye sleepy-headed Christians. . . .' That was God's message to me, and I sent my children to Sunday school . . . and from that time I have tried to follow Jesus, although I am afraid it has been very unworthy; but this I can say, and that is what I want you to tell any weary, tired woman or mother—never once all these years has God failed me. He has helped me in every trial or difficulty, and I praise His name for it. . . ."

The "words" which scandalised the elect were hugged to the breasts of such as these. Amid the clamouring of children and the quarrelling of neighbours and fellow-servants, they sit, some of them, after a day's charing, striving with the fiends that such weariness of limb and surroundings beget—whispering to themselves to submit—"He is here, I must submit as

Mr. Hughes did. Lord Jesus, I submit. Help me. Thou art here. Fill my heart with Thy love."

Such a soul told me that more than once lately she felt my father's spirit quite close to her, and was refreshed and reinvigorated thereby. When the souls of others shall accuse him of not having " built them up " in the days of their flesh, they shall not gain a hearing surely, amid the shout of these!

CHAPTER IX

DISCUSSIONS ON A BALCONY AND ELSEWHERE

"He broke the chains by which men were bound; he threw open to them the doors leading into the boundless freedom of nature and truth. But in the next generation he is idolised, and nature and truth as much forgotten as ever; if he could return to earth he would find that the crowbars and files with which he made his way out of the prison-house have been forged into the bolts and chains of a new prison called by his own name."

SIR JOHN SEELEY.

"'The Bitter Cry of Outcast London' awoke the metropolitan Churches as the scepticism of David Hume 'interrupted the dogmatic slumber' of Immanuel Kant. We realised that we were partly responsible for the existing sin and misery of London, and that we must do our share in the great work which demands the united devotion of all the Churches."

My Father's Introduction to First Report of
The West London Mission.

IT was in the vicinity of Epping Forest that my father's children first heard him speak forcibly concerning the Three Years' System. It must have been before Oxford even, where the matter first assumed serious proportions in his thought. They were lunching near the Forest, with an old school-friend of their mother's, when my father began on the itinerancy. "Wesley never intended it," he said. "It was an arrangement for his own times, when it suited a land of villages and small towns—not great industrial centres. He never intended its present rigid form, stifling our efforts and hampering the work of Christ." Somebody asked what was to be done. "Done!"—there was an expressive movement—"I wish we could utterly abolish it."

"Why don't you?" said another voice.

My father dropped his knife and fork. "It is impossible, impossible. You do not know all that you are suggesting.

190

Why, we should have to go to Parliament—the whole thing is so involved." Then followed mysterious hints about chapels and the poll-deed and land tenure, but it was the word " Parliament" that caught the fancy. So the Three Years' System had its ratification in that august assembly! How awe-inspiring that was! My father evidently was under the same impression, for he seemed anxious to impress the company with the awfulness of that which had been proposed. Some years after this, the family spent three weeks at Felixstowe, where my father had taken preaching appointments under an arrangement which enabled him to take his summer holiday. The Rev. James Ernest Clapham shortly appeared, and they walked and talked together, and appeared very cheerful. Later, it was found, he belonged to the Forward Movement. But previous to this my father had long conversations with Dr. Henry J. Pope. These took place at the Conference of 1884, just after my father had quitted the city of Oxford, and were intimately concerned with the Three Years' System. Systems provoke a diversity of comment, according to mood and locality. Epping Forest breeds a revolutionary tendency towards them, and the surging of the German Ocean exalts the heart, showing how infinitesimal a thing is trammel. But the precincts of a great authoritative assembly breeds another and very subtle attitude of mind. Dr. Pope and my father were nothing if not cautious, deliberative, conservative, alive to the value and significance of tradition, yet facing present facts and conditions. The nature of these has already been indicated. Methodism had been fatally crippled since the disaster of 1848, and was not taking her place in the arena of modern life or responding to its needs, and this despite the fact that the genius of its organisation was its adaptability. A large proportion of her workingclass adherents had already left her, and now the children of the middle classes, for whose peculiar benefit she was existing, were daily doing the same. The whole organisation needed rekindling.

To purify and spiritualise the life of the people, Methodism seemed first to have arisen, on that day when Wesley consenting to be altogether " vile," as he terms it, went out into the public highway to proclaim the gospel of Christ. Yet my father did not believe that Methodism was entirely for what are called the working classes. "Whoever says that," he exclaimed once in the *Methodist Times*, "is the deadliest enemy Methodism ever had." Nor did he think it should be given over to mission halls and popular forms of service—anything but that. But he did, for the time being, believe that for the sake of the people themselves, and for the Methodist Church, they were the first to be considered, and that the more educated needed bringing into direct touch with the lives of the majority of the English people—labourers toiling for their daily bread—and that until they were thus brought into contact with them their religion and their ideas generally would suffer enormously.

His experience at Oxford, where anything like Methodist activity had been given up as hopeless, served as an incitement to his sympathisers. These activities, coupled with his famous speech at the missionary meeting, brought him all at once into prominence, and the eyes of the community were fastened on him everywhere. So into the midst of the inner life of Methodism, my father, as the leader of the submerged Liberal section, suddenly entered. It was a shock to some that the family affairs should be examined into or made public at all. Families who have sunk in the scale do not appreciate the proclamation of the fact. To some, indeed, to whom the "preserve," as he called them, was altogether satisfactory, it was not only inexplicable, but it savoured of disloyalty. The articles soon to appear in the *Methodist Times*, entitled "Methodists! Wake up!" or "Is Methodism to be a Dying Sect or a Living Church?" and others of an equally breezy nature, convinced some readers that the sooner the writer was out of Methodism the better for its security. But as my father and Dr. Pope had correctly divined, these were the minority. Their finger was on the pulse of the Methodist people, who, as my father pointed out, had everywhere responded to a more liberal and aggressive régime. His opponents had always been a group of the older men, and these he would often succeed in winning over. Churches, as he once described them in a despatch of his in the *Methodist Times*, were to be no longer "rich men's clubs," but "camps." His glasses were rose-coloured and inclined to see the bright side of things, which was an invaluable quality, though it provoked inevitable comments. "All his geese," said the critics, "are swans." Perhaps so, but by this delusion of his, it was wonderful to what heights the geese would sometimes attain. It is to be doubted, also, whether others get out of their swans what he got out of his geese.

The circumstances were not hopeless, he insisted, provided that the Three Years' System could be modified in large towns, and indeed in all those districts where it was desirable that ministers should reside for longer than the allotted period.[1] It was the spirit of Methodism that mattered, not its minutiæ. Forms and methods must change with the times and the increase of God's purposes. Christ's gospel did not change, therefore Methodism need not, in its essentials. So he thought and planned, not only with Dr. Pope, but with whosoever else he thought might assist him. Deep within there was astonishment that more could not see eye to eye with him in this matter. The Rev. William Arthur, Rev. Dr. Moulton, the Rev. Dr. Stephenson, and the Rev. W. D. Walters, his fellow-candidate at Richmond, sympathised fully with him, as did a few also of the older men who remembered the days before 1848, and had not succumbed to its shadow. The supernumeraries (retired ministers), it has been pointed out, were more inclined to support the Forward Movement than contemporaries, because they remembered the more prosperous days before 1848, when Methodism, for all its periods of strife, was still vigorous and accomplishing her work in the world.

About the same time (the spring of 1885), a pamphlet, entitled the "Bitter Outcry of Outcast London," aroused the most reflective and compassionate spirits among the Churches, and led, among other things, to a great meeting at Exeter Hall, which my father addressed, with Lord Shaftesbury in the chair. As usual when on the platform, he was at his very best, and a Fidus Achates who was listening to him, recognised his leader at once. "That's my man," he said; and afterwards he became one of his most devoted helpers in West London. On this particular occasion, Lord Shaftesbury, misinterpreting something my father said,[2] interrupted him, but Fidus Achates,

---

[1] To many rural districts the itinerancy was still adapted.

[2] Some of the ideals of Socialism, my father implied, were also those of Christianity.

13

a very quiet and restrained man, jumped onto his seat, and cried, " Go on ! " That came to be the feeling of the great majority of the Methodist people, and more particularly of the humble and unknown among them.

It was first of all proposed that my father should start a mission in East London, which indeed was in accordance with his own feeling. His heart was stirred within him at the thought of the degradation and misery in the slums, which Christians, intent on singing hymns and the saving of their own miserable souls, had so long and shamefully neglected. None the less, he made certain stipulations of the following character. First, that he should have a free hand, and be responsible not to the District Synod (a Church Council resembling in its functions the Diocesan Synod of the Anglican Communion), but to a special committee appointed for the oversight of London work, and responsible for its actions to Conference alone, and to no other body. Second, that he should be at liberty to stay there as many years as he was able to carry on the work, and so long as he had the support and confidence of the Methodist Conference and people. In addition, suitable buildings were to be procured for the Mission, and the work was to be conceived and carried out on an adequate scale. The day of back corners and small things was over. The devil advertised himself, and the Christians must therefore advertise themselves, if they were successfully to cope with an age like the present. The work was to be maintained on the supposition that souls were attached to bodies, and for the comfort of these bodies—caskets of an immortal soul—it should be the aim of the Mission to make some provision. Body and soul were strangely blent and interfused in this life, and if men were to be saved, their bodies must share in the process. This may sound like the alphabet to the present generation, but when my father and his supporters first advocated it in Methodism, people were startled. He seemed to be contending, as much as anything, with the old coaching days, when the driver called for his glass, cracked his whip, and set out at the express speed of sixteen miles an hour, with the postilion jogging on in front, the conductor tootling the horn in the rear, and all in a delightful ignorance both of railways and the twentieth century. Who is there who has not loving feelings for the old coaching days, and does not like to read about them in the Victorian novels, of how Miss Lavinia drove from Newcastle to London and thought she had been half round the world, and how the Methodist preacher got in at the second halt, called for his glass, tucked his Bible under his arm, and went away to the next village to meet the classes of " The Society," while the driver cracked his whip, and the coach rumbled on its way as before. Beautiful days those were— simply made for a rigid itinerancy—and who shall dare to criticise the thoughts that belong to them !

Moderate men who did not actually resent the propositions, wanted to hear again of the matter, like the philosophers in the Athenian market-place, so that they might consider it in all its bearings, and accustom themselves to its novelty. Others, on the contrary, did not want to hear of it again—they had heard too much already. Two sections, in particular, opposed my father—those connected with London chapels, who feared the proximity of anything so attractive, and so likely to detract from their own particular operations as a great mission, and those who feared the result of any tampering with present polity. The first, despite the fact that the chapels were empty and unadapted to cope with the needs of the populace, insisted that Conference should consider their plight, and protect them from such a formidable rival. If these had been more willing to work in with the organisation he was contemplating—more willing to own themselves unable to cope with the stream of life seething in their neighbourhood under present conditions— both sides would have been saved a good deal of annoyance. More than one of those ministers who supported my father on this occasion eloquently urged the brethren to rise above local and petty considerations, and look the situation in the face. The fact that the people of this country were slipping from their grasp, and that Methodism would really not be much use without them, had not fully come home to many of their hearers. If a Circuit paid its way, and the chapel had the ordinary number of families and regular worshippers to enter into the traditional routine, people did not feel that any more was demanded of them. My father never could understand the opposition that his suggestions aroused. " Why do they object ? What is it ? " he kept saying to one in his confidence during the ensuing Conference session. Opposition seemed to shock and distress him, as savouring of lack of faith and unwillingness to do great things for Christ. But in the establishment of London Missions, which were permanent appointments, opponents thought they saw the thin end of that wedge which should come in and break up the whole. That, perhaps, was the real answer to my father's question, the basis of the opposition. His opponents did not object to missions and much that he was propagating, but to reform of any kind. Moreover, every controversy or debatable question in Methodism has an inner side known only to Methodists, so that they are often ill-understood by outsiders. The same, of course, may be said of all Churches and corporate bodies in general, but very specially of older Methodism, with which my father had such a lifelong struggle. The itinerant ministry stood for a manner of life and deeply engrained associations, and to tamper with these was as distasteful to the average Wesleyan minister as Disestablishment would be in a different way to many Anglicans.

Frequently in my father's controversies there is nothing more difficult to understand than what really was at issue —all that was in the minds of his opponents as well as in his. That they often imagined things were in it which were not, is easy to see. He was quite foreign to many of his opponents, and their understanding of the purport of his proposals grew with their understanding of his character. His advocacy of temperance and all other wild and unreasonable things prejudiced some, while others were certain he was the wildest Radical in the three kingdoms, and his way of talking and planning for Christ's Church struck them as embodying the same qualities as his politics. They failed to understand at first the intense spiritual enthusiasm which underlay his proposals. Dr. Osborn, for instance, who headed this section, spoke vehemently at Conference against intrusting a mission to one whose personal character so unfitted him for such a responsibility; and though he was interrupted in these remarks, his words showed something of the personal prejudice with which the pioneer of the Forward Movement had to contend.

The Conference of 1885, the first during which the question of the Mission arose,—for the London Missions were the pioneers of a whole series,—did not think good to grant the provision and powers for a mission in the East on the scale that my father demanded, so he refused to undertake it. But the Forward party, and all those dissatisfied with the scope of present undertakings, and desirous of new and greater things, still seethed and discussed possible contingencies. My father had no particular idea about his own future after the dropping of the East End scheme. One day, however, the Rev. R. W. Allen, who, as military chaplain, was living in the west of London, called to impart a conviction, which, he said, had long been borne in upon him. My father, he was convinced, should start and superintend a mission in the West End, on the lines that he stipulated. My father shook his head. " I have never," he said, "thought of that." "You must think of it, then," said Mr. Allen, and we and all the Forwards will back you through thick and thin, and send you there. Our Church demands such a centre, and it will catch the imagination of people and the world. You are the man, sir, and there are many in the West End who are in need of you and the kind of work that you propose. Pray and think over it, and then as a result decide to go." With some such remarks Mr. Allen departed, bent on rousing the Forwards, who speedily shared his opinion that my father should go to the West End, and urged him in like manner. But he still hesitated. "West London! West London!" he kept saying to my mother; " I cannot imagine it, or accustom myself to the idea. Such a thought has never come to me before, and indeed I do not feel I could undertake it, unless I had well-known and valuable support. Yet they all urge me. If I could have some such support, I think I might go. A wonderful opening, of course—wonderful; the very centre of the world's life, Bohemia, fashion, visitors and foreigners from all parts. A constant stream of our people from the provinces, whom we lose annually in that great sea, as well as another from our colonies and America, who would be impressed by such an undertaking, and whom we could stir to do likewise. But I could not do it alone, for I feel, you know, a certain diffidence . . ." Then later—"There is my lay agent here, and others, who I believe would come with us and assist. I believe Mark Guy Pearse to be the man I want. If he joins me, I will go." So he wrote to Mark Guy Pearse, who replied, saying that he much appreciated the kind suggestion, but did not see his way to accept it, and for two or three reasons. First, because he had decided to go and live in Cornwall, which he loved better than any place on earth ; secondly, because he wanted to be free to preach in different parts of England, and from time to time to visit the colonies ; and thirdly, because he was sure that where Hugh Price Hughes was, there really would not be much room for anybody else ! Hugh Price Hughes wrote back to say that there would be any amount of room, and he begged Mr. Pearse to seriously consider the situation and its responsibility, above all the openings, which he proceeded to indicate. He had now thoroughly warmed to the West End, believing it to be God's will that he should go there. "Come to tea with me," he concluded, "and see if we cannot talk it over and arrive at something." Mark Guy Pearse came to tea. He made pen-and-ink sketches for the children, which greatly impressed them, and then went upstairs with their father to the study. When he came down again it was all arranged. "You," my father said to Mr. Pearse, "shall edify the saints and I will pursue the sinners." Thus the joy of the Forwards was great, and they armed themselves to the teeth.

My father meanwhile prepared a speech to be delivered in Conference. This speech and the efforts of the Forwards completely captured the assembly, all the moderate men, who had been startled at first, voting like one man for the new campaign. Even Dr. Osborn, who had resisted up to the last because of his personal dislike and distrust of my father, succumbed to the new project in a way that is pleasant to relate, as it is a very pretty story. A committee was formed to prepare a special hymn-book for the Mission, on which both Dr. Osborn and my father sat. Close proximity seemed to have made a favourable impression on Dr. Osborn, for he came to feel that he had made a mistake, and that he did not quite understand either my father's character or the motives underlying his proposals. He found that this radical young minister read the hymns of the Wesleys and talked about the souls of men as if he were one of the Fathers. His manifest deference moreover, his desire to please, to take any suggestion, touched a chord in a nature not understood by many contemporaries, but which won the respect and affection of intimates. "Here, Hughes," he said, "take £10 for your Mission, and I hope it will be a great success." My father's hopes after this must have danced more than ever, and the discussions on the balcony outside the study window were felt to be distinctly thrilling. Dr. Lunn, who was about to start for India, was one of the group that sat wondering and planning as to the future—the great venture in which Methodism, my parents and Mark Guy Pearse, and several others, as it turned out, were to engage.

Mr. Pearse, it had been decided, was to preach every Sunday morning, and to assist in any other way that he chose, but to be free of the cares and responsibilities attending the organisation, as he had many other engagements over the country, and had promised to visit the colonies. As it proved, Mr. Pearse, by his loyalty and kindness to the Mission and the missioners, and his incessant proclamation of their work, did more than anybody to spread its fame among British people beyond the seas. His first feeling that there would be no need of another where Hugh Price Hughes was in charge, indicates how even the "Forwards" could misconceive their leader. His ability and power in debate, sweeping the way before him with a determination to carry his point, seems to have given an impression that he would not be easy to work with. He could not be content, contemporaries felt, unless he swept all before him, innovating ceaselessly, and caring little for the opinions and predilections of those associated with him. In the light of a colleagueship, which had never a ruffle, such assertions raise a smile.

The West Central District and its vicinity was scoured for a suitable house for the superintendent, till No. 8 Taviton Street, Gordon Square, was decided to answer the purpose in hand. My parents had lived in small two-roomed lodgings at the beginning of their married life, and had always found accommodation ample, whatever it was, being pleased with all that was provided for them. But my father felt that he must have somewhat larger accommodation in his new position, as it would have to be the centre of considerable activity, and many people would be passing in and out of his house. Round the corner, to my father's delight, Mr. Percy Bunting was living in Endsleigh Gardens. His name when it was mentioned on the balcony came out with the greatest gusto and carefully chosen eulogy. " And he sympathises with us and will do his best to help us. The services of such a man will be quite invaluable. I confess our good fortune quite overwhelms me." Mr. Bunting became treasurer and Circuit steward of the Mission, and, as my father was certain he would be, a most staunch and invaluable supporter. But that was not all. Round the corner again, in Tavistock Square, was his brother-in-law, Dr. Howard Barrett, whom he loved and esteemed greatly, and whose services—but here he dropped his voice, for he knew how he should appreciate them. He was the physician of the Mission, healing and invigorating the bodies of the missioners, so that the spirits within might wax strong and venturesome.

Round the corner again was Mr. Bamford Slack, the other Circuit steward, concerning whose coming there hangs a tale. My father met him at Barry Road at the time when Mr. Slack was living in lodgings, reading for the law. They went out for a walk on Peckham Rye, and my father told him all about the Forward Movement, and what the Forwards meant to do. In particular, he urged him to read the *Spectator*, and offered to lend him Green's *History*. At the time my parents went to West London, Mr. Slack, who was on the eve of marriage, was looking for a house. My father chancing to meet him out one evening, said, " Oh, you are looking for a house, are you? That's excellent. Get one in our neighbourhood. There are any number of commodious residences, Cubitt built, and within easy distance of omnibuses going to all parts of London as well as the Underground Railway. Above all, you will be able to help us in the Mission." After some delay he and his wife took a house in the neighbourhood of Taviton Street. A week or so after, some one called upon him and said, " You are Circuit steward of the Mission. I am so glad." " Indeed," said Mr. Slack, " I am so glad you informed me, because I did not know anything about it. Who told you?" " Mr. Hughes told me. He said you were going to render us the greatest service." To give the names of all who did the same, and justified my father's superlatives, would transcend the limits of any chapter.

Long before they came my father saw them coming.   He saw them as he sat on the balcony.   So it was impossible for moderate men to damp him, however much they might try to do so.   " But have you considered, Mr. Hughes—h'm—the full extent of the responsibility—h'm—you are undertaking— h'm ?   Then there are the means, the financial means, and the assistance of all kinds that you will be bound to require, if you are to carry out the schemes that you have undertaken."

" No, my dear sir, I can't say I have.   I leave the full extent to God, nor should I presume to take part of it."

Yet that which chiefly occupied the minds of dreamers on the balcony was the novel enterprise of a Sisterhood.   To quote my mother's own words :—

" My husband and I had long been struck with the way in which the Roman Catholic and Anglican Churches, and also the Salvation Army, utilised the services of its most devoted and capable women.   We felt that in Methodism there were many women equally devoted and capable, who would render untold service to their Church, and to suffering and outcast humanity, if some opportunity were afforded them of definitely organised work, to which they could devote their lives.   Without any thought of disparagement for the services rendered by humble women in the past as Bible-women, city missionaries, etc., we felt the time was come when women who had received the inestimable privileges of education and culture, were called to devote these great gifts to the service of the Church, and that they would be able to do a kind of work impossible to others.

" We felt it would be possible to organise a ' Sisterhood ' on a broad basis, including members of other Protestant Evangelical Churches, who were willing to work with us, in the spirit of John Wesley, who defined a true Methodist to be the friend of all, the enemy of none.

" Such a Sisterhood would, of course, be free from the objectionable vows and iron regulations that characterised such institutions in the older Churches, as much scope and freedom being given to its members as would be compatible with the harmony and efficiency of the whole.

" The whole idea was born of the ' Forward Movement '— the term ' Sister ' being used in its human and democratic sense, and not with an ecclesiastical signification.

"We wanted a band of large-hearted, sensible, capable Christian women to be a centre of service and help in the great whirlpool of West London life—not to look down upon miserable and distracted humanity from a superior height, but to place themselves by the side of the sinful and the sad. We wanted them to be 'the Sisters of the People'—the name which was afterwards adopted."

The great value of the Sisterhood was, as it proved, not so much in the work that the Sisters were able individually to accomplish, though this was considerable, but the impulse that its establishment communicated through Methodism, and as a result through Protestant circles generally. Sisterhoods, Brotherhoods and the like had become associated in the Protestant mind with lifelong vows, austerities, and other Roman accompaniments. Deaconesses, where they existed (my father did not fancy the title) among certain strong evangelical circles, were too restricted, too much under lock and key both as regarded thought and action, to attract the class that my parents had in mind.

A Sister who was successful in initiating several social enterprises was first introduced to my father at Brixton, where her wit and vivacity made her much in request in a gay and youthful circle. My father had observed the keen interest which she took in the poor, and in questions relating to them. One evening, at a party at the house of a friend, he was dilating on his plans for the Mission, when this young lady suddenly said, "When you start your Sisterhood in the Mission, will you accept me as one of the Sisters?" A roar of laughter greeted this inquiry, but my father replied solemnly, "Certainly I will; you are just the kind of Sister I want." Her friends could not believe that she was really in earnest, and surprise was great when she did actually join the Sisterhood, a month or two after it started. Her acquaintance could only remark, "She will not stay long." She stayed until she died.

In a cramping and fettered atmosphere such a development of latent capacity would have been impossible. The answer to my parents' critics was the personality they permitted. People tossed to and fro in the great sea of London life wanted personalities to lean upon, those who thought and felt as they did, not creatures formed upon a preconceived pattern. Sister Edith's family was Anglican, but she worked with the greatest delight among the Methodists with whom she came into contact. "They are so broad," she said, "in their sympathies. I have never met any people like them."

If the spectacle of the Sisterhood was to induce imitation, still more—as my father foresaw in the balcony—was the establishment of the Mission with which the Sisterhood was associated, and which, together with the other London Missions and that at Manchester, might be described as the first great triumphs of the Forward Movement in Methodism. Their establishment was the first wave of a great tide, which the following list will show:—

Name of Mission.				Year in which started.
East London	.	.	.	1885
Manchester		.	.	1885
Central London	.		.	1886
West London	.	.	.	1887
South London	.	.	.	1889
South-West London		.	.	1899
Poplar and Bow	.	.	.	1900
Deptford	.	.	.	1903

In addition missions were started at the great provincial centres — Birmingham, Edinburgh, Leeds, Liverpool, and Nottingham. A characteristic feature of the Forward Movement was the Bermondsey Settlement in South London, which worked on the lines of a university settlement, laying stress on social and educational work.

Each fresh wave, as it came rolling in after the first, was loudly acclaimed and trumpeted in the ever-watchful Journal. The editor was present at the inaugural meetings of the new mission, and cheered and aided the missioners in a variety of ways. Between himself and the superintendents there was always a special bond of fellowship, the newcomers regarding him as their leader and father, a position to which he was most fully entitled. It was his leadership, they say, that made the Forward party irresistible, and rendered action imperative. He fought in Conference for the necessary powers that such great undertakings involved, and championed, when needed, their promoters. The success of the first missions everywhere inspirited the whole party, and made the objections at first urged against the enterprise of no account. The prophet had proved to be right as well as irresistible. He had correctly read the signs and the times, divining how Methodism could best minister to the needs of great populations. But how altogether right he was, it needed the lapse of some years to prove.

The chief outcry of opponents was that the establishment of these great attractive missions would detract from the efforts and strength of the Circuits—the backbone of Methodism —where good men were labouring with none of the excitements and inducements attending the new enterprises. My father's reply, as at the beginning, was that so far from the Missions injuring the Circuits, they must only aid them. The tonic and restorative must finally permeate the whole frame, and no community could engage in a successful venture without communicating its benefits and the glow of its health to all its members. The enterprises for which the Forward party fought caught not only the imagination of the Methodist people, but that of other Churches and of many people who were not as a rule interested in religious undertakings. There was little wonder that members in Conference felt a natural hesitation at launching the enterprise in West London. Quite apart from local jealousies and the difficulties arising therefrom, was the game worth the candle? Only those who lived in London were aware of the unique difficulties, not only of religious work, but of gaining any hold on the populace. The Missions in the northern industrial cities knew nothing of that with which the London Missions had to contend. The elements in the former were not only far simpler and more congruous, but there was a distinct religious tradition, more often than not a Methodist one, on which to work, which was altogether absent in the Metropolis. Therefore nothing was more startling about the West London Mission than the temerity of its starting, which, in the light of its success and the developments that followed it, has been almost overlooked. It needed a man as bold and resourceful and sensitive to life at all points as the superintendent, to launch the vessel on what seemed so hazardous and uncertain a journey. The temerity—the boundless faith—of the undertaking, and the belief that all would be provided as the need should arise, was quite its most startling feature. No millionaire came forward to give the missioners a donation, nor had they any patronage in that great sea of human life on which the little barque set forth amid the good wishes, the criticism and wonder of onlookers. Of the leader it could be said that he expected great things, and he had them. I suppose his belief in prayer must have been a strong instinct with him at the first, seeing that when he could scarcely speak he was found praying out in the rain. The Mission, as it grew and developed, was by its varied elements to appeal to a sceptical humanitarian era, and by its fervour, mingled with a certain romantic ingredient, to suggest those characteristics with which the age of chivalry has been associated. But chivalry, and all that was in it—redress of the weak, and love of life and laughter—he claimed for the Church, wherein lay the distinguishing feature between his and other enterprises. It was the key as well as the struggle of his undertaking, which was throughout ecclesiastical. It was in his adherence to the Church (not Methodism or even Evangelicism, because the tenets which he stoutly maintained were common to all bodies of Christians, however differently expressed and accompanied) that he parted company with knights-at-arms, who in their chivalrous enterprises refused to keep the portals of the Church sufficiently in sight. Thus his chivalry, with all its designs, never interfered with his filial conduct towards his Church. He was ready at a moment to obey a decision of Conference respecting himself and what he should do.

About this time, before the Conference of 1886, there was a good deal of discontent with the constitution of the Mission House (the headquarters of the Foreign Mission work of Wesleyan Methodism), and there was some talk, on the part of the Forwards of course, that my father should occupy some official position there. In commenting on this, he remarked with a gesture, and to a listener's astonishment, that if such were the will of his brethren, he should have nothing to say on the matter. His one aim was to promote the welfare and the work of the Church of Christ. "But what will happen to the Mission?" said his companion. "Oh! some one else would take my place; I must go where they wish me." As it turned out, the brethren did not thus desire his presence, for they feared revolution if he came. So his plans were undisturbed.

Before passing to personal memories and impressions of the period, a few words must be said respecting a portion of the Forward Movement with which he was intimately connected, the Old Leysian Mission, whose new Settlement has recently been erected in the City Road. The Leys School was founded at Cambridge in the year 1875, with Dr. Moulton as its first headmaster, who left Richmond for the purpose. To bring Nonconformity, Wesleyan and otherwise, within the pale of the universities was an idea much advocated by the Forward Movement, and the earlier pages of the Journal bespeak the deepest interest, both in the foundation of the Leys School and that of Mansfield College at Oxford. While at Brixton my father came into contact with a group of young men who had just left the Leys, with whom he not only constantly conversed, but some of whom he "met in class" at their lodgings.

About this time, in connection with their old school, a mission was being formed in the East End by those of their number who had been responsive to Dr. Moulton's influence, which was very great over a large number of the pupils. Here, as usual, the Doctor and his former pupil seemed to be working in agreeable conjunction. Dr. Moulton, it was felt by certain of his pupils and their friends, had awakened them to spiritual life, but Mr. Hughes had first incited them to work for Christ's Church. As ever, it was the carefully prepared ground where he was most effective. The enthusiasm that he spread among them was not a transient flame, but one that endured for years amid many difficulties. "We have only to hear your father," they have said to his children, "to feel that we can do great things," thus betraying the secret of his power. The Mission was first situated in cramped premises in Whitechapel, where it was worked entirely by Old Leysians, and their sisters and friends. Its work resembled that of the West London Mission—i.e. it was evangelistic, united to a variety of social endeavour. My father throughout believed in the genuine nature of their efforts, displayed the keenest interest in all that they did, and always championed them at headquarters, when the necessity arose.

Particularly was this the case when the minister in residence
called upon him in 1899 to lay before him a scheme concerning a site in the City Road, where it was proposed to erect
premises containing full accommodation for a Settlement, such
as had been desired from the first, in addition to those for
the usual religious and social work. The advantages of a full
Settlement accommodation were manifest, and my father perceived them before they were enumerated. The sons of the
wealthy Methodists and other evangelical families, who went up
yearly to the Leys, were the future employers of labour, the
future members of learned professions, of municipal councils,
and of Parliament. By residing a year or two at the Settlement, and devoting their evenings, or more of their time as the
case might be, to actual personal contact with the people, they
must come to a greater understanding of their need and their
nature. The fault he found with so many journalists and
employers of labour of the present day, despite honourable
exceptions, was the fact that they lacked this individual
contact with the masses of the people, and the knowledge that
it brought. Now here obviously was a remedy to some of it—
a bridge between the classes and the masses ; and how excellent
a bridge, deeply rooted in the evangelical portion of the Universal Church !

The difficulties were the same as those that had attended
the starting of his own Mission. Those interested in City
Road Chapel complained of the proposal, because they said it
must have an injurious effect on the Cathedral of Methodism
in such close proximity to the proposed site. All this young
life, and these new attractive premises would draw off attention and interest from the ancient building in which the fathers
had worshipped, and which, but lately, their descendants had
taken such pains to renovate. Moreover, the elders asked,
"Where were the funds? With all these missions and funds
of various kinds, it was not to be expected that the Methodist
people would give any more. Why should there be another,
and a Leysian Mission?" Before he heard the objections, my
father knew them and had his answer—the old one. If they
wished the Cathedral of Methodism to be worthy of its
traditions, and to attract the attention of the world, for God's
sake let them encourage a Settlement of their best educated

young men and women in the immediate vicinity, so that when visitors came from afar to see the parent house, they could say, "Look out of the windows and you will see that the followers of Wesley are at it still. The bodies of the fathers are dust, but their spirit is undying and lives for ever." In the summer of 1904 the new edifice was opened by T.R.H. the Prince and Princess of Wales, and amid general rejoicing, though there was sadness behind it—particularly on the part of some. The two men, Dr. Moulton and Hugh Price Hughes, who had done more than any others to bring about that building, had passed from the earth, and the grave of the last was not long green. They were not there to smile upon them, and the imagination of some could not rid itself of their invisible presence and gladness.

CHAPTER IX

THE AGE OF CHIVALRY. ÆTAT 40–55. 1887–1902

"Some say that the age of chivalry is past. The age of chivalry is never past as long as there is a wrong left unredressed on earth, and a man or woman left to say, 'I will redress that wrong or spend my life in the attempt.'"   KINGSLEY.

"Like the missioners of the Teutonic peoples in the Middle Ages, we established a colony of workers in the region between Oxford Street and Piccadilly."

My Father's Introduction to First Report of The West London Mission.

IN September 1887 our family removed to 8 Taviton Street, in the centre of the west of London. As we listened to our father's characteristic conversation with visitors, it was brought home to us that, of all portions of the globe, the west of London was the one in which to establish a mission, and that Taviton Street was the best, if not the only street, in which its superintendent could reside. In those days it was gated, and there was a man in livery, who solemnly opened and shut the gates, and who, by his distinguished appearance, suggested the Duke, his master. The Duke and his brother peers, my father used to hint, were persons maintained by him and other good citizens. The gates were felt to be a great advantage, conducing to Sabbath peace and stillness in the street. "Not a sound," the superintendent would say at dinner, "greets our ears. We might be in the midst of the most delicious rural retreat, and yet we are in the centre of the greatest metropolis the world has ever known. Is it not extraordinary?"

None the less a roar, if somewhat distant, reached our ears. It was that of the traffic in the Euston Road; and my father's ear, at any rate, welcomed the sound. "Do you know what

14

Lowell called it?" he would inquire—"the roar of advancing
Time." In those early days it was doubtless as intoxicating
to him as the thunder of the waves to Ulysses; their mariner
souls knew no fear, and to greet the mighty tide of Time was
the prime motive of his generalship. To retreat from or
withstand it, as some captains of armies advocated, and as his
dear Tennyson, by the bye, in weak moments seemed inclined
to do, was utterly loathsome to him. He would have liked,
I believe, to erase "retreat" and "retrenchment" from the
English tongue. The tenor of his despatches was "Advance
all along the line," and when he started a mission magazine
it was entitled *Advance*, somewhat to the amusement of certain
contemporaries. Yet he chose the title gravely enough, for
the word was fraught with much thought and meaning to him
—more than people imagined. He must have often wondered
at this time at the levity of mankind, for, despite bursts of
buoyancy, he became perceptibly graver. He was now forty
years of age, in his prime, about to enter on that phase of his
career to which all the earlier portion had been subsidiary. As
to what he was, and what exactly he was doing, people's ideas
were often vague; but they were sure he was doing something
remarkable, something unexpected. Certainly his family did
not realise all that he was about. To their memory the household in Taviton Street resembled one swept by a whirlwind;
their parents rushing in and out of it at all hours of the day
and night, as did many others, who came apparently from the
four winds, tossed as they were by this elemental disturbance.

Neither of my parents, on coming to London, had any idea
of all that their position would involve. My mother, with the
coolness characteristic of her, imagined that my father would
gradually build up a congregation and a work in London. My
father, on the other hand, fully expected the rapid success that
his venture achieved. He had made his plans, enlisted Mr.
Pearse and the nucleus of the Sisterhood, and was certain that
they would have no difficulty in gaining the ear, both of those
in need of them, and of philanthropic and Christian people.
Only, as usual, time was omitted from his calculations. His
work in the Mission was never irksome to him, but other
undertakings which gathered in its train increasingly engulfed
him, so that, as years went on, he resembled one overborne

with the weight of his own endeavours.   Having once started, it seemed impossible to stop, so completely did he identify himself with the movements he had at heart.   People seemed to regard him as something made of iron, whose function it was to be turned on for the benefit of a cause.   After a few years he was seen to be sensible of the toils, struggling against them, but in vain.   He gloried in activities, but what burdened him at times past bearing was the continued travelling and the innumerable public meetings to get money for the Mission. He was not anxious to increase outside engagements, yet it often needed quite as much strength to refuse as to undertake these.   A Circuit or a cause was in a special plight, and he was implored to come and speak " just for once," to his perpetual embarrassment.   " My body," he would urge by way of apology, " cannot be in three places at the same time."

It was the rarest thing for him to dine or to have supper with a friend, and, on his own confession, he had no time to make new friends.   Dr. Lunn, who bombarded him in his study, was the one exception.   My mother would often see as little of him as anybody else, despite the fact that she was so closely associated with him in his work in the Mission. Pathetically she said, when they were down at Bournemouth after his illness, " It seems so strange sitting at home with him in the evening.   For months we seem to have only passed each other on the stairs ! "

Contemporary comments on this aspect of their life were remarkable for their singular lack of comprehension.   My mother flung herself into the work of the Sisterhood with a zeal equal to my father's, and the public rôle that she henceforward assumed was not undertaken merely to please my father—though, of course, it was partly so—but because she responded as he did to the spirit of the age, and conceived it as much her duty to undertake this work as my father did.

" I know we made mistakes in our first enthusiasm," she has said since, " but I cannot describe to you what it was— how we felt ourselves imperatively called to undertake the Mission and all that arose from it."

To both my parents the Mission and the social uplifting of the people that it stood for, were regarded in the light of one of those great causes for which men and women may rightly sacrifice a good deal more than household comfort. The children and household of Charles I. bore a good deal in order to uphold the Divine Right of Kings, and my parents thought they and theirs might well endure a little for the Divine right of helping their brother.

None the less, for all my mother's help, my father's life in London was at times a terrible strain, and would have been quite unbearable if he had not been a remarkably good sleeper. No sooner was his head on the pillow than he closed his eyes and went to sleep. This facility was strikingly illustrated when a colleague called late at night in great anxiety about something in the Mission, and was told to go up to his bedroom. He awoke as the colleague entered the room, asked what he wanted, adjusted the dilemma, gave some sound advice, and was off to sleep again before his visitor had left the room.

Without this constant recuperation he must have passed away even before he did. Not even the family knew how busy he was, and the numberless things that he had revolving in his mind, the number of letters he was daily writing, particularly to persons who had suffered bereavement. He would write to people whom he had not met for twenty years or more when they lost a dearly loved friend or relative; and when these were unknown or forgotten and worthy of notice of some kind, he would be careful to refer to them in the *Methodist Times*. He would come into meals with a book in his hand, and gave the impression of one who was incessantly reading. He read everything, from serious theological works sent him to review to the latest novel, and with equal enjoyment and avidity. Like Gladstone, it might have been said that the secret of his energies was his concentration on the object in hand. He passed from the committee to the book, and the book to the meeting, and from the meeting to supper and talk and bed, and did not let one process interfere with the other. He never opened the door in front of him without shutting to the door behind.

"Nobody," he would exclaim pathetically, "seems to understand how much I have to do, and how impossible it is for me to do more than I do do."

He was not satisfied at heart with his manner of life,

splendid and exhilarating as it seemed to many of his brother ministers. The fetters lay heavily on him for all his acquiescence in them. Without his enthusiasm, he could not have borne them, but " grace " sustained and uplifted him above the raging waters of a distracted life, and deep within was a calm that was as infinite.

In passing a member of the family on the stairs once, he murmured concerning Watson's poem on Wordsworth, " He says that we go to his poetry for peace. It is finely put; you must read it." His face, as he spoke, in its serenity and gentleness—that peculiar gentleness which always marked him when he spoke of the poets—was peace itself. His sermon on Christ's Peace was one of the most remarkable of all his discourses. " Christ will not," he said, "give you wealth or position, or troops of friends, or what the world calls happiness, but peace "; and, as usual, he had no words adequately to define or expound that peace. But that he participated in it must have been clear to many for whom Christ's peace could have no special import.

In the Mission that he started, and which embodied much of his chivalry, there was always from the first a certain rare and imaginative element that craved further development, and to which some of the unimaginative took great exception. A mission in the eyes of these was a " Mission "—

> "A primrose by the river's brim,
> A yellow primrose was to [them], . . .
> And nothing more . . ."

To my father it was a great deal more. It was not only his particular and especial crusade, carrying healing to the body and the soul of those who were in need of it in the heart of a great city, but an attempt to give a full presentation of what he conceived to be the essential teaching of Christianity, to give woman her full place in Church work, and to find a basis of Christian operation and teaching which should unite as large a section of Christendom as possible, to wit, that portion of it which falls between the extreme of Rome, on the one hand, and that of Unitarianism on the other. He knew that both of these contained saintly characters doing good work, for whom he had the highest respect, but he did not think they could work on Methodist lines, as he thought the others could. A Methodist, as he would tell companions on Hampstead Heath, where he used to expound these things, is one who is willing to model his life and belief on what is laid down in the New Testament, so there was nothing to prevent quite a number of people from becoming Methodists in that sense, or from working with Methodists if they preferred that way of putting it. Despite the fifteen hundred persons who joined themselves to the Mission Church, they were quite the minority of those who came under its influence. Persons belonging to other portions of the Universal Church, as well as those quite outside it, felt and still feel the influence of a movement, whose indirect results were equal to if not greater than its direct. Roman Catholics, members of the Greek Church, Unitarians, Protestants of all kinds, from Anglicans to the extreme evangelical sects, received help from the Sisters, attended and were benefited by the different services and meetings of the Mission, and remained members of the Church of their childhood. In all this, my father contended, he was strictly following Methodist procedure, acting in its spirit and in accordance with its traditions. Thus the broad and unsectarian principle was one of the first articles in which he trained his workers. " If a Jew or a Roman Catholic comes and asks you for bread and a cup of water, give it to him for Christ's sake, and let him know that it is for Christ's sake, not for any wretched fad or delusion of your own."

With such mandates he sent forth his first helpers into Piccadilly and Soho. An experience of his own was typical perhaps, as much as anything, of the attitude he encouraged. It was during the first year of the Mission, and certain can hear him speaking as if it were yesterday. He came into supper with brows knit looking deeply agitated.

" I have had," he said, " the most painful experience— most painful. It is so distressing indeed that I scarcely know how to relate it. I passed a public-house quite close here on my way back from Tottenham Court Road, and I saw that a commotion was going on, so I stopped to observe it. A hansom cab-driver had just come out—half-drunk evidently— and had managed to mount on his box. His wife, a slight, fragile creature, with one baby in her arms and another, half-unclothed, clinging to her skirt, was standing below." Here the speaker paused, and then resumed. "She wanted the man to give her money, and he would not, and at last it fell to quarrelling—and there she was shouting up at him—oh, it was most painful—till quite a crowd collected. Of course she spoke very improperly, poor thing, and there was the ragged child clinging to her skirt all the time. This went on for some minutes till the man drove away. I felt some one should go and speak to her, yet for some reason I could not. I shrank from it. So I turned on my heel and got as far as Gower Place, when I felt so ashamed of my cowardice that I had to turn back. I wasn't long in overtaking her, for that had taken place which I knew would happen." Here the speaker threw up his hands. "No sooner was the public-house out of sight than she had burst into sobs, and the wretched little children were sobbing too. Then I went up to her very quietly and said, 'Excuse me, but can I assist you in any way?' 'Thank you, sir,' she said, and looked up at me. She was Irish, as I had noted from the first. And then she began sobbing even more bitterly, but I spoke to her very quietly. 'If you will give me your address I know of a lady—a Sister —who will call upon you immediately and will endeavour to be of some assistance to you,' and she gave it to me. So I thought of Sister So-and-so—she is Irish, and was a Roman Catholic in her youth. She will know how to deal with the case." Then turning to my mother, "Can she, do you think, deal with the case immediately?"

My father's feelings towards the gates of Taviton Street were mingled, but at last the day came for them to be abolished. The inhabitants got up a petition to protest against this inroad upon their peace, and brought it round for him to sign. "How could I?" he said at dinner; "Jesus Christ would not have kept up those gates when hundreds of the people have to go a mile out of their way because half a dozen of us do not want to be disturbed."

"What did they say?" somebody asked.

"They told me they paid for it. Pay for it, my dear sir," said I.

"But they do pay for it, don't they?"

The speaker dropped his knife and fork. "Since the beginning of time half a dozen of us have been paying to keep other fellows out. Paying for it?——h'm. Do you think (fixing a withering eye on the speaker) that I should allow you to murder everyone in the street because you paid for the privilege? As I said to So-and-so—My dear sir, you are not entitled to pay. Are we by our filthy lucre to rob the masses of the people of their hard-earned leisure and make their life more insufferable to them than it is at present? God forbid! If you want to have perfect peace and quiet, go and live in the fields somewhere, where you are disturbing nobody, and where you can gratify your caprices to your heart's content."

It was suggested that Taviton Street was not a thoroughfare.

"Yes, but the other streets are, and the more avenues we have open the better. For myself, I want Taviton Street to set a good example and lead the rest. All the gates will have to come down everywhere, the poor must come through. In our selfishness we have kept them out long enough. As I said to So-and-so, if the drays do come thundering through the street at six o'clock in the morning, we must lie awake— that's all—or go and live somewhere else. I should be sorry for any one in Taviton Street to be disturbed at that hour, but I cannot see any way out of it except removal. The day has come when we must help the people by every means in our power—lie awake for them if necessary. So-and-so is in a great state because they are going to run trams in front of his house, and he says the neighbourhood will become intolerable. But I, as a Christian, could not sympathise with him. Think of the washerwomen and the girls with large parcels who will be able to pay a halfpenny and get a tram ride! What a blessed and glorious thought! I was very near bidding him praise God for it!"

Something resembling a family life was the centre and the inspiration of the Mission. The superintendent and his wife always breakfasted on Saturday mornings at Katherine House with the Sisters, when they would give and impart their news. My father would tell them what was going on in the world at large, where he was going, what he was intending to do, and often what he had been specially thinking and feeling. Perhaps a more transparent being never lived than the superintendent, and it was this transparency that delighted people. He dwelt in no impenetrable cloud. He assumed that others were interested in his concerns, as he undoubtedly was in theirs.

"Mr. Hughes was a most lovable man," wrote one gentleman at the time of his passing, and then stopped as if at a loss to say more.

My parents long remembered the eve of that first Sunday in October 1887 when they and Sister Lily, Sister Hilda, and Sister Katherine sat together in the dining-room of 8 Taviton Street wondering as to the morrow. On that morrow the West London Mission was to begin. St. James's Hall in Piccadilly had been taken as its headquarters, a choice which greatly delighted my father because of the strategic and spectacular value of its position. Would anybody come, and if so, how many? they wondered on that Saturday evening. What was the future to bring forth? "Let us pray," said the superintendent, and they were on their knees in that lightning fashion which was always demanded on these occasions. That first evening struck the keynote of the whole. Every special effort, every great need was always accompanied by prayer— often at midnight, when it was not possible to gather the missioners at those early morning hours that he loved. When he and the missioners were alone together there was never the slightest constraint about the proceeding, and it was the very reverse of that gloom which the pious sometimes think the only fitting accompaniment of their devotions.

"I was delighted beyond measure with *Little Lord Fauntleroy*," he would begin. "It is a most exquisite story, full of Christianity and the Gospel of St. John"—then bending forward—"The conversation between the boy and the savage old earl, his grandfather, when he tells him about his friends in America, is comic to the last degree. There was a certain grocer of his acquaintance—Katie, what was the name of that grocer?"

"What grocer?"

"Why, *the* grocer, Lord Fauntleroy's friend."

"Mr. Hodges."

"Ah"—slapping his legs—"that's it. Hodges. Well,

this Hodges "—then followed a graphic account of the sayings
and doings of Mr. Hodges, accompanied by much swaying to
and fro of the body, and interjectory laughter. "What"—
looking at his watch—"half-past ten! Let us pray."

"Lord Jesus Christ, who wast when Thou wert in the
flesh the friend of little children, and who art the same
yesterday, to-day, and for ever, make us more childlike, so
that we may understand Thee better, and by our love and
unconventionality commend Thee to this city of selfishness
and sin and sorrow. Grant unto us to leaven it with Thy
love—to break down the false and the evil in the hearts of
men and women, as Lord Fauntleroy broke down the false
and the evil in the heart of his savage grandfather. Make us
more willing to learn of Thee and from Thee—not stuck up
in our own conceits and opinions and delusions, but ready to
hear Thy voice and Thy bidding."

The last words were not unlike a species of arrows discharged into the breasts of certain of the kneeling company,
who could not rid themselves of the idea that Mr. Hughes
intended to depict their condition, and resented it accordingly,
though this did not in the least follow. One thought followed
another, and he was often believed to be implying certain
things when the idea of them had not entered his mind. It
was not till after years, when he had passed away from them,
that some felt how truthfully their condition had been depicted.
Quite early in the Mission a very faithful and esteemed Achates
was looking at the St. James's Hall evening congregation with
my mother, who, with the Sisters, went down early to speak
to persons known to them in the congregation, and to be "at
the disposal" of any who might wish to address them.

"What can we do, Mrs. Hughes," he said, "to lighten the
burden on Mr. Hughes' heart? I am sure the thought of this
service and its responsibilities must weigh very heavily upon
him." For Achates was able to look at the congregation with
something of my father's eye, and in not quite the same way
that most did. These came and noted the orchestra, listened
to its music, and marvelled above all at the attendance.
Persons wishing to secure seats would come two hours before
the time, and hundreds were nightly turned away. In the side
balconies were the rows of soldiers and policemen, and in the

front row of the end balcony the group of hospital nurses, for whom also seats were reserved. There would be waiters from the restaurant below near the entrance, with serviettes in their hands, and at the back of the hall a sprinkling of gentlemen in evening dress who had slipped in on their way to or from the club. The preponderating element, as in all his congregations, were the men, though the women were equally striking, and too showily dressed, some of them. The old and middle aged (sad and inscrutable-looking, many of these) were interspersed among the rows and rows of young men and young women, earning their bread and butter, and living solitary lives many of them, till the Mission came along and made a centre and a home for them. These last might be described as the main body of the congregation. A cheery element were good Methodists from the provinces and visitors from our colonies. This is not an exhaustive description, but it is a suggestive one, giving the main elements of a typical Sunday night congregation, as viewed by a keen observer, but not as we have seen by my father, and the one or two who were able to enter into sympathy with him.

On this gentleman's suggestion, it became customary for the missioners to hold a five minutes' prayer-meeting in the artistes' room, where they used to assemble just before the commencement of the service. This room thus witnessed a diversity of sights and personages during the last decade of the century—singers and instrumentalists of European reputation waiting and chatting there on Saturdays and Mondays, while on Sunday evening their place was taken by a group whose calling and supreme desire was not comprehensible to ordinary men and women of this world. No one was ever called upon to pray at this meeting, as the occasion was felt to be very solemn, and it was my father's desire that it should be entirely spontaneous in character. A Methodist minister who was once present (for it was the superintendent's habit to seize hold of any minister, Methodist or otherwise, whom he knew) related that no one would pray at all. My father seemed angry, and after asking several times, began to pray himself. "It was a revelation," said the minister, "of the purity of his wrath. In an instant it was transformed into the most selfless and passionate prayer." Neither his tradition nor his temperament led him in the direction of Quakers' meetings. Once when some one said to him that "the Quakers were a kind of spiritual aristocracy," he demurred and hummed, for while he sincerely admired them, his instincts were too ecclesiastic to admit of such a definition.

Before praying for the congregation, he was led by the instincts of his nature to sit unobserved among them—noting those who were about him, and regarding them with full friendly eye as they sat patiently waiting for the service, listening to the orchestra. Punctually to the hour, he ascended the platform, followed by the principal missioners and Sisters as well as visitors from the colonies and provinces, and gave out the first hymn, which was taken up by the whole congregation with singular unanimity. There was a lesson for the evening, and a hymn and two prayers—many announcements respecting operations during the ensuing week, and then the climax of them all, the collection, to which everything that had been said before was the prelude and explanation. Roman Catholic priests, who would occasionally be present, were struck by the forensic qualities of the preacher, greatly admiring his skill, and looking upon him not only as one who knew how to make announcements and explain the objects of a collection, but a Protestant who thoroughly understood his own business.

The sermons, to which these gentlemen, along with the rest, breathlessly listened—the adverb is not too strong—are not easy to describe. Everybody had to listen whether they agreed or not, though all sat motionless. Indeed, the whole atmosphere would often be highly charged, because people's natures seemed to be undergoing such struggles within themselves, and observers had only to look at some of the faces before them to realise this. Sad, bitter, defiant, certain persons would come week after week, as if there were no rest for them in this world, but sometimes, as they afterwards confessed, it came. A Sister was moved to speak to a girl who sat Sunday after Sunday and took notes. "I often see you here," said she, for she felt that this girl would like to talk to her, not that she was in need of it, but that she would actually like it. "Yes," answered the girl, "I am learning shorthand, and as Mr. Hughes has a very good delivery, I like to come and practise myself in the way you see. What he says is quite indifferent to me, as I believe nothing religious, having been trained from my youth to think and to doubt." After the Sister (who was discreet) had said a few words, they exchanged cards, and there began a friendship between them, which resulted at last, and after much prayer and conversation, in the inlet of light and hope to what God has made but which man does not always comprehend, a sceptical mind. During this process the Sister brought her to talk with the superintendent in his study, for he had many private talks with such persons.

On another occasion, a soldier who was half-drunk was reminded by my father's words of something that his mother used to say long ago. He was so pierced and sobered that he determined there and then to alter his manner of life and to submit to the influence of Christ. His companion, who was also stirred, could not see his way to doing so at first, but he went again and again to St. James's Hall, as if drawn by an invisible magnet. The words, and a strange constraining power which accompanied them, sank into him, so that, when far away from England, he at last yielded to their prompting and began a new life.[1] These are typical instances.

My mother, on being asked what she considered the greatest spiritual triumph of his life, replied, after several minutes' meditation, "That he was willing not to be a great preacher in the usual acceptation of that term. He had the power to be one, the force, and the intellectual equipment, but he was willing not to be — to make himself of no account, so that men should hear not him, but Christ." The magnitude of this sacrifice will be better realised by the ministry than the laity—all that it signified to a man of his powers. Indeed, it was a fairly widespread opinion among the ministry of his own communion that he could not preach, but the laity who went to hear him thought that he could. A friend of his said that he most admired him on an evening when Lord Rosebery came to hear him preach. On handing in his card, he was shown to a front seat, and was a listener to one of the simplest of my father's expositions. In order to let power go from him he had to obliterate something in him-

[1] The above was recently related to my mother by the matron of a military home.

self, to lay himself on the altar so that the fire was kindled. Lord Rosebery wrote to him afterwards saying that he had been much impressed by the service, and either on this occasion or some other, there was correspondence between them on the subject of Nonconformity. Indeed, in preaching as in prayer, he broke through routine, charging both with a spontaneity and a simplicity to which many contemporaries were unaccustomed.

The poor and ignorant after listening to him would sometimes present themselves to the Sisters the next day, asking for that sufficiency, that clothing and feeding in Christ, which his words had implied. While the quizzical doubted and wondered, the simple and weary of heart took what he said literally, so intense was the infection of his own belief, even when the nature of it was inadequately comprehended. The secret of my father's power was that *he* spoke, not his profession. Doubters and believers alike were caught in the same vice—he believed what he said. The Presence of Christ with His Church seemed to haunt him at all times, particularly on occasions such as these, and into the depth of High Anglican and Roman feeling on this matter he undoubtedly entered, as the following incident reveals. On entering a Roman Church in Italy on the evening of Christmas Day, he was visibly moved by the prostration of the congregation, their manifest belief that Christ was in their midst, however material and crude to his thinking the interpretation might appear. When he got outside he said in a low voice to my mother, " I understand this—I understand this. They have it,—the root idea." By this he meant that worshippers were there for the right reason, to feel the presence of Christ, and to meet Him there, not to hear a learned discourse or even to sing hymns, but to realise their Saviour as they could not elsewhere. Moreover, for all the mystical character of the main burden of his utterance, he never forgot that he was preaching in Piccadilly to tempted men and women. The conceptions of life with which West London abounded, and the thought of the evil and the anguish so close at hand was constantly present, a chord that vibrated in all that he said.

Listeners had to know a good deal of ordinary life in order to understand all that was in his sermons. He was unconventional, and yet he was restrained, knowing evil but not offending good taste. When he preached about the Prodigal Son or David, he seemed to some most impressive, as if he knew that the story of these two was eternal, and that the human race, despite all its other advances, had not got beyond their meaning yet. His sermons, he said, "came" to him, so that he had never any difficulty in thinking or planning for them. So full indeed was the week, of travelling, speaking, committees, and business, that people often wondered how he could possibly prepare for Sunday. "For some reason," he said, "I never have any difficulty. God, I believe, suggests the text to me, so I feel no anxiety on the matter, though I have not the time often to prepare as others do." This constant belief that God was with him, suggesting, sustaining, propelling, was a marked characteristic. At Conference he would use the phrase in a manner that suggested the mysterious references of Socrates to the δαιμόνιον. "God wishes me to-day to speak of this," or sometimes "I do not know what He wishes of me," or some other time "It may be His will that I do so and so." It was striking also that those sermons which showed least signs of preparation, and which seemed to some to bear the marks of lack of thought and time in preparation, were those which most affected people. On the other hand, those occasions when he had evidently spent more time in preparation, and which were specially striking for a depth and serenity of thought and feeling, and for quotations from thinkers or poets whom he loved (though few sermons passed without some such reference) were not as immediately and directly effective as the former. As the Sisters said, "They are above the people." Some responded—for he never preached without producing a visible result of some kind—but not as many as usual. Absence of visible response would distress him.

The sermons, so a Sister related, that most went home to people were those which laid stress on the fact that God's thoughts were not man's thoughts, and that by an infinitude of ways unknown to man He led him to Himself. The purport of his message was always "Submit to the process— submit to God in Christ," and as a sign of that submission he asked those present to stand or to walk out into the room behind the orchestra, so that certain of the Sisters and missioners might be acquainted with their decision. The motive of this lay in the desire to get in touch with his audience, so that those spiritually moved might not be left desolate and without those who could aid them. Romanism and Methodism are conspicuous in their effort to come in direct touch with the individual, but the Methodist inquiry room cannot be compared with the Confessional as is some-times ignorantly done. Persons entered his inquiry room without telling anything of themselves, save that they wished to lead a better life, and wanted to know the best way of setting about it. Sermons such as he preached, with winged appeals to the individual,—for there was a power in them beyond the words and himself,—were bound to be followed by such an institution as the inquiry room, for otherwise it would have been like writing on water. A congregation which scattered to the four quarters, certain never to return, had to be approached directly, if it was to be approached at all. Yet the direct personal appeal was never during the first service, but in an after-meeting when the majority had dispersed. It was the sanity, the almost military element in what he said, that went home to people, so that men and women would rise one after the other in response to his appeals, not as if they were doing anything unnatural, but what was inevitable and natural. He never demanded also that deep sense of sin, that overwhelming repentance for a past, which is insisted on by some missioners, and in defiance of what my father would call " the facts." All that he did insist on was that certain acts and methods of life should be abandoned. A sense of sin, of shortcoming, of imperfection is the flower of sainthood and a great character, or of reflexion and sudden insight into self. The thoughtless and the youthful suddenly arrested to serious thought—to a spiritual quickening—feel and desire something higher and better, but it is only after experience of that higher life that they begin to feel that personal un-worthiness and imperfection which is the characteristic of the Christian life. Some think this sense of sin to be as essential and inevitable to a renewed humanity, as others say the sacra-ments are to membership in Christ's visible Church. But the experience at any rate of the missioners in the St. James's Hall proved this not to be so, and that a sense of sin in the deep sense was the fruit not the germ of the spiritual life. Some would wake as it were, almost naturally, from a dream. A girl, who had been brought up from childhood to an evil life, submitted at once and without difficulty to my father's pleadings.

All who thus stood up in response to his appeal he noted, as did two others whom he had specially selected for the purpose—one of the Sisters, and a gentleman closely connected with the Mission. Both these were remarkable for their knowledge of the world and of persons, and for a tact and courtesy of demeanour which at once ingratiated them with those with whom they conversed. These two would walk quietly to and fro on the floor approaching those who had risen, and entering into conversation with those who desired it, or merely asking if they could be of some service. So invariably delicate was the penetration of these persons, and so intense the desire of many to be approached, that only once out of a period of fifteen years did either receive a rebuff. Their task was at first undertaken with diffidence, but it was for this diffidence that they were selected. When my father called upon those who had risen to go into the inquiry room, many would rise as these approached and silently follow, as if only desirous of some one to lead them. Each only addressed members of their own sex, and in the inquiry room the same rule was strictly observed. The Sisters were in charge of the women's room, and specially appointed missioners of the men's room. That each sex should minister to itself was a point on which he rigidly insisted. In inviting persons to enter the inquiry room, so as to inform the missioners of their decision and to seek aid in a better life, he also invited those who were conscious, as he had once been at Brighton, of the need of deeper consecration. He knew, from his own experience, and from observation, what a silent bitterness or rebellion in life may do to make good men wretched, and to impair the effectiveness of their endeavours. Thus a very striking feature were the ministers of religion and members of all Churches who came into the inquiry room to inform some missioner of deeper acquiescence in God's will, and to say a few words before going away. The great variety of persons who were moved by my father's Sunday evening sermons were noted by those who sat on the platform, so that often the gathering impression of what he said reminded of

15

nothing so much as corn bending before the scythe. Every face came to betray an interest of some kind.

On Mondays my parents always met the Sisters and missioners, and after prayer they would relate their experiences of the previous day, whether at St. James's Hall or the other services. The value of the Sunday night St. James's Hall service was without parallel both to the Mission and to himself. While recognising to the full the value of the work done in other halls, he laid stress on the fact that St. James's Hall was the centre of their endeavours, as it was, in a certain intimate and inner sense, of his own. The Sisters who knew him in this capacity, and who were aware of what he was doing in the world, said, " Nothing was as near to his heart as this— bringing individual men to Christ—for this was the end of all that he did and wished." Moreover, as one said, " It was of the greatest help to himself, and how great I can only see, now he has gone, and I am freer to compare him with others." Occupied as he was increasingly with affairs, and with great issues in the world, he might well have lost, as the prophets often do, that contact with the soul and with the individual life, which he never did, because he could not. For however busy the week, however involved in great questions, either ecclesiastical or political, he was bound to meet individual men and women on Sunday evening, and to encounter the realities of that life which is lived above the parties and turmoil of the world, because all men can participate in it. The boy who lay in an agony on the Welsh shore was with him to the end, and he could never get far away from him. Indeed, not many Sunday nights passed without his telling that story, so that some wondered, both at his simplicity and his power of telling the same thing many times. His social work and his various innovations were supported by certain of the professionally religious, simply because of the Sunday night service and its undeniable results. However they might criticise him and what he did, this aspect of him always remained, condoning the rest. Without such services also my father himself would never have consented to uphold the rest of the Mission, for that would have been to deny both his own calling and his own conception of the Christian religion. Nobody in Methodism believed more in a system, in organisation, than he did.

If he appeared to fight such it was only because he wished to strengthen it, to adapt it for new conditions. He was a great believer in organisation, not only for social but for the most intimate spiritual need. He found in his own Church, as a means of directly reaching the spiritual life of the individual, the "mission preacher," or "revivalist," as he used to be called, and that which has sprung up around him—the inquiry room and its methods. He took up both against inner predilections, and a certain fastidiousness of taste, and clung to both throughout life, intent as he always was on modifying and improving that which he found. His aim was to remove those accretions and accompaniments which rendered these distasteful or unsuited to the times.

In the first place, by devoting his own strength and powers to that of evangelical preaching, he raised the status of the evangelical preacher. It was unconscious, and therefore the more effective, though he would consciously do so when he showed a hesitancy to admit young men of "zeal," but who lacked parts, into the lay order, or *vice versâ*, by encouraging preachers everywhere, ministerial or lay, to take every opportunity of reading and improving their minds. He always maintained that to be a mission preacher needed all the brains and intellect that a man possessed, and that so far from disqualifying him for that position, as some ignorant persons thought, it gave him one of the highest qualifications. To those who sought to excuse themselves from the toil of thought or study on the plea that they wished to be mission preachers, he would say sternly, "If God has no need of your brains, He has still less need of your ignorance!"

He was quite conscious throughout life that he had assumed a rôle which the world and many of the religious were in the habit of looking down upon, and he would reveal his consciousness of the fact by humorous allusions to the view that such took of him. "Tell them that your father is a poor preacher of the gospel and does not know any better," or "What can be expected of a Methodist minister who dares to tell men and women that Christ saves them from their sins!" Certainly he coveted at times the scorn of the world, as the following instance shows. He had recently passed, so he said, a public-house, outside which certain

loungers were chatting and smoking. In front of him two
Salvation lasses were walking, at sight of whom the loungers
fell into revilings, crying out and overwhelming them with
abuse and ridicule. " And when I passed," here he paused, as
if the shame of that moment had not yet left him, " they never
cried out at all at me, but let me pass on in silence. Those
poor girls they covered with abuse, but for me they had not a
word. I confess I was ashamed to follow them, feeling unworthy of Christ in that my presence could not evoke scorn for
His sake. Why was it? Why was not I permitted to bear
what they bore?" Perhaps it was small wonder that some
did not know what to make of him or of such exclamations,
which sounded like anachronisms in the modern world. Such
fervent words, such a continuous consciousness of the presence
and person of Christ, befitted the saint of old time rather than
the perplexed modern, striving amid a great twilight to do
his task before the darkness. Yet while they thought faith
dim, and the Christian saint, as tradition has conceived him,
a figure of the past, many walked to and fro in their midst
as conscious of the life and message of His Son as any of
the early or middle age, seeing only in the modern world
a fresh phase of that existence to which He would reveal
Himself.

It was characteristic of him that he strongly resented the
idea that evangelistic services were for uneducated persons, or
indeed for any one section of humanity—which seems to be
the conception of some. He always remembered how the
artists and writers of the fifteenth century had received inspiration at the Duomo, when Savonarola preached to the Florentines
—for to his thinking Savonarola was an evangelical preacher,
and St. Francis and many others whose names figure in history.
It was the spirit with which he was concerned as ever, not its
letter or the form that it assumed in different ages. While he
used prevalent terms, it was certain that he endowed them with
a wider content than many of his contemporaries, and that by
evangelical preaching he denoted that direct untrammelled
appeal to the heart and conscience which may be communicated
in a variety of ways. Yet, whatever the particular method,
it is always a direct challenge to all present, in that it is a
portion of the preacher's experience, not something received

or expounded, but that which he has felt and that which he believes. Such preaching is not confined to any particular communion, though it may be at certain epochs. In addressing the newly ordained ministers as Ex-President, he described, perhaps more graphically than on any other occasion, his idea of what evangelical preaching should be. " Regard yourselves," he said, " as advocates for Christ. He is the Prisoner at the bar, and your audience are the jury. According to the nature of the jury and the circumstances of the case you will frame your address, but always with the one end in view—the cause of Him who is bound in your midst awaiting the verdict of each of those whom you are addressing. You may touch on a variety of themes and in a variety of methods but always with the same object—to move the will and the conscience of your audience on His behalf."

To attempt to give any account of those who he himself thus moved, and the number of them, would transcend the limits of any biography. For he was always Christ's advocate wherever he was—preaching or not preaching—and that for a period of forty-two years, during which he came into contact of various kinds with many thousands, always with the same object in view, but a different method of procedure, because the jury and the circumstances of the case were different. Of the number and character of those who experienced " illumination," " decision " in its different degrees and stages, as a result of his ministry at all times, it is quite impossible to form any conception. The letters at his death spoke of " thousands mourning him all over the world," of " thousands who had deeper communion with God, deeper hope and faith," because of him ; and perhaps these letters more than anything else would reveal to readers what he was in the spiritual life and aspiration of men and women.[1] He said once to his children when they were talking, " You must be quiet for a little. Do you know that I am writing words on which the welfare of thousands depends ? " This caught their attention, and they would relate it with smiles, for they knew that nobody else would have put it in quite that way except himself. The use of the word " welfare " was so characteristic. Not the " spiritual life," or

[1] "I have heard the fishermen round Solway Firth talk together of him," wrote a correspondent at the time of his death.

the " aspiration," but the substantial, concrete word " welfare "
—that which is generally applied to physical conditions. As
he wrote or spoke, amid criticism or contumely, he foresaw in
vision that which God should achieve through him.

At times he lacked insight into individuals. Men and
women owned that he believed what they made themselves out
to be, rather than what they were. This was partly the
simplicity that underlay a many-sided nature, and partly a
result of the hurry and stress of his days. For masses of men,
for the man as a citizen, as a member of a profession or church
or nation, he had an eagle eye indeed, and his intense sympathy
and tender-heartedness made him the true interpreter often of
crises in the individual life. Yet to the eyes of those about
him he would fail to detect the true calibre of men and women
who came into his path, overestimating some individuals and
underestimating others. He generally overestimated. One of
the missioners writes :—

" I was always so much struck by Mr. Hughes's gentleness
and tenderness for the feelings of others. He was so eager to
think the very best of people, and could not bear to attribute
an evil motive. Indeed he often suffered himself, because too
beautifully simple to read in anybody else the mixed motives,
which found no place in his own composition——but oh, people
didn't believe it ! I remember one day when I was declaiming
about some local temperance secretary whom I wanted to
have put out of office, how he just weighed up everything, and
begged me to be patient and make allowances for the character
of the man before his conversion. This is years ago, but it
made such an impression on me at the time and was so typical
of his spirit . . ."

My father always passionately contended that the Christian
religion was not ethic and never could be. Thus he had
continuous arguments with certain people who refused to
believe in others, because their spiritual fervour and insight was
not supplemented by corresponding ethical virtues. Ethical
uprightness, without the distinctly Christian and mystical
element, was often, I think, alien and repelling to him, so that
he preferred a faulty and irritating " Christian " because, at
moments at any rate, he did believe in something higher than
himself. On speaking to him of some who lived strenuous

THE AGE OF CHIVALRY 231

lives of high reflexion and usefulness, he would say, " Do you
not detect something missing in their very virtue, which
proclaims the absence of its Christianity?" Christianity, he
would argue, was neither conduct nor consistency, though these
were implied in it—it was a new life—a leaven struggling
amid a very imperfect and alien environment. The fact that
many of the degraded and the least perfect embraced Christianity, was to its honour in that it could take some kind of
root even in the most degraded soul, though here again he spoke
of Christ not Christianity; " for the centre of our religion," he
would say, " is not a creed or a tradition but a living Person."
Ethic may be largely the result of heredity, training, taste, and
temperament, as many say it is, and such combinations without
distinct Christian love and charity and humility were very
deficient to him. On the other hand, he would notice the
presence of Christian graces in those who did not profess
Christianity, but such he would designate as " unconscious
Christians," repelled by the unworthiness of those professing it.

A Brotherhood organised on the same lines as the Sisterhood was one of the many dreams which he was never able
to accomplish. The organised work among men did not,
except in one or two notable exceptions, approach the organised work among women. Such organisation would only
have been possible with a Brotherhood—professional as the
Sisterhood was professional. Invaluable assistance was
rendered by men in their leisure hours, but with all his
appreciation of such services he wanted gentlemen of leisure as
impassioned in the service of the Church and the community as
were the ladies who had joined the Sisterhood. If he had had
the necessary leisure such a Brotherhood would undoubtedly
have been formed, but such institutions, as history shows, need
time and attention. His idea was as follows : that " the
Brothers" should promise to devote themselves for a certain
number of years to social and religious work, and should for a
stated period form a community submitting to its discipline.
Such a community would have corresponded to High Anglican
and Roman institutions without any of those accompaniments
that he found to be objectionable. Few knew how he longed
for the service of the best and most intelligent of the lay
manhood, and how he continually deplored his inability to

carry out such a project. For a short period, indeed, he managed with Mr. Marden's assistance to hold a class for men, which was largely and representatively attended, but an increasing press of engagements made it impossible for him to continue this.

It was his habit to welcome a variety of "personalities," especially those who overflowed with novel ideas and daring suggestion, and who possessed gifts and accomplishments of any kind. "The basis of the Mission," he said a few months before he died, "is that the conventional and the unconventional work together." The unconventional were simply indispensable in his eyes; they gave the "phase of social Christianity" which the Mission expounded, a grace, a daring, an elasticity, a certain picturesqueness which was in his conception a most vital element. The absolute trust and confidence that he reposed in those working with him—particularly his ministerial colleagues—induced those who were associated with him to give the very best of themselves. His colleagues were free to employ their own methods, provided that after a reasonable period they proved successful in them. "Make any experiment you choose," he said to his early workers, "but if it fails drop it like a hot potato." "Nothing was more astonishing," one related, "than the confidence he placed in us. When anybody undertook that anything should be done he assumed that it would be, and had no further anxiety in the matter." Such a system was not without its defects, but they were outweighed by its great advantages—the immense appeal to what was latent in persons, and the giving of self that this involved. In particular, it was beneficial because it enabled him to depute work to others when necessary, a faculty which stood him in good stead, as he became increasingly concerned in a wider ecclesiastical life than that of the Mission. "The secret of success in work is to depute portions of it," he was in the habit of saying, and he would regret the inability of others to do the same thing. Thus in the atmosphere of trust and equality that he infused, each could bring their own particular gift to the commonweal.

On the first Christmas in London, at the suggestion of the evangelistic agent, "a dinner for the lonely" was held at

Lincoln House,[1] for persons in business who could not return home, but who were only too delighted to pay two shillings and sixpence and have a merry instead of a sad Christmas. The missioners and their families used to be present at these parties, and would take part in amusing and entertaining the company. My father sat smiling and talking with Mr. Pearse at the head table, chaffing those who sat near him, and afterwards, when the guests went upstairs, he read aloud one of Tennyson's Idyls—" Geraint and Enid " was his favourite. Mr. Pearse was the life of the party, reciting Cornish stories to the intense and transparent delight of my father, who always took the greatest pleasure in his colleague's utterances. " I never hear Pearse," he used to say, " without finding something intensely suggestive in what he says."

One of the beautiful suggestions of a Sister of the People, was the Guild of the Brave Poor Things, suggested by Mrs. Ewing's story, an organisation which has since spread to other parts of the kingdom. This Sister on visiting a cripple boy who was derided by the cruel, because thoughtless, youth of the neighbourhood, bethought herself of Mrs. Ewing's story and was able to infuse into him that heroic spirit, that zest in suffering which is perhaps the greatest attribute possessed by human beings. The medical director founded a home for the dying.[2]

A colleague suggested the Social Hour in Prince's Hall, Piccadilly, after the Sunday evening service at St. James's Hall,

[1] Lincoln House, Soho, had a romantic history, which my father loved to detail when he brought visitors there to tea on Sunday afternoons. In 1680 a colony of merchants from the Levant had settled in the neighbourhood, and the church built for the Greek form of worship gave its name to the street. Later, Joseph Wedgwood used to exhibit his pottery in the house in question, including the magnificent service which he made for the Empress of Russia, which Queen Charlotte herself came to inspect. Later, Sir Thomas Laurence built his studio on the top floor and painted ladies of fashion who came sweeping upstairs, which are full of strange rustlings to this day. More recently, the Jews held a free school in the premises, to be superseded by the Austro-Hungarian Club, whose evil practices were notorious even in Soho. With the advent of the missioners the name of John Wesley's College was affixed to the door, and the babies of the Crèche took their afternoon nap in the studio where Sir Thomas Laurence had painted ladies of fashion.

[2] Perhaps in no other department was there so apt an illustration of the catholicity of the Mission as St. Luke's Home for the Dying. The Jewish rabbi, the Roman Catholic priest, the Anglican clergyman, and Mark Guy Pearse have all ministered to the different patients.

so that the Sisters and missioners might enter into conversation with the young men and women who thronged their services, or with any others who might wish to speak with them. These are typical instances of individual contributions to the work and programme of the Mission, and they are only one or two out of many. As the superintendent regarded these contributions, he could not resist exclamations of pride. Many people did not like to hear him exclaiming in that manner; they said he did it too often. But he could not help himself when such people of genius came to assist him. Why there was the Sister in charge of the Crèche who positively cast a spell over the babies at two o'clock in the afternoon and sent them all to sleep. He had never heard of such a thing before, and he thought the public ought to know and wonder at it too! His attitude to the Press was a novelty to many religious contemporaries. Christian people, he used to say, had not only failed to read newspapers as they should, but to make use of them in an age when they were closely intertwined with the general life. Representatives of the Press were always welcomed by him, and missioners were early instructed to show them every courtesy. His understanding of journalism sprang partly from the fact that he was a journalist himself. " He always knew," interviewers would say, " what made good copy."

In the Rescue work my mother in particular took interest, and in order to reach the class among whom one or two of the Sisters laboured, a special effort was made during the winter months, when about a hundred women and girls were invited to what was called a midnight supper. My father did not at first attend, and when he did so it was a manifest effort. A Sister who was present related that he sat at the back of the room, almost obscured in the corner, from whence he watched the proceedings, so visibly affected that it was quite painful to see him. At last he beckoned to one of the Sisters to approach him. " Speak," he said, " to that poor girl over there. She looks so despairing." The ghastly supper doubtless suggested to him, as much else in life did, that whole of which the particular item under observation was but a significant portion. About the same time the Drunkards' Dinner was held, though it was not necessarily more drunken than the supper previously referred to. The Temperance question entered into every department of the work, and often to workers seemed the only question. The side of life with which the Mission and the Sisterhood dealt and deals cannot be portrayed either by reports or social statistics, and seems to need that vivid and passionate apprehension of things human and suffering which belongs to the pen of great French writers.

What may be called the civic side of Christian effort on which my father had always so insisted, was a marked feature of the Mission. Two of the Sisters became Guardians of the Poor. When one of them stood for St. Pancras, an "unconventional" Sister went about with a handbell in a cart through the Cleveland Street district in which she worked, with a great placard inciting the inhabitants to "plump" for the new candidate. The present superintendent,[1] also at my father's instigation, sat on the Borough Council, and was for some years chairman of the Health Committee. It was this recognition of the civic and municipal side of London life that struck outsiders, and which was increasingly an important aspect of successful Christian work in the Metropolis. That preaching in the open air, which had first become habitual with him at Oxford, was continued unabated in the west of London, in the neighbourhood of the different halls and centres, and particularly in Hyde Park and at Epsom Downs during the Derby week. A spot would be selected not far from the grand stand, and the lay agent and his helpers, by unfailing good-humour and the singing of hymns, would attract the attention of passers-by. The addresses were short, the lay agent related, and concerned with the love of God. On his return he would vividly repeat all that had occurred, how people looked and what they said, while the superintendent listened eagerly, laughing at anything that amused him, and uttering prayerful exclamations at any incident which showed that a man or woman had listened to the message of Christianity and taken it to themselves.

The sad side of all these activities, religious and social, was the strain of their financial support, which never ceased to burden him. Indeed, it was the ever-hovering nightmare of his life, which he would occasionally forget, but from which he

[1] Rev. Charles Ensor Walters.

was never entirely delivered. His own Mission naturally was
the peculiar object of his forethought and anxiety, but he
would continually hold meetings in the country with the other
missioners, to obtain money for all the London Missions. His
friends would say to him at times, " Is it necessary for you to
do this? Surely one in your position and with your varied
responsibilities, should be spared tramping about for the convenience of other people and their work without neglecting an
obvious duty?" But he had always the same answer to make,
that he could not refuse to go. This showed not merely his
loyalty to the connexional principles of Methodism, but the
fact that he was never centred, as he well might have been,
on his own particular share in a great work. A colleague to
whom he was much attached, and who had aided him in the
Mission for some years, said, on hearing of his death, " It's
the financial strain that killed him. He could have borne the
rest, but that finished him."

At midnight at the approach of the anniversary season, a
bowed figure would be seen sitting over the study writing-desk
inditing laborious letters to persons who might be moved to
assist the work, and to launch it into another year. No one could
interrupt, for it was a task that had long been postponed, and
which had to be accomplished. Every now and then he would
pause as if unable to continue, but after a space the pen would
be again taken in hand, and the writing would continue, but
always with the same unaccountable difficulty, as if it was all
the writer could do to complete his task. " Everybody thinks,"
he would exclaim, " that I like asking for money because I am
always doing it. God knows I hate it, and I detest it more
and more—particularly when it comes to writing private letters
to men." Perhaps the inherent irony of the situation affected
him as much as anything—that ministers of Christ should be
at their wits' end in London for a paltry £2000 or so. He
invariably used those words when speaking of sums of money
that he required—" paltry " or " trifling " or " small." It was
the result of a comparison—a constant comparison in his
mind—between what he saw people to be spending on themselves, and that which they spent on philanthropic objects or
the Church of Christ.

No one spoke more plainly to the rich on the subject of

giving, and was more respected in consequence. His anxiety that the rich men of his own communion should give largely either to his work or that of others was in large part for themselves—for it was from that aspect that he generally spoke of it. Not once did he say, but many times, that the curse of the Methodist people would be their wealth, thus echoing John Wesley's fears on the matter. "Unless we can induce dear So-and-so to give, his salvation is at stake," or "There is poor dear So-and-so, a charming fellow, simply rolling in wealth, and unless God can move his heart to give, I do not know what He has in store for him, or what will happen to him." Or again, "He is such a dear friend of mine but he does not give as God has blessed him. He thinks he does I don't doubt, but he is deceiving his own soul in the matter. Do not let us speak of it as it is very painful." "The love of money," he would continually quote, "is a root of all evil, and the poor may love money just as much as the rich." In the world of affairs also he found that it was the love of it which most opposed his ideals—not the love of money necessarily entertained by bad men, but by good. His keenest critics agreed that he was absolutely delivered from the love of it himself, and it was that which entitled him to speak as he did, and to obtain the respect that his speaking accorded. As if to prove one of his favourite maxims, that to be brave in doing what a man thought right was highest wisdom, his own Mission as well as his larger enterprises in Methodism received aid from time to time from a little group of rich men at whose generosity to himself and to others he wondered. "The same names," he said, "are always on all the lists, and the more I think of their devotion to Christ, and the way in which they account themselves His stewards, the more I admire them. God knows I should not like to be rich, for I doubt whether I could resist the temptation as they do. It is so subtle, so gradual often, that men do not see how their spiritual life is becoming paralysed by it." Yet it was not the rich who helped him to share what he would call "an intolerable burden," but the poor—the business girls and domestic servants in the classes of the Sisters, and struggling men and women all over the country. These saved from their pittances, or collected a few shillings from friends and employers, and sent them to him. The evenings of arduous days would be spent in making articles for sales of work, and at times of special effort they would astonish the superintendent when their contributions were repeated to him. On one occasion a young girl in one of the Mission classes visited from house to house in a very fashionable quarter. In every case she insisted on seeing the master or mistress of the house, so that she might personally inform them of a special Mission that the superintendent was about to hold in the Prince's Hall, Piccadilly. "I just told them," she related afterwards to a Sister, "what Mr. Hughes was going to do, and that I had come to bring a personal invitation from him." In the evenings, she confessed, she had been prostrate, what with fatigue and nervous exhaustion, and that she had lain trembling at the thought of the morrow. "I do not quite know," she continued, "how I got through that week, but God gave me strength. Mr. Hughes said we must not be content till the rich and the fashionable came to hear and receive the message of Christ, and that we must each do our share in the great work. It was laid upon me that this was my share." As the superintendent listened to the story of what she had done he wiped his forehead more than once, and kept exclaiming, "I could not have done it! I could not have done it!"

The efforts of children were also peculiarly touching to him. The little niece of one of the Sisters made some articles for a sale, and derived £10, 10s. as profit, which she sent to him for the work. In answer he wrote in his own hand as follows :—

"8 TAVITON STREET, GORDON SQUARE, W.C.,
"July 8, 1893.

"MY DEAR LILIAN,—I have been in Ireland, and since my return have been so busy that I have had no time between breakfast and midnight to write anything myself, or I would have written before now to thank you with all my heart for the great help you have given me. You and your schoolfriends have done a most beautiful work for the little children and the sick, whom Jesus specially loves. I do not think you could have done anything that could give Him greater happiness. I have paid your money into the bank, but I am sorry to say that I have been so busy that I have not had time to get a proper receipt, which, however, I will get and send you to-morrow. Please give our warm thanks to your schoolfriends, and Miss Dewhurst and Sister Lily, and your five helpers, and your father and mother, and all the kind people who came and made your bazaar so great a success. Five guineas have gone to the Crèche, where they will enable us to wash and dress and feed and amuse and teach many babies for many days. When you come to London (as everybody does) some day you must visit the Crèche. The other five guineas go to help and comfort the Brave Poor Things, some of whom are blind, some lame, and some deaf, and all in some way suffer greatly. But such kindness as yours gives them more happiness than you can imagine. You shall see some of them, too, when you come to London; and when you go to heaven, Jesus will Himself tell you that He was as much pleased as if you had given it all to Him. Please give my kind regards to your father and mother and brothers—have you any sisters? I think you have one. But I live so far off that I really cannot remember how many of you God has sent among us.—I am, dear Lilian, your grateful friend,

"H. PRICE HUGHES.

"Miss Lilian Thompson."

He was supposed to know little of children, but up and down the country he was the hero of some of them. Those who heard him as boys have told also of the impression that his sermons produced upon them, so that in some cases it affected the course of a whole lifetime.

One man and his wife, in particular, caught the chivalry of the age. They had saved up a certain amount of money, and were intending to spend the remainder of their lives in the suburbs. But after hearing my father preach the first Sunday, they felt unable to do so. He had come, he said, to be at the disposal of "the people," the lonely and the needy in this great city. He wanted others to join him, and they felt they must respond to his call. So they went to live in a mews instead, and gave up Sundays to entertaining lonely young men, always housing any persons for whom the Sisters could not for the time being find a home. This "applied Christianity," as my father called it, was emulated by other

members of the Mission, who prized opportunities of aiding
others at their own personal inconvenience. In such they
were told consisted Christianity, and they were amazingly
ignorant of it some of them. To give up a bed to one
wanting it, and to sleep on the floor, was deemed a privilege
by many young women in the classes of the Sisters. Stories
such as these, which the Sisters and missioners would tell him
at odd moments, or when they came to consult him in his
study, were the flowers in his pathway, in whose fragrance he
detected a foreshadowing of that golden age when men should
dwell in peace because in brotherly love. Indeed, in that
sympathy with humanity and its infirmity, which made the
Mission beloved by those who do not always love missions,
there was from the first a note rare, because so refined, so
intuitive. Missioners found their work full of problems, and
in early days particularly were continually consulting my
parents as to what should be done and advocated in any
matter. Each human being was considered not as a " case,"
or one who was in misfortune of any kind, but as an individual
soul. To one who was bedridden and in continual pain, a
gentleman connected with the Mission used to go and play his
violin, and that seems to represent more than anything else what
the Mission was like, and the spirit in which it was conducted.

The Journal and the Mission magazine *Advance* continually speak of praise meetings and love feasts[1] at Wardour
Hall. The difficulty of the work and the sadness of the lives
of the congregation seemed to necessitate such acts of jubilation. My father, undoubtedly, greatly enjoyed a love feast,[1]
and the recital of spiritual experiences, which is their characteristic. On whatever committees and various business he
had been engaged during the day, it never lost its charm,
and up to the very last he would laugh at some naïveté
in an " experience."[2] Wardour Hall[3] (now pulled down for

[1] Wesley revived the ancient ἀγάπη, or love feast, of the early Church.
[2] A friend of my parents who was present on such an occasion, and who found it
difficult to believe in anything at all, was not a little stirred by what she saw and
heard. " They have so little in this world," she exclaimed, " yet how real their
religion seems to them, as if it were something tangible that gave them happiness
amid all the unhappiness."
[3] Wardour Hall was made over to the West London Mission by the courtesy of
the Congregationalists.

several years) is always spoken of by its adherents as " Old Wardour," with a certain accent of regret and tenderness in the voice, which bespeaks allusion to the days that are gone. Those who simply look at the photograph of the square, ugly, old hall, and who never had the privilege of toiling day and night in its vicinity, of entering public-houses, and incessantly patrolling and singing in its streets, of ladling out soup from the soup kitchen, and helping to make drunken men and women sober, do not understand the romance of the title. As in the Oxfordshire villages, my father would chaff Fidus Achates at concerts and praise meetings, and the sad mothers in the gallery would rock themselves in their delight. " Ain't he lovely ? My dear, ain't he lovely ? " one of these was heard to say to another *à propos* of my father, when he was making a particularly lively and characteristic speech. Amid the joy-lessness of their lives, religion meant mirth, sobriety, and kindliness. They looked forward to it some of these poor souls, as some other people look forward to the play. " It's so lively and cheerful. There's so much going on," one poor woman was heard to say. When harvest festival came round there was always a surprise of some sort. One year there were live sheep bleating in a pen just beneath the pulpit, and always such a mass of flowers and vegetables, that there was scarcely room to breathe for the people squeezed in to look at them.

What haunted my father as an ecclesiastic was the neces-sary universality of the Church of Christ, and that her secret lay in the appeal to different classes and environments, and by a variety of method. In this he differed from many con-temporaries, and from those denominations whose ideas were bounded by a certain class, either the middle or the upper or the lower, and who were mutually intolerant of each other's practices. His struggle with the missioners from the begin-ning was to get certain of them to countenance one another, and to embue each with the necessary universality of the Christian Church.[1] They thought of him as one who recon-

---

[1] With all his sympathy for unconventional methods he disliked extremes, and would speak of them with distaste. The method of morning worship that was personally preferable to him was always that of the Liturgy, and it was a desire to profit by its discipline that led him to adopt the experiment of a liturgical service at

ciled them with each other, for it is the mote in the eye of brother and sister saints that is the difficulty. In the end it gets to look quite like a beam, and his incessant struggle was to prove the mistake. He fought to the teeth also any spirit of sectarianism in the Mission itself, by which any one group could think itself the most or least important, and thus separate itself in thought and spirit from the other groups. The main interest of each must be the welfare not of themselves but of the whole Mission of which they were part. Thus he rejoiced in collecting them all together and impressing upon them that spirit of loyalty and participation in the whole life of the Mission which must underlie not only the efficacy of their endeavours, but the depth and fulness of their own spiritual life. Nor did he stop here, in that he insisted, like a true Methodist, on the Mission itself being but a tiny portion of the varied activities and life of Methodism, of whose various needs and achievements he would delight to remind missioners. Moreover, Methodism herself, he undertook to remind Methodists, was but a portion of the larger life of the Church, and he did not confine his message to Methodism, but proclaimed it to the other Christian communions, as will be seen.

His interest in the musical efficiency of services was as keen as it had ever been. How the idea of an orchestral band was first suggested to him is doubtful. It was in part the result of conversations with Mr. Heath Mills, who had been organist and choirmaster at Richmond College, and with whom he early formed a friendship. Later in his early Circuits he would ask Mr. Mills to come down and start musical societies, or to hear his choir, and when it came to sitting in a balcony and planning for a band, it never occurred to him to do without the advice of Mr. Mills. Mr. Mills, moreover, gave more than his advice, he gave himself, and became the Musical Department incarnate. Friends listening to the orchestra would say to members of the family, " They are not all amateurs, are they ? " " No," would be the answer, " professionals take the

---

Craven Chapel during the time that that building was in the possession of the Mission. He had no wish to force a liturgical service upon those who did not appreciate it, but to make provision for those who did. He never forgot the few—their taste and spiritual need, and as years went on experience made him increasingly mindful of them. Only the few, he perceived, could help the many.

leading parts." "Oh, (then after a pause) they are paid?" "Not for their services — only the fares and incidental expenses." "Dear me, that is very kind of them. How did the Mission get to hear of them?" "They are friends of Mr. Mills," and with that they had to be satisfied, though it was no easy matter to slake the curiosity of some. After some time, however, they troubled the family no further, and for the good reason that they were endeavouring to get bands themselves. Upon this my father commented, "Have you noted how people first criticise and then imitate us? Indeed, I often wonder myself at the absence of any deviation in this compliment that they unwittingly pay us. Even when they leave the Mission on any pretext, they establish themselves in the neighbourhood, as if unable to escape the fascination of our operations. Are you not often struck by this?"

Of the conversations between my father and Mr. Mills the following may serve as a sample :—

"There will not be any difficulty, I suppose, in inducing members of your profession—those I mean among your immediate clientèle—to give us their services at a minimum charge? The leading parts, as you say, must be taken by professionals, and I am just a little anxious about securing these and satisfying their legitimate demands. The amateurs, of course, with your numerous clientèle, will be only too delighted to have such an opportunity, but "—

"Oh, I shall manage that, Mr. Hughes—I shall manage that!" Mr. Mills would burst out. "There's no fear on that score. We shall be able to satisfy them. As long as they can put in an appearance on Sunday evening and lead the rest we shall not ask any more of them."

"Besides," my father would continue, "You might represent to them the entirely undenominational character of our work, as well as its social and philanthropic side. Our efforts, too, among a foreign population such as Soho, must appeal to a cosmopolitan and warm-hearted profession."

"Warm-hearted, sir! the warmest!" Mr. Mills would cry, mopping his forehead as he did so. He was always doing that, as if he could scarcely support the tropical tenseness of his anxiety. To soothe this the superintendent thought to be his peculiar province, and nobody did it as he did. During the early days of the Mission in particular the two seem to memory almost inseparable, Mr. Mills constantly drinking tea with the family and talking about instruments in the study. Indeed, there was no restraining the passion for stringed music that swept the household and its immediate entourage. Mr. Mills procured a suitable instrument for all who desired to master its intricacies, for there was a widespread feeling that life was not worth living unless one could play on a stringed instrument of some kind. The superintendent, indeed, at this time digested such a knowledge of French horns, violins, and the like, and the secrets associated with them, that he would surprise listeners in after years by some musical technicality which had been stored with all the other data at the back of his mind. Thus nobody understood the Musical Department but the superintendent—the difficulty and indeed exhaustion of orchestrating hymn-tunes far into the night, and the hopes and fears attending the first performance of an overture. "Well, how did the rehearsal go?" he would inquire on Fridays, after the Executive Committee, where the musical director sat eager and attentive with the rest.

"Pretty well with the first violins and 'cellos, the flute and piccolo excellent—particularly the bars in the allegro,"— here he would hum them,—"but the second violins very poor —shocking. Have not got them to the scratch yet. No confidence, no precision of attack."

"Ah, precision of attack!" the superintendent would exclaim with sympathy, "that's so important. How can you remedy the defect?"

"Well, sir, I might get So-and-so to come and back them up. Two or three who knew their business might"—

"Exactly, ask them. Don't trouble about the expense, as I cannot have the message of the gospel misinterpreted by the second violins."

Perhaps no words would express the look which the musical director would direct at the superintendent at such moments— how he hugged such sympathy to his bosom. When the evangelistic and social department were trampling upon him and excluding him and his from the kingdom of heaven by their method of talking about them, he would ponder that glorious intimacy betwixt the gospel and the second violins.

"I think it is in imagination," the superintendent would gently remark; "no slight was intended. Your anxieties and toil of late may have rendered you hyper-sensitive. Your profession "—

"Oh no, Mr. Hughes, it is not that," he would exclaim, mopping his forehead; "I wish I could think it, but I cannot. They don't see that an *esprit de corps* is the very basis of a successful orchestra, and that we have not merely to do with fiddles but human beings. Machines don't come to play them. Now the other night "—and he would relate the incident that had distressed him.

"I will bear that in mind," the superintendent would remark, "and impress upon them all the services that are rendered by maintaining an *esprit de corps* in the band. Now about the annual band dinner, are the arrangements satisfactory so far?"

There was a point in the Sunday evening service when the conductor of the orchestra turned round on his velvet seat and looked anxiously yet expectantly at the superintendent. The notices were being given out, as only the superintendent, all agreed, could give them out. The evangelistic department —the relief, the children's work, the meetings for the week— were all having their share, and the conductor would listen with approval, for no one rejoiced more than he in the manifold departments of the Mission, as he had fully and reverently imbibed the superintendent's teaching on the matter. None the less, he expressed an undescribable blending of emotion, anxiety, and confidence, and each the sweeter for the other. At last, it was the turn of the Muses. "On Saturday night, our friends in the orchestra, to whose services we are so deeply and increasingly indebted, will give us their weekly concert in the Prince's Hall, Piccadilly — just opposite. The pro-gramme will be unusually attractive — unusually so. . . . Having said so much, there is no need to dilate further on what we shall miss if we are not all present. I shall be there as usual, and in the interim while the artistes are having neces-sary refreshment, I shall give my usual résumé of notable events of the week. Now all that remains is to announce the collection. The claims of the Mission were never more urgent than they are this evening, nor were the opportunities for doing

Christ's work in the west of London brighter and more numerous than they are to-day. Let each bear in mind their share in what is being done, and give as God has blessed them. Many who give copper could give silver, and some there are who are thinking of giving silver and could afford gold. Do not listen, I beseech you, to the promptings of habit, but those of prayer, and as you shall be moved in your heart, give freely and spontaneously to our work among the suffering and needy." During the early portion of this peroration it was impossible to describe the smile that broke round the lips of the musical director, and the glances of triumph and affection that he would shoot at the various professional gentlemen as the superintendent enunciated their names. His ear would be bent lovingly in the direction of the latter and the face became increasingly a benediction, and a benediction that could not be suppressed—irradiating every feature. When it came to the collection, he would straighten himself, elevating his eyebrows and glancing round like a father. "My children," he seemed to say, "have your score ready, so that we move the hearts of this congregation as Mr. Hughes desires." When it came to the words, "needy and suffering," his bâton would be raised in a kind of elation and his glance swept every row. "See," it said, "we are included in the kingdom, and it is ours to proclaim the gospel." At the professional leaders the eye gleamed, "On you alone I rely, and with what confidence," and to the amateur young ladies in the second violins, "Courage, all will be well." Then when every eye was riveted upon him, a sudden pointing, swift and imperious, of the bâton, and the first long notes of Handel's *Largo* would greet the ears of the congregation. It was to be doubted also whether he or they could have got through the Saturday evening concert without the superintendent.

"Innocent recreation," the latter would say, "is a necessity for life, and I rejoice to show my sympathy with it by being present this evening. Those who have reason to disapprove of much of the entertainment provided for young people in this city must, in some way, make good the deficiency as our orchestra is enabling us to do this evening." The quality of the singers and the various performances would be discussed, both before and after the concerts, by the superintendent and the musical director. At one time Sullivan's music was much in vogue, and in the Lake Scene of *William Tell* the eyes of the superintendent would dance with pleasure. But at last a Sunday evening came when there was no conductor in the velvet seat, only a bâton. It was draped in black, and the superintendent looked sad and grave as he took his stand just in front of it. The first violin gave the signal, and with the whole audience standing, the orchestra played the Dead March in *Saul* to honour a hand which would never wield a bâton any more, and whose eye would never sweep the second violins, and give them courage to interpret the gospel. Was he listening lovingly as of yore to the testimony of the superintendent, as he told the congregation, not of a musical director and the services of an orchestra, but a Christian character? So suddenly the end came, something gripping at the heart, just a moment in which the lips had framed "Jesus," and then had closed for ever. Mournfully they followed him to his grave, the orchestra and all the departments, for there is a music which no instrument made with hands ever emitted, that which proceeds from a sensitive and noble soul. Greatly devoted, greatly Christian, Mr. Mills ranks among the pioneers of the Forward Movement, which was inextricably bound up, as its critics early denoted, with the playing of bands.

The first service of the West London Mission was conducted by Spurgeon, who preached in St. James's Hall on a Friday morning, 21st October 1887. The following letter, which is *à propos* of this, will prove of interest:—

"WESTWOOD, BEULAH HILL,
"UPPER NORWOOD, *Sept.* 2, 1887.

"DEAR SIR,—I have to preach at Hinde Street on Oct. 11, and I greatly wish you could utilise this because I am going away on Nov. 7, and till then every day is engaged.

"I cannot do more, I ought to do less. I am greatly indebted to you and Mr. Pearse, and must do your bidding, but the notice is so short, and the day requested is at a time so pressed, that I must beg you to be merciful. If the 11th cannot be used, I must get off other engagements, and preach as you desire: *but please no bands of music.* What are you going at? And you a Methodist!—Yours truly,

"C. H. SPURGEON."

CHAPTER XI

INNER SIDE OF THE AGE

" There cometh a woman of Samaria to draw water : Jesus saith unto her, Give me to drink. . . . Jesus answered and said unto her, If thou knewest the gift of God, and who it is that saith to thee, Give me to drink ; thou wouldest have asked of him, and he would have given thee living water. The woman saith unto him, Sir, thou hast nothing to draw with, and the well is deep : from whence then hast thou that living water ? . . . Jesus answered and said unto her, Every one that drinketh of the water that I shall give him shall never thirst ; but the water that I shall give him shall become a well of water springing up unto eternal life. The woman saith unto him, Sir, give me this water, that I thirst not, . . . And upon this came his disciples ; and they marvelled that he was speaking with a woman."
Gospel according to St. John.

UNDERLYING the various characteristics and institutions of the Mission were two great ideals which possessed the superintendent, and which he impressed upon all who came into contact with him, — his ideal of holiness, and his ideal of woman.

Walking once across Dartmoor he said that the ideal life on earth must be a purified and deepened form of the old Greek conception—the sound life in the sound body. This holiness meant to him anything but that other worldliness of which George Eliot had accused Nonconformity, a criticism which rankled and to which he often made reference in the Journal. Nor did it mean a despising of the good things of this life when providence scattered them in life's path. To consecrate such to highest uses was different to thrusting them aside, and despising both them and the obligations that they entailed. Very far was it from any form of asceticism. In Professor James' recent book on *Varieties of Religious Experience*, the " hectic experiences " of various of the " underfed " saints, detailed at some length in one of the chapters, quite disgusted him. He could not tolerate the thought of their " morbidity," the more so because it accompanied such undoubted devotion and an abandonment to the highest conceived service, which was often missing, he feared, in the modern Protestant world. Holiness consisted in spiritual and mental healthiness—a full and harmonious development of man's nature, and, as far as possible, full physical efficiency. The athletic saint was a great delight to him, and there were times when he longed for a whole army of them, ready at a moment's notice to leap a five-barred gate or conduct a prayer-meeting. If the saints could only practise and excel in such vigorous performances, he would laughingly indicate, it would have a beneficial effect, not only on the Anglo-Saxon public, devoted like the Ephesians of old to the worship of Diana and kindred deities, but on so many of the saints themselves. He told men and women to cultivate and then consecrate their gifts—the gifts being of a great variety in his eyes, and distributed among every class of person. If speech, art, letters, social and civic position, were to be laid on Christ's altar, so equally were the cleaning of pots and pans and the blacking of boots. The writer is not quite sure that the mystery connected with the right performances of these latter did not, on certain occasions, appear to him more profound than that which is usually associated with the former. Persons who could deal with refractory window blinds, produce scissors and mend bicycles at the required moment, filled him with something approaching to awe. These oiled the machinery of existence and redeemed the first-named, himself among the number, from a helplessness that was too hideous to contemplate. Yet for all his sanity of conception, as regards holiness and its full-bloodedness, the roots of it lay deep as that of any accredited ascetic or mystic. Both in himself and the missioners he was always trying to embed the moorings of their faith—to hew deeper in that rock on which Christ had built His Church. Their house would withstand the rains and storms, and become a refuge for themselves and others, just in proportion as they entered into communion with Christ.

With not a little anxiety he was always trying to ensure this, especially during the first few years of the Mission, when he had a comparative leisure, which his later life rendered impossible. Thus he no sooner heard of any one versed in the spiritual life than he asked them to come and address the Sisters and missioners, and his continual desire for the Mission was that there should be a deepening of the spiritual life. Some Anglican Evangelicals were starting a yearly Holiness Convention, about the time the Mission was started, and he was not a little interested in the innovation. He himself had derived such benefit from a Holiness Convention at Brighton, that the trumpets of the Journal blew lustily by way of salutation, and then as suddenly ceased. The editor was disappointed, for the atmosphere was not breezy and invigorating as he had hoped it would have been. There was too much hymn-singing and splitting of straws, too little recognition of the civic and virile qualities of Christians. With all his respect for the piety and labours of many of those present, he could not accord with the tendency of their thought or with certain traits in their conception of Christ and the kind of service that He required from men in this world.

On one occasion when he had been walking and conversing a good deal with a fervent Evangelical and a most courteous and delightful Broad Churchman, he suddenly fell into a reverie concerning them. The latter appeared to him simply overflowing with the milk of human kindliness, but as ignorant on matters ecclesiastic and profoundly spiritual as a babe unborn. At last the remark escaped him, " I wish that by some process we could produce an amalgamation of both of them. How delightful it would be ! "

None the less, the idea of the Convention was an admirable one, and in the year 1892 he determined that the Sisterhood and the principal lay agents should retire from the world awhile to meditate on the deep things of the Spirit in a village at the foot of the Cotswold Hills, where one of his colleagues had recently been instrumental in the purchase of a Convalescent Home. But he refused to designate this retirement by the title of Convention. It was, he said, to be a " Retreat," and caused strong shivers accordingly among certain staunch Protestant sisters.

" What in the world was Mr. Hughes after now ! People would think that they were becoming High Anglicans and

Roman Catholics!" Psychically aware of the shivers, he insisted the more. A Retreat it was to be, past hope and shadow of turning and to all futurity. It was felt in addition that he was consciously reacting against current conceptions of the "Holiness Convention." Nothing could have been more vigorous than his method of alluding to it, more cognisant of earthly detail. Brakes would meet them at the station at such an hour, the train quitting Paddington at another hour.

Very particularly he begged them to lay aside any distracting thoughts—anything which might divert their attention from the spiritual and eternal themes to which for four days he wished their minds to be continuously directed. In order to set them an example, for he had no right to demand a personal sacrifice on their part without fully sharing in it himself, he pronounced his intention of not looking at a daily paper during the days of the Retreat, an intention which he fulfilled to the letter. The extent of this sacrifice perhaps even the missioners scarcely realised save the one or two who shared his keen interest in affairs. Some boarded in the Home, others in rooms in the village, and certainly from that early hour in the morning when they rose and sustained themselves with the inevitable cup of tea, till the evening when various of the company took the air on the downs, no opportunity seems to have been missed of united worship and meditation.[1] Dr. Fairbairn had just published his *Christ in Modern Theology*, and my father took the opportunity of giving a digest of its contents—an art in which he excelled. If his swiftness in assimilating and then transmitting ideas was remarkable, his power of imparting those ideas to others in as palatable a form as possible was equally so.

The lay agent said on his return—with the peculiar chuckle and rub of the hands which phases of the super-intendent's methods always caused him—"There's nobody

---

[1] The diary of one of the Sisters shows the order of the day to have been as follows :—

"7.30. Tea.

7.40–8.15. Prayer-Meeting.

8.30. Breakfast.

10.30–12. Session.

12.30. Dinner.

2.30–3.45. Session.

4. Tea.

7–8.30. Session.

8.45. Supper.

9. Family Prayer.

10. Bed.

10.30. Lights out."

who can dose like him. He gives the pill, but oh, he does not forget the jam! We swallow the pill and never taste it, because of all the jam he's put with it." When my father's digest of his work was reported to Dr. Fairbairn, he said, "There is no man in all England who could do it better. His gift in that direction of assimilating a book and then giving the heart of it to others, is very remarkable." The following year he gave a series of lectures on the Atonement, which caused a good deal of interesting discussion.

That which was not intellectually apprehended was to my father but half apprehended, and he would often say that a man needed all the brains he possessed in order to understand the Christian religion.

The Friday evening devotional meeting he would describe as the "pivot" on which the Mission turned, and in his addresses he liked specially to dwell on the "new love" which Christ had bequeathed to His followers—a love transcending (though including) that of husband or wife, father or mother, brother or sister. Only by loving could Christians hope to follow Christ and help others. One Friday evening after a very busy day spent amid committees, he delivered a peculiarly thoughtful and beautiful address on the inner and mystical side of Christianity, which surprised Dr. Lunn, who had been with him throughout the day. Where and when he had found time to prepare such an address his listener could not divine. For the last few days he had been by his side sharing in all that he did, so he knew how each hour had been filled to the brim without any opportunity for the preparation of such a discourse. When the service was over, as they were walking homewards, he asked the superintendent when the points and illustrations in his address had occurred to him.

"As I was walking with you up Gower Street this morning, the idea and main outline of what I was going to say flashed across me," was the reply.

A gentleman who had listened to him many Sundays was greatly surprised when he happened to hear him addressing one of the society classes. Was it possible that the fiery saint with whom he was acquainted, whose coat of mail, he thought, rendered him impervious to certain aspects of religion, was really speaking before him in those gentle, measured accents?

The Sisters, previous to their formal admission into the Sisterhood, always had a special talk with him in the study, consulting him as to their difficulties—particularly as to intellectual doubts of any kind.

The extent to which he solved doubt of various kinds never will be known. His most striking effect was over those who never communicated their doubts to him. Mental outlook and circumstances so differ, and reserve with some human beings is so intense, that to speak of what haunts and perplexes is often an impossibility. Such would speak to him about politics, or Methodism, or the County Council election, or the weather, and would go away reassured. To feel his presence and personality was to sight dry land. He certainly proved his own favourite maxim that salvation comes by the Holy Ghost, in that doubts, to which there was no immediate response, were felt to be solved in his presence and in the contemplation of his life and activities. As a young man at college he used to contend that all questions should be subjected to the "dry light of the intellect," and this was always a strong instinct, but in after-life he found himself influencing men and women in ways that he had not anticipated.

One of the missioners writes :

"How his very presence seemed to bring one near to Christ ! It was easier to work, to pray, when he was near ; he seemed so to lift up life, and help us to realise its dignity and grandeur, and the great importance of 'buying up the opportunity,' as he loved to put it, and doing 'just what Christ wanted.' How often do I remember his saying, when any difficulty arose : '*Oh*, but *you will do just what Christ wants.*'

"Then, the reality of Mr. Hughes's simple faith was as a blessed beacon-light—a great standby—to those who—

> ''Mid doubt's shivering night
> Wage silent, strenuous, mental fight.'

I am surprised no one seems to have touched upon this point ; one felt that he had faced the problems of the times, and fought his own way through, and that it was safe to trust what he said.

"When beset with difficulties myself, how easily have I

listened to him, and felt as I listened that there were truths which could not be shaken and did remain. It used to be such rest to listen, and no one, it seemed to me, could unveil the beauty of the salvation of Jesus Christ, or usher (for there is no other word) the seeking soul into the kingdom of heaven, like Mr. Hughes."

It was the younger ministry with whom he would talk on speculative matters, and his influence in this respect cannot be overestimated. A very kind correspondent from America, the Rev. H. W. Horwill, has written as follows. What he writes may be taken as typifying a great deal that my father did, and which will never be known.

". . . I was particularly interested by the remarks of a young minister who testified to the individual help he had received from Mr. Hughes, though they had never met. It seems that while a student in the Drew Theological Seminary in New Jersey, he was troubled by certain theological diffi-culties, and wrote for advice to Mr. Hughes, who, though very busy, replied quite fully. The correspondence, as I understand, continued a considerable time, until the young man's doubts were quite cleared away. At Washington, again, a minister of the M.E. Church, once a Wesleyan minister in England, spoke of help received from Mr. Hughes in a long conversation on theological questions. This minister was then a student at Richmond, and went over to Brixton Hill one Sunday to seek the solution of some problem. Mr. Hughes talked the matter out with him while walking to an appointment."

This must suffice.

Surrounded as he had been from his youth by intelligent and capable women, it was scarcely surprising that he deeply entered into the enlarged ideals of the age respecting the sphere of woman, her education and capacities. He used to say that when much else in the latter portion of the nineteenth century was forgotten, this singular social phenomenon would be remembered as a landmark in the history of humanity. A few months before he passed away, a companion read an article in the *Quarterly Review*, the gist of which was after-wards repeated to him. For the first time, this article con-tended, women had moved outside their assigned sphere, without any slackening of the moral ties which had hitherto been an invariable accompaniment of such an advance. The movement, particularly on the educational side, was essentially that of the upright and thoughtful middle class, and bore their impress throughout. The upper classes, who had generally been the only class to participate in the tide of feminine aspiration, were, with one or two exceptions, almost untouched. After listening to this summary, he exclaimed characteristically, " Ah ! Nonconformity has had a good deal to do with it." By this he meant that the religious life of the class which had produced this movement had acted as a restraining and elevating force. The Puritan tradition, which had always been preserved by the great English middle class, had dominated its latest development.

When one of the Methodist Synods elected a woman to sit in the Representative Session of the Methodist Conference in 1894, there was a good deal of perturbation in circles connected with that assembly. Would she go or would she not ? was the question passed from lip to lip. Women as class leaders were eligible both for the Leaders' Meeting, the Quarterly Meeting, and for the Synod ; but since the days when Lady Huntingdon sat in conference with the Wesleys, the idea of a woman taking part in the proceedings was something unheard of. Yet as members of Synod they were entitled, so far as the letter of the constitution went, to election with the other laity, and to a share in its proceedings. So novel, so amusing, was the idea both to men and women, that it was freely rumoured that the Synod in question had elected this representative in order to see what would ensue, and as a thoughtless echo to the aspiration of the age. The question of the admission of women into municipal councils or as accredited members of the ancient universities, and as holders of the parliamentary or municipal franchise, had already stirred the public mind, and it was therefore part of the general tide in affairs that a wave of it should assail even so conservative a body as the Wesleyan Conference.

One thing was certain, Hughes would charge in full defence, and the critics prepared themselves for those agreeable if diverse sensations which chivalry always arouses in the human breast, however debatable its aims. Nor were they

disappointed.   The Journal immediately emitted sparks
destined not so much to discomfort opponents as to kindle
the courage of the lady in question.   That singular apprehension of detail in a crisis on which stress has been laid, led the
editor to see two things very clearly.   First, that the critics by
their ridicule might prevent the lady in question from taking
her election seriously and presenting herself at Conference;
and second, that supposing she had sufficient Christian grace
to pay no heed to such witticisms, she might naturally shrink
from being the only woman in an assembly of men.   Did she,
therefore, feel such diffidence, so natural a timidity?   The
trumpet blew encouragement.   Let her put Christ's Church
and her work in it, before her own personal feelings, for she
would not long be alone.   Others would soon join her.   Let
her not desert her post because there was only one to guard it.
However lonely and disagreeable, it would soon be over.
Persons who based their criticisms of the notes in the *Methodist
Times* on the assumption that the editor was only considering
the case in point, as to whether or not women should be
eligible to sit in ensuing Conferences, failed to understand
that which they criticised.   The vision was prophetic.   The
Methodist Church had to face a new social ideal of the sex—
the ideal which had been born with the age, just as she had to
face other ideals and conditions of the era.   The form in which
the Church did so—the particular occasion—was a trifle to one
standing, as the prophets do, outside time—conscious of certain
facts and ideals rather than of any particular date or occasion
at which they can be said to be perceived.   The occasion
under consideration was symbolical, fraught with immense
issues.

At the Birmingham Conference in July 1894 where this
lady in accordance with the desire of her Synod consented to
be present, there was a good deal of excitement.   The Representative Session had no sooner opened than a resolution was
brought forward, challenging her election and her right to take
part in the proceedings.   To this the general feeling proved to
be opposed, as savouring both of lack of courtesy to the lady
in question, and to the Synod which had elected her by a large
majority.   My father's aim, in which from newspaper reports
he seems to have been alone, was that the presence of a woman

representative from the Synods should be passed over without comment, and that the business of the day should proceed as usual. He dreaded the quite unnecessary agitation, for so it appeared to him, which would ensue, if her presence were thus taken note of. Doubtless he was haunted by the mystical saying that in Christ Jesus there is neither male nor female, and that in an assembly of the Church it would be as well not to insist on those essential divergences on which the world laid such stress.

But the feeling of the assembly was unanimously against this proposal, in that it considered the introduction of a woman into their deliberations a constitutional innovation that could not be overlooked in the manner suggested. The complexities of the case from the constitutional side were not inconsiderable, and there was some difficulty in disentangling the variety of resolutions and amendments which were put to the assembly. On the one hand, there was the personal side of the case—as to whether or no the lady in question should take part in the proceedings and give her vote with the rest, and the more general question as to whether or no women should be admitted in the future. While there was a desire to evince courtesy to the lady in question, and to respect the decision of the Synod which had elected her by a large majority, there was also a fear that thus to admit her would be to create a precedent and to hamper discussion of the matter in the future. Finally, a carefully worded resolution, which permitted her to attend the present session as a species of concession to the special circumstances of the case, and not as the result of an election, which the Conference had declared valid, obtained the vote of a large majority, and the resumption of the order of the day. During the year a committee appointed by Conference sat to consider the question in all its bearings, of which my father was a member, and found the following resolution (16 voting for, 12 against):—

"The Committee, having considered in all its bearings the question of the election of women representatives to the Conference, reports that, in its judgment, it is not probable many women will be so elected ; but in view of the great services which women render to Methodism, of the increasing activity of women in all spheres of life, and of the fact that women are already eligible for every other lay office in the Church, the Committee recommends that, after due process of legislation, the Conference should permit the election of a woman representative to the Conference when, in the judgment of any District Synod, such an election would serve the best interests of the work of God."

At the Plymouth Conference in the following August my father presented these findings to the Representative Session, and made a speech of some length, to which the assembly was this time willing to listen, giving vent to those expressions of disagreement, concord, and amusement which it often evinced when he spoke. He closed his speech as follows :—

"... I do not suggest that we should go as far as John Wesley, and allow women to enter the Pastoral Session. But look over the agenda of the Representative Session, and you will find there indicated many spheres in which women may exert their influence. For instance, our Foreign Missions, in which women take part, some of them going to the ends of the earth ; Home Missions and the great development of the Sisterhoods ; the questions of Temperance, Social Purity, and Education—the majority of those who educate the youth of this country are women ; the question of the maintenance and the education of the children of ministers. Surely there is nothing more appropriate than that a few women should have a voice in the decision of matters of this kind. . . . No one really in touch with modern life, who knows the great part woman is increasingly playing in public life all over England, will, I am convinced, disagree with me. There is nothing more prejudicial to our best interests than that at the present time we should impose any disqualification upon sex as such. As to the sending of unsuitable women here, I confess that I have sufficient faith in the wisdom of the Synods to trust them not to send women here unless they are fit to come. For the sake of peace and quietness, and to prevent an agitation, I hope the Conference will consent to the proposal I put before it. (Great applause.)"

Opponents then spoke at some length, some seriously and others less so. The witty opponent said a good deal, and, among the rest, that supposing women did come they would not affect the tenor of their deliberations, for their admission would merely resemble the insertion of poppies in a cornfield Finally, an amendment hostile to the resolution of the special committee was carried by 18 votes only, which displayed a striking amount of liberality in an ecclesiastical council.

The traditions of early Methodism and the status that has always been given to women in Church work must have accounted for an opposition which was much less than it would have been elsewhere. No other ecclesiastical assembly of the time appointed a committee which advocated the admission of women into their annual deliberations. Though many objected, and strongly, in that taste and feeling rather than principle or reason, cried out against the innovation, they might have objected much more than they did.

The fashion for opponents was to treat the matter as a temporary affair, a sign of the erratic disease of the time which time and nature would soon adjust. My father's amusing mistake lay, they thought, in considering it a tide rather than the illusory foam of democratic unrest.

What was striking in his attitude was the distinct aggression that he advocated on the part of women, not for themselves but for Christ. He insisted, for instance, that it would be false modesty which prevented the lady elected by the Synod from taking the seat in Conference to which that election entitled her. If an uncomfortable discussion ensued she must submit to that discussion for the sake of Christ and His Church. Natural and instinctive feelings must yield to higher, and she must not listen to those who lay down false because narrow and unimaginative definitions of what is " womanly " and what is " unwomanly."

The women whom he admired among contemporaries were Florence Nightingale, Josephine Butler, Catherine Booth, and Mrs. Besant. They had felt the new " social love," and were typical, he thought, of the best things women had felt and done during the century. Of them all he seemed to admire Mrs. Butler the most, because no one had sacrificed more for other women than she had. She had made herself of no account, and had submitted to the cross and the shame. Catherine Booth, he writes in the Journal at the time of her death, the present generation could not rightly comprehend, because their eyes were too blinded by the mists of prejudice to conceive of the heart and mind that was in her.[1]

It was the humanitarian and democratic element in Mrs. Besant that attracted him, as well as certain emotional and sympathetic elements in character which appealed to him in the autobiography published some years ago.

---

[1] With Mrs. Butler my father had a lifelong friendship. With Catherine Booth also he had some personal acquaintance.

In a Sunday afternoon address on the Mystery of Pain, he spoke of her as follows :—

"I would rather be an atheist like Mrs. Besant than so hard-hearted that I was not affected by the misery and trouble around me. The next best thing to Christianity is atheism, in the form in which it is presented by that noble woman. Her atheism is the result of the tenderness of her heart. She is so distressed and horrified by misery, she compassionates her fellows so much, that she flies to that painful extreme. I would rather be in the position of one who has become an atheist through compassion for his fellows, than one who has been so selfish that he has no pity and no love for any one. God grant that if there are any such here, they may now accept the explanation which Christ gave."

Florence Nightingale also had felt a Divine call, something beyond herself, and had raised the whole status of the nursing profession. "Previous to her coming," my father would exclaim, "Sarah Gamp reigned supreme, and nursing was the profession of any uninformed woman who had nothing better to do." By laying down her life and giving up her best days to the nursing of suffering men, when such an occupation was deemed vile and unworthy of a gentlewoman by our grandparents, she opened up a road for those who should come after her, and brought honour to Christ, succour to humanity.

The equality of the sexes, sanely conceived, he believed to be as much an outcome of Christianity as the necessity of keeping one's temper, and returning good for evil. In literature he preferred the larger and more aspiring types, the unorthodox, to the orthodox and quiescent. Thus for all his deep acceptance of some of Tennyson's lines, it was Browning's women, their freedom, their lack of trammel, their large and vigorous outlook on things, that attracted him, particularly in later manhood. There was not a picture in all the long gallery of the latter which he did not like to look at and think about. From the little factory hand, Pippa, singing to herself in the morning her pure and joyous song, past the little Duchess who runs away with the gipsies because she cannot support the cramping conventionality of her surroundings, and that Last Duchess, who died in them (oh, how he understood these, his whole soul was with them!), right up to the Greek girl Balaustion, aglow with the intellect and the imagination of her race; he was with them all, thinking and feeling as the poet dictated.   Of course he loved Balaustion the best, partly because everything happened just as it should happen to her. Browning's "By the Fireside" and Mrs. Browning's "Aurora Leigh" were great favourites of his.   Of the latter he said, " The woman question is better solved here than anywhere."

In speaking of a lady who agreed with him in many matters, but not in certain things affecting social purity, he said in a low voice: " We cannot expect her to feel as we do. She made a 'mariage de convenance,' and never loved her husband."   Indeed, he became hyper-sensitive on the point, and traced everything down to people's marriages.   Contemporary love affairs and their tangles evoked groans.   He longed to be present and to untie the knots.   Often he would say of men and women that he knew, " Oh that I had been present just to say the word and to explain."   He knew he would have been given the necessary intuition—the right word.   In more than one case, he hinted, he had been successful, but further he would not divulge.

On one occasion he was talking to a young girl about the Mission and his work among the poor, and as she appeared responsive, he inquired, " Do you think you would care to be a Sister ? "

His companion hesitated before replying, and then said, half-apologetically, " Well, Mr. Hughes, I should, but—but I am going to be married."

" Ah," he said quietly, " there is nothing like that for a woman.   You have chosen the best "—and then with characteristic delicacy he changed the subject.

At other times his intuitions caused him pain.   A young girl had just called asking him to officiate at her forthcoming wedding.   After seeing her to the door he went to the window and watched her down the street.   " Poor thing," he kept ejaculating—" poor thing."   When he used that adjective it was in the tender inexplicable sense in which it is employed by the Welsh and the French.   This surprised one who was present, because the young lady's fiancé was considered in every way desirable, and there was every prospect of her happiness.   When asked why he thus apostrophised her, he answered, " Oh, woman is far away the best and man is not worthy of her."   Something he had seen in her hopes and fears which pierced him. Even when he thought a marriage to be right he was troubled during the wedding ceremony, so conscious was he of the fateful issues involved. At funerals, on the contrary, he was comparatively cheerful, for he could not think about funerals just as other people did. He loved right marriages because they made for the highest development of human life, and therefore for what the prophets desired in Church and State. Arrested development either in man or woman was grievous to him. A man said to him once, " I have a low opinion of women, Mr. Hughes, and don't think much of them."

" Ah, my dear sir," he replied, " is that so ? I am very sorry for you—very. Your experience must have been very unfortunate to make you speak in such a manner. Let us talk of something else." Another time a man came to him and said, " You are acquainted, Mr. Hughes, with many good and pleasant women, and I am wondering if you would recommend me one for a wife, as I wish to marry immediately." Such arrested development he found it difficult to comprehend. " I longed," he said afterwards, " to kick him out of the room." The development of women at other times struck him as arrested. He would experience surprise when he heard some underestimating the cares of maternity, or when he heard others speaking about men in terms that were so uncomplimentary as to be unfair to them. " It will pass," he would say, " it will pass. It is an inevitable revulsion from former slavish ideas, and the natural and full Christian view must again assert itself—still it is regrettable." Woman, he believed, was so close to Nature, that when she revolted from it, there was a very good explanation, and one into which it was worth while to inquire. So he was tender to her and made every allowance.

People noted a contradiction at times in his remarks on the vocation of women, but the contradictions were entailed in the subject. With one of the Sisters I can remember his having an argument.

" Well, Mr. Hughes, I have been thinking that quite possibly I may have to retire from the Mission. My mother is getting older, and I think it will be my duty to go and help my sister, who, for all I know, may have to leave home also."

" I do not understand you," would be the answer, " or that it would be your duty."

" Of course it would.   Nothing comes before a duty to parents."

" There again I disagree.   Christ comes first."

" Yes, but what can come before a daughter's duty to her mother ?   Christ could not wish otherwise."

" Oh, you inform me.   I thought," he said, " that whoso did not hate mother or father was not worthy of Him, by which He meant that His service and His wish for a human creature, man or woman, came before any one else's wishes at all.   A woman is responsible to God, not to her relatives."

" Oh, that's all very well—but a woman's mother is quite different to anybody else."

" Certainly, I agree, a mother has a special claim.   Under most circumstances it may be Christ's will that a daughter specially tend her.   But it's not His will in every case—circumstances differ.   What sickens me is the miserable inconsistency of the thing.   Again and again I have come across parents who have resisted to the teeth any project by which their daughter could serve God and humanity instead of themselves, not allowing her to perform the simplest duty to herself or to others.   Yet no sooner does a fellow come along from the antipodes, of whom they know nothing save that he has plenty of money with which to ruin himself and others, than they let her go off without a word, duty or no duty.   If they did not call themselves Christians, it would make the matter so much simpler.   As the world conceives of duty, they are discharging it to the letter, and everything would be clearer if they would own themselves the children of that world whose dictates they obey.   Of course it is often unconscious, they have excellent intentions, noble qualities, and are sincere often in their love of Christ, so long as it does not interfere with social and financial considerations.   What is required is clarity—the nurture and development of the logical faculty.   Professing Christians should really make a special study of logic."

" Do you think, Mr. Hughes, that you are logical ? "

" Certainly.   Indeed, that is what differentiates me from so many dear brethren—they are not logical and I am."

On another occasion somebody told him of a remark which had been made to some young girls, and which was to this effect, that they were not "the kind" to work in a mission. For reply he almost ground his teeth. That was the devil in all ages. The world to have the first-fruits, and then when little was left save what it thought to be the rind, it was to be given to Christ! Small thanks!

He persisted in regarding the life of a woman as a serious and important thing, whatever its circumstances, and he would use terms concerning it that were quite frightening to the average woman, such as "service," "career," "sphere," and what not, so that she trembled to hear him at times, not recognising herself. To those who seemed the most foolish and irresponsible, he would yet apply these terms, seriously considering that which they could effect. Indeed, his profoundest impression on certain women was that he took them seriously, when others did not do so. When they volunteered an opinion or said what they really thought, he gravely listened. In particular, if they asked a question or wanted to be clear on a point, he was at their service. He did not give her special directions for the cultivation of womanly virtues, assuming that she possessed them, even when she might not appear to do so. What he did inculcate was courage and heroism, and the daring that will embrace a high ideal. There was one thing in particular that he did not want a woman to do, and that was to shut herself up in a garden, however fair, religious, or intellectual, and to shut her ears to the misery and evil of the world. When she did that, he did not say that he was disappointed, but something pierced him because of the ideal that he had for her. Yet he knew that women were different, and had that "sanctified common sense" which did not expect the same "service" from them all. A certain lady whom many thought to be frivolous, took him into her confidence, explaining the object of her life, which was to make a delightful home for her sons. She wanted them to feel that the home was the place where they could be happiest, and where they would always like to return. Thus, when others in his presence spoke of what they considered her frivolity, he always corrected them at once, laying stress on what he knew to be the aim of this lady's life.   On another occasion he was talking with another minister about Methodism, and with the advent of afternoon tea the ladies came in to join them.   The minister who was talking to him, and who was very courteous, noted a certain surprise, perhaps weariness, on the face of the ladies, and said to my father, despite his frowns and raised voice, " Come, come, Mr. Hughes, we must not worry the ladies with these dull affairs."   Like a sledgehammer came the reply, " If the ladies, my dear sir, have not sufficient Christianity and sanctified common sense to take interest in matters of moment affecting the Church of Christ, it's a sad thing both for them and the Church. . . ."

On the other hand, it would be a very incorrect notion that my father talked over Methodist sub-committees before all manner of persons indiscriminately.   The ladies in question were all relatives of those who spent a great deal of their life in such committees, so he thought it quite in keeping that they should listen to something about them.   One who so adored chaffing others and who loved to find out, and to elicit what interested them in life, was far from lacking sociable qualities. All over the country when he was staying at a house for a few hours, the women welcomed his coming, and loved to listen to his conversation.   The thoughtful enjoyed his visits and so did the lively—though the terms are not mutually exclusive. In banter and a war of words, he was a worthy antagonist, and his conversation, full of what was going on in the Church and the world, caught the attention even of those who cared least for either.   If the hostess intimated that the gentlemen had best be left to discuss matters, he would smilingly intimate that man had made a great mess of society and the world, and that it was high time for woman to come and help him. Nor would he suffer any woman present to make a remark that contradicted the Christian conception of equality.   If a man also made remarks or implications of such a description, he greeted it with smiles and satire.   " The orient, my dear sir, is the only place for you.   You really should go there, where you will find the subjugation of the sex complete, and your views in the matter entirely respected."   This remark was made with such peculiar goodwill that it evoked laughter on all sides, just as when he said to a woman, "Hug your chains; slaves adore to do that."

My mother sat on the Executive Committee of the Women's Liberal Federation, and on her return from its meetings my father would closely question her as to what had taken place, for in all its proceedings he was deeply interested. He had always been an upholder of the parliamentary franchise for women. He perceived also, and strongly, that the woman of religious tradition and refined environment was bound to take her sister of the labouring classes after her. For her lot certainly needed amelioration, though she might not feel her deprivations as keenly as many women of the middle classes had come to feel theirs. The new social ideal of woman had come in with Democracy and was its offspring. In the selflessness of the whole movement lay its salvation. When a Women's Industrial Council was formed for the protection of women workers, he took a prominent part in the inaugural meetings along with other philanthropic men and women of the day. After he had gone, women used to say, "We miss the way he had of speaking to us. Others do not think of or talk to us quite as he did." While he counselled aggression for the Church of Christ or some great cause, he was far from approving certain individual forms of aggression. "Poor things," he would exclaim, referring to a certain type of woman, "they have gone too far. In their revulsion from man's oppression they have tried to imitate him." He was very sensible to feminine charm. No one had a greater admiration for the distinctive womanly qualities, or was quicker to note their absence.

His almost invariable effect over a woman was that she read books and became more reflective. He considered reflectiveness a womanly quality. In an age when the higher education of women was opposed and ridiculed in many quarters, he was always sympathetic, and ardently so, from the outset. Not a word would he suffer in his presence that disparaged the intellect of woman or the attempts to give her fair opportunities for its development. As an instance of the prejudice of mankind, he would quote the following: "When I was a young man, a distinguished member of the University of London said in my hearing that sooner than see his daughter take an academic degree he would follow her dead body to its grave." He would often quote this à propos of the granting of degrees to women at Oxford and Cambridge, and when he read of the refusal to do so, he would exclaim : "The people of this country will not stand their nonsense much longer." "They are mediæval," some one would remark, "and it is not possible to override their prejudices." "We shall have to override them," he would cry out ; "if they cannot be sensible, they must be forced into sense, and the matter taken out of their hands." The Journal crackled and sparkled over every indication of the intellectual advance of women, and readers seemed to hear the editor laughing as he wrote. He said once not long before he died, and as the result, evidently, of not a little rumination : "It has not yet been decided as to what is the best education for woman. The course prescribed for man may not be the one best suited to her particular capacities. We are still in the experimental stage." Yet he objected to doors being closed to women, in that by liberty, he thought, they could try their powers and see what it was they could best do. Only one woman out of a thousand, he argued at Conference, might have a particular capacity, but in that she had it she was entitled to make use of it. Nor did he take Ruskin's advice and suggest her exclusion from the problems of theology. Indeed, he would beg some women to take an interest in it, suggesting books and grappling with the prejudices they had formed against that science.

In 1898 a Women's Congress was held at Westminster Hall, to which representatives came from all parts of Europe and America. Since Siebert had built the first chapel there had never been quite such a thing on the banks of the Thames—women of all nations come to discuss and to report progress in the education of the young, in philanthropic work, in literary effort, in the drama, and a great variety of endeavour.

The Press took some notice of their presence, but the world generally hurried by the Thames quite unaware of it, and little realising, my father considered, all that it implied. On a Sunday evening during its session, he preached about it. Perhaps there never was a sermon more sympathetic to the new tide of aspiration than his. He began by paying it

reverence, by recalling great names, great examples, by bringing home to his hearers all that which this unique assembling
went to signify and to show. As he spoke, the spirit of the
age as expressed in woman seemed to come incarnate before
him. He beheld as it were a single form, and fell to addressing
it. " I know the travail of your soul, and that which you have
desired to see—the toil of brain and heart, the intellect and
the philanthropy and the nobility that has gone to gain what
you have gained; but I tell you before God and before man
that you will fall back to where you were, that it is mere
writing in water, unless you raise yourself in Christ Jesus.
In Him you must do it, and to Him." Not once did he say
this, but many times, and always with a passion—an accent
of pain—that was certainly not comprehensible to the majority.
One thing was wanting, and that was religion, and without
religion their bright hopes and noble endeavours would be
dashed to the ground. Was it to be the old tale over again—
heroic dreams, mayola—because humanity would not accept the
highest discipline, the discipline of Christ Jesus ? The authorisa-
tion of a teacher is that he understands something of those
whom he teaches—their struggle and aspiration. This struggle
and aspiration is nowhere better expressed, it is said, than
in the last scene of one of Ibsen's plays. To read this, so
encompassed with his markings, is to hear him speak again,
and to remember how well he understood. The final action of
the heroine, the leaving of her own home and children, is so
strongly opposed to the deepest instincts of a woman, that
many have seen in it this and this alone, while the whole aim
of the writer of the play and of those who understand him,
is not to lay stress on, or indeed justify what she does, but
simply to show why she did it, what was the train of emotion
and reasoning that led her to such a step, so opposed not
only to the general ethic, but to natural instinct. In a conversation with her husband at the close she makes clear why
she did it, what had impelled her in so extraordinary an act.
Much of what she says is heavily underlined by my father,
and the markings in their apprehension of certain points of
view are those of a woman, and in two places particularly so.
The man who has lost humanity and individuality just as the
woman, and who has become an embodiment of social force

and social convention, says to her, " Before all else you are a wife and a mother." " That," she replies, " I no longer believe. I think that before all else I am a human being, just as much as you are—or at least I will try and become one. I know that most people agree with you, Torvald, and that they say so in books. But henceforth I can't be satisfied with what most people say, and with what is in books. I must think things out for myself and try to get clear about them." This is the first passage that is heavily annotated, and the second is even more so.

> " *Helmer*. I would gladly work for you day and night, Nora—bear sorrow and want for your sake ; but no man sacrifices his honour, even for one he loves.
> " *Nora*. Millions of women have done so."

Here he understood her best of all ; that the markings and much that is remembered of him goes to show. Those who have seen the play performed say that the most impressive and tragic moment is the sound of the door shutting after her. It conveys as nothing else does the reality of a fact—that which is irrevocable. My father after reading the play late one night, said, after shutting the book, " The door closed— that was the climax of the whole." Indeed, to imagination she becomes no longer a woman of flesh and blood, but a personification of the spirit of the time going forth to seek and to know, so that she procure that which she shall dearly buy. Few helped, few understood, but one, a bond-servant of Jesus Christ, met her at the threshold so that he might arm and bind her as he was armed and bound. What to her was horror and agony was to him horror and agony. Indeed, he wept with her. When to her was cause for smiles, he smiled also and urged her spirit forward in all fair and high undertakings, never allowing her to lose heart, never exhorting save to what was worthiest of her. He saw her instinct and perceived that it was good, for whatever else was wrong the instinct was correct. Close on her disappointment in society was dissatisfaction with herself—with that which society had made her. She did not reason or argue but apprehended that something in herself was wanting, and when she shut the door of the doll's house behind her, it was to prepare herself anew for the task that was hers, which she suddenly realised she was unable to accomplish.

My father's understanding was the more marked, as the religious personalities who had fascinated and penetrated the best life of the age did not understand quite as he did.

At his death they said he will be remembered for his work in connection with Methodism and the Free Churches. He should also be remembered as the friend and brother of women, for that is what he would have wished.

CHAPTER XII

HOUSEHOLD LIFE

"From what great perils, on his way,
    He found, in prayer, release ;
Through what abysmal shadows lay
    His pathway unto peace.

God knoweth : we could only see
    The tranquil strength he gained :
The bondage lost in liberty,
    The fear in love unfeigned."

WHITTIER.

ABOUT this time much was said at the table of the poet Shakespeare and artists in general. My father thought some of his listeners were infatuated by them. "It is the prophets, the men of action, who have saved and inspired humanity. What has Shakespeare done for the masses of mankind? St. Paul now!"—Something in the faces of those present must have struck him, for he paused to look at them before continuing—"St. Paul," he repeated, "has entered into the hearts and consciences of tens of thousands of men, who have never read a line of Shakespeare."—"I can't hear what it is you are saying, dear." "I wish you would cultivate the art of distinct enunciation." "Oh—Ah—But that does not in the least affect what I was saying—the issue you refer to is another one altogether." "There is nothing like keeping the mind clear and unbiassed on these points, and resisting violent prejudice." "Of course," he would continue, "If So-and-so's an artist, there's nothing more to be said. Socrates, Buddha, and Moses were not artists, for mere art cannot save us. I agree that a just appreciation of what is beautiful is one that should undoubtedly be encouraged, and with much of what you feel and say I am in entire sympathy. No one believes more than myself in the important place of art in religion and life. It's your violence in the matter that I deprecate. Pass the mustard."

For a certain period neither St. Paul nor the prophets could be mentioned without the most violent emotions rending the bosoms of certain present. St. Paul fought for the universe with Shakespeare and the poets, and won, leaving, it must be confessed, some youthful hearts to the vanquished. Yet the allegiance of the apostolic vindicator was not what might have been anticipated, considering his way of expressing himself when he asked for the mustard. It must have been one Sunday morning, after the sermon was completed, that a member of the family, on entering the study, observed him deep in one of Knight's editions of Shakespeare, in bright red volumes, which he carefully preserved.

On looking over his shoulder, his visitor observed that the drama on which he was intent was *Love's Labour's Lost*. "Can you tell me," he said, "out of the depths of your fierce wisdom what they are all after? What are they all about, do you know?" The question ended in a half-sigh. "My opinion is that you are all strange creatures, the whole lot of you." The unfathomable wizardry of the great poet dwelt to my father in his comedies; the tragedies, the histories, those an honest humble-minded man could understand—but those tortuous comedies!

The subject haunted him, as did the fact that one whom he knew should spend so much time in perusing them. My mother related that, seated in a brake laden with that majority of mankind who knew St. Paul (or thought they did) and not Shakespeare, he would begin on the subject. "So-and-so (mentioning the Christian name of the person in question) has read every word that Shakespeare ever wrote—every word. Marvellous thing, is it not? I confess I feel quite taken aback by it. Every word that that mighty poet ever penned. Hamlet, Hamlet, my dear sir? Hamlet—a mere drop in the cup! Everything that hand ever deciphered So-and-so has read. Do you know that we are all Hamlet, you and I and every one in this coach? A great German critic said that he is every one of us. Hamlet is the result of a profound investigation into the nature of us all. But I can never forgive the fellow for the way he treated that lovely darling Ophelia, *never*. Do you know (bending forward) that Shakespeare never created a villain? Hamlet's father, for instance, he finds him praying, and he was a great sinner. But why he killed them all off at the last in that way I cannot imagine. Poor deluded So-and-so thinks it beautiful, but to me the whole business is too summary."

Conference was meeting that year at Birmingham, and my father happened to be in a brake because he found it imperative to visit Stratford-on-Avon. Outside Ann Hathaway's cottage he plucked a diminutive leaf, and, putting it in his purse, kept it for many months till he remembered to give it to the Shakespeare lover of whom he had been talking. Hamlet, for all the foregoing criticism, fascinated him greatly, so that he often wondered over him and pondered his sayings. King Harry with his "once more into the breach, dear friends, once more," was not nearly so attractive. In particular, he contended that Shakespeare despised the crowd and had never properly depicted one—a point which was disputed.[1] To visit places of interest when he happened to be in the neighbourhood he found to be a duty. Previous to inspecting "Burleigh House by Stamford Town," he read Tennyson's poem aloud at breakfast. His first reading to his children was at Oxford when he used to read *Brer Rabbit and Brer Fox*, as if anxious to find some one who could share his laughter. He also liked to read any special article that he had just written, or a passage in a novel, or a poem that had struck him. The first chapter of Sheldon's *What would Jesus do?* moved him, and he came and read it aloud one Sunday afternoon.

There was a certain routine about my father's days despite their variety of endeavour. He was down to breakfast somewhere about 8.30, and was always exceedingly punctual at that meal. It was only in quite the last days that he at all slackened in this respect, and it was that as much as anything else that denoted the change in him. All the newspapers and letters used to be in a pile beside his plate at the end of the

[1] In reading of Tennyson's last hours, he was surprised that *Cymbeline* was the last book in the poet's hand. "Why should he look at *Cymbeline*?" my father kept asking. "Why should he want *Cymbeline* just then?"

table. There was the *Times*, of course, the *Standard*, the *Daily News*, and the *Daily Chronicle*; various representative religious papers, such as the *Tablet*, the *Church Times*, the *Outlook*, and the *Christian World*, and on Saturdays the inevitable *Spectator*, which he read religiously throughout life from cover to cover. Of the *Pilot*, when it appeared, he was a great admirer, a friend sending him a copy every week.

The later sympathies of the *Spectator* he deplored, while admiring its high tone. There had been days, he used to say, when it was full of hope and confidence and liberal sentiment, in touch with popular ideals. Now—since the Irish question —it had taken a new turn and was becoming distrustful of the people and out of touch with them.

In particular, he enjoyed the articles on natural subjects, such as birds and fish and the various aspects of outdoor life, which are such a feature of that journal. Such articles were "delightful"; for his hankering after natural science and his interest in what he could hear and learn of it was never quenched. He gave out once with the greatest solemnity that he and my mother intended to procure a microscope, and to indulge in some scientific observations, for which she had an aptitude. Of the *Times* newspaper he was also a diligent reader, though diligent is scarcely the adjective; he devoured both it and all the other papers.

His punctuality was noted, and he was never known to be late for an engagement. He liked everything to be done decently and in order, but strongly objected to any such method being introduced into his study. This was so littered with books and papers that it was difficult at times to find a seat. As regards food, he had very simple tastes, and he ate little, taking what was provided for him, rarely making any comment.

In this respect he would sometimes surprise the servants, who knew the strength of some people's feelings on these matters. He came in once at an unusually irregular hour, and there was some difficulty in procuring him a meal. The potatoes did not arrive till the meal was finished. " I will take the will for the deed," he remarked with a smile.

When visitors were present his absorption in the papers was relaxed. He had to absorb the visitors, and if he had a special affection for them, he liked, independently of the process of absorption, to hear what they had to say, and to chaff them and ask questions. Later also as his children grew up they had matters to relate, which, to judge by his method of listening, it was imperative for him to hear. But the papers generally won the day, and there were few breakfasts in London when they were not the principal item in the bill of fare. In due course came family prayers, which were, on the whole, the most remarkable and spontaneous of his utterances. Anything more natural, more supremely part of a person's self, it was difficult to hear. They followed in his mind quite naturally from the perusal of the newspapers, so that listeners could often tell what he had been reading, and what he was going to do during the day. In times of exceptional stress, it was the only index as to the day's programme, as it was to the contemporary state of Europe and London, and his feelings on the point. He never prayed without specially alluding to the poor and the suffering and the sick; and in later years, after his father's first serious illness, to those "who were appointed to die." Nothing ever befell him, or those near him, which did not enlarge his sympathy and his vision, and teach him something new. His references to those "who serve in this house" sank deep into wondering hearts, and mysteriously interpreted the routine of the day. This, coupled with his general behaviour, and his known alliance with the forces of righteousness in London, made the servants attribute a special efficacy to these prayers. "You'll soon be better," one would say by the sickbed of the other; "master prayed for you this morning." They never forgot his words. One on leaving entered into that hand-to-hand struggle with evil forces in which some are so incessantly engaged. The thought that Mr. Hughes had prayed for her sustained her strangely, making any form of defeat not to be thought of. On meeting one of the Sisters some years afterwards, she confided what my father had been to her, which was in due course repeated to him. He was within a few weeks of passing away when he heard it, and was more than ever inclined to attach a high importance to what are called the little things of life. "It is the greatest consolation to me, and I am filled with thankfulness to God," he kept saying as he walked along the

Surrey lanes. "I was very surprised too, because I thought nobody ever liked my prayers, and that they thought them altogether odious." Family prayer is in the necessity of the case a delicate matter, particularly in a state of society which is, in certain quarters, highly conventional.

Next to his prayerfulness those about him remembered his humour. Certain people when they heard others talk of his vehemence and zeal and evangelicism, always felt as if he were being murdered, and it was impossible to say why—as if something that had breath had been strangled. As a matter of fact, his vehemence and zeal would never have maintained the Forward Movement; they did part of the work but not all. Vehemence and zeal may drive men into the kingdom of God, but they do not keep them there. Human nature may admire and revere vehemence and zeal, but it does not necessarily love them. In satire and irony—those terrible weapons of the prophets, those which they use when beset by the sections—he was sparing. It was in him to be both satirical and ironical, and he could be, but his use of them was very sparing. The writer can only remember the gentlest use of them—an irony that was stingless. Wit, the war of words, was his passion. To repeat to him a *bon-mot* or a good tale was to seriously contribute to his pleasure. No man was ever quicker at seeing wit or appreciating it, either in a book or a person. Indeed, a *bonâ fide* wit was one to whom he would love to pay honour, allowing no one else to lead the conversation, and by his smiles telegraphing appreciation to those sitting with him. Many odd moments in his life were spent in tripping up others in their speech, and in extracting from them expressions and opinions which were out of keeping with their characters, and it gave him such immense pleasure that it was infectious, and persons were quite pleased to find themselves tripping.

His exquisite feeling for the value of what is implied in words and turns of expression gave him a rapport with much that is in the French mind, and perhaps his art of condensation as a journalist.[1] A leader on Mr. Stopford Brooke's

[1] Some of the *Dolly Dialogues* of Mr. Anthony Hope charmed him. "I thought at first," he said, "that they must be the work of a Frenchman." All whom he met he would greet with the eager question, "I say, have you read the *Dolly Dialogues*?"

Browning that appeared a week or two before he died, was commented upon by a critic as containing much in a short space, and this was typical of a good deal that he wrote. He loved epigram too much perhaps for certain minds, who denote unfairness in that which is epigrammatically stated. Remarks such as " If Cleopatra's nose had been a shade longer, the history of the world would have been different," were a poignant pleasure to him, in that such suggested so much else that was not implicitly stated, and served as a type of those fine issues on which the trend of affairs and of lives may turn. Deliberate exaggeration or overstatement was a characteristic form of his humour. One day, as he was walking through the squares in a London fog, he met an acquaintance, to whom he exclaimed, " Why don't the aldermen of the city of London pick their brains and rid us of this nuisance? We ought to hang one daily till they hit on a remedy." His listener expressed heartiest agreement, and went on his way diabolically smiling, as did my father. Both derived inward solace at a vision of substantial aldermen suspended in mid-air because they could not stop the fogs. At other times, listeners would be taken aback and appear scandalised at his statements, which was a pleasure to him. His perception of the incongruous in persons and things was both his delight and his power, in that it was a great social quality, allying men to himself. Humour may unite or may estrange; his united. He seized on points that the generality could see, and never hurt by his laughter. Rather he seemed to be indebted to a person and to be laughing with him as the result of the peculiar affection that he bore him. As his blows as an antagonist conveyed no sting, so was it with his laughter. He was for ever laughing, and the laughter was infectious. Those who think of that laughter, so mirthful and spontaneous, are often reminded of that verse—" The bruised reed He shall not break, and the smoking flax He shall not quench." The most sensitive could have lived with him for years and never been injured by what he said. Thus, persons who felt themselves of small account would be particularly happy in his presence because they felt that here was one who took account of them. Only persons who were despised quite knew the depths of his tenderness.

Why certain evoked this humour never will be known save that it was a sign of special affection. Stout persons in particular had small shrift at his hands. Indeed, members of his family would speak to him seriously on this matter. "You really should not carry on so about it. You will become fat yourself one day as a punishment." "God forbid!" he would exclaim; but it made no difference, and he was off again with the next stout individual of his acquaintance. Indeed, the stout were to blame. They hung about him and so appeared to enjoy his remarks, that it was small wonder he went on making them. I have seen men and women quite flattered because he spoke of them as stout and middle-aged! In particular, he allied himself to crusty persons whom others found it difficult to get on with. To extract smiles from these against their will was his peculiar delight. Some of his acquaintances chiefly knew him as the exchanger of sallies, and on all varieties of subjects—their profession or accomplishment or particular manner of living and thinking. The power came in that the sallies, for all their froth, were yet serious—the excrescence of a deep sea. The remarkable thing was the amount of seriousness that he got into that light-heartedness, ready at a moment's notice to take a person in earnest. Many would not be as near the kingdom of heaven as they are unless he had joked with them. As a companion and conversationalist, he purified the springs of laughter, and that was almost as wonderful as the zeal, earnestness, and vehemence about which so much has been said. When a person looked serious at the mention of him, it was known that they had no real knowledge of him. When they betrayed enthusiasm of any kind, either friendly or hostile, it was certain that they had felt him. When they smiled it was seen that they knew something of him. Moreover, this laughter had its subtle aspects — these which were not communicated to the many but the few. He knew, for instance, the feelings of ecclesiastical opponents about him, and could describe these with smiles which betrayed sympathy. He knew what Bohemia thought of him—the Bohemia of the West End—the exact significance of its shrugs when he charged against some tradition or foible to which it was attached. The wits he understood thoroughly, and contained a silent admiration when they turned a good *mot* — not mere ridicule and non-understanding, but one that was really acute. So disposed was he to take all men well that they really had to go out of their way to offend him. A Metropolitan journal on one occasion assigned flowers to well-known public men, and decided, with what it considered some wit, on that flower which suited Mr. Price Hughes—a white one, they said. But the object of their witticism, so one related who was by him, appeared quite pleased at what he regarded an honour. His bone of contention with the great public schools was, that while they gave men courage to face a cannon, and incited to various virtues, they did not give men courage to sport a flower that he was proud to wear—even when it was offered him in jest.

To those who studied the incessant drama of his personality, this was the eternal puzzle—how these two forces could run together in harness as they did—the Hebraic and prophetic, with what might be called the Hellenic, the French, and the laughter-loving. Concentration did it to a great extent, for in his charges he could leave all laughter and lightness and incongruity behind him, and make for the object in view with a white heat and an impetus that was the astonishment of beholders. Then it was that his strength was manifested—the strength that could bear all before it. In a recent and fantastic novel,[1] there is a closing passage in which two forces are described—" two lobes of the same brain "—who are about to go round the world on the performance of the same quest. One, the spirit of seriousness, carries a sword; the other, the spirit of laughter, carries a halberd. If one thought haunts the reader's mind more than another, it is that the truce suggested will not be concluded on equal terms. One will choose the path and the other will follow him. In the life under consideration, despite all its instinct for the fine poising of elements, and the pervading vitality that made each portion vociferous to live, the sword-bearer took the lead, and was well in the advance dictating to his follower. This unequal truce was part of the struggle and the story of his life. Stress has to be laid on that side which was willingly subordinated, because lives should be interpreted by what is

---

[1] *The Napoleon of Notting Hill*, G. K. Chesterton.

submerged, not only by what they did and were, but by what they were never permitted to do and to be.

Who does not feel in that grim old tale of the driver and his children pursued by wolves, a certain explanation of human life? In order to reach the end, something precious has to be flung to the wolves who would obstruct its progress. Strong drivers are discerned by their power to strangle what was theirs and cast it from them. Yet one portion of his life he could not part with, because it would not leave him—the child of delight and laughter who beheld with God that creation was good and that for joy of it the mind of man has pictured the morning stars singing in unison.[1] So passionate was his desire to reach the goal—so consuming his purpose—that he had it in him to cast overboard even more than he did. Yet this portion of his life, though half-strangled, would not let him go, clinging about his neck till the goal was attained. Often it seemed as if it must go with the rest. The cruel wolves of the world's need leapt up with open jaws, and it was almost lifeless in the grip that would extinguish its life, but it never ceased to have life of some kind, and to importune him for it. Thus they ended their grim journey unseparated. Then it was seen that God sent that child to cling to him, for he could not have made that journey without him. It made it harder for him and those looking on to follow and understand, but it made the journey what it was.

His vehemence created a treadmill whose incessant and laborious turning men came to take for granted. From his labours he would sigh for what seemed the greater repose of other men, yet no sooner had he participated in this for a space—a study—a pastime—a voyage—than it became repose and delight no longer—transformed by the vehemence within him to something as arduous and exacting as the labours he had recently quitted. At his death they said, "Surely he is evangelising a planet," but the dreams of the saints, and his among the number, were for a repose of some kind. The sayings of our Lord lead fancy to picture a transformation of rôle in a future life, where the great combatants shall surely rest awhile, and the others fall to the evangelising.

[1] These last words were a favourite phrase of his in sermons.

By temperament and instinct, he was socially fastidious, and delighted in the society of cultivated persons. Grace of person and accomplishment were noted and appreciated by him. His beau-ideal would have been a salon of scientific and literary people who possessed that indescribable lightness and ease in the interchange of idea which is thought to be Celtic rather than Teutonic. Yet even the salon, the most exclusive of groups, would not have fettered him. He would have broken out from its conventions somehow, and started a forward movement and a new fashion. On one of the exceedingly rare occasions when he dined out, he went to a particularly stately banquet where the guests were entertained with music during the courses. On his return he appeared impressed at the munificence and display, as well as with the kindness he had received, and the interesting conversations with those present, though, as he expressed it, " there was a terrible aspect to it all," and that " we should thank God we were not rich men." Its soothing and pleasing effects seemed so felt by him, that he dreaded what must be an inevitable result on men and women. Yet through it all was a great kindliness. Idlers and exquisites, cultivated and uncultivated, he would allude to in ironic strain, yet nobody on the other hand could more enjoy himself in the society of individuals who might be supposed to fall under these epithets.

For the poet of Democracy he had varied feelings, as the following incident revealed.

It seemed good to him to read selections from Whitman's poems to a member of his family, and his joy in doing so was of the most jubilant and transparent character. Personally he did not altogether approve of the " barbaric yawp " of the American poet, though in portions he found that music of the storm and the elements, and the brotherhood of creation, which could not but play on a soul so attuned to them. Moreover, he discerned, as our most fastidious critics have, the ring and the metre of true poesy, and loved especially, " My Captain, oh, my Captain," " The Prayer of Christopher Columbus," and " The Song of the Redwood Tree." To hear him read the last was very moving, because he seemed to have a special affinity with it—his fingers turning to the page almost involuntarily. On one remarking to him that

lines of Whitman's had a certain haunting music hard to
explain, he instantly agreed, saying, " Yes, I know, I know."
"For instance," continued the one who was speaking—

> " I never walk under certain trees
> But large and melodious thoughts descend upon me."

" I know," he said, " I have thought of that line too."

Such, I think, would be a just description of many of his
own thoughts.   But with all his appreciation, something rough
and of the new world half-shocked a scholarly and conservative taste that delighted in the exquisite form of Tennyson,
and grieved over the irregularities even of his beloved
Browning.   " Whitman," he would say in the Journal, " has a
glimmering of Democracy, but he never understood it as
Mazzini did."   Something of such fastidiousness he imagined to
be in his listener, hence the intensity of the joy in dismaying
its inmost sensibilities, either of metre or thought.   As if to
sugar what he felt to be a considerable pill, he feigned a
certain sympathy with the outraged feelings of his companion,
recoiling in a species of horror from the revolutionary utterances which he declaimed, and hesitating before turning a
page, as if he dare not proceed any further with what was so
manifestly outrageous.

> "Till with sound of trumpet
> Far, far off the daybreak call—hark ! how loud and clear I hear it
>   wind,
> Swift ! to the head of the army !—swift ! spring to your places,
>   Pioneers ! O pioneers !"

he shouted, and then banged the chair on which he was
sitting, as if to emphasise a consternation that could not be
contained, but laughter betrayed him.   He hugged himself,
and continued :

> "'What to such as you, anyhow such a poet, I ? therefore leave my
>   works,
> And go lull yourself with what you can understand, and with piano
>   tunes ;
> For I lull nobody, and you will never understand me.'

Do you hear that, you must take yourself to piano tunes and
not stand any of his blasphemies.   I scarcely dare read this

to you, it is too awful for vocal utterance, but we'll get through it somehow, and drown it with piano tunes :

> "' To you, ye reverent sane sisters,
> I raise a voice for far superior themes for poets and for art,
> To exalt the present and the real,
> To teach the average man the glory of his daily walk and trade.'

Ah, have you realised that impiety, the average man and the average woman the centre and the inspiration of poetry and endeavour? Have you realised it, I say? No, you cannot; you do not understand Christianity sufficiently. Oh! oh!"—

(Companion) "Yes, but the average man and the average woman . . ." For reply he shook his head and rocked himself. He heard not one reply but a thousand—all the universities, and the parliaments, and the town councils, and the distinguished people criticising and crying down the average man, and what he meant and Christianity meant, and all equally ignorant of that which they ought to know.

Sometimes he would wait a moment in mock deference to a question or an inquiry, and at others he would hurry on as if they were bound to an awful and inexorable wheel whose every turning should reveal a fresh depth of an abyss. "The Prayer of Christopher Columbus" and "My Captain, oh, my Captain," served as an interlude, my father bowing with much ceremony, as if on behalf of himself and the poet, when his listener expressed commendation. Then the inexorable wheel began turning again, and they hung shuddering over the abyss:

> "O something pernicious and dread!
> Something far away from a puny and pious life!
> Something unproved! something in a trance!
> Something escaped from the anchorage and driving free."

He turned the page, when something caught his eye which appeared to create in him a horror greater than any to which they had yet penetrated. He blanched, and paused as if unable to utter the blasphemy the poet was about to put in his mouth. Then gathering himself together as if for a final effort:

> "Come, Muse, migrate from Greece and Ionia,
> Cross out, please, those immensely overpaid accounts,
> That matter of Troy and Achilles' wrath, and Æneas, Odysseus'
> wanderings,
> Placard 'Removed' and 'To Let' on the rocks of your snowy
> Parnassus."

"Parnassus to let!" Then his joy broke loose, the book falling on the table, seeing that the abyss was sounded and that there was no need of further blasphemy. "Parnassus to let!" he exclaimed again amid the intervals of a mirth that was in keeping with the sacred hill. At one moment he thumped his listener on the back, at the next he shook her and then subsided into his chair, making the ceiling echo with exclamation at the vision that the words had conjured. All the might and power that had described and given glory to the ancient world, yea, and more than that, at the service of the future, of the good days that were coming! For the kingdom of the Son of God should rise, not upon the giants, but upon the average men and women of the race. As often with him, he had passed beyond the bourne of time, and stood independent, viewing that climax of creation whose advent he so passionately saluted and prophesied, and in which in Christ Jesus he already participated. All his great hopes and ideals for the future were grounded in Him. A member of the family, who had heard the noise upstairs, burst open the door in amazement. "What is the matter?" she exclaimed. "What in the world is the matter?" For a minute her sudden appearance added to the frenzy, and then in an instant all was still. The ceiling stopped echoing, the various objects of furniture resumed their former complacency, and my father was looking at her with much calmness through his glasses. "Matter?—everything. 'Parnassus is to let!'"

What impressed men was the variety of subjects on which he could dilate, and even if he were not conversant in a matter or an aspect of life, he was aware of its existence and intent on knowing more concerning it. A better listener never lived. In an argument in particular it was often impossible to refute him. A friend (an electrical engineer) said:

"I was trying to prove to him something about the electric tram system in a certain town, but he would not agree, and, upon my word, he knocked my argument into a cocked hat, and I had not a word to say. Yet I was in the right and he was in the wrong."

A friend of the family, thoughtfully listening to this remark, said, "Are you quite sure you were in the right— that his knowledge in that particular was not superior to yours? My husband, who has lived all his life in Ireland, used to discuss Irish matters with him of a local as well as a general character. On one occasion my husband said something concerning a particular neighbourhood, and Mr. Hughes expressed surprise. 'Why,' he said, 'that was not so in 18—. Why has such a change been necessary?'"

This knowledge of detail—indeed the reserves that could be summoned to storm any position—bewildered certain people. They thought it almost uncanny. Some said, " There is nothing he does not know about,"; and others, " He has no need to know about a subject in order to discuss it. He will prove his point just the same." Again, his immense vitality— his way of dealing with a subject—was such that it became a permanent portion of a person's consciousness and reminiscence. They could listen to him and take in what he said when they were too weary to listen to others pleading the same thing. With those who had the misfortune to be parsons or the members of connexional committees there was small hope that he would talk on anything but ecclesiastical subjects. With those who were not thus circumstanced he sought for a topic which he divined to be their main interest, so that he might learn from them. With scholarly men or those of any literary reputation this humility sometimes led to underestimation of his powers. He feared almost to give his opinion or to intimate any proficiency in the presence of such, not à propos of political matters and the Church of Christ, but à propos of purely scholastic and literary matters in which he felt himself curtailed. For the sake of the persons with whom he conversed listeners used to wish that he had been less reticent, for " their soul's enlightenment," to quote a phrase of his own. When he did enter into such a discussion with equipped persons, the pressure at which he lived and thought would sometimes put him at a disadvantage. When quite a child I remember a most vehement discussion between him and a headmaster respecting Dr. Abbott's views concerning the resurrection of our Lord. My father had arrived at some conclusion in this matter which his companion did not consider justified, and in the metaphysical regions into which they ascended, my father, so far as I can remember, by the sound of it and the comments of other listeners, was hard pressed and scarcely at an advantage. But this same gentleman entertained high views of my father's scholastic powers, quite apart from any of his other qualities, and intimated an appreciation of them during the last visit to Grindelwald that was pleasing to one who had voluntarily laid aside the ambitions of youth.

There were two trees just outside his study window, whose tender leaves in spring used to tremble and shiver in the morning sunlight, and on these his eyes were often wistfully fixed. " Often," said his secretary, " in the intervals of his thought or writing, he would look out of the window at those trees, and his face would become strangely illuminated, and so he would remain for some seconds; I often noticed it." In their leafy network he saw the Golden Age, and as he poured forth his soul in the notes of the Journal or in prayer his eye kindled at the vision. It was characteristic that he was not rendered dreamy but reinvigorated. None the less he would often comment on their beauty as he left the dining-room with the *Times* newspaper under his arm : " A lovely sight, is it not? We are very privileged to have such a sight in the centre of London."

Animals as well as human beings were objects of interest and at times of his affection. The rabbits which his sons kept in the backyard had an interested spectator in the master of the house, who in intervals of his toils would observe them with rapt attention from the study and dining-room windows. Of birds he was particularly fond, and at one time used to feed a pigeon from the study balcony which came there daily for the purpose. Any book or article on these was particularly delightful to him, and he admired that work of Ouida where she compares birds to the thoughts of God, and pleads against those cruelties which fashion perpetrates. Yet his romance with the animal kind was bound up with a cat of illustrious lineage, whose admission into the household he secured in the following manner :—While staying with one of his sisters he visited a family honoured by the presence of this race whose lineage this family eagerly expounded, producing written matter—so his children were told—to corroborate their tale. Either the ancestor of the line had been present at the Flood, or a connection, so that in either case the length of the descent was unimpaired. A scion of the race shortly arrived in Taviton Street, my father preparing the household for some days for the event, and unfolding the tale of the lineage. Like most that was old and holy, it came from the East, and was a type of Persian, not unjustly designated "blue Persian," and a species, so it was said, that is almost extinct. After deliberation it was decided to call it Chin-Chin, which had the advantage of a certain Oriental flavour, and which was suggested to the family mind by a popular ditty of the day. The master of the house at first objected, thinking that the title lacked dignity, but in the end the concordat was too strong for him, and he would address it not by the double epithet at first proposed, but by the single title of "Chin." The animal was a very beautiful one; and as it grew in stature, and lay licking itself in the sunlight, curled in attitudes of Oriental grace and repose, my father would often watch and comment upon it, occasionally making some cautious advance which he trusted would be of an ingratiating character.

Years ago in the *Strand Magazine* he had read an illustrated article on cats which never ceased to haunt his memory, because in this article their conservatism and their aristocracy had been demonstrated in a very striking manner. "Never," would he say, "till I read that article did I begin to understand the cat. A cat is intensely reserved, and cannot be known at once, nor does the cat easily evince affection to all and anybody as the dog, but only to those one or two whom after deliberation she favours with such affection. The cat is not understood by us as yet, and the remarks that foolish people make concerning her are born of ignorance." Thus his advances to the animal were tentative, and of a success that surpassed his hopes. For as he sat writing notes in the study it was a usual sight to see the blue Persian sitting on his shoulder, curling his tail into the air, as if sharing in the triumph of his thought, and purring vociferously in sympathy with it. When visitors came, he turned round his chair slowly, so as not to incommode the blue Persian, and did not desist in paying those attentions which were necessary to the Persian's peace of mind. As he returned from showing a visitor to the door, the animal would spring upon his back, which he would immediately bend so as to form a meet resting-place, and with much slowness and discomfort make his way back to the study. The sight of this would arouse the curiosity of members of his family who knew how much had to be done in the day, and how little he could afford to lose the time. Passing him once in this posture one of them had the irreverence to remark, "Why don't you let the cat down? it's a great hindrance." The creature who had mounted on his shoulder breathed disdain at the question, curving his tail in a manner that bespoke volumes. Gently soothing the Persian with his hand, he thus replied: "For some reason the animal has taken an extravagant affection to me, and I dare not repulse it. It follows me everywhere, leaping upon me, invading the study at all times, so that I am really quite helpless in the matter. Strange, is it not, that it should have singled me out of all of you in this manner?"

Later, when the family went away for the summer holiday great precautions were taken to ensure the safety of the sacred Persian, who, alas! evaded them, so that on their return the household was bereft of his presence. The master fixed the members of the household with his eye. "I told you," he said, "that this would be the end of it. Knowing how you all profess to adore animals, I did my best to procure you one, and now you have allowed it to be stolen! I always knew it would be so, I always feared it," and sighing, he went up to his study. The loss of the blue Persian was so keen that for years it was never referred to. No other animal ever had the same entrée to the study, and while plebeian cats of uncertain ancestry, who seldom ventured above the lower regions, gave consolation to those who would take it, they had none to afford to the master of the house.

The catholicity of his heart and mind are nowhere better attested than in his book-shelves. One of the books is uncut, Goethe's *Hermann and Dorothea*. My father's niece was breakfasting with him some weeks before he died, and an animated discussion took place upon the poet Goethe, my father denying his democratic sympathies, or any large apprehension of the people and their need. His visitor had quoted this idyl in refutation, laying special stress on its melody, simplicity, and charm. My father shrugged and appeared dubious, but none the less took to heart everything that was said by an opponent, and quietly in the city one day bought Macmillan's edition with notes, so that he could "attack" it with the latest explanations. The *Confessions of Augustine* stand in their place, and were a favourite. Books treating of the conditions of the life of the people, of Temperance Reform, and the problems of economics, are not as indicative of their owner as the poets, the novelists,[1] and the historians. A handsome edition of the Platonic Dialogues recalls his love of Plato. Among modern philosophers he liked to dip into Bacon and Kant, and in later years was reading Lotze with particular interest.

After breakfast he would continue reading his papers, and when the secretary arrived he would dictate notes and letters. Then visitors would come—a long stream—ministers, his own assistants and those belonging to all Churches, particularly, of course, to the Free—rich men, poor men—in the very early days, beggar men, though these were shunted off as soon as there was an organised Relief Department. All manner of people must have come to see him, but the rush of his life did not enable him to tell us about them. Something was always happening to engross his attention, and he had the habit also of dismissing things from his mind after he had dealt with them. He said once, a few days before he passed away, "I wish I had kept some record of all the people I have met." Colonials, coloured ministers [2] occasionally, young ministers in doubt and difficulty, workers in need of encouragement, in fact, the strenuous and religious of all classes gravitated there as if by a natural attraction. A distinct class were the Press repre-

[1] Some of George Meredith's novels he read with particular pleasure, with the exception of *Diana of the Crossways*. "I cannot," he would exclaim, "get beyond the dancing and jigging of that first chapter." During the last days of his life he eagerly cross-examined an admirer of the novel, and had decided to make yet another attempt. Mr. Watts-Dunton's *Aylwin* he read with interest; and such delicate pieces of work as Mr. Barrie's novels would move to admiration. Shorthouse's *John Inglesant* he would describe as "one of the most fascinating pictures of the seventeenth century that was ever penned." To Inglesant himself he would never accord admiration. Any novel of note my father was certain to have read. He did not merely greatly enjoy reading them, but he felt them to be a mirror of the times, and therefore profitable.

[2] When "coloured brethren" came to St. James's Hall my father would be careful to show them every courtesy, asking them to pray, and going out of his way to make them feel at home. "Dean Stanley," he said once, "used to say that St. John's Gospel would never be properly apprehended till the negroes were Christianised."

19

sentatives, who came to ask his opinion on contemporary events.

Lord Halifax came to see him on some matter, and he was much impressed by the visit. "We agree, you know," he said, on coming down to dinner, "in essentials. He is a deeply spiritual man, and has been speaking most beautifully to me on the fundamentals of Christianity. Outsiders do not know how united Christians are. He gave his experience, in fact, just as if we were in class. I told him that we had been holding a class meeting." Another time a certain Father O—— came to visit him, producing apparently the same concord.

Scarcely a day must have passed without attending a committee, either in connection with his own Mission or the public life of London, and increasingly those connected with Methodism.

The feeling of the children during the early years of the Mission was a puzzle, the more particularly as friends, and sometimes relatives, indicated by head-shakings and other times by emphatic remarks, that the household was on its way head-long to ruin. Some ridiculed it, and on all sides their manner of living appeared to create consternation. Increasingly it was brought home to them that their parents were not like the rest of the world, and that their father in particular was the object of much criticism. A certain bewilderment ensued. Which was right, their father or his contemporaries? In that period of *Sturm und Drang* he literally seemed to make persons bristle at all points, and people would speak their mind to the prophet's children, if they could not get at the prophet. It seemed to be a form of relief to them, and the writer can recollect the following remarks:

"Tell your father to mind his own business! I'll never look at the —— paper again," and so on. Their very appearance indeed was sufficient to provoke vehement utterances. "God," one intimated, "never intended such goings on, and, above all, such a household!" "What did our parents mean," said another, "by giving up all their friends?"

Elderly ladies did not seem to have it in their vocabularies to epitomise my father, but they wept over my mother, and prophesied a speedy death. A few like their grandmother treated the prophet's children with consideration. The writer was sitting beside her once when someone said, " Well, Mrs. Barrett, what do you think of this West London Mission of Mr. Hughes'?" With a cough, she replied, " It is somewhat early to form an opinion." Then smothering a smile, " The preparations appear to be conceived on a peculiarly gigantic scale!"

His interest in the Trafalgar Square imbroglio, and his sympathy with the workmen in the various strikes that occurred about this time, particularly stirred the general animosity. Yet high above all waved the banner of Home Rule, and the hatred in which the Irish Methodists held him impressed his children not a little. His words and manner led them to understand that these thirsted for his blood, and that they loathed him unspeakably.[1]

Political matters were always familiar ground. The various European Powers gained distinct and portentous personalities, exciting a variety of emotions. Vast undeveloped Russia panted to get to the Black Sea, but the English, in their absurd fear of her and their anxiety concerning India, insisted on preventing so reasonable an ambition. None the less she must one day occupy Constantinople; on that he insisted.

They often confuted opponents by repeating their arguments to him. In return they received a volley, for he could not accord them the tolerance he did to others. After thus standing their ground they plucked the arrows from their own breast in order to plant them in that of the foe.

His attitude to Germany was that of unloving admiration, but he thought that the Emperor and Mr. Chamberlain were the two cleverest men in Europe. When the Emperor Frederick died, whom he so revered, he shook his head over the known military character of his son, whom he none the less held in a growing admiration. Dearly he loved to read how he rose betimes, hastening down to address his sailors in the ship while his relatives were yet abed; and for

---

[1] As a matter of fact, when my father went to Ireland as Wesleyan President, the old-fashioned ultra-Protestant Methodists were enchanted with him. "We could forgive anything," they said, "in a man who preaches the gospel as he does!" One of the most faithful and gifted of the nursing Sisters was an Irish Methodist who was first attracted to my father's work by reading the *Methodist Times* and its Home Rule policy.

all his mediæval inability to understand the word freedom, it
was impossible not to admire the man and his strength and
variety. With regard to a certain Imperial Bill before the
Reichstag, which was being much opposed, he remarked, " The
fellow's right, you know, but they have not the sense to see
it!" His parents had been in advance of their time:
Germany was not yet fit for their régime. The German
people as such did not take his fancy, but England must
increasingly ally herself with them, a conviction which was
much intensified by the reading of Mr. Kidd's *Social Evolution*.
Germany, like England, had accepted the Reformation, and
stood for the future and for progress. France, on the contrary,
had not done so, and was declining daily, and in that he loved
that country he incessantly belaboured her. Her successive
national actions made her sink lower and lower in his estimation, but he always remembered her struggle for the Golden
Age, and was sensible of the charm and vivacity of the race.
Their gesticulations, the subtilty and music of their language,
the apparent delirium of their manner of taking life, greatly
appealed to him. " Europe," he used to say, " has been
monstrously ungrateful to her." He longed, as he said at the
missionary meeting, for the conversion of France—for the
spread in her of " joyous primitive scriptural Christianity,"
unallied to the sacerdotalism of Rome, which made religion
hateful to her manhood. The fact that she was the first to
herald a new and better order by the Revolution made him
all the more desirous to consummate that end.

Austria, for all its crushing of national liberty, was spoken
of with compunction. The personalities of the Emperor and
Empress were mysteriously entwined with it. The spectacle
of an empire that had once been so mighty, dismembered
within one lifetime, appealed to certain compassionate elements.
Such a proud race they were too, and the mother incessantly
mourning the death of her son. Sorrow upon sorrow seemed
to have descended upon the house of Hapsburg. A great
friend of my parents, and latterly of their children, was an
Austrian lady—the Baroness von Langenau — who passed
away three months before my father, and almost as suddenly.
Hers had not been an ordinary career. Brought up in the
exclusive circle of the Austrian aristocracy, she married, whilst

still a young girl, a distinguished member of the diplomatic
profession, who was appointed Austrian ambassador to the
Hague and St. Petersburg successively.   Later she became a
lady-in-waiting to the Empress of Austria.   The death of her
husband, and later of her only son, whom she had long nursed
vainly but devotedly, left her unusually sad and lonely in a
frivolous and heartless society.   The old questions became
intensified, and her despair reached a species of agony.   One
evening she entered, she knew not why, a little Methodist
chapel in Vienna, and the words that she heard there answered
her agony and assuaged it.   They lived as her thirsty soul
lived, and told her of a Saviour who could appease its craving.
Having " found peace " with the Methodists, she determined to
join that communion, and came to London to ask counsel of
the Wesleyan missionary officials with regard to some property
that she wished to make over to the Methodist Church.

She called upon my father and told him her story.   In a
moment he divined and understood.   The life that went before
—the simplicity and the healing power of that message—the
ostracism that her course meant in an exclusive, chiefly Roman
Catholic society—her desire to do something for Christ in
helping the Methodists in the city.   She herself, nominally a
Lutheran, had lived outside all so-called religious influences,
till she came into contact with Methodism.   Protestantism
on the Continent, on its ecclesiastical side, as my father used
to express it, with gestures that bespoke the intensity of his
feeling, was crushed, cold, formal—in fact, " dead."   It could
neither captivate nor impress men and women.   The picture of
the little Methodist chapel in the great capital, bent for the
most part exclusively on the things of this world, and a great
deal of it a very evil world, moved him, as did the lady
before him.   Perhaps that was his greatest power—that of
comprehending the main facts, persons, and situations in a
moment, whereas the majority of mankind seem to take many
moments.   Men, too, often seem to live in the backyard of
their own ideas and predilections, and if anybody appears
altogether alien to these, their first instinct is to assume a
hostile attitude, whereas men of my father's type seem to
welcome such an advent, if it is only for the sake of the
opening they afford into alien realms.

She was one of those sensitive beings, hedged from their birth in an exclusive circle, who, while they appear to the unknowing to live in a position of great freedom and affluence, are helpless and enchained as a bird in a cage. She could find her way about in most European tongues, for she was a born linguist, and, in addition, she was a woman widely read, versed in affairs and remarkably intelligent. With these qualities she was extraordinarily simple and unassuming. My father not only helped her in the matter in hand, but she became a most faithful friend of my parents through the remainder of her life, visiting them yearly either in Switzerland or London, and taking the deepest interest in the Sisterhood and the Mission. A beautiful pearl necklace, for which she had no further use, she sold for the benefit of the Mission, as she did other valuables for the Orphanage in Vienna that she started and maintained. She became friends with one or two of the Sisters and others, and regarded her yearly visit to England as a kind of homecoming, when, after months of difficulty and persecution in intolerant Vienna, she could live and breathe among spiritual sympathisers.

Her elasticity of mind was perhaps her most remarkable characteristic, for, much to my father's amusement, in her old age, she became a partisan of the Socialists in that city, so he would exclaim with pretended horror, " Baroness, Baroness, you are actually worse than I am ! Do you realise that even my villainy does not approach yours ? " One of the many anecdotes she used to tell made a great impression on him. A certain Roman Catholic ecclesiastic was asked in her presence at a reception in Vienna as to what he would feel if Jesus of Nazareth were suddenly to appear on earth in their midst ?

" I should be terrified ! " he answered, with great spontaneity. " God forbid ! I should not know what to do ! "

My father was much startled at the incident, and at first would scarcely believe it. By nature he was inclined to believe the best of institutions, unless he knew to the contrary, and most certainly of persons. Slander or other disadvantageous stories he always received with the greatest incredulity. The Baroness once spoke quite casually of a well-known fact concerning a foreign royal personage, and my father seemed both grieved and astonished. "I never knew that," he said; "I never thought that."

Another interesting figure of this time is that of Mr. Jacob Holyoake, the well-known Secularist leader, who was brought into connection with my father in a somewhat interesting manner. A shoemaker in Soho who had been an atheist, on account of the lack of sympathy and compassion on the part of average orthodox Christianity, became converted shortly before his death. This was partly owing to his wife, who was a professed Christian attending the Mission, and very largely to one of the Sisters who visited their home and revealed Christianity to him in a new light. My father participated in this drama, and was present during his last hours. The whole incident so stirred him that he determined to write a little account of it, and to publish it in book form under the title of *The Atheist Shoemaker*. In doing so, he invented fictitious names for the two Sisters concerned, so that they might be spared painful publicity should such publicity arise. He was careful also to pay full tribute to the noble qualities of the shoemaker which he possessed previous to his acceptance of Christianity, to wit, the gentleness and tolerance that he had always displayed towards his wife, bringing her and taking her back from Christian services, in addition to a rare rectitude and honesty. But he could not see Love or Immortality in the universe; and considering all things, it was small wonder that he could not. For many years he had been half-starved, and he died before his time because of it. At the same time my father portrayed with all the vivid emotion of which he was capable the various stages of the struggle which had preceded his surrender to Christ, especially the last, when he lay pale and perspiring on his pillow. The roar of the London traffic below, he noted, sounded oddly and inharmoniously in the chamber where a soul was having its last struggle in this world.

There was a good deal of stir at its publication, particularly among pronounced Free-thinkers. Mr. Bradlaugh in his paper, the *National Reformer*, published a courteous note asking for the name of the shoemaker, which my father refused, " judging," to quote his own words, " that the relatives of the deceased and other people interested would not care to have their names in print." Mr. Foote, in the *Free-thinker*, transgressed the rules of courtesy altogether, and doubted my father's veracity, calling the book "A lie in five chapters." To such an accusation my father naturally could make no reply, for, as he replied in a letter to one of the London journals, if he were a liar, as Mr. Foote declared he was, it would be useless to open a discussion, since nothing he said was to be depended upon. None the less Mr. Foote pursued him for full five years, intent on picking a quarrel with him; at the end of which time my father thought it best to call in Mr. Holyoake, whom he knew to be a gentleman and one devoted to fair play. He had already met Mr. Holyoake at a reception at Lady Aberdeen's, where co-operation was under consideration, and had conversed with him on this theme. Mr. Holyoake had also formed a favourable impression of my father. On one occasion Mr. Gladstone had made some reference to John Wesley's ministry, to which my father had taken exception, and at a Sunday afternoon Conference he vindicated Wesley against this charge, to wit, that he had looked for sudden conversions rather than for the steady development of Christian character. For what, my father asked, were the class meetings and all the rest of the paraphernalia of Methodism if not for this latter purpose? Mr. Holyoake, who was present, was struck with the speech, and wrote a résumé of what he had heard, which he enclosed in a letter to Mr. Gladstone.

Early in 1894 he came at my father's request to see him, and consented to sift the affair for himself. My father's grace and ease in explaining matters impressed him, so he afterwards related. The result of Mr. Holyoake's investigations was entirely favourable to my father. He considered a Celt and an ardent Christian had described that last struggle in a way that might be expected of him; but that the people had actually existed, and that each of the events described had actually taken place, he was convinced, and sent the report of his investigations to the *Free-thinker*.

In his opinion, he told me since, my father was "shamefully and unfairly treated." However much he personally might differ from some of the author's opinions, he read *The Atheist Shoemaker* with respect. He was much struck by the full appreciation of an atheist's virtues, who is described in the book as " the noblest type of English working man," as well as other generous tributes, to wit, that " nothing was more beautiful in this man than his chivalrous and romantic love for his wife, which overflowed into a tender solicitude for the rights and happiness of her sex "; and, again, as possessing " an eloquent tongue, inspired by a keen intellect and a tender heart."

Indeed, the comparison between the author's fervent Christianity and equally fervent appreciation of an atheist's qualities, struck Mr. Holyoake so much as to cause him to ask in his contribution to the *Free-thinker*: " Why is it that Mr. Hughes, with more fervour of piety than most clerical adversaries of scepticism, is more discriminating and tolerant than they, I do not understand, though I have esteem for him on that ground."

In the course of his investigations Mr. Holyoake visited Katherine House, and was both pleased and impressed with what he saw, as well as with the two Sisters who were mentioned (under assumed names) in my father's story.

" I have seen and conversed separately," he writes, " with Sister Beatrice and Sister Ethel, from whom Mr. Hughes derived many of his statements. I was shown the private diary of Sister Beatrice, giving contemporary and documentary evidence of the minute accuracy of her statement. Their entire veracity seems to be unquestionable. They had not only sincerity, but that cultivated sincerity which is without exaggeration. They said Mr. Herbert [1] had a vivid faculty of speech and a brightness of conversation which compelled interest and attention. Of that they must be good judges, for their own grace and precision of speech showed that they understood those qualities."

He came to dine with the family once or twice, and my father was delighted with him, only sore at heart that Christians should alienate such a man by their folly. Mr. Holyoake went to St. James's Hall, and sat in the top gallery. He was much struck by my father's reading of the Parable of the Prodigal Son, which he had heard read for the first time in his life, he said, as it ought to be read. He had Bright's freshness, he thought, in the reading aloud of Scripture. Comparing him with Chamberlain as a speaker, he said that

---

[1] The atheist shoemaker.

the statesman lacked his passion.   My father was often thus
compared in his debating capacity, more than one versed in
parliamentary debates assuring me that he had no rival in
this department except Mr. Chamberlain.

When the Mission held its annual soirée at St. Martin's
Town Hall, Mr. Holyoake was always invited, and would sit
and converse with the sisters whom he knew.   He said he was
sorry that *The Atheist Shoemaker* was out of print, as it was
the first historic instance of Christian concession to the ethics
of heresy.   A Christian minister, he thought, had never done
such justice to the virtues of an atheist.   The Mission also in
the absolutely unsectarian character of its charity appealed to
him very much, and was phenomenal in his eyes.   No community of Christians he had ever known or heard of had distributed relief to the body without inquiry as to creed, and with
no *arrière pensée* of proselytism.

The most intimate and familiar figure of London days is
that of Dr. Lunn.   During the first year of the Mission he
was in India, experiencing many things and forming ideas on
what he saw, but suffering greatly in health, till his life became
almost unbearable on account of the repeated attacks of fever
that the climate engendered.   In such a state he wrote to
my father asking his advice about returning, to which my
father sent careful replies.   The wish of his heart to have
Dr. Lunn with him as colleague should he return made him
all the more insistent in giving reasons for Dr. Lunn's
remaining.

In the spring of 1888 he wrote strongly urging him to
stay, if it was only for the sake of his sympathy with the
native movement in India.   The enforcement of the Contagious Diseases and the Cantonment Acts in India, and the
agitation that arose in consequence, in which he was taking a
leading part, had stirred him to deep, though perhaps temporary, despondency concerning "our rule" in India.   At
other times he would speak of it as the greatest blessing
the country had ever known.   Dr. Lunn, however, cut the
gordian knot himself and returned home.

He was appointed as colleague to my father in the
West London Mission, which position he occupied till 1890.
Throughout this period he was constantly at my father's side,

helping him, not only in the strictly devotional and spiritual side of the work, but, as my father had expressed it in his letters, "in fifty ways"—in the great social and philanthropic movements which he had at heart, in the *Methodist Times*, and his other enterprises.

Unfortunately, as it turned out, this colleagueship was too soon to terminate. What was called the missionary controversy in 1889 broke off co-operation with Dr. Lunn, which, if it had been continued, must have made a considerable difference to his life and health. In particular, Dr. Lunn used to insist on his taking a long walk on Saturday afternoons, and it was on these occasions that they fell to discussing many matters connected with their Church and, in particular, foreign missions.

"NATIONAL LIBERAL CLUB,
"WHITEHALL PLACE, S.W.,
"*March* 22, 1892.

"DEAR MR. HUGHES,—After I return from the North a week or two or three hence, I will report myself at Taviton Street.

"Some of my friends speak evilly of you, as you may hear. But in their Halls in Manchester, in the Hall of Science and elsewhere, I have stated the grounds of my respect for you as a matter of justice.—Yours very sincerely,

"G. J. HOLYOAKE, Brighton.

"On Mazzini and on Profit Sharing I read the *Methodist Times* with pleasure."

"62 PENTONVILLE ROAD, N.,
"*May* 4, 1899.

"DEAR MR. HUGHES,—At 12 o'clock last night I told Mr. Bunting I hoped to meet him to-night, at your and Mrs. Hughes's Reception. Lest I do not I send a line to say I am obliged to return to Brighton this morning, on business of our Liverpool Congress next week. Still, if I can, I shall return, as I want to see with mine own eyes that you are really well again.—With real regards to Mrs. Hughes and yourself,

"G. J. HOLYOAKE."

CHAPTER XIII

DARK DAYS AND A VISIT TO THE NEW WORLD

" That is why Reform, full of questions of expediency and policy, in detail, is, in the gross, not a question of expediency or of policy at all ; . . . They will admit much of my theory, but then they will say like practical men that the ignorant classes cannot understand affairs of State and are sure to go wrong. But the odd thing is that the most prosperous nations in the world are both governed by the masses—France and America. So there must be a flaw in the argument somewhere. The fact is that education, intelligence, wealth, are a security against certain faults of conduct, not against errors of policy. There is no error so monstrous that it fails to find defenders among the ablest men. Imagine a congress of eminent celebrities, such as More, Bacon, Grotius, Pascal, Cromwell, Bossuet, Montesquieu, Jefferson, Napoleon, Pitt, etc. The result would be an Encyclopædia of Error. They would assert Slavery, Socialism, Persecution, Divine Right, military despotism, the reign of force, the supremacy of the executive over legislation and justice, purchase in the magistracy, the abolition of credit, the limitation of laws to nineteen years, etc. If you were to read Walter Scott's Pamphlets, Southey's Colloquies, Ellenborough's Diary, Wellington's Despatches—distrust of the select few, of the chosen leaders of the community, would displace the dread of the masses. The danger is not that a particular class is unfit to govern. Every class is unfit to govern."

Letters of Lord Acton to Mary Gladstone.

YET the *raison d'être* of what among Methodists is known as the Indian Missionary controversy was far from springing entirely from these conversations. Discussion concerning the best method of propagating Christianity in foreign, particularly Eastern countries, was occupying the minds of the religious world generally, articles on the subject appearing in various well-known periodicals. This, apart from any other special consideration, would have induced my father to invite discussion on this topic in the *Methodist Times*, which existed, as its first leader expressed it, to provide " a perfectly independent organ in which any intelligent and courteous writer may freely ventilate his opinions. We have nothing to conceal, and are more concerned for the safety and wisdom which free discussion brings, than for the triumph of our own convictions. . . . Our columns are freely open to those who differ from us. We shall always try to secure a full and masterly statement of the views we oppose. We wish our readers to hear both sides. We believe that a policy of secrecy and reticence, however innocent, is a mistaken policy, and one increasingly apt to do endless mischief. We shall therefore take care that any matter of importance is frankly discussed, and that the Methodist people are made acquainted with all they have a right to know."

But there was also a special consideration which made anything like abstract discussion of the subject in his Journal under his auspices partake of the character of distinct reformatory proposals. In the first place, dissatisfaction with the Mission House was rife at that time, as already intimated, and any movement toward complaint or reform was necessarily looked for in my father's direction, the leader of the Forward party. Any pronouncement or article in his paper was bound to bear a significance that it would not have borne in another paper. He had already been successful in introducing reform or modification, or whatever men chose to call it, in the Home policy. Seeing his power, his vehemence, and his increasing following, many were quite prepared for a descent on Foreign Missionary policy. They wanted, as my father wanted, some kind of free discussion—not revolution, setting aside the wisest and most expert opinion, not even necessarily a reformed or modified policy, if that were understood to be undesirable (though he, rightly or wrongly, thought it to be desirable), but what he used to describe in the Journal as a " ventilation." Because he was greatly misunderstood, the writer has ventured to touch on what may be still a delicate matter, despite the lapse of some years, and the signs of new interest in missionary work which Methodism is at present witnessing. This policy of " ventilation " was one of the main things he instituted in Methodism, and which made him so approved by some and disapproved by others.

In the first place, he thought it a necessary acclimatisation to a democratic era. While loyalty and subservience to estab-

lished authority must be absolute, as it is with the British
subject, he thought that a citizen when he happened to be a
Methodist minister or intelligent layman, should be as open to
fairly discuss the policies of his Church on suitable occasions,
as he was open to discuss those of the British Government,
without being vetoed or suspected of disloyalty. Such freedom
does not always necessitate the reform and change that its
opponents fear. Existing systems may be strengthened by
discussion, as Free Trade may be more securely established
by the present agitation.

Secondly, as a direct consequence of this attitude of mind,
he believed it was the best means of uniting, animating, and
spiritualising Methodism—for the spirit meant to him, as it
did to the Greeks, the wind (τὸ πνεῦμα) blowing in through
open windows. It was the main body of the ministry and
people in Methodism who must finally support the great
missions and undertakings of their Church, both at home and
abroad, and without their interest and enthusiastic support
advance could not be made. His own home policy, the great
popular missions, were in particular the child of the people,
and depended upon them daily for sustenance. This should
be the case, he considered, with foreign missions. Good heavens,
was his thought, how he had perambulated the country week in
and week out for home missions, preaching and speaking and
discussing their policy without end in the pages of the *Methodist
Times* and elsewhere ! He did think it would be a good thing
to have some such campaign for foreign missions, something
daring, novel, gigantic, unconventional, so that the old interest
would be more than revived, the papers full of foreign
missions, and the missionary meetings full too. The mist of
the fifties and sixties, so it appeared to many, had fallen nowhere more heavily than on foreign missionary activities, and
lonely missionaries as they saw the home department resusci-
tated, longed for a little of the enthusiasm and support which
was lavished upon missioners at home. My father was, on
his side, more than anxious that some of this zeal and enthusiasm should go to the " foreign brethren," and that ardent
desire underlay all his so-called " interference " in their affairs.
Yet, rightly or wrongly, he did not believe that the foreign
work, any more than the home work, would win any con-

siderable popular support without " ventilation " and modification in its existing régime. The missionaries themselves, he
thought, would benefit most by such " ventilation." Individuals
among them would be able to make suggestions and criticisms
regarding the present régime, as he and others had done about
the home policy.

In the third place, he believed that " ventilation," apart
from any other consideration, was the best policy even from
the point of view of the most conservative and unbending of
the fathers. I can remember the immense satisfaction with
which he would regard Hyde Park, and its variety of platforms and speakers, on a Saturday and Sunday afternoon.
" There they all are," he would say, " Republicans, Socialists,
Free-thinkers, and all the rest, having it out, feeling ever so
much better for it, and asharm less as mice in consequence.
Now, in France or Germany, or any of the other Continental
countries, they would not allow them this airing, with the
result that the Socialists are a distinct social and political
menace, as they never are here."

A person, he thought, who can make suggestions and air
his grievances in a community without arousing a suspicion of
disloyalty will remain a loyal member of it, while one who is
suppressed seldom does so. In the desire to suppress certain
opinions and criticisms that did not meet official approval, lay
the mistake of the first half of the century, and the root of the
Fly Sheet controversy, and to mend it the *Methodist Times*
had largely been started.

And there was a fourth and greater reason which underlay
all these, a passion for the extension of Christ's gospel and
Church. Where usage or tradition had left a stone or a piece
of red tape that retarded its progress, he wanted that stone
removed and that piece of red tape untied. As, in vision, he
saw Christ's gospel sweeping over the whole home country, so
did he see it sweeping unimpeded over the East and foreign
lands. His own extraordinary vehemence and passion swept
him on to a mountain top, and, as it seemed to certain onlookers, blinded him in its whirl and cloud to near issues, to
various aspects of a complicated situation, and made him forget
strangely enough practical exigencies. The ordinary, certainly
the selfish mind, would have seen them at once, but mountain

tops in the age of chivalry quite obscured personal considerations. The curiously simple and unsuspecting element in him, which opponents could never associate with his vehemence and vast designs, was never more manifest than in this particular crisis. He went into it with the careless recklessness of a boy, as generals on these isles have often been in the habit of doing; but when they have been successful, they conceal, like Mrs. Gilpin, a frugal mind. He had certainly concealed such a mind in his home policy, his conclusions and suggestions being based on years of experience and observation. That he should possess an equally frugal and prepared mind with regard to foreign policy, did not seem necessary when he suggested to Dr. Lunn an embodiment of his views and impressions respecting Indian missions in a series of articles in the *Methodist Times*, and so start the ball rolling for foreign missions as other balls had been started rolling for home enterprises of various kinds. An editor whose function it is to set balls rolling is undoubtedly responsible for the rolling of them, but there is no need for him to possess expert knowledge about every subject that is admitted into the columns of his newspaper. He does often need courage— but that this editor had in abundance. This was why, perhaps, he set so many balls rolling, not because he wished to roll them, but because they came his way to be rolled.

What my father overlooked then and always was the force of his own personality, which permeated his newspaper more perhaps than any of his other undertakings, and in this particular instance he also overlooked his leadership of the triumphant Forward party, which gave any suggestion or article under his auspices a peculiar significance. If certain politicians were to edit a newspaper, not even the most rigid Conservative, or Radical, would be deprived of his sleep for fear of a revolutionary or reactionary proposal. They would turn over on their side knowing that it belonged to the abstract realms of pure idea, about which sensible men need not distress themselves in the very least. But let the newspaper of another prominent politician contain such a proposal and they will lie awake half the night, so assured are they that the editor means business, and that something awful is going to happen. My father if he had been a politician would certainly have been among the latter order, though it took him quite a considerable time to realise how terrific and dangerous he was. When he did he curbed himself yet afresh. Thus when it was suggested to him that the articles signed by a " Friend of Missions " would create a considerable stir—not to say animosity—he shook his head. Discussion, of course, they would excite, but that was what he wanted. He was living in a tremendous rush and whirl at the time—chivalry in that year being strained to its farthest bounds, and its propagator fighting in at least six places at the same time, as the reader will see when the next chapter tells him further about these years of 1889 and 1890. In the midst of this war with the heathen—literary, political, and otherwise—it was tempting to dream of the extension of Christ's Church far away in the dependencies of the Empire, and to do anything that might make the dream a reality—to overlook all questions affecting personality as completely as he overlooked his own. The extension of the visible Catholic Church touched the springs of poetry in him. This was one of the things that made him inexplicable, as it touches the springs of poetry in so few. He dreamed of Christ's Church and gospel allying itself in all climes with the needs and hearts of the people, and he wanted this to come to pass with the least possible delay, so that sorrow and superstition and despair might flee away, and that joy might descend on the heart of the toiler, and the night of his weariness break into morning. Meanwhile the present articles would raise a discussion, which was what he desired.

As he was advised to do so, the articles were shown round to some friends in Methodism, who read them previous to their publication. The side issue concerning rupees and stipends, etc., he had first hesitated to bring forward, but his vehemence and his own preoccupation with considerations of policy and system rather than persons, led him into the strategical error, for so it proved, of retaining them.[1] The whole expected

[1] Dr. Lunn entertained criticisms in the first place respecting the educational policy that had been established by Dr. Duff, and which had now been in vogue for many years among Indian Missions of all communions; and, secondly, about what he and others thought to be an unnecessary separation between the missionaries and the natives, the missionary being inevitably under the present system, so he thought, too much identified with the British ruling caste. As a kind of corollary from this

20

discussion turned on these clauses and certain unfortunate methods of expression, arousing the intensest bitterness as well as odium towards him and the writer of the articles. The Indian missionaries and their friends read the criticism on an existing system as a personal attack upon themselves, and they did so not without reason, for both my father and the writer of the articles had overlooked what struck outsiders, at any rate, as an important aspect. Missionaries, if any, belong to the universal Church of Christ. On the field, startling as it may appear to supporters at home, they must quite forget sometimes whether they are Methodists or Baptists, or even Anglicans. They belong to the whole Church of Christ, and are its pioneers. Their position, therefore, is peculiarly delicate and honourable, and never more so than in 1889, when there was a widespread apathy concerning missionary work — a general disposition to doubt its desirability, and in India particularly to seize any handle that could be used against the missionaries, both on the part of a careless society and that of a hostile native press.

The articles in the *Methodist Times* were commented on widely, and were used by opponents of the missionaries for their own purposes. Men and women also who are far from home and friends are necessarily peculiarly sensitive, reading between the lines of a criticism that which its framers never intended to imply. Yet the advance of knowledge in this era and the growth of democratic conceptions do not permit either doctrines or policies or systems to occupy an unassailable position which it is impiety to examine into, to question or to touch. But as advance is essentially slow—each generation surely being but a wave in a full tide—not even generals are

he suggested a reduction of stipend, based on certain calculations on the relative value of English and Indian money, and on the income paid to Salvationist and Roman Catholic missionaries. He did not advocate this latter income, which he thought insufficient, but a *Via Media*. The Commission to which reference is made in the text published findings which denied the accuracy of these observations and the calculations and the conclusions to which they had led. Criticisms of various kinds respecting the existing system and headquarters were shared by other missionaries than Dr. Lunn, and indeed this was so well known that certain told the writer that they thought the earlier articles had been written in the interest of many of the missionaries, and that it was not until the unfortunate insertions respecting the question of income and the use of certain expressions, that they perceived that a blunder had been committed, and that dissension of a disagreeable nature would ensue.

always called upon to hurry. Nor did my father hurry thus in other matters, for his reserve and conservatism in certain respects was quite astonishing. But in his passionate desire to help to bring about what he considered at that time necessary reform in foreign missionary policy, he did not sufficiently consider the how and the when and where of introducing it, which, as Aristotle said, are essential to practical wisdom. It was a remarkable mistake for one who was so possessed of that particular kind of wisdom, but there is never a wise man who does not once make a blunder, and the greatest generals are prone to miscalculation. The forces are calculated for and against—the heavens are read with the same certainty as formerly—a shower at the most is predicted, and lo! 'tis a storm and a hurricane.

No sooner did they see their mistake than my father and Dr. Lunn offered to withdraw certain phrases that had given offence, but they were told that this was insufficient, and that the " charges " contained in the articles would have to be fought to the hilt, and confuted in front of the Church and the world that had heard them. Then when a special assembly of Indian missionaries was convened at Bangalore, and two of the ablest of their number were selected and took ship to appear before a Special Commission at the Mission House in London, the full extent of their strategical blunder was brought home both to them and the Methodist people at large, for the missionaries had decided that they must be publicly cleared of the imputations brought against them, and that only thus could they be reinstated both to the world and their brethren. Thus the discussion that was to bring fresh life to foreign missions, and to stir up the Methodist people to interest and generosity, was to end in a most painful Commission,[1] to clear, as the missionaries said, their characters from the charges which had been brought against them. Issues concerned with policy and régime which were the motive of the publication of the articles, simply dwindled away before the distressing incidents of that Commission, these greater issues occupying but a brief portion of its sitting, and amid conditions that may well be imagined. The strong family

---

[1] The Commission sat in the early summer of 1890, and sent in its report to the Bristol Conference of that year.

feeling of the Methodist people was up in arms on behalf of
missionary relatives, as were the ministry generally touched to
the quick at what they considered a distinct act of disloyalty.
The intensity of bitterness that he aroused among a section
my father never understood. In the first place, he could not
conceive, judging from his past efforts on their behalf, how it
was that the missionaries or their relatives should ever think
of him as anybody but their best friend. However mistaken
or misled they might suppose him to be—a supposition to
which he was accustomed—he could not think of their regarding him as actuated by any but the most brotherly motives
towards them and theirs. " To think," he said once to a friend
of his, " that they actually believe that I want to deprive them
of any comforts or necessaries, that I of all men under heaven
desire to effect such a thing, and that that is the object of my
existence." Indeed, the situation was not without its poignant
note of irony. The more intelligent and zealous among
Wesleyan missionaries in India, as elsewhere, had looked upon
my father as their great champion, particularly since the day
when he cleared a great debt for them at the Annual Missionary Meeting. Moreover, before this as a youth of twenty-
two at Richmond, he alone in Methodism had publicly
championed their cause and dared to evoke the displeasure
of the authorities. With much that was in his designs they
perhaps had more sympathy than the home ministry, and the
most painful item of a painful business was that a champion,
and those for whom he fought, found themselves at what
seemed to the world direct enmity. Certainly there had been
a terrible mistake somewhere, a terrible misunderstanding.
Seeing that even on Arthur fell confusion, still greater was that
which fell on the onlooker. Friend struck friend, for " to be
wroth with one we love doth work like madness in the brain."
One thing was certain, that nothing would induce the editor of
the *Methodist Times* to swerve as much as a hair's breadth
from his loyalty to Dr. Lunn, in his contention that he was
justified in giving his impressions and speaking his mind,
and in his absolute belief in the nobility and integrity of
his friend, in which those who knew the latter ardently shared.
His position, therefore, was one of peculiar difficulty, and how
difficult none but himself knew.

r="

Of all his qualities that which most baffled opponents was his humility. They told him, with considerable directness, what they thought of him and his conduct, and he took it like a child who had been chidden. If the *Methodist Times* had a right to speak directly and to express that which it wished to say, so he felt had those who criticised it. Thus caught though he was in the toils, his loftiness and purity of character struck home even to men who most deeply resented his conduct, and who considered that they and their cause had been cruelly wounded by it. A nature clear as a brook leaping over Welsh hills, and reflecting in its limpid depths the light of heaven, is somewhat disconcerting when it is found to be the possession of a redoubtable opponent as revealed in particular in the close quarters of private conversation. "Why wasn't I told that?" he would exclaim hastily. "Somebody should have told me that before; why wasn't I told?" Indeed, sitting by his side, opponents realised that they had been friends from the beginning, only that a slight misunderstanding had arisen between them which no one regretted more than himself. On the other hand, he fought in the Journal persistently for the writer of the articles, and his right to say that which he had said, while he set forth the circumstances which justified him.

The close of the Special Commission, which was conducted to the satisfaction of the missionary representatives, if such a term can be applied to so sad a business, in that it cleared them of that which they considered had been alleged against them, was not the end of the difficulty, though it might well have terminated at this point, seeing that all acknowledged a blunder of some kind had been made, and that the missionaries themselves had obtained the vindication which they desired. In the *Methodist Times*, also, my father reiterated the desire that the matter should drop, accepting the findings of the Commission, because he was a loyal son of his Church and exceedingly anxious that bygones should be bygones. Yet the bitterness among a certain section was of the quality which cannot be appeased, but which increases with the days. My grandmother was in the habit of attending a ladies' committee with a clock-work regularity, but about this time she ceased to do so. "Really," she said, "their conversation and accusations are such that I do not feel I can go again at present." That her son-in-law was rash and had monstrous and impossible designs she did not doubt, but that he was what the committee said he was she had known him too long and too well to believe, nor did she care to listen to it.   The writer has heard also of persons who cancelled acceptances of invitations to dinner because my father was going to be present.   It was therefore scarcely surprising that the agitation went dragging on through two Conferences, coming to a head in 1890 at Bristol, when Dr. Moulton was elected President, and was again in a position to befriend his former pupil.   From my father's correspondence at this period it is evident that he regarded much of the controversy as a last effort of the reactionaries against the Forward Movement.   Those who clung to the old order and feared the new were bound to gather themselves in one last desperate resistance against the leader who had made a strategical blunder and given them, so it was felt, considerable provocation.   All the old intense clan feeling—it is difficult to know how else to describe it—was up in arms, determined to avenge itself.   The displeasure, as was inevitable, mainly vented itself on the writer of the articles, and that Conference should by some disciplinary measure avenge the honour of the ministry generally and the missionaries, was felt to be imperative.

My father insisted, as he had from the beginning, upon identifying himself absolutely with his colleague, the writer of the articles in question, declaring that any mark of displeasure or dishonour meted out to him would be meted out to both of them.   Mr. Mark Guy Pearse, whose loyalty to my father was always splendid, here joined the fray and expressed the same determination as my father had done.   Dr. Lunn, on his side, seeing the odium which had been aroused against my father and the difficulties that his continuance as my father's colleague in the Mission would involve, sent in a resignation of his position to the authorities.   The Conference which met at Bristol, therefore, with Dr. Moulton in the chair, had to choose between the honourable retirement of Dr. Lunn from the Mission, or the resignation of the three ministers in charge, which at one time seemed imminent.   There was a strong feeling against this honourable retirement, and a wave of anger against my father. A vote condemning his conduct (which was afterwards withdrawn through the efforts of friends, who did not want such a vote to appear in the Conference Minutes) induced my father also to send in his resignation to Dr. Moulton, an act which evoked a very pleasing incident. One of the elder ministers— a former missionary—Dr. Jenkins, and one greatly beloved of Methodism, on hearing what my father had done, penned him there and then the following affectionate note :—

"CLAVERHAM HOUSE, CLIFTON DOWN,
"*July* 29, 1890.

"DEAR BROTHER HUGHES,—The President gave me to read your letter to him intimating your wish to *resign*! I must leave any conceivable right I have to suppose that any words of mine will affect your judgment at this crisis. But I know you are a genuine lover of Methodism, and for her sake I entreat you to listen to your friends, and they are legion in the Conference, not to take this step ; and something bigger than Methodism, which you also love and delight to serve, the Church outside us. For its sake keep to us. I would not speak thus if I were not assured that Methodism is your place. My prayers have been going up that the step you have contemplated may be averted.—With Christian love, affectionately yours,

"E. E. JENKINS.

"Rev. H. P. Hughes, M.A."

He disapproved of the articles, but he understood, as everybody did not, the dreams of the editor, and like many of the elder missionaries he knew his love for their cause, and honoured his gifts and enthusiasm. This piece of spontaneous recognition of his toil and services for Methodism, when many seemed to have quite forgotten them, must have been very pleasant reading to my father ; indeed, it was a most graceful link between new and old and therefore particularly valuable to the representative of the new. There is no apostle who does not lay claim to some kind of succession, and it was this recognition that the hearts of the fathers afforded him which was his main credential as well as the sign of his strength. He kept few letters, but in searching through his desk, my mother came upon this one, which shows the value that he put upon it. A good many besides Dr. Jenkins doubtless regarded the prospect of my father and Mr. Pearse leaving Methodism with dismay, though they did not tell him so. Certainly my father so regarded it. He scarcely spoke, was pale, restless, fidgety, and very quiet. The household at the time seemed to be undergoing a species of nightmare—not a waking reality at all. There was nothing joyful and eager about this contest —it was the very reverse. As to what it was exactly his children were very vague, and their father did not enlighten them as he did on political subjects.

A Methodist minister who was anxious that my father's biography should be as free in speech as the subject of it, said, " Now if your father said anything against a Methodist minister put it in. Don't mind what anybody says." The writer, after much searching of memory, is reminded of the poet in *Alice in Wonderland,* who could not chronicle any clouds in the sky because there were none to view, or any birds because there were none to fly. My father did occasionally comment on a Methodist minister—he could have stopped breathing more easily than he could have stopped commenting on persons and things—but I never heard him say one word against any of them. On the contrary, listeners were always given to understand that Methodism and her ministry was something quite flawless and exceptional, and even at this time when he would have been expected to indulge in personalities, he did not speak with resentment of anybody. Even in earlier days, he would say of a certain old minister, now passed away, who loved him little and opposed him constantly in consequence, " Poor old So-and-so, he is over-due in heaven." Thus my father's behaviour by no means gave the impression that he had anything to complain of in Methodism, though others thought he had, and importuned him to leave it. Seeing that he would not yield—for it was evident that he had only to receive some general sign of esteem from his brethren to consent to remain in their midst—they went to my mother begging her to use her influence. She knew and had marked the bitterness and the pain, but declined, just as she had declined to influence him against Temperance when she was a young wife at Brighton. Where other women would have lost control, she redoubled it, and she knew why he had retained Dr. Jenkins' letter. So the family, watching their parents as in a nightmare, had a distinct presentiment that they might shortly be going out into the wilderness, but where and how imagination refused to picture.

It may be observed of generals that the last quality to desert them, even in the darkest moments, is that of strategy. Napoleon at St. Helena conquered Europe in his mind's eye, and sat with its map on his knee. In like manner did my father one day grip Dr. Lunn by the arm. "Lunn, if we have to go out, we must join one of the minor Methodist bodies, unite all of them, and then make overtures to the Wesleyans." [1] Dr. Lunn had received an invitation to the chaplaincy of the Polytechnic, for his singular success in the Mission, and the affection in which he was held by its members, was noted by many outsiders. On the consent of Conference to his assuming that post instead of being drafted to some solitary Circuit far removed from his friends and former labours, his two colleagues consented to continue their labours in Methodism and the Mission. The few friendly to my father, and very particularly men of moderation and statesmanship, fought for the *status quo*, however distasteful the price. The ultimate settlers of all disputes nowadays—the mass of the people—were present in spirit if not in body. Outside those circles previously mentioned—officials and the relatives of missionaries—were the mass of the people hearing vague rumours of what was going on in headquarters, and not a little perplexed. Over the counter and by the fireside, they questioned and wondered. Indeed, it is easy to imagine the scene. What would be the end of it all? Even Fidus Achatēs did not know, only he felt sure that the editor of the *Methodist Times* was born to astound. His mother said with authority when they had time to sit down for a minute or so in the evening (after washing up the supper things), "I can't think that Mr. Hughes wants to bring charges against the missionaries. That does not sound like him somehow. Don't you remember that speech he made at Exeter Hall, and all the money he collected; and how he said we ought to think of them toiling and suffering at the ends of the earth and do something to encourage them and make their work easier?"

To which the sister of Fidus Achates would reply, "He's

[1] In a conversation with my mother, at this time, he spoke of entering the Presbyterian ministry, should he be forced to leave Methodism.

not making charges, mother. He has not anything in his mind against anybody, but he wants the Church and the world to be different, for he does not like them as they are. So he speaks out plainly, and all the while he's not thinking at all about the people and the things that we think he's thinking about."

At which the father of Fidus Achates would shake his head and remain grumbling: "He should have looked before he leaped, that's my opinion. What does he know of India and what's for the good of those who have toiled there all their lives—how can he know better than they? That's what I want to know. Things there, they say, are not like things here, and if things are to be looked into and brushed up, it should be done careful by them as knows. All the same I don't fancy Methodism without him and Mark Guy. They'll be making a new sort of Methodism somewhere else, and it seems to me there will be many as would like to be in it." At which the daughter would continue: "And Mrs. Brown, she's taking on awful, reading the papers and crying when you speak to her. Mr. Hughes so stirred her up and made her feel such shame for herself that she won't have a word said against him. And when her son-in-law was round he said, 'Why, mother, not even Hugh Price Hughes can always be right'; and she said, 'Get along with you and don't dare to say that again'; so there's no dealing with her. And her husband said, 'Come, come, he's never spoken a word to you. He's not your friend!' and at that she said, 'He is, and of thousands more the whole world over, though he don't know it. Nobody will know all his friends till the Last Day!'"

Thus the relatives and neighbours of Fidus Achates had one mind in the matter. They were puzzled, but they believed in Hugh Price Hughes—not his opinion on every matter, but himself. While Conference was sitting at Bristol they had an opportunity of showing their belief. At a great meeting in the Colston Hall one of the speakers referred accidentally to his name (not in connection with the contemporary crisis), and in a moment the assembly sprang to its feet and waved their handkerchiefs for five minutes, just as they do in great political gatherings when a leader comes to address them. The fluttering of those handkerchiefs—Mrs. Brown and her family and all the persons who sympathised with her—

were distinctly perceptible in the atmosphere of Conference. The time had gone by when any assembly, ecclesiastical or otherwise, could afford with profit to take no note of those handkerchiefs. For better or for worse, it had gone by. On the day that was to decide matters, he went with my mother and Dr. Lunn, Mr. Heath Mills, and one of the Sisters to Epping Forest, and there, lying on the grass and plucking the leaves, he tided over the hours, while the others talked in snatches. Not the least anxious among the observers of the controversy were the Sisters and missioners. Was the Mission, they wondered, to come to an end, and this new portion of their life to cease almost as soon as it had begun? But these were fears merely, and fears that were not to be justified, for on their return a pile of telegrams was lying on the hall table. All was well at last; Dr. Lunn was to accept the chaplaincy of the Polytechnic and my father and Mr. Pearse could remain in the Mission and in Methodism. The nightmare was at an end, and the valley into which it had thrust him vanished with it. As of yore he walked on the mountain top greeting the first faint lights of promised dawn All with him took deep breaths—shook themselves and awoke. So far seemingly from being dejected by the temporary submersion, it appeared to inspirit him. To the Rev. W. D. Walters, his faithful friend during this period, and with whom he constantly corresponded, revealing his hopes and fears, he wrote as follows :—

"BISHOP'S TEIGNTON, SOUTH DEVON,
"*August* 18, 1890.

"DEAR MR. WALTERS,—I was very glad to hear from you. I do not know how to express properly—I cannot indeed express properly—my deep sense of gratitude to you for your kindness. You have been a true and great friend to me, and, God helping me, I will repay you your kindness and affection. I am distressed to think that you should have suffered in any way from the troubles of the passing hour. I am delighted that you are elected to go to America. . . .

"The more I reflect, the more I am convinced that all that has happened will prove to be for the furtherance of the gospel. We shall have a good year. I fancy I detect a note of anxiety in your letter, but I think there is now no occasion for it.   The people are more with us than ever.   We shall get all the money we want.

"I have booked all the dates you name, including the new one for Hull.   I am keeping myself free to go with you whenever you want me. . . .

"I am greatly indebted to you and Mr. Bunting for the cheque you have collected.   I believe that the attack on me has only brought out the strong sympathy of our people with the London Mission.   I am convinced that the reactionaries have made a great mistake.   By going too far they have already created a reaction in our favour.   We must take full advantage of that everywhere.   There is no occasion for discouragement.   I am sure you may be of good cheer.

"I shall be in London from Thursday, September 5th, to Monday, September 8th.   If in town, you might see me then. —Yours very gratefully and affectionately,

"H. PRICE HUGHES.

"Rev. W. D. Walters."

The letters received by him at this period showed that he represented a body of opinion when he seemed most solitary.

"WESLEYAN CONFERENCE, OLD MARKET STREET CHAPEL,
"BRISTOL, *August* 1, 1890.

"MY DEAR FRIEND,—My heart has been with you in your great trial, and I can't forbear writing to assure you of my love.

"I think you have acted wisely in not coming to Bristol, but I hope you will be at your post at Nottingham.   Don't let this upset or disturb you.   You are enthroned in the hearts of the people, and you can therefore afford to let the attacks of the few pass by unnoticed.   You have the faculty of winning the hearts of all who are associated with you, and that is a priceless gift. . . .

"I hope you are going to take a good long holiday.   *You* must not break down, for the hope of hundreds of us is in you.

"I hope Mrs. Hughes keeps well, and that you obey *her orders* in all things.

"Don't trouble to answer this.   I only want you to know that I am ever—Your faithful friend,

"CHARLES GARRETT.

"*P.S.*—Kind regards to Dr. Lunn."

"8 TAVITON STREET, GORDON SQUARE, W.C.,
"*July* 27, 1890.

"MY DEAR ALLEN,—Your very kind letter is much appreciated by Mrs. Price Hughes and myself. I fully recognise the kindness to me personally which was exhibited both in the course of the debate and in the vote at its close. I think that Dr. Rigg and some others have behaved very handsomely in the closing stages of this long and miserable controversy.

"I cannot help resenting the injustice of stating that I had made charges which I never made, and which I have emphatically repudiated from the first. But I take that in conjunction with some of the speeches and the final vote. I am very thankful that we have saved Lunn. He is a most affectionate and loyal Methodist preacher. God blesses his ministry conspicuously and constantly. I think he will yet prove this to all men.

"Mrs. Price Hughes has, as you anticipate, been greatly troubled during this long controversy. But it has been an immense help to me that one so good and so specially conscientious has approved of my course from first to last.

"Time will remove many misapprehensions.—Yours very gratefully,

"H. PRICE HUGHES."

Thus, like Browning's hero, did he march breast forward. For, in a certain sense, he had experienced a victory. The fact that Methodism could hold him and was going to do so, despite every appearance to the contrary, caused persons to wonder. In a certain sense it was the hour of his triumph. No *faux pas* on his part could prevent the inevitable issue of the lengthy struggle, that Methodism was no more to elude his grip in the lifelong wrestle that he had with her, than any of his other combatants. He offended her dearest prejudices, but she struggled in vain. Yet he was far from being conscious of this at the time. What he did think was, as he had good reason to, that he was through by the skin of his teeth. If so, the greater deliverance and the more reason to give thanks. So on he went breast forward. To opponents I fear it seemed a species of triumphal march. On he goes, they thought, rejoicing, recking little of us on whom in his strength he has trampled, and in so thinking they deceived their own souls. Browning's warrior marches forward undismayed, but it is not told what wounds he bore—rankling, as they must, long after the hero, by his martial appearance, strikes onlookers as scathless. 'Twas very deep, this wound. By such scars are enthusiasts shaped to their task—reminded of the flesh and blood in which it must be wrought.

A general who has made one serious strategical mistake will either lose heart for strategy altogether or never make another. To that latter order my father belonged. The mistake was the finishing stroke of his strategy, which became after this increasingly redoubtable, because, along with the power to act, he came to see more and more the diverse aspects of a situation. His tendency became increasingly not merely to base his operations on a portion of the field, but to be conscious of all the results which a particular movement might entail. Where this apprehension is developed early in life it seems to impede action, but where it gradually evolves from a series of convictions and acts, as it did with my father, it aids it. As previously shown, he took one thing at a time in his youth, and was in no hurry in certain ways, despite his appearance to the contrary. That which was set before him and that which he saw were the determinants of his views and actions. "To see one side strongly," as he replied once early in life to a friend who thought him one-sided, revealed his instinct in the matter. This proclivity was just the necessity for the early portion of his career, particularly as it affected Methodism. To put on blinkers and charge was a necessity if the feat could not be managed any other way, and it was by this insistence in overlooked aspects of things that he set the Forward Movement in motion. It was when he touched on the condition of the Church in the East that this method of strategy proved to be insufficient, and gave the opponents of reform a manifest advantage.

Two articles that have recently appeared in the *Hibbert Journal* on the subject of Indian Missions, indicate afresh and very clearly the complexity of the subject which had to be faced. The writer of the first article makes some of the criticisms that appeared in the *Methodist Times*, and the writer of the second, in a very striking defence (which is the more striking in that imperfections are admitted as well as the advisability of modification in portions of the existing régime), proves how the previous writer based his criticism on certain districts, not on an impartial survey of the whole field, while he lays stress on the fact that a great work has already been accomplished, whose result, particularly in its indirect and unseen aspects, has yet to be seen. To put it briefly, chivalry went out this time against a continent, and a continent, so his opponents said, of which he was imperfectly informed. Thus it was intimated that he would do well to confine his schemes to the western hemisphere, which was vast enough to contain those revolutionary projects on which he brooded. Though such projects were sufficiently conspicuous in his conversation, they were not his characteristic when it came to action. In this connection it is only necessary to cite his attitude towards the three years' system in home policy—that which he used to say, and that which he actually proposed and effected. A locomotive, before starting on its journey, gets up steam, and those who approach certain systems seem to be under the same necessity.

A missionary said to the writer, " If he had had the opportunity of really seeing that which is being effected, of seeing something of the working of that policy which he condemns, he would have become its most enthusiastic supporter." Yet in the same breath he spoke of him as a revolutionary, and as one who had at all costs to be prevented from controlling the affairs of foreign missions. Indeed, to critics as well as opponents, he appeared high-handed, springing proposals upon the public in much the same way as Mr. Gladstone from an imperious solitude had sprung Home Rule upon the country. His mistake, so he afterwards admitted, lay in allowing that to be proposed to the public which should have taken the form of resolutions in committee. Yet, for all this seeming high-handedness, this volcanic atmosphere, for so it appeared to many, the whole *raison d'être* of the controversy lay in nothing but this desire for ventilation and in the popularisation because the free discussion of the missionary cause.

If he had considered his own personal interests he would have let the matter alone altogether, and if he had considered the personal feelings of others, he would not have committed the mistake that he did. As usual, he was bound hand and foot to a cause, and his ideals were imperial, because he thought of Christ as Imperator and claimed empire for Him. In this conception of Christ as Imperator lay the *raison d'être* of missionary enterprise. In his missionary enthusiasm, indeed, lay one of his greatest divergences from the age, for the latter part of the century cannot be described as enthusiastically missionary in the sense that he understood that term. The perplexities and uncertainties of the thought of the time had made themselves felt in all departments of the Christian Church, and in none more than in the support of those activities where certitude of belief and depth of enthusiasm seem to be great essentials. In this, again, his finger was on the pulse of the age. The free discussion that he wished to provoke, for such discussion is enlightenment, would have given opportunities for an exposition of the missionary cause that it was not the object of the special commission to supply. A new generation needed not only a fresh expression of certain doctrines, but an expression, suited to its spirit, of the missionary motive and necessity. Such a generation is awake as it was not formerly to the realities of Western civilisation and what may coexist with the profession of the Christian religion as well as with that of other religions. It is more imaginative than it used to be, and more perplexed. It seeks for enlightenment that it regards as impartial, and obtains it from literature of various kinds. The East, it believes, has something to give to the West, for missionaries and travellers have told them so, and it cannot but be interested to know how Christianity is spread and taught, and how the religions of the East are approached. Yet it was not in any intellectual exposition of the import and value of foreign missions that my father put his trust, but in a great crusading impetus born of the Spirit of God, which should send men and women to the east of the world, as it had sent them to the east and west of London.

Revivals of any kind did not originate, he believed, through intellectualism, but through something unseen and compelling blowing upon the thought and aspirations of men's lives, and turning the tide of them in the direction that it would. Disquisitions did not send men to found the first settlements of the British Empire in the reign of Queen Elizabeth. None the less the outburst of adventure and maritime enthusiasm had its roots in years of silent investigation, by which the mind of man had been deepened and broadened, and its powers led forth to survey fresh fields. Such an outburst in the adventure and ardour of his spirit he seemed to anticipate, as he was wafted on wings which soared above present contingencies.

Before he conversed with Dr. Lunn he had his own views concerning the propagation of Christianity in India, and had long considered, rightly or wrongly, that the educational element was too preponderant, and that the simple and democratic preaching of the gospel, which was more in accordance with the traditions of Christianity and our Lord's commands, was not sufficiently conspicuous in the present régime.

Opposed to him and those who thought like him, was a body of expert opinion which held that he, and those of his thinking, were unacquainted with the complexities of the situation, and with the fact that the Eastern mind may need training in certain directions before it can enter into the Western acceptation of Christianity. A companion spoke to him once with enthusiasm of St. Paul's discourse at Athens, but he replied without enthusiasm to the effect that if the apostle had preached the gospel in the Acropolis as he did else-where, without any special effort to understand the particular mental attitude of his hearers, but only to deliver his message as he felt it and knew it to be, he would not have been so unsuccessful as he was reported. Often also he would exclaim, " Oh that I could go through India with an inter-preter, preaching Christ ! "

In an annual sermon preached to the London Missionary Society in 1889, a year before the articles appeared, he ex-pounded what he considered the successful missionary method, from which the following quotation has been taken :——

" . . . . And I venture to say here, in the presence of many learned theologians,—and I hope they will not be very much shocked, and, if they are, I must still say it,—that, so far as my knowledge of real Christianity goes, no human being was ever either reasoned into Christianity or reasoned out of it. I believe that no man was ever saved by a process of ratiocination. It is as the result of the direct personal intervention of the Spirit of God in the soul, by a divine illumination, by a revelation of Christ, that men are brought back again to God and their Father. I have no

21

doubt that this audience will thoroughly agree with me that we cannot be saved by sacraments. Are we equally agreed that we cannot be saved by syllogisms? I say that neither by sacraments nor by syllogisms can men be saved, but only by the power of the Holy Ghost. The most perilous delusion that possesses many educated men and women in the present day is the delusion that Christianity is a matter of opinion ; that to become a Christian means merely to accept certain opinions ; and that to give up Christianity means to reject those opinions. . . . The Christian ideas which will regenerate human society are rooted in the Christian life. My whole contention this morning is this, that the new ideas of Christianity, which, as I said at the outset, will accomplish all our hopes for our family, for our nation, and for our race,—these new ideas spring out of the New Life. That New Life never has sprung out of them, and never can. But this New Life,—which will necessarily create the new ideas of unselfishness and of highest happiness achieved in accomplishing my neighbour's good, —how is it to be communicated to me? By the miraculous personal intervention of the Holy Spirit. Does the doctrine which I have now laid down teach that there is no scope for the intellect in Christianity? Certainly not. I hold strongly with Dr. Fairbairn that the adequate intellectual expression of the truths and principles and purposes of the Christian religion demands the highest intellect that God has given to man. And in that very epistle to the Corinthians to which I referred you, St. Paul, while repudiating human learning as the cause and condition of salvation, proceeds at once to add, 'We speak wisdom among the perfect' (1 Cor. ii. 6). When the great power of God has laid hold of the human heart and regenerated it, then you have endless scope for the development of all those great ideas which spring up from the New Life, the Divine Life, the Life of Christ communicated to you, and for their embodiment in all the policies of States and all the institutions of human society."

Such words were not the result of instinct or of opinion or bias, but of experience, and it was inevitable that he should look out on life and its problems through the eyes that it brought. What he saw went to form great convictions, and to these he sacrificed most that he cared about.

A just presentment of what was vital in his attitude to this controversy must include the following considerations. First, that so long as the world needed to have the gospel preached to it, he would have considered himself free to discuss the best way of doing it, and to criticise existing methods with a view to improving them. Further, the continual growth and acclimatisation of his mind to fresh aspects and wider views of situations does not allow indiscriminate insistence on any particular opinion that he may have expressed in the heat and difficulty of his position. He would have been the first to own error or limitation of view when he perceived such, for to the end of life he retained the somewhat rare faculty of perceiving what he had not formerly perceived. In other questions he struck men as modifying and indeed contradicting former advocacies; and on the great question of missionary method and organisation he might have similarly struck them if he had lived to aid these as he desired. What is ever worthy of admiration, despite any mistake or misunderstanding into which, in the eyes of some, he may have fallen, is the spirit of the venture, that he thought methods for the propagation of Christ's gospel could be improved, and that he was willing to utterly sacrifice his own interests so as to secure what he considered their greater efficiency.

A mistake of any kind is always a revelation of character, and it revealed his in a variety of lights. It showed, among other things, that while there were wonderful moments when he understood humanity, there were equally wonderful moments when he did not. In great schemes individual men and women would become non-existent to him, *i.e.* they would exist only in relation to the schemes, and with the sensibilities that sprang from such relationship. Thus it never occurred to him that the missionaries would resent the articles, and when it was suggested that they would do so, he at once contradicted the remark. In arguments he would often be the same, and whoever the person with whom he was talking. The fact also that the majority of mankind are not anxious for reform was surprising to him, and his knowledge of the average state of mind seemed to come more by experience than divination. Thus the shock of these months permanently affected him, making him not less ready to act when the necessity arose and bold in doing so, but with the disposition to reflect and halt that sprang from a deeper insight into the average human instinct.

It is probable that those in the Church who play the part of pioneer, and know the difficulties of such a rôle, will, as time goes on, be among the greatest disciples and comprehenders of Hugh Price Hughes. His intensity of spirit, his enthusiasm, and the breadth of his outlook, were so essentially missionary that in many ways it was easier for men on the foreign field to understand him than men at home. A conception of the essential unity underlying the divergences of the Church of Christ and an understanding of alien streams of thought and conditions, is an outcome of missionary labour, and therefore of his. The Methodist Church never had a greater missionary than he. The old missionaries, like Mr. James Calvert, who had sailed over seas to unknown islands to carry the gospel of Christ to those that knew Him not, loved and understood him. They belonged doubtless to a different order, an older generation, but certain kinds of spirits are contemporaries. They cannot wax old, for the nature of the hope and the fire that is within them. Such saw his aims in home policy better than they at home. To both Christ was a great reality, appealing not to one order of men but to many, not necessarily through one channel but through many. The following letter has therefore a peculiar interest :—

"WESLEYAN M. MISSION HOUSE, INDUS (NIGAM),
"GADAVERY VALLEY RAILWAY, DECCAN, INDIA,
"*October* 6, 1903.

"DEAR SIR,—I enclose with this cheque for . . ., contribution to the H. P. H. Memorial Fund from my wife and myself. Mrs. Winters had once the well-remembered pleasure of being his hostess in Monmouthshire. My only meeting with him was in St. James's Hall, when I received from him great kindness and consideration. But I met him weekly in the *Methodist Times*, and that weekly meeting built up in me, as years passed me here in India, a profound respect and reverent love. I came to look on him as the embodiment and inspiration of all that is best in modern Methodism. Week by week, in lonely and not easy labour among Indian Pariahs, there reached me from him, through his paper, some small measure of the inspiration, the enthusiasm which he diffused and kindled so marvellously in the home Churches. I shall be ever his debtor, and hold his memory in grateful affection. I recall, as I think of him, passages from *Rugby Chapel*, which so well described him as perhaps they have described no one else. His harvest is not all gathered yet, and it is not in England only. "The world was his parish" indeed, and over it all his harvest grows still. With exceeding thankfulness for my debt to him I send you this small contribution, and am, sir,—Yours very sincerely,

"CHARLES T. WINTERS.

"J. Bamford Slack, Esq."

He marched "breast forward" the easier and forgot his wounds because he was so forgiving. This was not a virtue; it was his nature. He was made so. As an antagonist it was his most baffling quality, and certainly it was one of the most striking of his characteristics. One of his sisters used often to say, "I have never met a person who feels so deeply as Hugh does and who can forgive so absolutely." When asked how this was, he would reply that he could not remember long enough to be unforgiving. Forgiveness with him was a mental incapacity to harbour certain feelings. He forgave his enemies because he could not do otherwise.

In the autumn of this year, 1890, he was all eagerness to see the New World, to which he was about to pay a five weeks' visit as one of the English representatives at the approaching Methodist Œcumenical Conference in America. Previous to departure with my mother and a small party of friends, he dictated a book of fourteen sermons in one week to his secretary, Mr. Parker. At various times he published four volumes of sermons at the instigation of Dr. Lunn, and not without hesitation. The speed at which his books were written made literary finish impossible, as he was aware, but the excellence and suggestiveness of the matter struck thoughtful men in Methodism and outside it.

"HAMPSTEAD, *April* 4.

"MY DEAR HUGHES,—One hurried 'God bless you' for your book. Anything more clear and pointed and hard pressing on the facts I have seldom seen. I do indeed thank God for it and you.

"Thou almost persuadest me to be a Methodist. But instead of that I hope you may persuade all Methodists to be as yourself.—Yours ever,

"R. F. HORTON."

"Mansfield College, Oxford, *May* 11, 1888.

"Dear Mr. Price Hughes,—I have owed you a letter for some weeks past to thank you in particular for *Social Christianity*. It is a living book; the spirit of its maker lives in it. It is an admirable specimen of how the truth that does not change may be applied to the changed problems of our day. Would that every man who is privileged to speak the great message might do it so vividly and well. But now having discharged my conscience on one point, I have to appeal to you on another. Will you come to our help, and be in our chapel and pulpit in our first term the representative preacher of Methodism? The 3rd or 4th Sundays of November will suit us, or indeed an earlier Sunday were it to you more convenient. If you can give me alternatives it would be more agreeable, but I shall take the day that will suit you best, if it be at all possible. Be sure to come. You know Oxford; Oxford people know much of you. Come to our help.— Believe me, sincerely yours,

"A. M. Fairbairn."

A series of articles on his American impressions denote the usual keen observation and mental activity. He questions and converses with all whom he meets, and is swift, as usual, in drawing and expressing conclusions. In particular, he takes pleasure in the Conference at Washington and in the discussion of those great questions in which the Methodist people were interested. On American journalism he cannot help animadverting :—

"The impression which a European gains of American journalism is that this light-hearted and prosperous people have never yet taken life quite seriously enough. Having obtained without effort and without delay the most prolific and splendid heritage that God ever granted to mortals, they are in danger of acting like all spoiled children. No doubt the awful sorrow of the great war, of which we find many monumental traces everywhere, brought out the serious side of American life, and was overruled for good. But everything is so extremely in favour of the United States that it is difficult enough for this privileged people to avoid the intoxication of success. It is not unnatural that Europeans, who have passed through centuries of strife and suffering, and who have had all the realities of life presented to them in their sternest forms, should be a little irritated at the superficial flippancy of the ever-prospering Yankee. But those who take the trouble to look a little below the surface can find an extremely kind and tender heart as well as an astonishing intellectual versatility. Nevertheless, I already realise why Matthew Arnold, when he came here, dwelt so much on conduct as the essence of life, and why Mr. Herbert Spencer, with that keen vision of his, said that the one peril of the United States was, that amid unprecedented commercial prosperity they might not sufficiently realise the importance of personal and national character. But it is surely the mission of the American Church to guard against this inevitable temptation, and they will have no excuse if they fail. Religion here is free, and the ministers of religion are treated with great respect everywhere. A small but significant illustration of this has just come under my notice. The great railway companies in this part of the continent furnish all settled pastors with a ticket, which enables them to travel everywhere at half-price. This offer is not given in response to an appeal, but is gratuitously sent at the beginning of the year to every pastor. On this continent ministers of the Prince of Peace have the same facilities for railway travelling that are given in England to soldiers in the British army."

Perhaps my father never had better listeners and sincerer admirers than among this " light - hearted and prosperous people." His personality and command of language made a great impression upon them. At every turn he displayed what they are pleased to call a " live man "; his trick of putting things causing reflection. What startled them were his descriptions of the advance of British Methodism and the inauguration of the London Mission. Americans, he insisted, did not realise how behindhand they were.[1]

" If we could stay here for many months," he writes in the Journal, " we should not be able to accept all our invitations." Nothing surprised him more than the great distances on that continent. He had no idea till he got there how long it took to get from one place to another. That was why he could go to comparatively few places, he explained. At Boston he stayed with Bishop Hamilton, whose society and hospitality both my parents greatly enjoyed. The bishop, in his anxiety for the comfort of his guests, was found one morning bearing off their boots in order to clean them—a bit of New World courtesy for which the Old has hardly a parallel. As regards the literary associations of the city, I do not think they ever

[1] Some of his most characteristic conversations were conducted with Americans, who delighted to listen to him even when he attacked Protection. He was a great Free Trader, and would argue *in extenso* on that theme. What seemed to offend him in Americans was their ideal of personal piety, which was " shallow," he said, and not to be compared with the English ideal. What pleased him was the special honour in which, he thought, the American mother was held.

specially appealed to him. I never heard him quote Emerson, though Lowell he greatly admired.

The humour of Americans he much appreciated, and would often repeat stories illustrative of it. A negro service which they attended in the South much impressed both my parents. " One old woman suddenly commenced leaping from her seat high into the air like a kangaroo. It was most extraordinary," he said. At Washington he went to White House and shook hands with the President, " a gentleman in plain black clothes, unguarded, holding out his hand to us all." That sight seemed to impress him more than anything in America except the Pilgrims' Rock at Plymouth. Yet with all the courtesy of his hosts, and the superior advantages of a democratic country, he was quite impatient to be back again in the city which he loved, and to which his life was given.

CHAPTER XIV

CITIZENSHIP IN LONDON

" Oh, clear-eyed Soul !
        That saw the light undimmed above the mists
        That blinded worldly eyes because it knew
        The rule of Right one with the law of God."

" In evangelical circles the recoil from the collectivism of the Latin Church has been so great, that the teaching of orthodox pulpits has become excessively individualistic. The manhood of England has been largely alienated from the organised Churches because we have been so absorbed by the interests of the individual soul as to neglect the woes of society, and so preoccupied with the delights of heaven as to overlook some of the most urgent duties of earth. As Mr. Ruskin has well said, 'If our religion is good for anything, it is good for everything.' If our religion is not a conventional sham, it is as suitable for Monday and Saturday as for Sunday. The ethical teaching of Christ is applicable to business, pleasure, and politics, as well as to prayer-meetings and sacraments. The great defect has been our failure to apply the principles of Christ fearlessly and thoroughly to the daily lives of men and peoples."

My Father's Introduction to the First Report of
The West London Mission.

ON one aspect of the age of chivalry comment has not yet been made, and it was the aspect in which many Londoners best knew Hugh Price Hughes. In that period for the first time the Metropolis entered into some kind of municipal consciousness of itself. The so-called City of London had survived in its centre, as a historic memorial, with its peculiar usages and privileges, but it was a mere pin-point in the vast conglomeration of cities within cities which stretched for miles around it, in ignorance for the most part of their own interests or each other's boundaries.

The formation of the directly popularly elected assembly known as the London County Council, was the realisation, in

part at any rate, of the dreams of thinkers and reformers, who
had long advocated some kind of unification, and certainly
so able and representative a body had never before sat to
consider the needs of the Metropolis.   Its first session took
place in 1888, the year after my father came to London,
and 8 Taviton Street throbbed with the event.   While the
spectacle of Professor Green sitting in the Oxford Town
Council had moved my father to enthusiasm, still more did
that of Lord Rosebery, Sir John Lubbock, and John Burns
sitting on the new County Council for London.

The new County Council and the Parish Councils introduced in Sir Henry Fowler's Bill six years later (also a
" famous victory "), seemed to stand as a kind of expression
of and incitement to the ideals of a group of patriotic and
unselfish citizens, who gave the Metropolis in their imaginings
and teachings a certain corporate form, a tangibility which in
its previous undefined vastness it had hitherto lacked.   Of this
group my father was one, its not least remarkable feature
being the leading place assigned to certain ministers of religion.
Lord Rosebery, who was the first chairman of the new Council,
began to speak of the disconnected millions of all nations
and creeds, as statesmen and writers have spoken of Paris or
Edinburgh, or, in older days, of Rome.

Writers and statesmen had also written of London in days
gone by, but literary tradition was associated with the small
area called the City, or with some suburb or neighbourhood
that had completely changed its character.   Even Dickens,
who had written with more vividness and accuracy than any
other writer of the London of the early Victorian era, was out
of date.   Whole localities had undergone transformation since
his day, not to mention a leap of millions in the population.
My father would often remark on the changes that he had
seen in its thoroughfares, and listening omnibus drivers would
nod their heads in profound acquiescence, verifying what he
said, and producing fresh instances of the rapidly changed
and changing city in which they were driving.   For with the
new municipal régime transformation and improvements went
on apace.   When anyone compared London with any of the
Continental cities to its disadvantage, my father would always
exclaim, " Oh, but you don't know how it is being improved,"

and he would quote what his friends the omnibus drivers had told him. Thus beyond even reflective circles, London was felt to be in some kind of transformation. Her face was changing.

The great force that throbs during all those years is this same magic London. My father was always full of it. When he came back from a journey or from a holiday abroad, his head was out of the cab window, recognising and drinking in familiar sights and sounds, like the hero of a novel when he returns to his native village. "Oh, I delight to be back in London," he would say. Everything paled and fell into shadow before the mighty import of that name. The word "season," as used by society, filled him with a spirit of disgust. "They are a drop," he would say, "in the ocean. What difference does it make to the real inhabitants of London!" "Is it not good for trade?" somebody would ask. "No, anything but; most pernicious—ruins it, in fact; the whole system is loathsome." Once, at any rate, he must have walked in Hyde Park at this period, for he said that the sight made him deadly sick, and that he always did his best to avoid the place.

After "Home Rule," no burden of his prophecy so impressed listeners. Home Rule, indeed, came to be a spectral apparition, compared with this beating, full-blooded, ever-present, mighty Being which my father called London. It figured in his speech, his sermons, his work, so that all other life seemed petty compared to it.

What was the Being exactly? Very clearly, it was not the Being about which many others spoke—a place where there were shops and places of amusement, and a great crowd. It partly stood for great historic associations, and for a place where the morning papers came first thing, so that a person felt in touch with everybody and everything—an excellent spot in which to observe an interesting planet. But that was not the London about which he spoke in St. James's Hall, or wrote with such fire in the Journal.

The key was first supplied by an incident which impressed itself on memory, and which at the time was not understood. Once in quite early days, on the top of the tram going up to Hampstead Heath, he pointed out a row of grey houses and artisans' model dwellings on the side of the road. " Every window," he said, "represents human beings. I often think of the life and suffering that they all mean. The thought of what may be going on within haunts me."

If it had been on the Thames, and he had pointed out the Houses of Parliament, and the Law Courts, and the great houses that adorn its banks, it would have been easier to understand. There was life to wonder and dream over indeed. What is fair to look upon, or historic, appeals to the imagination of youth; but in those vistas of grey undecipherable households, what was there to arouse emotion or sentiment? The lives within were surely grey and undecipherable, not striking, dramatic, full of colour and wonder, like those of whom the poets and novelists told. Gradually it came home, impressions linked themselves. It was the people of London about whom my father and his coadjutors and the Sisters supremely cared.

It was not the people who came up for the season and drove about the park (though many of these needed profoundest sympathy), nor was it the governors of the Empire and its litterateurs in the West End (they were a " mere handful " and " a minority "), it was the people in the grey undecipherable dwellings, stretching by the thousand to all points of the compass. The houses and the foot-passengers seemed to suggest the advance of that democracy about which he had dreamt as a young man, and concerning which he persistently warned his own Church. Thus the pages of the Journal during the early years of its existence bespeak a writer both brooding over and possessed by such a conception.

Nothing more clearly illustrated his attitude than his reflections in the year 1892, on the occasion of the death of the Duke of Clarence, a short time before his eagerly anticipated marriage. The dormant emotionalism of the Metropolis was stirred to its depths. Neither the daily press nor private individuals seemed to find sufficient means to express their grief and sympathy. Numbers, quite outside any society pretensions, went into mourning, and the very sweet-shops made sweets in mourning colours. That my father entered into the tragedy was evident, for he spoke with suppressed feeling of the bereaved mother and bride. Yet, in the depths of his heart, he half-deprecated, half-envied, all this nation's treasure of emotion and sympathy poured upon a princess, however much she might need and merit it. The day was surely coming when the passionate sympathy and under-standing accorded to the griefs of princes and princesses—the few—would be lavished upon the joys and sufferings of the dim millions, which art had not consecrated. Like Whitman, he wanted some master of the imagination who should illumin-ate and embalm the joys and sorrows of the multitude. So readers of the Journal were surprised, or the reverse, according to their knowledge of the editor, when an imperious leader appeared one Thursday morning entitled " Wanted a Poet."

The reason why he accorded sympathy to writers with great circulations in England, and to Tolstoy and Zola (in his later novels) in Europe, was because they had written for the needs of the people, and felt great social sympathies. They had a gospel not only for the individual and the privileged individual, but for society at large. He would say of such— a favourite saying of his—" the iron has entered into their souls." That was often his answer to what appeared highly reasonable remarks. The later novels of Zola—*La Débâcle*, *Lourdes*, *Paris*, *Rome* — he appreciated because the writer suffers and feels for the starved, the houseless, and the toilers. His marvellous descriptive power took such a tender tinge when it dealt with these. Into the soul of Tolstoy also the iron had entered.

With Mr. Hall Caine, the novelist, he had some interesting correspondence, which appears at the end of this chapter. The publication of his novel *The Christian*, based on many years of study of life in West London and Soho, caused considerable sensation, sections of the public denying the cor-rectness of the picture, saying " the colouring was too high." This, my father emphatically denied, maintaining that what Mr. Hall Caine saw and reported was seen daily by his agents and the Sisters. Society did not like the bare naked truth of things, and he for one was glad that they should see it for once. The persons who so sorely resented the process were evidently in the greatest need of it.

Victor Hugo's *Les Misérables* seemed to be his favourite novel. It appealed to him and moved him to the core, as perhaps no other novel ever did. He read it in a species of agony, yet the exclamation would burst from him at intervals, "Victor Hugo really knew the meaning of Christianity; I am sure he was a Christian; he really understood it!" Zola's realism was by no means approved of by him, nor was it possible that one so idealist in his conceptions of life and its great issues, so fastidious in taste, should approve of a writer who read men and life on their lowest side, and did not hesitate to show it. Speaking of one of his earlier novels, he said, "I really could not read it, it was so unspeakably loathsome, I flung it from me with disgust." Of course my father was by no means alone in his passion for the people. Others very different from him in their habits of mind shared it also. But there was a peculiar Hebraic intensity in his passion which few understood.

What of the soul of this people? Like the old prophets, he longed for the days when peace and righteousness should abound and the sound of lamentation should be heard no more. Oh, that lamentation, long agonised, reiterated, and the sin and selfishness that lay at its root! In an age when, among refined circles at any rate, it was not fashionable to estimate unduly that element in affairs, and when the mention of the word sin would bring a smile to certain lips as an old-fashioned conception which the modern world had long left behind it, he was torn within at the sight and the approach of evil. This old-fashioned abhorrence of the social atmosphere and tenets of life that make unrighteousness possible, accounted for much of his denunciatory language, which opponents, with justice, sometimes considered unprovoked. But in the light of things as they are, a light which the common judgment is apt to set aside, many of his strong utterances should appear in a wonderful, not to say highly reasonable, light. This does not mean that he did not at times overstate views, or that all his inferences on a subject were always justified. If he had graduated the scale more, it would have been more telling in certain instances. But such criticisms—what are they? There are thousands who can nicely adjust and dissect the blame attaching to social evils, by their fireside, to one who will go forth and denounce it, and insist that justice shall be done.

It was that quality more than anything else that made it

the age of chivalry. When anything was done contrary to its knightly code—women dishonoured or youth imperilled— his action recalled those impetuous figures of romance who are galloping down the highroad before most people have taken in the news. A fig for caution and prudence, for the taunts and exclamation of the concourse lining the route—for the effect produced on powerful persons—for what was really the most moderate and therefore, so they said, the wisest course to take.[1] That is always the way of love. When the child cries, the mother does not listen to the advice of the sensible people standing by who say that the child has nothing to cry about, but she runs to the child. That little group of persons who manage to see Lazarus and his relations at the gate, and to give them something more than the crumbs, really get to feel for them with something of that unreasonable feeling that the mother has for her child. Between them and the onlookers there is something irreconcilable, and no amount of argument can heal the breach.

How he managed in those charges to evade the law of the land was sometimes startling, but he did. His father, an anxious observer at times of his son's conduct, would often say, "I am always expecting Hugh to do something fatally rash, but he never does." To many of his contemporaries, indeed, he appeared to be for ever not only standing on a precipice, but inducing them to jump over it with him. It was just this staying power in rashness, the look that he some- how managed to give before he leapt, that was the uniqueness of him. It reminded of a mettlesome steed with the light hand of its master on the bridle, who would draw him up on his haunches, sooner than let him get out of bounds.

A leader that he wrote *à propos* of the imprisonment of Mr. Stead entitled, "The Justice of Mr. Justice Lopes," has been mentioned as perilously near contempt of Court. If he was on the right side of the law, it was by a hair's breadth. In any case, the law showed no inclination to extend its mighty arm in his direction.

On this occasion, as on others, he remained curiously unscathed. Men wondered at it. The things that ought to

[1] After he was gone people used to exclaim, "Oh for an hour of Hugh Price Hughes!"

have befallen him did not. He appeared to come forth from each fray only the mightier for impediments that had been thrust in his path. His strength was seen to consist in a terrific power of appealing to certain sentiments in the bystanders. So it came to be felt that he was one of the strongest and most forcible religious personalities living. People speculated sometimes as to what would have happened, if all that force of his in appealing to the underlying moral sentiments in men and women had been directed, say for his own personal ends, or to sentiments nearer the surface than the often submerged moral.

Observers noted that he was for ever permitting the reining in of that fiery steed of a man's wishes and inclinations, and praying God that he might be saved from caring a jot about anything tending to personal aggrandisement. He had seen into himself as a youth, and since then, and he trusted to Christ to cleanse and purify him. Hence a deep humility that often surprised people. " You ought not to have said that to So-and-so," some one would say, in a position to thus address him. " You don't know all the circumstances of the case, and it sounded unjust and will give people a wrong idea."

" What were the circumstances ? "

Then later—" Well, I will speak to So-and-so on the matter ; I am very sorry to have misunderstood or misrepresented the case in any way—very, very sorry."

Thus his heart, for all his seeming imperiousness, was very humble as he rode along into the highway, and though several men did not accredit him with that humility, they did feel the purity of motive which it engendered.

If that intense realisation of sin helped to arm him for the contest, so also did it send him out upon the field. At times the weight of what he saw and heard and felt weighed upon him past bearing. " I wish," he said once to the present superintendent of the Mission, as he met him in Taviton Street, " that we could start a guild to agonise over the sins and sorrows of London." Perhaps the aspect of the street and the neighbouring squares, so suggestive of the four-walled respectability of the middle class, had something to do with the remark. He grasped a companion once by the arm and exclaimed with a gesture that swept the neighbourhood, " They never see realities, these people, never "—an assertion which he repeated with the profoundest conviction. Sweeping his listener with his eye, he continued, " From time to time, Death enters into their midst, when they have some contact with reality, but only then. It is the one occasion." The assertion was undoubtedly sweeping, and if the listener had been intent on what my father would have called " technical details," exceptions might have been mentioned, but it would not have interfered with the significance of the remark, and the criticism of British four-walled life that it implied.

To his spirit apprising and weighing what observant eyes so continuously looked out upon, the bevy of children and their chattering elders closing the square gate behind them, seemed at times to be removed from the great actualities. For the most part, he felt, they knew not the things that pertained to their peace. He lived essentially among classes of men and women, and his judgments were passed upon them, not the individuals, to whom he was surprisingly lenient, and by whom, to quote the family's view of the case, " he could be easily taken in."

The individual was a creature struggling, however vainly, amid the toils of environment ; but the class, its predilections and its selfishness, its social atmosphere, was something to be attacked, and without mercy. The mention of any individual chattering lady would recall him to a land of query and tender surmise. Some of the gentlemen also with whom he was personally acquainted who lived in squares were most excellent of their kind, possessing virtues of heart and head which he would have died to maintain.

If only members of the classes whom he arraigned could have been brought up before him one by one, and either, by the aid of a judicious interpreter, or still more in their own tongue, have given an account of their struggles from the beginning, he would have been a most sympathetic listener, their dauntless champion against the critics who understood them not. At the same time, in the weekly issues of the Journal, he would have discharged a whole battery instead of one cannon at the particular section of society to which they belonged. Many people are misunderstood in the world, but

22

social reformers most of all. They keep watch at Gethsemane while the rest sleep.

In 1890 there was a struggle in connection with the London County Council, whose inauguration he had so welcomed and whose proceedings he had followed with the closest attention. This attention was part of the puzzle of contemporaries. What business was it of his? To such queries he never replied, leaving it along with other questions to that future state of existence when there would be "added illumination." Certainly from his method of procedure he seemed to have no fears but that the "added illumination" would only go to prove his favourite maxim that everything was everybody's business, particularly in municipal affairs. His zeal, indeed, in this latter was so intense that witty journalists queried, "What would happen to London and all of us if Mr. Price Hughes were not here? We should go to the dogs every one."

In 1889, Mr. John M'Dougall, since Chairman of the Council in 1902, but then a private member, took action as a member of the Theatres and Music Hall Committee in regard to the character of entertainments given at the Music Halls, which created the most violent opposition and ridicule in polite as well as in less fastidious circles. Performers, Mr. M'Dougall alleged, made additions to the songs set down on the programme, which were of a highly objectionable character, so that a modern "Colonel Newcome," with all his love of a good song, would have marched out his young son almost at the beginning of the performance. Not that the social reformers in this case had much thought of the good Colonel, though he occurs as a parallel.

My father, at any rate, who early leapt into the lists, was thinking, not of Colonel Newcome, but of the artisan and the toiler in the indistinguishable dwellings to which reference has been made, and very particularly of his sons and daughters —also toilers. While still in their teens, these add their quota to the family revenue. On coming out of work at night they are as eager for amusement and relaxation as their youth and cramped conditions entitle them to be, and the streets and places of amusement are their one outlet. Any historian of the "people" of London in this age has to deal with the growing popularity of these places of amusement, their growing importance in the life of those whose early imagination is fired and moulded by what they see and hear within them.   Each Music Hall has to apply for a licence to the County Council, and the question which arose in 1890 was whether the licence should be granted in those cases where performances had been of the questionable character indicated, and later, whether or not intoxicating drinks were to be sold in the promenade.   The alleged delight of these places of amusement lies in the freedom that it allows to tired business or working men.   Smoking is permitted, a man is free to yawn and stretch his legs and to go out and to come in just as he pleases.   The entertainments are short, varied, intended to amuse, and no strain is made upon tired brains.   In fact, to many an Englishman, whether he would class himself with the people or not, the Music Hall form of entertainment seems to be a necessity when he lives in a city.

It was no wish of the group of social reformers indicated to interfere with the class of entertainment that the needs of the populace demanded.   If a minority had tastes which considered certain representations vulgar, or not calculated to edify the minds of onlookers, this was their way of regarding it ; but the populace was entitled, so my father and his friends considered, to see and hear anything that would give them pleasure, provided that nothing was said or done that was distinctly pernicious.   That was his sole contention, an atmosphere not of refinement or elevation, but, as far as possible, of purity, of that atmosphere which the middle classes of England have so wonderfully infused into their home-life.   By the way Mr. John M‘Dougall and his friends were lampooned and attacked they might have wished to deprive the average Englishman of every form of recreation and music.   Persons who previously had not cared in the least to exercise themselves concerning these pleasures suddenly took up arms in defence of them.   As for milk-livered Puritanism, it was the curse of the community, and it was high time that the fellows who fostered it should get back to their psalm-singing.   Moreover, they were misinformed absolutely.   That which they represented to take place, did not.   The milk-livered in consequence left their psalm-singing, and attired in strange habiliments, paid visits to the places of amusement under consideration, so as to see with their own eyes, and hear with their own ears, what went on, and thus bring personal testimony to strengthen their case. They thus added spying to that of their other iniquities.

Nothing was lost upon my father. Every nerve was strained to catch what he regarded as a form of interpretation of the people of the great city. Not all of it, he thought, interpreted them; that was the devil's version of the case. Christ saw them as sheep without a shepherd, and the shepherd must weed out the poison from this particular pasture. For himself, with his fastidious taste, mingled though it was with that broad perception of the comic in things which appeals to elemental persons, he would have wished the pasture otherwise, but that was neither here nor there, while average humanity, thanks to unfaithful shepherds, remained as it was.

The opera in Naples where the fishermen and their sweethearts came to hear the singers, and fill the place with their plaudits, or the old Greek theatre in the open air, was more the thing, he thought. He never went to a theatre in London, deeming it incompatible with his position, and with what was to him the very intricate question of what is called the stage problem. "The worst account I have ever heard of the stage is from people on it," he would say. The present conditions of life on the stage from all he could learn of it were far from satisfactory, but he was very guarded on the point, not laying down rules for others in the matter. For the dramatic art, apart from its contemporary conditions, he had undoubtedly the intensest appreciation, responding to it with the intensity of the Celt in such matters.

Among personal deprivations, that of witnessing fine plays finely performed was undoubtedly one. He would comment with admiration on Sir Henry Irving's elevating influence on the modern stage. Towards the end of his life he said, "What a pity it is that I cannot witness plays such as those performed by Irving and Tree. They would divert and instruct my mind and be such a real recreation to me.

"A busy person like myself is just the one who would greatly profit and be diverted by such plays—greatly." The idea seemed to strike him as something altogether fresh in the horizon of fact. Yet he would none the less say, "The London stage is one. We cannot differentiate." Despite all his love of drama in its true sense, he was deeply aware of what he considered its seamy side, as well as of the travesty of true drama that many modern Londoners go to see. His perusal of the newspapers, and his wakefulness regarding all that persons had to report on the matter, made him form his own conclusions. The answer given to all in the Mission who inquired concerning theatre-going was as follows:—"If you find it a hindrance to your communion with Christ, you ought not to indulge in it." There were times, undoubtedly, when his contact with the London stage in its wide sense and its reality made him assume an uncompromising attitude, while at others the innate love of drama and a desire for a high form of it in this country, would lead to a remark so appreciative as that just quoted. "It wants altogether putting on a different basis," he would exclaim; "the State ought to take it in hand." A well-known stage-manager once sent him an invitation to a play of a religious character. He mentioned the incident as one half-pleased, though most clearly it had not entered his head to accept it. If there was one saying of the Apostle Paul which he rated higher than the others it was this, "All things are lawful unto me, but all things are not expedient." For himself and the missioners, there was, he considered, one answer—the weaker brother and sister, for whom society in its various forms cared so little. For the same reason he abstained from wine. The result of his influence on people was to lessen their participation in such things, not because he forbade or opposed it, but because he gave them something else to do and to think about. Fidus Achates said to a friend, "I never used to go to London without hearing Irving, but now I cannot find the time." He shifted the proportion of men's desires and estimates, making that of much account which was hitherto nil, and *vice versâ*.

His conclusions on those evenings in 1890 when he came face to face with the amusements of the populace, might have been summarised as follows: "Pasture they must have, but weeded of certain poisonous growths." Then, "May we professing Christians of London suffer torment, if we don't speak up and uphold M'Dougall in this matter, though all the rascality of the place make waxen images of every one of us, and burn us in effigy seven times over! The early Christians gave their bodies to be burned for His sake, and we are too thin-skinned to abide even a jeer, and so occupied in our business and pleasure and household matters and good works and what not, that we do not discern His Spirit going forth to war, nor do we follow in His train. For Christus is Imperator in places of amusement as well as in places of worship, and we must not keep Him from His kingdom." Such reflections were communicated to the Journal, whose artillery was in full action. Once indeed it seemed that he would get involved in a libel action, but with his usual good fortune he just escaped doing so. As if to justify the taunts of certain of his opponents, he took care that the praying and psalm-singing should be unabated. Doubtless he considered that such a campaign would not only be a failure without it, but one on which human beings could not dare to venture without invoking the Divine aid.

One Friday night after he had been both beseeching God and exhorting the missioners on this matter at a late prayer-meeting at Lincoln House, his colleague, Mr. Mark Guy Pearse, suggested that a meeting should be held on the following Friday, at St. James's Hall, to support Mr. John M'Dougall in his campaign. My father at once adopted this suggestion, and said to his younger colleague, " Go first to the Bishop of London and ask him to take the chair, and if he cannot, ask Cardinal Manning or Archdeacon Farrar." Whereupon his colleague sped from his presence, and he has thus reported what ensued. The Bishop of London, the late Dr. Temple, a great Temperance advocate and a friend to all good causes, did not feel justified in accepting the leading position involved without first consulting some of his clergy, who should, he thought, be considered, before the official representative of their Church plunged into such a controversy, when much was being said on both sides, and of a violent character. The Cardinal said, " If the bishop has a reason against taking the chair I have eighty. For I am fourscore, and an old man, and in my time I have done what I could for London and her people. This is not a position for me." Archdeacon Farrar also declined. When Dr. Lunn returned with these replies, my father stifled an exclamation. "Fetch me," he said, "pen, ink, and paper; if Manning will not, the bishop must."

Without hesitation he indited an epistle to his Lordship, the purport of which was something as follows: One primate in Christ's Church did most heartily implore his brother of London in remembrance of their ever victorious Head and of those great and signal gifts in His service, for which his brother of London had so long been distinguished, and in the keenest appreciation of which he now wrote to add yet another service to their long and valiant roll. The writer prayed Almighty God that he might take the present crisis in affairs to heart, and despite the hesitation that prudence might well necessitate, to cast it all to the winds in defence of the moral welfare of the thousands of the city, which the official representatives of Christ's Church were there in a very special sense to guard. Let him not fail, but give his imprimatur to what Christians were praying for, amidst the opposition of the upholders of iniquity. Let the Church of Christ speak now with no uncertain voice in the thick of the fight, when her voice heard by all might rally good men under her banner to insist on purity, and to sweep away all that would hinder the youth of the great city from being acceptable in Christ's most blessed sight. The letter is not word for word, as no copy of it has, unfortunately, been preserved, but that this was the main purport his colleague is able to verify. In any case he thought it, while he wrote it, which is the main consideration.

The bishop read the letter carefully, and then said, "I cannot promise to be present in the chair on Friday night, but so far as my own personal wishes and desires are concerned, I shall be. You can give it out that I hope to take the chair"; and he did, which showed that the one who received the letter was as much in the age of chivalry as the one who wrote it. My father knew that this was so when he called for the pen, ink, and paper, for in crises he generally knew to whom he was writing and talking. Thus the whole episode is a singularly pleasing one. The meeting was largely attended both by the milk-livered and their opponents, the former showing themselves possessed of a strength of muscle that considerably impressed those who had not previously regarded them in that light, and of which more hereafter. Suffice it to say that those who tried to interrupt the speakers rapidly found themselves in the cool night air, and at liberty to air their objections to their hearts' content.

This indomitable attitude on my father's part, which caused such a stir both on this and other occasions, was his continuously, ever since the days when he had burst into tears on the platform at Dover.

The trend of public affairs would from time to time reveal him in this ever-watchful, uncompromising attitude; it was an attitude and a warfare maintained throughout life. After the release of Mr. Stead, a society was formed by citizens who took such things to heart, and who endeavoured to maintain and protect the moral well-being of the community. With the inauguration of this society my father had a good deal to do, and he sat on one committee formed specially for that purpose in London, as did my mother. The Journal was ever in the arena echoing, perhaps as well as any contemporary paper, the sentiments of the group to whom allusion is made. The degree of force in the editorials always depended on the circumstances of the case. When he felt the world to be unusually scornful and apathetic, and the saints absenting themselves from the contest, under the pretext of false modesty, or the satanic plea of attending to their own business and nobody else's, his denunciation was unstinted, and the superlatives in which he found relief, unbounded. A New Zealand Methodist newspaper commenting on what it considered the "hysterical" character of the Journal at times, remarked in explanation that nobody can recite "The Charge of the Light Brigade" unless they see the battalions of the Russians, a gift in which the editor was never deficient. No one knew the enemy better than he. The shrug, the smile, the sophism, inflamed him as he wrote. The youth of the community would drink in what they said, and the devil be securer than ever. Everything was explained, glossed over, except the great What Was, the hideous facts and realities of the case, which the superficial were so careful to avoid, while the enemy entrenched themselves, misleading the public. Thus he flung superlatives, instead of arrows, into their midst. Yet few men were less stirred by personalities in great contests than he was, for when he fought he was hugely impersonal. A figure or figures appeared on the ramparts of that which he was attacking, and the artillery played freely in their direction. That was all. If they manned such ramparts or appeared to do so, they must take the consequences, and friends or relatives would have formed no exception. Yet, on the other hand, when certain accusations were common property against a well-known member of the Radical party, he refused to condemn, till the Courts had given their anticipated decision, restraining his own party in the usual manner.

The efforts and watchfulness of this party, of which he was one, were not limited to the Metropolis, but extended over that Empire of which it was the centre. Whether they ever made a mistake—and in all great and complicated ventures mistakes must be made—was of slight import compared with the presence of that religious spirit which underlay their endeavours, and particularly his. The indirect result of their endeavours was probably equal to their direct outcome. It was not only that the entertainments in Music Halls were perceptibly weeded of decidedly objectionable features; but West London knew that this party was in their midst, and wrestled with them. One who was intimately acquainted with the fashionable Bohemian side of West London life said of my father, " He has not only organised a great work among the very poor, but he has been a voice crying in the great wilderness of London, ' Repent !' Fearlessly and bravely, in the very midst of the cultured classes, he has denounced the sins which are the very ruin of modern England, and the pitfall of our nation." That was the true description—"a voice crying in the wilderness "—so that whatever men and women did and thought, they could not but hear it.

A tenet which he held in flat defiance of the general opinion was that men in public life, and leaders of parties, should be men of spotless reputation. Indeed, his influence in public affairs, and in representing sections of the community, may be said to have reached its visible climax in such an insistence, for it was then that he impressed the world, which venerates force and power of any kind, even when it greatly dislikes the form of it. Yet few would have foreseen that the

man to insist on the abdication of the leader of the Home
Rule party would be Hugh Price Hughes, conspicuous among
the Protestant ministry in his support of the Home Rulers and
their leaders. The memory of this period is a vivid one. Mr.
O'Brien's imprisonment and subsequent release in the spring of
1889 again brought the banner of Home Rule to the forefront
of the family horizon, and there was joy accordingly. Despite
the fact that Mr. O'Brien and his partisans had appeared amid
acclamation in the neighbourhood of Euston Station, while the
family decked in green watched the triumph from Endsleigh
Gardens, a cloud seemed to have fallen on their cause—the
rage of opponents reducing itself to vague threats and imputations, a knowing something that they would not reveal. The
Times newspaper, also, had been violently engaged in piling
on the clouds which had suddenly and wondrously dispersed
owing to the intervention of Sir Charles Russell, who had
"smashed Pigott to bits," and proved the whole accusation a
forgery and a hallucination. Thus rejoicing had redoubled.
Parnell was blameless, a meet leader, when suddenly the
heavens began to darken again and the heads of opponents
to wag with unmistakable significance. On an afternoon in
November my father was pacing up and down the dining-
room in Taviton Street, with Dr. Lunn as usual in attendance, and their conversation was not of the missionary
controversy, which was then waging, but of something quite
different.

The situation was as follows. The divorce suit in which
Mr. Parnell was co-respondent, and which had been hanging
over him for nearly a year, had occupied the Court for two
days (November 15–17), with the result that his friends had
feared. Their leader did not attempt a defence of any kind,
and the political world was thrown into considerable agitation.
The Irish, as was natural, were determined to stand by him at all
costs, while the Liberals were in some quandary and uncertain
as to how to act, for the General Election was at hand, and
they did not want to lose the votes of the large body of
citizens who would deeply resent Mr. Parnell's retention of the
Irish leadership. Yet, on the other hand, he was acknowledged
by all to have done splendid service for the Irish party and to
have been a magnificent leader, and it was felt that his abdica-

tion would seriously affect the prospects of Home Rule.   The Liberals were thus in a state of hesitancy waiting for some pressure from without—some act on Mr. Parnell's own part which should relieve the situation.   By Mr. Gladstone and those in his confidence a letter from the Irish leader was hourly expected announcing his resignation.   Some temporary withdrawal from public life was urged by certain of his own followers, who pressed upon him the wisdom of such a course, which would by no means preclude, they felt, a return at a later date, when the public mind had recovered from the shock of recent disclosures.   Home Rule had produced such cleavage, such political passion in the community, and Mr. Parnell himself had latterly in particular been so constantly before the public, that the crisis was exceptional, and one which without definite action of some kind it was impossible to tide over.   Opponents did not conceal their exultation, and politicians looked anxiously towards two classes—the Romanist leaders in Ireland and the Nonconformist leaders in England.   These were known to have scruples on such matters, and the general public, as well as the wire-pullers, were awaiting their verdict—the sound of those voices which lead and express the views of masses of men in a democratic era.   Mingled with the general feeling of consternation at the duplicity which the Courts had revealed, there was among men of any sensibility a compunction for the offender, a feeling that there were elements in the case which rendered it exceptional. Many also, while rejoicing unfeignedly at the discomfiture of a party, were too much aware of the general life and its problems to lay special stress on the present one.   Such was the state of men's feeling as my father walked up and down the dining-room on November 17th, the day when the Court gave its decision.

Parliament was to open in a week (November 25th), and the evening papers were circulating the news.   The current caricatures of my father always represented him with something of a distracted appearance—eyebrows knit to excruciation, and the look of one who was fighting foes within as well as those without.   Certainly he was thus that afternoon, every line and movement betraying that distress which the popular imagination had accorded him.   As he paced up and down, his eyes

fixed on the carpet, he repeated with almost dirge-like monotony a phrase which was soon to become general, " Parnell
must go.   We cannot help it, but he must go."   From time
to time he stopped at the window, surveying the opposite
houses with unseeing gaze and lost apparently in prayer.
Full well this time he saw the enemy charging, for there was
that in his humanity which charged with them—so he prayed.
Men of heart and conviction do not give their support—moral
or active—to a man and a party without sharing in the dismay
that accompanies their sins and calamities.   Tragedies are
great in so far as they engulf those who are not immediately
concerned with them.   What men would say he already heard,
and he wrestled with them in advance.   Of Ireland as yet he
scarcely dared to think, save that the cup of her sorrow was
one drop the fuller.   " Parnell," said his companion, " will fight
to the last.   He will never retire."   " What, what ? " said he,
and stood facing the window again.   Then, as he paced, came
a repetition of the dirge, " He must go ; it is terribly distressing,
but he must go."   As he walked, it was observed that he
gained in collectedness, in determination, as if, despite the distress which still devoured him, he was increasingly able to
articulate his thought.   " If necessary," he said quietly, " everything must go.   What are parties and causes compared to an
issue like this—the establishing of Christ's kingdom ?   If we
once let this principle go, and allow men convicted of these
sins to assume honourable and leading positions, what is to
happen to us, our youth, or anybody ?   The whole atmosphere
will become vitiated, and righteousness an impossibility.   Unless we speak out plainly now there will be loss untold, the
social atmosphere more vitiated even than it is at present."
That entity which few understand, but which is so powerful in
life, the social atmosphere into which men and women are born,
was the goal of many of his endeavours.   The leader who
must go stirred compassion greater than the public divined,
but the thought of the public life, the public tradition, which
mould men and women from their youth up, heartened him
for a thankless task, one of those tasks that men get through
somehow, and then never refer to again.   Many considered
his action at this crisis the most striking of his whole life, and
would refer to it with pleasure ; but he never did.

On the Sunday afternoon that followed this eventful day, he was announced to speak on the matter of the moment at St. James's Hall. The public attention was focused upon him as a likely exponent of the religious view of the case, and the Journal, which circulated his views, made the leap in circulation that it always did when some great issue was at stake. Undoubtedly by that Sunday he was at white heat, for he increasingly realised all that was involved in the question of the moment. That public life should be animated by Christian ideals was one of the leading principles of his career, and he saw that principle in jeopardy. While the lorn figure on the ramparts tore him, he was given the strength to proceed because of the pleas of those who came forward to support it. " What in the world has it to do with Ireland or Home Rule ? " said these ; " all that business is his private life, his own concern, not ours." So their counsels heartened him, giving him the strength to go on. The audience that afternoon, always remarkable for its representative character, was more than ever expressive of that diverse life which flows in West London. Politicians and journalists were there in rows, and so was Fidus Achates. Nor were they the only element, for there was an unusual and a sinister one. This my father swiftly detected, and the slight twitching of his features was noted by one always quick to read them—the evangelistic agent. In a moment he was by his side.

" What's the matter ? " said he.

" These Irish ! " was the answer ; " I am afraid they will make a row."

" No, they won't."

" How do you know that ? "

" Because they'll be like lambs."

" Yes, but "—

" My class are here." [1]

" Ah, that menagerie—they understand—are on the alert ? "

" Teetotallers all, sir, and only thirsty to show Irishmen the way to Piccadilly."

---

[1] The members of the society class of the lay agent represented a variety of the callings of mankind, including that of retired prize-fighter. After meeting the class on one occasion, my father exclaimed to its leader, " What a menagerie you have here ! " By that name they generally alluded to it.

" Where are they ? "

" Where they are placed, sir ! Have no fear but deliver the message."

The lay agent, after repeating this conversation a few months ago, became lost in reminiscence, and when asked, " And he did deliver the message ? "

" He did ! " he said, and shrugged.

This conversation with the superintendent was one of those pieces of pantomime which from time to time took place between the superintendent and the principal missioners, and, not least, with the lay agent. My father would never have addressed such a meeting without knowing that all the necessary preparations had been made, and the lay agent never doubted but that the speaker would deliver the message. Yet it was necessary for the heartening of both of them to have these conversations, in which either knew exactly what the other was going to say. All that each waited for was some variation of the accustomed phrases, some fresh version of the old part. They were continually assisting at fresh combinations of old circumstances, and it behoved them at each combination to play their little pantomime, which never failed to bring sustainment.

My father's description of himself during the speech that followed might have been that of a man with his back against a wall, who was conscious that God was with him. Critics felt that the instinct of the advocate, always so marked, now stood him in good stead, as did his power of concentrating on one supreme aspect of a subject. Nor was it the Irish leader who was the prisoner at the bar, but Christ Jesus. Somehow He was to be delivered from obloquy, and it was uncertain whether the speaker saw anybody clearly but Him.

As was usual with him, he did not address his remarks to the gallery. It was often noted that while he was one of the most popular preachers and speakers in England, his language and thought was always that of a cultivated man, and that he aimed at taking the gallery with him, rather than playing to it. On this particular occasion he quoted what others had to say on the matter, particularly those who did not think like him, and by some power that was given him, visibly [1] moved the audience to take that view of the case that he took. By presenting to them various aspects of the subject, he moved them to see that there was one higher and more convincing than all the rest.

After quoting from the Psalms and Matthew Arnold, he referred to the traditions of that party to which he belonged, " moved " from their " wicked slumber by Mrs. Josephine Butler a quarter of a century ago." Then he said :

"No one can suppose that I have any pleasure in dealing with this case. I have stood on this very platform at Mr. Parnell's side rejoicing at the vindication of his character from the infamous charge of Pigott the forger ; and if he had been able to vindicate it now, we all should have rejoiced more than we did then. Further, if he had retired quietly and promptly from public life, we would have spread the mantle of silence over him, and not uttered a word to add to his humiliation. I have a right to speak as a friend of the Irish people. I have made sacrifices for their cause ; and although I have never declared myself on this debated issue on this platform, it is a matter of public notoriety that I have been for some years past an enthusiastic Home Ruler.

"I do not underestimate the immense and unique services which Mr. Parnell has rendered to the Irish race. I say that it is to their credit that they should be grateful to him, that it would be truly disgraceful if they were not grateful, and that they should show their gratitude in every legitimate way. But there ought to be two limits to their gratitude. It ought not to exceed their patriotism, and it ought not to exceed their faith in God. I am extremely anxious to put before you the strongest expression of the view, which it is my duty to denounce. I received yesterday a letter from a Roman Catholic priest in Ireland, which I will read to you."

The writer urged that political and national necessity made it essential for the Irish people to pardon Mr. Parnell. He wrote with much courtesy, closing as follows :—

"I had the pleasure of seeing and hearing you on one occasion. It was at an Exeter Hall meeting some years ago, when Mr. Stead also spoke. I admired your eloquent zeal in denouncing (in spite of interruption too) what goes on in India. But is not your great and powerful nation, are not your successive national governments, the culprits whom you denounced? May I lightly mention this matter without offence, in order to convey to you the

---

[1] One who was present writes in the *Methodist Times* : "I had the opportunity of sitting beside Mr. Price Hughes on the platform at St. James's Hall on Sunday afternoon, when he delivered the address on Mr. Parnell's case. I was very forcibly impressed with the enthusiastic agreement of the great audience with Mr. Price Hughes when he urged the vast importance of demanding that the leaders of our public life should not be immoral men."

delicate position you can't help occupying in teaching us. We are grieved enough ; pray do not take any part in injuring us more by attempting the impossible—that is, to separate the Irish people from the leader, whom his own unique qualities and the course of events have made for the present the very embodiment of the Irish cause itself."

My father replied as follows :—

"My answer to this Catholic priest shall be given in the form of a touching incident which occurred at the height of the Civil War in America. The slaves were greatly depressed because the tide of the war seemed to be running fast against the Abolitionists. There was a great prayer-meeting in one of the American churches. In the midst of their depression an aged woman rushed into the aisle and shrieked out, 'Is God dead?' The whole attitude of the meeting was changed in a moment. They realised that theirs was a sacred cause, and that if they still believed in God it was impossible for them to despair. My Catholic correspondent has written as though God were dead. To him I say, 'Oh ! my Christian brother, if your cause is of God, what have you to fear? Suppose Mr. Parnell died to-morrow, Home Rule would not die. A cause so legitimate and so sacred does not depend upon the life of any man. Put your trust in God, and not in Parnell.'"

Next he considered the plea that the question was one in which the English people had no right to interfere, because it concerned the Irish exclusively. To this he replied that the Home Rule party was necessarily one and indivisible, and that the English section could not rid themselves of their responsibility in this matter any more than the Irish, seeing that the Home Rule cause was fought in an English Parliament and on English platforms. Then he took a third plea, that of certain Socialists who contended that an artificial state of society was the root-cause of this and similar calamities. To this, again, he did not attempt any dialectical response, but swept it aside with some emanation from himself that was not dialectic. "I am fighting," he said in effect, "for a party that has striven without ceasing for twenty-five years, and there are certain points of view that we repeat to you that you be perfectly informed, but we cannot reck of them." He closed with four passionate appeals : the first to Mr. Parnell himself; the second to Cardinal Manning to use his influence with the bishops and clergy of the Catholic Church of Ireland ; the third to Mr. Gladstone to exert his " unique and unparalleled authority "; and last to the Irish people themselves.

"... Here we must leave it. We love Ireland. We passionately desire her well-being ; but our first obedience and our highest devotion must be to God. We have sacrificed much for Ireland. She is entitled to many sacrifices at our hands ; but there is one thing we will never sacrifice, and that is our religion. We stand immovably on this eternal rock ; what is morally wrong can never be politically right. . . ."

The power was not in the words, which are quoted from a newspaper report, but in something that rang through them. As he spoke, pale, yet determined, he was continually interrupted from all parts of the hall, and to every interruption he had a reply. It was these replies that impressed listeners. " Of course," said one who had no previous knowledge of the speaker, but whose connection with the case had led to his presence in the audience, " those interruptions were prepared beforehand. No speaker could have answered them off-hand in that manner." All my father knew was that voices interrupted him, which he answered immediately, producing silence or laughter. In an appeal to the Irish people some voice shouted out defiance. " Is that the voice of Ireland ? " he inquired oratorically.

" Yes ! " came the answer.

" It isn't the right brogue," was his quiet response, and he returned so quickly to his theme that he had scarcely time to feel the convulsion of the audience. In a few moments other voices were assailing him, and in the interests of those who joined him with their back against the wall, he cut them down one after the other with a light flashing sword that was given him, and went on. At last there was silence altogether, the sword and the powerful teetotallers working in a unison that was marvellous to behold. The lay agent regarded these latter as arteries coursing through the body of the audience, charged to communicate with its extremest members. Orders, he said, should be as simple as possible, so that repetition could only enhance their significance. " I am visible to the view," he said, " and you will keep your eye on me as I move quietly from one part of the hall to the other. When I hold up one finger, it is one man ; when I hold up another, it is two men ; and when I hold up another, it is three men. One finger, one man ; two fingers, two men ; three fingers, three men, according to the article under consideration. Now,

23

hearties, to your posts, keep a good look out, and don't forget the hymn-books." The mingling of comic with tragic elements was strangely typified that afternoon, for it was certain that there were no happier mortals in Piccadilly than those Christian teetotallers greedily eyeing their prey as they awaited the signal to fall upon it. With them for a season the struggle of terrestrial life was resolved into blissful concord, and it was impossible to say which they enjoyed most, the sight of the superintendent of the Mission whom they were assisting, the hymns which sang of themselves, or the sight of discontented gentlemen waiting to be shown the way to Piccadilly. Their condition indeed defied description, except that it was not of a kind to bear repetition. Once before God had been good to them, and it was not to be expected that more than two such occasions would be given to undeserving mortals. Yet these Irish, they felt, were not to be compared to those members of " the profession " who had swelled the audience on the previous occasion when the bishop was in the chair. There was that in their display of chains and rings, they remembered, which made the mouth water, and there was not a portion of the sleek frames which did not seem specially adapted to the fists of teetotallers. For Pat there was more compunction ; still if the joy was not quite so unbridled, it was none the less celestial. That problem which the speaker was painfully solving in his own person, the concord of that weakness incidental to humanity and the grace of God, was in them most harmoniously established.

My father often rejoiced over the prowess of his stalwart confrère. He loved to think of it. Gentlemen of the profession brought into close contact with the muscle of psalm-singers, Irish Romanists in the grip of members of a Methodist class meeting. Two fingers raised in mid-air by the lay agent meant the stealthy advance of two of them, with that gliding undulating motion which characterises the cat when she descends on her prey. So swift was it, that they were sure to be in time to hear the following conversation conducted in low and distinct tones. " I shall be obliged, sir, if you will sit down ! "

" Begorrah, but I stand till I fall ! "

" As a friend, I advise you to sit down ! "

" 'Tis a free country ; a man has a right to use his voice ! "
This would be said with expletives.

" On Monday, my friend, you will have. This man has
taken this hall to give his opinion on Sunday. You come
and give yours to-morrow."

" I am here to do it this afternoon."

There was a flicker of the lay agent's eyelids, and two
stalwarts were flanking him on either side.

" I am sorry to interfere with your plans, but I am afraid
you will do it in the mud of Piccadilly Circus."

Then since all Celts are bold to speak as to do, this one
would turn on him, and squarely too ; but he had not reckoned
for the two merry gentlemen on either side of his opponent,
standing like statues, but with eyes gleaming queerly at the
corners. The gentleman in their midst was in the act of
raising one finger in the air in a manner both solemn and
ominous, and by a thrill on the part of the statues it was
evident that some addition to the force was anticipated.
" Good afternoon, sir," said the lay agent, for the Irishman
had resumed his seat. Of all the figures that afternoon his
seems the most pathetic—the least without hope—yet it is im-
probable that his sufferings were of the order of the speaker
who felt himself to be fighting with his back against a wall
and God with him. For some to appear as censors of their
fellow-men either in the matter of morals or pleasures may
be sufficiently easy, but to those truly convinced of sin in
themselves and others, it is not so. Perhaps such a conviction
is the only thing that makes men charitable—not indifferent,
but charitable. They who discipline humanity impose no
more stringent discipline upon it than that with which, in ways
unknown to others, they discipline themselves. It is the
apprehension of this discipline—the stigmata of the modern
saint—which makes men and women listen, for these are so
entitled to dictate to them. Those who often heard my
father both preach and speak say that they never heard him
to greater advantage than on this occasion, and that it was
a spectacle which will ever live in their memory. What it
was exactly they could not define ; but it was its sublimity which
held them, something human in fetters, and against great odds.
What he was attacking in such campaigns he knew

full well, and that it was not what he was supposed to be attacking, which must have been a consolation to him. Great realities he knew himself to be dealing with, not only the expression of an outraged Puritanism, and he was obdurate and unflinching accordingly. Still, certain rôles there are which are not pleasing to men, and so many that he assumed were pleasing to him, that he was more fortunate than many others. One narrow in outlook, with forbidding conceptions of the Christian religion, would have minded less that pinnacle of austerity on which certain contemporaries made no ado about placing him. Press cuttings were sent him most mornings, and he knew what was thought of him. His speech that Sunday afternoon—reported at length in the Press throughout the kingdom—was considered by the Irish members and the lobby of the House, generally, to have decided matters and opened the sluice-gates.[1] Nonconformity rose in arms throughout the country, and the Liberal leaders were deluged with letters from their supporters and constituents. Almost immediately Mr. Gladstone wrote his letter to Mr. Morley, breaking his alliance with the Irish party so long as Mr. Parnell was leader, and a short time later Mr. Parnell himself broke with the majority of his followers.

It was when Mr. Parnell went to Ireland to fight the election at Kilkenny that my father's distress at the situation became acute. A Celt under emotional tension has a logic of his own, unerring as lightning, but too like fork-lightning to be understood of the Saxon. A man, however, at variance both with the dictates of general morality and of prudence, who stands with his back against a wall, fighting for what he regards as his life-work, appeals, however unjustifiably, to the human heart. My father in particular was distressed at the spectacle. After reading once of a convict who had escaped from Dartmoor and who was hiding somewhere on the moor while the keepers and hounds were in full cry, he said, " It is horrible. I cannot bear to think of it. To think of a

---

[1] For the part played by my father in the Parnell episode, see Barry O'Brien's *Life of Parnell*, vol. ii. pp. 246, 247, 267. " Despite the warning note struck by the Rev. Hugh Price Hughes, who really must be regarded as the English hero of the struggle, the Liberal leaders believed at first that Parnell would not have to be sacrificed, but gradually they began to waver."

man hunted in that manner!" and something of the same emotion was stirred by Mr. Parnell's Irish campaign. Both from the platform of St. James's Hall and from the Journal he had earnestly and courteously besought Mr. Parnell to retire. Finding this in vain, he attacked the Irish people, and said they were immoral to support him. Such things, he felt, ought not to have been allowed, and the Irish should have prevented it. Not unnaturally he was assailed at once for the use of such an expression, and in the next number of the Journal he wrote to explain that he had never made a charge of any kind against the Irish people, which was quite true. He was very sorry also that he had been misunderstood.

At the same time a great contention was going on in the columns of the *Times*. It was a journal which he read increasingly, for he saw that it represented the average English opinion on many matters, and had a unique influence in the country. On this particular occasion several well-known gentlemen, who were ill at ease both with the position of Mr. Parnell and the Irish party, and very particularly with my father, whom they considered to be largely the cause of it, were airing their grievances in the hospitable columns of that newspaper. He was not long in entering into the fray, and in a short time there was a regular *mêlée*, his correspondents finally attacking what they considered to be the evidences of the Christian faith, and my father replying to them with characteristic vehemence. Then they veered from this, and not without smiles, evolved between them the phrase "Nonconformist conscience" as a missile which should express their contempt both for his conduct and that of his associates. Instantly he snatched it to his breast. "I thank you," he said, "for that word," and began proclaiming it throughout the land. The more he talked and thought about it, the more glorious it seemed to him, and everywhere he was saying to Nonconformist friends, "Let us see that we are worthy of this title which has been bestowed upon us," so that the original framers must have almost regretted their venture. Whenever anything happened that was dishonourable, or when persons of distinction associated themselves too conspicuously, as some thought, with horse-racing, or when liberties were attacked, he did all that he could to drive that conscience into the com-

munity, and while everybody laughed a good deal and some
shrugged, the British people took to it, considering all things,
surprisingly well.   It became a recognised force in affairs, and
was respected as such.   Even solemn academic journals came
to say, after the first outcry, that the Nonconformist conscience
was " an admirable and indispensable element in the community," and when that is conceded by an academic journal,
there is not much left to ambition in this world.   They in
literary balloons also were having their laugh at what was
going on upon the earth, and half-approving evidently, despite
their smiles.   Altogether it was a famous victory, and he grew
more hopeful and buoyant than ever, the recent reverse of
the missionary controversy, and the subsequent deliverance,
adding a peculiar zest to his emotions and undertakings.
Yet that phrase, " Nonconformist conscience," creating smiles,
annoyance, or admiration, as the case might be, and which
became a byword, was born of travail, and to show it this
chapter has been written.   Thus did Christ say that His
Cross would draw all men unto Him, for it is the crucifixion of
self which has power for salvation unto humanity, and the
salvation is greatest where there is much to crucify.

Of all the things said against my father, this seems to have
been one of the most common, that he was " political," meddling
in those things in which a Christian minister had no concern,
and using his position for advocating or denouncing matters
which did not fall within his province.   Perhaps there never
was a Christian citizen or minister who cared more for politics
and was yet so aloof from its party aspect.   He never went to
political meetings or supported Liberal platforms, and only
attended a debate in the House two or three times in his whole
life.   Taking to heart, as he did, the great humanitarian and
social causes which were identified for some years with the
Liberal party, it was astonishing how he kept himself free from
any party imbroglio, or from that fine network which will commit
men to parties.

Only on one occasion does the writer remember his
taking any part in what might be termed political affairs,
and that was at a private dinner at the house of a Liberal
member, where several leading Nonconformist ministers and
others were invited to meet a political leader, so as to suggest

some compromise with regard to the breach which the Boer War and Imperialism had caused in the ranks of the party. Since many Nonconformists had objected to the war, attempts at Liberal reconciliation could not well take place without some consultation of their leaders, for in past years Nonconformity had been the backbone of the party. My father's speech was admired by those present as a model of tact and ability—that tact which springs from a full understanding of circumstances and the persons involved. He was the more admired, as leaders of various kinds had spoken of him with scant courtesy during the recent cleavage, and it seemed as if in his little address to that company he was anxious to atone for their slips in charity, by making none himself. On returning, he gave a full and glowing account of what had taken place, apparently delighted at having even some slight share in the many forces and incidents that go to make up a reconciliation. He laid stress on the fact that the dinner was private, as if to intimate that if it had not been so he would not have attended. This is the only instance of what is termed "party" intervention that can be quoted.

His consolation, undoubtedly, lay in the freest criticism of the drama. For every crisis he had his own explanation, his own opinion as to the nature of what had been done, and what with advantage could be done. It was therefore not surprising that he was credited with being bound up with the Liberal party when he was not. Other ministers felt as he on certain political matters, but men did not suspect them of party sympathy. His way of stating things, of concentration for the time being on a particular aspect of a question, caused people to attribute opinions to him which he never possessed. On the platform he would deal with certain great social and humanitarian questions, which entered the arena of affairs, but in his strictly ministerial character, in the pulpit, his aim seems to have lain in excluding everything but those deep questions for the individual soul on which it is the duty of the Christian minister to insist.

Yet the silence of a large portion of the Christian ministry on matters of great social import had, my father thought, a disastrous effect, in that it alienated them from the leaders of Democracy and the most philanthropic and ardent minds of the day. So he had determined, as he sat planning on the balcony at Brixton, to conduct a series of Sunday afternoon conferences on social subjects at St. James's Hall, and thus attract that class in the Metropolis who were interested in social and philanthropic subjects, but repelled by the Christian Church because she took so little public part in them. When he would say, at one of these conferences, " we can never be said to do the will of our Father on earth as angels do it in heaven, if we do that will only in certain times and at certain places," the assembly would burst into clapping of hands, and it was all he could do to keep from laughing aloud. " Many of these fellows," he would comment afterwards, " *think* they have rejected Christianity, but there they were rapturously applauding it." The more he showed forth its essential tolerance and compassion, the more delighted and at one with it they appeared. At the same time he perceived such outbursts to be out of order, and if any saints known to him happened to be present he surveyed them with keen and affectionate glances to see how they were supporting the ordeal.

When he brought friends he always warned them, " You may be startled, but my audience this afternoon contains queer brethren, who are accustomed to give vent to their feelings. They are quite ignorant of Christianity—most of them owing to our misrepresentations—so when they hear an exposition of it for the first time, they cannot resist showing rejoicing in the manner that is customary to them. You must not be startled. You may even find it somewhat exciting. Some have told me they do, but in any case there is no need for alarm, and I hope you will not resent it. If you can conveniently stay to the evening service, you will perceive a cathedral calm, and so carry away a better impression of us."

Yet for all his anxiety to explain himself and his designs to the saints, the venture was keenly criticised by some. " How can he," they said, " risk such a priceless opportunity of saving souls." They wondered also what he was thinking about, and declared it to be against their principles to have party politics dragged into religion. At times he must have found current criticism a little confusing, and certainly calculated to minister to his perception of the incongruous. It was not so long ago that certain people had criticised him for direct methods, shrugging at his incapacity to preach those good and solid sermons which won the approval of the wise. To be accused of neglecting to preach the gospel must have sounded strangely to him, as did the injunction that he was apparently never to address an assembly without aiming at individual conversion. At the District Synod in particular he was attacked, and the old wonder came over him. "What have I done; why did they do it?" he would say to one or two sympathisers. After years of service in the Christian ministry, he was yet so mistrusted as to be accused of introducing party issues and neglecting high spiritual considerations. The world did not make this mistake concerning him, for there were many who were not only absolutely ignorant of his political views, but good Conservatives, who were quite nonplussed when it was insisted that he did not belong to their party.

In these afternoon conferences he confined himself to the portrayal of great citizens whom he admired, and whose moral worth was attested by opponents as well as followers, or to those social reforms and crusades which, though they may be temporarily associated with one party, stand apart from and above all parties in the eyes of their chief promoters, *e.g.* temperance reform, social purity, just hours and conditions for the labouring classes, the evils of war, the promotion of the public health, and the well-being of children and animals. His aim was to indicate the spirit that should animate the discharge of civic duties and the selfishness and disloyalty to Christ that was implied in their neglect. He dealt entirely with the religious, moral, and humanitarian aspects of the case. Particularly was he anxious to make the people (the inhabitants of indistinguishable dwellings) realise that Jesus Christ of Nazareth was their Friend, and that His life on earth had a special significance for them.

There was therefore something remarkable in the delivery of such addresses as "Jesus Christ and the Masses," "Jesus Christ and Social Distress," "The Supremacy of the Law of Christ," "Christ the Greatest of Social Reformers," on a Sunday afternoon in Piccadilly, not in academic, obscure, or hushed phrase, but in quite forcible, unmistakable English, and in a voice that could be heard from all parts of the hall. The thought would be culled from the reading and experience of his lifetime, but he was such a remarkable filterer of thought, that everything he said struck listeners as not less lucid than suggestive. Like children, he thought, the common people often understood the sufficiency of the gospel of Jesus Christ more quickly than those who were esteemed their superiors. "They really think," he used to say, "that He meant what He said." The poor had less to substitute in its place, and by the "realities" with which they contended, and the sordidness of their surroundings, more quickly realised the need of the spiritual. His passionate sympathy with the masses of the people led him to adopt a very decided attitude in some of the social controversies of the time—controversies which are, and were, quite distinct from political issues, though my father used to consider that they underlay and must ultimately determine these. He would object to the definitions of parties that are given in history books as out of date. "The real dividing line," he said at this time, "will, I think, be increasingly betwixt those who are in sympathy with the masses of the people, and those who are in sympathy with wealth and privilege."

It was his interposition in these great social and industrial strifes, and his intense force of feeling in the matter, that seemed to invoke the ire of many contemporaries, and the disapprobation of the Synod. When mass meetings were forbidden in Trafalgar Square he was indignant, just as he had been, many years before, when a similar privilege was forbidden in Hyde Park. The attitude of the journalistic world roused his ire. "We wish," he wrote in the Journal, "we could induce the editor of the *Times* to read Canon Westcott's recent volume of sermons on Social Christianity." About the same time he urged with prophetic irony that persons in positions of responsibility should pull down the buildings of the Bible Society to prevent the circulation of Scriptures, which favoured the just claims of the masses. "Far-sighted upholders of the ancien régime," he added, "have generally favoured such a course." His platform utterances on the needs of the masses were felt to be singularly allied to his manner of life, both as it was shown in the Mission and the prominent part that he took with Cardinal Manning, Dr. Clifford,

and one or two others, in the settlement and pacification of
the great industrial strikes, for which those years were remarkable—particularly the dock labourers' strike, when decided
sympathy was felt in many quarters with the demands of
the men, and which provoked a good deal of strong feeling
among opponents.   When the national strike of coal miners
took place, he was in such sympathy with their demands, that
one of the Sisters was allowed to devote herself to the care of
the miners' wives, who came to collect money for the strikers.
On such occasions the Lord Mayor would summon an arbitra-
tion committee, and my father would have opportunities of
sotto voce conversations with the various ministers of religion
and employers of labour who sat upon it.   Not the least
interesting were those with Cardinal Manning, whose urbanity
and tact were noted.   "When I was young," the Cardinal once
said, "parents brought up their children. Now it is the other
way about, children bring up their parents."   His listeners
loved that mot and often repeated it.   Every strike, when the
demands of the strikers were legitimate in his eyes, and they
generally were, was watched by him in the Journal with the
keenest interest and encouragement.   Despite the manifest
chaos that such warfare temporarily produced, the editor
could not but manifest a certain rejoicing that the people
at last were rising and demanding what both justice and
humanity, not to mention Christianity, demanded on their
behalf.

The assembling of the Trades Union Congress caused
him exultation. Yet he did not think Trades Unions to be
perfect more than any other human institution, grieving indeed
over some of their tendencies.[1]   Nothing was ever more pleasing

[1] An article in the *Times* gave facts concerning the Bricklayers' Union, in which
it was attested that workmen, however skilful, were forbidden to lay more than a
certain number of bricks per day. "It is terrible," my father said, "terrible. If
the working men become selfish and lazy, not making the very best of the capacities
God has given them, they are simply committing suicide. However, they are merely
following the example of their employers, those who formerly had all the power in
their hands. The working men in their ignorance are selfish as these were. At
first, poor fellows, they abuse their privileges and misuse them." Then with
increased emphasis owing to a remark of his companion, "Nothing whatever can
excuse a man from putting forth his best powers and capacities, from working to his
utmost, and no trades union in the kingdom has the right to prevent him from doing
so." His condemnation, as ever, was tempered with compassion.

to him than that the working men should regard him as their friend and representative. " I don't know how it is, but these fellows seem to regard me as some sort of champion of theirs," he would remark with smiles. As their representative and champion, he combated the compensation of licensed victuallers out of the public money—he and the missioners, and the brass band and numerous temperance societies and trades unions marching in procession to Hyde Park to demonstrate against the Government's proposals, to which " the publican was neither legally nor morally entitled." They reached Trafalgar Square just a minute or two before they were expected, which gave my father the opportunity of jumping out of his carriage with greater nimbleness than usual and taking his position near one of the lions, where he spoke to the crowd for two or three minutes, and appeared to be expressing himself with more than customary force. When he came back, he had the look of one from whom a great load had fallen. " That's what I have been longing to do all my life. At last I have done it." The lay agent explained afterwards that the excess of punctuality had been arranged beforehand with this end in view. " Why, I could not hear a word you said," said a Sister from Yorkshire. The superintendent looked at her speechless, what did that matter when he had gratified the ambition of a lifetime.

But with all his insistence on the message of Christianity to the body, and, therefore, to those classes who are most in need of that portion, he never omitted its message to the mind. Many of his conferences on Sunday afternoon were peculiarly addressed to the thoughtful and the doubting, particularly two of them on the novel, *Robert Elsmere*, which had caused considerable sensation in literary and religious circles on its appearance. Its interest to my father lay, as it did to Mr. Gladstone, in its "faithful and vivid revelation of the literary scepticism of the time," as well as the " deep insight into human character," which distinguished so many parts of the book. His answer to its arguments was the same in essence as that which he gave to the gentlemen who had criticised the evidences of the Christian religion in the columns of the *Times*, and had accused him of harbouring a " Nonconformist conscience." The following quotation, though it cannot epitomise all that he said, will give an indication of its drift :—

" I, too, in all humility, speaking on behalf of millions of men and women in all lands, testify that their hearts and my own have experienced the Divine change to which Augustine and Gordon, and Maurice and Newman, and Chalmers and Wesley, were never tired of referring ; and yet to this living testimony of the Christians of every age *Robert Elsmere* never once refers. This book attacks the outworks of Christianity ; it never so much as discharges a single shell at the citadel. It is not a question of documents. It is a question of living men and living women, who realise in their own souls the presence of the Divine Christ. Squire Wendover might argue for fifty years, but his arguments would never produce the slightest impression upon such Christians. Robert Elsmere abandoned Christianity at once because he had never understood it, never experienced it, never realised it as it is realised by all those whose Christianity is not a hope or a mental conviction, but a fact and a *life*."

The fact that the literary and academic world of his day knew so little of the great body of Christian experience, of the motives and hopes and struggles of genuine Christian lives, indeed of what was life to them and the one thing in their lives, was continuously noted by him. Unbelief had its problem in this respect, he thought, as well as belief. Sceptical circles had certain names whom they quoted, and a certain experience culled from their particular coterie and reading, but it was not an experience, he considered, drawn from close contact with, or a wide knowledge of, humanity, and it certainly took little account of the saints and their lives, whether in the early Church or of modern times.

Perhaps this was why he made such a point of referring to the latter and delivering addresses on them from time to time in St. James's Hall—his range being a very wide one. Father Damien, Catherine Booth, St. Francis of Assisi, General Gordon, John Wesley, Cardinal Newman, and John Bright, were all equally entitled to appear on his calendar. His remarks about people when they died were often different to what was generally being said, as if he saw deeper into the secret of their lives than most. Of Queen Victoria, for instance, when everybody was saying the same thing, " that she was an excellent wife and mother, and had established the throne in the respect and the affection of her people," he said what seemed to him individual in her—that she had suppressed her own desires and claims to what she conceived to be the good of her people, continually and silently yielding to encroachments on royal prerogative.   He would remark, for instance, that in surrendering the sovereign's position as head of the army, Her Majesty had been willing to suffer a possible lowering of prestige in the eyes of continental relatives.   Commenting on the death of Spurgeon, he said his scholarship had been underestimated, and that he possessed the largest library he had ever seen in a minister's private house.

His addresses on Buddhism were interesting, because of his admiration for Buddha and much that was in his religion, along with the passionate conviction that it was fragmentary and impotent compared with the completeness of the gospel of Christ.   *The Light of Asia*, which had revealed the spirit of Buddhism to modern England, could never have been written, he used to say, by its gifted author, unless he had been imbued with the gospel narrative.   In an address on the philosophy of Schopenhauer he said, "Europe will have to choose ultimately between Christ and the philosophy of despair."

Another discourse was on Giordano Bruno, the monk of the Renascence, who attracted him, and of whom he liked to speak.   On Bright also he was happy, quoting the Essays of the Quaker, Jonathan Dymond, which had made such a turning-point in the life of that statesman, and which he urged the young men and women who were present to procure and read. Other characteristic discourses were on the Greek and Roman conceptions of life, as well as a denunciation of prevalent militarism.   Most elaborate and thoughtful perhaps of all were the discourses on Mazzini and Ruskin, and the poets Tennyson and Browning.   He would get through a great deal of reading in a short space of time before these expositions, making use of what great critics had said, though their thought would become so part of the ever-active mint of his mind, that every explanation and statement would bear his own individual impress.   It was a matter of rejoicing to him that the two great poets of the era were men of stainless reputation, and who, while differing in much, were alike in their singularly high conception of marriage, and in the happiness of their own wedded lives.   To a companion he exclaimed when speaking of Tennyson, " There's no nonsense here of Art for Art's sake, or the impossibility of artists having the same moral code as other men. This great representative poet crumbles all such talk to dust"; and, as he thought of it all, the Knights of that Round Table and Arthur with them, beside whom the poet himself was entitled to take a place, he gloried exceedingly. An interesting element of this and of all his audiences, were the men of business who listened with curious attention to what he had to say. The fascination seemed to lie in the fact that he continually contradicted what were supposed to be some of their favourite maxims.

His faculty of fashioning and modelling the ideas of men almost against their wills was quite extraordinary. A person said to a member of the family, " The talk in your house is regular nonsense." " What portion of it in particular?" was the response. " Oh, all of it; there's no sense in it." Further illumination a listener could not gather, so that it was not possible to do more than gently deprecate such an assertion, long habitude to these having fostered a certain humility. It was not so long after that, and shortly after my father's death, that this critic was saying to someone, " I can never be quite the same again. He has taught me that there is something more in life than getting on and making money." Between these two conversations, he had become a listener to my father's discourses, and had come to closer personal quarters with him. His case was typical of many.

The modern aspirations of women was the subject of a series of addresses, and in his discourses on Browning he spoke on marriage. As he began, he observed half-suppressed smiles and titters on the part of many amongst the audience. There was clearly an impression that the subject chosen was scarcely a serious one, and that it would form an agreeable relaxation after the high matters of social and philosophical import, to which their attention was generally called. What pierced was that certain whom he knew to be earnest Christian men and women, dared to join in the veiled titter. He stopped short and looked at them. There were moments, all agreed, when he was terrible, and this was one. So Arthur might have blazed across the round table at some unworthy knight. " Is our everlasting vulgarity," he asked, " to prevent us from ever realising the sacredness and solemnity of marriage? Lives are either cursed or glorified by it. Yet even Christian men and women cannot hear it mentioned without breaking into puerile and unseemly mirth." One who was sitting by him related that the smiles froze upon the faces of his audience, and that as the speaker continued, each seemed to hold his breath as if spellbound by the awe of that rebuke. When a few minutes later he said, " Young men, young women, for God's sake be careful whom you marry," there was that " cathedral calm " that always reigned during his exposition of great Christian mysteries.

As was well discerned by a sympathetic brother-minister, the Conferences were undertaken at immense personal cost. What most failed to see was the restriction that he laid upon himself, and that he was still the ambassador in bonds just as he was in the evening. He no more allowed the subtleties of intellect or the fancies and predilections of self to have their sway than he did in preaching a sermon. When he spoke of Schopenhauer's system, of Buddhism, or of the condition of the labouring classes, he was equally conscious of giving not so much a personal opinion as a message, and nobody would see that it was a message. Constantly they spoke to him and of him as one tossed by the desire of innovation, or of promoting the interests of a political party, without seeing that nothing so demanded a sacrifice as a message. Gradually he learned not to heed merely smiling when people mentioned what they thought to be his opinions. Those journals which were the expression of the typical Bohemian West End life, gave glowing tributes to his insistence on the social applications of Christianity. Seeing that he denounced what are deemed to be the special vices of this society, this testimony was very striking, as well as suggestive of what the world can respect. Even the journal of his own communion, which represented the older school of Methodism and was naturally critical of his personality and designs, wrote at his death as follows : " It would be impossible to enumerate his services to the cause of morals in this country. He has exerted a purifying influence upon the manners, the pleasures, the literature, and the social customs of the day "[1] (*Methodist Recorder*). Liberty, it has been said, is maintained by constant vigilance, and so he thought was the purity and righteousness of a community or a city. He was for ever on the alert, particularly in the *Methodist Times*, and to a degree that most could not comprehend.

His sympathies were not confined to London, but went out to persecuted European peoples, and to those who suffered injustice the world over. The Semitic strain in his blood seemed to give him comprehension of those persecuted peoples who lift appealing hands to heaven, and rendered him non-comprehensible to certain sober contemporaries. He seemed able to feel in himself what it was to be a Jew, or a Hungarian, or a Pole, or an Armenian. The national music of the second in its drama and despair touched deep chords, and one of his delights was to hear a friend sing Hungarian songs. The writer recollects his face as one described to him Tchaikovsky's symphony written to celebrate Napoleon's defeat in 1812. As commemorative of a defeat of Napoleon, it had a charm outside that of the music, for he regarded the great Corsican as a species of Antichrist. On his sympathetic attitude to the Jews reference has already been made, and this was an element in his advocacy of Captain Dreyfus. He was also much to the fore in a movement in London which befriended the persecuted Russian Jews, when he addressed a great meeting on their behalf. He did not allude to the Christianisation of the Jews, probably because he felt that so long as Christendom persecuted them, it was not likely they would favour the Christian religion.

He was also active with tongue and pen on behalf of the Russian Stundists, who resembled the Methodists, he said, and who were undergoing persecution for their convictions.

It was part of his intense practicality in political as well as ecclesiastical affairs, to offer some kind of solution to a problem.

---

[1] Alluding to the public life of an English city, a correspondent writes that there is a change for the better, and the presence of wider and more unselfish ideals. "On inquiry," he continues, "I find that a little group of young men who came under Mr. Hughes's influence are the cause of the innovation." This is only one out of similar instances.

24

It was no good saying the present was intolerable unless a person had something to offer in its stead. This was very manifest in a great meeting held in the City Temple to protest against the continuance of the Armeinan massacres. Dr. Parker spoke first, and his address was one never to be forgotten, the passion and the power much affecting his listeners. When the Doctor had sat down my father rose to his feet and in a very clear and energetic manner began to intimate that course which, to his thinking, the Great Powers might with general advantage pursue. He quoted precedent, but always with a view to the present crisis, neither taking his audience back to past history, so as to unfold a tale of European shame and responsibility, nor in the least appealing to the emotional aspect. His appeal, while it assumed a certain moral judgment, was entirely to the understanding. This crisp, keen deliverance fell somewhat flat on an assembly stirred by Dr. Parker's oratory, and they did not applaud it as they had the previous speech. A friend remarked in a significant manner that it was "very clever," but with the implication that something was lacking. Yet the poetry and the passion, however differently it might clothe itself, was equal in both, which Dr. Parker himself was foremost in recognising. Observers particularly admired his advocacy of the Armenian cause, because it cost him not a little. When he held a conference on the subject on Sunday afternoon he did not spare himself in getting up the necessary details. The morning was spent in reading harrowing accounts of witnesses and survivors, and he said it had been an agony to him. It was no exaggeration, because he hated painful details of all kinds.

To the end of his life he was the member of many anti-societies, and for all his constructive and disciplinary tendencies could not resist a certain warming of the heart towards an agitator. To one who, fearing the perpetration of a public act of cruelty towards animals, wrote to him as the most likely person to take the matter to heart, he replied immediately, " I am glad to see that you have already entered the noble army of agitators." He was a member of the Society for the Prevention of Cruelty to Children, of the Humanitarian League, of the Anti-Vivisection Society, and,

worst trespass of all, of the Anti-Vaccination Society. All
these societies flooded him with their publications, often
appealing to him to speak at one of their meetings or to
give them his support in the Journal.

For his anti-vaccination principles some of his friends in
the medical profession never forgave him. Even those most
indulgent towards him said, "We cannot understand—h-m—
how a man like Mr. Hughes—h-m—so clever and thoughtful,
and with such a wide experience of life—h-m—can take the
attitude that he does in this matter. It is astonishing to me."
"There are two great tyrannies in the earth," said my father
to one of his daughters; "one is the clerical profession and
the other is the medical. Your sex is to blame. You have
bowed and fluttered before them since the beginning of time,
with the result that there is no limit to their pretensions.
You might as well question or resist God Almighty as dare
question or resist one of their decrees." For this reason my
father, on his own confession, came to strongly suspect either
profession, where they contended for or resisted—*qua* profession
—any issue. "Individually (speaking of the medical profession) I believe it to contain the most delightful, high-minded,
unselfish and excellent of men, but their Trades Unionism
binds them hand and foot. They cannot help it, poor things,
they are bound to grovel before the god of professionalism.
There is no tyranny to be compared with that of the professions."
Certainly if any one did his share in his day of bowing before
loved members of a beloved profession, it was my father. With
them he was as clay in the hands of the potter, commenting
on the wisdom of the decree, while he submitted himself to it
with an obeisance that was Oriental.

At meal-times he would say to shocked visitors: "I
believe less and less in this tomfoolery of medicine. Ah,
modern surgery, that is a different matter altogether—Oh,
wonderful, of course. I was only reading about an operation
in one of the medical journals the other day, which is really
productive of benefit and health to the race; but all this other
business quite sickens me." As likely as not a neat white
paper parcel from the chemist's would appear a few minutes
later—"Ah!" The parcel would be undone and a portion of
its contents carefully measured into a glass.

" Have you shaken it as Howard says you are to shake it ? "

" Yes, I have shaken it."

" Give it to me," and he would quaff it reverently.

The imprimatur of the beloved physician plus the inherited instinct of the race that a glass of medicine must do it good, were too much for my father—tomfoolery or no tomfoolery. Medicine taking had been from the beginning, and seemed, judging by the signs, likely to continue unabated, but vaccination, together with blood-letting, was one of those temporary expedients, he considered, which one generation passionately advocates, and at which the next smiles. His first distrust, not of clerical and medical men, but of their profession, arose in their attitude towards Mrs. Josephine Butler's campaign, of which he was such a champion. Previous to this, his natural intellectual deference towards specialistic opinion, and his love in particular for medical men—of whom his own father was one—would have led him to assume anything but a doubtful attitude towards professional verdicts. But this shook his faith, placing what were to him supreme moral and spiritual considerations at variance with the wisdom of the professions. Later, the fact that medical men themselves began, to his thinking, to shift ground, as well as the evidence of those who had suffered under and resented vaccination—led him to adopt the anti-vaccinationist attitude, and to become one of the champions of that society. The findings of the Royal Commission, and still more, Dr. Russell Wallace's book, *The Wonderful Century*, added strength to his convictions. That, so far as the writer knows, is the account of an advocacy which surprised and angered many contemporaries.

Another of the great anti-societies to which he belonged was the Peace Society. The earliest memories of the writer are associated with his denunciations of war and the existing European armaments. " Carlyle," he would say, " gave us the only just definition of war—a group of men dressed up in red coats sent to the other end of the world to kill another group of men dressed in another colour whom they had never seen, because the journalists and politicians of the two countries had some disagreement which they wanted others to settle instead of them." On the St. James's Hall platform he would denounce it as among the most deadly of the great social sins, and would give almost as much offence, to some people, as when he advocated the claims of the masses.

" It is detrimental to the community," escaped him once at breakfast, " to keep a portion of its manhood in idleness."

" You cannot call it idleness ! " exclaimed his listeners.

" Of course I can. It is idleness."

" Oh ! " was the answer ; and then that charged silence which he knew so well how to interpret. After a pause he would resume, " You probably misunderstand the meaning of the word ' idleness ' in its economic sense. Idleness as used by social philosophers means ' unproductiveness,' and has none of the implication which you attribute to it. The essence of logical argument, as the philosopher Hobbes expressed it, is to arrive at an understanding of the true meaning of terms."

" At a common understanding of their meaning ? " somebody would remark.

" At an understanding," he would continue, " in which the thoughtful can concur. Now reflection inevitably suggests that the profession of arms cannot be maintained without loss to the crafts and professions and art—certainly the art of the community. Art and letters are always the product of eras of peace, and I am surprised that such passionate ' artistes ' do not evince more insight in the matter. The great thing is to calm the mind, and in cloudless serenity to arrive at the true perception of these things. . . . Ah, that has always been alleged by a section, but Professor T. H. Green of Oxford, on the other hand, maintains that all the virtues to which you refer can be attained by a full citizenship in a peaceful community. The preservation of life and the pursuit of athletics as practised by the Greeks—in artistic moderation, not in the wholesale and barbarous fashion of modern lunatics —affords full scope for the hardihood and unselfish qualities to which you refer. . . . Butchery inspire the artists did you say ? What have we come to ? They will have to answer at the Last Day—the whole lot—if they cannot find anything better to inspire them. Slaughter and blood has been the burden of their song long enough, and they have so bewitched us that we think we are doing God's service when we cause misery to our fellow-men. Of course there are occasions when Christian men are bound to fight, as in the American War and wars of deliverance, such as the Italian struggle against Austria ; but the whole idea is the deadliest delusion on which in days to come the race will look back with horror and astonishment."

"You think then," his listeners would ask, "that a day will come when wars will cease? So-and-so was saying the other day that they are a necessary condition of life in this world."

"A necessary condition? as if any evil were necessary. Only the devil insists on their necessity. Christ does not. He has come to vanquish darkness and suffering, and to bring light and joy to mankind."

"Righteousness," my father used to say, " is generally the plea and the emanation of the weak and unknown." Yet sometimes, as in the old Puritan tale, God sends them a champion—Greatheart—to remind the world of their cause. What they lisp, he proclaims on the housetops, and that which they dumbly advocate, he champions and stoutly maintains. Social amelioration, in whatever form, is the cause of women and children, and their champions are for ever laying about them on the attack, in that they are for ever on the defence. By their great voice and presence they cheer Christiana and the children and their defenders on their way to the heavenly city.

The following letters will prove of interest. On one occasion my father had a conversation with Mr. Gladstone, who was dining at the house of Mr. Percy Bunting. This made a deep impression upon him, as he said afterwards that he felt he was conversing with a really great man.

"At other times," he added, " I have spoken with those who held high positions and who were reputed to be great, but they did not impress me as such. Mr. Gladstone did."

My father would often say, " Though Nonconformists have been among Mr. Gladstone's principal supporters, he has never understood Nonconformity." At Mr. Gladstone's death, he said, " He was the greatest and most typical Englishman of our time."

" 1 CARLTON GARDENS, *Ap.* 29, 1892.

" SIR,—I am so convinced of the high aim of your leading article of yesterday, that without vouching any matter of opinion, I send you a note of my recollections of the C. D. Acts, of course not infallible, but very different indeed from yours. It is not for publication, but simply for your consideration.—I remain, yours faithfully obediently,

" W. E. GLADSTONE.

" The Editor, *Methodist Times.*"

" 1 CARLTON GARDENS, *May* 3, 1892.

" REV. AND DEAR SIR,—When I wrote to you I had not the least idea whom I was addressing, and I am much obliged by your letter.

" The first of the two questions for Ireland which you raise has given rise to much difference of opinion ; we shall do our best in the way of reconciling duty.

" With regard to the second, I am only anxious that the case should be beyond all doubt, not however forgetting that superfluous assertion sometimes lets in doubt.

" I think you may read with interest a speech by Mr. Oscar Browning which I enclose. It was made without any communication with me. Without doubt you would be free to reprint anything you think material.—Yours very faithfully,

" W. E. GLADSTONE."

" 115 BRISTOL ROAD, BIRMINGHAM,
" 28/3/91.

" DEAR MR. HUGHES,—It is a very great encouragement to me to learn from your generous article in the *Methodist Times* of this week, that in your judgment my little book is likely to be useful. As the shadows lengthen and one anticipates the end, so much that one has done seems to have been of no effect, and one is grateful for the hope that all one's work is not wholly worthless.—I am, yours faithfully,

" R. W. DALE.

" Rev. Hugh Price Hughes, M.A."

TYNEHOME.
LYNDHURST GARDENS,
SOUTH HAMPSTEAD. N.W.

Feb 25/96

Yes, my dear Friend,
you are

"Our firebrand",
I thank God for your
zeal. Burn on!

affectly yr

Joseph Parker.

Rev Hugh Price Hughes MA

"THE CITY TEMPLE, HOLBORN VIADUCT, E.C.,
"LONDON, *June* 6, 1895.

" MY DEAR FRIEND,—My sexton has just observed a
painful paragraph in the *Chronicle* about your health.   I
cannot believe it.   I don't want to believe it.   The Mission is
yours, and in all the thoughts of Israel you are the one man
to handle it.   Have a colleague if you like, but do not give
up your primacy.   We hold you in loving honour, and for
your great and precious ministry we thank the Head of the
Church.—Ever affectionately yours,

" JOSEPH PARKER.
" Rev. Hugh Price Hughes, M.A."

"14 LYNDHURST GARDENS,
"SOUTH HAMPSTEAD, N.W.,
"28/10/1901.

" MY DEAR PRICE HUGHES,—We have a little club of ten
ministers meeting once a month at each other's houses.   To-
day the club met at my house and eagerly and unanimously
accepted my suggestion that we should write to you and
assure you of our united most hearty interest in your work
and all its widespread influence.   My dear friend, it gives me
the greatest pleasure to convey this expression of brotherly
feeling, and to give you every assurance of our united and
cordial affection.   We think of you often, and we thank God
for your noble testimony and your self-sacrificing labour.
' Be strong in the Lord and in the power of His might!'
And as for your future, leave it in His hands whose eyes
watch all our ways.   God bless you, strengthen you, renew
all the sources of your power, and in the end—far off—give
you the crown He has enabled you to win.—Ever affectionately yours,

" JOSEPH PARKER.
" Rev. Hugh Price Hughes, M.A.,
" 8 Taviton Street, Gordon Square, W.C."

"HAMPSTEAD, *July* 24.

" MY DEAR FRIEND,—I cannot read about the Aquarium
without thanking God and congratulating *Methodism* and the
whole Free Church.

" It is a splendid move. The policy is at once heroic and practical. This action ought to wake up all Churches to 'attempt great things' in the name of the Immortal Cross. It makes me almost young again, though I am so weak and woebegone with pain and fear.

" Excuse a tired but still willing hand, and believe me.— Ever affectionately yours,

" JOSEPH PARKER.

" Rev. Hugh Price Hughes, M.A."

Written in reply to my father's letter on the death of Mrs. Parker.

"14 LYNDHURST GARDENS, SOUTH HAMPSTEAD,
"LONDON, N.W., *January* 28.

" MY DEAR FRIEND,—This is the only available paper for the moment; pray excuse it. The truly fraternal and comforting letter which you addressed to me so kindly was deeply appreciated by us *both*. She is not here, she is risen; and for the moment the valley shuts out the sky. My warmest thanks to yourself and to all the brethren. I have no words. My soul is bowed down in heaviness.—Affectionately yours.

" JOSEPH PARKER.

" The Rev. the President of the Wesleyan Conference."

"PARK GATE HOUSE, HAM COMMON,
"*July* 14, 1894.

" SIR,—I have read with much interest and pleasure a recent article or letter rather of yours, which, in its outspoken and large-minded views on the subject of the turf and its evils, commends itself to everyone. I have long wished to have a conversation with you on that and other subjects. Would it be too presumptuous of me to ask you to favour me one day with a visit here should you at any time find yourself in this vicinity.

" I am aware that your life is a very busy one, and that your time is valuable to yourself and others, but should you be able to spare a few hours any day before 28th July, or any day later on in August, it would be the height of interest to me to see you, and to hear your views on so important a subject (I know that my husband, Lord Charles Beresford, fully endorses all your views), and one in which I am so much interested.

"This place is within easy reach of London. It is easy to get here from Richmond Station or from Mortlake, if you feel at any time disposed to see me and to stay to lunch and dinner.

"Hoping that you will pardon me for addressing you thus without having had the previous pleasure of your acquaintance, —I am, sir, very faithfully yours,

"MINA BERESFORD."

From Mrs. Henry Fawcett to a member of the family at the time of my father's death.

"2 GOWER STREET, *November* 18.

"It seems so lately that I saw you that I hope I am not intruding on your great sorrow in writing to express some of the deep sympathy I feel for your mother and for you all. Your father's death is a very great loss, not to you only, but to London and to England. He was so fearless and outspoken, and dared to think for himself, that one always watched for his voice as the voice of a real leader.

. . . .

"Believe me, with deepest sympathy, especially for your mother,—Yours very sincerely,

"M. G. FAWCETT."

"THE WALSINGHAM HOUSE, PICCADILLY, "*October* 23, 1897.

"DEAR MR. HUGH PRICE HUGHES,—I thank you very sincerely for the strong help you give me in your article in the *Methodist Times*. It is admirable in itself, valuable as the utterance of one who knows the West End so well from the point of view of the missionary, but most of all important to me as a clear-minded exposition of the motive of the book.

"The article is highly suggestive, and there are many things I could say about it. I could tell you stories of the music hall, and of the 'screw' that is being put upon certain of its people to deny that they have any knowledge of me—of my experiences of Soho, too, and the boycotting which I have to submit to on many sides. These, however, are personal matters, and only of consequence so far as they show that the book has touched life near enough to draw blood.

"As to what you say of the 'antichristian asceticism' which is sweeping over one part of the Church, I don't know if you have heard that ——, who established a Brotherhood, has just resigned his position of superior and abandoned the vows. This fact is not, I think, generally known, and I should shrink from any public mention of a circumstance which might naturally draw attention to the teaching and chief character of my own book. —— is by no means John Storm, though some of his Brotherhood appear to think he sat for the portrait.

"To this fragmentary and too personal note of thanks I feel tempted to add that in my boyhood I saw much of the Methodists in Liverpool, was a member of a class at 'Wesley Chapel,' and, I think, in early manhood, chairman of the Young Men's Society there, where one of my younger associates was 'Harry Lindsay,' known to me then by another name.—With kindest greetings,

"HALL CAINE."

"1 WHITEHALL GARDENS, S.W.,
"September 29, 1899.

"MY DEAR MR. HUGH PRICE HUGHES,—Do you ever go to the theatre? If so, would you come to see *The Christian* on its opening night, October 16? We are to have a dress rehearsal on Wednesday morning next, and I am wondering if you have an hour or two to spare out of your very busy life.

"The essence of the play would probably be done between 12 and 2 o'clock.

"I shall enclose the new preface to be published next week. —With warm regard,

"HALL CAINE."

"GREEBA CASTLE, ISLE OF MAN,
"September 9, 1901.

"MY DEAR MR. HUGH PRICE HUGHES,—I don't think I can be mistaken in thinking that, although you are off duty and forbidden to work, an article on my book in the *Methodist Times* is from your pen. Even if your hand did not write it your spirit runs through it, and my personal gratification is the same. I cannot easily say how much it stirred and stimulated me. I was trying not to listen to the poor little grudging squeals of the minor critics when your article came with its breath of mountain air, straight from the place where my motive had been born. It did me good. Since then a good many writers have followed where you led, and one or two fine minds (Ian Maclaren's, for example) have given independent expression to the same general thoughts.

"The problems you deal with are the great problems of the time. Is Christ the lawgiver for the nation as well as for the individual? Or is the prayer 'Thy kingdom come' a thing that takes no account of the eternal life of man? Did Christ come to save mankind as well as man? These questions carry us far. They cut at the root of all that is pagan in our national life. Perhaps they cut at the root of national life itself, and show that it is only a stage in human progress. Nothing seems clearer than that Christ asserted the rights of the individual soul, while paganism denied those rights. For lack of space I am not making my meaning clear.

"I trust you are recovering and enjoying your holiday. Don't think it necessary to reply to this. I am also overdone, and ought not to put pen to paper.—With warmest greetings,

"HALL CAINE."

"GREEBA CASTLE, ISLE OF MAN,
"*September* 10, 1901.

"DEAR MR. HUGH PRICE HUGHES,—Since writing to you yesterday I have received from Italy a copy of the Vatican organ, *La Voce della Verita*, for September 2, containing enclosed passage which will interest you, in view of what you lately said in the *Methodist Times* on the ethical exposition of the Lord's Prayer, in the Evangelical Free Church Catechism, in its relation to the material as well as the spiritual life of man. Is it not wonderful that after two thousand years this prayer should be seen in its social bearing? Or, rather, is it not strange that its social teaching has been so long obscured?

"Last night I dined with a group of Catholic ecclesiastics of various degrees, and the talk turned on Wesley. I described the expansion of Wesleyanism as indicated by the surprising chart which the *Methodist Times* publishes this week. Then I gave a little account of a prayer-meeting of five old men in a disused chapel just under my house here at Greeba—the sincerity, the devotion, the fervour, the language of Scripture, the complete absence of the forms and ceremonies that usually accompany the approach to the Almighty.

"I wish you could have heard what the priests said of it all—how they spoke of Wesley and the great man's great secret of employing the laity, and then of that scene of the five old men. I went home saying, 'There is the soul of the Catholic Church and there is the body of the Catholic Church, and the soul is indeed Catholic, and it is divine, and it will live for ever. It is only the body of it that makes and keeps us Protestants.'

"But you are right—it will always do so. The Church is not only Catholic, it is and ever will be also Roman.—With kind regards,

"HALL CAINE."

CHAPTER XV

HOLIDAYS AT GRINDELWALD

"The Church's one foundation
Is Jesus Christ her Lord:
She is His new creation
By water and the word:
From heaven He came, and sought her
To be His holy bride;
With His own blood He bought her,
And for her life He died."

THE reader may well ask whether my father ever took a
holiday. He undoubtedly tried to, for at the rate at which
he lived, recuperation became an increasing necessity. A
month in summer and a fortnight at Christmas, with a few
days in spring, was the yearly allowance during these years
of stress. But to the ordinary way of thinking he did not
employ these periods as holidays. In the first place, he
took books with him and wrote articles for the Journal, as
well as various letters that were on his mind. Even if he
were freed from this latter, the books were always there, and
not least the people with whom he conversed and swung into
his orbit. More than all, his active brain militated against
repose and made it well-nigh impossible. The health resort
of Huntly, Bishopsteignton, was a favourite of his, where the
kindness of the proprietors enabled him to spend short restful
holidays. On one of these occasions he persuaded some of
the visitors to take an interest in the villagers, and started a
Sunday afternoon service.

In the drawing-room in the evening games were played,
charades in particular, in which he took pleasure, though by no
inducement could he be got to take a part in the performances. Picnics by land and sea he would also enjoy when

his writing permitted, but nothing was more delightful than a long walk across the moors. Then he could rouse his family and friends at the witching hours that he loved; this reveillé gave a zest to the day's proceedings, of which he would not have been deprived for worlds. " Time to get up. Breakfast will be in half an hour. It is cloudy now, but it will be glorious presently." Then away across Dartmoor with some parson or other in tow, and an undaunted strategy.

He loved conversing with all manner of persons, but I do think he preferred a parson to any other. There was so much that he could tell him. Increasingly he loved their company. So it was scarcely surprising that August from 1892 onwards became apportioned to Grindelwald and what were called the Reunion Conferences, inaugurated by Dr. Lunn in 1892.

The previous Christmas Dr. Lunn had met some leading clergymen of various Churches at the Bear Hotel, Grindelwald, and in the evenings when the day's amusement was over, they had fallen to discussing questions relating to their common faith, and particularly as to wherein lay their divergences. Perhaps there is no greater reconciler than actual personal intercourse, and ecclesiastics, in particular, seem to have the most erroneous opinions concerning their brethren whom they have not met. So the result of these conversations was so interesting and unanticipated that Dr. Lunn decided to repeat the experiment in the following summer, and hold a regular Reunion Conference, to which the bishops and leading prelates of the Anglican Church and the leaders of Presbyterianism and English Noncomformity were invited.

The pill, moreover, of ecclesiastical discussion was to be embedded in the jam of mountain excursions and occasional evening programmes, in which instruction and amusement were mingled, alternated with serious theological discussions. Leading ministers who consented to read papers or deliver lectures were invited to come out to Switzerland as the guests of the originator of the Conference. The contemporary press alluded slyly to the spectacle, Mr. Gould's pencil producing some of his inimitable caricatures. The journals of the Metropolis took a good deal of notice of my father. He was the great belligerent of the rights of Nonconformity, not only as the possessor of a "conscience" whose dictates should not be overlooked, but as entitled to a social, civic, and ecclesiastical recognition, which he considered had till lately been denied them. "I don't know how it is," he exclaimed to a companion one day, " but it seems ingrained in English blood, this accursed snobbishness. The best and most Catholic cannot rid themselves of it. The Baroness told me a story that I could scarcely have believed but for her emphatic assurances. She met B——, a well-known clergyman of the Anglican communion, a most devoted Christian, at Vienna, and told him that she intended allying herself with the Methodists in England. This holy man—for whom I have the highest respect —was quite horrified. ' Baroness,' he said, ' it is impossible ! I assure you, no one belongs to the Methodists in England. They have no standing whatever.' ' Surely,' I said, ' you have made a mistake—not So-and-so? Why, he fraternised with me only lately, and appeared to possess the most Catholic sentiments.' But she insisted to me that he showed the greatest consternation when she evinced her determination of coming over here and joining us. The very air is charged with this social virus, and we take it with us wherever we go, in addition, I know, with certain fine qualities. The generality, indeed, are quite unconscious of it."

When Lord Hugh Cecil remarked in the House that he would have no objection if certain of the Nonconformists could sit among the peers spiritual in the House of Lords, the press and literary Bohemia seized upon my father as a likely wearer of the episcopal robes, and chuckled hugely over Mr. Gould's presentation of the espisode, as they did over his delineation of what was called " The Parsons' Picnic."

Certainly it was a varied spectacle, calculated in some ways to meet all my father's inclinations for the queer and picturesque brethren. To those first Reunion Conferences in 1892 and 1893, when the curiosity they excited was still fresh in a portion of the public mind, all the free lances as well as some of the dignitaries came. Conspicuous among the latter were the Bishop of Worcester, Archdeacon Wilson, Dean Freemantle, Père Hyacinthe, Prebendary Webb Peploe, Professor G. T. Stokes of Dublin, Pastor Theodore Monod, Dr. Stephenson, who with my father represented Methodism, and last but not least Dr. Berry of Wolverhampton, whose

25

meeting with my father was to be of much moment in the
world of Evangelical Protestantism.   But perhaps the most
picturesque of the brethren in his eyes was Père Hyacinthe,
the celebrated preacher at Notre Dame in Paris, who had
abandoned the Papacy, left Rome, and joined the Old
Catholics.   He was both an orator and a Frenchman, a quite
irresistible combination, and my father clave unto him.

Nobody knew how he had become conversant with the
French tongue, as he had never had an opportunity of doing
so.   From his youth up he had read French and understood
it when it was spoken.   Though he did not speak it fluently
himself and with no pretensions to accent, he yet seemed to
be able to express a great deal that he wished.   His gestures,
his determination that a Frenchman should understand him,
as well as something electrical and sympathetic which existed
between them, made mutual comprehension a comparatively
easy matter.   A French professor was living at the châlet
where my father was staying, who was unusually gentle in
manner and profound in thought.   I can only once remember
him being roused, which was during an argument on the
Woman question.

The professor raised his first finger and said that " woman
could not assert herself or demand a right because, as soon as
she did so, she ceased to be herself—to be woman.   In so
doing she overstepped her domain, her sovereignty ceased—
it was not her "—

He stopped here, partly because his English could carry
him no further, and still more because my father interrupted
him.

" Who are you to say what her domain is, and how she is
to assert herself?   It's a matter for her to decide, and the
God who made her with faculties, and the desire to use them,
whether man likes it or no."

" But," began the professor, " she cannot as woman "—

" But she can," said my father ; " I tell you she can, and
has, and she's not going to stand any of our humbug any
longer."

The idealism of the professor was no longer to be contained in Saxon limits ; he broke into French, my father
listening carefully and breaking in as before.

If the conversation had continued for weeks, they would not have got one whit nearer agreeing with each other.

One Sunday evening Père Hyacinthe preached, a proceeding which, apart from its striking character, inevitably reminded of Hans Andersen's story of the Emperor's Invisible Clothes. Just as all had to appear as if their eyes were entranced with the alleged royal garments, so on this occasion all present fixed their eyes on the Père and wore a look of the acutest comprehension. No man cared to own to his neighbour that he had not been entranced by the preacher's oratory, or that lack of familiarity with the French tongue had prevented him from grasping its import.

My father, who understood the discourse better than his family, recited its gist, which was an impassioned declaration of the essential universality of Christianity, of the wideness of its embrace. Its arms were open to all races of men and creeds too, for that matter, in that Christianity was the arched roof of a cathedral that enclosed them all. The translator smiled, noted the periods, spoke tenderly of the beautiful spirit that had animated the discourse, but regarded it as no more practicable than he did the polite suggestions of Broad Churchmen.

None the less his mind was busy devising possible *rapprochements* in a disunited Christendom. He seems to have felt, increasingly, about this time that he had a special work to do in such a direction, and that his ecclesiastical endeavours would be his chief service to mankind. His views of the special work and the constitution of Methodism led him to devote much of his mind and energies to those constitutional measures and ideals which he considered necessary to its full and unimpeded working. But both his mind and his energies soared beyond Methodism. He was essentially, for all his impassioned bias for his own communion, a member of the Universal Church, and profoundly interested in it. Moreover, ever since Oxford days, when he had felt the strength and attractiveness of much that belonged to the High Church ideal, he had been led to criticise not only the attitude of Methodism but the other Protestant communities, who had from time to time withdrawn from the Established Church of this country. Fighting each for a particular liberty

or aspect of truth, they had forgotten that the fold was one,
and that there was one Shepherd.

The immediate question was this.   Could these various
communities come to some ground of understanding with the
Protestant Mother Church of this country?   The Lambeth
proposals he considered to be more generous than Nonconformity had yet recognised.   So he spoke at the Conferences
as follows :—

"The Lambeth proposals, I entirely agree, contain great concessions,
which we ought fully to appreciate.   In the light of ecclesiastical history—
and unless we know something of it we are scarcely in a position to understand this question at all—it is an astounding thing that the bishops did
not insist upon infant baptism, and that the Athanasian Creed is not so
much as mentioned.   When we remember again the controversies of the
past, it is remarkable that they did not insist upon the Liturgy, nor even
mention the Thirty-Nine Articles.   If their predecessors had been willing
to make these concessions in the reign of Charles II., instead of passing
the Act of Uniformity, Dissent would never have assumed its present
dimensions.   If this spirit of compromise had existed two hundred years
ago we should not have been face to face with the difficulties which concern
us now.   But it often happens that if compromises are not made at the
proper time much more is required ; but when we consider the number of
ministers expelled by the Act of Uniformity, who had never even theoretic-
ally rejected Episcopacy, the position of the Anglican bishops at present
is a very hopeful fact.   You must remember, too, that these proposals are
only the first step made by brethren who, I firmly believe, would go
farther if they were encouraged by reciprocity on the part of the Nonconformists, who have never yet responded to the proposal.   We cannot
expect the clergy of that ancient and mighty Church to make every
conceivable concession until we are prepared to indicate the same spirit ;
and if the first step came quite spontaneously, without any offer from us,
I think it is a splendid example, which, with due regard to our conscientious
convictions, we ought to follow.   They insist upon the authority of Scripture,
and throw tradition overboard.   That is a point upon which we are all
agreed.   They put in the Apostles' and the Nicene Creeds.   I do not know
whether they would insist upon the Nicene Creed if we are prepared to
accept the Apostles', but I must say it is a very small demand to be made
by a great historic Church, because these two Creeds at any rate include
scarcely anything except a statement of plain and indisputable historic facts
which are the foundation of Christianity, and which involve scarcely any
theological differences.

"Then they assert the necessity of two Sacraments.   I do not understand why Mr. Aitken brought confirmation into his proposals.   I do not
know whether the Episcopacy involves the rite of confirmation.   ('No.')
Then we need not be troubled with this difficulty, because I am sure
Mr. Aitken would be satisfied with anything that would satisfy the Episcopal

bench. But, personally, confirmation in the evangelical and Protestant sense in which it is held by thousands of our brethren, is no alarming feature to me. I have always held that something corresponding to confirmation is necessary in all Churches which believe in pædobaptism—that at the right time young people in the Church should be brought face to face with their baptismal obligations. If Nonconformists believe that, there is no question of insuperable difficulty, and nothing to lead us to hold up our hands in despair."

Another time he spoke as follows:—

"I should like further to emphasise the absolute absurdity of the proposal that the Reunion of Christendom can ever be achieved by the capture of individuals. There are some who think that if they can persuade evangelical Nonconformists, by individuals or by families, to go over to the true Church of God, in this way gradually the object in view will be accomplished. The thing is mathematically impossible. There is no time to do it, and the number of ministers believing that theory is too small to enable them to carry it out. I stand here with careful computations which were brought before the Œcumenical Conference, as the representative of twenty-five millions of Methodists. Can you ever bring them one by one into any Church in the world? Of course there are always a number of Methodists who prefer to become Churchmen, and if it does them any good, we do not object in the least degree; but it will never make the least appreciable difference. Some of our brethren of the Church of England are not so anxious to make the necessary concessions because of the delusion that they are emptying other Churches. There never was a greater delusion since the world began. There are fifteen millions of Congregationalists, fifteen millions of Baptists, and an equal number of Presbyterians in the English-speaking world. We evangelical Nonconformists represent per head three times as many persons as the Anglican Church. The highest computation I have ever heard of the Anglican strength is twenty millions, and the lowest computation of the Nonconformist bodies is sixty millions. I merely mention this, not because it is an indication in the least degree that we are right—because the right often lies with the minority—but to show that it is a hopeless enterprise to suppose that by merely stealing one sheep here and another there you will empty these gigantic folds. If real union is to be secured, it must be of an organic kind. The great Churches are prepared on both sides to make concessions. It is quite possible that I have gone much farther than many Nonconformists are prepared to go at present, but I have not said it suddenly or hastily, but after twenty years of prayerful reflection and study of the Word of God, and I am extremely hopeful for the future. There are, of course, great differences on both sides, and I pray God to give us patience and mutual tolerance, so as to bear with many things we do not like, and at least to make an effort to understand one another. In Christ we are essentially one. Let us so abide in Him that we may ultimately become ecclesiastically one." (Applause.)

The great line of demarcation he knew to be the Anglican interpretation of the Apostolic Succession, and so the discussions abundantly proved. "Rome does not recognise the Anglican succession, or they ours," he would say. Another time, after pondering this question, he remarked with the suppressed gleam and the gravity that denoted the humorous perception of things, "Well, we are all in a great quandary, and how we are to extricate ourselves—let alone the Almighty—I cannot see. Unfortunately, He has tied up His grace with the bishops, and is altogether helpless without them!"

The recognition of the validity of the orders of ministers, who, like himself, had not only undergone a long and trying probation, ending with a solemn ordination service, but whose ministry had been blessed everywhere by conversions and incitements to higher living, of which this book and others have told, was to him vital. In its defence he would have fought till the millennium. As well might St. Paul have said he was not an accredited apostle because his apostleship rested primarily on the vision God gave him, and the work he did among men, rather than on the reception St. James with the eleven had accorded him at Jerusalem. The passage where St. Paul exclaims, "Am I not an apostle? am I not free? have I not seen Christ Jesus our Lord? are not ye my work in the Lord?" (1 Cor. ix.), would be quoted by him as a vindication of such a position.

There was a certain urbanity in my father and the bishop (during the proceedings) that bespoke a discussion of ideals and probabilities, not present contingencies. For all the solemnity of an occasion unique among Protestant divines, and the sincere desire to find and enlarge common ground on the part of those present, there was a feeling that the issues were speculative and therefore not vital—the good humour of my father and the bishop being quite delightful to contemplate, coupled with the gentle thrusts that they could not resist giving one another. During the discussion on Episcopacy, Dr. Perowne said, "Even Mr. Price Hughes, I believe, gives us his imprimatur on this point. Episcopacy is valuable, I understand" (with marked emphasis), "for aggressive purposes."

Prior to my father's speaking there was a species of wink among certain good Nonconformists. Now, they seemed to say, our great gun is going to boom! But it did not: the bugle instead blew peace and fraternity. "My lord bishop," I can remember him beginning, "when the question of reunion of the Churches in this country is mooted, there is ultimately but one basis, one meeting ground, that we could all desire, the Mother of us all." This speech, I think, was intended for his own Left as much as for the bishop. To bring them into line was always the problem of his strategy, and he was as much distressed sometimes at their behaviour as they were astounded at his. Certain Anglican clergymen were even more astounded. "Till to-day that man has been my *bête noir,*" said one to Dr. Lunn; said another, "It was worth travelling half across Europe to hear that speech."

One of my father's contentions was that Episcopacy had been a fact not a dogma in the Church since the days of St. John; he could not understand why certain brethren shuddered at the thought of what was a *sine qua non* of anything approaching reunion, such as the present discussion was contemplating, though as regards the nature of such an Episcopacy, and the method of securing it, he had, needless to say, his own peculiar and carefully thought-out views and opinions.[1]

The argument used by the bishop at the September session, that an Established Church was desirable because it conduced to the religious sense and life of the State, did not affect him. He was too ardent for that, both in certain religious views regarding the Church, and certain Liberal ones regarding the State. Like many spiritually minded men, he hated any view or state of things that permitted the clerical profession to be taken up by men because it was advantageous and "eminently respectable." Ingrained in him was the Methodist idea that the minister is "called" to his vocation.

In the notes of the *Methodist Times,* despite all appearances to the contrary, he was impersonal, attacking ramparts, but in actual intercourse he was much swayed by the personal

---

[1] All pastors of the United Church, he suggested, should be elected by the adult members of the Church, male and female. The bishops should then be elected by the pastors and lay representatives.

element, careful not to offend unless necessary, and courteous to a nicety. A staunch Presbyterian gentleman who appeared before the Mansion House Committee at the time of the Gas and Coke Company strike, on which Cardinal Manning was sitting, boasted to a member of the family of having addressed the Cardinal as " Sir." " You wouldn't catch me," he said, " calling him Your Eminence ! "

" I am distressed to hear it," said my father. " Very rude, very shocking." No doubt it was this gentleman's opposition to the demands of the men, and a lack of anything approaching true sympathy with them, compared with the very different demeanour on the part of the Roman Catholic dignitary, that helped to make him sore for the outraged dignity of the latter. Yet it was a very characteristic observation. He had far too much respect for the etiquette of his own branch of the Church not to respect it in that of others. He thought, moreover, that a careful etiquette and procedure within due bounds was most salutary in all departments of life, and not the least in its ecclesiastical side, where it was not difficult to shock him. Ministers of whatever Church who played practical jokes and made themselves look ridiculous, were not approved by him, however much he might approve them in other respects.

Nothing angered him more than persons who entered solemn assemblies, like the Reunion Conclave at Grindelwald, with a view to make light of, or to cast ridicule on, its proceedings. An irreconcilable High Anglican or Baptist he would listen to with distinct approval. They cared—were in earnest—saw the reality of life and religion and its issues. But witty persons, who with their tongue in their cheek, or something like it, set the whole assembly laughing at the wrong moment, were, for the time being, absolutely loathsome in his eyes ; nor had he any words strong enough to describe or condemn their conduct. By grace the most charitable of men, he would scarcely have been so, if he had followed primitive promptings, so was it his very nature at times to take strong likes and dislikes, and to resent those who offended his sense of what was fitting. That the courteous and conciliatory attitude of Bishop Perowne was not echoed by his fellow-Churchmen was made only too manifest by the reminders of the Anglican

Press when it commented on a feature of the Sunday that closed the Conferences.   The bishop administered the sacrament to all who had taken part in the proceedings, an act which much scandalised certain of the Establishment at home. To consent to preside over a group of leading Nonconformists was one thing, but to publicly partake with them of the rite which Christ had bidden His followers everywhere to celebrate in remembrance of Him, was something too much to be expected in an age of enlightenment.   At any rate, as my father would have put it, the two sides had seen something of their respective frontage.

The aspiration after reunion, of reversion to parent sources, was not confined to the leaders of Nonconformity; it was in the air.   High Anglicanism was again stretching out arms to Rome, seeking for recognition, and both Mr. Gladstone and Lord Halifax were taking a prominent part in the movement. In 1887 the latter went to Rome to obtain an audience of the Pope with this end in view.   In fact, the most unexpected feet were turned Romewards, including those of a prominent journalist, whom the world had never suspected of harbouring such desires.   These and other signs did not escape the religious leaders at Grindelwald, and in 1895 the Conferences exercised themselves over a new problem, which rose as follows : Pope Leo XIII. had written a letter to the English people—*ad Anglos*—which had provoked a variety of comment.   To this letter Dean Fremantle drafted an address which he submitted to the Marquess of Ripon, and then brought with him to Grindelwald.   The Conference appointed a committee, consisting of Dr. Pope, President of the Wesleyan Conference, the Archdeacon of Manchester, the Moderators of the Church of Scotland and of the United Presbyterian Church, Professor Lindsay of Glasgow, my father, Dr. Lunn, and the Dean himself.   After several sessions, the committee finally agreed upon an address, which was signed by most of the foregoing and several leaders of Anglican and Nonconformist thought. The address itself, after a courteous reference to the Pope's appeal and an expression of sympathy with his letter, affirmed that the signatories also deplored the present divided state of Christendom.   At the same time, they could not but recognise that " existing divisions arose in defence of vital elements of apostolic Christianity and scriptural truth." They affirmed that there was " a real spiritual unity underlying all our differences, and manifesting itself in the prayer and praise of a common Christian life, in the numerous signs of a common Christian experience, and in the signal blessing which the God of all grace has bestowed upon every fragment of the divided Catholic Church." The address concluded by affirming that our Lord Himself was the only possible centre of Christian unity.

With this document duly framed and signed, Dr. Lunn was despatched to the Eternal City, where it was submitted to His Eminence Cardinal Rampolla, who had it translated by English-speaking fathers and submitted to the Pope.

The Pontiff declared that the address contained so many heretical sentiments that he could not receive it officially, but he courteously offered a private interview to the bearer of the document. This he did not feel justified in accepting. None the less, the bearer had several interesting experiences, dined with Vatican officials, and returned well pleased with his visit, which he related in full, to the undisguised delectation of my father. As my father listened, he was led to reflect increasingly on the policy of Rome, and the manner in which she had profited by the enthusiasm of her most ardent spirits.

One day at Grindelwald, when he was out with a Broad Churchman, whose society he found very delightful, he began descanting on the Pope's wisdom in this respect—no personal Pope, of course—but the traditional policy of the chair of Peter. " Now in Anglicanism, for instance, or Methodism, or any other of the Protestant communities, if a man comes along full of the zeal of the Holy Ghost, willing to lay down his life for the advancement of the Church and humanity, and to use any method, conventional or unconventional, in the achievement of this purpose, he is scowled at, looked down upon, tied up here and tied up there, so that in the end if he wants to do his work in this world he has to clear out of Methodism or any other ' ism ' altogether. But the Pope, on the contrary "— (here my father raised his voice, as his companion was struggling with some unruly roots which he wanted to put into a basket)—" the Pope, on the contrary, welcomes him, ties a rope round his waist, and gives him more or less *carte blanche* to do as he pleases—*i.e.* he founds an order, and so keeps both himself and the whole concern alive. Oh, if we could only imitate his policy in this respect, the whole world might be at our feet. Have you not pondered over that, over the astonishing instances that the mediæval Church affords of this piece of far-sightedness?" Apparently his friend had not pondered—he was still tugging at the roots, and his mutterings when audible did not express any special jubilation at the spectacle of the mediæval Church and her orders.

My father denounced mediævalism, while he was attracted by certain of its phases. Indeed, he himself was not unlike a humanised Peter the Hermit, everywhere inciting men to crusades, not for the restoration of the Lord's burial-place, but for that of His nature and His ideals in the poor, the outcast, and the erring of society. As simple and tense and vivid seemed his faith as romance has portrayed theirs. When he actually visited the sepulchre in which he believed the Lord to have lain (he did not accept the traditional site, but took General Gordon's view, and had an animated contention on the subject), he lay full length as gently and reverently as the knight of the legend who has visited the spot of his desires. "My Master lay here," he murmured; "see, I stretch myself where He lay." Always His figure haunts him as he wanders through the land where He walked. At a bend of the steep and dusty road along which he is driving he descries a turbaned peasant climbing up the hill. "So He must have walked," is the instant thought. "Shall I ride where He toiled? God forbid!"—and in a moment he leaps from the carriage and finishes the ascent on foot. In the great metropolis of the West Christ is equally present, toiling, suffering, rejoicing over one sinner that repenteth. The most lovable, he is also the most solitary. He leans on no man, is dependent on none. "Thou, oh Christ, art all I want"—it is the refrain of life, the refrain with which he would fling himself into eternity. "Since I have Thee, what is there to lose—what can any man do unto me since Thou art here. What would'st Thou, Lord. What shall I say, whither go, what do? If I die 'tis gain, for I see Thee; if I live 'tis but to serve Thee!"

A little book to which he was attached contained the devotional exercises and experiences of one Brother Laurence, a monk residing in Paris, who was in the wont of practising and inculcating, as he expressed it, "the practice of the Presence of God." Like other Christians of the era, my father was possessed with the idea of the Universal Church, which is supposed to have been more clearly conceived in mediæval times because less rich and varied, than the period following the Reformation. "If Christians were united, what would become of us!" he read once as a boy from the pen of an opponent, and never forgot the exclamation. He often said: "If Cardinal Newman, the Archbishop of Canterbury, General Booth, and the President of the Methodist Conference, were locked up in a room and told they must not come out till they had arrived at a vital point of agreement with regard to the Christian faith, they would be released in two or three minutes."

That the various Protestant bodies should unite and enter into their responsibility as a recognised and integral part of the body catholic became a leading idea both of his and of Dr. Berry's, whom he met at Grindelwald about this time. Their conversations up winding ascents revealed two minds at once delighted and surprised with each other's ideas. A prophet enamoured of liberty and of Democracy each had expected to find in the other, but scarcely a High Churchman in addition. "I take it," began the Doctor—and my father inclining his head would smile at the true ecclesiastical ring of the takings. The deep valleys and peaks of the Bernese Oberland unfurling itself before them appeared to incite yet farther in their review of what men have called Christ's temple on earth. Each peak almost might have stood for a corresponding eminence in the history of the Churches; Greece and Rome, and the varied field of modern Protestantism seemed to lie at their feet like the smiling valleys echoing with the roar of some molten ice rivulet, or with the cannonade of the falling avalanches. To the mind not occupied with ecclesiastical matters, such absorption appeared strange. "Does not the view strike dumb," a companion would say to him. "How little all else seems in comparison!"

"It's your mind that perceives the view. You are greater than anything you see."

This was only an aspect of the analysis of the situation, but the speaker thought that aspect ought to be insisted on.

Whether Dr. Berry was present or not, these mountain conversations invariably tended to an ecclesiastical turn, nor did the proximity of a historic lake, the following summer at Lucerne, tend to digression from the central theme. It simply went over bodily with the mountains, and became part of the chart, as at Grindelwald. Yet the party were far from forgetting Schiller and William Tell, who figured in the interludes, together with various personages present on whom my father vented his witticisms. The climax of the day's programme was tea at four o'clock at some spot marked for the purpose on the shores of the historic lake. The necessity of reaching that spot without fail at the hour designated was impressed upon the party at the start, and somehow clave to their memory more than any of the events of the day. All else was subsidiary to this climax. First an eminence had to be scaled, from the summit of which climbers were watched with anxious eye. " Ah, poor thing, poor thing ; just a hundred paces more and then the end of all your woes. Courage, courage! Do you want my assistance? Now for the tug. There's my alpenstock. Hallelujah! You have scaled the height, and now you can rest for evermore!" No climber was ever deceived! If the ascent had been necessary, still more was the descent for that inexorable tea at four o'clock at some spot overlooking the lake. Persons strove against this decree of the Fates, but in vain. Why not five minutes past, or ten minutes past, or even a quarter past, and a saunter down inviting slopes? To their questionings they obtained no detailed response, but the intensest impression that to resist what had been decreed was both shame and ruin—shame to them and ruin to the day's undertakings.

At tea they were incited to admire the view. " Why don't you allow your soul to expand at the vision of it?" followed by reference to what the speaker conceived to be the idiosyncrasies of the party, to which some would respond with vigour. Sallies that were unusually salient he would greet with applause. " Well done, indeed! I could not have put it better myself. As in all else, wretch that I am, I bow to your superior learning and eloquence. Now, honey or jam, which will you have? Take your share now, as Mr. S. I understand is going to consume the whole pot as a protest against the divine rage that I have excited in his bosom. What's that—Miss P. is going to—what, what? . . . Well I never—what are young women coming to next," etc. Then out came the watch—" Now we have no time to lose. The boat goes at five fifteen precisely." By this time all doubt and smouldering mutiny had ceased. Everybody hurried their operations as if there were no other boat on the lake, inciting each other if any showed a tendency to lag behind in the race. On one memorable occasion a gentleman of the party just got on board by the skin of his teeth, and my father never forgot the incident. He watched his haste with keenest enjoyment from the side of the vessel on which the rest of the party were duly drawn up and stationed. " John Gilpin was not in it, my dear sir—not in it. Where were you, and how in the world did you elude our notice? Tell us now, when you feel a little better, and the fair have ceased to palpitate on your behalf. I had no idea that we had such an athlete in our midst. The forward movement of that leg was magnificent, only you should have looked a little less disconcerted. When you run next, my dear fellow, wear the look of a victor, not of a fugitive!" Such displays would cause him laughter for days after their occurrence, and at the end of a week the recital of it was so splendidly conceived, transformed, and coloured that everybody would come crowding into the room to hear him tell it again.

It was so difficult to focus my father's attitude on various matters that there were often the wildest rumours concerning him—to wit, that he was about to return to the bosom of the Anglican communion, or that he was a member of the Society of Jesus, acting in the interests of Rome. On reading the former assertion once in the columns of the daily newspaper, he could not resist a two-edged piece of criticism in the notes of the Journal. How, in the first place, could he return to the bosom of anything on which he had never rested; and why, in the second place, did not his friends suggest a return to the bosom of the Greek Church? That would sound so much more romantic! When the question of Count Tolstoy's excommunication from the Greek Church was mooted, and passionately repudiated by prophets in the wilderness and others, he maintained a marked silence. At last he said, " The Greek Church cannot do otherwise.   You are not aware of the difficulties of the situation."

Dr. Berry one Sunday preached a great sermon on the New Jerusalem, based on its description in Revelation, with a gate to the north, and a gate to the south, and a gate to the east, and a gate to the west.   Each of the great gates stood for the Church of those peoples inhabiting that portion of the earth to which they pointed, the westward gate representing the western churches and so on, and a great deal else which memory cannot recall; but though the gates were far apart, and the roads leading to them different one from the other, they all led to that heavenly city into which the gates opened.

Other people beside my father and Dr. Berry had their dreams and particular conceptions of the visible Church at this time.   Mr. Stead was full of what he called a " Civic Church," which shocked my father not a little.   " The idea is beautiful," he said, " but to call it a Church is a misnomer."   At Lucerne one day Mr. Stead came to lunch, and was careful to address him as " Bishop," whether as a tribute to his ecclesiastical proclivities or to what he considered his autocracy, is not known; but it was probably the latter.   In his train also came Mr. Benjamin Waugh, the founder and secretary of the Society for the Prevention of Cruelty to Children, and he kept everybody entertained by the hour by the narration of the exploits and victories of that gallant society.   My father considered him the " queerest and most Christlike brother " he had met for a long time, but quite ignorant concerning the true nature and signification of the visible Church.   An even " queerer " brother in his eyes was Mr. Richard Le Gallienne, whom he met at Davos one summer, and to whom he took a great fancy, I might say affection.   The length of that writer's hair caused him diversion, as did the length of his own eyebrows supply fuel to the mirth of Mr. Le Gallienne.   On Mr. Le Gallienne proclaiming himself a pagan, my father drowned him with a negative.   "You are not a pagan," he shouted; "never let me hear you say it again."   This writer always presented my father with copies of his books (of which *The Religion of a Literary Man* interested him specially); and on another occasion he attended the Sunday evening service at

St. James's Hall, and then accompanied the preacher home to supper. Relatives or friends who would be present at his Sunday service and then relate their impressions, afforded him the greatest delight. It reminded of an eager child who wants others to come and see what he is doing and building up in the corner. Despite his solitariness of spirit in many ways, he was immensely dependent on sympathy, and the more so as he himself was often attacked and misunderstood. This need for sympathy himself often made him deeply intuitive of the feelings of others, and when he perceived himself to have failed in such intuition, his distress was great.

The following is a case in point. During the first Reunion Conference there was a young Irish lady staying at the same châlet, who experienced the deepest amazement and then wrath at what were evidently "the opinions of English Non-conformists." They were not only at variance with all that she had been taught to consider desirable, but they verged on cruelty when they advocated Home Rule in Ireland. Like many questions on which people feel deeply, her tongue failed her in argument, and she would close a passage of arms by saying that she would rather die than see Ireland given over to the populace and the priests. At meal-times it was her fate to hear assertions to which there was no means of reply-ing, and during which she would clench her teeth, as people did sometimes when my father happened to be saying some-thing counter to their predilections. On one such occasion she retired to her bedroom and burst into tears. The occur-rence was repeated to my father, and caused him the acutest distress. The "opinions of Nonconformists" henceforth under-went considerable modification; assertions turned out to have quite a different complexion to that which might have been supposed, and there was not a rule that had not its exceptions. The references to the army were particularly guarded, as the young lady, like others in the world, took what my father had to say against that institution (uttered from Pisgah heights, where brotherly love begets a certain ferocity of sentiment) as an indictment against her own relatives in that service. As for the "banner," he absolutely ceased to wave it altogether. When reproached on this subject, he answered with much sorrowfulness, "Do you not see how helpless I am—how tongue-tied? That poor girl was found weeping in her bed-room the other day at something I said,—I am sure I don't know what it was,—so I have been feeling much distressed that any remark of mine should cause her suffering. Evidently I am such an awful monster that the quieter I keep the better, particularly about Ireland. Like all the Orange Protestants, she is absolutely mad on this subject."

From the above it may be seen that the effect of the Grindelwald parties was not limited to projects of reunion. It brought people of all degrees of opinion and environment into personal contact with each other, with the most benficent results. My father became not only better acquainted with certain Anglican and foreign clergy, such as Père Hyacinthe, but with those Nonconformists whom he regarded as " extreme " in certain ways, and with whom he afterwards came into closer rapport in the work of federating the Free Churches.

Yet the Anglican benefit in this direction seems to have been greater than the Nonconformist. My father at any rate had mingled with men of other Churches from his youth up, and was well informed both of the history and leading men of Anglicanism, while they on their side were often amusingly ignorant of Methodism and other portions of Nonconformity. One clergyman's wife said to my mother, " I had no idea before I came here that Nonconformists were so religious. I thought them very clever of course, but I did not think they believed anything ! "

The possession of any social graces on the part of Non-conformists seemed also surprising to them, which recalls the answer made by an Irish Canon of the Anglican Church to one who made the following inquiry : " Now what kind of fellow is this Price Hughes ? "

" Well, he is a most charming person (pause) to meet. Quite a delightful companion and talker."

" Really "—which being interpreted meant—" You don't mean it ! "

The personal element was undoubtedly strong with my father, as it is with everybody. Often when he was denouncing classes of action and persons, his children would interrupt him with, " But So-and-so, father ? She's not that," or " He's not that."

26

" Oh, well," was the answer, " there are special circumstances in poor So-and-so's case. Besides, that does not detract from my main contention." A marked trait was his insistence on what he would term the " earnest Christianity" of many of his opponents, either in Methodist or other Churches. Having shown what he considered the shortcomings and " delusions " of their policies and opinions, he would always close his remarks by saying reverentially, " Of course So-and-so is a very earnest Christian." Even when commenting on a political leader so opposed to him in mind and temperament as the late Lord Salisbury, he was careful to pay this tribute. A deputation, of which my father was a member, waited on his lordship, when Premier, with respect to a proposed Education Bill.

His extreme sagacity seemed to impress him as much as anything. " There he sat immovable," narrated my father afterwards, not without enthusiasm, " and nothing was lost upon him, not a word. He contradicted me once before I had finished my sentence—' I beg your pardon, my lord,' said I, ' but that was only a comma. If you will permit me, I will continue to the full stop.' "

" Oh, I beg your pardon, I beg your pardon," he said.

" I took care to rub it in well. ' Can you imagine, my lord,' said I, ' either yourself or one cherishing your convictions forced to send their sons and daughters to a *Baptist* school, to receive instruction from the hands of *Baptist* teachers, in the *Baptist* acceptation of Christian doctrine, and to be given to understand from their *Baptist* instructors, perhaps by some of their *Baptist* associates, that attendance at the *Baptist* mode of worship in the *Baptist* chapel, would be of greater benefit to them both here and hereafter than if they attended the services and ministrations of the Parish Church?' I threw gusto into the word Baptist each time that I said it, as I knew he hated them worst of all of us, and I thought that the determined reiteration of the word might help to bring the case home to him, and the feelings of certain Baptists in our villages. He was very near squirming."

The evident sagacity of one whose policy he deplored in certain directions seemed to strike my father. It was the necessary " audacity," not statesmanship, that he thought his lordship lacked. " Why have not men more courage," he often asked, and many in the Cabinet, and out of it, suffered, to his thinking, from that complaint. There was always one summary when speaking of his lordship—" He is an earnest Christian and a most devout member of the Anglican communion."

That earnest men, however divergent in views and environment, should come to some understanding of each other, is surely a triumph and touchstone of pure goodness. This, and this alone, may well atone for the ridicule which greeted the promoters of the Grindelwald Conferences. The loftiness of the discussions, the deep interest of what was said, the courtesy and spirituality of the proceedings, sank into the minds of most who were present. These perceived that Christians who appeared to have the most divergent views were yet bound by a common faith, whose obligations they could realise in the " ampler, purer air " of the eternal hills, as they failed to do in the closer atmosphere of the valley. Henceforth charity was deeper, the outlook wider. My father's optimism was in particular intensified. The contention of his speeches throughout was that some form of reunion was an actual possibility. When speakers contended that sectarianism and discord were unavoidable in the Church of Christ, and a necessary accompaniment of earthly existence, he would repudiate such ideas as contrary to the teaching of Christ. In private he would employ the strong language that he loved and say such teaching was " of the devil."

In the summer of 1894 his nervous exhaustion was felt to be serious. The terrible strain of 1889 and 1890, the years of the Missionary controversy, added to the efforts expended on launching the Mission and in various public matters in London, had left their mark upon him. It was felt that a long holiday was necessary, and this a little group of Methodist friends undertook to ensure. The proximity of Grindelwald to Italy, where my father was as usual spending August, was felt to indicate the nature of the holiday proposed. In the land of blue sky and *dolce far niente*, it was thought he would obtain the rest and refreshment that both body and mind alike craved. To visit Italy, moreover, had always been one of his dreams, and very particularly since my mother's visit on a previous Easter to its principal cities—so to Italy they both went.

CHAPTER XVI

ITALY, ART, AND ST. FRANCIS

"Oh, Francis, never may thy sainted name
Be thought or written save with soul aflame,
Nor spoken openly nor breathed apart
Without a stir or swelling of the heart."

" I myself had a deep conviction throughout my visit to Italy that it was not a mere journey for pleasure or even for health, but that it was a rare opportunity of enriching my mind, and qualifying myself for better service at home."

Extract from my Father's Italian Journal.

ITALY was a true holiday to my father, as no one doubted who saw his face when he left England, and its serene and unclouded aspect on his return. To the generosity of these friends he owed not only deep delight but the strength which he afterwards brought to arduous ecclesiastical toil. In addition to books bearing on the various cities and their history which they contemplated visiting, he thought some knowledge of the Italian language desirable, so he procured a grammar and sat in the corner of the railway carriage " muttering Italian verbs," as my mother expressed it in one of her letters.[1] While at Rome he derived much profit and delight from the society of Mr. Piggott, and through his advice was enabled to obtain a complete library of Italian masterpieces at a moderate price. The exultation with which he indicated this goodly row was almost fierce. " The best are all there—do you comprehend it, I wonder ? "

---

[1] His secretary relates that he never in later life made one of his frequent visits to the provinces without taking a German and Italian grammar at the bottom of his bag. They were there as a matter of course, though it must have been seldom indeed that he found time to look at them.

Italy held to him two saints whose shrines he was to reverently visit, the founder of the Franciscan Order and Joseph Mazzini, whose tomb he said "he kissed—no one else's." Yet in the Journal he confesses (after apologising for excess of sentiment) that he similarly saluted the name of Savonarola on the walls of his cell at San Marco.

His visit to Assisi he described as follows :—

" How shall I describe the emotions with which we approached Assisi ? M. Paul Sabatier's *Vie de St. François d'Assise* had filled our minds with the most romantic anticipations. I confess that I had sometimes suspected that the brilliant pen of one whom I am now so happy to call my friend had invested Assisi itself with an imaginary glamour. But it was not so. Apart from its delightful associations with sweet St. Francis and St. Clara, 'the sweetest flower of St. Francis,' Assisi is one of the most beautiful spots I have ever visited. Planted romantically on the steep side of a huge projecting buttress of the Apennines, it is visible far off as the train winds down from Perugia. The vast fertile plain stretches in all directions, to be finally enclosed in hills of every picturesque shape. Assisi itself is embedded in lovely olive groves and vineyards, and the air is ever filled with the exquisite perfume of flowers and aromatic plants. St. Francis was born and nurtured amid all that is most beautiful, romantic, and delicious in sunny, radiant Italy. What he would have said or done amid the gloom and fogs of northern latitudes it is impossible to imagine. But no one who has visited Assisi and studied his life can doubt that his lovely birthplace and home coloured his temper and creed.

"As soon as Assisi appeared to our outstretched heads, we also saw its most conspicuous building—the vast church and convent which now enshrine the ashes of the most popular champion Rome ever had. . . . After an Italian dinner in the hotel, a young English artist who was staying at Assisi said to me, 'Do you know who it was who sat on our left at dinner?' 'No,' I replied. 'It was Paul Sabatier,' he answered, to my immense surprise and delight. The next morning, of course, I appeared with my octavo volume of the great Life in my hand, and, as soon as the illustrious man was seated, I told him with what intense pleasure and profit my wife and I had read his book. He was very affable, and in a short time we were as friendly as if we had known one another from our youth. He accompanied us to the Church of St. Francis to point out a figure of the saint by Cimabue, which he thinks gives the best idea of him. He also took long walks with me about Assisi, and we discussed a multitude of questions. I was delighted to find that he shared my high estimate of St. Clara. He was staying at Assisi in order to bring down his history of the Franciscan movement to the death of St. Clara. We talked much of the religious future of Italy and France. I found that he heartily endorsed the principles of 'the Forward Movement,' and he became greatly interested in our West End work. I am hoping to have the great happiness of seeing him in London next spring."

Yet Italy was not merely sacred to him as the home of saints and great men, but as the home of the arts. As a young man, he had not impressed beholders with a comprehension of the divine frenzy, but in later years he was always striving to develop unsuspected portions of his mind. Concert programmes in a friend's drawing-room had a fascination for him, and the name of one composer in particular — one Wagner.

"Why are they all mad about him ? " asked my father.

Then it was that his sisters-in-law took compassion upon him and gave him Mr. Forsyth's *Religion in Recent Art* to read, which did not merely reveal Wagner and the pre-Raphaelites in a new light, but commented on the "unloveliness" of the religion of many Nonconformists. The dismay that he shared with the author at a fact that could not be denied quickly communicated itself to the pages of the Journal; not that he felt the dismay for the first time, but it was brought invincibly home to him. The students in the Wesleyan Colleges, he exclaims, should be trained to appreciate art, and to realise its blessedness. John Wesley, he admits in another place, had no adequate sense of the beautiful, and the Methodist Church had suffered in consequence. "It is high time that those of us who represent the glorious Puritan tradition should remember that there is such a thing as the ' holiness of beauty ' as well as ' the beauty of holiness.' Our great representative, Milton, was keenly alive to the beauty of nature and of music, without abating one jot of his adherence to a lofty ethical code. We must be equally sensitive and responsive to the beauty with which God has filled the world. We must approach the True through the Beautiful, as well as the Beautiful through the True."

This fact always haunted him, particularly after his visit to Italy, and he wished that he could find a remedy and make the " Forward Movement " develop in that direction, as it was bound to do, if it was to entice mankind as it should. Something was wrong somewhere. Cromwell was the maker of modern England, and the most powerful and righteous ruler that had ever regulated our affairs; yet youth instead of adoring him and loving his memory as it ought, was mad after the cavaliers and their lovelocks. The literary artists were to blame here. They wrote in such an enchanting manner about high-born youths and fair ladies that voracious youth loathed everybody who opposed these; and the dramatic artists too, they were to blame—silks and satins and sentiments and graces, against men who sniffed and talked with a drawl. "Why do they never draw a picture of a scholar and a gentleman like Colonel Hutchinson," he once exclaimed, "who delighted in music, and was the father of charming daughters." "It's an everlasting Princess this, and poor my Lord Duke that, while those who have founded our liberties are of no account and go to the wall." "Oh," he exclaimed another time, "that would be a great deed, to write a play on Cromwell and his times, and to portray him worthily." "Even some of the members of the House of Commons, who ought to have known better," he added, "made a fuss about erecting that statue of Cromwell—and when they did they stuck him down in an obscure corner where nobody notices him—he who made them what they are." "Oh, the folly of mankind!" And the root of it all lay with the writers of romances and plays! So he grew not only to love art more and more, but to fear it, for he saw its powers, which at times struck him as terrible.

He wondered sometimes how much his great ecclesiastical opponents owed to those qualities which art had glorified. If a man took Newman's arguments and conceptions of the Catholic Church, for instance, what did they possess as an argument and a conception to bewitch portions of mankind? It was the literary style of their exposition that explained the witchery and the secret, and on that he exclaims when he comments in the Journal on the Cardinal's death. It had intoxicated generations of journalists and literary men.

A lack of musical training in early youth was always lamented by him. "If you will only practise I don't mind what you do," he would say to members of his family, whom duty required to perform on the pianoforte in the room adjoining his study. "Even your scales soothe me." When he saw any member of the household going to a concert, he would exclaim, "Lucky dog! I must wait for my music." Yet on one occasion the first violin of the Mission was electrified to see the superintendent sitting in the balcony of St. James's Hall at a Richter Concert.

On another occasion he went to the Leeds Festival when he happened to be in the neighbourhood, and on another to the Handel Festival at the Crystal Palace, where he was not a little impressed and stirred. He was a good deal nearer the apprehension of certain artistic circles and its life and charm than contemporaries imagined, though he would fight them as well as anybody else to the death when it came to questions of social morality. The opening chapters of Mr. du Maurier's *Trilby* entranced him. " It is the first portion—the description of Bohemian life in Paris—that is excellent," he said ; " it falls off at the end." The fact that one so skilful as the author with his pencil should attain celebrity in addition by a product of his pen appeared to impress him. Of his society sketches in *Punch* he was always a great devotee, and he would spend Christmas evening poring over " Things one would rather have left unsaid," Mrs. Ponsonby de Tompkins, the æsthetic craze, and all the rest. At dinner he would lead the conversation with éclat, but afterwards he would relapse deeper and deeper into the mint of that artist's delicate humour till he fell to mutely turning the pages, the silence never being broken except by " Would you kindly pass me the next volume? "

About the time of the Missionary controversy he happened to be reading the libretto of Wagner's opera, for there were great plans abroad. One of his sisters (Mrs. F. Webb-Peploe), a lover of art and Wagner, was doing her best to persuade him to accompany her to the Bayreuth Festival in the summer of 1892. As my aunt had considerable determination, and my father needed little persuading, their visit was accordingly arranged, and took place to the great satisfaction of all concerned.

My aunt's impressions of my father at this time are reported in her own words:

"I attended the Wagner Festival at Bayreuth in 1891, and directly I heard that an extra Festival was to be given in 1892 (to satisfy the discontented members of European Wagner Societies who had been unable to obtain tickets in 1891), my first impulse was to persuade your father to make a pilgrimage to Bayreuth with me. I felt so strongly that here was dramatic art in a form which would appeal strongly to your father's dramatic instinct, and without the distasteful accompaniments so often found in English theatres.

"You will remember how we left you all at Grindelwald and started off for Bayreuth, Dr. and Mrs. Lunn, your mother and father and I. We witnessed four of the eight great works of Wagner, namely, *Tannhäuser*, *The Meistersingers*, *Tristan and Isolde*, and *Parsifal*. The first we heard was *Tannhäuser*. You know the various arrangements of the Opera House, and how everything is planned to permit the operas to be heard and seen to the very best advantage.

" Before each Act, three weird trumpet-calls sound, the audience moves on, and the doors are locked. Not the Regent himself would be admitted as a late comer, so absolutely is music the dominant interest here. And within—all combines to deepen the expectancy—the darkness of the house ; the hidden orchestra ; the intense quiet ; and then falling upon the solemn silence the strange beautiful overture of *Tannhäuser*. How can I better describe to those who knew him the effect of *Tannhäuser* upon your father than to say that for the first and only time in my experience, he was perfectly still. As I had foreseen, here was dramatic art that satisfied him, for with strong artistic instincts and a great love for the æsthetic side of life, he always needed what children call 'a moral.' He was Hebraic to the backbone. Under the art, underlying the beautiful, some defined moral teaching. Were it not so, then for him, the production, be it play, book, poem, or picture, was incomplete. *Tannhäuser* satisfied him. In it he saw life as he ever viewed it, not on the surface, but in its depths, good and evil in deadly conflict, the evil terribly fascinating, terribly strong, but yet (he never doubted that) the good stronger, the good triumphant.

" As I sat beside your father I was conscious again and again, without a spoken word, that he was stirred to the depths.

" Later we saw *The Meistersingers*. You can realise how in that comic pendant to *Tannhäuser*, your father rejoiced in the underlying nobility of Hans Sachs and the way in which Wagner himself evidently learned to love him, true man under his many oddities and affectations. This proof of the nobility of man as such illumined the play for him. But *Tristan and Isolde* quite failed to attract him. You remember how the unlawful love of the two was brought about by means of a magic love potion, all guilt being removed from its victims. This unreality spoiled the opera to your father. The needed moral was absent. There was no freewill, and no responsibility, and, consequently, it was 'unreal.'

" ' Why should such an artifice be employed ? ' I remember his questioning, as he compared the rendering of Wagner with those of Tennyson and Matthew Arnold, and we wondered what was the original conception of the story in the Welsh Mabinopon. I remember, too, his waxing extremely merry over the exceeding corpulence of Kurwenal, whose size I have scarcely ever seen equalled, and whose romantic part in the play went strangely with his unwieldy form.

" *Parsifal* impressed him greatly, but again there was a flaw. It seemed almost a caricature on the ' old, old story.'

" The washing of the feet of Parsifal by the repentant Kundry especially aroused his remonstrances. Why should Wagner borrow so largely from the details of the Bible story, and make what must necessarily be a poor imitation ? And yet he felt it was an impressive fact that one who made no profession of belief should go to the old familiar story for his scenes, and base the last of his great works on the divine watchwords of 'pity' and 'service.'

"But interested as he was in the works he saw, your father never again experienced the unmixed pleasure of *Tannhäuser*, where he saw depicted, with the magical adjuncts of music and song, the great struggle of right against wrong in which he himself ever fought, through good report and evil report, with changes of opinion but never change of principle, ever subjecting his natural love of art and culture, of 'sweetness and light,' to the greater object of the world's needs."

Tristan and Isolde confirmed him in the belief that the Germans were the most sentimental people on the face of the earth. " There are no words," he would exclaim, " to describe it —none. For three mortal hours they were at it, shouting at one another without apparently experiencing the least fatigue in the endless unfurling and enunciation of their emotions." Another musical drama at which he was a rapt and most devout listener was the performance of Bach's Passion music on Tuesday in Holy Week at St. Paul's, which he managed on one occasion to attend. Another time he went to the performance of the *Antigone* of Sophocles, by the boys of Bradfield College, near Reading, which he thoroughly enjoyed, interspersing the proceedings with lively and characteristic comments. Yet performances were never so interesting to him as those who went to view them. During the performance his eye was fixed on the actors and the text, but in the train and in the brake along the dusty road, and during every possible interval, his eye was glancing over and sweeping the assemblage. Were they on the side of Antigone or that of Creon? Did they advocate nobility and audacity in human affairs, or the reverse of these?

He had no doubt that the generality, for all their charm and fluttering and wonderful learning, would be on the side of Creon—a decision which he communicated to a member of his family who strove against it. " But how can you tell?" she asked. " I know," he said, " because they always have acted in that way and taken that side. Haven't you read any history, child? Your ignorance is astonishing."

But as Art and Music, when they sought to interpret the life of our Lord, had in his eyes a special significance, so equally had Drama when she makes the same venture at the Bohemian village of Oberammergau.

For some time he hesitated to witness what might jar both sensibility and religious feelings, but friends again came to the rescue, and swept him thither one summer holiday. He was completely captivated, both by the reverence and singular power of the performance, as well as the devotion of the simple Roman Catholic villagers.   Some of the most vivid articles he ever wrote were those in which he related his impressions.   But it was Italy that revealed to him the highest religious art.   Perhaps his devoteeship surprised even himself; he had scarcely expected it.

The artists for once were doing their duty, blending that which was highest with that which was most attractive. Particularly was he satisfied by one of Raphael's pictures, of which St. Cecilia is the principal figure.   The saint and her companions, who are richly attired, are looking upward rapt in the strains of music which proceed from the angelic choir. " You see," he would say, as he pointed out its beauties, " that there is nothing ascetic about the saint and her companions. Both their appearance and their clothing represent a full and richly endowed life, which prefers the harmonies of heaven to those of earth, which latter are not inconsiderable, as you see by the profusion of instruments scattered around."

Torn by a hundred impulses, he wrote weekly letters to the Journal.   These, so far as the revelation of a religious personality is concerned, should rank as some of the most interesting which have ever been written by a visitor to Italian cities.   They reveal an ardent supporter of the evangelical portion of Christ's Church, distressed at much that he saw, yet keenly alive, as always, to the strong points and vantage ground of ecclesiastical opponents.   Where Rome was or is strong, or regenerating, or politic, he is the first to own it. Where it strikes him, as it generally does in Italy, as corrupt and deficient in spirituality, he is equally swift and to the point in commenting upon it.   The classic and old pagan life with which the country abounded increasingly stir disgust at the heathen excesses of mediæval asceticism.   That the radiant idea of the healthiest paganism should have been supplanted everywhere by bowed and bleeding figures, denoting an idea of life and religion both stunted and hysterical, cut him to the quick.   How all that played into the hands of those outside the Church! Such wandered through a score of Italian churches, and called what they saw Christianity, regretting (small wonder) that health and joyousness in art which did not struggle forth from all this death in life till after centuries of darkness. Thus:

"The apostles of the first Christian centuries rejoiced in the Gospel of the Resurrection. They did not dwell sentimentally and morbidly on the sufferings of the Son of Man. Those sufferings were ineffable and inconceivable. They were over for ever. It was their privilege to rejoice with Him who was now 'alive for evermore.' The dead Christ has thrown a sepulchral gloom over Latin Christianity; and, on the one hand, has produced an unnatural ascetic piety, and, on the other hand, has driven men to find in a healthy and radiant Madonna[1] the consolations and the inspiration which they could not derive from a dead Christ. It is an astounding fact that I have not yet seen or heard of a living Christ in any of the countless churches of Italy. Everywhere the Son of God is either a helpless babe or a dead man. But where is my risen, glorified, omnipotent, ever-present Saviour, whom St. John saw on Patmos, and with whom every Christian may have living 'fellowship' every day? Oh, my Roman Catholic friends, 'why do ye seek the living among the dead?' Is it because the realised presence of the living Christ would leave no room or sphere for Madonna, or saint, or angel, or priest, or pope, or any other 'vicar'? He promised that He Himself would be ever with us. Why, then, do you everlastingly present Him to us as though He were dead? He is not dead; He, and He alone, is here and everywhere. Unless your Madonna and your saints and your angels are both omniscient and omnipresent, I do not see what security you have that they can either hear or help you. I, at any rate, rejoice in the living presence of a risen and reigning Christ who Himself answers my prayers, absolves my sins, purifies my heart. What more do I want? 'Thou, O Christ, art all I want.' And for long centuries, Christian art itself being witness, the primitive Christians found, like me, everything in 'Jesus only.'"

The darker side of the life of St. Francis, the reputed rolling in thorns, and the practice of daily austerities, is distressing to him, but he consoles himself with the reflection that it was in the times, but not the man, and was the survival

---

[1] A conversation with one who was formerly a Roman Catholic gave him new insight, he said some years later, into the adoration for Christ's mother that is so conspicuous a feature of Latin Christianity. "She is a woman, they feel, and therefore able to understand and compassionate man's sin and weakness as even Christ her Son cannot. It is a terrible error, but his explanation interested me." The presentation of Mary at the Oberammergau Passion Play so moved him that he expressed indignation with Romanism, because by its excesses and Mariolatry it had forced Protestants into averting their eyes from "the saintly and beautiful life of the mother of Our Lord."

of heathen ideals of God, which Christianity had not yet transformed. The hills and vales of Assisi, the woods of La Verna in whose recesses Francis had prayed and worshipped, took the saint into their chorus, and endowed him with their gladness and their music. That the birds, his "brethren," alighted on the saint's shoulder, my father was inclined to believe, because there was always a basis of truth in even the most extravagant legends. George Sand, he argued, had an extraordinarily attractive influence over animals.

Yet as he returned from La Verna, he could scarcely enjoy the glorious scenery because of the well-meant and superstitious tortures of the Franciscan monks, who are in the habit of kneeling three times a week round the spot where the saint received the stigmata, and scourging themselves with iron chains as the five lamps, symbolical of the five wounds, are one by one solemnly extinguished.[1] Only the gallop down the winding roads to Bibbiena and the glory of the setting sun alleviates the painful impression. Dr. Pusey, he exclaimed, must have introduced far more of this thing into England than he imagined. Yet the devotion, the utter renunciation of self that lay behind the immolation of mediævalism, modern as well as ancient, moved him exceedingly.

Especially was this so when he saw the room formerly occupied by St. Clara and her companions, whom he reflected "were some of the most beautiful, refined, and wealthy ladies of Italy."

"God forbid that Protestant Sisters should ever be doomed to such repulsive quarters; but it was a vivid illustration of the heartiness and utter self-sacrifice with which women gave themselves up to the Mediæval Church and to Christ. They would undoubtedly have been healthier, happier, and more serviceable if they had enjoyed plenty of simple, pleasant food, and slept in bright attractive bedrooms. Christ could not take any pleasure in quarters to which we would not doom the most degraded criminals.

"But when I think where sweet St. Clara lived, and ate, and slept, and prayed and planned, and ruled for forty and two years, I can only pray again that I and mine and all who are associated with me may abhor 'needless self-indulgence' as much as Wesley did."

Moreover, the procession of the monks at La Verna whose

---

[1] Like Mons. Sabatier, he was inclined to think that the evidence in favour of the stigmata is "simply overwhelming."

self-imposed tortures so distress him, is "very mediæval and romantic." It takes place twice in the twenty-four hours down "the long curved gallery," on the edge of the mountain, the procession chanting as they move. Rome's use of the picturesque he thought quite admirable when it was not material and repulsive. Her harping on the physical sufferings of saints, and, most of all, Our Lord, distressed him. It was not His body that suffered so much as His spirit, His mind, His heart. Let Christians reserve their tears for His poor, His little ones, and so share what was His real agony.

Nothing in Roman Catholic Italy seems to have impressed him more than the great Benedictine Monastery of Monte Cassino, half-way between Rome and Naples. The situation, its history in Western civilisation and letters, its library, its associations with St. Benedict, the founder of monastic law and his sainted sister, Scolastica, all powerfully appealed to him, as did "an extremely devout and courteous English monk," who showed them over the institution. In the Journal he writes :

"I cannot speak too highly of his manifest spirituality or of his kindness. There is no space here to describe the church, the monastery, the library, the printing office, the cells and memorials of St. Benedict. That I hope to do at length elsewhere. It must suffice to say that the church is more splendidly and sumptuously decorated with marbles, gems, and precious stones even than St. Peter's at Rome, and vies with the Certosa di Pavia itself in priceless magnificence.

"Popes and emperors have vied with one another in lavishing upon Monte Cassino every species of wealth and privilege.

"In the library there are no less than eight hundred diplomas of charters and privileges accorded to the abbey by popes, emperors, and kings. Once, as our young Benedictine guide proudly and bitterly reminded us, the Abbot of Monte Cassino was the lord of all the country round as far as the eye could reach, and the abbey had immense wealth. Now the abbey is stripped of all its possessions, and the monks themselves are there on sufferance as the guardians of the National Library and the tutorial staff of the large public school—a sort of Italian Eton—which is established in one wing of the vast edifice. The most interesting spots were the crypt under the high altar—cut out of the solid rock—the cell of St. Benedict, and the other chambers of the primitive monastery, which in 1880, on the fourteenth centenary of the birth of St. Benedict, were covered with most beautiful frescoes by German Benedictine artists. However much we may differ from some of St. Benedict's views, no one who knows anything of modern history can forget that he was one of the holiest men of the Christian era, and one whose gigantic influence is stamped upon every country in Europe.

My heart was greatly moved when I entered the little cell in which he prayed, wept, thought, planned, and organised for so many years. An amusing incident occurred when the tour of inspection was over. I expressed a wish to see an inhabited cell, and the good monk took me to his own. When we were alone, judging, I presume, from my ministerial dress, he asked me if I was an Anglican. I said, 'No, a Methodist.' Then I proceeded to enlighten his ignorance on the subject of Methodism. I told him I was one of a great community of Evangelical Christians spread all over the world, although organised only in the last century, and already numbering at least thirty millions. 'Then,' he exclaimed in surprise, 'you are more numerous than the Anglicans?' 'Certainly,' I replied, 'not in England ; but in America and the colonies and the world at large.' 'I have heard,' he proceeded, 'that John Wesley was a very good man.' 'So good and so wise,' I added, 'that he has not yet been properly understood and appreciated even by those who profess to be his followers.' 'Tell me,' said my guide, 'the names of some of your ministers.' Before I could reply, he said, 'I have heard of Spurgeon.' Spurgeon, I explained, was a Baptist, and was now in heaven. 'Then,' he added, 'there is Mr. Parker in London.' 'Dr. Parker,' I replied, 'is a Congregationalist.' Dr. Parker may not be displeased to hear that his fame, although not his degree, has travelled as far as the great Benedictine monastery in the south of Italy.

"My guide evidently thought it time to leave the selection of names to me. I spoke of Dr. Moulton, and his European fame as a scholar. I said he had been one of the revisers of the New Testament. I was just on the point of going on to mention Mr. Arthur and Dr. Rigg when, to my immense surprise and amusement, the Benedictine said, 'There is a Mr. Price Hughes who is surely one of you.' I burst into laughter, and confessed that I knew him, and, in fact, that he was just then in a Benedictine's cell! After having been found out in this curious way, I told him much about our work in London, and my wife's Sisterhood, which interested him greatly. His permanent residence is in Rome, and he pressed me to let him know when I reached the Eternal City, which I shall certainly and gladly do. I hope to renew his acquaintance next week. After bidding our courteous and interesting guide farewell, we set out in the bright fresh air to catch the morning train for Naples and Rome respectively. The drive down the zigzags was delightful.

"As it was a Saturday, we were fortunate enough to see in Cassino, at the foot of the mountain, such a sight as Mr. Gutteridge informed us we might have spent months or years in Italy without seeing. It was market-day, and the peasants in the picturesque native dress, which is, unfortunately, abandoned in the cities, were congregated in hundreds. It was a vivid bit of old, mediæval, rural Italy which will be a very happy memorial of our last hour with friends who have made our visit to Naples so happy."

There, as at Assisi, he is struck by the lack of honour paid to women in the Roman as well as in other portions of the Christian Church.

"My wife and her companion cannot so much as enter the monastery, while we gentlemen could not only see all over the convent at Assisi, but saw certain apartments which the ladies were not permitted to see, namely, the cells occupied by St. Clara and her original companions. All the pilgrims visit the church and tomb of St. Francis, which is enclosed in a building of the most exquisite architecture, enveloped night and day with music, and surrounded with paintings of all the Italian masters from Cimabue downwards."

He felt with a "distinguished critic" that all artists of renown have prostrated themselves here in succession. But all that is mortal of "his best friend, his wisest counsellor, his greatest human comforter," lay "in a silent and empty church."

"In the very centre of the nave a huge flight of steps leads down to a crypt under the high altar. In that you stand in darkness. Presently a nun, concealed behind a grating, draws up a screen, and there, in an inner chapel lighted with candles, lies the actual body of St. Clara, still clad in the very habit she wore when alive. How her frame has been preserved for so many centuries I cannot say. But there—slightly shrunk, in an attitude of profound repose—lies all that is mortal of one of the best and holiest women that ever lived. I greatly resented the fact that, with all the reverence paid to her memory, she does not receive even at Assisi a grateful recognition proportionate to her claims. . . . Scarcely yet, either in Church or in State, is woman properly appreciated and reverenced. When will those who bear the name of Christ treat women as He did?

"The more I learn of the early history of the Franciscan Order the more I am convinced that, beautiful as was the character of St. Francis, the character of St. Clara was even more beautiful and more lofty. She never faltered, she never succumbed to the Pope. Poor St. Francis, worn out by unnatural asceticism, and subject to the gracious infirmity of excessive amiability, allowed the government of the Order to pass out of his hands, and, with only a faint protest, permitted the Pope to shatter his ideal and revolutionise the organisation. He died, as Sabatier has so conclusively shown, a disappointed and defeated, almost a broken-hearted, man. But St. Clara, with all her humility and gentleness, was inflexible as steel when principle was concerned. She never swerved from the original vow of personal and collective poverty. And when the Pope himself visited the nunnery and offered to absolve her from the primitive Franciscan vow, which prohibited collective as well as personal wealth, the brave little woman—although St. Francis was dead, and all the men in the Order had succumbed to the Pope—answered firmly, 'Holy Father, I shall be glad if you will absolve me from my sins, but I do not wish to be absolved from literal obedience to the command of our Lord Jesus Christ.' O holy and brave woman! Well did one of the earliest annalists of this Order, with a play upon your name, exclaim respecting you, 'Clara nomina, vita clarior, clarissima moribus.' I was very glad, with these convictions, that our first visit was made to the convent of St. Damiano. Passing beyond the city wall at the Foligno gate, we descended the steep hillside for half a mile, and there, embowered in trees, we found an insignificant, time-worn building, over whose portals were printed these thrilling words : 'Questo è il primo convento di St. Chiara.' (This is the first convent of St. Clara.) Here she founded the Order of 'Poor Clares,' here she lived for forty-two years, and here she died."

In studying the Forum at Rome, he is similarly struck by mementoes of distinguished women :

"Nothing interested me so much as the temple and residence of the Vestal Virgins. How astonishing it is that women occupied all through the history of Rome a position of such commanding influence and authority ! These Vestal Virgins were the earliest nuns in European history. Their uniform has been imitated by the Roman Catholic Sisterhoods. No one can visit the remains of these old nunneries of ancient Rome, or examine the uniforms of the abbesses or sisters superior, which are still extant in statues, without realising where Rome borrowed her Sisterhoods. It is a pity she did not at the same time limit her vows to a term of years, as did the Vestals, and also give her nuns a similar amount of ethical and public work, together with complete freedom from masculine control. The Vestal Virgins of old Rome were not placed under the thumb of any priesthood. They were allowed to govern themselves, which piece of information will be very gratifying to the advanced ladies of to-day.—ROME, *October* 20, 1894."

The melancholy and vastness of Rome, the looming shadow of the Papacy, and the relics of epochs impossible even to imagine in so short a space of time, depress and thwart him. The memories of Rome, he writes, are too vast and too numerous. Yet his journals denote the keenest interest in the Forum and in all mementoes of the late Republican period. He is particularly impressed by the site of the Senate, which for hundreds of years had ruled the world.

In Florence he is happier :

" Her life at its prime is not too far away to be out of touch with living issues, and it is not too complex to be grasped. Moreover, Florence is not a city of the dead. It is not overshadowed either by a vanished classic paganism or by the papal ghost of that dead pagan world. The golden age of Florence belongs not to ancient but to modern history, and her heroes were not fatally out of touch and out of sympathy with the modern life. Her Catholics were anti-papal, her artists were anti-pagan, and her statesmen were, with all their inconsistencies and vagaries, anti-tyrannical. Florence was, indeed, as Shelley sings, the Athens of the Middle Ages, and her streets are crowded with the masterpieces and the memories and force of the most brilliant periods of human history. Florence is neither heathen nor clerical, but intensely human and liberally Catholic."

27

Here Dante[1] had lived, whom from this period he intermittently studied, and Savonarola and the great painters. All that he felt about these others, or indeed Italy in general, was never adequately shown by anything he wrote with his pen. The glowing of his eyes and the play of feature in conversation were always the truest index to what was in him, particularly with regard to literary and artistic subjects. Apart from the fact that his genius was that of the speaker, not of the writer, his writings were always written under pressure, and bear throughout evident signs of haste, both in the impressions denoted and the conclusions to which they lead.

His motive for writing when he could ill afford the time is found in the first letter:

"It has been strongly pressed upon me that those whose importunate kindness has compelled me to take the longest holiday of my life would like to know how that holiday is being spent. And, indeed, I can think of no other way in which I can reach all of them, and in some slight degree indicate how deeply my wife and I value their sympathy and their prayers."

As he continued writing the journals and was told of the increasing interest that they evoked, he wrote even more fully as to friends and well-wishers, who were anxious to have even a hurried impression of what he was seeing and doing. They were never intended as subtle, literary disquisitions, but for the eyes of those who wished to know what he was thinking and feeling, just as if they were walking beside him.[2]

Lack of leisure to see and study all that he desires is continually felt by his readers. "Why," he exclaims in one place, "are all these masterpieces thus crowded together in one country, so that they come to be as silver in the reign of Solomon, and nothing accounted of because of their abundance? There ought to be a greater dispersion of them through the cities of Europe."

---

[1] He would eagerly question students of Dante and read the books that they recommended him. After Browning, he was the favourite poet of his later days.

[2] When it was suggested that the letters should be put into separate book form, he replies that if he has time to complete and revise the letters he will do so. But that time was denied him, and they break off when he is in the midst of describing his Venetian experiences. They were continued after his return to London, and must have been written under considerable difficulty.

Elsewhere he writes :

"As to Tintoretto, of whom we saw much all over Venice, and of whom you can see nothing except at Venice, I feel almost unable to speak. Ruskin says he is one of the greatest artists the world has ever seen, and there is no doubt he does everything on a colossal scale. His Paradiso, for example, on the east wall of the Sala del Maggior Consiglio, is the largest oil painting in the world, and I do not know how many hundreds of figures it contains. The spectator is bewildered, overwhelmed, dazed, and only some, who, like Mr. Ruskin, have time and money to spend years in the study of individual artists, will be able to comprehend Tintoretto.

"The haste with which he worked, and the vast spaces which he covered with his creations, give him a unique place in the history of art. He is altogether too much for ordinary mortals, and, moreover, so many of his paintings are put where they can never be seen, that altogether the effect is irritating and disappointing. You have a peculiar impression of something very wonderful and almost superhuman ; you feel that you have been gazing, not on a picture, but on an entire art gallery, and one which you have most imperfectly seen. This is supremely the case with one who, like myself, has comparatively poor sight, and can only examine these miserably placed and fading pictures with an opera-glass, which necessarily concentrates your vision on one small fragment of a gigantic production. Tintoretto evades my powers of observation.

"Perhaps, if I am ever able to visit Venice again, and to give a little more attention to his vast works, I shall be better able to understand the superlative opinion which Ruskin has formed of them."

Quite the most striking feature of my father's sayings in these letters are their singular independence. He is constantly reading and quoting from established critics, opinions with which he disagrees. If he likes a certain master he says so, and sticks to it whatever the predilections of critics, nor does he prostrate himself before those whom they have singled out for prostration.

At Venice he gives his vote for John Bellini, "the best and the greatest Christian artist of the Middle Ages," and is surprised that Ruskin, despite some sentences of the highest eulogy, does not say more about him and give the same minute study of his works that he does to those on roofs. There must have been some very subtle sympathy between the soul of Bellini and that of my father. When at Venice he did not give himself "any peace until he had searched out and pondered every picture of his in the city."

It was their intense and reverent Christianity, mingled with classicism, the harmonious development of power, that so strongly appealed to him. John Bellini, amongst all the distractions of the pagan influences of the age, never departed from those distinctly Christian subjects in which he had been trained in his youth.

He delights in nothing more than in the portrayal of the Mother and the Divine Child, and in noble and beautiful figures, apostles, and saints in attendance upon these. His Madonna is quite different from the Madonnas of the other painters, and my father thought that none of these had conceived her more finely and fittingly than Bellini. He was thinking, my father felt, when he was painting her, not merely of some beautiful woman whom he admired, but of the Mother of our Lord, and he conceived her as a noble, simple, dignified creature, who does not care in the least about admiration for herself but wants it all for her Son. "She offers her Son," as Mrs. Oliphant expresses it, " to the worship of the world." Yet she is perfect womanhood, tenderness and strength in every line. Looking tenderly, after his return, at a photograph of one of Bellini's Madonnas, he said, " I prefer her to all of them. She looks such a good mother." The angel children who surround the central figures, lost in contemplation of the Saviour of the world, were also a very endearing expression of the master's genius.

The work of Giotto and the early painters he admired, because Ruskin and Browning between them unveiled their greatness to him. He read *Old Masters in Florence* again and again in that city. The stiff Madonnas, the monstrous babes, were made credible and significant to him through Browning's eyes. Great and mighty, he felt, was the launch that they made into the new and unknown, the fresh aspiration after a higher perfection; but it was that launch he admired, not the Madonnas—centuries could not have made him do that. So strong in him was the instinct for success in achievement here and now, that it entered into all his partialities. In a high religious sense, and in moments of exaltation, such as the great poets could produce in him, he understood failure, but not normally. Where he saw it in the life of others, it was a perplexity and distress, and one from which he involuntarily turned.

Another painter whom he saw with Browning's eyes was

Andrea del Sarto, whom he loved as much for himself as for his pictures. A personal touch or intimation could win or repulse him quite incredibly. The perception or the intimation even that a person was misunderstood or unfortunate made him a friend at once. Andrea's tragedy, springing from his marriage with a beautiful woman who is both selfish and soulless, with the results in life that the poet depicts, invested every work of his with a certain pathos. My mother said that when he read the poem to her in Florence, where the artist had lived and suffered in obscurity, he could scarcely get through it for the choking that overcame him. Like the artist, he seemed to find it hard to feel otherwise than half gently towards the woman. No other poem seemed to reveal his tenderness and humility as this did.

"Is it not awful?" he would exclaim. "Do you understand? She brushed with her dress a picture on which he had expended his soul and months of toil!" How different it was with himself, that was the inmost thought suggested rather than expressed. Raphael enchanted him, though he cannot refrain from exclaiming:

"In Raphael the Renascence dominated Christianity, Athens was stronger than Jerusalem. Art triumphed over ethics." "It is very beautiful, it is bewitching, it has rendered immense service, but divorced from the righteousness of the Puritan, the Renascence has doomed the Latin races to sterility and defeat."

"Mr. Benjamin Kidd is right—the secret of human progress is character, not intellect and beauty unnaturally separated."

This is interesting, because it was one of his dreams that Jerusalem should conquer Athens, and that they in the market-place should listen to St. Paul. When this amalgamation took place, the expression of Western Christianity would be complete.

Da Vinci's Last Supper and Ghiberti's Bronze Gates of the Baptistery at Florence were objects of careful and por-longed study. Of the first he writes: "You should seat yourself in front of the vast painting, and with the assistance of an opera-glass study every face." Goethe's description of the picture moves him. The artist surely could have attained no greater triumph than to bring home the sacredness and tragedy of the scene to "such an unregenerate pagan" as the poet.

He said this smiling, because he admired Goethe as a literary genius, and was not a little attracted by his richness and classicism, yet there was that in Goethe that he loathed.

The poet's love affairs, and his manner of describing them, were too much for him. "There he was everlastingly at it," he would exclaim, "and only thinking of himself. While his countrymen fought and bled for the independence of Germany, he was calmly developing himself, and writing his plays and poems as if there were no such thing as liberty and patriotism. How different was the Puritan poet Milton, who left the world poorer, perhaps, by an immortal work because he cared for liberty and the struggle of his countrymen to attain her."

Of the Battistero he writes:

"Now can you believe that we spent three busy hours in looking at three bronze doors? Can you credit that of Londoners, at the close of the nineteenth century? But it took Andrea Pisano twenty-two years to make the first door, the oldest of the three, that on the south side. Was it too much to devote a single hour to a masterpiece which kept a great artist busy for twenty-two years? It consists of twenty panels, representing scenes in the life of the Baptist. . . ."

Dissentient veins would lead at times to unexpected exclamations. "Oh!" he cried once, "that I had known 'Praise-God-Barebones!'" but why, he did not explain. He had probably been listening to something very dilettante, and had invoked Praise-God-Barebones as a form of relief.

The genius of Michael Angelo awed him, it was sublime, awful, like the peaks of Switzerland, but he did not love it as he did that of the Bellinis, or Raphael, or Andrea del Sarto. Moreover, the solitude and agony of Buonarrotti's soul during so many years of life he could not bear to think about. "If only he had met Vittoria Colonna before," he muttered, "he ought to have met her; why was it that they were so long apart?"

His humanity delighted in the great sculptor's latter days, more than in any other portion of his career. The two friends who had sat in the Rospigliosi Gardens at Rome, exchanging the high converse and sympathy that their natures craved, caused him to glance affectionately at the gardens in question, and to allude to the two who had once walked there, as if he had some special intimation concerning the friendship of noble souls so above the ordinary apprehension.

Of Fra Angelico he says :

"There is a standing controversy between my wife and myself about Fra Angelico. She has a boundless admiration for him ; I profoundly appreciate his sweetness, his gentleness, and his deep spirituality, but I must confess that he seems to lack manliness. All his angels are young women, and all his men are effeminate. He appears to possess none of that healthful manliness which so manifestly redeems the painting of Giovanni Bellini, for example, from the impression of weakness and effeminacy ; and yet I am so conscious of the dear and glorious qualities of Fra Angelico that I am half-ashamed of myself for having expressed this opinion either to my wife or to the public."

Sandra Botticelli is something of a mystery, and perplexes him. On a person expressing fervent admiration for the works of that artist, he would be seized with boundless curiosity to know the why and the wherefore. The bizarre and undefined realms, where genius seems to cast aside its bounds and revel at will, were not always to the liking or understanding of a taste so allied to the presentation of what was healthful and fair.

Thus in descanting on the sculpture in the Naples Museum he writes :

"I was, if possible, even more delighted with some of the bronzes. The Narcissus, the Dancing Faun, and the Resting Mercury are surely the *ne plus ultra* of the ancient sculptor's art. I dismiss the Dancing Faun, because I do not like the subject. A faun is a grotesque and odious creature—the 'missing link' between man and beast—which happily does not exist in the world of reality. Why should artists waste their priceless gifts over unnatural absurdities? But who can imagine anything more lovely to the eye than the Narcissus or the Resting Mercury? These beautiful youths on the one hand and the lovely Psyche of Capua on the other represent the most refined and exquisite types of human physical beauty that the mind of man can conceive."

It may seem strange that the art which represents still life should possess a peculiar attraction for one whose instinct appeared so much opposed to such. But it had, and increasingly. The perfect poise and serenity which distinguished the Greek mind found its plastic expression in sculpture, and in that it did he was bound not only to admire, but to examine and understand. On returning from Italy he brought with him a couple of terra cotta statuettes (the Narcissus and the

Resting Mercury), at which he would often glance affectionately. The sight of their perfect proportions soothed, and he would have liked to live in a house adorned with statuary. His love for sculpture had in it another element—a rebound from what came to be an increasing eyesore in the paintings of the old masters. The Papacy had appropriated these, embracing them with some of their favourite conceptions, but the sculptors of the age of Pericles breathed everlasting defiance to the Vatican and all its accompaniments. In the Vatican picture gallery he said feverishly to a companion, " Let us get to the sculpture, for there is so much artificiality here that it sickens me. When we get there we shall breathe more freely." Even Raphael's St. Cecilia was not entirely pleasing to him. When he was pointing out its beauties one of his children would ask, " Which Pope is that who stands on her left looking at her ? " " Oh, my dear child," he would answer, " what does it matter ? In a delusion so gigantic that it is carried on from generation to generation, it really comes to be infinitesimal as to who in particular is chosen to maintain it. What good can it do you or anybody else to know either his name or his number. Look at that fine thoughtful head of St. Paul."

He insists in the Journal and elsewhere that the Papacy was an excrescence and not a fundamental element of the Church of Rome. " Those who cannot perform this piece of separation," he writes, " are ignorant of the A B C of ecclesiastical history." The doctrine of the Papal Infallibility was a modern accretion, and was the invention of the Jesuits in modern times. The origin of the Papacy itself was pagan, not Christian, and had its roots in that Roman Empire amid which Christianity took its rise, so that its early institutions were framed on Roman models. " That was a sad day," he exclaimed once, " when Constantine established the Christian religion in the Roman Empire. I wish he had not."

From Rome he writes :

" Nothing is more significant in thoughtful Italian travel than the extent to which Catholic Italy, in the best sense of the word, is not only free from the inventions and corruptions of the Papacy, but is strenuously opposed to them. The Catholicism of the best days of Florence and Venice is as different as possible from the Catholicism of Naples. The hero of Florence is Savonarola, whom the Pope murdered, and the hero of Venice is Sarpi, whom the Pope tried to murder. How is it, then, that the Papacy has always apparently triumphed over the Liberal section of the Latin Church? Because the ecclesiastical caucus has always been controlled by the Vatican. The administration and the discipline of the Latin Church have been for a thousand years in the hands of the Pope and of the Ultramontane ring, which in the last resort controls the Pope himself. It is an awful illustration of the power of organisation. Organisation won in the Franco-German War, and is now winning in the war between Japan and China. In the Society of Jesus Ignatius Loyola subordinated everything to organisation and discipline. He was wise in his generation."

On arriving at Venice he had no words to express his emotion. His delight, indeed, at unexpected or beautiful sights resembled nothing so much as that of a child. The pigeons who flock the piazza in front of S. Marco, and perch all over my mother while she feeds them, he finds a most curious and entrancing spectacle.

"They are, if possible, even tamer than the pigeons that trot about in front of the Guildhall in London, and they are much more numerous. Tourists purchase little bags of corn, and the moment they begin to empty the bags in the Square the air is filled with the rushing noise of many wings, and hundreds of pigeons fly to the spot from every point of view."

The Church of S. Marco does not carry him away at first as much as my mother had hoped, but bit by bit it grows upon him, particularly when the Presbyterian minister (Dr. Robertson) gives the benefit of his explanations.

"It is only when the symbolic significance of S. Marco is realised that its true glory dawns upon the mind. The building is so strangely different from the Teutonic cathedrals—it is so Oriental, so Arabic, so opulent—that it is with difficulty that a Teuton realises it is a Christian sanctuary. But once we have overcome this preliminary obstacle, it grows continually upon the mind and heart. Its ornamental structure vividly reminds the student of history that in the hour of her greatness Venice had the most intimate relations with Constantinople and the Orient.

"Dr. Robertson began on the outside, and explained to us how intensely evangelical and how essentially Protestant this ancient building was. It is defaced and damaged now by vulgar and gaudy mosaics illustrating Mariolatry and the extravagance of modern Romanism.

"The Ultramontanes seem to have lost altogether the artistic refinement of the great ages of modern painting, and there could be no more painful contrast than that which exists between the gaudy mosaics of to-day and the reverent and devout mosaics which formed the original structure of S. Marco. Dr. Robertson pointed out how everything everywhere in this building led up not to the Church but to the Bible, not to Mary but to

Christ. It is a true monument of Venetian Christianity which has always been strongly opposed to the Papacy, because truly Catholic."

It was a pity from one point of view that he could not content himself with gliding in a gondola or wandering over S. Marco, and watching the pigeons in the piazza. But the various objects of environment incited as ever his unslaked mind to fresh fever. The gondola becomes a place in which to rest while he is being conveyed from one place to another.

"The proverbial skill of a London cabman is really nothing in comparison with the way in which these gondoliers, young and old, dodge by one another, and twist round corners. They go literally within half an inch of one another's gondola, but never touch. A bump would be a fatal defect in the soft, silent, warm progress of the Venetian canals. As the gondolas and barges move quite silently, and many of the canals are at right angles to one another, there would, however, be terrible collisions did not every gondolier utter a sharp musical cry as he approached a corner. They can stop their long gondolas in a minute, and move them right or left as easily as I move my pen. In the narrowest and most crowded canal you soon come to feel that collisions are out of the question, and you glide in and out as securely as though you had the whole place to yourself. Our first destination that lovely morning was the Church of S. Maria Formosa to see the St. Barbara of that fine artist Palma Vecchio. This picture has been often photographed, and is a superb specimen of one of the noblest types of Venetian beauty—healthy, warm-hearted, and regal.

"An additional interest clings to it as it is really a portrait of the artist's own daughter Violante, who was beloved of Titian. She would have been an ideal mate for him."

. . . .

"The next day was again most beautiful and very warm. It is difficult amid the wet and gloom of London to realise that as late as the 17th of last November I lounged in an open boat on the Adriatic, in the lightest summer costume, with my umbrella wide open to arrest the excessive rays of the sun. With Baedeker's excellent map on my knees, I was able to direct our venerable gondolier with perfect ease. We rowed round the Giudecca, an oblong, outlying island of Venice, and came back to our hotel on the Grand Canal in time for luncheon. In the afternoon, just as the sun was declining, we ascended the Campanile of S. Marco, from which you have a glorious view of Venice and the lagoon. It is impossible to describe a sunset on the Adriatic seen from that conspicuous tower. The natural beauty and brilliance of Venice are lit up with almost all the colours of the rainbow, and every romantic and picturesque feature of the neighbourhood is enhanced until the hushed spectator begins to doubt whether he is really looking at a city of mortal men, or at some imaginary scene in the *Arabian Nights*. I quite agree with Mr. Hare that this should be one of the first points visited in Venice. It is only from this spot that we have something like a bird's-eye view of the intricate plan of the wonderful water-city. You see Venice and its islands, and the Adriatic, and also the chain of snowclad Alps which bound the horizon on the land side. It is very easy to climb, as the gradient is so gentle that there are no steps. At night after dinner, as on most evenings, we roamed for about an hour through the intricate labyrinth of little streets."

His delight in the natural beauty of Italy is very marked, and breaks out in the midst of all kinds of dissertations. At Vallombrosa, for instance, he writes:

"We visited these glorious woods in the very time described in the words of Milton. I have never seen anything so beautiful of its kind. The pine forests are more magnificent than any I have ever seen in any part of Switzerland. The trees are immense—so tall, so straight, so symmetrical. The contrast between the dark pine and the rich autumn gold of the Spanish chestnuts which abound on every side is simply indescribable. We wandered for hours in all directions, through the woods and over the hills, watching the charcoal burners at their work, catching the leaves as they fluttered down from the trees in the very exuberance of our health and joy, and then talking or meditating on the strange reverses of human fortune by which the great monastery, once one of the mightiest in the world, has now become a school of forestry; and the sacred wells, to which thousands of devout pilgrims once came from all parts of Europe to be healed, are to-day visited only by the swiftly-darting lizard, and listen only to the buzzing of insects and the crackling noise of grasshoppers."

The same delight is apparent in the drive from Salerno to Amalfi. "So many things combine to make the road from Salerno to Amalfi peerless." While art and nature exercise their spell, it was inevitable that he continually returns to the religious condition of the country. He expected more of Romanism—it is corrupter, less spiritual even than he had anticipated. In a Franciscan church the verger burst out laughing because my father thought the monks were in the habit of preaching.

"'But,' I said, 'the Franciscans owe everything to preaching. Why don't they preach now?' He burst into peals of laughter, and said the monks in the present day had no time to do anything except look after their dinner. He used words somewhat more expressive and less elegant than these. Here there was a man who had equal contempt for the clericals and anti-clericals, and yet he could never pass an altar without bowing to it, and he was the official custodian of the sanctuary. He was a typical modern Italian, utterly sceptical as to real spiritual Christianity, but extremely devout and fully alive to the tangible perquisites attaching to the Roman Church as a real and powerful Corporation."

My father is horrified here not at the monks whom the

verger had sweepingly condemned, but what was evidently an average attitude of the lay mind. Just as in London he had talked with people of all kinds, and endeavoured, as a friend put it, " to squeeze them like sponges," so he did in Italy, and nothing in the life of the streets or of the persons whom he encountered, seemed to be lost upon him. A slipshod christening ceremony, where the mothers lounge and gossip among themselves, causes him dismay, and a festa in Venice provokes the following comment :—

" There is something quite pathetic in the way in which the public of Italy, as of England, avail themselves of the slightest occasion of holiday-making. There was nothing specially attractive or intelligible in walking across the bridge of boats, going into a crowded church, and then walking back again ; nevertheless, thousands of persons did it out of curiosity, or because it was a slight change from the monotony of daily life. All round the Church of the Salute were costermongers loudly hawking candles, sweetmeats, nuts, and other trinkets, as in an English fair. No doubt the children enjoyed the sweetmeats, the crowd, and the lighted candles in the church.

" In the church itself there was an entire absence of devotion or reverence. The people stood about in crowds, watched their neighbours, talked to one another, and then went out. Even those of them who may have supposed that there was some advantage in what was being done at the altar, evidently thought that it was being very successfully achieved by the priests without any assistance from them, and that they would be benefited enough by it if they simply bowed their heads when the bell rang and the host was elevated. The modern Italian Catholic has no more to do with the efficacy of any service in which he takes part than the Englishman suffering from any disease has to do with the process by which the chemist makes up the prescription which the doctor has given him. The patient stands listlessly by while the chemist, with pestle and mortar and measuring glass, makes up the medicine. When that is over the patient pays for the medicine and swallows it, and the thing is done. He generally has no idea what he has swallowed. He has simply taken what his doctor told him to take, and there it ends for the present. This is the attitude of the Roman Catholic worshipper in Italy, even when he takes it seriously. But the majority of those who go, do so out of mere traditional habit, and have no real interest in what is being done."

Protestantism—whether in the form of the administration of the Holy Communion to soldiers in Rome, or in the Presbyterian community at Venice, where he and my mother gave some account of the Sisterhood and the Mission (which they did on one or two occasions)—is naturally very close to his heart. Yet it is difficult to say what interests him the most.

It is not some things in a place, but everything that he sees there. Curiously enough, while at Venice, he saw the present Pope, who was entering the city for the first time as Patriarch.

A " violent Ultramontane letter " that he had just addressed to the Venetian clergy, provoked the deepest popular indignation, so that the town council on meeting had decided that no public municipal reception should be accorded him.

"As I said in my last letter, tens of thousands of circulars had been distributed in the streets passionately imploring the people to illuminate their houses, and to put carpets and other decorations out of their windows. As far as the illumination was concerned, the appeal fell so absolutely flat that the project was at the last moment abandoned. As regards decorations, I carefully examined the palaces and public buildings as we wound along the Grand Canal. There were a few carpets in the windows of the Venetian aristocracy, who, like the old nobility of Rome, adhered to the Papacy, and have not yet accepted the new order of things.

"But with these trifling exceptions there was an entire absence of the usual indications of public approval. Those who remembered the visit of the King of Italy a few months ago were greatly struck by the startling contrast. Then every house was decorated, the state barges of the municipality were all in evidence on the Grand Canal, and the whole population gave signs of pleasure and loyalty."

The appearance of the Patriarch impressed him favourably.

"I was quite close to the Patriarch when he arrived at the landing-stage. He had a pleasant and amiable appearance ; and I could not help thinking that even now if the old Latin Church of Italy, instead of sacrificing everything to its political ambitions, would really devote itself to the spiritual service of the people, it was not yet too late for it to render immeasurable service to God and man. At present everything is subordinated to the hopeless and impossible task of recovering the temporal power which is gone for ever."

That is very characteristic. The distinguishing feature of his strategy was that no situation ever appeared hopeless. Just as the crippled state of Methodism when he was a young minister, and the constant withdrawals from its membership, could not depress him, but only spurred to fresh effort, so it was in his view of the Roman portion of Christ's Church. There was plenty of room for a Forward Movement, if only she would cease caring about present emolument and present power.

Revolving these things, he went to hear His Eminence

preach in the Cathedral next morning, when he pronounced as follows:—" He (His Eminence) delivered a sort of allocution which contained no reference whatever to the gospel, but was full of excellent worldly ethical advice." On leaving Venice they visited Verona, and so returned to London, which he loved, he writes, "more than all the fair cities of Italy." He loved, I think, what was to be done there, for certain portions of his nature always craved Italy; the warmth, the climate, the various many-coloured life, the cafés, the art, and the associations were distinctly missed by him long after his return. A continental Bradshaw caused him sighs, and he exclaimed laughingly more than once, "Oh that a devout woman, full of days, would go to heaven and leave me a fortune so that I might run over to Italy!"

Both my parents had written letters about St. Francis of Assisi and their impressions, and my father particularly had made intimations which seemed to point to a new campaign founded on the main conceptions of the saint. Poverty was his bride, so the saint had said in his quaint picturesque way, and he had trampled down this accursed money-getting and money-thinking under his feet. So what was wanted in London at that very hour were men and women filled with the self-sacrificing loving spirit of Francis and Clara, content to have only the necessities of life so long as they could have communion with their Saviour and with suffering humanity as they did.

Thus it was felt that my father was returning as a species of Franciscan reformer to further transform both the missioners' manner of life and his own. Thereupon, it occurred to the Sister in charge, who came from Yorkshire, and one or two others who were nothing if not practical, that they should show their appreciation of Francis and the new campaign by giving him a true Franciscan welcome. "We will have supper," they said, "not in the dining-room but downstairs in the kitchen."

"Moreover, we will not have any pudding or butter or coffee, as we generally do, but just brown bread and water, as Francis would have approved, on the wooden kitchen table." An Irish Sister and another, as fond of a joke as herself, dressed themselves in a hood and cowl, and ushered my parents downstairs to the kitchen on their arrival. My father was mystified, and my mother bubbling with inward mirth. Downstairs the wooden table, uncompromisingly set with a loaf of brown bread and a jug of water, helped to solve the enigma. The Sisters, who were ranged round the room, could not long keep their countenances, but soon fell into as much merriment as the saint and his disciples were reported to have done over their repasts. My father, however, would not allow himself to be amused, but tried to restrain the general mirth, checking his own perception of a humorous situation. "Let me beg of you," he implored, "not to laugh." Perhaps nobody ever knew how he feared ridicule, not for himself, but for those causes in which he believed.

Enthusiasms, spiritual awakenings struggled to light amid indifference and ridicule, and he always feared lest he should unwittingly yield to these stifling influences of which the world is so full. If he had met the child, St. Teresa, tottering forth on her quest, he would have taken her by the hand and led her home in duty bound, but how gently, with what sympathy, with what promises of aid and encouragement when the right time should come.

On one occasion a boy of twelve was pointed out as having already made up his mind to be a Wesleyan minister. He regarded the child at once with the most serious and affectionate glance, and patted him on the shoulder. "I don't think I was much older than you when I first began to preach," he said; and he began to talk to the child, listening to him as if he had been twice his age.

So he implored the little company at Katherine House not even to laugh, however innocently, at anything connected with Francis and the revival, which under God he had been the means of introducing into the Christian Church. Certain aspects of the saint's life he deplored, but those were temporary, belonging to the times, not to the man. Then he bent forward, and, with his eyes far away, began to talk about Francis and Umbria and all the wonderful stories concerning him and his first disciples.

The first adherents, among whom were labourers, learned men, poets, nobles, soldiers, and every variety of persons (he spread out his hands as if to include them all) had gone hither and thither preaching the gospel of Jesus Christ, just as the early Wesleyans had done. Only (here he smiled) the early Franciscans had gone about in Italy among a people peculiarly sensitive to beauty and soon to break forth into a wonderful outburst of art and literature, and in the dawn of it these early disciples had shared. All their asceticism and heathen conceptions could not prevent that. Why, the very songs that they sang, as they wandered barefoot in their brown, rough habits from village to village, were the beginning of Italian literature. Francis himself was a model of grace and courtesy, with those exquisite manners of the best Italian society that many modern English people would do well to imitate. On that he laid stress.

What a heroine was Clara when she went stealing through the wood to La Portiuncula, however mistaken, and how hard was her lot compared with that of Francis! The very animals came into this Forward Movement to offer, as Clara had done, their services to Christ — and the queer brethren like Fra Ginepro, as well as the more decorous and learned. For once, moreover, and this was the secret of his joy, the artists and litterateurs had done their duty. The painters had vied together in honour of Francis, and Dante had placed him in the fourth circle of his Paradiso.

Surely there was something strikingly individual and romantic he and they could do in the spirit of the Italian saint in the midst of the terrible distress and riches of London, that should show all men that they were Christ's, and that they cared for Him and His more than for any miserable conventionality and wretched piece of lucre. After that he said, " Let us pray "; and they prayed together with the Sisters about St. Francis and Italy and London.[1]

---

[1] Their children's ideas of Italy were limited to the pagan era, and a welcome was therefore accorded at Taviton Street of a strictly classic nature. The two younger placed a laurel wreath on each of the travellers' brows, hailing them with suitable remarks in the Latin tongue which had been prepared by their elders for the occasion. My father's delight was manifest, as was his gravity. When my mother wished to remove her wreath he said she must on no account do so. Then when all were settled to the meal an oration was given, saluting the travellers and reminding them of their wonderful journey, "more wondrous far than that of Æneas in his wanderings among the dead that be departed." "Surely they had held communion with these," etc. etc. "We have," my father cried, whereupon the names of the mighty were enumerated. "And what ground had they not traversed, sacred with what

To the reader it will doubtless appear that my parents and those who were with them had already given all that they well could to Christ and His service at the close of the nineteenth century. But love ever longs for deeper sacrifice, more passionate giving. It is not content even with what its own conviction knows to be the most excellent and effective way. At the starting of the Mission my father had insisted that proper accommodation should be provided for all the missioners, so that health and effectiveness on their part should be maintained, a stipulation which the strain and stress of their life abundantly proved to be necessary. Workers must live in the first place, and be effective, healthy, and good-tempered in the second. Ladies did not come to the Mission to sweep floors and cook themselves scanty meals, but to help the people of whom they were the sisters—a help which involved more care and thought and time than outsiders imagined, and which made them very tired sometimes. My father himself once wrote: "They are true sisters of the unprivileged and disinherited—as ready to make a bed, cook a dinner, scrub a floor, or nurse a baby, as to minister to the higher need of the immortal spirit."

As a matter of fact, the Franciscan spirit had never been absent from the Mission, and it may compare in several particulars with the old Italian order. The singular enthusiasm and devotion which filled the early workers, the twofold message which they carried to the people, as well as the variety of character in their own dispositions and service, included a recognition of the joyous, romantic, and artistic side of life. In addition, they were both great beggars.

A certain likeness also in the spiritual history of St. Francis and my father has probably struck the reader. The depth of their conversion and the desire that followed it, not to save their own soul but to do something for Christ and for man, bear strong points of resemblance, as do their extraordinary enthusiasm and power of communicating it to the

dust," etc. In the Forum the travellers were reminded they had stood at the threshold of Cæsar's house, and had gazed at the place where Vesta's sacred fire had never ceased to burn, etc. That very spot had they seen from which Cicero had spoken with eagle glance. Here my father, despite the order that he was bent on maintaining, could scarce contain himself. No words can describe how his eyes gleamed, and how affirmation was on the point all the time of bursting from his lips.

most various persons. In particular, that personal, intimate love that my father had for Jesus Christ at the close of the nineteenth century was just as vivid as that held by Francis in the thirteenth, and is destined to produce more widely reaching results than most are aware. Italy and her life and politics, past and present, receded into the inner portions of my father's mind, as did the new love for the arts which she had awakened within him. Their shadow lay across his path, though he could not turn to look upon it. But the spirit of St. Francis and its message pursued him to the end.

"HOTEL DE PENSION SUBASIO, ASSISI,
"26 *Mai* 1898.

"MON CHER AMI,—Je vous ai écrit déjà deux fois sans recevoir de réponse. Serai-je plus heureux cette fois?

"J'ai découvert et je viens de publier la Legenda anti-quissima S. Francisa Assisiensis, faite par frère Loen son disciple préféré quelques mois après sa mort.

"En voulex-vous un exemplaire? Je serai heureux de vous l'envoyer en souvenir de notre rencontre à Assise.

"Le vrai S. François nous y est rendu, celui d'avant la canonisation, et on m'écrit de partout que ce livre deviendra populaire et aura une influence morale, religieuse et sociale sur notre fin du 19e siècle. Encore ce matin c'est la pensée que m'expriment deux hommes très différents,—M. Réville, et le P. Hyacinthe Loyson.

"Cette publication aura du reste une heureuse influence sur les Romanisants en les obligeant à venir sur le terrain scientifique et historique. Dans les jours ténébreux que nous traversons je crois que l'apologétique protestante doit se renouveler et que son devoir est moins d'attaquer l'erreur, que de faire éclater une vérité plus haute devant laquelle l'erreur se dissipera tout naturellement.

"Veuillez présenter mes respectueux hommages a Madame Hughes et me croire.—Votre cordialement dévoué,

"PAUL SABATIER."

CHAPTER XVII

THE CATHOLIC IDEA OF THE CHURCH

ὥσπερ ὅπου ἂν ᾖ Χριστὸς Ἰησοῦς ἐκεῖ ἡ καθολικὴ ἐκκλησία.

St. Ignatius.

I. *A Federation*

THE period after the return from Italy early in 1895 is associated with what may be called the distinctly and strenuously ecclesiastical portion of my father's career. Hitherto his most striking service had lain in the propagation of chivalry by establishing a Mission, calculated to meet both religious and social needs, and to induce imitation in all parts of the English-speaking world, and in attacking face to face the great social evils of his day.

Yet at no time had he been without absorbing ecclesiastical interests and endeavours, particularly in later years, but the general public did not know of them. They saw in him the Christian prophet and the philanthropist, and knew nothing of what had been forming itself all these years in the recesses of his mind—a mind which revolved round everything that daily experience brought it, and not least round the projects of his own chivalry.

But from 1895 onwards, his own and what he termed the evangelical portion of Christ's Church came to the front of his endeavours, and increasingly absorbed him. For many years he had been foremost in exploits of chivalry through both good and ill report, and now, though his sword was still in its sheath ready to flash forth as of yore at anything that it deemed just provocation, it was the sword of the leader, whose mind by dint of long service claims the Council, rather than the field, as the scene of its principal operations.

To mark off so many-sided a life into exclusive stages is manifestly impossible, but each portion has its predominant characteristic, a main outlet of its energy, for with all the variety of his interests he was never lost amid them. There was always one predominating over the others, engrossing him above all the rest.

In early childhood it was games in the playground; then his first vivid realisation of spiritual life and its accompanying activities and desires. Later, mental pursuits and their wide engrossing life, and later again the simple preaching of Christ's gospel and His constraining power on those who heard it. Inevitably there followed a duel between this simple evangelistic side and the mental energies, not quite lulled for many years, though he acquiesced in the abeyance of the latter in the spiritual crisis through which he passed at Brighton. That there should always be something of this duel, however profound his acquiescence in this sacrifice of purely intellectual pursuits, was a necessity both to his work for the Church and his influence in the world. With all this early duel, putting it out of sight altogether and leaving the profoundest impress on his character and outlook, was his singularly happy marriage and the years of companionship with one who not only possessed the complementary qualities to his own, but who increasingly grew to understand him and the work that he had to accomplish. God's will concerning him became her meat as it was his. He was to do it and she was to help—how much in those early years of struggle and hope, when the home joys and cares were all in all to both, she did not divine. My father's absorption in the home is shown clearly in the letters from which extracts were given at the close of an earlier chapter. He is never away but he longs to return—and, indeed, that was always so—but in later years it was a very large home, to which many were admitted. Even Conference, where he finds it hard to write, because he is so interested in "important discussions," is a species of banishment which he quits at the first opportunity. None the less, even in those days, he was part of its life—present at its discussions—commenting, reflecting on all that passed.

From Oxford onwards his attention is first seriously

directed to the contemporary condition of his own and kindred
Churches, and to the conviction that in chivalry, in its widest,
deepest sense, lay the cure for the present inertia, the present
isolation of the Christian Church from much of the life and
needs of the world. Democracy claimed it of her far more
than mediæval times, that democracy which, ideally conceived,
was, for all its first threatening appearance, a direct outcome of
the life and teaching of Him who was known to the men of
His day as a village carpenter, and who had once and for
ever glorified the life of the average working man, lighting it
up with heavenly meanings. "Christ and the People" was
the watchword of the Mission to which from 1887 onwards
he devoted so much of his time and energies, as it was that of
his most militant chivalry. But underneath it all two great
perceptions were gaining definition: first, how terribly the
people were in need of Christ, and of men and women entirely
animated by His sympathies and His ideals; and second,
what all men come to be increasingly conscious of at one
time or another, in all departments of life, that their days
are as grass, and therefore many of their endeavours. That
nothing blooms and fades in the universe without giving its
contribution to the general life and divine purpose, is increasingly the ardent belief of the religious; but side by side with
this, as an instinct of life itself, is the desire to perpetuate its
spiritual forms.

Every great spirit wishes to work that which will endure
after the bodily form has crumbled into dust. They say with
justice, "What is the good of the little I have done if others
after me do not add to it?" So great men do not so much
accomplish things in their own day, as they prepare the way
for others to accomplish who shall come after them. That
undoubtedly was the light in which my father regarded his
endeavours; for from 1895 onwards he was increasingly constrained to devote his mind and his energies in a strenuous
effort to adjust Methodism to the new era, by humanising and
spiritualising it, and to achieve what he regarded as even
more important and far-reaching, a federation of the various
evangelical denominations, on a practicable basis, alive at every
point to the needs of democracy, yet a conscious portion of
the Catholic Church of Christ, enriching herself with the

memories and tradition which the consciousness of such a descent entails. The Church as the perpetuator of good works and of the faith by which those good works have been wrought, does not seem to have caught the popular imagination. With the prejudices which resulted he was continually at war. As a leader of chivalry he laid hold of the popular mind, but his ecclesiastical labours outside ministerial circles and a group of the Methodist laity, were quite unknown to the generality. Indeed, those who associated with him in his directly chivalrous and spiritual endeavours, grudged the time given to what appeared non-vital issues. In reality it was the greatest period of his life, so far as the development of his own faculties and the breadth of his outlook were concerned. Impetuous and brilliant youth, maturity with its deep heart, poured the fruits of their zeal into the harvest of his mind. To certain of his brother-ministers he was mainly an ecclesiastic, and they were as little conscious apparently of the other portion of his life as certain circles were of his ecclesiastical interests and endeavours.

He who at the beginning of his career had appeared to many as a free lance, was to mould himself more and more into the history and shaping of those religious communities with which he was associated. But very few saw all that he intended, and still fewer divined the width of his mental survey. Dr. Parker, who had a faculty of understanding my father, was heard to remark at this time that " Hugh Price Hughes' brains were simply invaluable to the Churches with which he was associated." The strategical mistake of the Missionary controversy would have been an impossibility at this period, when he looked both behind and before, pondering and considering the various aspects of questions. Not the least striking feature of this era was his own acclimatisation to an environment in which he had always been something of a foreigner—scarcely understanding contemporaries or they him. My mother relates that in earlier days he would often exclaim to her, " I don't understand them—I cannot ; I don't know what it is, but I feel differently constituted from them." This was not merely applied to his ecclesiastical contemporaries, but to the sober Englishmen among whom his lot was principally cast. The blood of the Hebrew and the Celt militated against the slow and deliberate working of the Anglo-Saxon mind. Vehement and passionate speech seemed at times to repel, not to win; while he was often sensible that the minds and prejudices of contemporaries were distinctly alien to him. That he could charm and lead them on occasions was undoubted, but he was conscious of misunderstanding, of having things put down to him which he did not intend. But in this latter portion of his life he became wonderfully acclimatised, understanding not only the fine shades and sensibilities of Methodism, but those of the English character as a whole. Certainly he gained much from his impact upon the Anglo-Saxon mind, as it displayed itself in its most immovable forms in Methodism, the defect which Dr. Moulton had noted in his youth being cured by time—and wounds. He learned to put a break on his own faculties, and the faculties greatly benefited. A Celt who perpetually flings himself against sections of the British mind immensely gains by the process, and might make the nearest approach to omniscience that is possible in a mortal. It is doubtful whether any other religious system would have laid hold of my father and he of it, as the Methodist. As earlier chapters show, it appears Saxon to the roots, with all the Saxon strength and Saxon power of affiliating complementary and helpful elements. Both were immensely indebted to each other, my father to Methodism and Methodism to him.

In their struggle it did seem at moments as if one must let go the other, yet some common instinct on either side would always prevent this from taking place, for neither could accomplish their work without the other. Again, the general public, particularly the more thoughtful sections, accorded him a hearing which they did not in his earlier days. Instinctively, the best Englishmen, while often the propagators of chivalry themselves, suspect any one who makes, so they think, too open a profession of it, and who is unduly vehement in its service. The silent arduous performance of duty often seems to attract them, rather than the knight-at-arms who comes breathing desperate enterprise, glory, and redress. Such, they say, cannot last long. But if he display that pertinacity and devotion to duty which is their admiration, they will accord him in the end, what all men desire, justice—and as no other nation can

—the nation which goes out to cheer a general who has lost its battles.

Yet my father lived more than ever, so far as his mental life was concerned, in a world by himself, though he touched fellow-ministers at a variety of points and spoke freely to them. But not to any one did he ever reveal his whole mind, because it was not in his power to do so. Nobody who possesses a mind at all can do so. Over a point at issue he would talk most openly and unreservedly, but it was the point at issue, not the fabric of his designs, which was half-merged in dream, as are all vast undertakings. At the same time he was keenly sensible of the limits and complexities amid which it would have to take form. The Federation of the Free Churches in particular touched his imagination as it did that of Dr. Berry, to whom probably he spoke more freely concerning his ecclesiastical ideas than to any other minister. His contribution to this movement—leadership one may fairly term it—was that which he regarded as the chief work of his lifetime, for he believed that in the future it would have the greatest and most varied issues, and be the most abiding of all that he had wrought. In Methodism there was much wealth of religious life, which needed "reanimating" or "organising" for the service of the community. Yet how much more was there need of the same process in Nonconformity as a whole, so that all its branches could use their treasure for the same end, each supplementing the other, and contributing, by its distinctive strength and gifts (whether of intellect or zeal), to the common weal! The zeal and compact organisation of a united Methodism allied with the intellectualism of Congregationalism, the rugged independence of the Baptist communion, and the lofty spirituality [1] of the Society of Friends, formed an ideal combination which should be endowed throughout with a true sense of their place in the Catholic Church and the heritage that he thought they could claim in it. Yet my father in these dreams did not take much to himself. He felt himself to be a plain man with a capacity for organising armies and making them move in the only possible direction.

That Nonconformity contained leaders far more learned and

[1] These qualifications are not intended to be mutually exclusive but suggestive of the leading characteristics of the communions in question.

spiritual and competent than himself, he was fully assured, but he wanted their talents to be made the utmost use of, to find the widest possible field. He was not asserting himself, but the contrary; for these years were full of drudgery, of endless committee work, in which for the hope that was in him he delighted exceedingly. He did not make a fame for himself so much as he helped to assure it for others. No one could envy him his task—the task of securely federating the Evangelical Churches; for it is the adverb to which he may lay special claim, and the particular manner in which the amalgamation took place. Among the leaders of Non-conformity generally, there had been a growing desire for several years towards some form of *rapprochement*. For the longing after some visible form of reunion, so manifest in large portions of Christendom, was nowhere more felt than among a little group of Christian ministers, who became increasingly conscious amid whatever divergences that in essentials they were in vital agreement—and not the least—in a passionate acceptance of the principles of the Reformation. But it was confined to the leaders, to those men of large sympathies and outlook, who, in various ways, had come to reflect on the contemporary situation, and, most important of all, to know each other. My father, before he went to Grindelwald, where he met Dr. Berry, belonged to this group; for ever since the days when he had tried to re-establish the work of a Congregationalist Church at Dover, he had known and conversed with ministers of other denominations.

So, as early as 1890, when the question of reunion was so to the fore in men's minds that even the Missionary and the Parnell controversy could not banish it from my father's, he wrote to Dr. Guinness Rogers asking him to contribute an article to the *Methodist Times*, and thus set the ball a-rolling. Dr. Rogers' article suggested a Nonconformist Congress based on the lines of Church Congresses, as the best means not only of fraternisation and of *rapprochement*, but of the maintenance of those principles and forms of religious worship which many of their Christian brethren seemed determined to attack, not to say suppress. The article was defensive rather than constructive, though it was not purely so.

The response was immediate, half a dozen representative

ministers writing in the next issue of the Journal,[1] the editor, in particular, demanding why the more recent forces in the army of Christendom should be in so disorderly and disunited a condition. " Protestanism is a mob," he could not refrain from exclaiming while turning over in his mind the elaborate organisation of Romanism, though he would lay stress on the fact that this organisation was far from securing true unity. What distinguished him throughout the whole campaign was this highly developed ecclesiasticism in which perhaps only Dr. Berry fully shared. An annual gathering of Nonconformists for purely " consultative and fraternal intercourse " was only a small part of that which was in his mind, but it was a portion of his thought, so he welcomed that and every similar suggestion.

It was not till he met Dr. Berry in 1892 that he met one whom he at once recognised as the constructive genius of the movement, and who was able to regard it in quite the same full manner as he did. The form of the *rapprochement* was undoubtedly shaped on the Swiss mountains. Without Dr. Berry or my father, if it is possible to imagine the movement without them, a *rapprochement* of some kind would undoubtedly have taken place, so widespread was the feeling among ministers of all kinds, but it would have been a *rapprochement* on different lines. It would probably have resulted in a loose yearly gathering of some kind, the import of which would have come home but slowly, if at all, to the public mind and the Nonconformist people. Moreover, it would have been of very different import when it did come home, as the sequel will show. To put it plainly, Dr. Berry and my father were convinced that the Federation must recognise itself to be a conscious branch of the visible Catholic Church, with the dignity and spirituality pertaining to such full membership. Nonconformists were not entering the New Jerusalem through side gates as certain contended they were, and as some of them had almost come to believe, but through one of the great accredited gates which St. John saw in that vision which Dr. Berry liked to preach about.[2] Those who

[1] The Revs. Dr. Clifford, F. B. Meyer, B.A., Dr. Stephenson, Dr. Townsend, Dr. Keen, Dr. Watts.
[2] See Chapter XV. " Holidays at Grindelwald."

enter a city by a historic gate along a well-worn road should, if they are wise and devout pilgrims, my father thought, reflect on those who have gone before, and on certain habits and beliefs and observances which were essential to their progress, and which could not altogether be lightly laid aside. No wisdom of the race but has its meanings for all time, its part in the great whole. As citizenship and all that citizenship involves is but entering into a heritage, so, my father thought, was Christian Churchmanship, in which certain new-comers possessed of full civic claims have the richest, because the largest, heritage, if they will only enter into it—not disdain and overlook portions of it, because of the shortcomings of previous generations and the slowness of the working of God's purposes. My father claimed, that is to say, as did Dr. Berry, that certain Nonconformist bodies were an accredited portion of the visible Catholic Church, just as many contemporaries claimed the same for Anglicanism.

The main basis of their contention has been indicated in an earlier chapter, that the presence of Jesus Christ in the hearts and lives of men, and His transforming power, was the only foundation on which His Church must rest, together with a reverent use and observance of the sacraments specially ordained by Him. My father here was not considering conditions of salvations—simply conditions of membership of the visible Catholic Church. How he justified himself in this contention is not at all the subject of this chapter, which is personal, not ecclesiastical. Suffice it to say that while my father made personal experience the touchstone of Christian Churchmanship, he was aware of another aspect of the case, which, though of minor importance in his eyes, he knew to have an important bearing—to wit that documentary evidence which authorities on such matters can alone grapple with and determine. Here, as elsewhere, he quoted the early Fathers, and on one occasion indulged in a lengthy discussion on the matter with a courteous Anglican clergyman in the columns of an evening newspaper. But the main point for the present volume is that he did claim such membership for himself and for those who were in communion with him, though excommunicated by the Roman and Anglican Churches. Other Nonconformists, if they had claimed this membership had been very reticent about it, or they had not thought it worth while or indeed desirable to assert it. " We all belong to the invisible Church," some would say, and then leave the matter. Thus Christian Churchmanship in the full sense had been half-suspected, half-overlooked by many Protestants, on account, as my father thought, of the extreme individualism that certain forms of it had engendered. Undoubtedly my father, like other Nonconformists of the time, thought it an excellent thing that they should all meet and combine as often as possible, but he thought more than that. They were to meet and combine not as Congregationalists, Baptists, Methodists, Presbyterians, and Quakers, but as Free Churchmen, and thereby hangs a tale.

At the same time that my father and Dr. Berry were conversing in Switzerland, other ministers from their point of view were conversing at home. In the city of Birmingham in particular, two or three such ministers, noting the small proportion of the population who went to church, laid their heads together, and decided as wise men have decided from time immemorial, that three are better than one, and that it would be a good thing to join hands in their efforts to leaven a great city. Having found such an opportunity, they quickly communicated what they had achieved to their friends and acquaintances in the ministry and out of it, which further set the ball a-rolling and people discussing. Indeed, among leaders everywhere there seems to have been a remarkable unanimity regarding some form of closer association and co-operation. This unanimity was very striking and indicative of a new order of life in Nonconformity—more elastic, zealous, and imaginative than the old. The conditions of modern life, the increased facilities for meeting and exchanging ideas, and the increase of education were reaping their inevitable result. The desire to join hands in some way or other was anything but a sign of weakness; it was rather the first symptom of a new strength—the first sign of a serious grappling with the problem of the times. The story of how it all came about, how the old barriers and misunderstandings melted away before the new spirit of fraternisation, and the desire to meet the world's need, could well occupy a chapter by itself, which someone one day, who remembers this great wave of Christian brotherliness, might very profitably describe. So much is said of the disagreements of Christians, that an account of a time when many of them were willing to pass over old differences and to forget minor divergences, should be a very pleasant page of ecclesiastical history, and one which the Free Churches may well remember with pride.

The present generation, in these days of increased fraternisation and unity, is in danger of forgetting, say—thirty years ago—when Methodists, Congregationalists, and Baptists each lived severally apart, and looked at one another reproachfully from a distance, as if they quite resented the fact of each other's existence. My father, toiling more than ever in his study at 8 Taviton Street, became after 1890 increasingly the confidant of the instigators of the new movement, in which numbers of the leading laity, as well as the ministry, at once joined.

All that took place before the First Constitutional Congress of the Federation in 1895 this chapter does not undertake to tell, for it is not a history of a singularly wide and influential movement in which many able men, both ministers and laymen, took part, but of one man who was inextricably bound up with it. Previous to this Congress my father and Dr. Berry had, by their unexampled toil and thought, constituted themselves the leaders of the Federation. Many aided, as I have intimated, but none bore the burden and the heat of the day as they, and for the following reason. Any movement or project in these days depends for its final sanction on the suffrages of the people. For the leaders of Nonconformity in Switzerland and elsewhere to draw up schemes of Federated Churches or forms of *rapprochement* was "magnifique," but it was scarcely "la guerre." "La guerre" commenced when Dr. Berry, my father, and the organising secretary, the Rev. Thomas Law, traversed the country from end to end to obtain the suffrages of the Nonconformist electors.

Now let the reader here imagine the average religious person in an English town, of whatever denomination, Anglican or Nonconformist. If they do take a special interest in religious or public affairs, it is often largely a parochial one. To look at wide issues, to care for what does not appear to personally affect them and their relatives and friends, is not an easy matter to the average man or woman intent on the struggle for existence, and bounded by local ties and predilections. The value of modern Imperialism to many lies in the wide sense of citizenship and public interest, which that and nothing else has opened to the average citizen. But in 1893 and 1894 when my father and Dr. Berry conducted their campaign, they had not even the outburst of imperialistic feelings, and its consequent enlargement of vista, to aid them in their laborious undertaking. My father in particular hated travelling, and suffered nervously from his long train journeys, to an extent that was sometimes quite unaccountable to those who accompanied him. Perhaps no one ever knew what he suffered and feared at times on taking a journey. It was so unreasoning.[1]   Like some unwilling and uncomplaining horse,

[1] Though he never missed a train in his life, he seemed to always imagine that he was going to do so, and a journey where he could not sit facing the engine and in a corner seat was a torture to him. Naturally in his travels, arrangements would be made for his comfort, but these did not at times prevent distress on his part and the passing of comments which were unkind because thoughtless. It was an infirmity doubtless, but it was not more. Yet when he was in good health, and with congenial companions, he often made very pleasant journeys—for instance, when he was travelling to Conference, or in company with Dr. Berry or Mr. Law and other friends and colleagues.

The writer would notice how the porters simply flocked around him at the station, as if aware that here was one who greatly needed them. Many on the line would know him, and he would exchange salutations with them, always expressing gratitude for their services. One day a guard was unusually considerate, quite charming in the eyes of his family, who were the object of his solicitude, and after he had gone my father said with a smile and a nod that explained all, " The man's a Methodist." On one occasion the officials failed in performing a desired service—a tea-basket was not in readiness, and he had to go on without it. The feature of the occasion lay in the opportunity that it gave his oratory—the whole carriage, which consisted of strangers, was in a few minutes deeply interested in the matter and throbbing with him.

The locomotive and its accompaniments he seemed to regard as powers of darkness which lay outside his control. By much studying of Bradshaw he endeavoured to follow their movements, but the study of them did not appear to give him that satisfaction which other studies gave him. When he took express journeys the Bradshaw and his watch would be continually open at some wayside station through which the train flashed, and on the Continent he was even more restless. A scene at a Swiss station comes vividly before the writer. The train was expected in about twenty minutes' time, and he was standing on the platform awaiting its arrival with the luggage beside him. The other travellers on the platform did not share his anxiety, lounging and laughing and gossiping as if there were no such thing as trains in the world. After looking at them for some moments, with a face in which anxiety, distress, and envy were curiously mingled, he burst out to his companion,

my father had yoked himself to the public service, which did not spare the whip of criticism when he indulged in what it regarded as meaningless fears and antics.   The inmost feelings of public benefactors, as well as of horses, might prove startling if they could be revealed.   But my father had come to regard the various causes in which he engaged as his own life, and while he smarted under the whip which descended, he knew not why, he did not question its legitimacy.   No campaign, despite the physical distaste of the incessant travelling, was more to his heart than this, more part and parcel of his inner spiritual life.   In the unfortunate Education controversy amid which this book is written, an impression has got abroad that the Federation of the Free Churches was anti-Anglican in its origin.   My father, at any rate, who took a leading part in its shaping, had no such idea, and always opposed any attempt in this direction.   Meanwhile the unhappy circumstances of the hour as well as remarks prompted by that bitterness and intensity of feeling which accompany it on both sides, tend to propagate so false a notion of what led to one of the most beautiful events and alliances in modern Christianity.

In an article in a current number of the *Contemporary Review* he described the character of the movement, from which the following quotations are taken :—

"The title is 'The National Council of the Evangelical Free Churches. 'The Churches constituting the local Councils entitled to representation on the National Council are the Congregational and Baptist Churches, the Methodist Churches, the Presbyterian Church of England, the Free Episcopal Churches, the Society of Friends, and such other Evangelical Churches as the National Council may at any time admit.' With respect to the title, I need call attention only to the clause which asserts that the Council will heartily welcome the co-operation of any Episcopal Church which is not

---

" How do these people manage to get to their journey's end and to catch their trains at all? I must say that it passes my comprehension. Do you know how they achieve it ? I, poor wretch, strain every nerve, and then I only do it by the skin of my teeth." Despite the keen criticism of conduct that the remark implied, it was charged with a certain longing to be released from the fiery wheel of his energies, that longing which was characteristic of his later years. This debility was partly inherited, as neither of his parents could travel happily, and was partly a result of the overstrained conditions of his life.

The fairy tales which depict to childhood one growth of the forest envious of another, the pine sighing because it cannot partake of the life of the fern and *vice versâ*, have their counterpart in the life of humanity.

subject to the authority of the secular power, and which enjoys that complete self-government which is essential to the full discharge of Church duties. This movement, therefore, does not represent any antagonism whatever to Episcopacy as such. The true nature of modern Dissent as expounded by Dr. Guinness Rogers, Dr. Berry, and others, is very much larger, more comprehensive, and more catholic than views which have sometimes prevailed. The promoters of this movement will be only too glad to co-operate and to combine heartily with any Churches, however constituted, which are absolutely loyal to the Head of the Church, and which are faithful to what we regard as the fundamental ecclesiastical idea of the New Testament, namely, the real, uninterrupted, and perpetual presence and supremacy of Jesus Christ in the midst of His own Church.

"The Constitution defines the objects of the movement in the following terms : '(a) To facilitate fraternal intercourse and co-operation among the Evangelical Free Churches. (b) To assist in the organisation of local Councils. (c) To encourage devotional fellowship and mutual counsel concerning the spiritual life and religious activities of the Churches. (d) To advocate the New Testament doctrine of the Church, and to defend the rights of the associated Churches. (e) To promote the application of the law of Christ in every relation of human life.'

"With respect to the first of these objects, we can only say that we are beginning to realise that our divisions have been a greater evil than we supposed. Isolation from our fellow-Christians narrows the mind and chills the heart. We have all been much more bigoted and sectarian than we were aware. It is only in the comprehensive, many-sided life of a Catholic Church that we can perceive the difference between the essentials and the accidents of the faith, and that we form those larger and deeper conceptions which harmonise varieties of truth.

. . . .

"Whenever we discover in any group of associated Christians unmistakable signs of supernatural grace, whenever such an organised group is instrumental in the conversion of sinners and in the edification of saints, we have decisive evidence of the presence, approval, blessing, and imprimatur of Jesus Christ. Conversion and sanctification are miracles, are divine facts ; they can never be achieved by the instrumentality of unauthorised persons. They can be sacramentally realised only through the channel of recognised and legitimate sacraments. Wherever these things take place Christ is, and Christ sanctions the worship and the service, and who shall take upon himself to deny the authority and the validity of that of which Christ Himself approves? It seems to us that the fundamental delusion underlying much of the literature of exclusive and schismatical Churches is the absolutely unproved assumption that our Lord did once for all constitute a cast-iron ecclesiastical polity, from which there was never to be any departure without the sacrifice of spiritual life. There is not one single sentence in the New Testament which intimates that Christ or His apostles did ever construct an unalterable system of that sort. History and reason are both opposed to the assumption that the organism of the visible Church was never to adapt itself to the changing conditions of life and service. Christ did not abandon His Church when He had established it.   He remains in the midst of the Church, animating and inspiring it as at the beginning, and leading it from time to time to such modifications of ecclesiastical organisation as the changing circumstances of the centuries may require.   In the absence of any positive statement to the contrary, either by our Lord or by any of His apostles, there is no decisive test of a Christian Church left, except those signs of divine grace and those seals of divine approval to which exclusively Jesus Christ Himself and His apostles referred inquirers and critics.

"We have just had a striking illustration of this fact in the language which Lord Halifax found himself compelled to employ in reply to Leo XIII. The Pope, with 'infallible' authority *ex cathedrâ*, has proclaimed to all mankind that the Church of England is no Church at all, that her ministers are impostors, and that her sacraments are delusions.   It is to be hoped that such a *reductio ad absurdum* of the clerical, as distinguished from the scriptural, method of discovering the true branches of the Catholic Church will open the eyes of Englishmen to the folly of the clerical method. . . . Lord Halifax seemed to realise this when, replying to the direct and cruel blow of the Pope, he said, with gracious simplicity, that the Pope must be mistaken, as he and all whom he represented had been converted through the ministry of the Anglican clergy and were now edified at her altars. That is a decisive reply to the folly of the Papal Bull ; but it is curious that Lord Halifax does not seem to perceive that we of the Evangelical Churches are able to make a similar reply to his when, like the Pope, he proposes to excommunicate us, and to place us and the millions whom we represent as completely outside the true Church as the Pope places him.   Our ministers and our sacraments have precisely the same spiritual attestations and sanctions as those which he properly claims for the ministry and sacraments of the Anglican communion."—*Contemporary Review*, March 1897.

Thus peace and brotherly love—vast and lofty conceptions of the Catholic and Apostolic Church and its work on earth—filled the minds of Dr. Berry and my father in their tour of this country.   Dr. Berry was the architect of the temple.   He taught the import of federal unity, of the relation of the different states to one another, of the impossibility that the good of one state should mean the detriment of another, of the nature of supreme Congress and of the local Councils sitting in each town. Together with my father, he laid stress on the increase in strength and effectiveness of Christian work that such councils and united endeavour must everywhere ensure, as well as on the absence of that waste and friction in effort which had been so distressing and spiritually degenerating in the past.   All must unite in impassioned membership of Christ's world-wide Church, and join wherever they could with fellow-Christians in

29

that leavening of the world and society which two thousand years ago He had committed to their charge.

My father's special contribution was the advocacy of chivalry, the nature of which has already been sufficiently indicated. As Free Churchmen, he insisted, they could propagate it, as Methodists, Baptists, Congregationalists, and Quakers could never hope to do by themselves. On what enterprises of social welfare, he urged, might they not embark, both as regarded the amelioration of the public life in cities and villages as well as in the reclaiming and aiding of lost and suffering individuals. Oh, they might testify to the reality of Christianity, the working reality of it, and so commend it to the hearts and consciences of men! Let them hate sin as Christ did, and spare no effort to shed abroad love and righteousness in the lives of their neighbours, not by preaching and praying and sighing after it only, for these had their place, but by actual practice and endeavour in daily and public life, particularly public. Then he gathered the whole discourse into a nutshell, as was his habit, and closed as follows:—" Vote and act in public life and in business just as if Christ were by your side. In no other way can you prove the reality of your Christianity, and the work to which I believe God has specially called Free Churchmen." [1] His power of gripping an audience, of forcing and rousing attention and interest, never perhaps stood him in better stead. He would repeat also stories of the work of his own mission, and tell his audiences how happily and successfully liberal Anglicans, Congregationalists, Baptists, Presbyterians, Salvationists, Quakers, and Methodists worked together in West London. In this manner, then, local Councils were established.

In addition to arousing popular interest and support in the movement, he was always a prominent and keenly

[1] Mr. Nix related the following as illustrative of my father's method of addressing audiences and collecting the information necessary for doing so. On arriving at the house where he was to spend the night, he entered into conversation with the hostess. Amid talk of a quite general character, he extracted from her various items respecting the chapel where he was to speak, and the traditions, religious or otherwise, of the town. " So when he came to speak in the evening," said Mr. Nix, " everything was pieced together in his mind like a puzzle solved, and the audience would stare at him in astonishment, for he was speaking to them as if he had lived in the neighbourhood since the year one ! "

interested figure at the committees and assemblies of various
kinds, so frequent from 1890 onwards, in which the details
and character of the Federation met with the most ardent
discussion. Though in general assemblies he would dominate,
as will be shown, he seems to have reserved a peculiar
strength for committee work, in which his zeal and grasp of
detail astonished beholders. His absorption in what often
appeared mere minutiæ was felt to be astounding in the case
of a man who swept people after him like leaves in the
wake of the wind, and who was generally regarded as an invincible fighter and champion, a brilliant journalist and speaker,
rather than one whose abilities, at any rate, were never at
greater advantage than in a committee. Methodism knew
this,[1] but it was something of a surprise to members of other
Nonconformist Churches. A sub-committee, so far from boring
him, appeared to be his passion. To say that every detail
interested him is incorrect; he simply revelled in them all.
How he felt always and thought as he sat with so many of
his dear Cromwellian brethren, and what they felt always and
thought concerning him, history unfortunately cannot accurately
relate. Her muse never does relate what she reasonably might,
being the most prudent, undoubtedly, of the nine. But the
spirit of divination, which is nothing if not audacious, endeavours
to supply her omissions. In a word, it was increasingly brought
home that the writer of the " Notes " of the *Methodist Times*,
who thought nothing of charging the bench of bishops when it
roused his anger, might really have been a bishop himself by
the way he went on! They would never have suspected him
of it! Still he could charge like any Ironside when the need
arose, but in the intervals there was a distinct suggestion of
mitre and crosier.

[1] My father's opponents in Methodism used to say that they were contending
with two distinct personalities, which were so divergent that they could not associate them with each other. In addressing Conference and other ecclesiastical
assemblies, the Celtic and the idealistic element was sometimes inclined to be in the
ascendant, so he would impress certain of his opponents as entirely impracticable.
In committees, on the other hand, the Semitic element was always in the ascendant ;
and he would be as keen a business man as any of his opponents, conscious seemingly
not of ideals and probabilities, but only of the actual facts and possibilities, and
what could be obtained from these.

Mr. Law, in speaking of my father's contributions to the Federation, said, "He
was our best business man in committee."

His intellectual attitude also caused them a certain amount of query. " How far had he thought ? " " Did he think ? " Strange to say, he was also wondering as to whether the average Nonconformists thought of the inevitable result of the policy some of them were so bent on pursuing. If they did think just a moment of what it would entail in the everyday world of affairs, they would accept what he was advocating. But though full mutual understanding was scarcely possible—when is it ?—there is no pleasanter portion of my father's career than his dealings with Free Churchmen and their treatment of him. To agree with him always was an impossibility ; continually, openly and unreservedly they disagreed, but admiration, recognition of his services, they gave freely, and where the relationship was at all personal or intimate, an unbounded love.

Two of the most generous and understanding tributes accorded him were from Dr. Clifford and Dr. Guinness Rogers, in a few words at the Free Church Congress of 1903. Dr. Rogers paused before commencing, and when he did speak said, " If it had not been for Hugh Price Hughes we should not have been here at all." [1] The sentences that followed had an import beyond their verbal expression, nor were they chosen with a view to it. They were far also from anything approaching eulogy. " This is not the occasion," the speaker intimated. " Time must bring that, the years with their perspective." He—we—were too near the figure to do it justice, to understand it and all that it had wrought. Suddenly he changed, and the remarks became personal, familiar, as if the speaker were no longer able to repress the reminiscences which would have choked him if he had allowed them full utterance. " Of course I did not always agree " (and he half smiled) " with him,—but "— and he never explained what was in that " but." It was one of the longest words in the language, the audience felt, containing in it all that Hugh Price Hughes was to the speaker and the Churches. " One time," he continued, succumbing altogether to those reminiscences, " everybody was speaking against him. Nobody

[1] One who visited Dr. Rogers on the day of my father's death said he had not seen him so shaken since the death of Dr. Dale. " Hughes," he said, " was such a lovable man." Clifford's tribute also on the following Sunday was full of insight and affection.

seemed to agree with him, nor did I. But one Sunday night I went down to St. James's Hall, where he was preaching, and walked straight into the vestry, and I said, " I have been reading and hearing all the things they are saying against you, and I don't see with you myself, but I want just to shake you by the hand to assure you "— And again to listeners he did not appear to finish, nor could they get beyond the shake of that hand, which seemed the grip of a common faith. It recalled to certain, as it did to the speaker, that boundless faith and belief in the Unseen which characterised him whom flesh should no more behold. The vision of it indeed caught the speaker to heights where he smiled as Hugh Price Hughes had done at the disquietude of Christian men concerning the waves of that deep in the serene hollow of His hand.

What did it matter whether Moses wrote the Pentateuch or whether he wrote anything, or who wrote this document or who wrote that, or whether the documents were not written at all. What did it matter after all, in the face of Jesus Christ of Nazareth, the Saviour of the world, living to-day in His Church and in every victory of the Cross over sin and selfishness in the lives and ideals and purposes of men. That, listeners felt, was the very crux of the Credo, that only portion with which a Christian could presume to face death and life as Hugh Price Hughes had faced them. There was no more after that, but it was one of the longest eulogies ever heard in the Church of Christ. Dr. Lunn, who followed him, spoke as my father's most intimate and loved friend would be expected to do of a side not generally known to the world at large, of his love for theology, and the special gifts which enabled him to develop an ecclesiastical structure in a young organisation.

All this was most admirably put and true, but the majority of the listeners did not comprehend it as they did the former. The people think of him as Hugh Price Hughes, not as an ecclesiastic or a student of theology. The Church Triumphant may give him the mitre and crosier one day, that day the old artists and saints used to dream of, but to the people he will appear strangely in it!

So in several distinct ways my father shaped and left his impress on the Federation. He everywhere advocated and aided in the construction of a local Free Church Council, which

should unite the Nonconformists of the locality in the promotion of the spiritual life of the Christian religion.   With their
formation was bound up the constitution of Congress, which
from 1895 assumed a more elaborate and strictly representative basis.   So far it had consisted for the most part of
enthusiastic assemblies of leading Nonconformist ministers and
their supporters, and was not a strictly constitutional and
representative assembly as it is at this moment.   On what
basis should delegates be elected to attend the Supreme Council
of the Federation?   That was the knotty point of the second
Congress held in Leeds in 1894, some months before my
father went to Italy.   It was strongly felt that each of the
Federated Churches should elect their representatives, and
send them as such to Congress.   By this means it was
contended the election of the most suitable would be best
secured, and each confederate would thus be enabled to voice
its own interest and feeling in the Supreme Council of the
Federation.

But against this proposition, which was earnestly advocated, my father offered a determined resistance.   The basis
of representation, he held, must be territorial, not denominational.   Nottingham, Birmingham, Leeds and all the other
English towns and groups of villages which went to form their
parochial system, must send Free Churchmen to the Congress,
not Wesleyan Methodists, or Primitive Methodists, or Congregationalists, or Quakers.   Everything hung on that—on
that spirit of unity and catholicity that such a representative
basis would ensure.   In no other way also could they show the
world that Nonconformists were one.   He wanted delegates to
forget when they were in Congress whether they were Methodists or Baptists, and to think of themselves as members of the
evangelical portion of Christ's Church elected to represent their
particular parish on the Supreme Council and nothing else.

He was convinced that, apart from the wider and more
catholic outlook involved, such a representation would be a
far wiser and more prudent polity.   The sectarian differences
which they wished so much to avoid, and which they simply
must if their Federation was to be at all durable, would be
best avoided by such a course.   Delegates would not then be
committed to the particular policy or interest of an individual

communion, which they could scarcely fail to be if they came as its representatives. Freedom of discussion and the atmosphere of unclouded fellowship so essential to their meeting would be ensured by non-sectarian representation. Moreover, there was the divine practical aspect. If representation was denominational, and the various central bodies, *e.g.* the Methodist Conference and the Congregational Union, had to give their adherence and elect representatives, some denominations might take half a century in sending their quota. The Free Church Council of every " parish " which would consist of Nonconformists kindled to catholicity, must send their representative to Congress. He felt the crisis to be a most critical one, colouring the whole future of the Federation and the ecclesiastical history of Great Britain. For the sake of God and humanity let them adopt the attitude and standpoint of Catholic Churchmen, and eschew any spirit of dissent or sectarianism. In such a manner the " bishop " spoke, for it was in such a character that many of his brethren must have seen him at such moments. But " bishop " or " no bishop," they felt that what he said was good, and voted for territorial and non-sectarian representation. Doubtless it was against the grain to some, but they did not intend to impair their Federation.

As a result they empowered Mr. Law to establish local Councils throughout the country, and it was after his return from Italy that my father and Dr. Berry were able to assist him so materially in the way indicated. Immense stress was laid by my father on the formation and work of these local Councils, for they necessarily were the key of the whole. Supreme assemblies, where leaders, lay and ministerial, could congregate, were all very delightful and interesting in their way, but it was not the principal scene of the new operations and the new fellowship, even if it was their most imposing display. Right away in the towns and villages of England among the main body of the people, the Federation should do its greatest work,[1] strengthening, encouraging, and inspiring

[1] Let the reader imagine the effect of such Councils, say, in the rural districts of old England. He should think of the new interest, the new sense of strength, that such a union with fellow-Christians tends to create—not to mention the educative and spiritualising influence of men and women realising themselves a portion of a very

those of the people whose religious life and inspiration was derived from the evangelical portion of Christ's Church.

The value of Congress, he saw, lay in its effect on the various delegates, bringing them into touch with each other and their leaders. He hoped that it would send men and women back to their homes charged with fresh inspiration, hopes, and ideals for everyday life—domestic as well as civic. So all through the nineties Mr. Law was continually ascending the staircase of 8 Taviton Street, and confering with my father about the local Councils and the affairs of the Federation in general. The little room which they took in Farringdon Street as the centre of their operations was as dear to certain of my father's fellow-workers as the office of the Journal in Fleet Street. The small beginnings of a great movement or venture haunt memory, because then association is closest, and the first ideals seem freshest and least impaired.

About the year 1893 something occurred which will not only reveal my father's character very intimately, but which caused at the time a great deal of discussion and free criticism respecting Nonconformist leaders. The programme of Dr. Berry and my father was so wide and social that it seemed calculated not only to appeal to but to include religious-minded people who did not accord with them in the expression of certain Christian doctrines. Thus it was scarcely surprising that the Unitarian body offered to join with them in social enterprise, and indeed to be admitted within the pale of the Federation. The rejection of their services and alliance was keenly criticised by an age which lays stress on Christian deed rather than on the exact nature of Christian thought. What did it matter, it was pretty widely demanded, when each denomination was avowedly free to pursue its own ideas and tradition? Because the belief of one concerning the Trinity

large army charged with aiding the weak and the establishment of righteousness. That they are by any means perfect councils cannot be maintained ; like most that is earthly, they are very imperfect ; but they have this ideal and a new enthusiasm in life which has its roots in the Church of Christ. It is the mass of the people, the traders, teachers, agriculturists, who benefit by the Federation, the army of toilers who are more dependent on such organisations in their religious life, and the widening of their ideals, than more leisured and privileged persons imagine. My father's model was his own Mission, with its various clubs, guilds, etc., whose leading ideas several Councils have begun to imitate.

was not the same as that of the others, what difference did it make to the elevation of mankind through religious influence on which both were equally bent? Assuredly they were narrow and intolerant as the rest, and Hugh Price Hughes most of all, for he in particular was inflexible, insisting more than anyone that their admission was an impossibility.

What made my father's attitude in this matter inflexible? Many, doubtless, thought him narrow and intolerant, and lacking in width of sympathy and any depth of imagination.

But neither of these suppositions was true. It was the depth of this latter which dictated his attitude, and the wideness of his sympathies which helped to make him so inflexible, because he was fighting against them. If he had been less wide in sympathy and understanding he would have been a more amicable fighter.

As he would have declared with truth, he was indebted to the writings and example of great Unitarians from his youth up. But all this could not alter his conviction that they could not belong to the Church of Christ. He was not dreaming of a loose federation, of religious and philanthropic bodies, but of a close federation of a portion of the Catholic Church linked in the depths of its thought and feeling to earliest times. Their position evidently was misunderstood, and he was very sorry for it, more than he could say, as he hated to have to appear to repulse those whom in many ways he so much admired.

The feeling of listeners desiring federation in great social and ethical issues, might be thus expressed : " Must the Catholic Church be everlastingly repelling those who cannot think exactly as she does? Shall we not be sinning against His spirit in rejecting those who are so willing to enter into His ideas and purposes, even though they do not think of Him as we do? Must we, like the disciples of old, repel those who would touch the hem of His garment? Besides, is not each confederate avowedly free to pursue its own ideas and tradition and to join in those great issues which Christendom has in common? Moreover, it is often metaphysics, not the heart, that separates them from us and our beliefs. That world's need also of which you speak so much—what of that? Could not we set an example to that Catholic Church in which you are so concerned, of joining hands with those who can aid us in so

many ways, and who are so noble in their manner of life?
We, as the last branch of the Church Catholic, ought to be
the most elastic and imaginative, not like our mediæval predecessors."

This was the feeling, undoubtedly, of some evangelistic
Christians, while the outside world was more outspoken and
less understanding in its comments.   In the first place, my
father was most passionately a Catholic Churchman, and would
have felt quite at home with Anselm and Augustine in some
ways.   In the second place, he was not fighting for a doctrine
of the Church of Christ so much as for something else which
transcended any doctrine.   As he heard and read what men
said concerning what he regarded as the chief article of the
Christian faith,—the reality of the Atonement of Jesus Christ
and His resurrection,—he must have often felt himself a boy
again on the Welsh shore.   "Lord Jesus, save me from my sin,
from that which separates me from Thee.   Cleanse Thou me.
Help me, as Thou alone canst help and cleanse."   Browning,
who expressed so much that was in him, also expressed that
agony as nobody else did :

> "O Thou pale Form, so dimly seen, deep-eyed !
> I have denied Thee calmly ; do I not
> Pant when I read of Thy consummate deeds?
> And burn to see Thy calm pure truths outflash
> The brightest gleams of earth's philosophy?
> Do I not shake to hear aught question Thee?
> If I am erring, save me ! madden me !
> Take from me powers and pleasures ! let me die
> Ages, so I see Thee.   I am knit round
> As with a chain by sin and lust and pride ;
> Yet though my wandering dreams have seen all shapes
> Of strange delight, oft have I stood by Thee—
> Have I been keeping lonely watch with Thee
> In the damp night by weeping Olivet,
> Or leaning on Thy bosom, proudly less."

The agony was past and the sun shining, while the waves
crept forward and broke into foam on the shore below.
"Lord Jesus, I submit.   Take me as I am.   Use me as Thou
wilt."   He fought for that boy as well as Augustine, which
gave such strength to his convictions.   He knew in himself
the depth of the humility and the passion, and the aspiration and the love which belonged to those two names,

Christ Jesus, and none other. It was life and death and immortality, all that had been, and all that was to come, the meaning and the outcome of living. It was the burning secret of unnumbered souls who for all their diversity of tongue and condition were one in Him. It was the sun gilding and warming the peaks of life as they stretched into the vista of eternity. It was hourly and unseen communion with One who never let him go despite shortcoming, and in whose mingled agony and joy over creation he faintly shared. As in Browning's poem, He swept him along through the universes, leading him into all of them, yet never forsaking him, so that the "Christmas Eve" must have seemed almost a personal experience. This consciousness of the united testimony of the universal Christian Church for two thousand years regarding the great essentials of the faith was always very present to my father, and led to his insistence on personal experience as the ultimate touchstone respecting the value of religion.

In such a manner and for such reasons was he inflexible.[1] Though certain, while profoundly agreeing with him and his interpretation of the Christian faith, were yet unwilling to appear uncharitable to those whom they regarded as noble members of the kingdom, the general feeling was strongly with him. As usual, also, immediate practical issues were on his side. How could those who denied His atonement, and, some of them, His resurrection, join in the united worship of the federated Churches, in its hymns and prayers and sacraments, especially in the evangelical missions, which were early associated with them, and conducted throughout the towns and villages of the country? Putting aside the feelings of the average member, the thing was a manifest impossibility. Besides, it would have opened them to misconstruction, particularly to other branches of the Church Catholic, who would not interpret such inclusion as charity.

---

[1] Perhaps a saying that is attributed to Charles Lamb will reveal to some minds something of that for which my father was contending. Charles Lamb had been speaking of the great spirits of the past, and the instinctive effect that they would produce if they suddenly appeared in the room where he and his companions were conversing. "If William Shakspere came into the room, we should all stand up," said he, with his characteristic stutter. "If Jesus Christ came into the room," he added, "we should all kneel down." The full recognition of such a distinction, my father could not imperil.

II. *A Catechism*

That my father saw this clearly was certain—probably
more clearly than anything else so far as policy was concerned.
As he sat in ecclesiastical council he could not wean himself
from the habits and outlook of long service, so that he was
obliged to see things as they take shape in the field, and to
give his counsels accordingly.   When to startled beholders he
appeared to don the red hat, it was fairly certain that it concealed a helmet.   For instance when the brethren of the Free
Churches met and clasped hands, regaling themselves with
hymns and thanksgiving in the valley, amid much contentment
and brotherly love, he could not but be aware that other
Christian brethren in the Anglican communion were on one of
the neighbouring hilltops bent on operations which must, he considered, interfere with the Free Church operations in the valley.

That this consideration lay at the back of his propositions
is not maintained, for their motive was embedded in the
depths of his religious and mental being, but he must have
none the less been conscious that they were preparing for all
possible emergencies.   The reader is here besought to pardon
the phraseology of the age of chivalry, which is the only
phraseology that can exactly express my father's feelings at
this point.   From the very beginning undoubtedly he had had
the idea of digging a deep entrenchment, and so defining the
theological whereabouts of the Free Churches and their exact
position.

Yet it would be impossible to describe the exact processes,
mental and religious, which led him, with all the adjuncts
of an invisible episcopacy, to insist on the compilation of a
Catechism which should represent the convictions of the
whole Federation of the United Free Churches.   " It must be,
brethren," he said in effect ; " our leaders must meet and arrive
at a common definition of their faith.   It is no good singing
we are united, and clasping each other's hands, if we don't
show some signs of it in verbal expression—in the language
and methods that are understood on the field.   Heaven doubtless comprehends our agreement, but earth does not ; and one
of the purposes of our meeting in the valley is to show forth
in the planet where we now happen to be existing the under-

lying unity of Christ's Catholic Church. By such means we shall not only edify ourselves in that we shall be led to see more clearly into the depths of our faith and our agreement therein, but we may also edify our brethren on the hilltop yonder, who will see how closely allied we are with them in thought and feelings on many essential matters." And it came to pass that the fathers listening saw that it was good. Few things struck the fathers more than the excessive nimbleness begotten by chivalry in the field. Lightly and persuasively he stepped in and out amongst them, taking each by the hand and leading them to that business on which his heart was set.

In plain language, my father summoned a representative Committee for the compilation of a Catechism at 8 Taviton Street. Some time previously he had asked Dr. J. Oswald Dykes to compile a draft Catechism, knowing that none of the leading ministers of the Federation had greater learning and understanding for this purpose than he. The vista of theology and history which such an undertaking opened up simply inflamed a mind ever eager to find outlet for itself, and devoted to a wide philosophical study of theology. The devotion of the early Fathers to the exact and full presentation of the heart and issues of their faith seemed to be echoed in him, as well as a delicate and full recognition of the progress of contemporary religious thought—that progress which consists in response to the Zeit Geist and in our time to the liberating influences of science. To enter into the arena of philosophic and scholastic pursuits had not been his, but like one banished from the land which is dear to him, he was always gleaning the latest news concerning its doings, following in a general way their nature and issue. From one traveller from its bourne he would derive as much as other men get from twenty. It was a necessity, and his own swift mind aided him in the process. What gleanings they were, to be sure, anything but the dream of his college days, yet quite sufficient to enable him to discern the lie of a Catechism and the difficulties of its course.

His reading, which was always varied, had none the less a predominant philosophical and theological tinge. His own strong personal taste made philosophy in its widest sense his favourite study, particularly in later years. " Poetry for youth," he would say; "philosophy for age." The Catechism was not only the latest verbal deliverance of Christendom respecting its belief and the heir of the ages of Christian thought that had gone before, but it brought to him visions of her future, of the children who should be instructed in its simple grand formulas, and who would thus enter into the treasury of the past, as all do half-unconsciously. Under the shadow of its freedom—that freedom for which the Fathers had fought—the children of the twentieth century should be reared, imbibing even in infancy that wide charity which had characterised the wisest Christian thinkers. The formulas which should haunt memory should be those expressive of the deep religious thought and feeling of past time, as well as the latest outcome of a more enlightened ethical teaching. It was the graving in permanent stone of the endeavours and designs of his life, but nobody except one or two seemed to see its practical and poetic side. Dr. Dykes saw it, of course, for he was a Scotsman in addition to being a theologian, and knew how the first sentence of the Shorter Catechism could sink into the innermost portions of a man's memory, remaining there when he is under the impression that he has long forgotten it. My father must have thirsted for the presence of the Presbyterians within his entrenchments. The Established Church of Scotland, being allied to the State, could not rank with the confederates, and the Free Kirk and the United Presbyterians preferred, with the instinct of nature, to cling to their mother rather than to join those with whose tenets and feelings they found themselves in so much accord. The Presbyterians, like the Cromwellians, were always very gracious to my father. Wesleyan ministers who have travelled in Scotland relate that people there know the names of two members of their Church, Hugh Price Hughes and Mark Guy Pearse, and that round these twain, and the Mission connected with them, their thoughts concerning Methodism obstinately revolve.

The size of the Catechism Committee that gathered in the dining-room of 8 Taviton Street impressed the family as much as any intimations of its business. The wonder was the walls did not give way, so packed was that room, some members of Committee being almost in danger of falling out of the window. At a certain stage of the proceedings tea was brought in, which my father dispensed. The fact that he thus officiated impressed the family imagination more than the fact that he was chairman of the Committee, and that, as the maid expressed it who brought in the tray, " he was a-leading of them."

The main items of the Catechism my father himself briefly described in a current number of the *Contemporary Review*, from which the following quotations are taken :—

"Just as the pupils of eminent sculptors do a great deal of the rough work of hewing the marble into something like its final shape before the sculptor himself takes the block minutely in hand, it was thought that some of the younger and more promising men of the Evangelical Free Churches might save the time and shorten the labour of those more responsible persons who give the new Catechism its final shape. It was not found possible, however, to carry out this idea in its original form, and the more responsible representatives of the movement have been active members of both Committees. I happened to be President of the National Council at the time the project was started, so that I became *ex officio* chairman of the first Committee. I was subsequently made permanent chairman, as I had all the threads in my hand ; and, finally, my distinguished friend, Dr. Mackennal, who was for some time secretary of the Committee, having found it increasingly difficult to attend meetings in London and to keep detailed records of the proceedings, I was appointed to his office as well as my own. As chairman and convener, I have attended every meeting of the Committee, and have been familiar with every detail. The Preliminary Committee, meeting at intervals of about six weeks or two months, spent two years in revising the original draft.

"For upwards of thirty years the leading Presbyterian theologian of our country had been unconsciously preparing for his great task by a special study of the great Confessions of Faith prepared during the Reformation era. When Dr. Dykes appeared for the first time, manuscript in hand, at the Catechism Committee, I exclaimed, 'Well, Doctor, you have undertaken what no man in Europe has dared to attempt for three hundred years.' Every one who has any historical knowledge of theology, or any imagination, can realise the almost insuperable difficulties which surround the preparation of the draft of a new Catechism. Of course there have been innumerable alterations in detail, and we are much indebted to Dr. Dykes for the humility and sweet reasonableness with which he has permitted us to criticise and alter his questions and answers. But the general structure remains what it was. . . . Our object was to express, not the peculiarities of any particular denomination, but those fundamental and essential truths which are common to all the great Evangelical Churches, truths which both unite and transcend all our varieties of opinion. In such an enterprise, representing not only one but all the Evangelical Churches, it was obviously essential in some instances to find language as many-sided as the language of Scripture itself. . . . It will also be noticed that the estimable Society of Friends is not represented on the Catechism Committee. It has been understood from the beginning of the movement in which our brethren of that communion have been most prominently and actively associated, that with respect to the sacraments we should 'agree to differ,' as Wesley and Whitfield agreed to differ on some profound aspects of the Calvinistic controversy."

Then follows a list of the framers of the Catechism.

"The representative theologians in the foregoing list were appointed not by their own communions, but by the Committee of the National Council. In the strictest sense, therefore, no communion is responsible for this Catechism. These theologians have prepared it on their personal responsibility. As in the case of the revision of the Authorised Version of the Bible, it carries no official weight; it depends for its acceptance upon the extent to which its authors command the confidence of their various communions, and yet more upon the extent to which, after due reflection, the Catechism commends itself to the general approval of Christian men. At the same time, he must be a very ill-informed person who fails to realise the significance of a Catechism approved by such names. No such combination representing so many Churches has ever before prepared or sanctioned a detailed statement of Christian belief.

"It will be noted with interest that two of the theologians who took part n preparing this Catechism are laymen. . . . It is a mere accident that the great majority of the compilers of this Catechism are ordained ministers of religion. It is due to the obvious fact that separated ministers have the time, aptitude, learning, and other qualifications for a work which peculiarly belongs to their profession. Very few laymen have either time or opportunity, in the busy world of this century, to qualify themselves for such work, which is partly technical, and which requires extensive familiarity not only with the Bible, but also with the processes of human thought through all ages, and with similar undertakings in the past. At the same time, the presence of at least two influential laymen on the Committee demonstrates that no professional class has an absolute monopoly in the scientific interpretation of the Holy Scriptures or in the exposition of convictions which arise in the hearts of all men who have personal experience of the gospel of God. I ought to add in this preliminary explanation that the National Council undertook this great work not merely, perhaps I ought to say not mainly, in order to demonstrate the unanimity of theological conviction which now characterises the great Protestant Churches, but in response to an urgent and ever-growing appeal for a new Catechism that was catholic rather than denominational, and that was also up to date, up to date not in the sense that any ancient doctrine is or could be superseded, but in the sense that catechetical statements should be expressed in modern language rather than in obsolete terms which involve risk of ambiguity and misapprehension.

.   .   .   .

"The first question and answer are—Question : 'What is the Christian religion?' Answer : 'It is the religion founded by our Lord and Saviour

Jesus Christ, who has brought to us the full knowledge of God and of Eternal Life.' This question strikes the keynote of the new Catechism. We begin, not with metaphysical abstractions, but with the incarnate Christ ; and our object is to discuss, not a verbal creed, but a living religion.

. . . .

"It is obvious that this Catechism is prepared to meet the subjective wants of the human heart, as well as to state the objective facts of an historical faith. It will also be noticed that in our numerous definitions of the Deity the historical rather than the metaphysical order has been followed. We begin by defining the Eternal Father as revealed to us in Christ. We then describe the historic facts of our Lord's Life, Death, and Resurrection, summing them up, it will be observed, in certain essential clauses of the Nicene Creed. Then we speak of the Holy Spirit, whose existence is the final disclosure in the gradual revelation of truth respecting the nature of God. Thoughtful persons will also note that in speaking of the Holy and Blessed Spirit we have avoided that unhappy addition to the Nicene Creed which the intolerance of Rome, in its incapacity to appreciate niceties of profound truth, attempted to force upon the Eastern Church at the cost of the first, greatest, and most permanent of all schisms. While not doubting for a moment the double procession of the Holy Spirit, we agree with the Eastern Church in the conviction that we ought not to compel any one to use in relation to the mystery of the Divine existence any expression not explicitly found in Holy Scripture.

"In our fundamental definition of God we have taken care to say that ' He is Love,' thus removing one of the greatest blemishes in the Catechisms of the past.

. . . .

"In Question 13 the new note in the best evangelical teaching of our time is emphasised by the statement that Christ is not only our Saviour, but also 'a perfect example of what we ought to be.' I quite agree with Dr. Stalker that the imitation of Christ has not hitherto been sufficiently prominent in the thoughts of Protestants ; but Dr. Stalker himself must be satisfied with this plain statement. The ceaseless intercession of our Lord, which is caricatured in the bewitching service of the Mass, and which is often overlooked in Protestant thought, is taught very emphatically in Answer 16. The most suspicious evangelical Christian will find that the definitions of repentance and faith unmistakably protect us against the delusions of a dead orthodoxy. The fundamental truth of Calvinism is again brought out in the answer to Question 23, where it is declared that we are enabled to repent and believe 'by the secret power of the Holy Spirit working graciously in our hearts, and using for this end providential discipline and the message of the gospel.' Reference has already been made to the striking feature of this new Catechism, which consists in a careful Christian interpretation of the ten Jewish commandments. Let me especially emphasise sub-question and sub-answer (viii.). Even our Socialistic friends ought to be satisfied with the lofty Christian ethic which declares that the eighth commandment teaches us 'to be honest and fair in all our dealings, and in no wise to take unbrotherly advantage of another by fraud

or force.' All who ponder the far-reaching significance of this last clause
will agree that it embodies the highest Christian conception of honesty.

.   .   .   .

"The next section of the new Catechism is the one which will probably
excite most attention and interest. Many of us have long felt that the attitude of Protestantism in relation to Romanism and Romanising Anglicanism
has been far too negative, critical, and destructive. As my eminent friend
Dr. Berry has insisted with splendid eloquence on many a platform during
the last few years in this country, it is high time for us to become definite,
positive, and constructive. The Committee unanimously agreed to state the
doctrine of the Church in the following significant question and equally
significant answer :—
    "Question : 'What is the Holy Catholic Church?'
    "Answer : 'It is that holy society of believers in Christ Jesus which He
founded, of which He is the only Head, and in which He dwells by His
Spirit ; so that, though made up of many communions, organised in various
modes, and scattered throughout the world, it is yet one in Him.'
    "It will be noted that this definition makes no reference whatever to the
metaphysical abstraction entitled the 'Invisible Church,' which was invented
in the sixteenth century. Of course we all believe in the 'Invisible Church'
in the sense that the Church Triumphant in heaven is a part of the true
Church not visible on earth. As we often sing :

          'One family we dwell in Him,
              One Church above, beneath,
          Though now divided by the stream,
              The narrow stream of death.'

    "But in Protestant controversy the 'Invisible Church' is used in a totally
different sense, to describe some Church of which every believer in Christ
is a member, even when he totally neglects all the duties and obligations of
practical fellowship with his fellow-Christians. London swarms with ecclesiastical vagrants, who flatter themselves that because they believe in Christ,
and are therefore, according to their own notions, members of the 'Invisible
Church,' they suffer no loss by holding entirely aloof from the organised
fellowship of every Christian communion, and by refusing to bear any of
the burdens or discharge any of the duties of the Christian sanctuary.
Anything more entirely opposed to the original purpose of Christ or the best
interests both of the individual and of human society, I cannot imagine. I
am deeply thankful that the Catechism Committee, without attempting to
define or to discuss any 'invisible' entity, have limited themselves to defining
that real, practical, visible organisation which exists on earth and does the
work of Christ on earth. If we had nothing in existence here except the
so-called 'Invisible Church,' which is so dear to well-meaning, obstinate,
and self-assertive Christians who resent the discipline of co-operation with
their fellow-Christians, the powers of evil would not have much to fear. We
frankly accept the Church which was organised by Christ and His apostles
as a visible, audible, and tangible society ; and at the same time, without in
any way destroying the existing ecclesiastical organisations which are

required by the varieties of the human mind, we proclaim the true bond of ecclesiastical unity. The Church is one neither in the Pope nor in the Sovereign, but in Christ Jesus, its Divine Head and Lord. The great movement which has produced this Catechism is itself an illustration of that ancient catholic truth. We are obviously one, not only in external co-operation for defence or attack, but in doctrinal conviction and spiritual aspiration. And it is well to remember here that we are a majority of those inhabitants of England and Wales who make any profession of religion. In the English-speaking world we are an overwhelming majority, representing at least two-thirds of all who speak the English tongue and profess the Christian religion. Under these circumstances, thoughtful persons will estimate the significance of our recently discovered unity. The visibility of the Church is expressly reaffirmed in the next question and answer.

"Question : 'For what ends did our Lord found His Church?' Answer : 'He united His people into this visible brotherhood for the worship of God and the ministry of the Word and the Sacraments ; for mutual edification, the administration of discipline, and the advancement of His kingdom.'

"The burning question of the right of any particular organisation to call itself a 'Church' is faced in Question and Answer 35. Question : 'What is the essential mark of a true branch of the Catholic Church?' Answer : 'The essential mark of a true branch of the Catholic Church is the presence of Christ, through His indwelling Spirit, manifested in holy life and fellowship.' In a word, we accept the most ancient definition of 'the Catholic Church,' the most ancient because it is the definition given by the apostolic Father who invented the expression. In his letter to the Smyrnæans St. Ignatius says : 'Wheresoever the bishop shall appear, there let the people be ; even as where Christ Jesus may be, there is the Catholic Church.' (ὥσπερ ὅπου ἂν ᾖ Χριστὸς Ἰησοῦς ἐκεῖ ἡ καθολικὴ ἐκκλησία.) Some Anglican scholars and theologians, unfamiliar with every Christian communion except their own and the Romanist, seem to be incapable of conceiving any Church in which an episcopate does not occupy the same position that bishops hold in the Anglican and Roman Churches. They imagine, therefore, that St. Ignatius could not have meant exactly what he said, because in the context he contends that no Eucharist, Baptism, or Love Feast is lawful in the absence of the bishop or one whom he has appointed to conduct the service. But that statement is equally true to-day of the 'superintendent' or 'bishop' of a Methodist 'circuit' or 'diocese.' It is simply a question of Church order involving no exclusive claims on the part either of an ancient Greek 'bishop' or a modern Methodist 'superintendent.' The very passage I have quoted above expressly asserts that the bishop *may* be present without the people, but that Christ *cannot* be present without 'the Church' being present also. The Free Church Catechism declares in harmony with the New Testament and Christian Antiquity, that the only final and decisive proof that any organisation is a real 'Church' is the unmistakable presence of the miraculous grace of the Holy Spirit manifested in the conversion and sanctification of men. This proves that Christ is really present, that He gives His *imprimatur*, His sanction, His approval, and from the *imprimatur* of the Supreme Head of the Church there is no appeal either to Canterbury or to Rome.

. . . .

"The ancient and Catholic doctrine is reasserted in Question and Answer 40, where it is stated that 'the decisive proof of a valid ministry is the sanction of the Divine Head of the Church, manifested in the conversion of sinners and the edification of the body of Christ.' It will be noted that the commonly but most unjustly called 'Zwinglian' view of the Lord's Supper is repudiated again and again in our statements about that divinely appointed ordinance. In Answer 41 it is asserted that the sacraments, 'when rightly used,' 'become a means to convey' the grace of God 'to our hearts.' And in Answer 47 it is said that they 'who in penitence and faith partake of' the Lord's Supper 'feed spiritually upon Christ as the nourishment of the soul, by which they are strengthened and refreshed for the duties and trials of life.'

"The closing questions and answers teach the doctrines of the Last Things in devout and scriptural terms which must command general assent. I confess that the rock on which I feared we should be split and wrecked, even within sight of port, was the definition of baptism. Remembering the terrible controversies of Pædobaptists and Anabaptists in the past, my fears were not unnatural. I thought we should at least be compelled to give two alternative answers, although that would have been exceedingly objectionable. However, we found a formula of peace in the statement that the Sacrament of Baptism signifies 'the washing away of sin and the new birth wrought by the Holy Ghost in all who repent and believe.' This is not an unreal, verbal compromise, but an honest statement of truth believed by all. My friend Dr. Clifford and I do not differ in the least with respect to the Processes of divine grace or the evolution of the life of God in the soul, but only with respect to the precise point in the evolution at which the rite of baptism should be administered—in other words, what stage of the work of the Spirit of God baptism specifically symbolises. It is a curious fact that the greatest difficulty we experienced was one which nobody would have anticipated. It was in formulating such a definition of the Resurrection of the Body as would exclude no orthodox opinion, and to which we could all agree. The curious reader may ponder for himself the finally unanimous answer. It must not be assumed from our ultimate unanimity that we had no difficulties. Again and again we seemed to have reached an impassable mountain of difficulty. But, with mutual goodwill and prayerful patience, we persisted in testing every side of the apparently inaccessible Matterhorn until we succeeded in scaling it.

. . . .

"I might further illustrate the comprehensiveness of the Catechism by pointing out that for the first time—as might be expected from stalwart Free Churchmen—we define the relations of the Church to the State and of the State to the Church.

. . . .

"We have long borne the reproach of unnecessary and endless division. We bear it no longer. The centrifugal forces of excessive individualism, the

reaction from centralised, clerical despotism, have spent their strength. The centripetal forces of vital and brotherly Christianity have resumed their genial sway. To those who can 'discern the signs of the times,' this little Catechism is, as Carlyle would have said, 'significant of much.' Before we are twenty years older, all men will realise that it is one of the most wonderful and far-reaching facts of 'the wonderful century' now hasting to its close. *A Domino factum est istud: et est mirabile in oculis nostris."*
—*Contemporary Review*, January 1899.

In the first of the above quotations the reader will note a reference to the Presidency to which he was elected in 1896 by the first Council of the Free Churches of this country. The year before Dr. Berry had assumed the Presidency of the annual assembly, for in that it was not a regular representation it can scarcely be defined by its later title. Thus my father was first President of the Free Church Council, and in that position delivered an address which, for its statement of the Free Church aim and the defence of its position, was much admired. It was entitled "Democracy and the Twentieth Century," and maintained that the Federation was a response to the needs and hopes of a democratic era. In substance it was a repetition of much that has been quoted already. About this time both in public and private he was continually expounding what he regarded as the scriptural definition of the Catholic Church, which he would regard as one of the greatest needs of the time. Many of the laity may have wondered at his insistence, but for the younger ministry, particularly in his own branch of Nonconformity, the stress that he laid on this and other ecclesiastical details was of the greatest importance.

In the world of the Churches, as indicated, the question of the apostolic succession and of the nature and boundaries of the visible Catholic Church was one very much to the fore, and the younger ministry of all denominations were bound to be affected by it and to question concerning it. The insistence laid by Dr. Berry and my father on what they termed the " scriptural definition " was therefore most timely from the point of view of Nonconformity. The younger ministers in Wesleyanism looked upon my father as their champion in all such matters, and both by his conversation and correspondence he would act as their sustainer and encourager. One of them said (and I believe it to be the feeling of many), " He was so certain that we belonged to the Catholic Church and that we had a great work to accomplish. I can never forget his teaching and the impression he made upon me." His certainties respecting one or two things were so great and deep-rooted that they were infectious, and had the strongest effect on those with whom he was brought into contact. It was in his insistence on the catholicity of the Federation that his special contribution lay, for it was the basis, as shown, of the constitution that he gave to it.

In particular, his quotation from St. Ignatius—that "where Christ Jesus may be there is the Catholic Church"—is worthy of insistence, because in it he proclaimed that doctrine of tolerance which his whole life had gone to show forth. In making it the great watchword of the Free Churches he enjoined upon them a tolerance so great and startling that many did not seem to divine it.

Since Christ was with men wherever His ministers or sacraments led them to newness of life, all communions, from Rome to the Society of Friends, were equally intimate with Him wherever this condition was fulfilled, and merited that consideration and courtesy which attached to fellow-members of the Church of Christ. The fact that some of these did not accord their fellow-Christians the recognition which Free Churchmen thought they ought, did not alter to his thinking the superior claims on courtesy and tolerance necessitated by a wider definition of the Catholic Church. The Roman Catholic who saw Christ Jesus present in the unity of the Papacy and those who submitted to it, or the Christian who could only truly behold Him within a certain order of ministers and amid certain specially performed rites and sacraments, or in the absence of these, could not be expected to exercise the tolerance and fellowship of one who said, "These are but minutiæ, different methods by which Christ communicates with the soul. We have strong reason to prefer our own, but seeing that Christ Jesus does thus communicate with our fellow-Christians, in ways distasteful to some of us, we are bound to evince towards them every courtesy and consideration." The keynote of Dr. Berry's discourses and my father's was never " Christ Jesus is with us more than the rest," but always " He is with us and the rest, provided that there is not perfunctory entrance into routine, but some participation in His life." Undoubtedly my father laid such stress on this definition because he foresaw that on a right understanding and practice of it, however difficult at times, the future of the Free Churches would depend. By their superior toleration and catholicity they could win the approval and support of men, and enter into that depth of devotion and width of interest and sympathy which make Christian communions beloved. This was the more striking as it was not as easy for him to be tolerant as it is to some ; indeed it was difficult. He was a born fighter, and felt strongly his own point of view as well as the cause of those particular denominations with which he was associated.

One contribution he gave to the Free Church movement was never adequately realised during his lifetime, in that most took it for granted. This was his gift as a public speaker, as a debater, and as one who understood profoundly the value of procedure and order in a great public assembly. His genius lay in managing assemblies without appearing to control them. A colleague who would often sit next him at public meetings said that he felt him playing at times with his audience. Indeed, his power and ease in addressing popular gatherings was an essential to his life-work, and without this power and ease it could not have been accomplished. None the less it was not in his addressing of great meetings that he displayed his greatest power, but in the management of what was mainly a professional assembly, and which was therefore not inclined to be overruled. Feeling ran high in the clerical world in his later years, and it needed exceptional qualifications to dominate any one of their gatherings. The Free Church assemblies applied the test, and witnessed the triumph of his gifts as a speaker and as the leader of men.

A story that best illustrates this is the following :—A lady, an Anglican, was visiting the family and accompanied my father to a great meeting at the City Temple, where several Free Churchmen were speaking. It was shortly after the great *rapprochement* that has been described in this chapter, and some of the speakers referred in somewhat strong terms to the Anglican Church, and were applauded by the audience in consequence.

When my father got up, he replied to these remarks on behalf of the Anglican Church, for so it struck the lady.

" She is an ancient and great Church," he said, " and we must
not allow ourselves to underestimate her in any way or to
speak slightingly concerning her.   We all know how glad we
should have been if she had been willing to enter our Federation, and that she has a great work and a great charge in this
country just as we have.   While seeing aspects of her which
we must deplore, we cannot but see that Christ is visibly
present, redeeming and aiding the lives of men."   In such
strains he spoke, and the audience listened respectfully, as it
always did to him.   On speaking to this lady at the close of
the meeting he said, " I am distressed that you should have
heard this—very.   I hope it has not hurt your feelings very
much, and indeed I would not have brought you if I had
known."

He had evidently been eager to introduce her to the
Federation and the charity of Free Churchmen, and was not a
little disappointed that it was not forthcoming as he wished.
His independence in an assembly struck onlookers.   He respected its laws, but for some purpose of his own, so that often
he seemed not to sue for sympathy but to command it.   Persons who introduced proposals at the wrong time and in the
wrong manner would provoke comment at their lack of skill,
though he admired their courage.   Because he wished assemblies to follow his wishes, he knew that courage was not the
only requisite.   In particular—and perhaps this was the inner
secret of his power—he was a great spiritual force in their
midst, and was remembered as such.   His presence tended to
the elevation of assemblies, and the one or two whom he met
at all intimately continually repeated to the writer what he
had dinned into their own ears, that the aims of the Federation were before everything else religious and spiritual, not
sectarian or defensive, and that for this end it had been
brought about.   The things of the Spirit were known to weigh
more with him than any other consideration.   His past, the
weekly Sunday evening services which carried on its traditions,
his insistence on Christian principle in all the relationships of
life, and the varied elements of his personality, invested him
with a dignity to which the most divergent were quick to feel
and to respond.

When President he would brook neither clapping of hands

nor noisy demonstration of any kind, laying stress on the fact that they were not a mere irresponsible assembly—" a fortuitous concourse of atoms," as he once expressed it—but a body of delegates met to discharge a grave ecclesiastical function. In particular, he always endeavoured to sustain that lofty interest in public and civic affairs which was distinct from party and temporal issues. The Church of Christ he felt, in a democratic era, must take great social questions to heart, but they must do so in a lofty, religious, and catholic spirit. Nothing distressed him more than the absence of this. In his Presidential address he insists on the fact that the movement was not political, as that term is usually understood :—

"In the first place, and emphatically, it is not a 'political' movement in the sense in which that greatly abused word is usually employed. Unhappily the word 'political' has come to mean in this country party-political, and is used to express those subordinate and passing issues on which good men are divided. The word has lost the sublime significance which it had in the vocabulary of Aristotle. I am afraid it is too late to redeem it from base associations, although it is obvious to all capable of the most elementary thought that everybody who is not an absolute anchorite, living in a cave far from the busy haunts of men, must inevitably be a politician. The relations of husband and wife, parent and child, master and servant, are essentially political. Every act of social life has its political side. In that true and proper sense it is impossible for any human being, except an anchorite, to escape from politics. But in the ordinary and vulgar sense of the word there is no trace of 'politics' in this movement. I do wish to emphasise this, because the only rock upon which we may be wrecked is the possibility of misapprehension or prejudice or error here. Every true Church ought to be comprehensive enough to provide a home for men of every shade of political opinion." [1]

---

[1] From Rome, also, in October 1894, my father writes: ". . . when from this great distance I longingly and lovingly watch the course of events in England, and notice that representative Nonconformist authorities are disposed, for example, to boycott publications which advocate novel views of property, I express no final dogmatic opinion, but I tremble. I am anxious; I cannot help saying to myself: 'I wish every Nonconformist official could see what I am now seeing every day. We must not allow our Churches to be identified with party politics, and in the twentieth century party politics will not be Whig or Tory, Liberal or Conservative, but Collectivist and Individualist. Woe to the Church that commits itself either to the Collectivist or to the Individualist side ! Private men, and even ministers in their private capacity, must do what they think right. They commit nobody except themselves. But our Churches as such must not take sides, must observe a strict neutrality, must be as impartial and comprehensive as the Bible, or they will be involved in a greater disaster than that which has stunned and paralysed the Roman Church in Italy.'"

If my father were asked as to wherein lay the chief contribution of the movement to the Christian life of his time, in the strict practical side and apart from the question of ideal, he would have replied that it was twofold—first, in the compilation of a United Free Church Catechism, and second, in the establishment of Free Church parishes throughout England and Wales as a result of the formation of those local Councils to which allusion has been made. By this division he claimed not a benefit to Nonconformity alone, though it was that, but to the Christian life of England. Speaking from the standpoint of the addresses at Grindelwald, he would point to the fact that, while the Established Church and much of literary tradition recognise one communion for Englishmen and none other, there are, happily or unhappily, rightly or wrongly, as men may regard it, multitudes in England and Wales who lie outside that particular communion and show no signs of returning within its fold, in addition to that very large element which lies outside the Churches altogether. Nonconformity existed, therefore, as a great fact in the national life, influencing and determining its future. To ignore its presence, and to treat every attempt on its part at wider usefulness as a species of insubordination against the Establishment, was not merely a deficiency in courtesy, he thought, and the toleration that springs from such, but a lack of all statesmanship, whether civil or ecclesiastical. He was keenly aware that the Non-conforming Churches had suffered from absence of centralisa-tion, and that thus much of the Christianity of this country had been impeded and stifled by local jealousies and over-lapping. Without any regard for each other or the general weal, Nonconformist chapels would spring up in the same street, and had thus begotten, not merely a tragic waste of Christian effort, but a narrow sectarian life, which had in part justified the criticism of Matthew Arnold, and of that world of culture which saw through his eyes.[1] In an article in the *Encyclopædia Britannica* he writes thus :—

"... A striking feature of this movement is the adoption of the parochial system for the purposes of local work. Each of the associated Churches is requested to look after a parish, not of course with any attempt

---

[1] My father's comments on the extreme unfairness of such criticism have previously been cited.

to exclude other Churches, but as having a special responsibility for those in that area who are not already connected with some existing Church. In the great cities, especially in London and in the counties, local Councils are formed into Federations, which are intermediate between them and the National Council. The local Councils do what is possible to prevent over-lapping and excessive competition between the Churches. Large circulating libraries are already established for the benefit of ministers in villages and country districts. A considerable literature has sprung into existence, con-sisting of numerous periodicals, hymn-books for special occasions, and works of different kinds, explaining the history and ideals of the Evangelical Free Churches. . . . The primary object of the whole organisation is to reach the masses of the people who are not yet attached to any Church. . . . The Catechism represents the creed of not less than 80,000,000 Protestants. It has been widely circulated throughout Great Britain, in British Colonies, and the United States of America. It has also been translated into Welsh, French, and Italian. This movement has spread to all parts of Australia, New Zealand, South Africa, Jamaica, the United States of America, and India. . . ."

A guiding also of religious life, for which Hugh Price Hughes was so largely responsible, was bound to recognise from the first the contributions and the capacities of English women. Women of note and philanthropy sat on local Councils, spoke at the annual Council, and were enthusiastically received and listened to.

The verdict on such endeavours lies not with the members of any one Christian communion, but with the average citizen. That which Dr. Berry, my father and their sympathisers worked for has yet to reap its harvest in the national life, in the forma-tion of such a religious and social environment as shall permit wider ideals and a wider usefulness than has hitherto been possible to many men and women. My father used to say that it would take fifty years before the significance of the Federation was perceived by English people.

His efforts after Christian reunion were expressed in military phraseology—"effectiveness," "co-operation," an inevit-able expression on the lips of a man of action; but his longings, his root impulse in the matter, was that of the Christian mystic. He regarded the Church as St. John did as the Bride of Christ, and he witnessed with anguish her dismemberment, her hourly betrayal, for so it seemed to him at times, of her Divine Head. Few suspected that a man so teeming with practical suggestion and with the military method of expressing his thought, nursed in his heart a world of glowing imagery, seeing not so much the people who passed him in the street and who came to see him in his study, but great shapes and forms who brooded over and explained them. If the dead over whom he pondered had suddenly appeared and walked beside him, he would scarcely have experienced surprise, for he was one who seems to have perpetually felt in himself the result of a great spiritual illumination—a continuous awakening from illusion to reality. In very truth at times the shapes of men of old seem to have stalked beside him as he walked and pondered.

Christ's two great apostles, St. Paul and St. John, and the great figures of later times, St. Francis, Oliver Cromwell, John Wesley, John Henry Newman, were moving and living in the affairs and aspirations of men. He spoke of them familiarly, almost saw them and conversed with them, so close did this intimacy appear. This world of glowing imagery in which he moved and had his being, particularly in its religious depth, was one necessarily shut within himself. Thus his ideal of a visible Church that was one in Christ Jesus is communicable to those who can enter into that mystical depth of religious experience which he enjoyed, and who have an imagination which so pierces the forms of Christian worship that it is not bound by them. At times in his reflections he would take his children up into his thought, asking them what sounded like riddles. "Define," he would say, "philosophy." To every answer he shook his head. "No, you have not got it; that is not the best definition." After a long pause he would relieve their anxiety. "Plato gave the best definition. It is to see the one in the many and the many in the one." Undoubtedly at such times he was thinking of the Church of Christ, pondering his definition of it. The value of ideals consists not in their immediate practicability, but in the fact that they are given. When they are great they influence those who appear most opposed to them as well as those whose instincts lead to a swift sympathy with them. Wesley naturally was the supreme influence in my father's ecclesiastical thinking.

Maurice and Westcott had a great influence upon his theology. From Newman he disagreed widely, but cherished a deep admiration for his saintliness. Great ideals are never given to one communion but to all, for they cannot be contained by one. Thus it would seem that the labours and comparatively early death of Dr. Berry and my father—due in both cases to toils which were too great for them—would not be without their fruitage in the general life of Christian men. Thoughtful opponents, while rejecting certain of their conclusions, and not seeing eye to eye in various matters, will be unable to escape the gracious emanation of their charity, the imperial character of their conceptions, the depth of their devotion—a devotion which could not brook any but the widest religious life and the deepest and fullest communion with the Saviour of men, a communion they believed which could not be attained without a far wider fellowship (κοινωνία) than is at present enjoyed by the average Christian. Already, despite seeming strife, there are signs here and there of a new order of Christian, deeply feeling and responding to the needs of the times, and for the sake of the Churches themselves willing to overlook certain necessary divergences and to meet on what my father always contended was a great common ground. Two Free Churchmen proclaimed this ideal not to a college common room or a group of cultured and sympathethic minds, or in a book, which is the general method, but over the length and breadth of England and Wales, to packed audiences of men, women, and children, whose habits of mind and life would not seem to invite ecclesiastical disquisitions. Whatever the indirect influence of what they proclaimed and accomplished, its direct result must be on those communions with which they were so closely associated. "Ideals," as Lightfoot finely said, "are prophecies which work their own fulfilment."

"38 COLLHURST ROAD, CROUCH END, N.,
"*October* 4, 1898.

"MY DEAR MR. PRICE HUGHES, — Twice over this summer I have been tempted to trespass on your leisure by sending you a word of cordial felicitation; first on your deserved elevation to the seat of honour in your own branch of the Church; and again when your friends were congratulating you on your 'silver wedding.' But I felt it was little business I had to intrude on so busy a man.

" Your new circular letter with the Explanatory Note just gives me the excuses I wanted, and I hope you will allow me to say that no one has more sincerely rejoiced over both incidents in your useful career than I.

" But to business.

" This preface to the Catechism is to be over your sole signature as our chairman, of course, so that you alone can be held responsible for what it says. All the same, you would not send it round your Committee, if you did not want our frank suggestions, so I give them with all freedom.

" 1. In the opening sentence as well as throughout I miss any allusion to the purpose of the Catechism as a manual in the instruction of young Free Church people. At the least, I would insert after the words 'a new Catechism' these 'for the instruction of the young,' or the like. It is all very well to go on to say it demonstrates our substantial agreement. But that is the one thought of the closing paragraph, too, and is amply emphasised. What you nowhere hint at is our hope that families and schools will use the Catechism for catechetical teaching. Surely that deserves even more words than the few words I venture to suggest. A word about the need and the importance of such teaching would not appear to me out of place. For it is surely out of that this work has sprung, not primarily to be a quasi-creed for Free Churches. Considering the attitude of our Congregational brethren to creeds, indeed, I should be thankful to gain that end *without calling too much attention to it!*

" 2. As a matter of printing, would not the names of the Committee be less confusing to the reader and more agreeable to the eye if put one above another, somewhat thus ?—

" '*Congregationalists :*—
          " Rev. A. C. Berry, D.D., etc. etc.
          " Rev. A. Mackennal, D.D., etc. etc.'

" By the bye 'E.P. Assembly' and so on, after Monro Gibson's name, should be 'E.P. Synod,' and, if you are puting such things in, I, too, happen to be an ex-Moderator of it.

" 3. For perfect accuracy, would it not be well in the last

paragraph to insert after ' directly or indirectly ' the words—
' the beliefs of ' and so on ? It may be objected to your
statement that we had no mandate to represent the millions
of our people, either directly or even indirectly, in this business,
but no one can say we do not represent their fundamental
' beliefs.'

"4. I hesitate to offer any more verbal criticism, as the
phraseology is rightly your own. If I did so, I should gently
chasten these very strong phrases—' almost numberless ' in
end of par. 1 ; ' quarrelled with ' in par. 3 ; and ' internecine '
in the next line. But this is higher criticism of what is after
all a matter of style.

"I trust the business arrangements which have deferred
the issue of our work are by this time well advanced, so that
we may hope to see it in the hands of the public ere long.

"Believe me to be, with very pleasant and fraternal recollections of our joint labours—Ever most truly yours,

"J. OSWALD DYKES.

"Rev. H. Price Hughes, M.A."

"THEOLOGICAL COLLEGE,
"GUILDFORD STREET, W.C., LONDON,
"January 10, 1899.

"DEAR MR. HUGHES,—Thanks for your reply to my last
by card.

"Since then I have found opportunity to read your article
in the Contemporary. Apart from your references to myself
which are much too flattering and kind, I feel bound to thank
you for so fully and carefully introducing our work to the
reading public. Of course I do not say I entirely agree with
every word, or that there are not things on which I should
express myself otherwise. That is very natural in a man of so
much colder temperament than your own. But I do feel you
have added by your admirable article to the already heavy
obligation under which you had laid us by your presidency of
the whole work.

"I am particularly grateful to you for pleading for time
and reserve in the expression of criticism. I have already had
examples how unfavourably even friendly critics may express
themselves on a first hasty consideration of it. I expect we

shall have to be prepared for a good deal of adverse judgment
—and little enthusiasm—at least at first.

"Before I close I cannot forbear to add a word on the
very shabby and poor form in which it has been issued; even
at a penny something better in appearance might have been
obtainable. Its appearance, too, with no recognised publisher's
name attached, is not in its favour!—Yours truly,

"J. OSWALD DYKES."

CHAPTER XVIII

THE CATHOLIC IDEA OF A CHRISTIAN EDUCATION

"For as the body is one, and hath many members, and all the members of the body, being many, are one body ; so also is Christ."

First Epistle of St. Paul to the Corinthians, xii. 12.

"The great object in trying to understand history, political, religious, literary, or scientific, is to get behind men and to grasp ideas. Ideas have a radiation and development, an ancestry and posterity of their own, in which men play the part of godfathers and grandmothers more than that of legitimate parents."

Letters of Lord Acton to Mary Gladstone.

YET, while my father was absorbed in the inner and spiritual side of this ideal, the presence of Christ Jesus in His Church from Greece and Rome down to the diversity of Christian communions in the modern and western world, which have come to number many thousands, he did not forget the other aspect of the movement which so far has received the maximum attention—that Nonconformists were not only Churchmen, but Free Churchmen. The following paragraph in his article in the *Contemporary* is unmistakable enough :—

"We must be positive and constructive. In our own time we are known mainly by three names—Protestant, Nonconformist, Dissenter. We are proud of all three. We still claim and vindicate all three. But they are all negative. No doubt they present certain aspects of positive truth. We are Protestants, because we protest against any one coming between us and our Lord Jesus Christ. We are Nonconformists, because we refuse to conform to a schismatical Act passed in the degraded reign of Charles II., which would have placed us in a position of schismatical isolation from the majority of our fellow-Christians. We believe that there is a sin of schism, and that the very worst form of schism is to pledge ourselves never to enter the pulpits of our fellow-Christians, never to recognise them, and never to meet them at the communion table of our Lord. We are also Dissenters, because we dissent from the strange and anti-scriptural doctrine that the Church

31

should be subject to the authority of the State.   It seems to us as monstrous
that the State should domineer over the Church, as that the Church should
domineer over the State.   It would be thought monstrous if we proposed
that the President of the Methodist Conference should nominate the members of Her Majesty's Government.   But surely it is equally and more monstrous that the members of Her Majesty's Government should nominate the
President of the Methodist Conference.   The Church has the same right as
the State to be self-governed.   Both are of God, both have their own sphere,
and the only Christian doctrine of their relation is expressed in the famous
formula of Cavour, 'A free Church in a free State.'   I suppose that no
genuine student of Scripture and of history can deny that both presbyters
and bishops were elected in ancient times by the Church, and not only by
presbyters and bishops but by the laity as well.   Of this fact there is indubit-
able evidence, but it is an unworthy quibble to contend that the legitimate
share of the laity in the election of the clergy is in any sense expressed by
an arrangement which places the election of the chief officers of a great
Christian Church in the hands of the party politician, whatever his character,
who happens, for the time being, to be the Prime Minister of England.   We
quite admit, however, that after we have thus vindicated our title to those
three names, we are open to the criticism that each of them is a negative
one, and that we are bound not only to inform the public what we are not,
what we do not, and what we will not, but also to state positively what we
are.   We now agree to say in the first place that we are 'Churchmen.'   It
is an injustice to state that the original Congregationalists came out of the
Church of England because they were capricious and wilful and self-
assertive, and because they put the whim of the lawless individual before
the authority of the Church.   They came out because they were 'Churchmen,' and Churchmen so pronounced and so strong that they suffered the
loss of all things rather than tolerate any arrangement by which it seemed
to them that the authority of Christ and the rights of the Church were
sacrificed."—*Contemporary Review*, March 1897.

Yet here again he was not a Free Churchman in the
superficial sense that the general public sometimes interpret
that term.   He was a Free Churchman, as certain very devout
High Churchmen might term themselves Free Churchmen,
resenting any control of the Church, save that which its own
constituted authorities impose upon it.   A Church, to his
thinking, was highly disciplined, both as to expression of
belief and as to the nature of her action and influence in the
State.   A free community, like a free person, meant the recognition of an internal discipline, far more stringent than that
which was imposed on communities of persons more outwardly
shackled.

Certainly, as an ideal, he did not believe in an Established
Church, accepting Cavour's principle; but his acceptance of

this ideal did not make him forgetful of the rights and susceptibilities of fellow-Christians who differed from him, or,
particularly in later life, of the complexities attending most
situations. The prophets are doubtless intended to ignore
these complexities—they must, but ecclesiastical councillors
cannot. This he increasingly found. His influence in the
Federation was exerted to keep any proposition for Disestablishment, or any proposition that might savour of
hostility to other Christian communions, in the background.
"No Christian communion," he was in the habit of saying in
private, "would profit more by Disestablishment than the
Anglican. Moreover, certain of the High Anglican party
would not mind in the least. In their intense spirituality
they do not care about such minutiæ, and it would not affect
them." When speaking on this matter, he always based his
criticism of a Christian communion from what he considered
to be its own standpoint. For instance, all his ire with the
Papacy and its accompaniments was from what he considered
the point of view of the Roman communion. Without it, to
what depths of spiritual life might she not attain; what a
removal of the gibes and accusations which Protestants now
brought against her! His attitude to Anglicanism was the
same. Severed from the State, to what heights might she not
reach, while she could free herself from those accusations and
calumnies with which outsiders were in the habit of reproaching
her. Nobody resented more than himself a manner of referring
to Anglicanism which sometimes characterises extremists in
Nonconformity on this matter. *À propos* of Disestablishment
of the Church in Wales, he wrote in 1892 in a current number
of the *Review of the Churches* :—

"It is with the greatest reluctance that I have consented to say anything
at all about the Disestablishment controversy. Although I have long been
persuaded by my study of the Bible and of ecclesiastical history that the
present method of union between the Church and the State tends to make the
Church worldly without making the world Christian, I shrink exceedingly
from a controversy which cannot be conducted without causing deep pain to
some of the best Christians. . . . If the prominent representatives of the two
sides of this question could meet together to compare notes and to define
their terms, much good might follow. There is not the least doubt that a
great deal of the bitterness already evoked is the result of extraordinary
misunderstanding, leading evidently to misrepresentation and injustice. We

had an almost comic illustration of this a few years ago in London. Dr. Parker invited a few of us to speak on the subject of Disestablishment in the City Temple. I well remember the amazement of the author of the Bampton Lecture on Dissent at what he regarded as the almost incredible moderation of Mr. Guinness Rogers and myself and other dreadful characters. That distinguished clergyman, who had even undertaken to give the world an authoritative account of the various forms of Dissent, was under the delusion that the Voluntary Churches desired not only to deprive the Episcopal Church of all her sanctuaries, but actually to take legal steps to destroy her ecclesiastical unity, so as to impose the Congregational system upon the Anglican Church by force of law! He had been misled by some purely tentative and unofficial suggestions which the Liberation Society had unfortunately published. We were able at once to reassure him on that point, and to make it quite plain that no sane person had the least wish to impair, much less to destroy, the corporate unity of the Episcopal body in this country."

Then, *à propos* of an article by an Irish Episcopalian, he writes amid other criticisms :—

"Surely it ought to be remembered not only that extreme sentiments uttered in the heat of debate are repudiated in cold blood even by the men who uttered them, but also that the advocates of a great religious idea must not be held responsible for the casual expression of irresponsible supporters. Moreover, when Parliament comes to settle any controversy, the opponents of change have a large voice in the decision, and every such controversy must, in the very nature of things, end in a compromise which gives a wide berth to the 'falsehood of extremes.'

"One of the great difficulties of the Welsh controversy is that English and Irish Episcopalians are able to interfere. If the Welsh people themselves were allowed to settle this question, the whole controversy would be at an end in forty-eight hours. Those outsiders who assume the responsibility of encouraging their Welsh co-religionists to keep up a useless struggle are taking upon themselves a very grave responsibility. As a Welshman, I am intensely anxious that the bitterness which now exists in my native land should cease. But, like every other Welshman, I am well aware that there is only one possible way of doing it, and that is by Disestablishment, which I sincerely believe will be a greater blessing to the English Church in Wales than to any other community of Christians. Welsh Episcopalians are for the time being sacrificing the substance of spiritual prosperity for the vain shadow of political ascendancy. Of course they do not realise this, or they would not do so. But I am confident that twenty years after the controversy is over they will all admit that those who insisted upon Disestablishment were their true friends. Even now they should dismiss the absurd fear that there would be the least attempt to deprive them of their churches or of the life interest in endowments to which they are entitled. The Nonconformists of Wales desire to treat them with the utmost consideration and generosity. Even if it were otherwise, their English friends would be sufficiently powerful to protect their legitimate interests.'

His aim throughout life was to associate, not dissociate, Christian men, and for this reason he did not encourage any act of aggression in his own lifetime on the part of Free Churchmen, though in theory he was an advocate of Disestablishment.

These considerations lead inevitably to a very interesting aspect of his life—his attitude to the Education controversy. To many contemporaries this was a puzzling one. Anglicans, after hearing something he had said, would think, " Here is a friendly fair-minded Nonconformist." Then a few days later, after reading a further statement of his opinions, they would exclaim, " Certainly he hates us ! " In the north of England he met on one occasion a wide-minded Anglican, and had much pleasant conversation with him. Shortly after, this clergyman happened to come across a letter of his in the *Times*, and he laid it down with a shake of the head. " I cannot," he said, " follow him here." Visitors and acquaintances who were struck by what they considered my father's width of view would at times experience a shock when they heard him on this controversy. There was an intensity about it, a note of bitterness almost, for which they were not prepared.

Certain Nonconformists, also, were not much surer of him in the matter.

In what lies the answer to the riddle?

In an answer which, like the sermons of old time, might be comprised under three headings. First, it is clear that in the conflicts of every life there is a twofold element, one that belongs to a man's ideal, and another to his flesh and blood, and arising out of these a third, that which he can attain towards his ideal while yet in the bonds just signified.

Now my father's ideal in this matter was something very great and consistent. It sprang directly from his definition of the Scriptural Catholic Church—from the rooted conviction of his life that the Christian Church must accept the necessary conditions of a Democratic era.[1] The flesh-and-blood element was more transparent, easier to see and understand, and not

---

[1] The Democratic era which the Revolution had heralded was a great test, he believed, of all branches of the Church of Christ, demanding from them, as the Reformation had done, a certain self-discipline. Each must make material sacrifice in order to attain spiritual gain.

nearly as important as his ideal, so that shall be first spoken of. The attraction that certain elements in Anglicanism had for him from his youth up was obvious, and the words with which, as President, he welcomed the Anglican deputation to the Wesleyan Conference were one of his sincerest utterances :

" We never forget that the divinely appointed instrument in the establishment of this world-wide Church was a distinguished clergyman of the Anglican communion, and we know full well no Church in Christendom has produced more learned theologians or more eminent saints than the Church which you loyally represent this morning. Indeed, there is no more exquisite or heavenly form of piety on earth than the refined and cultured goodness of the best Anglican type."

But, on the other hand, his very love and appreciation for much that was in Anglicanism, his very affection for members of her communion, made him all the more keenly resent other aspects not of her individual but of her corporate character. If he had lived as some others have been content to do, in a 'small world, doing the duty that came to them, he would not have resented the exclusion of Nonconformists from much that was fair and of value in the national life.

The social slight, which until recently was such a feature of English life, was keenly felt by him on behalf of those orders which he represented and whose claims to recognition he continually championed. At notable State functions of various kinds he would exclaim, " Why are the Nonconformist leaders never asked ? They have a right as well as the others." He resented also the ecclesiastical assumptions of Anglicanism. In one of the articles in the *Contemporary Review* from which quotations have been taken, he wrote :

" We Evangelical Free Churchmen have many grievances against the Church of England. She has treated us and our fathers with studied and systematic cruelty ; but we should deem ourselves foolish and wicked if for that or any other reason we denied that she was a true branch of the Catholic Church, that she had rendered long and valuable service, and that she included within her communion some of the greatest saints. Upon the Church of England has rested from age to age the unmistakable blessing of God ; and that fact, and no mere speculative, doubtful argument from ancient and contradictory documents, is her true claim to the confidence and affection of the people."—*Contemporary Review*, March 1897.

As usual, he attacked not contemporary individuals, but ramparts on which they appeared. Indeed, his quarrel at times with Anglicanism seemed to be with nothing visible, but with her history since the days of Elizabeth, and her attitude towards those who had not conformed to her usages. Somebody would make a remark about Anglicanism in the reign of Queen Victoria, and for reply he would begin talking about the reign of Charles II., for the two in his mind were vitally connected. It was here that he identified himself with many in Congregationalism. He felt in his own flesh and blood the treatment of those from whom they came and for whom they cared. On one occasion he attended a meeting at Hyde Park to commemorate the death of Penry,[1] and spoke from a cart with Dr. Clifford and other ministers to pay honour to his memory, and with no desire to recall ancient grievances. Neither individuals or communities, he thought, should foster these.

Thus Guy Fawkes Day and its celebration would always provoke his ire as an unreasonable and absurd observance of something which should long have been forgotten and which was only provocative of unchristian feeling towards Romanists.

Yet phases of his conversation and incidents like that just quoted revealed the keenest participation in the history and the struggles of Nonconformity. Incidents also in his own personal experience, and those known to him, rendered him very vehement, at times, in his method of expression, not in public (for his sense of responsibility made him exceedingly careful on those occasions), but in private conversation with friends.

In such conversations there were three subjects on which he sometimes seemed unfair—the Anglican communion, the University of Oxford, and the French people; and each so tore him that at times he scarcely knew what he thought of them. The love that he had for each made it impossible for him to mete out fairness to them. On the other hand, no one could plead or vaunt the claims of any one of them better than he.

Speaking of the parochial system to an Anglican friend at Dover, he said, " It is perfect, as an *ideal* that in every village and town in the kingdom there should be a Christian gentleman in charge of the spiritual and higher interests of the population."

[1] An Independent, who was put to death for his convictions in Queen Elizabeth's reign.

In such a strain he would go on till put in mind of those instances of lack of charity which so often came under his notice. Once in the earlier portion of his career he had baptized a child of a village carpenter, and the Squire and the vicar had together succeeded in starving the carpenter out of the village because my father had baptized his child. On another occasion a vicar tried to persuade a dying Wesleyan known to him, a good and simple woman, that salvation would not be hers unless she joined the true Church, that is to say, the Anglican communion. If such incidents had not unfortunately been typical of a number of others for many years past and all over the country, the impression created on his mind would have been of a less painful character, for he absolutely identified himself in this and in other respects with brother-ministers who had a good deal more experience of such things than he had. For instance, when addressing the Wesleyan Conference as President, he says, *à propos* of the fact that Methodism is a living branch of the Catholic Church of Christ :

"I entirely agree with Dr. H. J. Pope that the real founder of Methodism was not John Wesley, but Jesus Christ. The great Dr. Beaumont, whose courtesy and great gifts, whose splendid preaching power, whose prescient statesmanship we are at last beginning to recognise, once used a clever and striking illustration of Wesley's relation to Methodism in a great debate in the Conference of 1834, when discussing Methodism and the Church of England. 'Mr. Wesley,' said Dr. Beaumont in the discussion, in which all the great Methodist preachers of the day took part—'Mr. Wesley was like a strong skilful rower ; he looked one way while every stroke of the oar took him in an opposite direction. He never resolved that he would go no further from the Church.' Let them read the invaluable publication of Dr. Rigg on the subject. To say that John Wesley never left the Church of England when he ordained bishops for America, presbyters for Scotland, and presbyters for England, is to talk meaningless nonsense. I know he was very reluctant to do so, but his extreme reluctance only proved that he was the unwilling instrument of the Divine purpose. The unmistakable will of Christ overcame even the intense preferences and prejudices of John Wesley. Almost every day I receive from some brother in a country circuit, a copy of some tract or pamphlet issued by the vicar of the parish, full of quotations from every period of Wesley's life, indiscriminately mixed up, stating that he never left the Church of England, and that Methodism ought not to leave the Church. What is the use in wasting time and money in circulating literature of that kind, which only proves one thing—Methodism is not of man but of God, and it is high time we ourselves recognise that fact frankly, openly, and fully."

"You have no idea also," he would say at other times, "of what is going on all over the country, and of what I am continually hearing in our committees." Recollections of his life, as previous chapters show, were of the pleasantest relations with Anglicans, clerical and lay. In his work in the Mission, he was on the friendliest terms with the neighbouring clergy, and at anniversary meetings Liberal Anglicans would often be on the platform. At his death it was quite in keeping with this aspect of his life that the vicar of the parish, a High Churchman, went out of his way to pay honour to his memory, causing the bell of the parish church to be tolled as soon as he heard the news, and attending with other Anglican clergymen the Funeral Service at Wesley's Chapel. But in his own flesh and blood my father bore the reproach of his people, their suffering at times, for it has been that in England, particularly in villages and small country towns. To be a "Dissenter," to quote a phrase which is not now current, has been to put human beings outside the social pale, outside that free intercourse with their fellows and with the national life which a democratic era claims increasingly for all varieties of men and women.

So his loyalty to his order seemed at times the very fibre of his being, the rule of his existence. Yet it was startling how little he allowed flesh and blood to dictate his policies.

In the Journal undoubtedly he spoke his mind, and when a Government Bill appeared that was hostile to the interests and claims of those whose cause he advocated, and to whom he belonged, I have seen his eye flash and his whole frame express intensest distress and indignation. People could not understand it. When the Education Bill of 1896 appeared, a relative saw him walking along one of the Squares looking the very picture of anxiety. "Thinking," said this relative, "that Hugh had lost his nearest relative, I crossed the street to ask what was the matter with him. For reply he muttered, 'Oh! this unspeakable Government and the wretched Bill they have had the audacity to introduce.'"

"What Bill?" asked the relative.

"The Bill that would blight the Christianity of this country if they can ever pass it, which I doubt. The wretched little Baptists are to be instructed in one corner, the wretched little Anglicans in another, and the wretched little Methodists in another."

Yet to those who knew this intense feeling on the matter, nothing was more striking than the manner in which he curbed and restrained it on those committees and gatherings of various kinds in which the Bills were increasingly discussed. So marked, indeed, was this moderation of attitude, particularly in his latter days, that he was noted by his opponents as being the most amenable to compromise. "No one among the Nonconformists," said the Bishop of London, "was more anxious to come to a settlement than Mr. Price Hughes." And on his own side there was often keen criticism on account of this concilatory attitude. The explanation of this lies, like everything else in his life, in his ideal, which was greater even than the loyalty which made the grievances of Nonconformity those of his own flesh and blood.

All during his life he laid stress on the existence of a great common element in Christianity, and the best way to secure belief in it, he thought, was to bring up children to realise that there was such a common element. His exclamations just quoted with regard to the Bill of 1896 explain his whole attitude. Under the arrangement that the Bill proposed, the earliest impressions of children would be that there was something differentiating them from their fellow-Christians, not something uniting them.

However much the different denominations in their necessary accentuation of different aspects of the faith forgot their fellow-Catholics, as the good and zealous often did, the State schools should remind and embue them once and for ever with their common Christianity. If he could have trusted the Anglicans to ensure this, he would have troubled less about their having the main control of State-supported schools. He recognised, undoubtedly, that they had a claim on the community for their past services in education; for one who felt so keenly the claims of his own religious order was in a position to understand those who made similar claims on behalf of their own orders. In the midst of the School Board dissension in the nineties, he wrote as follows in the *Review of the Churches*:

"I have always been aware that the educational arrangements of the country are not yet in a state of stable equilibrium, and that the compromise of 1870 ought to be revised as soon as the sectarian parties are sufficiently magnanimous and sagacious to think more of the interests of Christianity than of their particular sectarian objects. But I greatly regret the method, and the agency, by which this momentous national difficulty has been reopened and forced upon the public attention. I had hoped that, at some convenient time, there might be unofficial and amiable conferences between the leaders of the great Christian communities, with a view to discover quietly and calmly how far they were agreed, and where they really differed. Such conferences might lead to a compromise that would settle the question for generations."

Educationalists who were by no means prejudiced in favour of Nonconformity would say to him: "How is it that you Nonconformists are letting the teaching profession slip from your hands? The Anglicans have captured all the posts worth having, and you are rapidly being pushed out of the profession. Why don't some of you do something?" Such remarks he would receive in silence. He knew undoubtedly that such was the case, that, increasingly, educated and qualified Nonconformists found it difficult to obtain good scholastic posts; but his fear of dissension, and of impairing the interests of Christianity at large, made him silently submit to a state of things which he was assured was continually on the increase.

All his life he had been toiling and wearing himself out for greater Christian concord, and he knew that such a controversy must for the time being strike a great blow at all his efforts, Indeed, it is sad to think that his latter days were thus clouded, and if faith had not pierced the clouds, he must have felt even sadder than he did.

When he thought it necessary to defend Nonconformity, and what he regarded its just claim, he would do so, however distasteful to him, and seemingly destructive to the efforts of his life. Yet, he would have said, he was fighting not so much for the rights of Nonconformity and any immediate result, but for the Catholic Church scripturally and comprehensively defined, for that atmosphere which would induce religious equality, and lead ultimately to goodwill, not divergence between Christians. Undoubtedly also his attitude was intensified by the claims and practices of the Romanising section of the Anglican communion, but he was not in the habit of making the charges and complaints that were current at that time. He saw clearly that certain practices were helpful to certain Anglicans. Nonconformists must accord that respect for the practices of others which they asked for their own, though from the point of view of a Church established to maintain the principles of the Reformation, he regretted the innovations and practices of so large a number of her clergy.

Yet underlying all his profound disagreement with High Anglican definitions of the Catholic Church was a great admiration for the self-sacrifice and devotion of some of them, and a keen perception of the fact that Christ Jesus was visibly present with them in transforming power. "The High Anglicans," he has said to companions more than once, "really understand conversion." So, while many recriminated and deplored, he ruminated in silence about the course that circumstances dictated. What one communion left undone the rest must endeavour to do. In the silences he became possessed by a conviction that the maintenance of the principles of the Reformation must depend on the Free Churches of this country, and in what a spirit has been shown, not sectarian and unenlightened, but comprehensive and imaginative, not afraid to borrow and learn from a great variety of sources, mediæval as well as modern, and to enter into all that heritage which Free Churchmen in their Catechism claimed for themselves. "The Reformation," he would say, "brought tolerance into the world. The early Protestants did not understand it, but we later ones must endeavour to do so."

The only charge that I ever heard him bring against the "Romanisers" was that of intolerance. "They have not the chivalry to let us alone. Why do they wish to take the members of our congregations from us? I cannot understand it. We never think of interfering with them and proselytising as they do." To the Churches also who accepted the principles of the Reformation was surely entrusted the teaching of the Bible and its propagation throughout the world.

The fault of Protestantism, he used to say, had been, first, the failure to apprehend tolerance, and second, the substitution of an infallible Bible for an infallible Pope. Christians should read the Bible with their understandings, not like parrots. The Higher Criticism, which so many ignorantly feared, would only lead to greater understanding of the Book of books, to deeper reverence and love of it. All that was essential and vital remained, and the fears and flutters respecting the date and authorship of certain portions on which the learned were necessarily in some disagreement, he could not understand.[1] The result of Higher Criticism and its investigation was to make the Scriptures ten times more precious and illuminating. " There is no doubt," he would say, " that certain parts of the Old Testament are simply incomprehensible without it. What Christians must be got to see is that the reality and test of their religion lies in the life, in men and women who are quickened by Christ. The Old Testament, when properly interpreted, is full of value both to the mind and the spirit, and the New is most precious of all. But even in that is not found the foundations of our faith, though it contains un-doubtedly the argument for Protestantism, so that it is the text-book in our divergence with Rome. Christian experience was prior to the writing of the New Testament, and produced it." Thus he would talk.

At Oxford he had reiterated what he believed since Brighton days—that in Scripture was contained the great common element of Christianity, which was taught in a satis-factory manner, he considered, in the Board Schools. That weak places might be found, he was aware, just as there were Christian ministers in every communion who did not preach the gospel as he thought they might. Yet he never judged a ministry by those weak places, for he did not think it fair to them. He believed if only simple biblical instruction could be agreed upon, the seemingly careless and half-hostile element in society would be won over to the side of the Church, because all agreed, whatever the diversity of opinion concerning author-ship and the correctness of certain details, that it was the Book of books, and for literary strength and sincerity and beauty quite unsurpassed. Should the Christian Church in all her communions be reasonable in the matter, not claiming

---

[1] On one occasion, at a comparatively early date in his ministry, he was present at a gathering of evangelical ministers of various denominations. Several who were present confessed to a period of inward perturbation and no little shaking of their faith when the "inspiration" of Scripture first came to be questioned. My father was greatly surprised at these confessions, and said both then and afterwards that he could not understand the necessity for the agitation which his brethren had ex-perienced.

more than she ought in a State-supported school in a demo-cratic era, all he felt would be well.

As a leader in this controversy he had a twofold fear. First, that the extremists on either side would play into the hands of the secularists by demanding in State-supported schools what a democratic era could not accord, and second, that the extremists on his own side would, in revulsion against the "clericals," side with the secularists, and ask too little, instead of too much. For there was one party with whom he had no manner of sympathy, and that was the secularists, as well as the avowedly indifferent element which said, " A plague on both your houses! The one thing we can do is to banish religion and Bible-teaching from the schools altogether—that is the only way to keep the peace." It was because he feared such a solution, and was so intensely sensible of what the ordinary man and woman thought and felt in a democratic era, that he took part in a controversy which was the most personally distasteful in which he engaged. The Christian Church, he considered, had a right to insist on Christian teaching of some kind in State-supported schools.[1] The exact kind was just that about which much of the contemporary divergence lay. England and Wales owed all that was best in them, he thought, not only to Christian ideals, but to the Scriptural Catholic Church, a debt which all her sins and shortcomings at various epochs could not obliterate. When men ceased to owe anything to the religion of their mothers, or to the ideals and influences of Christianity, then they could begin talking about banishing Christian teaching from the schools.

When he came to Taviton Street, the "alarums" and "excursions" of the period were associated with the London School Board, on which sat two valiant protagonists of the clerical party—Mr. Diggle and Mr. Athelstan Riley. At this time also it became the fashion, as shown, for certain ecclesi-astical opponents to continue their discussions in Switzerland, so that it was quite a surmise as to whether two opponents

---

[1] He was liberal in the insertion of conscience clauses, and would have advocated a full consideration for the just claims of Jews and Freethinkers. He would often remark that even pronounced Freethinkers liked their children to have a Christian education.

could long differ in this country—so irresistible was the general tendency to arrive at amicable settlements in Switzerland. Thus it was quite in accordance with the prevailing fashion, that Archdeacon Wilson, Mr. Percy Bunting, Dr. Lunn, Mr. Athelstan Riley, and my father found themselves in close proximity in the summer of 1895, and they no sooner thus found themselves than they set about framing a concordat— the object of universal desire. It was a critical as well as an interesting position. What would either side concede to the other—the representative of extreme Anglican clericalism to the representative of the Nonconformist clergy? My father was willing to allow the teaching of the Apostles' Creed in State-supported schools, provided the clergy would consent to the establishment of a universal system of Board Schools. It is needless to say that the *rapprochement* was eagerly watched by adherents on either side; and certain, on hearing of my father's concessions, were filled with anger against him, saying that he had betrayed his own party, and was nothing but a " clerical " in disguise himself. Feeling thus, they betook themselves to the columns of the daily press, and did not hesitate to give expression to their thought.

Meantime my father and Dr. Lunn, after the exposition of this concordat, had parted company with Mr. Athelstan Riley, and were driving down the valley of the Inn towards Innsbruck, talking as they often did on political themes, and in particular on Home Rule and Mr. Chamberlain. In the midst of this animated discourse they were enabled to obtain copies of the daily press, which they instantly proceeded to devour. Both read in silence, as they well might, for there was a good deal to interest them. Suddenly my father made an exclamation in that swift flashing up of wrath which reveals the heart of a leader. " If they go on in this way we shall have to change sides ! " Dr. Lunn's paper almost fell from his hand.

" What do you mean ? " he said.

" I mean," said my father very quietly, " that if men of our thinking begin to care more for wretched party and sectarian issues than for the whole Church of Christ and the teaching of the Christian religion in our schools, we must go over in this matter to those who do care, however much we may disagree with them on other issues."

Seeing Dr. Lunn's continued astonishment, he added :

"Chamberlain went over on the question of Home Rule, and I, if it comes to secularism and the abandonment of Christian teaching, will go over to State-supported Denominationalism."

What angered him was not the adverse criticism of friends, for to this he was accustomed, but the fact that his critics consisted of two parties whose union he simply could not brook —a section of his own party and the secularists. If one or the other had attacked him singly he would have thought far less of it, but it was their agreement which caused him distress. Moreover, he knew exactly what his ecclesiastical opponents would think and say about it, and the knowledge did not afford him pleasure.

There is, and always has been, so strong a body of feeling in the Free Churches that absolutely accorded with him in this matter, as revealed for instance in their last Council (1904) when an overwhelming majority voted for universal scriptural instruction in State schools, that he never at any time had to practically contemplate the course he suggested, but the suggestion showed what he was prepared to do in defence of distinct religious teaching in State schools ; and, coming from one so loyal to Nonconformity, so passionately devoted to its claims, it goes to show the depth of that participation in Scriptural Catholicism which he spent so much of his life in proclaiming. As usual, he did not ask of men what he did not demand of himself.

None the less was my father anxious, for he knew, as already intimated, the resourcefulness of ecclesiastical opponents, and it was with the greatest apprehension that he opened the morning papers in March 1902, when the outline of the present [1] Education Act was made known to the public. After the silence he took a deep breath, groaned, and knitted his brow. The pallor which was often characteristic of him in those days—for it was near the end of his life, when he was wintering at Bournemouth—seemed intensified. When he got out on to the cliff he expressed one or two opinions about his ecclesiastical opponents—not individually—for as individuals he considered many of them charming, but collectively.

[1] October 1904.

Clearly the Government knew what it was about this time, for whenever his companion asked a question or made a suggestion, he answered the one and poured contempt upon the other. Oh! it was clever—that was the implied admission of all he was saying and confuting—it held out a hand to the educationalists, because it gave some kind of co-ordination, and they were so desperate, and had so long hoped for and despaired of reform that they would clutch at anything that was given them, even though it was far from what they had a right to claim or what they desired. Then it made a bid for the Socialists and Secularists and humanitarian group because it municipalised the education authority, and at that he ground his teeth again. For he was a centraliser in that as in every other matter, and wanted an education authority that should be elected *ad hoc*. Then, and this was the cut, it was very unfair to the Nonconformists, and yet it bribed them. On the one hand, it imposed upon them as citizens a special rate to support schools that were not under full public control, and what some of them felt even more, it imposed in actual effect, though not in so many words, a religious test on the teaching profession. My father and the other leaders in Nonconformity had already realised that the teaching profession was slipping from their grasp, and this part of the Bill seemed to bring home the fact that it had indeed, and that unless they made a stand of some kind their religious influence in this country, and their tradition of religious equality, would be practically nil. The religious communion that captivates the early youth of a human being, that surrounds it with its own particular atmosphere, may be regarded as possessing that human being in some form or another for the rest of his natural lifetime. That Nonconformists would thus think and reason the Government had foreseen, so it bribed them, introducing provisions which appeared to have that effect, *e.g.*, that if a number of Methodists, Baptists, or Congregationalists, or Roman Catholics in a certain area petitioned the proper authorities, they also would obtain State aid for the erection of schools, as the Anglicans were doing, or if such schools were already in existence, State aid on the same conditions that the Anglicans obtained it. They could therefore promulgate their own

32

particular tradition and establish their own tests as the Anglicans.

It is doubtful whether any portion of the Bill was as distasteful to my father as this portion, for it must have seemed to him the reversal of that spirit of charity in the Christian Church which he had all his life endeavoured to promote. Every denomination over the land would strive to perpetuate its own particular tenets and be jealous of its neighbour, so that there would be no such thing in England as State schools where side by side children could imbibe the common elements of Christianity. The tendency of such an arrangement, he felt, must be towards the greater separation of the denominations, not the promulgation of the common elements of the faith. In ideal and intent, Liberal Anglicanism or Liberal Nonconformity might undertake to diffuse a full exposition of the Christian faith, and to refrain from that exclusiveness and lack of charity which had dismembered the Church in all ages, but in his heart he dared not trust either of them—not in the main control of State-supported schools.

He did not object to the Act as a Free Churchman merely, but as a citizen, for the dreams of Dover were equally involved with those of Oxford. To unite the watchwords of Democracy—Liberty, Equality, and Fraternity—with the watchwords of the Church of Christ had ever been the struggle of his life, and it was never more difficult than at this juncture.

The Romanists he seems to have considered little in the matter, because he thought them very well able to look after themselves. They naturally were in favour of the Bill, and had powerful supporters. The Roman Church also was ancient and full of tradition, arousing a sympathy and interest in certain circles, which Protestant Nonconformity did not ; that element of romance which artists and litterateurs in the usual fashion had accorded, gave her a hold on those large sections of humanity who are easily stirred by what is picturesque and emotional, and not inclined to examine into underlying principles. Indeed, he regarded her as in danger of getting too much rather than too little. The proposal to erect a Roman Catholic university in Ireland at State expense was one at whose " audacity " he never ceased to wonder, and which he vigorously opposed. At one of the Conferences at Fulham, a bishop present remarked of a certain proposal, "What of the Romanists? I cannot think that this will be accepted by them."

With a smile my father replied, "I do not think, my Lord Bishop, we need agitate ourselves about them, because they are so well able to look after themselves." He saw the expelled French orders establishing themselves all over the country, and the communion generally finding a pleasant asylum in a free country, which at present was undergoing a certain reaction from the previous suspicions concerning it. The educated and fashionable world was curiously lenient and respectful towards Romanism, particularly the London press and Bohemian circles generally, so he entertained no fears but that any just demand of theirs would have the fullest consideration. It was the younger and democratically governed Churches that those in high places did not understand or care for, and on whose behalf he felt indignant that March morning. The right persons had a faculty of coming to him at the right moment, and it was scarcely surprising that he almost fell that morning into the arms of a leading Congregationalist minister who was visiting Bournemouth. They had not conversed long before they became possessed by a passion to see the draft of the Bill. The initial step, they agreed, was a thorough comprehension of the draft, which this minister promised to procure from London on the first opportunity. On its arrival, my father gave himself to the digestion of its contents, and sat down to write laborious and closely written epistles to certain Free Church leaders.

The underlying difficulty of the situation lay to him in the Wesleyan attitude in this matter, for their tradition, as already indicated, is not the same as that of the other branches of Nonconformity. Wesley himself had set the example of building and maintaining schools, and down to this day there are some Wesleyans who believe in denominational teaching, and prefer to send their children to those institutions which are controlled and permeated by their particular communion. At the same time the original catholicity of Methodism is so far preserved in them, that Anglicans and Nonconformists constitute a number of their pupils, their parents having full confidence, both in the Christian charity and the comprehensiveness of a religious régime which can include various shades of the evangelical tradition. Many Methodists therefore favoured Government Bills which gave State support to denominational schools, and were not in the least inclined to approve of the more democratic methods which other Nonconformists favoured. Indeed, a section was as eager as the Romanists to propagate its faith by building schools with State aid, and not at all in love with my father's particular methods. "Children, if they are to be good Wesleyan Methodists," such said, "must be instructed from their infancy in Wesleyan Methodist schools, by Wesleyan Methodist teachers, and by Wesleyan Methodist ministers of religion."

Theirs, in short, was what is termed the extreme ecclesiastical view, and they were as opposed to my father's more democratic views, as any High Anglican or Romanist, perhaps more so, in that he belonged to their own communion.

Of denominational schools, even when erected at the cost of the Church, it cannot be said that he approved, though he would speak with commendation of such institutions in Methodism, and would fully recognise the value of that which they achieved. In such matters a man should be judged by what he desired for his own children, and he certainly never evinced any eagerness to send them to a Wesleyan institution. Where the educational advantages were greatest, where there was an absolute religious equality, the children of Jews, Agnostics, and all shades of Christians meeting on equal terms, there he thought the charity of Christ could best be imbibed.

Thus it was his views respecting education that made him such a democrat, such a participator in certain traditions of Nonconformity, for in the Wesleyan tradition on this matter he cannot be said to have shared. Yet he himself went to a denominational school, and in some sense may be said to have benefited by it, in that a spiritual crisis took place in a sympathetic environment. But, on the other hand, he never ceased to inwardly regret the deficient educational equipment of his youth, and what he believed to be the inevitable narrowing influence of such an upbringing, both mentally and spiritually.

The Imperial idea of a university—varieties of mental and spiritual growth meeting and clashing—constituted, he believed, the true atmosphere of education and mutual understanding.[1] He resented on behalf of Nonconformity her exclusion, till quite recently, from the universities, and the warping of her life that this isolation had produced. God, he did not believe, had tied up His grace any more with denominational schools than He had with episcopacy or any other ecclesiastical system. In times past, denominational schools, certainly in Anglicanism, which had struggled and toiled to educate the villages in the past, and Methodism in more recent years, had done splendid service to the community; but those times were past, and an Imperial era demanded Imperial ideas, both in the Church and in education. What was excellent for one generation and its needs was not necessarily excellent for the next. The ripening of choice spirits could be performed in the open air amid the free breezes of heaven as well as in hothouses, and the Almighty knew better than man how to rear and prop those spirits whom in any way He had finely touched. If He wanted to make a man a good Methodist or Baptist or Anglican, He would, whether he was in a denominational school or not. The Church had its distinctive work for individuals, and so had the State school. Thus throughout this anxious time, conscious on the one hand of an approaching crisis in the life of the Churches which nothing could tide, and, on the other, of rapidly failing health, he was entertaining hopes and fears respecting approaching Conference which should decide the Wesleyan attitude towards the present Bill. The Liberals and Forwards were naturally strongly with him, and the air as usual was alive with rumour when some engagement was on hand. Moreover, as with many of their engagements, it was to end in a victory, so that the fears of their leader proved themselves to be without foundation in fact.

At the same time he was fully conscious of the difficulties of his position and of the susceptibilities of Wesleyan Methodism. Anything in the nature of violent resistance or seeming antagonism to the Anglican Church was distasteful to it, and while he personally felt bound in the interests of Noncon-

[1] Yet this conviction was one of principle rather than innate instinct. He feared often to submit youth to a variety of influence, but his belief that it was the best thing in the long run, and God's will would always triumph over any hidden anxiety.

formity and as a Nonconformist to side with the methods adopted by other Free Church leaders, he was careful throughout to consider as far as he could the feelings of that communion which he represented.

Passive resistance was the traditional method by which Nonconformity asserted its rights, and that it should be resorted to seems to have been the instinctive and unanimous decision of its leaders. A deputation which waited on the Liberal Peers received the following reply from Lord Rosebery:

"I am not myself in favour of a refusal of the payment of rates, but then I am not in your position. I confess that if the Nonconformists of England submit tamely to the enactments of this Bill, I will not say they will be weakened religiously, but I will say this, that, in my judgment, politically they will have ceased to exist."—*December* 8, 1902.

This disinterested verdict shows the gravity of the situation, how it seemed to them not a fight for privilege or even justice, but for very existence. My father's own opinion respecting the rights and advisability of passive resistance the writer does not know, as he never spoke concerning it, merely stating that, in company with other Nonconformists, he had decided to adopt it, an intention which he publicly announced. One thing was certain, that he would not have enjoyed it or any of its accompaniments. But feeling, thinking, leading as he did, he was bound to resort to it, and had, indeed, little choice in the matter. It was the weapon of defence that was customary and traditional, and as instant and united action was imperative, he seized upon the instrument that was likely to secure this.

Moreover, some organisation was necessary in an age of combination, where individual efforts and actions are apt to prove ineffective. Thus, Mr. Law, the secretary of the Federation, was continually passing up and down the stairs of 8 Taviton Street and discussing with him that form of combination which should advocate and protect passive resistance. My father was most anxious that this combination should not be identified with the Free Church Council. That the Federated Free Churches should be identified with a movement that, however conscientiously undertaken, was political to the general thinking rather than spiritual, was not at all to his liking. On the day that he died, Mr. Law submitted to him a scheme for the formation of a Passive Resistance Committee which should be independent of the Federation, so that it would be impossible to identify the two. After careful listening and some discussion, he gave his sanction to the scheme. Perhaps no one more than himself dreaded the effect on his own side, the hostility to Anglicanism and the sectarianism that such strife was almost bound to beget, for a season at any rate, and perhaps more than that. His own work was bound to be undone for a time, and to be misunderstood of the public. Scriptural Catholicism, the apprehension of Christian fellowship (κοινωνία), was bound to suffer, and therefore the world. Thus a strife that he sanctioned, and whose participators may rightly claim his benediction, was bound to be hateful to him, and to evoke an attitude which struck many as inconsistent. In the London press and its cartoons he rightly figured with Dr. Clifford as the champion of Nonconformity, while he wrote in the columns of his own Journal with an occasional acerbity which disturbed, as we have seen, kindly Anglicans with whom he had just been conversing. Yet the pungent ink in which he dipped his pen (to quote an American bishop's criticism of him) owed its pungency, not so much to unregulated feeling, as to dismay at the present situation.

As a matter of fact, failing health, perhaps innate distaste, necessitated his taking a less active share, though his lifelong identification with the educational struggle identified him with this latter stage in the public mind, which he scarcely lived to see.[1] If he spoke of one thing more than another during those last months, it was of a compromise, repeatedly saying that Englishmen respect nothing more than this, and that such must be the issue of the present struggle. He knew quite well the indifference of a large section of the public, and that it desired nothing so much as a treaty of some kind. Though he had pledged himself to passive resistance, he never seemed to contemplate its actual occurrence, always hoping that some form of settlement would render it unnecessary.

---

[1] The detailed solution of the religious difficulty he did not live to formulate, for the struggle in his lifetime was still in its initial stage. He rather laid stress on what he thought to be guiding principles, and proclaimed these to his generation. On what would have been the detailed application of these principles at any crisis it would not always be easy to pronounce, so sensible was he of modification in circumstances and so various were the considerations which dictated his course.

An enforced holiday gave him greater opportunities for the display of that Christian fellowship which he had always advocated ; and it is unlikely that he ever before met so many Anglicans or was so friendly with them, paying visits to friends and relatives, and everywhere entering into the friendliest relations with those whom an outsider might have imagined him to be most at variance.

In particular, he took delight in informal meetings at Fulham Palace, where the Bishop of London invited a few Nonconformist and Anglican leaders to meet together, with a hope that they might see their way to arrive at a settlement of some kind.[1]   The alleged quarrels in the Christian Church are often as misleading to outsiders as those in politics.   The opposite front benches are pretty sure to be on good terms, whatever the political jealousies of their followers in the country, and one good effect of the present disturbance has been a closer fraternisation amidst leaders, so that the world has beheld in the Church that which it has seen too seldom, certain fighting to the hilt for conviction and for those whom they represent, but not yielding one whit in charity and sympathy to all men, including those most in opposition to them.   One, at any rate, for all the passion of loyalty and conviction that we have indicated, was " aloof" from this as well as other parties.   As ever, in this struggle he seemed to be treading a *via media*, ready to throw up what was nearest and dearest if the welfare of Christianity and the whole Church was at stake.

One incident in particular made a lively impression. The month after the appearance of the Bill witnessed not only agitation in certain circles, but several changes in the constitution of the Bill itself during its passage through the House, so that, while these modifications could not satisfy my father's party, they were highly distasteful to his Anglican opponents.   Thus those " sections " of human beings with whom the writer has described him as for ever contending, were particularly stirred, and waylaid, as usual, the prophet's friends when they came across them.   They spoke, they said, not for themselves but their relatives, and it must be owned that the sensibilities of these were excessive.   One

---

[1] It was characteristic that at these meetings he was remembered, not only for his counsels and his conciliatory spirit, but for the effervescence of his wit.

had been dining only lately with an Anglican clergyman who had expressed the hope that Mr. Price Hughes was not among opponents in this matter, that he surely was too wise and wide-minded. So far, this clergyman said, from gaining anything by the Bill, he and his party had irretrievably lost by it. Schools which they had formerly entirely controlled were in large measure passing from their hands, and that if it were not for the educational efficiency of the country, they would never have submitted to such a sacrifice. Indeed, the more a friend of the prophet listened, the more there seemed to be confusion on all sides.

The modifications introduced into a Bill that was not uncomplicated at the outset, tended to make it a test of the intelligence, so that a great many who were, as they said, quite unable to comprehend it themselves, suspected those of their number who pretended to such a comprehension. Some said that the only alternative was the dismissal of Christian teaching from the schools altogether, while others said that anything would be better than this, and that the safest and simplest course seemed to be to support the Establishment. Then fresh sections arose, saying that the Bill, when it was put into operation, might have quite the contrary effect to what was supposed, and that no one could say whether Nonconformists or Anglicans would be the most benefited. At last a member of Parliament, and a great admirer of Mr. Balfour's, told a member of the family that my father had not grasped the import of the Bill, which was not only of advantage to the country but to the Nonconformists, and that he greatly deplored his misconceptions in the matter. This great concourse of opinion stirred not only reflection but curiosity,—given certain occurrences, what would be the attitude of one of the principal opponents of the Bill? One question, in particular, demanded an answer, and as my father was taking up the evening paper preparatory to going into the study, it came out like a discharge of ammunition.

"If you had to choose between banishing distinctly religious and biblical teaching from the schools and what is called a clerical and Anglican monopoly, which alternative would you choose?"

He expressed no surprise at the suddenness of the demand,

but received it with the gravity with which it was uttered—much as if an archbishop had come to deliver an "ultimatum."

"I should," he said, "choose the Anglican monopoly," and then paused a moment as if viewing in his mind's eye the nature of such a crisis and the attitude of friends and opponents. In this controversy, as in every other, he submitted to a discipline that transcended that of party.

Nothing in public life was more to him than the cause of the Free Churches, that is to say, of much of the organised Christianity of this country, for to them he had given his life-blood, in that he lived and died toiling and planning, not for one, but for all of them. He believed, with other Nonconformist leaders and certain outsiders, that the Act in its contemporary form must tend to the cramping if not the crushing of Nonconformity, and thus to the blighting of all those hopes which he had formed for it and which had underlain the endeavours and the toils of his life. He believed it also to be deleterious to the interests of the whole Church, because it was non-democratic in the first place, and because neither Anglicanism or Nonconformity could live unto themselves. What was injurious to the one was also, to his thinking, injurious to the other, or he would not have felt and written as he did. Therefore the greatness of the sacrifice must be fully perceived, both what he was ready to demand first in himself and afterwards in others. In thus choosing the lesser of two ills, for so I think he regarded them, he looked British democracy very squarely in the face, and saw it as it was, not as it might be, or even as it is supposed to be. He perceived its possibilities—all that was dormant and great in it, but he also saw that it was very drunken in many quarters—seldom at a high state of living either in spirit or body or mind, and often in great misery. For this misery he would have said there were many causes, but principally the lack of self-discipline, that discipline which Christianity enjoined. Indeed, his feeling seems to have approached that of our Lord's parable, where He said it is better to pluck out the right eye and go maimed into life than to descend whole and unimpaired into the fire of that anguish which is not quenched. Humanity, he thought, often did that; it refused to be maimed, and had reaped anguish for itself in consequence; and what he feared for people and persons in a democratic era, was that they would go the way of the rest, sacrificing the greater interests to the lesser.

A Bill that led to what he considered clerical monopoly in State-supported education, Nonconforming or Anglican, was to his thinking an arrow in the bosom of Democracy and as such a wound to humanity, to what it had achieved and wrought. Yet it was not in his eyes as great an ill as a Bill which should deprive children of Christian education altogether.

CHAPTER XIX

THE CHAIR OF JOHN WESLEY

" Lord, grant us eyes to see and ears to hear,
    And souls to love and minds to understand,
    And steadfast faces toward the Holy Land,
And confidence of hope, and filial fear,
And citizenship where Thy saints appear
    Before Thee heart in heart and hand in hand,
    And Alleluias where their chanting band
As waters and as thunders fill the sphere.
Lord, grant us what Thou wilt, and what Thou wilt
    Deny, and fold us in Thy peaceful fold :
    Not as the world gives, give to us . . .
Inbuild us where Jerusalem is built
    With walls of jasper and with streets of gold,
    And Thou Thyself, Lord Christ, for Corner-Stone."
                                    CHRISTINA ROSSETTI.

EVER since 1896, when he had been President of the Free
Church Congress at Nottingham, the Wesleyan Presidency
had become a query in my father's mind, because it had also
become a query in the minds of others. The triumph of the
party that he led—the " Forwards "—was now assured, and
the only motive that could keep him from the Chair, as he
knew, was a personal one. Many felt, both outside and inside
Methodism, that it was high time for the leader of the Forward Movement, who had done such service for Methodism,
to occupy the Chair of John Wesley. Comment was freely
passed, outsiders either wondering why he was not President,
or, more frequently, assuming that he already occupied that
position. A young minister wrote concerning him, " He
brought honour to the Chair of John Wesley "; but my father
saw it contrariwise. In earlier years he had never entertained
any confidence respecting a possible Presidency, though the

humble, in the various Circuits, would echo the prediction of the old women who had listened to his first sermon.

As the years went on it did not look much like it, particularly after the Missionary controversy. But the triumph and popularity of the Forward party and his own position in London and the Free Churches, brought the Presidency to the fore, so that, for two years before he was elected, it was eagerly anticipated by his supporters, and frustrated by his opponents. My father was aware of this opposition, as no attempt was made to conceal it. The prophets are the prophets, and Democracy is Democracy, and not all the perfumes of Arabia can sweeten them to some!

In the late October of 1897, my grandfather passed away, leaving a blank that was never filled in the life of his eldest son. Living far from his home, and engrossed in the toils that increasingly fell to him, he had little or no time for the correspondence in which he had engaged as a younger man. None the less his father was very often in his thought, and their affection for each other was deep to the last. During all those years, when the path of my grandfather's life was dipping into the valley of the shadow, and he found himself, through declining health, unable to resume the offices and occupations which were the essence of life to men of that family, my father was praying for him after breakfast in Taviton Street as he prayed for his mother, at this time also an invalid. Ever since boyhood he had leant on the strong, tender-hearted man in the quiet country town, who had never ceased to think of him and his, and plan for their well-being. Instinctively my father turned to him in times of difficulty, and was never disappointed. The savings, which care, not stint, made the necessary accompaniment of a temperate life, were directed as much to his son as his daughters. "A Wesleyan minister," he used to say, "cannot make money or properly provide for the future."

As he walked the streets of Carmarthen in these latter years and the country roads of the neighbourhood, he would be greeted in the sing-song of the Principality by a good Wesleyan as follows: "Eh, doctor, but your son will be President. Indeed now he will. What with the preaching and the newspapers you will see him yet in Mr. Wesley's Chair."

To which my grandfather would answer gruffly, " Too rash, too rash, they'll never make him President."

To his native town my father was always the preacher. The other rumours concerning him were a mystery. Good souls went up by excursion trains to see London and hear "Hugh Price." After much perambulating of the neighbourhood of Paddington Station to see the city, and an excursion to the Abbey at Westminster on the part of the more venturesome, they presented themselves at St. James's Hall, Piccadilly, for the great event of the visit, which was duly described to friends in the market-place on the following Saturday. My grandfather drank in these accounts, and the more he heard the more determined was he that wild horses should not drag him to a service at which his son presided. Good Heavens! he would not be in the place five minutes before one of Hugh's retainers would be dragging him to the penitent form. In 1897, after the meeting of Conference, good Wesleyans would stop him in his walk, remarking, " 'Twill be next year, doctor. Mark my word." Then he would shake his head as he always did, and in the autumn he died. Yet it was his face his son saw, when he rose from his seat on the floor in the following August, and walked on to the platform to occupy the Chair of John Wesley. It was doubtful, indeed, whether he saw any other face at first but his—the face of one who had not lived to see his rash son President. The thought pierced him, and in his speech from the Chair he told the Conference that it had.

For several minutes after the announcement of his election there was an uproar, many of those present breaking into wild cheering. It was felt to be a great moment and a triumph, and it was. It was not so much a triumph for him, though it was that—as the installation in the heart of Methodism itself of a new and wider spirit—old in its fervour and intensity, but sympathetic to the needs and questionings of a new era. This new spirit was not, as my father had contended in the pages of the Journal, mission halls and brass bands, but something deeper and wider than any methods which circumstances might dictate.

About the beginning of my father's Presidential speech he said quietly, " I am not afraid of any one of you," and from the benches on the floor there rose a murmur that was half-sympathy, half-amusement. He had sometimes doubted, he said, whether he would ever be elected to sit on the Chair of Wesley. It was the first honour also that his own Church had ever paid him. The general opinion, including even that of some of his supporters, concerning the opening clauses, seems to have been that the address was lacking in modesty, and with a personal note too much in the ascendant. The opinion of others again, particularly those outside Conference whose cause he had championed, was one of pleasure that at last he should be saying something personal on a platform and something that concerned himself.[1] If they recognised the humanity they rejoiced in it, particularly those who could look to the beginning of his career and see how in all points his humanity had been straitened for the sake of others. Moreover, there is another explanation. These words were far from being the fruit of the moment, but had long been the subject of meditation and prayer. To enter the supreme office of his communion with all its spiritual responsibilities was bound to affect such a nature, and to lead to that self-examination which he thought to be a necessary prelude. The higher the office the more stringent the self-discipline, and feelings of resentment which might be justifiable for ministers on the floor were not possible, he thought, for the minister who sat in the Chair of John Wesley. Nothing, he felt, however justifiable, must cloud the serenity of his mind, though how to secure this serenity was difficult. Prayer revealed the solution. In his inaugural address, while the ex-Presidents and officials were sitting behind him, and the brethren on the floor in front of him, he would lay bare to them some of his thought. If he had expressed such feelings in private to friends or relatives, many of his listeners would have understood him.

[1] My father's personal sensitiveness, strange to say, was greatly underestimated. Many believed that he cared little, if at all, for what others said or thought about him, when, as a matter of fact, he cared increasingly. This sensitiveness did not diminish as it often does in life, but rather became keener. During these later years one of his sisters remarked after a visit to Taviton Street, "I am sorry to see that Hugh minds what people say about him. He used not to." A lady who was staying in the house a few weeks before his death related her surprise at this aspect of my father's character. "Before I came I thought he was a public leader who lived on platforms and in causes, and was untouched by anything outside these. But I was not in the house a few hours before I realised my mistake. I never beheld a gentler and more deeply sensitive soul."

Because he did it in public and on such an occasion they could not follow him; it was too audacious, too unconventional to suit the general taste. Nor did they perceive that his fearlessness and sense of honour made such an occasion the only possible one for expressing his inner feelings. Members of his family who read the Presidential speech, heard it as Conference did for the first time, and were quite surprised to find that he could criticise anything his brother-ministers had omitted to do for him in the past. To so loyal a Methodist minister it was the only possible opportunity of expressing these feelings.

Yet the speech was far from bearing a purely personal aspect. Listeners were probably more conscious of this aspect than he was, because what is most personal escapes men without their knowledge. His ostensible and stated object was the vindication and true explanation of the Forward Movement, which had never been properly understood, he thought, either by Conference or the world. The world not only identified him with it, but spoke of him as its leader, even its originator, which was the most terrible mistake of all. What man ever originated the love of God? All that he and his followers had been allowed to do was to dispel certain mists which had hidden the surface of things. Their hour was brief, but that which they showed had been before them and would survive them. What was it in definite terms, he asked, that they had shown? The love of God was too vague, too all-embracing, it wanted defining. If he had not been in an ecclesiastical assembly, he might have begun an exposition of Browning,[1] but as he was in an ecclesiastical assembly there was only one thing he could do, namely, to give what he and Dr. Berry had given all over England—a scriptural exposition of the Catholic Church—and in a manner that should befit the assembly he was addressing. This portion of his address was much appreciated, as were his references to what he considered the particular rôle of Methodism among Christian communions.

Quite the most marked trait of my father's occupancy of the Chair was his insistence on the devotional character of the proceedings. The short religious service which preceded

[1] Browning, he used to say, was the poet of the Forward Movement.

the morning session, which had hitherto been inadequately attended, to the grief of some of the elder ministry, was reinstated, so to speak, by the President. Dr. Rigg, Dr. Jenkins, and others of the fathers were invited to deliver short homilies, and the courtesy evinced towards those who had previously been opponents was generally noted.

" Am I not fortunate," my father exclaimed some time afterwards to a youthful companion at the foot of a Swiss mountain —"Am I not fortunate ? I have lived to see my opponents become friendly to me, and former misunderstandings passed over. Look at So-and-so and So-and-so. Nothing can exceed our goodwill and brotherly love. I should be very thankful to God."

The year of his Presidency is associated with two great campaigns, in each of which he took of necessity the leading rôle, perambulating the country on their behalf, just as he had done for the great Missions and the Federation of the Churches. The first was the consummation of that policy of aggression which he had done so much to inaugurate. If he had impressed anything upon Methodists, it was that they should be as ready to lavish money on paying off debts and building new premises for furthering the work of Christ's Church, as they were to beautify and enlarge their own houses and places of business. They had always been a liberal people, as far as the necessities of the Church were concerned, and he appealed to that tradition with quite extraordinary results, so it appeared to onlookers. The great Missions were a direct outcome of this, and throughout the country where Methodists were feeling their influence, attempts were being made to clear debts and erect new premises where necessary. Yet with all these it was not felt that Methodism was properly equipped, in her various departments, for the new century on which she was entering. Men began to feel that an Imperial era demanded great centres of activity and outlay, as well as designs and policies that were in keeping with such an epoch. Means should be raised, not locally, and in a series of fits and starts, but comprehensively, in one simultaneous and sustained effort.

The origination of such a scheme sprang from Mr. Perks, and the President echoed the suggestion, and gave it his most

33

vigorous benediction.   The Presidential idea of a benediction was intimately connected with the drawing of a sword from its scabbard.   Mr. Perks' suggestion was as follows : — That a million Methodists should contribute each a guinea to a Twentieth Century Fund, which should be divided among the different departments of Methodism, home and foreign, providing each with adequate means for suitable premises and various forms of extension.   The committee which sat to consider and apportion the scheme, and of which my father was a member, resolved on a building in the West End of London, which was to serve a twofold purpose ; fiirst, as a church house, a centre of Methodist enterprise, and a meeting-place for Methodists all over the world ; and second, as a centre of that evangelistic and social enterprise which the West London Mission had inaugurated, and which it should in future occupy.   As my father walked to and from St. James's Hall, he used to muse like the poet of Democracy on all that was "to let."   Here a fortress and there battlements, yonder outposts, and here a camp, and so should Babylon be stormed by the two-edged gospel of the Son of God.

A new theatre testifying to the wide-awakeness of men in business made the mouth water ; another opportunity snatched from Christians who feared " outlay " and advocated " retrenchment."   In passing the Empire Theatre one day, he startled a minister who was walking with him by exclaiming, " That's the place I want to get hold of," and for full half an hour he dilated on its capabilities as a centre for the full application of the gospel.   If men in London would not go to church, and they clearly would not, the Church must come into their midst, assailing and persuading them in any place where they would listen to her.   No one ever studied thoroughfares and sites and their peculiarities more than he, and it would perhaps be quite truthful to say that he was never without some imagined centre, some base of operations, with which to beguile his walks through the city.   Few things were more indicative of him than his manner of walking.   At times he would appear to be brooding, his head bent and his eyebrows, by dint of their unusual length, looking as if they were fiercely knitted, and then in a moment he would lift up his head and quicken his pace, every portion of his frame betraying a certain muscular exuberance, a springiness which was seldom equalled in a man of his age and toils. With difficulty he would keep himself from bounding, his feet having that distaste for the cramping earth which some of the old painters portray in their canvasses.

The building that he desired for the West London Mission was to be called after the apostle that he loved, St. John, and not a site was to let but his eye commanded and scanned it with a view to the exigencies of a building dedicated to the lively memory of that saint. The raising of a Twentieth Century Fund brought St. John's Hall within the sweet realm of immediate realisation; and the Mission Church, in common with every Circuit in Methodism, was canvassed on behalf of the Fund. Ministers all over England and the Principality received instructions from the President to use every effort to raise a generous quota from their Circuit, and in keeping with its resources. An historic roll was to be drawn up, on which the names of those would be inscribed who for the glory of God had contributed or collected one guinea for the furtherance of the gospel of His Son at the beginning of the twentieth century. This historic roll would be preserved henceforth in the archives of the Methodist branch of the Church Catholic. All the saints might contribute, he said, whether in the flesh or out of it, for their children could give a guinea in their name and so inscribe them in the roll-call of the people called Methodists. Moreover, let them not interpret the word "Methodist" too narrowly, and without the exercise of the imaginative faculty. Many in this country were indebted to Methodism, who did not call themselves by that name, or actively associate themselves with its worship. How many in all grades of society traced their holiest memories and impressions to some soul who had imbibed the quickening influence of the great religious revival! Let such, in their name and for their sake, make this roll still more precious, and the proposed fund, whose progress was so keenly noted by other churchmen, one step nearer its completion.

A feature of the historic roll on which the originator of the scheme laid stress was the deference that it paid to the principle of equality. The amounts contributed were not recorded, but only the names of the contributors ; so that the old woman who had scraped her guinea together in her stocking, and the rich man who had given many guineas, ranked side by side without distinction. As far as possible, Mr. Perks desired equality of giving, so that all might feel an equal share in the undertaking. A guinea, he felt, was within the compass of all. But in connection with this equality of giving there arose, in course of time, a divergence between my father and the originator. It was the sustainment, the completion of the effort, that he knew would be the pull. The first plunge, when everybody was warm to the work, was as nothing to the final tug up hill, for which he at the outset prepared himself. Any bias in favour of equality should give way, he felt, before the exigencies of the hour, and the necessity for the completion of the task. Besides, what an opportunity for the rich men and women of Methodism to pour forth their treasure for Christ's Church. How could they better evince the reality of their religion and their gratitude to God than giving after the manner of His poor. He knew the sacrifices these were making all over Methodism. One old woman, one of the Sisters told him, was denying herself her afternoon cup of tea so that she might contribute to Christ's treasury ; and were those rich in this world's goods to be for ever debarred from making the least personal sacrifice in His name ? At the Burslem Conference, two years later, when it seemed likely that a special appeal to the rich men of Methodism would not be made, a younger minister was enabled to get a glimpse of him while he thought himself unseen. His hands were nervously locked, and his lips moving as if in prayer. Perhaps it was small wonder that when he sprang to his feet he was irresistible, no man having the power to stay his path, to prevent him from demanding for Christ what he believed to be His. The scene that followed resembled that of the great missionary appeal many years ago, save that those sitting behind him on the platform shared the emotion which swept the assembly. " There was hardly any one in the chapel," said one who was present, " who was not weeping." A layman present rose and promised £20,000, and so led the way to a series of efforts which in 1904 witnessed the completion of the fund.

But the Chair of John Wesley did not only spell that self-discipline which the occupier had been spelling all his life, but it made an admission which he had also been making all his life. When anybody asked him concerning the comparative ineffectiveness of professing Christianity, he had always one answer, "the character of professing Christians." He knew that whatever preparations the Church might make for an Imperial era, they were useless unless, to quote his favourite phrase, the Christians were "fully consecrated."

In addition to the necessary travels of the year, he intended to undertake a yet further one for the holding of "conventions" all over the country, in which he would appeal, not to the ordinary congregation, or even to members of the Church, but to those who held office within it—the staff in all its branches. So in the course of a second speech from the Chair he spoke as follows:—

"If those of us who have the same burdens and responsibilities were to spend some time in rejoicing in the love of God and realising the presence of Christ, we might obtain the blessing of the Almighty for ourselves. As far as I understand Church history or the New Testament, the special Pentecostal blessing of God is bestowed on us, not when we are alone and separated, but when we meet together in one place with one accord.

. . . .

"But there is one difficulty in the way, and that is, many of our class-leaders and local preachers live in remote villages in country circuits, and they may not be able to bear the expense of the railway journeys so as to be present at the meetings. But I am quite confident that our laymen in the different centres of this country will be exceedingly glad to form a small fund to meet the small expenses. It would be an unspeakable calamity for any poor brother, who has had to fight a desperate battle in a distant village, to be prevented from once in his life meeting a multitude of brethren in some central place, because he could not pay the railway fare ; and those of us accustomed for many years past to promote gatherings of this kind, know how greatly encouraged the poor brethren are to find that they are not alone after all, but that they belong to a large army, and that there are multitudes besides themselves engaged in the same work. . . . I am quite sure if we feel that the set time has come to promote a deepening of the spiritual life of all our Churches, that we shall be able to achieve more in this way than in any other. We have had many controversies during many years past, in which I have taken some humble share, and we have had difficulties and we have had discouragements. We have not made such great progress as I could wish. Some of the social and ecclesiastical and spiritual signs of the times are not encouraging. But it is my conviction, so far as Methodism is concerned, that there is a turn in the tide."

Preparations were made in every district for the President's visitation, and the most able and thoughtful of those holding office prepared papers on matters touching Church procedure and the best method of living the Christian life. At the various sessions the President gave a suitable instruction or exposition, infusing into the whole procedure a memorable devotional atmosphere, which was marked by a profound stillness, showing the deep impression on many present. This visitation, exhausting as it undoubtedly was to a frame terribly overtaxing its strength, was none the less a singularly pleasant recollection. He enjoyed his high office despite all its wear and tear, and particularly his visitations among the people for whom he laboured and whom he loved. Pastoral work, for which latterly he had had so little leisure, was always a delight to him, and letters that testified to help received on these occasions he much prized. The variety of the President's correspondence—the humblest writing to him as a friend—impressed the writer when dealing with some of his correspondence. Yet the chief interest of the Presidential Conventions lay in the fact that he knew such methods to be comparative failures; for, effective as they were to a certain extent, among the Methodist people,—as were the United Free Church Missions effective in their particular capacity two years later, —it could not blind his eyes to the fact that neither conventions nor special missions, in the accepted sense of those terms, had a hold on the popular imagination. He looked not so much for any special efforts peculiar to the methods of particular Churches as some great Renascence in the spiritual life which should kindle them all.[1]

Some Traditions of the Chair.

"Projects for great and sudden changes are now, as ever, foredoomed to fail, and to cause reaction. We are still unable to move safely, if we move so fast that our new plans of life altogether outrun our instincts. It is true that human nature can be modified; new ideals, new opportunities, and new methods of action may, as history shows, alter it very much even in a few generations. This change in human nature has perhaps never covered so wide an area and moved so fast as in the present generation. But still it is a growth, and therefore gradual; and changes of our social organisation must wait on it, and therefore they must be gradual too. But though

---

[1] See close of Chapter XVI. on the spirit of St. Francis and its message.

they wait on it, they may always keep a little in advance of it, promoting the growth of our higher social nature by giving it always some new and higher work to do, some practical ideal towards which to strive."—Marshall's *Economics of Industry*, Book I. chap. iii.

In a great communion whose life is manifold there are necessarily divergent points of view, and a forward movement will appear differently to different minds. It must be opposed as well as followed, criticised as well as admired. Some will do their work in the world by opposing it, just as others do their work in the world by advocating it. Much of the history of the Forward Movement, *i.e.* of the Methodism of the latter portion of the century, is necessarily contained in assemblies and committees, and no interpreter could write adequately of this portion, unless he had been present in these assemblies and was familiar with the personalities and circumstances involved. There is one name which, by its distinction and its unique position in the Methodism of the century, must be mentioned, even in a life that does not pretend to be ecclesiastical.

" There is one minister in Conference," said my father once to a member of his family, " who knows the exact import of all that is passing, and whither each proposition and detail is tending. That man is Dr. Rigg. He misses nothing." [1] Thus around his name and my father's the history of modern Methodism revolves, and the history of modern Methodism in detail and on its ecclesiastical side has yet to be written. In the letter at the close of this chapter, which my father wrote concerning Dr. Rigg, readers will note the sentence: " I am deeply grateful to Dr. Rigg for the courage and energy with which he has invariably supported every proposal and every movement which has tended to deepen the spirituality and to promote the aggressive and missionary work of Wesleyan Methodism."

Thus, in what all Methodists would agree to be essentials, they were agreed. Indeed, the evangelistic aspirations and endeavours were the connecting bridge between him and others whose thought differed widely from his. Methodism

---

[1] To listen to Dr. Rigg and my father as they debated in committee was, hearers related, an " intellectual pleasure." Despite their differences of mind and method, the two debaters were wonderfully well matched.

owes its birth to a great evangelical revival, which is the greatest of all its traditions; and by my father's unflinching adherence to it, he not only bound himself to the history of Methodism for ever, but he also bound himself to those who were most opposed to some of his advocacies. Whatever their divergencies, they spoke the same tongue, and neither could get away from the other. There is in Methodism a *lingua franca*, and it can be explained and defined to no one who has not been bred in it. Along with this is a chain of associations and sensibilities which no outsider can possibly divine, and it is this incommunicability which constitutes its charm. On inquiring into the origin of this peculiar possession, it seems to lie as much as anything in that deep Christian fellowship which the Methodists seem specially to understand and practise. As the ancient world said of the early Christians, " See how they love one another," so could the other Churches say of the Methodists. Undoubtedly they are angry with one another at times, and say so, but this fellowship is at the back all the time.

In Yorkshire an observer noted that when any Methodist wanted to speak his mind against another, he looked round the room and said in a sepulchral voice, " Are we all Methodists ? " When he was assured that no stranger was present, he would say what he desired. Thus anger with them will often conceal love, and they are angry often because they love. It is like a family who, while privately aware of each other's foibles, are immensely proud of one another, and when it comes to facing the world will do so shoulder to shoulder. In their hearts they know there is no family like them, and that in the very failings of their relatives there is something superior to the virtues of others.

Perhaps the most striking example of this in my father's experience was a visit that he received while at Brighton from the aged Mr. Dunn, one of the three ministers—Everett, Griffiths, and Dunn—who were expelled at the time of the great rupture fifty years ago, when Methodists were certainly very angry with one another. He was a very old man when he paid the visit, and he much impressed my father by his saintliness. His interest and concern for Wesleyan Methodism, which, in the eyes of many, had treated him very badly, seems to have been extreme. The tears rolled down his cheeks as he said that he had reason to hope that better days would come to Methodism, and that his listener would be the means, under God, of healing the breach, which he deplored, and of introducing a new and happier order. As my father was then little past his twenty-sixth year, the prophecy was remarkable, and must have haunted his imagination not a little. Years after, as he was walking on Hampstead Heath, he recalled the incident and told it to Dr. Lunn.

With these associations and sensibilities my father had from time to time to come into conflict. None the less the conflict was more apparent than real, a commotion on the surface of things rather than beneath. The deepest note of that fellowship he never violated, because he was true to what was deepest in its tradition. His grief at having to come into contact with it was not fully estimated by some Methodists, nor did they know the sacrifice involved to such a Methodist as he was. It may sound incredible but it is true, that nothing personally was a greater sacrifice than the obligation to incur those misunderstandings and slights which the rôle of pioneer necessitated. The letters of leading Methodist friends were treasured by him, and he would be quite in a flutter of delight if one of them paid him a special attention, or showed him an act of kindness, however slight. He greatly benefited by the fellowship and free-masonry of Methodism, and, without them, he could never have done what he did. His whole appeal was to the connexional principle, not to what was temporary or incidental, but to what was comprehensive and profound. He served Methodism also the more in that he served Christ first.

On the education question my father found himself at variance with Dr. Rigg and a body of opinion which was strong, because traditional, in Wesleyan Methodism. Since the days of Wesley, schools and colleges had been maintained by his followers, and it was the struggle of the conservative party to preserve these intact, just as it was with the Anglicans. At the creation of the School Board in 1870 a proposal was made to transfer Wesleyan schools to that body, and with this proposition began the struggle of the present liberal party in Methodism. Where ministerial sensibilities were so much concerned, feeling was bound to run high. None the less my father showed in this matter, as in others, a disposition to compromise, which was noted with different sentiments by both sides.

My father always spoke with pride of the debates in Conference. "Nobody," he used to say, "can debate like an assembly of Methodist ministers, for the average debating power is so high. All who are present have a gift of utterance of some kind, seeing that their very profession depends largely on the power to express themselves. The House of Commons is nothing to it." It is scarcely surprising, therefore, that the standard in such an assembly is unusually high, and that young ministers are often nervous before rising to address so critical an audience. A remark of my father, as President, alludes to his plight and emotions on the first occasion when he rose to address the Conference:

"I will say now what I said the first time I ever dared, with trembling legs, my knees knocking together, to speak in this august assembly, 'Wesleyan Methodism lies in the hollow of our hands.' The ministers of this Church can do anything they like with their Church. If you put your hearts into this movement or a similar movement, you can overcome every difficulty and carry everything before you, and it is for us as the pastors of the Church to do everything that may be wisely done in order that we may prepare for the new century on which we are about to enter."

That he was thus agitated is not easily believed, but it was a vivid presentment of what a born speaker felt when he rose to address Conference for the first time. Of all the endeavours and victories and routs of the year, Conference was the climax, and everything led up to this. For about six weeks before his annual departure to that assembly, Conference scintillated in the air. His projects and hopes were not stated, but were seen to be contained within him. About Conference there was always a mystery as of a life lived apart, in which the ordinary world could not share. Affairs municipal and political, matters connected with the Mission, he would speak of freely in that they were open to the ordinary apprehension, but not Conference. Rightly to perceive the full import of any of its deliberations needs unusual qualifications, a knowledge of its history since the days when John Wesley vested his powers in a hundred ministers, not to mention a full participation in the Methodist fellowship and its subtle associations.

What my father felt to be the difficulty and solitude of early years was revealed by the following remark :—" At last I observed a group who silently rose and supported my propositions. They never spoke or agitated in any way, but rose in company, quietly seating themselves after they had demonstrated in my behalf." The group who thus silently rose consisted of young ministers, and with them, he felt, rested the development of the Forward Movement and the maintenance of its traditions. His belief in young men and what they could do for the Church and the world was often attested. Thus at the Passion Play at Oberammergau he was distressed that Christ's immediate followers should be represented as reverent seigneurs, and that St. Peter, who had first protested his love, should be portrayed by a very respectable and cautious disciple. His own presence was so singular an inspiration that he had only to touch younger men on the shoulder, or to say a couple of words, in order to make it felt. At the time of his death also elder ministers had one unanimous testimony in their letters, that he had made it easier for young ministers to speak in Conference.

The " Minutes " of Conference my father read and marked repeatedly, with an absorption that was striking even for him. To a young minister who found him thus engaged he said eagerly, " Well, what do you think of the Minutes ? "

" I am afraid I have not read them, Mr. Hughes."

" How's that ? "

" They don't interest me particularly, and I have so much else to do."

" You astonish me," was all my father could exclaim. Then after a pause, " How strange, how very strange ! " Bewilderment had rendered him pensive. The decisions of the Supreme Council, under whose cognisance came all the affairs of Methodism, were to him food for reflection that was both tender and keen, and it had never occurred to him that all other ministers did not feel about it quite as he did. For all the reserve attendant on this portion of his life he none the less dropped hints to the family at table. When he was elected a member of the Legal Hundred, the fact was duly impressed upon them and explained. " No proposition can become law," he said, " until it has received the separate assent of the Legal Hundred. Thus all the measures passed by Conference received from it their final ratification. No assembly of Conference is also possible without the Hundred, who form the quorum, and its first duty every year is to fill up the vacancies that may have occurred by death or retirement. Without the full Hundred it would be impossible to elect the President, or to proceed with any of our business." Thus the family were early impressed with the dignity of the Hundred.

But later even this dignity paled before the responsibilities of the Stationing Committee, and the delicacy of the duties with which it was charged. " This is a most anxious time," he would say, " for many of our ministers, and some are eagerly awaiting our decisions. You cannot imagine our difficulties and the private correspondence that it entails—our anxiety to do our best for all." Here he would sigh and knit his brows, like a father who is anxious about the placing of his children. Sometimes he gave listeners glimpses into the life of Conference that were charged with severity and gloom. There was a roll-call at the beginning of each session, and if any minister had incurred debts, or in some other way infringed the code of high living, he had to answer to his brethren as they sat with the Hundred.

Such occasions, they understood, were exceptional, though they had from time to time arisen. But even here justice was tempered with mercy. On one occasion it was perceived that a brother had mistaken his vocation. The Stationing Committee with fatherly anxiety had done all that they could to procure him a Circuit, but his ministry was not edifying, and no Circuit desired his services. Thus the brethren had to inform him of their decision, and it was a most painful task. One or two who were intimate with him would rise on such an occasion and with tears in their eyes plead with Conference on his behalf, mentioning his wife and children, and Conference would weep with sympathy also, but its decision was inexorable. Edification and the effective preaching of Christ's gospel was the first necessity, and compassion had to assume a secondary place.

There were brethren also whom my father desired to aid in some way, both for their own sake and that of Methodism. " I am most anxious," he would say in a low voice, " that

So-and-so should be elected into the Hundred. I should like him to have that mark of esteem."

Individual ministers would find a brother indeed when they came to see him on any personal matter. The place that he won in their hearts was not divined by outsiders, who imagined him a somewhat solitary figure in Methodism, often at variance with his contemporaries. But this again was illusion. He had a following which was openly devoted to him, and many of those who resented portions of his policy cherished admiration and affection. "A most fascinating man," they would say, divided between dislike of his ideas and a secret liking for himself.

The letters of some of these opponents, and still more their faces and words when they visited the house after his death, were sufficient indication of the place he had occupied in their lives. "I cried like a child," wrote one with whom he had sometimes disagreed on minor matters. "My chief desire for the next life is to meet him again," wrote another. "I disagreed with him again and again and again," wrote a third. Yet there never was a minister, he added, who had so disturbed Wesleyan Methodism, and who was more sincerely mourned at his death. Even those who personally liked him the least confessed themselves overwhelmed at the receipt of the news.[1]

If one fact more than another was intimated to the family during the year of Presidency, it was that the President was *ex officio* chairman of all Methodist committees, including that which regulated the affairs of Foreign Missions. Here a laugh would escape the President, and of purest glee. What an opportunity for dissipating former misapprehension! For several years he was assistant to Dr. Rigg so long as he retained the chairmanship of the Second London District Synod, and after his Presidency he himself became permanently its chairman. The substitution of the term "District Synod" for that of "District Meeting" was his own suggestion, and the substitution of the term "Wesleyan Methodist Church" for

[1] At the funeral service at Wesley's Chapel, the President of the Conference spoke on behalf of the Methodist people when he said, "We loved him with a strength that we hardly knew." "He often fought some of us," he added, "and his blows were hard, but they were always straight."

that of "Wesleyan Methodist Society" was another innovation
on which he would lay stress and comment with pleasure.
An interpreter could write many pages, not on the great
measures in which he was interested, but on the smaller.

That he should be the champion of the Welsh ministry in
their demand for a national assembly, was natural. A Welsh
minister related that his last words in the last English Conference that he ever attended were, strangely enough, connected
with Carmarthen, his native town. Equally characteristic was
his advocacy of the full status of coloured ministers.

An advocacy with which he was conspicuously concerned,
and which was carried on throughout his career, was connected
with the character of Conference, whose Representative Session
includes laymen as well as ministers. The Hundred with
their absolute powers had loomed large during the first three-
quarters of the century, and while the other ministers were
gradually admitted to their deliberations, forming the present
Pastoral Session, there was a great discussion and no little
excitement before the laity were admitted into the supreme
assembly and allowed to express their opinion and give their
vote with the rest, a concession which took place in 1878.
Hitherto they had sat in committee for the control of finance
and in various of the minor assemblies, as the times had not
been ripe for further participation in affairs. A portion of Dr.
Bunting's great contribution to Methodism lay in a singularly
clear conception of the pastoral office, its privileges and responsibilities, a conception which remains to this day, and in
which my father to a certain extent shared. The Wesleyan
estimate of the pastoral office has always been a distinctive
feature, and has allied her rather to Anglicanism than to Nonconformity. At the same time my father believed that the
pastoral idea had been developed at the expense of one that,
to his thinking, was greater and more comprehensive—that
whole body of the people for whom the Church existed. The
following sentence of a liberal minister, Dr. Beaumont, who
lived in the first half of the century, was often in his
thought :—

"The people are as essential to the idea of a ministry as the ministry is
essential to the idea of a Church. We cannot exist alone, and we must not
act alone."

Thus he believed in admitting the laity, whether men or women, as far as possible into the counsels of the Church. Men, he believed, in a democratic era—particularly Englishmen who have long been accustomed to govern themselves—would never become Christian Churchmen, and take their share in its life, unless they had a legitimate voice in its affairs. The Church also must benefit, because laymen had a less biassed outlook in many ways than the ministry, and by their knowledge of affairs were peculiarly fitted to render service in the initiation of great schemes and in the discussion of novel enterprises. The settlement of 1878 was still unpleasing to the laity, as the Representative Session did not sit till the close of the Pastoral, when measures had already been introduced and discussed. Although these were resubmitted for discussion, they inevitably bore upon them the stamp of the previous debate, so that neither advocates nor critics felt the field clear before them.

The Representative Session should sit first, it was felt, so that ministers and laity might share together in the launching of important debates. Many of the laity also thought that they were entitled to their share in the election of the President, which must, they considered, be granted them, if they were present at the opening Conference when the Presidential election took place. The clear apprehension of this desire by the pastorate, and a distaste for the further extension of lay privilege which they thought to be already quite adequate, induced a strong resistance to this demand, which found its champion in Dr. Rigg, as the other side found a champion in my father. That the laity would ultimately obtain what they desired must have been the conclusion of prescient observers, who none the less welcomed a stemming of the tide, which the pastorate was successful in effecting.

By what was called "The Sandwich Compromise," which was the achievement of Dr. Rigg, the Pastoral Session still opened the proceedings of Conference, but adjourned after the first week for the Representative Session, which was thus interposed like a sandwich between the two sittings of the pastorate. While such an arrangement had its advantages from the point of view of statesmanship, it had certain

practical inconveniences which ensured its temporary character.   Ministers who did not sit in the Representative Session
were kept waiting about during the week of its sitting, and
the arrangement, as could be expected, was still unpleasing
to the laity, who were deprived of that share in the opening
business which they desired.

In 1901, the year before my father died, a further position
was captured by the liberal section, who destroyed the
" sandwich " arrangement, completely inverting the old order of
the sessions.   For the first time in its history Conference was
opened by ministers and laymen in company, but at the cost
of a compromise which represented the last and determined
stand of the conservative and clerical section.   The Pastoral
Session was still to retain the privilege of the Presidential
election, because it would choose the President a year in advance,
electing in its separate session the occupant for the Chair
of the ensuing Conference.   At this compromise my father
clutched, amid the open discontent of a section of his followers,
who complained as usual that he led them to an imperfect
victory.   The least understanding of his opponents, on the
other hand, noted with approbation a willingness to compromise, which partially absolved what they regarded his other
errors.   Several ministers were unable to understand his
advocacy of the lay cause, because they perceived those
ecclesiastical sensibilities in which they shared, nor could they
see the benefit that would ensue from an inverted order of
sessions.   The question seemed to them one of convenience for
the most part, and by no means worthy of the stress that he
and others laid upon it.   His answer to the latter criticism is
contained in a letter which he wrote to Dr. Townsend, *à propos*
of Methodist union :—

"PENRHEOL, BARRY, CARDIFF,
"*September* 9, 1901.

" DEAR DR. TOWNSEND,—If nothing more were possible,
I think a union between you the Free Methodists and the
Bible Christians would be a great blessing, and I see no
difficulty in the way.   But I am *very strongly* of opinion that
a general union would be far better.   We shall never rest
until that is achieved.   And in the meantime smaller fragmentary reunions will be a waste of time and strength.   It

would be wiser, I think, to wait a few years and do as they are doing in Australia. Let us see what will be the effect of the remarkable conversation of last Friday. I shall fill the next issue of the *Methodist Times* with it. It is a great step in advance. I have no doubt that a majority of our laymen are already in favour of union, so are many of our ministers. But we have only *this very year* gained the crowning victory of getting the Representative Session to meet first. That breaks the neck of the difficulty. Many of our ministers felt that very deeply, although most of them reconciled themselves to the change very magnanimously at last. I do not think it would be politic to trouble Dr. Rigg's party again, so soon after that great defeat. I believe that if you will wait a few years, we shall take the initiative, as some of you suggested, and as I think we ought to do. I should be very sorry if attention were diverted from the larger issue by any smaller enterprise. We have everything to gain by a little delay. With returning health I shall be delighted to do all I can with voice and pen to promote the great enterprise of universal reunion throughout the British Empire and the mission field. Let our people feel the full effect of the Australian reunion. One of my own chief objects in going to Australia was to report to England the result of union there, and to begin a campaign when I returned. But events are anticipating me. The higher our aim, the more it will appeal to sentiment and enthusiasm. I think a little patience now will help the move-ment.—Yours very sincerely,

"H. PRICE HUGHES.

"The Rev. Dr. Townsend."

Many in Conference came to silently admire one who continually strove with its predilections, paying the tribute that all men render to courage, but they should rather have admired him for the prayer that he prayed before he got there, for it was this: "From all my inborn instincts, good Lord, deliver me, so that I plead what Thou and not I myself wouldst have." It was the prayer of his life.

The laymen who could not respect the class that was set apart to specially minister to the Church and its peculiar duties and claims, was wanting in his eyes in a Christian

34

grace. Yet to the lay share in the election of the President he did not object, any more than he objected to lay representation in the election of bishops. But three great prerogatives of the Pastoral Session his instinct certainly claimed —the exclusive right to deal with questions of discipline, with stationing (*i.e.* ministerial appointments), and with all questions relating to the expression of Christian doctrine.

On being asked why he made such a point of the reservation of doctrine, he made the unexpected reply, that the laity were so conservative, and that if they were permitted to have a share in such matters, there would never be any advance. His real answer was contained in his article on the Catechism, where he explains the almost total absence of laymen in its compilation, by saying that few possessed the leisure or the necessary qualifications. Just as the average Englishman was specially fitted to render certain practical services to the Church, so did he think the ministry, by their training and bent of mind, to be specially charged with the interpretation of its dogma and doctrine. He knew there were exceptions to this, that certain laymen might be as versed in theology as certain of the ministry, but it was a very rare occurrence. The laity, if they happened to be of a studious bent, did not generally choose theology for their particular study. But he would not have excluded a suitable layman from discussions on this subject any more than he would have excluded a suitable woman from the Representative Session ; when he made such reservations he was thinking of the general rule, not of those exceptional cases which have to be decided on their own merits as they happen to arise.

Yet certain instincts in him were felt to be having free play when Dr. Rigg suggested that, in cases where it was desirable, chairmen of districts should be exempt from their Circuit duties, and left free to supervise the district as they were not able to do under the present régime. The phrase " separated chairman " quickly became converted into that of " bishop," whose duties it was seen to clearly resemble, and a regular hue and cry was raised among a certain section who deplored what appeared an unblushing assumption of clericalism. The *Methodist Times* blew the trumpet valiantly for Dr. Rigg and the bishops, the editor being strongly of opinion that

Methodist bishops would advance the cause of God and man, and that "for purposes of aggression" they were not only desirable, but an absolute necessity—a phrase, it may be remembered, which Bishop Perowne smilingly quoted at Grindelwald.

From the strategic point of view his position was quite comprehensible—because most, after reflection, could not fail to perceive that a district which was administered by one who had no other duty on his hands, was likely to be in a more satisfactory condition than a district which was administered by one who had the cares and responsibilities of a Circuit in addition to that of the more general supervision. Yet while Bishop Perowne had intimated that my father's approval of the Episcopacy was of the military order, he did not know him as well as certain Methodists did. The charge that "Mr. Hughes was succumbing to ecclesiasticism" was entirely true. A suppressed instinct had leaped out like a flame from beneath the coals—one of those instincts which cannot be described, but which are immediately divined. The Methodist bishop of his imaginings would have been aware of a special form of self-discipline, and, as such, of the special responsibilities and prerogatives of his office. Indeed, they would have clothed him in fitting garb, omitting none of those outward insignia that could contribute either to its picturesque quality or its essential dignity. They would have girt him with stalwart laity, the laity to elect him if need be, and frustrate all his designs as they sat with him in Council—if they could—and to be a thorn in his flesh till he died, so that he be saved from vain imaginings and all forms of self-assertion—yet with the full insignia of office which neither its holder or anybody else could afford to overlook.

The tongues of the interpreters here are not divining the possibilities of Methodism, but of certain unchecked instincts of the heart. The separated chairman of his advocacy would have been far removed from the mediæval bishop, and in strictest accordance with Methodist tradition and feeling. None the less he would have pleasantly approximated towards the former. The advocacy, however, was not popular in Methodism, despite two such powerful supporters, and it dropped into the limbo of measures that have yet to see the light.

His known feelings on this matter caused some to wonder at his impassioned advocacy for Methodist union, which seemed to contradict certain conceptions of the pastoral office. The secessions from the Wesleyan body were all more or less the result of reaction from its sway, as embodied in decisions of Conference, and each great group had abandoned in consequence what were regarded as vital elements in the pastoral tradition. None the less all were children of the same religious revival, and possessed those great common elements in apprehending the Christian faith which make them speak the same language whatever the divergences of dialect. Of this common possession my father considered it part of his task to constantly inform Wesleyan Methodists, and almost with the starting of the *Methodist Times* Dr. Jenkins contributed an article advocating Methodist reunion. The differences, constitutional and political, that had once divided Methodists into opposing groups, were now completely buried so far as the present generation was concerned, and it was time for a prescient statesmanship to call attention to this fact, and to advocate that further participation in fellowship which must benefit, not only Methodism itself, but, as a consequence, the world. To this point of view there seems to have been two main classes of objectors.

Those who thought the idea entirely impracticable and a species of fantasy on the part of its principal promoter, and others who, while they saw with him the removal of certain obstacles and the probable trend of affairs, were yet in no hurry to precipitate what would in good time take place of its own accord, if it ever took place at all. Reunion, my father saw, must become the talk of a people and a Conference before it can enter the realm of practical advocacies, and must be derided before it can gain serious consideration. In this proposition he had the sympathy of certain of the elder ministry, while many contemporaries entirely failed to accord it. Thus, while he often urged reunion both in the *Methodist Times* and in Conference, he would, if pressed, have replied that he was telling the Methodist people of a dream, rather than urging what was immediate and practicable, though he would speak in a manner that implied these. Difficulties, he thought, could be no more dispelled by thinking about them than the galleons of Spain which the winds of heaven dismantled and sank. Yet what men could do they should, so that they be found waiting and equipped when God breathed on the face of the waters.

At times his personal desire for anything would cause him to read the same desire in others. In visits over the country he would sweep several into the current of his thought and hope, and would return with the impression that a large number of people were participating in them.

His witty opponent, Mr. Watkinson, made an excellent mot once on this propensity. My father had been telling Conference that the whole Connexion was eager for reunion if only some feasible proposal could be adopted by the present assembly, and in sitting down he was immediately followed by his opponent, who spoke as follows :—

"When I was a boy I was taken by my mother to a ventriloquial performance. While the performance was proceeding there came a loud knocking at one of the doors of the hall, and then there was a noisy scuffle in the passage as if a mob were breaking in. Everybody was alarmed, and we thought there would be a panic, but there was no need. There wasn't any mob. It was only the ventriloquist."

Then he sat down amid the roars of the assembly, having frustrated the effect of the previous speech. On another occasion, it is fair to add, my father made an excellent mot with regard to his opponent. In a carefully prepared speech given by Mr. Watkinson, many allusions were made to the *Methodist Times* and the monstrous things therein proposed— a friend sitting below and passing up quotations from the journal in question. The delivery lasted for over an hour, and at the close Conference adjourned for tea. His brethren, so my father gave his family to understand, were not a little impressed, one or two coming forward to shake him by the hand and gaze sympathetically into his face. Amid intense silence my father rose after the resumption of the debate, and remarked as follows :—" I have only one criticism to offer with regard to Mr. Watkinson's moving address—I am sorry to find that he unduly confines his reading to one newspaper," and it was some time before he could continue, so were the brethren tossed on the great sea of their laughter. Having dissolved the impression of his opponent's speech, he proceeded with ease and amid the sympathy of his hearers.

My father's greatest triumph as a speaker in Conference was in the Pastoral Session when the question arose as to whether ministers in the foreign field should be allowed to record their vote in the Presidential election. For some time the assembly wavered, until my father arose to address it. When he did he appealed to Conference to recollect its dignity and that peculiar solemnity which attaches to an ecclesiastical election within a sacred building where all are gathered for the same purpose. Any tampering with this environment must be detrimental, he felt, both to tradition and the highest religious privileges and interests of the ministry. Certain instincts often repressed and held in check had their sway in him, and by the time he had finished he was surprised to see his audience standing on its feet—one or two *half* standing, as if resisting an act which they felt compelled to perform. Opponents, adherents, critics, moderates, waverers, were swept after him in one irresistible impulse to maintain the high religious character of one of the principal acts of their meeting, and to resist any measure by which ministers who were not present could claim privileges to which they were not entitled. An old minister said, on resuming his seat, to a friend of my father who was sitting beside him, " Dr. Bunting was never finer than this."

Part of my father's belief in Methodism lay in the fact that the English-speaking peoples could carry it with them wherever they went, and that while in the Metropolis and the south of England it was comparatively little known and esteemed, it was a great feature in the life of the English-speaking world. His heart and policy were continually at the ends of the earth with the people called Methodists, and because it was so, the Methodists at the ends of the earth came to perceive and to respond to the largeness of both. Notices in the colonial press showed that while these disagreed in certain particulars, they could yet take his measure as perhaps Methodists at home were not able to do. His grasp of what was fundamental and vital in Methodism, and his imperial ideas, appealed to British colonists, who have in their blood, many of them, the traditions of Methodism and Nonconformity, and are proud of the fact. Men and women living in a democratic atmosphere and in that perspective which perhaps the seas can only bring, saw what he was doing more clearly than some nearer him. The great essentials on which he laid stress were more to them than the washing of cups and platters and the letter of tradition. Visitors from the colonies speak of him with enthusiasm, though they never saw his face or heard him speak. The following letters will prove of interest :—

"HAWTHORN, *Oct.* 18, 1902.

"DEAR MR. HUGHES,—It was pleasant to get your letter and to learn by direct communication from you that you were getting back to working condition again. May God give you many happy years of glorious service ! That you could not visit us this year was a bitter disappointment to us in Australia ; and you may be sure that we watched every detail of your sickness and recovery with intense interest. You must come to us some day, and then you—and we !—will have a golden time.

"I am glad to say that Methodist union in Victoria is working out splendidly. I have always felt that, in the last analysis, the question of union was a religious question. We were divided because we had not enough of religion amongst us to keep the peace at our own firesides. And the attempt to unite was a test of our spiritual condition. Thank God we have met the test ! Union has evoked a wonderful manifestation of Christian temper in the uniting Churches, of chivalrous consideration and affection for each other. The very men who opposed union so long have done their utmost after union was finally accepted to make the union successful. We have no rebellious or unconvinced minorities !

. . . . . .

"With all loyal regards.—Yours ever,
"W. H. FITCHETT."

"8 TAVITON STREET, GORDON SQUARE, W.C.,
"*August* 18, 1902.

"DEAR MR. FITCHETT,—I had intended to reply to your very kind letter long before now, but as part of my cure has been to spend as many hours as possible in the open air, and I have been compelled to do a certain amount of work in my official position and as editor of the *Methodist Times*, the opportunity of writing to you never seems to have come.

"I cannot tell you how distressed I am at the failure of my health for many reasons, but for none more than that it has prevented me from at present paying a visit to Australia, which my wife and I were anticipating with great delight. I cherish the thought that this visit is not put off for ever, but simply postponed for a year or so.

. . . .

"The ministers have also placed a quite unprecedented number of young and progressive men in the Hundred. We are evidently entering upon a new era in our history. We have also secured, after two years of private effort and prayer, the Aquarium in Westminster, immediately opposite Westminster Abbey, the most magnificent site in London. Here we shall erect the headquarters of world-wide Methodism, and also provide the West London Mission with a permanent centre of work. Everything, therefore, in England looks very hopeful, provided we devote ourselves adequately to our Divine Lord.

. . . .

"I feel that I have failed to express to you strongly enough how disappointed I am that I am not now on my way to Australia. I hope that this visit is only deferred. I was greatly delighted when you were elected the first President of our United Church in Australasia. That most blessed consummation owes more to you, under God, than to anybody else, and I greatly rejoice that you have been able to render this immense service to Methodism and to Christianity.

"My eighteen months of comparative silence has been very painful to me, but it has taught me many things. I have specially prayed God to restore me to health for two reasons. One is that I may live to do something to revive and deepen the foreign missionary spirit; and the other is that I may be able to assist in bringing to England that Methodist union which you have happily achieved in Australasia. It had been my hope that visiting Australasia this year I could bring back to this country such a report of the success and blessing which have followed the union among you, that we might commence a definite campaign to promote union here.   I have never yet said to any one on earth what I now, in strict confidence, say to you.   It was the hope that I might hold up Australian Methodism as a model and an encouragement to British Methodism that has added a special element of distress to my disappointment in being unable to visit you at present.   Perhaps God may hereafter give me another opportunity.   Many years ago, the late Dr. George of Chicago, the founder of the Œcumenical Conference, implored me to devote my life to the promotion of Methodist union.   I received that thought from him as a Divine charge, and have always cherished it in my heart.   I now mention the fact to you, as I have said, in strict confidence.   I do not think that anything would be gained by giving definite publicity to this hope now; but I think the time may come in a few years, and I shall be unspeakably thankful to God if I can do anything here at all proportionate to the splendid work you have done in the New World.—I am, yours very sincerely,

"H. PRICE HUGHES."

"The Rev. W. H. Fitchett, B.A."

"HAWTHORN, *March* 18, 1903.

"DEAR MRS. PRICE HUGHES,—I enclose the last letter I received from Mr. Hughes.   It is a remarkable letter, and may be of use in the biography which is to be written. . . . Though the letter is written confidentially, I thought that death had cancelled the seal of confidence.   I told the Conference, what I believed profoundly, that not since John Wesley died has the Methodist Church possessed a man who was a more perfect embodiment of the central and imperishable characteristics of Methodism than your husband.   Thank God for his memory and work!

"Let me add how deeply the few lines you were good enough to write me have touched me.   Yes, his death is one of God's mysteries, of which only God keeps the key.   But there is no mistake, and no defeat, and no failure.   When we see it all in the light and perspective of eternity, see it as God sees it, it will be well.   Meanwhile may God wonderfully sustain and comfort you.—Yours ever,

"W. H. FITCHETT."

[1]"DE PAUW UNIVERSITY, GREENCASTLE, INDIANA,
"*Nov.* 24, 1902.

" . . . By the kindness of our mutual friend, ——, I wish to send you an expression of my deep sympathy with you in your unspeakable sorrow over the sudden departure of your great and good father. I never had the pleasure of meeting him in person, but I have read so much of his writing and I have learned so much about his wonderful work in London, that I feel that I knew him well, and I loved him heartily. I think, beyond all doubt, that he was the greatest man in all Methodism in the opening of the twentieth century. Such energy, such deep enthusiasm, and at the same time so well balanced with superior discretion. Surely he lives on in a higher sphere, and doubtless has taken rank already among the spirits of the just and the glorified, and some undertakings congenial to his nature still reward him and bless him for the mighty deeds of his earthly life. . . .—Very cordially,

"H. A. GOBIN."

Dr. Rigg, at the Conference after my father's death, paid a personal tribute to what after many years of observation in the public life of Methodism he discerned to be the inner nature of the man. Mr. Watkinson noted my father's sacrifice of scholarly ambition, when others talked only of his activities.[2] The greatest tribute ever paid him was that given in private by a Methodist bishop, for though he was not accorded the insignia of his office and went by a somewhat humbler title, he understood that inner discipline and that width of outlook which my father would have defined as episcopal. He had been talking of many things, and in particular of a certain day years ago when Hugh Price Hughes undertook to pilot his fellow-students to a church steeple which he thought it advisable for them to ascend.

"As we were coming down the ladder he was behind me," said the speaker, "and he was at me all the time. 'Go on, my dear sir, go on. Can't you perceive the hurry of the brethren

---

[1] Written to a member of the family at the time of my father's death.

[2] *Wesleyan Methodist Magazine*, January 1903. To converse with understanding opponents was often a peculiar pleasure. They saw the natural man as followers sometimes failed to do.

behind.' But what with fear of laughing and giddiness, it was impossible to move on. There was I, like grim death, hanging on to the ladder, and he treading on my hands all the time.

"'My good sir,' said he, 'this is the pace of a tortoise, not of a Christian.'

"'No Christian,' said I, 'should be expected to come down such a ladder.'"

Afterwards they had parted, for one went to India as a missionary and laboured many years against great odds. From time to time, also, they disagreed, and very strongly, though the speaker smiled more than once as he recalled past days. "What did Hugh Price Hughes do for Methodism?" asked his listener. "Ah," he said, and drew himself up as if to reflect. When he answered it was after some time, and it sounded like a prayer: "Jabez Bunting gave us our Constitution and laid the foundations of future progress. Hugh Price Hughes spiritualised us."

"HUNTLY, BISHOPSTEIGNTON,
            "*Jan.* 13, 1901.

"DEAR MR. WYNNE-JONES,—As I explained in a previous letter, I am unable, to my great regret, to be in London when Dr. Rigg receives from his brethren a unique but richly deserved tribute of esteem and gratitude. I am thankful, however, to have the opportunity of associating myself most heartily with what is about to be done. God has given us a succession of three very eminent men—Dr. Bunting, Dr. Osborn, and Dr. Rigg—who during the last century preserved the continuity and distinctive features of Wesleyan Methodism. Some of us have tried, in successive generations, to induce these three great ecclesiastical leaders to move a little faster with the times. But I, at any rate, fully realise the necessity for those conservative influences which have brought it to pass that desirable reforms are now being effected with practical unanimity and general goodwill. Dr. Rigg's erudition and long experience have always illuminated every subject he has discussed; and those who, like myself, have often differed from him, are, none the less, under great obligations to him for reliable information and wise counsel. Above all, I am deeply grateful to Dr. Rigg for the courage and energy with which he has invariably supported every proposal and every movement which has tended to deepen the spirituality and to promote the aggressive and missionary work of Wesleyan Methodism.

"I have greatly regretted the fact that Dr. Rigg has not written a life of John Wesley. I fear it is now too late to urge that great task upon him, but if I could have been with my brethren at the luncheon, I would have availed myself of that genial hour to try to extract from Dr. Rigg a promise that he would render to Methodism one other great service by writing an autobiography. He is the last link with a great age. No one else can ever tell us many things about the Methodism of the nineteenth century which Dr. Rigg *remembers*. He really ought not to take with him to heaven (on, I trust, the yet distant day when he is summoned there) the treasures of Methodist knowledge which he has accumulated during his most influential and illustrious career. Will my brethren kindly second this proposal of mine?——Yours very sincerely,

"HUGH PRICE HUGHES.

"Rev. T. Wynne-Jones."

[1] "HAZELWOOD HYDRO., GRANGE-OVER-SANDS,
"Nov. 20, 1902.

"MY DEAR MRS. HUGHES,——I scarcely know how to write you. To the fullest extent I share your sorrow. My sense of personal bereavement is intense and depressing, and public life can never be the same to me without your dear husband. No one, I think, understood him better than I did——no one more thoroughly appreciated and loved him. It was our good fortune to think alike on most subjects, and when we differed in opinion no cloud of misunderstanding ever came even for a moment between us. The memory of our intercourse will be a benediction and an inspiration as long as I live, and an additional burden will be felt by me in all public and Church work without his strength and help to fall back upon.

"I was hoping he might be spared to wield at a different stage of life an influence somewhat different, but quite as much needed and as valuable as this influence of his youth and manhood. God has willed it otherwise, and we can only

[1] Written to my mother at the time of my father's death.

silently submit and wait through the night of sorrow for the full revelation—until the day dawns and the shadows flee away.

" His life and work have marked an epoch in the progress of Methodism. His influence will be a tradition that cannot die. Others will feel its power and its spell for many years to come. The chapter in our history he has opened will not be closed by his removal, and in the years to come he will be seen to be greater even than the most of his contemporaries have felt him to be. Much as we should have liked to keep him, we cannot fail to see that the vigour, intensity, and enthusiasm that have prematurely worn him out have helped him to accomplish in the years spent on earth vastly more than most men can hope to do with the longest life.

.   .   .   .

" Yours very truly,
                    " HENRY J. POPE."

CHAPTER XX

THE IMPERIAL IDEA OF THE STATE

"A foolish consistency is the hobgoblin of little minds, adored by little statesmen and philosophers and divines. With consistency a great soul has simply nothing to do. He may as well concern himself with his shadow on the wall. Out upon your guarded lips! Sew them up with packthread, do. Else, if you would be a man, speak what you think to-day in words as hard as cannon balls, and to-morrow speak what to-morrow thinks in hard words again, though it contradict everything you said to-day. Ah! then exclaim the aged ladies, you shall be sure to be misunderstood. Misunderstood! It is a right fool's word." EMERSON.

THAT the ethics and politics of 8 Taviton Street should ever win the general approval, had never entered the imaginings of its occupants. Yet the victories of my father's chivalry as well as the weight of his ecclesiastical counsels had left their impress on large portions of the public mind, not escaping that most devoted to the worship of the Conventions. The goddess who rules these is exceedingly ancient, and large-hearted at the core, and no opinion is really offensive to her. If it be maintained long and effectively by a strong man, she will give him her benison like the rest, as the family perceived during the last two or three years of the century. There seemed to be a general rubbing of the eyes in the Church and out of it. "This man is not so bad surely as we thought? What strength and ability he has! We must look into it!" Then at the outbreak of the great Boer War, when many looked upon him with hope and many with anxiety, he nonplussed the general expectation and showed himself an Imperialist, and a supporter of what he regarded an inevitable conflict. Doubt turned into certainty on the part of several, and in their exuberance titles were accorded his name which the university had not bestowed upon it.

" And how is Dr. Price Hughes ? " has been asked by one who knew of him vaguely as a wise man. " I am so glad your father is so sensible on this matter—he is doing any amount of good." " How very clever and far-seeing your father is! I have been so interested in reading his articles." Even when the commendation was more measured, it was kindly. " I must say that I was surprised to see the side your father took, but I was very glad—very." The elders and fathers in Methodism, the missionaries, many of the ministry and his opponents in politics, smiled all over while they wondered. They had all taken a deep breath at the outset, not knowing exactly what was going to happen ; but now they resigned themselves to thanksgiving. Certain could have sworn that he would have split Methodism, exerting his influence over sections of the populace in a most disastrous manner. But, lo and behold! he was in their portion of the field charging from it in fine style, and while they exchanged smiles it was difficult to refrain from the stifled jubilate. Those who had been threatened with something resembling apoplexy, when they read former notes of the *Methodist Times*, now clasped that journal to their bosom. One Conservative gentleman related that, after hearing a Methodist minister speak in public on behalf of the Boers and against the British, he went up to him and shook the *Methodist Times* in his face. " Now, just you see what your chief says—read it when you get home, and for God's sake don't talk like that again." The reply of the minister, who must, and with reason, have been thoroughly indignant, was not repeated.

In all kinds of unexpected places the world over, the name of the great advocate of peace received the military and the popular approval. Never in the general estimation was his place surer or his abilities more highly estimated. Yet never, on the other hand, except in the Missionary controversy which was confined to Methodism, was he more bitterly attacked, and his name held up to greater opprobrium. That regiment, which he as much as any man had helped to train and to lead, turned from him with anger and dismay. Fidus Achates was writing to him from all parts of the country and the world, just as he himself might have done to a lost leader when he was a young man at Dover. The very phraseology that they used in places was his, and the sentiments as he read them appeared excellent, reflecting the greatest credit on the writers. He wrote brief and careful replies, but nothing that he wrote or said could account for his transformation—the desertion to the opposite ranks, for so it appeared to them. Year after year since he had first awakened them to life, they had read and smiled, criticised and gloried over the *Methodist Times*, and now it smote them in the face, like an east wind in a world which was upside down. " He should have died," some of them said ; " I would rather be reading of his funeral than what he's got to say to-day."

The fact that many members of the Liberal party and the most humane of the Christian ministry were of my father's way of thinking, did not in the least affect them or give them the clue to his attitude. Love of war, blindness, and greed of gold were the very elements of human nature, and they had seen the best men of their time yield to one or the other—but not Hugh Price Hughes. Not that most men by any means held such an explanation of his conduct, but he classed himself with the general ruck, which came to the same thing. Whether, he really had surrendered to the power of darkness, or whether with an innocence in keeping with that of a babe unborn, he had allowed himself to become the tool of the crafty, was a matter of doubt with them. His simplicity, remembered of old, revealed itself in that brief letter which did not exonerate him. Yet he was a perfect general, in the notes using all the old craft and strategy on the wrong side. Not only the Boers were under a delusion, but all their supporters. He sympathised with their sentiments, admired them, but was grieved that a confirmed prejudice against their country should lead excellent men into such violence and uncharitableness towards those whose views differed from theirs.

Then he began to explain the reason why he differed, which Fidus Achates sometimes in his rage did not care to read. He said, " I won't take the *Methodist Times* in any more. I have done with it and him for ever." Many like unto Achates— in that they acknowledged my father as their leader, though their knowledge of him had never been an intimate one— experienced varying emotions of astonishment. Without forgetting any of their respect for his character, they could not explain or understand its latest aspect. Some of the missioners, including his colleagues, were found among this number; and though their intimacy with him was too great to permit any cooling of it, they disagreed with him, however unobtrusive they might be with respect to their opinions. His Imperialism, even more than his ecclesiastical labours, lay outside their knowledge of him. To the missioners he was the inspired leader who led them to battle against the evil and poverty and despair of London, and who in private life talked to them of spiritual things which meant most things, and whose genial presence was too rarely seen these latter days, to make anything like divergence with it desirable.

There was too much of immediate moment to talk about without entering this dubious region of the war and Imperialism. In the dark December of 1899, when all hearts sank low, whatever their sympathies, it was pleasant to sit and listen to him amid the defeats of the forces and the general blackness of the horizon. " It always has been so," he said ; " this country has never been prepared,"—but like everybody else, he was vastly surprised. In the previous August he had assured his friend, the Baroness von Langenau, that the British force, on their arrival, would settle the whole matter in a few weeks, and the Baroness had utterly disbelieved him. At times of disaster and uncertainty and low spirits, many liked to be near him. His presence was the restorative. Nor had they any need of word of his mouth to feel its invigorating power. Belief and faith were his emanation, and to be in the room with him was to imbibe these. On some his effect was particularly marked. " Often I have gone into his study," said a young colleague, " exhausted in body, not to speak of depression, and the bracing effect of his personality on me was so extraordinary that I have stepped out into the street with glowing frame and new vigour. It was not only his effect on the mood and outlook of my mind, it was the communication of new strength to my limbs, and of zest to the flow of the blood through my veins."

When after weary months of anxiety and waiting a member of the family ran up into the study exclaiming, " Ladysmith is relieved! they are shouting it in the street!" he cried, " You don't mean it ! "—then when he was satisfied

35

of the truth, " Thank God! Thank God!" His joy was solemn and religious, as that which had greeted the return of the busybodies and the milk-livered to the County Council. To the ends of the world the bells of this glorious victory were pealing forth, and on every shore over which the eye of his mind roved, he saw the British peoples thanking God with him. For years he had been leading up to the present position, suppressing his instincts in the matter, just because he shared in many of the sentiments of the pro-Boers.

Long before he openly advocated Imperialism he was struggling with conclusions that he found it difficult to avoid. The struggle first assumed serious proportions at the time of the British occupation of Egypt. " France," he would say, " is enraged because we have not kept our word and evacuated the country." " Did we say we would do so?" a listener would inquire. " Well, I am afraid we did." Here a curious stillness would descend upon him, that fine equilibrium which belongs to the victim of two totally divergent forces equal in magnitude. " Unforeseen circumstances have arisen which made our evacuation impossible, disastrous for the country. We have undoubtedly conferred great benefits by our sojourn, —but poor France is mad with us. It is difficult to see how it could have been avoided—very difficult." Then came a long pause. " I do not see how we could have left her. It's a strange business the whole thing." In Brixton days when General Gordon, Gladstone, and Khartoum were the one topic of general conversation, he was curiously silent. The soldier who divided his time between saying his prayers and the profession of the sword, had a curious fascination for this upholder of chivalry, and he would always closely question those who had any special knowledge of him. His operations in China particularly interested him. There he was, putting all right, insisting on justice and mercy, and not asking a penny in return. During the last months of his life he was reading a *Life of Gordon*, and when his companion read how Gordon refused a large sum of money that the Emperor offered him, his ecstasy knew no bounds. A suffering frame again spent itself in that laughter which was his familiar. Here was Christianity indeed, undefiled and unmistakable. " Read it again!" he cried. " Fancy taking a decree and writing on the back of it. A general writing on the back of an Imperial decree, that he did not want any of the money an Emperor offered, and then sending it back to him!" Then to his companion, "Show me the book. I think you have made up that sentence about writing on the back of it."

Most of his great joys and sorrows were of an Imperial character, *i.e.* they did not affect him personally. He was for ever exulting and grieving over acts done and words written by those who were far away from him, and who did not know of his existence. He seemed linked, not only to the contemporary living, but to past personages, and those who were to come. Their agonies seemed to have entered his soul, and often he appeared to be participating in the better fortune of new eras. At Brixton, where the general criticism called forth loyalty to Mr. Gladstone and the Cabinet, into whose difficulties and point of view he entered, he none the less felt sick at heart at each delay. "One day too late— Oh, awful!" he would exclaim during that well-remembered reading—"Just one day too late. If he had been alive now he would have managed that South African business for us. It is the greatest possible disaster that we lack his services."

The South African continent was also largely responsible for my father's Imperialism. He could not but perceive that during the last twenty years it had been delivered, as countries are delivered, into the hands of the European peoples,—*i.e.* groups of these, whether they ought to or no, rushed in and annexed it. "There's a barbaric simplicity about the thing," he remarked; "you get up at four o'clock in the morning, arm yourself to the teeth, and run for your life, so as to get there before any other fellow. You then annex as you go, and if anybody interferes you shoot him." France and Germany had rushed in before the English people were sufficiently alive to what was going on. "Why were not we alive?" was the usual solemn interrogation. He shook his head and refused a response. When questioned concerning the evacuation of the Transvaal in 1881, he replied, "Mr. Gladstone made a noble mistake. Our ships were on the high seas, and the country would have been in our hands—without this agony and bloodshed. Mr. Gladstone did not foresee what would happen, and this act of self-suppression on his part—of deliberately abstaining from pressing an advantage on a foe who would have been helpless, is one of the noblest and most humane in modern history. The Boers in their ignorance have not the wildest idea of our resources—not the wildest. It has been a history of accidents. Majuba Hill was an accident." (Then came a description of the battle.) "One minute more and we should have captured the whole position. The Jameson raid gave us away hopelessly. That was the worst incident of the whole chapter."

His wrath at the Jameson raid, vented both in his conversation and the Journal, made his advocacy of the war which followed it the more inconsistent in the eyes of many. Fierce and swift were his emotions of the first few days of the year 1896, as details of the disastrous fight at Dornkop leaked out bit by bit to an astonished public. "The rascals," was one of his first exclamations, "cannot even fight. I expect they were in liquor at the time. As it is they have not only sinned against the etiquette of nations, they have disgraced us in the eyes of the world. In their wine and lawlessness they think themselves free to trample on any considerations of honour so that they may satisfy their glut for land and diamonds, yet, when it comes to the point, they cannot even fight." Certain listeners felt strong disapprobation, for the case to their thinking was not fairly stated. The German Emperor's telegram of condolence to President Kruger left him muttering. "It's like his impertinence," he said, "a youth to write and congratulate President Kruger on the failure of an expedition for which the British people are not responsible!"

As he warmed to his theme in Taviton Street, the audience listened with distinct approbation, for it was felt to be fairly stated. The "wine-bibbers," however, were not forgotten, for my mother, on joining him a day or two after in Devonshire, was charged with the following message, "Tell him that he may be glad to hear that the wine-bibbers fought —hours on end—and died fighting." There was no other message, and it was received in admiring silence. Dramatically, it was appealing, and he knew in what rage and joy it had been despatched. Besides, the joy was reciprocal, though he did not choose to own this, for no one had more duly and copiously imbibed the details in the morning papers than he had.

Later, when he had gleaned further information on the matter, he still spoke very strongly concerning Dr. Jameson's raid, which betrayed, so he and others considered, the just insurrection of the Johannesburg Uitlanders. Yet the ill-fated expedition did not assume in his eyes the significance and moment that it did in the eyes of many of his fellow-countrymen. It was one of those disasters that gave away and prejudiced a cause, but he was so accustomed to these and their results, from personal experience, that he was quite prepared for the indelible impression that it produced on the minds of the Continent and many of his fellow-countrymen. There was no more inconsistency in his denunciation of the raid, and his vindication of the war, than his opposition to the Temperance extremists, while he was an ardent advocate of Temperance reform.

The silent, subconscious process for ever observing facts and drawing conclusions, which led to the conviction that British rule was the best thing that could happen in this world to the dark races, was strengthened in a twofold manner. First, by his own visits to the Continent, and second, by a greater understanding of the English people, and their methods of government, which filled him with admiration, Ireland always excepted. For all his enjoyment of the insight into past history and art which these visits afforded, he was never in love with foreign Governments, and the régime and conveniences that they afforded to those living under them. Dr. Johnson himself could not have been more squarely British : "rags of newspapers—hideous system of luggage—engines puffing wretched smoke—no idea of personal liberty, still less of governing—ecclesiastical Protestantism in a wretched condition—the Pope everywhere producing bitter reaction against the Christian religion—and a general incapacity to manage people's own affairs, let alone those of others." Charms other nations had undoubtedly, he said, good points in which English people might well follow. They were more artistic, for instance, and amiable than we were — but oh for our Divine practicability—a British policeman who could regulate the traffic and point out the way !

He was never away from British Government but he sighed for it, and eagerly acclaimed his return to its enchanted area.   On returning from his tour in the Eastern Mediterranean in 1900, he said, " I have seen many fair and wonderful sights, but the fairest and most wonderful of all was a grinning Tommy Atkins at Alexandria.   I sighted him as our vessel was approaching the shore—grinning for all he was worth, and my heart leapt up at him.   Oh, my God, the wretched Egyptians have at last attained something approaching happiness in this world!   Everywhere, justice and the Pax Britannica.   The very donkey boys were full of it. They said to me, ' Wonderful! wonderful! a donkey boy and a cadi equal before the law!   Wonderful, wonderful!'   The Englishman, you see, in spite of his slowness, has grasped something of justice, and, being a bull-dog, does not let it go. Oh! it is marvellous—look at India and all these fellows. Peace at last after centuries, and the princes and potentates stopped from cutting each other's throats, and something like decent civilisation."   He had so much to say that he was breathless, and even then he could not say it all!   His mind, in its rovings and gleanings, saw the pioneers and bridge-builders and civilisers.   They were part of the vast landscape which he sighted at this time, and he could not put into words all that he beheld in it—the vistas that it contained to him. By forcible English, by humorous exaggeration, he tried to bring a little of it home to those around him, but he knew it was a difficult matter for those who had not exercised their imaginations in that particular direction, and he did not suppose for an instant that it was possible to convince them.   If the British also did not assert themselves in Africa, the Dutch or somebody else would do so, introducing their imperfect ideas of justice and government.

Therefore the spectacle of the barbarians at play at four o'clock in the morning did not upset him so much as it did some others.   At the worst they were somewhat tarnished pawns on the Divine Chessboard, the marble goddess of the conventions herself, moving from square to square as the Divine Finger dictated.   For all his active resistance to evil —the essential part he conceived of a Christian's duty in this world—he became increasingly convinced of a Divine overruling—of immense purposes in the history of the race, a conviction which his wide, various, and constant reading only tended to deepen. The gradual founding of our Empire —not of design, but by a certain impelling necessity—was not the least of that historical gleaning and reminiscence in which he delighted.

He had restrained delight in the most martial of our heroes. The coolness of the British Bull-Dog, his pluck and endurance, and the modest and unassuming way he performed feats that would make a Frenchman's hair stand on end, produced a certain elation. Quite his favourite incident was that of the British general, who, riding with his force to reduce a rebel town, could not resist the temptation of a particularly good mount to canter on ahead. Arriving at the gates of the town before his force were even in sight, he demanded its submission. The inhabitants, who were armed to the teeth, promptly refused. "Oh! very well," replied the general, "we must wait a little"; so, taking his umbrella and feeling for his pipe, he sat himself on the shadiest spot he could find in the vicinity, and awaited the arrival of his troops. The rebels, peering from their artillery at the figure smoking under an umbrella just outside their walls, were so over-awed and nonplussed at the extraordinary nature of the spectacle—the apparently invulnerable god waiting for his allies—that they capitulated before the British force arrived. Such a bloodless ending, due entirely to commanding personality, was naturally very delightful to my father, and he felt there was no need to restrain his instinctive joy in the matter, as he was so often obliged to do. It was his taking to Imperialism and its military necessities, as to the manner born, that so enraged certain of his opponents. If they could have felt him less at home they would not have minded so much. They overlooked the fact that he was restraining instinct with an iron hand—suppressing not encouraging the dictates of nature. Yet certain instincts of the blood will out somehow, grace refusing to tamper with their primitive intensity; and this democratic leader showed himself a British Imperialist to the finger tips, regarding the world, so it sometimes seemed, with the same imperious eye as the typical travelled Englishman of the period.

While the outbreak of the war in South Africa may be regarded as the inevitable and terrible climax of a long race struggle, at home it was a flashlight on the trend of a man's political thinking. The Imperialistic idea, common enough in certain circles, became the possession of the multitude, and each individual seemed to decide concerning the rights and wrongs of the war according to his acceptance or rejection of an Imperial mission of the race. A silent conclusion, long fostered in subconscious regions, became part of the political creed of many pronounced and intelligent Liberals. In great questions agitating the public mind, one is tempted to imagine that people first arrive at their conclusions and then find facts to justify them. Nothing proves to be more elastic than data, more accommodating than figures. All Little Englanders thought the war unjustified; all Imperialists thought it forced upon them, and my father among the number. He believed President Kruger and his oligarchy had been meditating and planning the overthrow of British rule in South Africa for years, and he felt bound to uphold the legislature which recognised the coloured races and had grasped something of tolerance and justice.

His Imperialism, like everything else, was part of his religion, and having accepted its application in the State as well as the Church, it was astonishing how every day and hour of the day added fuel to the fire of it. Opponents in an argument often wondered why so much that happened in the world proved his convictions. Having once after a silent subconscious process declared a belief in anything, he grew daily a more passionate and convinced believer. Time did not suggest queries; it dispersed them until a fresh revelation (and his landscape was always enlarging, not contracting) made him appear inconsistent to the earlier one. Looking back, I doubt whether he may ever be described as possessing a conviction or a belief; they possessed him, and that was why he was so successful in imparting them.

The writer is reminded of a cycle ride a year before my father died, when this possession by religious Imperialism may be said to have been nearing its zenith. By this time it could not be called British—it was Anglo-Saxon. Lord Rosebery was the exponent whom he most favoured, and he greeted, like his Lordship, a day when the British Parliament should steam across the Atlantic to join the Federated Imperial Assembly at Washington—that assembly which should uphold the Pax Britannica and put an end to bloodshed and anarchy. When his opponents said, " You, an advocate of peace and a member of the Peace Society, uphold this iniquity ? " he thought, " Yes, indeed, and a vaster Peace Society than you wot of, my dear brother. Our Society ranges the earth, and sends men to their deaths so that thousands unborn may have some chance of enjoying what you and I do." This Peace Society, moreover, was distinctly Teutonic in character and friendly to the Teutonic peoples, because these had accepted the principles of the Reformation. Here it was that the ecclesiastic stepped in and kept pace with the statesman, and the two being Imperialist to the core and believing in federation as the best and only means of attaining unity and concord, kept up a most harmonious duet, each supporting the other to a degree which, unless a person heard it, he would not have believed possible.

The causes of the war which his opponents took pains to bring home to him did not appear to him the true causes at all.[1] They were the accidents leading to the inevitable struggle. Neither again did the sins and errors of the British—of which he surely as much as any man was aware—including the affair of the raid, obscure to his eyes the good ground which underlay all the tangle and muddle on the surface, just as in his dealings with individuals he often saw their aspirations and better self rather than the tangle and the mud which struck other people.

His conviction of the inherent justice of the British cause was due as much as anything to the reports of the Methodist missionaries on the spot. It was hinted by more than one source that " Uitlander " relatives were to blame for his " shocking conversion," but he was in communication with missionaries before he saw and talked with relatives at all. He often said to the writer, " The missionaries say " this and that and the other, " and the missionaries support the British."

[1] Mr. E. T. Cook's *Rights and Wrongs of the Transvaal War* influenced him more than anything so far as written matter was concerned, as did Mr. Fitzpatrick's *Transvaal from Within*.

When opponents raged to him concerning the million-aires, who, in their eyes, were the prime instigators and causes of the war, he would reply with the great gentleness that he always displayed towards this class of opponent, " But, indeed, you are mistaken. The country is not peopled by millionaires. I know of good Methodist miners and any number of humble persons, who resent the injustice of the present intolerable régime as much as you or I would if we happened to be living there. Englishmen really cannot stand this kind of thing, and I don't see how we can expect them to. Look at this letter from an excellent citizen in Johannesburg which I received this morning." The " millionaire," to my father's thinking, unduly occupied the minds of his opponents. Like the Czar of Russia and the Emperor of Germany, they were but grasshoppers before the scythe of the Eternal Designs.

"Don't you see," an opponent would exclaim to him in all the rage of love, " that you are yoked to the gilded car of the millionaires, and that they are just driving you wherever they please? Don't you perceive that they are thanking their stars that they have muzzled you, and that the party which you have always led hitherto lacks your leadership?" "Which party?" he would interrupt. "Your metaphor in its zeal confuses me. I am still pondering over that glorious vision of the gilded car." "Why the party that has some regard for truth and justice and national righteous-ness, that regards God before the fear of man, and considers its duty to its neighbour as well as the scraping together of all the money it can lay its hands on." "And that party, you say, is now ruling all things?" my father would inquire. "Of course! It is dragging us after its chariot wheels into the most disastrous war since the Crimea, including advocates of peace like yourself. I have lived to see a good deal in my time, but I never expected to witness this disastrous regression."

"Do sit down" would be the answer.

He felt a great compassion for the speaker. As he said to the writer once, "I really am sorry for So-and-so and So-and-so. They think that justice and righteousness are absolutely in abeyance, and that money and selfishness are everywhere securing their own ends. Terrible for them, is it not? Thinking as they do, I cannot wonder at the darkness in which they find themselves. Kruger and his oligarchy are a species of helpless saint, and we are preying upon them in the time-honoured manner." Compassion gave way to thanksgiving as the seated opponent drew pictures of the scramble for new territory, particularly where there was a suspicion of diamond mines. "Awful!" my father would exclaim, his thought drawing a picture of the probable state of the country if Dutch, French, and German barbarians had been allowed to play unchecked by British rule and public opinion at home.

He was always dreaming of the peoples everywhere, and never more so than when he became a pronounced Imperialist and meditated concerning the Pax Britannica, which should protect them. At last the disciplining of the ruling castes would enable them to emerge into some freedom, some hope. As he listened to opponents, he seemed to be looking at many pictures and they at one. Why was it impossible, he wondered, for men to conceive of the British régime as a liberating one? There was Kitchener now in Northern Africa, spending eleven years in teaching Egyptians to ride and not to fear Dervishes. Eleven years ago, when an Egyptian saw a Dervish, he knelt down and prepared to have his throat cut. Now there was a chance for him, and none at all for the Dervishes. Just to think of it—teaching timid fellows to charge and fight on horseback against Dervishes—fellows who could not even sit in the saddle like a soldier when Kitchener first went out there! Quotations from the prophets and the New Testament on the part of a correspondent filled him with exultation. What foreign country was there that could boast such a religious public, so conversant with Holy Scripture, so intent on keeping barbarians and millionaires in their right place? Would France or Germany have allowed or harboured for an instant the intensely religious and noble demonstrations that were flourishing in the British midst? Then when writers went on to tell him that he as much as any man had trained them in their convictions, it was impossible to restrain a certain glow of satisfaction, just as Kitchener, when he looked at his Egyptian cavalry, must have felt that he had done something towards training the forces of the Empire and establishing the Pax Britannica.

Two things in particular, to my father's surprise, angered his opponents. The first was, that he evidently conceived of the Empire's forces—civil and military—as a gigantic mission, which was absurd. What the British Government wanted was a railway from Cape Town to Cairo—no nonsense about this civilising and humanising force. Well, such a railway, my father said, would greatly facilitate the " gigantic mission," and he was quite sure that no foreigner could build a railroad like the British,—they could do many things better than we, but not railroads. He had had experience of them. Africa could not escape railways any more than Europe, and for his part he liked to think of the British building them. " Oh, but it is dangerous," they would burst out; " this theory of yours that the British are to spread humane and democratic institutions, and are therefore morally justified in going wherever the Government wants them to go." " I never said that," he would interrupt. " You know my reasons for supporting an inevitable and defensive war. The British can no more leave Africa, with honour, to the Dutch and the foreigner, than we could leave Egypt and the wretched Egyptians to the Dervishes. I really cannot see your objection to conceiving of the British Empire as a humanising and civilising force."

" Oh, it is because they are all laughing up their sleeve at you."

" They may laugh up their sleeve till they are black in the face," my father would reply, " but if God chooses to make use of the British people in their sin and ignorance as instruments of His will, their laughing cannot much affect matters."

Another suspicion which made opponents very angry was that he conceived of an Imperial Anglo-Saxon Federation, with Methodism, a not inconsiderable factor in the religious life of each of its constituent states. Such a very innocent dream it seemed to him. Methodists never proselytised, were true to the principles of the Reformation and the necessities of an Imperial ecclesiastical organisation. He liked to think that Methodists had never persecuted their co-religionists, and informed his children of the same in a very emphatic manner. A pause revealed him struggling with a smile, and it was with a truly benign countenance that he added, " They have never had the opportunity." He was not sure that even Methodists could beat down the spirit of sectarianism and the lack of charity which was the curse of Christ's Church. Imperial Methodism undoubtedly, to his thinking, was curiously suited to the British Empire, but he was really not to blame for the suitability. If a person has two mental conceptions that fit into one another and answer each other's necessities, the conceiver is scarcely responsible for their homogeneity. The Christian citizen, having clearly conceived of a Federation which should benefit the race, could scarcely refrain from shaking hands with the militant ecclesiastic who, in his dreams of a Federated Christendom, was inclined to assign a leading rôle to his own communion.

In the notes of the *Methodist Times* he made clear that he supported the British on the following issues:—Firstly, That he believed the régime of Kruger to be reactionary, and opposed to those principles of liberal self-government which all the Anglo-Saxon nations had adopted. Secondly, He was convinced that the rule of the Boer meant licence for the drink traffic. Thirdly, He held that under the Boer the natives were in a condition of practical slavery, having no right to own land.

While many of his former friends and supporters were strongly and sometimes bitterly opposed to him on this issue, certain whose opinion and judgment he greatly respected felt with him, including Mrs. Josephine Butler, and persons as closely connected with the Mission and his political opinions as Mr. Percy Bunting, and many in the Christian ministry, at home and abroad. The depth of the resentment and dismay that his attitude towards the war excited among a large wing of his former adherents, may be traced perhaps to what they felt to be a new attitude on his part with regard to the workaday world. Some never could connect his Imperialistic dreamings with the passionate utterances of former years respecting war and its accompaniments. He himself saw no inconsistency, because he said with truth that while he respected the Quaker attitude he had never accepted it. None the less it was possible that his critics divined a change in tactic, of which he himself was scarcely conscious. He knew perfectly, as he listened to their most able exponents, that they were one at heart, each desirous of bringing about the day, when, to quote

one of his favourite sayings from Isaiah, " Sorrow and sighing
shall flee away," and when, to quote the Psalmist, " The voice
of complaining shall be heard no more in the streets."

But there was the usual bridge between him and so many
of his followers.   They wanted the whole loaf or nothing, and
he was willing for the half-a-slice if it came to that matter.
Always, they said, " He leads us to compromise and to one-
quarter of what he said he would."   Was this his last great
compromise with the world as it is, for the sake of that
practical effectiveness which was his supreme instinct?   For
years he had said, " How awful is the present state of affairs—
this European concert!   All of us armed to the teeth, all of
us clutching at everything we can get.   Militarism everywhere
blotting out the very sunshine that God sends upon the earth."
It was in his anti-militarism that he defied, as it were, the
very constitution of the world.   The marble goddess of conventionality might have forgiven him every other delinquency
but this one.   The dawn of the twentieth century witnessed
not what eager spirits a century ago had ardently dreamed,
and in whose dreams he, as a young man, had shared, but the
division of the world between highly equipped military powers
hourly on the alert and the defensive.

The gallant craft was not to finish its voyage before
resolutely breasting an ingathering tide.   Whence such come
and whither they lead, the prevailing darkness hides from the
view, but good men believe them to be of God.   Amid the
waste of wind and waters they hear His voice, and venture
where more timid crafts essay to plunge.   The Pilot whom
faith discerns they supplicate with tears.   " Not in such whirl-
pools, Master, was our craft built to plunge," and still with
bleeding hand He points to an invisible dawn.   'Tis the last
trial, and some it cannot break.   " Yea, Master," such reply,
" Thou art here, and that is sufficient for me."

If, indeed, such a compromise with the actual, as opposed
to the ideal, did actually occur, it but reveals fresh depths
of my father's faith, the greatest perhaps of his career.   Who
can imagine the unspeakable discipline of pioneers eking out
their existence on crumbs, and thanking God every morning
for His bounty; or of the general who seeing the extent of
the hosts sends his own regiment into their midst, saying,

"I have long beheld their work and much of it is good. Help to make it better." Men's course and fate, in Shakespeare's conception, is said to lie in the constituent elements of their character, and my father simply had not it in him to play the rôle of a Cato. It was too unpractical. If Cato instead of falling on his sword at Utica, in which the poets of antiquity so delighted, had survived, say, to found an order in Imperial Rome which should be an example to her citizens of Republican high living and austerity, it would have been far more effective, to my father's thinking, than falling upon his sword and thus depriving the empire of a most excellent citizen. One speaking to him once of Cicero, brimful of the humanity of his letters rather than the wisdom of his politics, was surprised by the following: "What a fool the fellow was." "Why?" "Oh, for not falling into line with Cæsar! He should have seen that was the only alternative, and how things must fall out." Another time he would say, "One empire after another developing, and then spreading its civilisation, has been the history of the world so far. You and I may not like it, but there it is. None of them can approach the British, and I don't suppose you realise in what a wonderful state of things you are living. Dominion after dominion has come—often without any deliberate effort on our part—into our possession. There has been nothing like it since the beginning of the world, and wherever we go there is the establishment of order and some kind of justice."

His mind became so possessed with these brighter aspects of Imperialism that it induced him sometimes to adopt a standpoint which must have amused friends as well as opponents. He was like one intent on reminding the nation of the ideal aspect of its mission. There were plenty to talk about the other aspects, and there was a danger in the pride and pomp and glare attending Imperial and material expansion, to forget that aspect on which he as a Christian minister insisted. So, while some shrugged and others raged, he charged oblivious of it all, caring supremely for what he would have termed "the soul of the empire," just as he cared supremely for the souls of her citizens. His method of aiding the life of the soul was by reminding men of its existence, and by writing in the Journal as if they were as anxious about it as he was.

At first some found this to be annoying, but as he was so persistent in thus regarding them it came to impress them in the end.

Readers were stirred to varying emotion by the editorial notes in the year 1900. Despite what the British at home regarded as decisive victories, the enemy were evidently bent on continuing a desperate resistance, a resolution which the editor deplored. The enemy had fought gallantly, he intimated, and had shown their strength, so that their opponents must always respect and admire them. Why prolong the inevitable sacrificing of precious lives on both sides, when there was only one ending to the present struggle? Capitulation at the right moment was the wisdom of gallantry to a foe like the British. Indeed, there was a certain tone of annoyance, as if expostulating with those who deliberately rejected benevolent intentions. Even the most moderate men, who were far too well bred to speak or think much of their soul, could not resist his interpretation of their own and British designs. It spoke for the dumb section of them, and in the depths of their being they preferred his interpretation to anybody else's. A glance at the notes of the *Methodist Times* did make such an one feel a better man somehow; and there was a curious pleasure in passing it to members of his acquaintance, as much as to say, " See what Hughes and I have got to say this week." In his comprehensive longings for the higher flight of the race he seemed at times to have taken white wings from his own shoulders and fastened them on those who, flap as they might, were unable to reach a higher altitude. " Try these, my brother," he seemed to say; " they will bear you higher than the others."

One of his children quoted to him from John Richard Green, whom he so much admired, where the historian says that the vision of a group of free Florentine citizens waving their hats in the piazza was sweeter to him than all the incense and glory that had belonged to world empires. He was so struck by it that he stopped walking and stared at his companion. " Exactly. Don't you see, you foolish child, that that's what it is going to be? Thousands of free citizens waving their hats in piazzas, and the Pax Britannica will see that nobody disturbs them at it—thousands and thousands and thousands of them, each in their respective piazza. That's the very thing we are aiming at—the very thing. Why are my children so foolish? Don't you see and comprehend it all?"

The lamentations of opponents over the loss of precious life, as well as over the general political horizon, were not always pleasing to him. They seemed to arise from the conviction that death in the cause of duty entailed loss—a conviction which he had always opposed. People would excuse courses of conduct in argument by saying, "A man or a woman must live, sir. What are we in the world for but to scrape together a living." "I beg your pardon, sir," he would reply; "we are not in the world for any such purpose at all, but to do God's will in Christ, and glorify His name, and if we can't do it by keeping our soul in our body, which I grant is the usual and right method, let us die, so as to glorify Him. Soldiers die daily for their country, and if we can serve Him better by starving for Him, let us do so. As you know, I generally advocate the contrary method—living as long as possible in a sound body—but not if the price of life in the body is the denial of Him." This clinging at all costs to terrestrial existence and bodily comfort, as if it were the end-all and be-all, distressed him as a denial of that invisible, which in Christ was so near to him. Thus the lamentations of some, when the defenders of a British armoured train suffered death at the outset, drew from him the exclamation, "These men died doing their duty, and war is war! We have entered upon it, and nothing is gained by being hysterical or pusillanimous." On the other hand, he hated militarism and the horrors of war as much as he had ever done, supporting the Imperial idea of the State, because he believed it to be the largest and most practical Peace Society that he knew of.

So when the Peace Society held meetings and were mobbed at the door, he was almost as angry as when persons advocated conscription. How he let loose the artillery of the Journal when they did that! He never made any compromise there, and it was with great delight that he found the prevalent opinion of military connoisseurs, immediately after the war, to lie in the direction of small highly trained proficient forces, rather than vast half-trained ones.

36

The attitude of a section who appeared to find a delight in bringing charges against British arms, he resented and strove to confute in the Journal. On the other hand, he was free in those criticisms which the length of the campaign and the lack of British preparations inevitably suggested, though none of these approached the revelations of the recent War Commission Report. The increased militarism in society and its members which a great war naturally engendered, were distinct causes of distress to him, however inevitable he might regard them.

One day as he was riding on an omnibus down Piccadilly, when the Park was alive with a vast military display, the idealist in him could not resist a shudder at the spectacle. " It is too much," he said, " too much. A certain amount we must have, but the community is suffering at present from a great wave of militarism "; and he would say the same when he came across military detachments on Hampstead Heath. Still more was he " horrified " (that was his expression) at the effect of the " wave of militarism " on certain individuals. A victory was a victory, and every good citizen thanked God for it ; but to go on yelling and shouting long after it was all over was not sufficiently in keeping with national humility.

The appearance of Mr. Rudyard Kipling's " Recessional " in the *Times* was greeted by him with rapture.

" The shouting and the tumult dies. Lest we forget. Lest we forget ! " he would read with delight.

Then—" He owes that poem to the Methodism in him. You may smile, but it is true."

It was noted that when persons of distinction obtained unusual commendation, it was due to one and the same cause. In commenting once on Her late Majesty, it was rather difficult to see how this could be introduced, seeing that none of the Royal line had been followers of John Wesley. As a matter of fact, this proved to be no difficulty. After the eulogy there was a pause, and the significant remark, " Her Majesty's nurse was a godly Methodist."

The terrible nature of my father's toils (the adjective is justified) necessitated another holiday which he had long been planning. At the end of the ex-Presidential year in 1900 he arranged to pay a six weeks' visit to the Eastern Mediterranean, and to visit Egypt, Sicily, Constantinople, Greece, and the Holy Land. Even Italy and its reading was not to rank with the preparations for what he gave listeners to understand was to be the greatest journey of his life. During the year he intended to reread at odd moments the great historians of antiquity, but as he was unavoidably pressed for time he should resort to the device of the unscholarly, and dive into translations. Jowett's *Thucydides*, Rawlinson's *Herodotus* and Fraser's *Pausanias*, in addition to other classical treasures, were eagerly eyed and procured. Inevitably the greater portion of his library was devoured during the voyage in question. While the company ran races on deck, my father, to quote his own expression, sat " perspiring over *Thucydides* " in the cabin below.

The thought of sailing past the isles of Greece, where Sappho loved and sang, with no responsive thrill to their undying romance, of sighting what had been Piræus with no mental picture of Themistocles who had built the walls, and the eager crowd who used to line its shores, came upon him with a kind of horror. When in calm weather and the consequent freedom from sea-sickness, he poured over Jowett's *Thucydides*, and listened to the laughter of the players on deck, he shrank from the thought of the present crew committing so deadly a sin, and his heart went out to them in their apathy and heedlessness. Somehow or other they must be got to comprehend—to respond. Some, he noticed, eyed him with suspicion, as if they suspected his faculties, because he was not as heedless as they were. That life which palpitates in books, unduly claimed, many thought, so sensible and indeed so genial a man. He would laugh with the rest, the centre of their mundane life, and then, like some prophet suddenly caught up on high, he would ascend into what he so often vituperated, " a literary balloon." Once there, it was quite impossible to make him descend till he chose to. The passengers doubtless regarded his absorption as ephemeral, but it was to be doubted whether his occupation appeared half as shadowy in their eyes, as theirs did to his.

These literary " possessions " often startled friends and acquaintances who expected better things of him. On one occasion my parents spent a week-end in the beautiful country house of a friend. It was summer, and the woods and fields were aglow with the first outburst of its life. Deep leafy glades and myriad forms of flower life beckoned to those leisurely strolls, which are the delight of country lovers. To stay within was felt to be little less than a sin, and members of the party had one main subject of wonder. Why did my father persist in staying indoors? In the recesses of the library he sat lost in Boswell's *Life of Johnson*, turning the pages with that care and avidity which characterise those who are getting up books for examination. On entering the house his eye had quickly scanned its shelves full of classic lore, and his hand had instantly clutched Boswell's handiwork. " I have always wished to read that book," he said, " and I am going to read the whole of it, if possible, while I am here." The vow was taken, and in cavernous depths he kept it. On a member of the family entering the room, he would exclaim, " Five hundred pages," and would continue reading. Indeed, at times his aspect was almost forbidding, so did he suspect intruders of foolish and nefarious designs. At tea he would relax to exclaim: " The comicality of the fellow is beyond words, and the way he treated the young ladies of his acquaintance is not the least portion of it,"—an instance of which he would proceed to cite.

So a distinct horror fell upon him as he sat devouring books in his cabin on the Mediterranean. He thought of all the English people who spent their holidays at Scarborough instead of cultivating their imaginations on the Mediterranean. The series of letters he was sending to the Journal would perhaps induce certain to follow his example, and he perspired and went on afresh. Under such circumstances it was scarcely to be expected that his letters when they appeared were as bright and elastic as his Italian epistles. Sometimes it was the quotation and exposition of authorities rather than himself —and the public, in foreign impressions, expect to view things through the medium of a personality which has well digested them. Yet to some they were intensely interesting. How absorbed he was in the Eleusinian mysteries, two or three numbers quite throbbing with their exposition!

On their return journey by way of Italy and the Riviera my parents stopped at Rome, and it was distressing to see my father's bodily exhaustion, though his mental faculties were more eager and vehement than ever. On arriving at the station, he grasped a companion by the arm, and without ado of greeting, began at once: " You cannot form any idea of what I have seen and where I have been. Rome, where you have been living, is modern, European. Only the other day I was galloping across the desert on the back of a camel ! "

" Were you really ? "

" I was galloping on the back of a camel. I have seen Athens and the great harbour at Syracuse, and Jerusalem which slew the prophets, and Nazareth, and only one-fifth of what I have seen has sunk into my mind. The remaining four-fifths I shall spend the rest of my life in absorbing. I shall not have another such journey till I go to Paradise."

It was then that one noticed the bodily exhaustion—the care and weariness on his face in repose. The next minute he was absorbed in the luggage ; but in the omnibus he began again on the impossibility of realising the East ; and, among other things, an account of a visit to a bazaar at Cairo which seemed to have greatly impressed him. " They gave me a cup of coffee and a stool, and there we sat facing one another —the proprietor and I exchanging courtesies through the interpreter — delightfully at our ease, delightfully leisured. Certain of our party objected to this method of bargaining, and wanted to settle the thing at once ; but I entirely differed from them, I thought it so picturesque. As I told them, we must cultivate an Oriental calm, and we do just the same thing at home—the maximum buying price of the public is ascertained, only in another manner. It's all quite fair, though I had a difficulty in getting certain members of the party to see it." Certain of the party had left them at Naples and gone home by sea, the rest would shortly accompany them. Next to the East, he appeared to be interested in that party and eager for its arrival. Not a site or a landmark that he passed could evoke enthusiasm from him, so distasteful apparently was the West and all traces of its modernism.

" There is the obelisk from the Temple of the Sun at Heliopolis which Moses is supposed to have seen," said his companion. " What more can you have than that ? " He disdained a reply. " By the bye," he said, " you have asked

Mr. Piggot to show us over the Forum and the Capitoline Hill. I am most anxious to see the new excavations. What, what, what's that? Of course we must see the Black Stone. When did you say it was discovered? Only the classical remains of the city interest me, the other portions sicken me."

A Protestant minister was awaiting him at the hotel, and before sitting down to dinner my father asked some one to look at the war bulletins. On hearing them, he stifled a groan. "I am afraid Mafeking will be lost—very much afraid." Then he took up his knife and fork, and said to the Protestant minister who was sitting opposite him, "Well, what about our work in Italy?" He ate, and knew not that he ate. "Ah! in Rome you say good, but why did so-and-so happen?" Then, after the answer had been given, "So Protestantism in" (mentioning the name of a place) "is doing fairly well. Oh! and Methodism?" He spoke with the usual emphasis and at some length. By the time he had finished his dinner he had a very fair strategic idea of the state of Protestantism in Italy.

The party which was expected arrived, and he greeted its members with manifest delight. One middle-aged gentleman, a Tory evidently, and a very pleasant one, called my father "Captain," and appeared to be on the most friendly terms with him. There were also some young ladies whose studies my father was marshalling, and he questioned them closely about the sights they had seen at Naples. Both the pleasant middle-aged gentleman and the young ladies seemed most grateful to him for his exposition of their tour, and for making clear and vivid to them all that he had done. "You should have heard him expounding Marathon," said the pleasant gentleman during the meal which my father took care they should procure. "Here were the Athenians, there the Plateans, there the Persians! I could see it all as if it were yesterday." "Do you mind, sir, rising for 7.30 o'clock breakfast to-morrow morning?" asked my father. "You must have a bird's-eye view of the city before we pass on; and I have made full arrangements, for I know how punctilious haughty politicians of your type are. If you were a humble Liberal now"— The haughty politician raised his hand to the salute, "Your servant, sir, and any hour you please." At this there was a chorus from the ladies, "Mr. Hughes, we cannot: it is impossible. "Very well then, 8 o'clock." The chorus fell to muttering, at which the pleasant gentleman cried out, "Come, come, not a word against the Captain, he has seen us through this business as nobody else could, and he shall see us through to the end."

"My only thought was," said my father gently, "that it would be a good thing to climb to the cupola of St. Peter's, and so have a view of this wonderful city and its environs while it is still clear and the morning mists have just lifted. I cannot help thinking that you will regret not having done so, just for the sake of making a slight effort. However, as you please. If you cannot, you cannot, and I should be the last to "— "Oh, Mr. Hughes, of course we will come," was the quite eager chorus. "Not if it exhausts you; but I am only so anxious that when you visit Rome again you may really be in a position to commence studying it." He said this with enthusiasm. "But I would not have you do anything that is distasteful to you." "Oh, Mr. Hughes, we would not miss going for anything. Indeed we would not."

After the ascent to the cupola the party patrolled the Sistine chapel, the Vatican galleries (sculpture and painting) and the Pope's library. A companion tried to expostulate with him once or twice, but he would always answer, "You don't understand the exigencies of a bird's-eye view." On arriving at the hotel they discussed the afternoon's programme. The party said they did not mind where they went as long as it was not the Vatican.

After dinner he came to a little gathering of friends living in the city. He was somewhat silent at first, but on being introduced to a young Italian lady, a very good linguist, he discoursed with her on the acquisition of languages, and of French and German in particular. Later he was overheard in conversation with three American ladies. He told them about America, and bade them be true to the principles of Plymouth Rock. If the nation were only mindful of the piety and wisdom of the Puritan Fathers, they could hope for a great future. His listeners appeared deeply impressed, and indeed they related afterwards that they were so. There was something in him that gave him a right to speak to people. He was so manifestly under control, an invisible discipline absorbing his speech and life. His alertness also for the sensibilities of his listeners, when he chose, was very marked.

Later he was pressed to give an explanation of the British cause in South Africa, for the benefit of the Italians present. He gave a compendious defence, which was interpreted, ending with an exclamation of surprise that Italian Roman Catholics could ever defend the Boers, under whose Government no Roman Catholic was ever permitted to hold office. He said this because he had been told that the majority present were Roman Catholics, and opposed to the British. A white-haired old man, who was sitting listening with the greatest attention, broke into a " Bravo ! " at the close, and came forward to grip him by the hand. My father seemed pleased, and they shook hands heartily. Only a few months ago this old gentleman related that he had never forgotten the speech. It was a revelation to him, he said, and he was thankful to hear the truth about the British.

On the next morning, which was Sunday and his last day in Rome, he preached at the American Episcopalian Methodist Church, making a deep impression on those present.

The text was that saying of our Lord's, which he seemed to prefer above all others, " I am Alpha and Omega, the first and the last . . . I am He that liveth, and was dead ; and, behold, I am alive for evermore, Amen ; and have the keys of hell and of death " (Rev. i. 11, 18). There were many references to the East, but nothing that he said could adequately convey an idea of the vistas before his mind. The preacher was dumb as usual concerning the real nature of his secret. It was the dumbness that held. In Carmarthen, when reference was made to a sermon that he had preached there not long before his death, tears sprang into the eyes of those in the room who had heard it. They did not know him at all. It was just the thought of the sermon. " He cannot always preach just like that ; it would not be possible," they said after this sermon at Rome. There is a C major in preaching as in life. He was insistent during those days in Rome that the rest of his life must be spent in " chewing the cud " of that which he had seen. His only desire for future travel seemed to be to revisit at greater leisure those places which he had so recently quitted.

This interest in foreign lands and foreign peoples undoubtedly affected his outlook.   In those periods in the history
of Europe, when the Church of Rome has been at her
strongest, he would have been at home in some ways in the
College of Cardinals.   At times, undoubtedly, they must have
gnashed their teeth at him, but at others some treating with
European Powers would have earned him respect and gratitude.
His policy was of a kind that needed a large field, and it is
possible to regard his mistakes and those designs in which he
could not get others to agree with him, as a natural exercise of
an instinctive faculty.   The following is an instance of this.
In the year 1900, in the midst of the Imperial period
described in these chapters, he was rushing into the house
amid the full stress of an overcrowded day, when he was
stopped at the threshold by a gentleman who sought an interview with him.   "I am extremely sorry—extremely," he
began, "but I haven't a moment to spare.   I am half-killed
with all that I have to do, and I have been at committees
since early this morning" (the gentleman handed him a letter);
"indeed, I have no choice in the matter; and there is endless
business and correspondence awaiting me upstairs, so that it is
quite impossible to see you to-day.   I"— (two words in the
letter had attracted his attention, and he paused, spellbound).
One of those words was the adjective "French" and the
other was the noun "priest."   In silence he finished reading;
then, sweeping his visitor with a glance, he said, "Come
upstairs with me.   I am most interested in what this letter
has to say.   Ah, here is Mr. Bunting who will join us."   All
at once he had become leisurely, deliberative, walking slowly,
and apparently reflecting deeply.   There was no such thing
now as urgent business and correspondence—they had melted
into thin air.   A moment later the study door shut with a
bang, and was not opened till two or three hours later, when
the conclave, still conversing, went out to a restaurant in the
neighbourhood, had their dinner, and returned to continue
their deliberations.   The gentleman who had thus suddenly
changed the course of my father's day was a former Monsignor
of the Roman Catholic Church, and he had come to report a
wide movement of dissatisfaction and revolt among French
priests.   The Monsignor's own history was a striking one, and

was repeated the next day to the family at dinner. He had been, so they were told, a most devout ecclesiastic of the Roman communion in the Far East, and, far from Rome, had grown up devoted to her usages, her simple piety, and her picturesque ceremonial. In such sequestered spots the life and exposition of the faith were at its best and purest, and the young priest had imbibed of these. He had become a Monsignor, and straight from this life and these scenes he had journeyed to Rome, ardent as Luther, and to be repulsed and horrified as he. "Then," said my father, "he saw the unreality and the workings of it all—the materialism and the absence of spirituality."[1]

Now Romanists who rejected the error and superstition which had mingled with the pure stream of the faith, did not like to call themselves Protestants. How could they? It was allying themselves with what was alien—foreign, associated with what we, as Protestants, could not understand. Yet because of this feeling on their part there was no reason why Protestants should not prove themselves imaginative, and advance to meet those who, in essentials, agreed with themselves. In a word, there was a great opening, if only Methodists could be got to see it. Current numbers of the Journal were aflame with the Abbé Bourier and the French Catholics who were in revolt, and his conversation and correspondence were aglow also. But despite these efforts his hopes were not fully realised, and his projects unfulfilled. Others apparently saw something of what he beheld, but not all. It was in these larger and more imperial aspects of strategy that he was by nature at his ease. He liked to deal with armies and on a wide field. To many, indeed, such conceptions would appear not only impracticable but positively undesirable—too tinged with that military conception of the faith which characterised portions of my father's ecclesiastical and civil thinking. Yet all such objections, to quote a well-known phrase, are "neither here nor there"; it is the effect on the imagination and the routine of statesmanship that makes such conceptions both practicable and desirable. My father's ecclesiastical biographer, in time to come, may estimate highly or lowly what he actually

---

[1] The Monsignor in question was ultimately received by the Bishop of London into the Church of England after a long period of waiting.

achieved in this and similar departments of his life. But he cannot annul the impression on the general mind and policy, in that he not only dreamt audacious dreams but set about realising them.

"39 CLARENCE SQUARE, CHELTENHAM, *Jan.* 4.

"MY DEAR MR. HUGHES,—I must tell you how very grateful I am to you for having in your New Year's leading article revived and insisted on the importance of the native question in South Africa. I may be a little fanatical on that subject; but it has all along seemed to me to be the crux of the whole situation. I think that the native population of South Africa is, in proportion to the whites, six to one, and yet how little we hear in certain parts of society (Parliament) of that mass of people. Some intelligent Imperialists, Liberals, like my kinsman Sir Edward Grey, fail to take in the thought of our great responsibility to the natives. I often think of what one of the Schreiners (now in England) said to me very solemnly and with conviction, ' I do not believe, Mrs. Butler, that this war will end until every rood of African soil which has been watered with the blood of murdered natives shall again be watered with the blood of the white man, for there is a Nemesis for guilty nations.' Observe the expression was 'murdered' natives, not natives killed in battle; and the speaker, who had spent much time in the Transvaal, gave me facts at first hand, things witnessed by the speaker. He said, 'A pious Boer, after reading the Bible and praying with his family at their first meal, would go out, and come in again to dine, his hands red with the blood of a poor Kaffir slave, whom he had flogged to death for some neglect of work; and yet he was pious!'

"The pity is that the blood of so many non-guilty men, our poor 'Tommies' and officers' blood, is watering the African soil as well as that of Boers. One of my sons was five years in South Africa before the war began. His account of the better tribes of natives—Zulus, Shaughans, Basutos, etc.—is most interesting. He says they rise morally at a cheering rate, if treated with justice as well as kindness. They have the keenest sense of justice, poor souls. Some Englishmen err in treating them with a vulgar familiarity, jocularly, and yet contemptuously. The native sees through that, and he does not believe in such men. My son had to go on an expedition into Mashonaland, and took with him some fifteen of his men whom he employed, leaving thirty or forty behind in a remote place, to guard his work and keep it going, and to guard also his hut, books, papers, clothes, etc. etc. He left them money enough to live for some three weeks. Accidents of various kinds prevented his return until a considerably longer time. He was distressed, thinking the poor fellows would starve, and that the strain on their honesty would be severe. When he returned, he found them all rather lean and hungry, but the place in perfect order; and all his property sacredly kept, and the work going on. When asked how they had lived, they said, on roots and wild fruit, and what birds they could catch. This shows that respect for a just master draws out the best qualities. These were not Christian natives, and yet how loyal, how perfectly honest!

"My heart bleeds for them, thinking of the horrid treatment they have so long undergone. But surely God will arise for His poor redeemed creatures, and a better day is approaching for them.

"I have not the least objection to your mention of me in your paper, nor to what you have said, only it is far too good. I am so keenly sensible of my many errors, and of the mixed character of much of my work in life.

"Of course I am writing personally to you now; but oh! I do beg you to bear in mind those poor millions of natives— you *will* do so, I know.

"Long, long ago I had a dream, in which I seemed to see Jesus Christ pointing from the Cross to a great multitude of lost women, in a kind of earthly hell, and then I dreamed that He looked at me from the Cross. That look was enough. Now when I think of South Africa and its myraids of 'lost' natives, it seems as if again He looked at me. Yet I can now do nothing actively. Will He perhaps suffer some word that I may speak or write to fall into the good soil of a good and fruitful heart, and bear fruit a hundredfold?

"I have been disappointed with the 'Aborigines Protection Society.' They have done a good deal of harm as well as good. . . .

" I have read with keen interest your comments on Stead's new departure, and I agree entirely with your criticism. I have just ordered a dozen copies of this week's *Methodist Times* to send to a few right-minded foreign friends.

" I have again inflicted too long a letter on you, and I fear I have mislaid your Bournemouth address.—Ever yours very truly,

" JOSEPHINE BUTLER."

"s.y. 'ARGONAUT,' *Feb.* 12, 1900.

" MY DEAR LUNN,—I am much touched and comforted by your kindly sympathy, and by the thoughtful way in which you promoted the expression of sympathy from the Free Church Committee, which also met me here. I have just written a reply to Dr. Monro Gibson's letter.

" Only those who have lost both parents can fully realise the sense of desolation which comes. At the same time I am very thankful to God who spared us both our parents until all their children were settled in life. I could not wish that the extreme feebleness of my bedridden mother should be pro- longed, and I am very grateful that she—who had dreaded death all her life—fell asleep in Christ so painlessly and so quietly at last. I cannot sufficiently thank you for all you have done for me in this matter.

" I am also much indebted to you for the interesting account of the Council Committee you have sent me.

" I am very sorry the South African War is to be discussed at Sheffield. Excellent Free Churchmen differ so deeply about that, that if I had been at the Committee I should have done my utmost to induce them to leave the subject severely alone. The War, Home Rule, and all topics on which we are not agreed, should never be touched. The one great peril of the moment is the perpetual attempt to drag such burning questions into our midst. Our business is to keep to the deep theological and ecclesiastical issues on which we are agreed.

" So far as the war is concerned, I wish you and all who agree with you could see the blissful results of British rule in Egypt, and could realise the effect abroad of the incessant nagging at your own great country, and the even more pestiferous whitewashing of one of the most cruel and mendacious military oligarchies that ever enslaved black men and outraged white men. Englishmen whose prophet is John Redmond are in a poor way. I have been working so hard to make the very most of the great opportunity which you have given me, that I have had no time to write before. But I have thought every day of writing to tell you how very kindly and thoughtfully your brother and all the officials have treated my wife and me. It was a *bitter* disappointment that you and your wife could not accompany us; and we have been much distressed to hear of your illness. But in your absence your brother has done everything to make this the most enjoyable and instructive tour we have ever had. I feel as though I had been to another university and received a totally new and additional education. I shall be very glad to golf with you. We expect to reach London on Thursday the 22nd inst. Your brother will accompany us through Italy, to our great comfort. With love to your wife and yourself in which Katie joins,—Yours affectionately,

"H. PRICE HUGHES."

CHAPTER XXI

FAITHFUL FRIENDS AND THOUGHTS ON CHRISTIAN DOCTRINE

> " That most closely we may follow Him
> By suffering, have all hearts of men allowed.
> Is suffering then more near and dear to God
> For its own sake than joy is? God forbid!
> We know not its beginning nor its end;
> Is it a sacrifice? a test? a school?
> We suffer. Why we suffer. That is hid
> With God's foreknowledge in the clouds of Heaven."
>
> H. HAMILTON KING.

IN March of 1901, while my father was conducting the United Mission of the Free Churches at Manchester, he was taken ill on the Monday morning after addressing crowded meetings on the previous Sunday. It was the beginning of the end, and, though the battle was not ended, the brunt of it, so far as he was concerned, was over. After that collapse he was never the same again, and though there were periods when he appeared to regain his former vigour, they were transitory.

Hitherto the strain of his life had only resulted in occasional nervous headaches, so that, compared to the general lot, his health had been exceptionally and indeed wonderfully sound. Had it been otherwise, he could not have lived the life that he did. Indeed, so exceptionally sound was his constitution that men always took it for granted that he would outlive them, and he had so worked himself into the thought of multitudes that they did not imagine life without him. Yet with the nervous collapse and the serious symptoms that occurred in March, it began to be felt that even his endurance and strength might be limited, and these fears gained credence when, six months later, the collapse was repeated. His hair, plentifully streaked with silver, was noted by persons who had not seen him for a season, as did the face, which by its various play of feature, had ever been the response to a manifold drama. In the early days of his ministry he had struck men as devoured by a flame, and his face, pale and ascetic-looking, his form, lithe and nervous, seemed the outward symbols of the fire that consumed them. Eyes early weakened by excess of study flashed kindliness behind glasses, which added to the impression that he was old beyond his years, although endowed with outbursts of youth that were astonishing in one so consumed with zeal and with toils. That such ebullitions could last long none believed, and most took upon themselves to tell him so. "You will burn yourself out. Living cannot be long at this rate." But he did live, and so soundly that study and enthusiasm seemed to promote living. The pale almost spare face became that of the fighter and the strong man — one who knew his mind and could proclaim it if necessary against the world. In moments of repose it could flash humour, reflexion, and affection, just as at other moments it could flash wrath and determination. This was how London knew him, and the aspect that most preferred to look back upon and to remember. Photographs taken after suffering had left their seal, were not admired except by one or two. Yet to bear the mark of suffering is to wear the seal of a great kinship, to understand what only a great kinship can teach.

It is certain that he never understood humanity so well as he did at this time. It is not in the thick of the fight that the blows are most felt. He would often say during these last two years that people did not realise all the trouble he was passing through, which was not merely physical, just as they did not realise what certain blows during the fight had cost him. The insight into individual men and women, in which he has been described as hitherto lacking, was deepened, and such a deepening, whatever its pleasurable surprises on the one side, was bound to be fraught with pain to one physically ill able to contend with the disappointment that such insight must also bring. His fits of depression seemed, no more than his joys, to be bound up with himself. The failure of the world, and particularly of the Church, to rise to certain of his ideals for them, would at times cause him the most poignant wonder and sorrow. So continuously did both blind their eyes to those great realities which so flooded his own life, that he could not understand why they were so blind to them, and how it came to be. Moreover, the disabling of any leader throws light on the army of his followers, on the aim and character of those who profess to admire him and to have adopted his designs. If there has been a petty jealousy, a silent criticism of any kind, it will spring to the surface now that his strength is no longer there in full force to quell them.

Such incidents are old as history. The world admires men for what they give it, and but rarely for themselves. His sublime selflessness had accorded with this, and, indeed, encouraged it, taking for granted that he should be esteemed for what he could give. Yet when he fancied that men considered his giving to be at an end, and that they were anxious to press on without him, it was then that the rub came. Perhaps also he began to wish that his silence might be a little more divined and understood—the silences that are the self. In later years he would often say to Dr. Lunn, "Nobody understands my silences." Many could not tolerate the thought of his outliving his public endeavours, of his becoming less conspicuous in London or the life of Methodism and the Churches. "It is better far," they said, "that he died when he did." Others again told members of the family that they should be thankful he was taken in his prime. In addition, it was shown how few really understood his life-work or grasped its extent and its meaning. His personality, and the contagion of his enthusiasm for Churches and causes, had drawn certain around the standard, who, while they spoke the same tongue, certainly did not mean by it what he did. Such searchlights there had to be. That men always show their truest selves in such moments, or that a leader whose nervous system has been spent truly judges the situation, the writer is not contending. Yet he is bound to feel more than the generality or even those nearest to him can divine.

My father's capacity for feeling had always been above the average, and at this stage it was terrible at times. He was not accustomed to lying sleepless at night, to forced inactivity, and to protracted pain, and this made it the harder. For years he had been a target for criticism, as shown, and though

37

certain criticisms found free vent at this particular period, they were really not different in character from what they always had been. It was the same thing over again; mistaken people did not understand the width of his outlook, and acted after their kind. The difference lay in himself, that he was necessarily inactive, unable to explain and dominate as he once had, and sensitive past thinking. He was so brilliant, so dazzling in some ways, that he had to pay more heavily than other men for a miscalculation or a misunderstanding. Men and women did not expect it of him, and they could forgive in others what they did not forgive in him.

The criticism concerning the Mission and his endeavours had always hovered round various contentions, and one in particular. It was not sufficiently denominational, *i.e.* not Wesleyan Methodist, to the thinking of certain of its critics. Their environment and conviction and quality of mind had led to one interpretation of Wesleyan Methodism, and my father's environment and conviction and quality of mind had led to another. He regarded Methodism as a uniting not a segregating force—something that was so aware of the need of men for Christ, and of the evil and misery of the world, that it made men join hands with whoever they could find to help them in ministering to its need. Yet, in the divergence of view that arose between him and others, now or at any time, it was seldom that there was any heart estrangement, though at times there might appear to be so. For the most part it was a question of mental outlook, or, in the wider life of Methodism, of party and political bias. Indeed, he perceived that this was so, and that men were not as estranged as they sometimes appeared. It was in periods of ill-health that it was difficult to remember this, and to estimate aright. The writer also has to note a curious coincidence which shows how the sections, while wrestling with the prophet, never defeated him at any time.

Hitherto he had, to the thinking of some, lacked a quality of charity, contemporaries complaining that "he attacked without stint and without discernment." Of the charity which springs from the heart, he had ever imbibed in abundance. The sight of a beggar, or a woman in tears, was insupportable, and he used to say that he could not refuse anything to either of these. In early days, before there was an organised relief department in the Mission, he was often sorely put to by an inability to refuse mendicants, even when he suspected their designs. Yet not all shed tears who well might, and not all who need alms ask for them. At times, in his compassion for what was manifestly crooked and awry in the world, he seemed to be almost wilfully overlooking certain considerations. Charity springs from the head as well as the heart, and its highest form is that which springs from discernment. Certain details and facts concerning individuals he always put from him, and there were problems concerning these which he would not face. That he acted thus was sufficiently comprehensible, for he had problems enough to face in the world at large. To see, too, much round the corner in things would have hindered him as a man of action, and his instinct seemed to tell him so, for he would sweep away considerations that seemed to others paramount.

Great generals are bound at times to do this, and it was often interesting to watch how he did it. In a sermon or a conversation something would escape him, and then he would thrust it from him, as one who is determined to reach a journey's end will thrust aside an obstacle that besets his path. His business was, not to look right and left and to distract himself at the point of view of bystanders, but to run with patience the race that was set before him. When details or a point of view helped him in that race he took note of them, but when they did not he thrust them from him. So successful was he in this that people did not always perceive that he had to thrust them from his path, and that more of his time may have been spent in doing this than anybody divined.

As this general neared the goal, and with slackened pace, he came to reckon as he had not formerly with that which thrust itself across his way, and to fill in on his map what had formerly been undefined and vague. In that he saw more deeply into the tangle of individual life his charity increased, because there was the necessary breathing space for a quality that had never been allowed to expand.

At last he faced certain aspects of persons and things, and perceived who had been near him in the fight and who far away. That men and women, even the best, were sometimes a strange medley, he increasingly perceived, and with wonder, with pain, and with gentleness. "So-and-so," he would remark, "has many excellent qualities, a great influence for good in many ways, but is still influenced at heart by worldly considerations." That careless talk of the tongue which so intensifies the pain of human beings caused him exclamation. Some one repeated to him a remark which had deeply hurt another. "Oh, why must they go on doing it!" he said; "there is enough misery in the world without such remarks to make it worse. Why are they so ignorant, and why do they do it?" Again, he seemed to perceive more clearly the struggles, not only of those who were exceptional in any way, but of people whom their fellow-men call ordinary. There was more repose in his society because at last he seemed to acquiesce in mortality in others. Certain persons did not feel that his expectations and ideals were less high and stringent, but that he had more sympathy with and a greater understanding of that which clogs their realisation. Hitherto, perhaps, he had seemed to some like a strong and tireless runner who swept all before him because he had not the infirmities of certain others. Now that he was stricken, he seemed nearer them, more allied to the general fate.

In these last days, also, his loneliness seemed intensified, and he fell back increasingly on the society of certain old campaigners—those who had exulted with him over the great victory of 1880. The fact that, after the outbreak of the South African War, he was a lost leader to a large number of those who had once followed him, the ominous approach of a great educational struggle in the Churches, as well as matters of dissension in his own communion, of which hereafter, were bound to produce their effect on one whose physical strength was more impaired than any supposed. Pathetically he writes to one of the Sisters at this time: "I had hoped that I was entering upon a period of rest and peace. But it would seem that my 'rest is in heaven, my rest is not here.' There seems to be no rest for me on earth." Besides, it is probable that he had reached a vantage ground and outlook from which few could understand or follow him. As the historian Green puts it in his letters: "What seems to grow fairer to me as life goes by is the love and peace and tenderness of it; not its wit and cleverness and grandeur of knowledge, grand as knowledge is,

but just the laughter of little children, and the friendship
of friends, and the cosy talk by the fireside, and the sight of
flowers, and the sound of music." His conversation often
seemed to re-echo this. Moreover, the loneliness and the
suffering were not all, for there was a good deal else, as his
face often went to show. A great wistfulness seemed to be its
pervading characteristic, a wistfulness which sprang, not from
any thought concerning himself, but from hope and anxiety
concerning the world and the Church, and a wonder as to how
long he would be permitted to play a part in either. The
world, for all his eager participation and delight in its affairs,
had always had a touch of unreality to him, and the unreality
increased. Yet he responded as ever to the life of humanity,
especially to its tender and incongruous aspects, its hopes and
its sadnesses. Thus laughter and sorrow seemed often to be
mated upon his face, and no high emotion or aspiration but
seemed to sweep it as a keyboard. Whatever was seen or
heard evoked response upon it, and he was always seeing and
hearing. Wrath was almost a stranger to it, and suspicion
had never at any time visited it. It did not show, as it once
had, that he had led and fought men; but one thing it made
evident, that he had suffered for them, that he had seen into
them, and that he hoped for them. At times it was a study
of thought and of conflicting thoughts, and at others of un-
dimmed happiness like a child without care.

No one had friends such as he had. On a morning in
the early summer, one of them, Mr. Henry Holloway, drove
up to the house, by special appointment, and had a conclave
of some duration in the study. At the close, my father
summoned the various members of the household into the
drawing-room, and thus addressed them: " I have just had
a most astonishing conversation—most. Indeed, I could
scarcely believe my own ears, and I don't suppose you will
believe your own either when I tell you about it."

" What was it ? " some one asked.

" I don't suppose you could form any idea. Not even your
wildest imaginings could suggest it to you. I don't suppose
you could any of you dream it even, fertile as you are in the
fabrication of midnight fantasy." Here he paused for a space.
Such a thought as suddenly breaking a piece of news to his

family had never occurred to him; it would have been a sin
against the established code in such matters.   If they ever
inquired concerning the text of a sermon or the gist of a
speech he took several minutes to inform them, for he loved to
hint a secret and then to gradually disclose it.   Seeing that he
had made a considerable impression, he continued : " The suggestion that Mr. Holloway made to me just now has quite
taken my breath away.   Indeed, I do not know what to think
or to do."   Here he smiled, and a laugh broke from him,
despite himself, so that the secret seemed about to break from
him also.   But seeing the faces of his listeners his brow clouded.

" Indeed, Mr. Holloway's proposition is of such a nature
that I do not quite see my way to accepting it.   I cannot
think what to do about it."

His brow clouded again as if in perplexity.

" At the time I agreed to it."

" Agreed to what ? " asked one more impetuous than wise.

" Ah, that is the question."

He clasped his arms and restrained as it were a rushing
torrent.

" You may well ask what your father agreed to ! "

Then perceiving that expectation was at its fever height,
and that suspense could not further be borne, he said gently :

" You know that for a long time your mother and I have
wished to procure a cottage within a suitable distance from
London, so that we might go down at the week-end from time
to time, but we found this to be an impossibility.   In the first
place, there was no cottage to be had, and, in the second,
we could not incur the expense of providing one.   Now Mr.
Holloway"—here he dropped his voice—" actually suggests that
he and a few friends shall build us a house—not a cottage, but
a house—in the neighbourhood of Haslemere, where we shall
not only be able to live ourselves, but if necessary to invite
one or two friends.   He quite scouts the idea of a cottage ;
that, he says, would not suit our purpose.   'There would be
no room, Mr. Hughes, for your family or your friends.   You
would not enjoy that.   You must have a spare room.'   And
upon my word I did not know what to say to the man.   The
generosity of the whole thing took my breath away, and I said
at first that I really could not accept it.   Indeed, I could not

reply to him. 'This is too much,' I said; and then he answered so modestly and simply, as if I were conferring instead of receiving a benefit, 'If you had been in business, Mr. Hughes, you would have made enough money to build yourself a house in the country for your old age.' Then he told me that he and his brother[1] had always had this intention to build me a house in the country after I had retired from active service, but that my illness had decided them to build it now. 'Why wait,' they said, 'till he is old. He will need it now more than then, and it may be a refreshment and delight to him now as it cannot be then. If he is to continue his work in London, a country home where he can find rest and fresh air may help him to do it, and lengthen his life at the same time. For the sake of the work, if for no other reason, you must let us show what we feel towards you. We regard it as a debt, you know';—and there I was speechless, scarcely knowing how to thank him. Then it was arranged. Your mother and I are to drive over to Haslemere to see a piece of ground that he has in view there. Now, have you ever heard of such a thing? Can you realise it?"

After exclamations and questions on the part of those present, he continued again, but as if to himself not to them:

"What have I done, I wonder. Other men and their families don't get houses in this way. How fortunate we are and beyond our deserts."

Such moments of true simplicity bewildered men. They could not associate it with the man of affairs. None the less it was at such moments that he was intensely himself. Later came the drive to Haslemere, and on the return the reiteration of the magic word "freehold." Later, again, visits to a house that was in process of erection, and visits fraught with consequence to the establishments of furniture dealers. Immediately on the return from these latter there would be a drive on the top of the omnibus, or a walk in Regent's Park, where, in answer to eager questionings, his children would tell him all —the nature of the deliberations, and the decisions to which they had severally led.

"Ah!" he would exclaim, "I see that we shall have a *bijou* residence."

---

[1] A few friends also aided in their scheme.

Then came altercations as to the naming of the house; he wanted to call it by an Italian name, and the family by a Welsh one.

" Let us," he said, " call it ' Quisisana,' because there health will be regained," but they strove against it, saying that it sounded like a hospital, and that people would neither understand nor pronounce it.   In the end, after a good deal of inquiry at authoritative sources, the Welsh words " Ty Bryn " (the house on the hill) were chosen, not only as expressive of allegiance to the Principality, but as amenable to ordinary pronunciation.   Around " Ty Bryn " all the brightness of his last days seems to have centred, and people could not long enter into conversation with him before he would begin to speak of it.   I can remember his clutching the arm of a Congregationalist minister as he led him down the lane to the house, and inquiring, " Now, do Congregationalists do this kind of thing?   Would they build houses like this for their ministers?   Such a thing would only be possible in Methodism. What?   What?"—

Nor was this, the house at Haslemere, the only instance of friendliness at a time when there was a good deal of private as well as public anxiety, and when there was bound to be a strain on his private resources.

A relative sent him a cheque for £100, which he begged him to accept for what he knew must be present need.   My father, however, in thinking over it thought he could do without it, and wrote back to say that he would prefer not to receive it for himself, but to give it to the Mission, which was needier than he was.

One wondered at his zeal, at his positive impatience to enter, as he termed it, " into residence."   " Why are you so anxious to go to Haslemere?" one of his family asked him. " Why?   So that we may rejoice," he answered, and then hugged himself at the thought of the bliss in prospect.   Every dear brother and sister whom he met, including his friends at the office, were invited to that house, till it seemed as if all the world were coming there.   From the beginning of his ministry he had always followed the New Testament tradition of inviting those whom he met to come and sup with him.   In the most stressful times of the age of chivalry some one would be announced in the middle of a meal. " Bring him in," he would ring out; and then, " Ah, my dear sir, delighted to see you, and if you are not a vegetarian, as I am beginning to think we ought all to be, help us to devour this sheep."

After the second collapse he was ordered to cease work for a year, and to give up everything except the editorship of the *Methodist Times*. On every other point except this the medical director was obdurate. His patient complied as usual without a murmur, but on the top of the omnibus he stifled a sigh: " You know, I suppose, that arrangements have been made for your mother and me to go to Australia this year. They were completed, all was in readiness, and now Howard forbids me to go, and I was very anxious to speak to our Australian brethren concerning the true meaning and import of Methodism —very anxious. I think they would listen to me. However, in the future perhaps God may grant it." The difficulty was to know what to do with my father and where to send him. At my uncle's in Wales, they had devised the temporary expedient of golf, and he had bought a thick volume concerning the game, which he was marking and studying. His knowledge of how to play was undoubted, as he told others exactly what to do, but it never captivated him as cycling did. Sometimes, too, the books would have their way—though every expedient would be devised to separate him from them.

Mr. Hall Caine had just published his novel *The Eternal City*, and had sent him a copy, which he was occupied in reading and reviewing. The novelist much appreciated his criticism, and wrote him a letter expressing his gratitude for an insight into the idea and inner import of that which he had written.

While he was thus occupied with reading and writing of various kinds at a table covered with papers—and " reserved," as he would assure the family, by their mother, for his special use—his fate was being decided by a council of war below, and he knew it. Without exaggeration, the eye of the family mind roved the habitable portions of the globe, seeking for suitable resorts and finding none. His Methodist friends, I believe, would have sent him anywhere and done anything to restore him to health. One of them drove up to 8 Taviton Street at this time and said, " Come away with me and let us leave everything and everybody behind us. It shall be the Highlands or the Canary Islands "—(he mentioned one or two places)—" just as you please, only let us get away. I am in need of a change too." My father thanked him repeatedly, but replied that other arrangements were being made for him. On his driving away he watched him with affectionate regard. " A most warm-hearted brother," he exclaimed, " full of generosity and fervour." The medical director barred cities absolutely, and shuddered at the thought of any place on the Mediterranean. Even islands he was dubious about—islands might contain buried ruins of pagan temples, which could be dug up and described in the notes of the *Methodist Times*. Whatever happened, he was not to winter in an interesting place, or in any spot that had historical associations. My father's brother, Mr. Arthur Hughes, solved the problem. " Hugh must go to Bournemouth. It's pleasant and warm there—with the New Forest close at hand, and more variety of occupation than most watering-places." During a walk the decision was broken to him, and he protested loudly, " I cannot and will not "; but by the evening he became both mollified and resigned. His companions drew enticing pictures for him, laying special stress on the reading room, on the concerts at the winter gardens, on the warmth of the climate and the perfection of the New Forest for cycling. My uncle addressed him, " It is decided then that you go to Bourne-mouth and live a normal life ? "

" A what ? " he groaned.

" A life like other men."

" What do you mean ? "

" A holiday as other men take holidays. My advice is, breakfast at your leisure—say nine o'clock, and then read the morning paper and have a turn at the golf links. Come home to lunch and go to sleep, and then go out again for a little walk, not too long—the pier, for instance, to hear the band "—

" The pier, to hear the band ? "

" Yes, the pier, to hear the band."

" I thought I was to cycle ? "

" You cannot cycle and play golf both on the same day. You can cycle the following day. Then have dinner and a good one, and play games."

" Play what ? "

" Games—draughts or chess or ping-pong or something."

" Well, I might do something at chess, perhaps. I was very fond of that game when I was a boy."

He evidently reflected over the latter advice, for before going to Bournemouth he went shopping with one of his children, and laid in a store of games. After he had been at Bournemouth some weeks, a member of the family paid a visit and found him enthusiastic. He was delighted with the place, had thoroughly reconnoitred it, including the topography, and was quite in a position to hold the town against foreign invaders. The rides in the New Forest particularly pleased him. After lunching at some picturesque-looking inn, he would pounce in the usual way on any books and papers he could lay his hand on. " You do not know," he would say in excuse, " what it is to edit a journal. The wretch can never miss a day's news, and must never get without earshot of it." It was the first time he was heard to refer to the editorship of the Journal as at all irksome, and later, at Haslemere, he said, " For sixteen years I have scarcely ever missed writing the leader and notes of the paper, and it becomes more of a grind than people imagine." Cycle rides by the sea with friends or relatives would be provocative of the strangest discussions, springing from the air rather than the minds of the riders. On one occasion my father was contending that salvation came from the Jews, while one of the riders cycled vehemently ahead declaring that it came from the Greeks—so vehemently, indeed, that the narrow way was lost and the Jews left in complete possession. I can see his figure now, bowed and convulsed with mirth at the cross-roads. The point was gained visibly and tangibly. " Oh, come back to the Jews," he cried to his discomfited opponent. " They alone can guide you."

" Another time he went over sands and cliffs and streams to Poole—a most circuitous and involved route—and one of the party, in a powdery sand, refused to go further because the cycle apparently was of the same mind. Though a quarter of a mile ahead, he came back like a windmill, gesticulating, waving, laughing, insistent.

" I cannot and will not go on ! "

" You shall and must."

" It is impossible ; let me stay here."

" No, I shall not let you stay here."

" I must stay here."

" Nothing of the kind.   Of course, you must "—

Some fury caught him—a moment, and the cycle had resumed its course.   The powder of that sand might have been asphalt.

At draughts in the evenings there were lengthy contests. My father became quite gloomy once because he thought he was going to lose, but the cloud dispersed and he came out victor in the end.   His reading was various as usual, and he was read to sleep more than once with Mr. Kidd's *Social Evolution*, but as the book was being read for the third time, no indignity was implied in such a use.

The elaborate annotation and care with which he read volumes that he was reviewing or expounding was surprising when one took into account the variety of his endeavours.   One day, on visiting Shelley's birthplace, he said he could not claim to be a great admirer of that poet, though he hinted admiration of the smaller poems.   One evening he read aloud Browning's " Childe Roland to the Dark Tower came," and on being asked for an explanation, he said, after a pause, " that ultimately we attain our ideal."   This was striking, as indicating his unquenchable optimism, this poem being often taken, I believe, as about the grimmest poetic expression of a man who has outlived his hopes and enthusiasm, and who, without solace or ray of light, sets his teeth for the end.   But my father, with his deep belief in Christ Jesus—the revelation of the love of God—saw in the gloom and terror of that poem only a stage in the progress of the soul.   Beyond that fight at the close, joy would break like the sun after a storm, and the ideal of the soul—some expression of itself—would come to it, because Christ Jesus was living for evermore, and in His hand were the keys of death and of life.   Facts, while they perplexed even pierced him, as they could not fail to do with his knowledge of life, did not make any difference to his belief.   He saw them in the light of that belief which possessed him.   The heathen raged and so did the pessimists, but the raging had no effect upon him.   The writer hesitates to speak concerning the intimacy betwixt him and Browning, for, though he never saw or spoke to him in the flesh, he had that curious intimacy with portions of his mind which exists between great poets and certain of their readers. His appreciation of other poets, even those whom one would have thought him least likely to appreciate, has already been indicated, but no writer either of prose or poetry ever entered into his life-blood as Robert Browning did. People knew that when they heard him read his poetry. Certain portions of the New Testament and certain poems of Browning—read by him—were unforgettable. He was of a piece with what he read, and became possessed, absorbed, forgetful both of his listeners and himself. Listeners wondered how commentaries led to an understanding of Browning. For those who had a spiritual intimacy they were useful as they were to my father, but they were not the open sesame. From the hour when he first diffidently took up the poet's works to the time of his death, he might be described as growing in this discipleship. The poet's death and the preparation involved in the consequent Sunday afternoon address, was undoubtedly a great impetus. How he found time thus to study him, nobody knew, but he did. In Christ Jesus he seemed at times to be living a transcendent life, not hampered, but vast, elastic, for all his great toils. The story of the Arab physician—"the picker-up of learning's crumbs"— who in his wanderings comes across Lazarus and reports his strange case to his chief, was a peculiar delight to him, particularly for the manner in which it is related.

    .   .   .   .

> " He holds on firmly to some thread of life—
> (It is the life to lead perforcedly)
> Which runs across some vast distracting orb
> Of glory on either side that meagre thread,
> Which, conscious of, he must not enter yet—
> The spiritual life around the earthly life :
> The law of that is known to him as this,
> His heart and brain move there, his feet stay here.
> So is the man perplext with impulses
> Sudden to start off crosswise, not straight on."

He remarked once musingly, after reading these lines, that the poet's suggestion seemed to be that Lazarus was not altogether benefited by his knowledge of that " spiritual life around the earthly." It disturbed the harmony, impairing his effectiveness. Men, like horses, evidently could see too much. Though delivered with unusual deliberation and a keen consciousness of the various aspects of the problem, it was a very characteristic utterance. " The Bishop orders his Tomb at St. Praxed's Church " was another that he liked to read. He would preface the reading of it by remarking, " Ruskin says there is more of the Renascence in this poem than in any book of his own on that period." That quality of the poet so often commented upon, that of seizing and piercing a phase of life in a few lines, was very attractive to him. It was delightful to hear him read anything so dramatic as " In a Laboratory " or " The Patriot." It is surprising that not more attention has been drawn to my father's dramatic powers as a preacher and speaker. " A Toccata of Galuppi's " was another in which he delighted. Of the poems treating of the love of man and woman, " In the Campagna," " Love among the Ruins," and " The Last Ride Together " were favourites. To his appreciation of the longer, more elaborate works, such as " The Ring and The Book," etc., reference is not here made. He read them to himself with care and eagerness, but when he read aloud he naturally selected poems suitable for that purpose and likely to appeal to listeners not familiar with the more difficult portions. Naturally those poems in which the motive is distinctly religious had a special appeal to him. " Instans Tyrannus," for example, caused him exultation, and always, when he had been reading, his fingers showed a disposition to turn the pages to " Saul." " But you have read that so often," a companion would exclaim. " Oh, I must read it again, because you don't understand it ! "

" We do."

" You think you do."

After he had read it, this statement was proved to be correct.

At Bournemouth one day, at a friend's house, a Congregationalist minister was asked to give some readings from Browning, which he did very beautifully. My father was also entreated, but he became seized with embarrassment. " I cannot ; I am not competent." As usual, he feared to assume any literary capacity in the presence of the élite, and unless he had been strongly urged, he would never have dared to read Browning aloud at all.

Nothing was more remarkable about my father than his refusal to limit his interests in any way.   He was not interested in most things but in everything.   Because he was interested in Browning and Lotze and theology, that did not prevent him from evincing the keenest interest in writings of a light and popular character.   As already stated, he had none of the disdain of a certain section for the popular writers; for despite his appreciation of literary subtlety and power, he loved to thrill with the unlettered multitude over the simplest stories of adventure and contemporary life.   Indeed, on railway journeys, I have even seen him absorbed in portions of *Answers*, which afforded apparently, like everything else, grist to his mill. While at Bournemouth, he was eagerly awaiting the last chapter of Sir Conan Doyle's " Hound of the Baskervilles," which was to appear in the next issue of the *Strand Magazine*.   On the day of its publication, which he had been anticipating like any schoolboy, he could not wait to return home, but insisted on going on to the pier.   Choosing a more or less secluded seat, he sat down with his back to his daughter, and told her not to disturb him till he had finished the tale and unravelled the mystery which had so long been perplexing him.

In walking along the street and on the tops of omnibuses he noted and drank in all that he saw, often turning over some incident in his mind and then suddenly commenting on it.   The writer has heard him complain of various things, but never that anything was stale or wearisome—sermons always excepted.[1]   The only line of Browning that he appeared to adversely criticise was where the poet exclaims, " How hard it is to be a Christian ! "   Why, it was hard surely to be any-thing else, to a thoughtful man—a Christlike Christian, that is to say, not a miserable caricature of one.

At Taviton Street about this time he was much confined to the study with what appeared to be an important document —indeed the family scarcely dared interrupt him.   A glance within revealed him stretched on the sofa intent on something which he was hiding under the coverlet.   At meals he

---

[1] "God knows," he exclaimed once with a groan, "that I cannot listen to a sermon, so that is why He has made me a preacher."

appeared abstracted, and they could have sworn that some document relating to Methodism was the cause of it all. In the evening, on telling him it was time to retire, the cause of this absorption was revealed. George Eliot's *Mill on the Floss* was slowly displayed to the view. He looked half-angry with them for seeing it—for knowing that the old spell was upon him.

"You like it?" one ventured.

"Powerful," he answered—"most powerful."

Then he sat up to deliver himself. "Of all the vile inhuman wretches that ever darkened the face of the earth, Tom Tulliver was most hateful to God and man. If ever there was a detestable, cold-blooded beast, that beast was Tom Tulliver."

"But he was very upright," one ventured, anxious to rouse him still further. "He paid the family debts."

"Paid the family debts! Never let me hear a child of mine offer that excuse again. It distresses me to hear you. I don't care if he paid the family debts a thousand times over. All I know is that he did not pay his debt to Christ and his sister. Even if the poor girl committed the sin she was tempted to commit, there would have been no excuse for him; but she did not, yet he dared to refuse to shelter her. Oh, the more I think of it, the more awful he appears to me, the more terribly in need of Christian mercy. And why Maggie fell in love with that fellow Stephen, I cannot imagine. He was quite unworthy of her."

"But she did."

"Well, I cannot think it fitting . . ."

"I am afraid also that there are many like Tom, professing to be Christian, and cold, hard-headed, upright, unsympathetic, treading the weak under foot in the gutter, and making religion hard and unlovely. Oh, I cannot bear to think of it, and I fear there are many of them!"

Speaking of Dickens' *David Copperfield* he would say, "That is a fine book; there is that old sailor, what's his name?"

"Peggotty."

"Ah, Peggotty, Peggotty, who kept the light burning. His daughter ran away with a rascal, and he used to say that the candle should be kept burning in the old pane of glass as if to say, 'Come back, my child, come back.' A splendid old fellow!"

A Tale of Two Cities was a great favourite of his, but with the exception, perhaps, of the *Pickwick Papers* he used to say that Dickens had thrown away great talents. "Why did not he employ them in describing great historical events, as in *A Tale of Two Cities*, since he had such a power for doing so, instead of writing about all those strange creatures,"—one of several contradictions to his democratic theories.

After breakfast at Bournemouth he would hand a companion the Bible, and ask for a few verses, almost always some saying or doing of our Lord. Then he would pray, not like a child, for he had suffered too much, but in as simple and profound a manner as ever. From thence he went to the reading room. Two events in the outer world greatly stirred him at this time: one was the illness of the young Queen of Holland, and the other was the 1902 Education Bill, to which reference has already been made. He was full of compassion for the former, and at certain rumours rife in the papers which stirred his most vehement indignation.

Dr. Lunn came down one week-end, and they wandered together over the sands, my father's whole frame bespeaking the intensest activity as he threw himself into the knotty question of the reunion of the Liberal party. It was impossible not to think that the pain and discomfort of the last weeks were rapidly passing, and that he would regain much of his former health and strength. Another time Dr. Pope came, and the experience of the Swiss mountains was repeated. Everything in the great globe went to rack, except Methodism. They wandered out on the cliffs, they had tea, they sat down, they had dinner, they sat down and then bade each other good-night, and it was all Methodism. Dr. Pope was straight from a work which was of the greatest interest to his listener—the greater co-ordination of the Methodist Church in the villages—her work having suffered hitherto through the isolation of chapels and stations. Methodist union was also touched upon. Dr. Pope mentioned difficulties, while my father became a pure idealist, and would not admit any difficulties at all. "Oh," he said, "we must sweep them all away, as well as all that weights and confines us in our three years' system!"

38

The youthful mood of Epping Forest was upon him, and he was neither cautious nor constitutional. Judging by many writers, humanity in its age loses the dreams and aspiration of its youth, but in him these grew in intensity, so that the dreams and aspiration of the youth were not to be compared with those of the man of fifty-five. Another day a Methodist layman—a very saintly man—came and talked so well and so long, that my father did not get a word in any-where. This visit much impressed him. Another afternoon a rich Methodist took him for a drive, and told him what a business it was to look after money, and to dispense it in the best way, my father listening with much sympathy and the heartiest agreement. All who came to see him or whom he came across he was delighted to meet, and full of appreciative comments about them after they had gone. That year Sir Horace Marshall, who was Sheriff of the City of London, had asked my father to act as his chaplain, so he expected, not without eagerness, to be present at the Lord Mayor's Banquet, and to hear the speeches which are such a feature of that occasion. In particular, he was looking forward to the Prime Minister's utterances, and when he returned he retailed them. The King's Levée also (the first after his coronation) he was careful to attend, and for reasons that have been stated.[1] Shortly afterwards he and my mother cycled over to visit one of his sisters (Mrs. Berney) in Wiltshire.

While staying with her he visited some of the villagers in whom she took an interest, and was particularly moved by a bedridden woman. Though a sufferer for many years, her words to him were not those of complaint but of thanksgiving. God, she said, had been very good to her, and she was full of rejoicing rather than sorrow.

Later in the year he visited his sister, Mrs. Frank Webbe-Peploe, in Westmoreland, who writes as follows:—

"Your father's last visit to us at Leck, in the autumn of 1901, will always be a most happy memory. He and your mother spent a month with us, and it was a particularly happy and peaceful time. When he arrived I was, of course, greatly struck by his changed appearance, and I

---

[1] As Wesleyan President my father had been introduced at Court. Nonconformist clergymen who occupied leading positions in their communion should, he thought, take their full share in the national life and in the obligations that such entailed.

felt that his mind, though it had lost none of its quick grip, was, for the time, tired.

"It was the first time for years that I had seen your father sufficiently at rest to enjoy him socially. We had friends staying with us during part of his visit, and they have a most vivid remembrance of his brightness and brilliance.

"I remember how, one night, he read Browning to us, poem after poem, and then pretended to be surprised when your mother and I objected to his turning to Tennyson!

"It was a time of great peace. The only daily paper he was able to see on the day of issue was the *Yorkshire Post*, which we used to hand him with great relish, and I think the bareness of the land in that respect was really good for him. Of course he had numerous London papers forwarded to him, but the fact of their arriving a day late had a distinctly calming effect. Outside, the Boer War still lingered, and the Education Bill held on its way, but in our remote country vicarage the strife of men seemed very far away. Several times your father told me how he appreciated having time to *feel* home-life, and how interested he was in his glimpse of the lives of country clergymen.

"He took a keen interest in our various interests. He gave my husband the latest *Dictionary of the Bible* (Hastings), which has been invaluable to him, and provided me with a Browning *Cyclopædia* to prepare for some Browning readings, while our little Gwen—his youngest niece—counts among her greatest treasures the *Tales of Ancient Greece* he and your mother gave her then."

An interesting episode of the early spring of this year was the meeting with the artist, Mr. Frederick Shields, which was brought about through a mutual friend.

A person who was present described it as the meeting of two who had very much in common. One said something and the other took it up and continued what he had said. Then they contradicted each other, and burst out laughing. In their conversation they glanced from topic to topic and place to place like a sunbeam shooting over a pool. Italy, the Orient, both were as near at hand as the objects lying about the studio, which were so quick to fasten the attention of one of them. Naturally Mr. Shields' designs and pictures were the most absorbing topic. My father admired in particular the fresco which depicts the quarrel of the Apostles when they strove with each other as to who should have the highest place in the kingdom.[1] A book lying on a table, when snatched

[1] Now on view in the Chapel of the Ascension. Our Lord's Baptism in the same series was a great favourite of my father's. "It's so original," he used to say.

up by hands practised in this species of pilfering, proved to be the Hymns of John and Charles Wesley.

"No hymns, you say, to be compared with them?" my father inquired. "Your favourite? That's the case with me, and I said so when my brethren elected me President."

The pages of the hymn-book fluttered like leaves.

"Now the fuss they make about these other collections is due to the tunes they have managed to get hold ot and keep to themselves. It's not their hymns, my dear fellow, but the tunes. People will sing anything if you put a tune to it."

They sat down and became absorbed in the structure and charm of Wesley's Hymns.

"So much that people sing now," said Mr. Shields, "has nothing in it and resembles a tinkling cymbal. What is there to compare to this? There is vitality, health, strength in these, something to sing about."

At this point I am sure my father must have informed Mr. Shields that the Methodist Church was contemplating a revision of the Methodist Hymn-Book—a needful weeding process by which the fairest flowers of the garden would only profit. He was sitting on the Revision Committee at the time of his death, and would report, as he walked along Gower Street and elsewhere, the extent of the clearage. Thus, except for flashes respecting Charles Wesley's hymns, the Pope, Holman Hunt, Michael Angelo, and the Rossettis, it was difficult to know what they talked about. Certainly there were confidences, and my father appeared much affected after his return.

"In years to come," he said, "they will go streaming into his chapel, admiring his work and never know what it cost him, how he suffered." The lack of sympathy evinced by many in dealing with an artist seemed to have been painfully brought home to him. Indeed, it was with difficulty that he could bring himself to utter the barbarous and callous remarks of prosaic persons. "Oh, it is awful!" he exclaimed—"awful. May God in His mercy deliver us from such unspeakable vulgarity!" Mr. Shields said, "I cannot remember what your father said, because his personality absorbed me—I knew I had found a friend." Every now and then my father would throw out a remark of Mr. Shields'—for instance—"When I spoke of him as being a religious painter, he at once repudiated the term.

' On no account,' he said, ' I endeavour to be a spiritual painter. Heaven save me from being a religious one.' He says that art should appeal to the spirit as well as the senses, and that any one who says that art has only to do with the senses is a liar, and the love of God is not in him." Then at some length he repeated Mr. Shields' views on these matters with growing rapture.

It was his intention to write about Mr. Shields and the Chapel of the Ascension in the Journal—an intention which the pressure of other matters—the Education Bill, and the case of Dr. Beet, and finally death—prevented him from carrying out. Doubtless he felt some diffidence, whatever his interest, in embarking on a subject which seems to require specialist knowledge. Yet the writer is none the less haunted by the thought that he passed away without performing an act of friendship which he most heartily intended to accomplish. He would have delighted to inform readers of the *Methodist Times* of the whereabouts of the Chapel of the Ascension, in the Bayswater Road, midway between the Marble Arch and Lancaster Gate, and intended by its designers to serve as a place of meditation and silence in the rush of the great city.

While much of my father's interest in Mr. Shields was that springing from spontaneous affection, it contained, like so many of his lively emotions, an element of statecraft. To understand something of it, the reader must imagine a Pope of the Middle Ages brought face to face with an artist glowing with the essential attributes of the Roman faith. Doubtless these often felt, as my father did, a grudge against those artists and writers who persist in leading men astray, confirming them in their prejudices instead of trying to lessen them. Like them, he brooded in secret over the ghastly powers wielded by irresponsible persons, and waited day and night to find one unto his liking, so that he might clutch at him and set him to work in suitable and conspicuous places. To be possessed by evangelical tradition and to combine with intense devoutness that touch of reverent familiarity which made Christ human and yet near, was what he desired to see in the works of an artist. His ideal of bliss on this earth would have been to set numbers of such painters at work on the great Methodist Hall at Westminster, and to have looked in

upon them, say, on breezy spring mornings on his way from a
connexional committee. Each he would have courteously
saluted, and each would have confided in him. " Ah! you
have been making progress." " The left wing of the arch-
angel is visibly expanding. I much admire that faint rose
with which you are tipping his plumage. It suggests, you
say—daybreak—? Ah, I must take a chair and sit down and
look at it." Then, in a low voice, " What about that matter
you were referring to the other day? Can I be of any further
service. They said what? Never mind what they said. Put
your trust in the Almighty and tell them you will not stand
any of their humbug."

In particular, he would have banished heathen delineations
of the hereafter as unfit for the brush of Christian art. He
could never forgive Michael Angelo for his delineation of the
Judgment, over the High Altar in the Sistine Chapel at Rome.
His mighty art had been used to enhance a theology which
had so terrified generations of mankind that certain had spent
their life in trembling at the thought of it, and in neglecting
many of their palpable duties, because they wanted by hook or
crook to make some way of escape. Besides, how had this
heathen encroachment misrepresented and checked the progress of Christianity? Noble and sensitive souls had grown
up to loathe the religion of their fathers and had become its
most violent opponents. The true purport and endeavour of
the Christian life had been lost sight of on account of the
diversion which a heathen idea of God had engendered. That
retribution had overtaken his generation I believe him to have
sincerely believed, nor did I ever hear him express surprise or
anger at the attacks on Christianity and professing Christians
which were pretty constant in his time. He would comment
as follows: " So-and-so, being full of the most beautiful ethical
and humanitarian ideals, which he derives from Christ, is attacking us Christians because we are not carrying them out.
With much that he says I am in entire sympathy—the rest I
deplore, because he writes, poor fellow, from depths of misconception and ignorance, knowing no more of Christianity and
the Church of Christ than if he were a babe unborn. But it is
greatly our fault, and we can only pray God both to enlighten
him and us."

It is scarcely possible, perhaps, for the present generation to understand certain circles of religious thought, even as recently as thirty-five years ago. When my father was a young man, an old minister said to him, "Hughes, preach Hell and its fire—that is the only way to impress and save the people," which recalls the following incident in his Dover ministry. One of the sons, at a house which he was visiting on Sunday afternoon, said with a smile to my father —half-satiric, half-indulgent—"Well, Hughes, what is it this evening at Snargate Street—a good dose of hell fire, eh?" With a smile, long remembered of those who saw it, he answered quickly, "Something sweeter than that, John." The saints as well as the sinners, he found, seemed to live in an unnatural gloom, and it was not only Achates-in-the-Fields to whom he administered vigorous consolation.

In one of the suburbs, he came back from his weekly devotional class with the tale of a certain lady who thought she had committed the unpardonable sin. He gave my mother to understand that in his desire to deal effectively with the patient he had administered a consolatory tonic, so vigorous as to savour of rebuke, leaving the lady in question in the arms of a fair friend who was to bestow soothing syrup after the tonic that had just been administered. "I did right, did I not?" he asked; "for really I thought it was the best way. There was that saintly woman trembling in every limb, because she thought she had inadvertently committed something for which God would never forgive her, and I was bound to reprove her for the blasphemy, though I felt very sorry for the poor woman—very—at the thought of her passing through all this unnecessary agony." Yet does a reader smile at what seems to him these old-world agonies; he never did. He knew they had their place and meaning like every other darkness through which the race has passed. He was ever the last to underestimate those agonies and heart-searchings which, from time immemorial, have been the prelude to higher life. I can remember his comments when one, quickened, she knew not how, and full of restless questionings concerning herself and her life, called upon the vicar of the parish where she was living, and was told by him that, as she was baptized and confirmed, she must be suffering from some enlargement of the conscience which must be lulled to its normal condition. "Just fancy," he exclaimed, "an 'enlarged' conscience, when the poor thing was longing for peace." While, on the one hand, no one was more opposed to the introspective morbid state in which certain professing Christians had fallen, or more vigorous in shaking them into health, he was far too much of a Catholic Churchman, too devoted to the memory of her best saints, to underestimate and not prize those periods of exultation and of agony which are the manifestations of the life of the Spirit. The effect of his preaching and presence, it must be remembered, was often to evoke these manifestations—not emotional demonstrations, as previously cited, but deeper thought, deeper feeling. At Brixton there was a gardener who experienced such joy when my father was taking the service, that he felt bound to swing his arms and leap into the air, retiring indeed into the adjoining vestry for that purpose, so that he might not scandalise sedate persons.

Later, I can remember my father expressing great regret at Mr. Spurgeon's attitude towards the doctrine of eternal punishment. At Conference also he distinctly enunciated his disagreement with those theologians of his own Church who disliked any tampering with traditional doctrine, and had written in defence of it. Moreover, at the Conference of 1902, the August after he met Mr. Shields, he defended Dr. Beet, whose case was arousing much feeling in Wesleyan Methodism, because it was a good deal involved, and by no means so simple as it appeared to the outside world. Dr. Beet had not only written condemning the doctrine of eternal torment, but he had supplemented this by certain views of his own concerning immortality, which were held by no other theological school. In addition, he was tutor at one of the Wesleyan colleges, and could scarcely be expected not to inculcate what he wrote.

A disturbance had arisen, and Dr. Beet had been summoned before a special committee. The whole matter was to be brought before the Pastoral Session, which should decide whether a teacher of such independent views could with advantage occupy the chair of one of their theological colleges. It has been generally admitted that it was my father's defence which retained Dr. Beet in his position. It was a matter that was bound to be involved, and to appeal differently to different minds, for it is seldom indeed that the bulwarks of tradition are first assailed in a manner that the wisest could suggest. Younger ministers who were in some perplexity as to how to decide in a case that presented complications, asked which side Hughes was taking, and, on hearing that he was going to defend Dr. Beet, determined, without further questioning, to defend him also. Of the many times my father had risen to address Conference, this, the last, seems to have been the most remarkable, on account of the singular character of the hearing that was given him. Old misapprehensions were losing their hold, and the silent exclamation (often repeated during this Conference) must have risen to the surface of many minds, " How ill he looks ! " His speech, judging by comments made to the writer, seems to have produced a certain awe—the fruit apparently neither of brilliance nor acumen, or even of that grasp of the subject, and the sensibilities of the audience, which must have been its dominant characteristic, but of a singular elevation of spirit which carried the day, because there was none to combat it from a similar altitude. As to the solution that was proposed and effected, the more liberal in the outside world could not be pleased with it, and indeed were not. The writer has come across correspondence criticising Dr. Beet's defender for half-heartedness. Opponents, on the other hand, remarked that the compromise was palpably illogical. My father, as usual, had made for a compromise, and compromises are not remarkable for their coherency. Dr. Beet retained his chair on the considerations cited below, and notably on those in which he pledged himself to abstain from teaching further, either by pen or word of mouth, his particular interpretation of certain doctrines.

The charges were as follows : [1]—

1. That Dr. Beet has violated a pledge, given at the Hull Conference in 1898, to withdraw the book entitled *The Last*

---

[1] " It may be stated that the discussion occupied three hours, that excitement necessarily at times was very great, that the findings of the Committee were considered clause by clause, that the leaders in Conference debates mostly took part in the conversation, that appeals for order by the President were distressingly frequent, but that in the end there was unanimity in accepting the findings of the Committee. . . ."—Extract from *Methodist Times*.

Things, by republishing the substance of the book in another book entitled *The Immortality of the Soul : A Protest.*

2. That Dr. Beet has published in the aforesaid book, entitled *The Immortality of the Soul : A Protest*, doctrines contrary to the standards of our Church.

The Committee finds in regard to No. 1 that Dr. Beet has not kept the pledge given to the Conference in the sense in which it was generally understood; but the Committee recognises the great difficulty and perplexity in which Dr. Beet was placed at the time the promise was made, and, while deeply regretting his action, regards it as arising from a serious error of judgment rather than from want of good faith.

In regard to objection 2, Mr. Wilson maintained that the teaching of the book is contrary to our standards—(*a*) In exalting the moral sense as an authority in matters of religious belief above Holy Scripture; (*b*) in regard to the immortality of the soul and the endless suffering of the lost.

As to 2 (*a*) the Committee finds that though his language was unguarded and liable to misconception, and some passages of his book seem to place the moral sense above the Scriptures, as an authority in matters of religious belief, Dr. Beet had no intention of doing this, and he emphatically denies that there is any real conflict between the two.

As to 2 (*b*) Dr. Beet stated before the Committee that in some small details his teaching contravenes the teaching of our standards, but that it is in harmony with the general system of doctrine that underlies them.

The Committee reports that Dr. Beet rejects, as without adequate foundation, the doctrines popularly known as those of " Annihilation," " Conditional Immortality," " Universal Restoration," and " Probation after Death," and maintains :

(*a*) That though the Holy Scriptures teach that " all souls will survive death " for a period to which no limit can be affixed, and that " utter, hopeless, and final punishment will overtake " the impenitent, they do not " assert or assume the essential permanence of the soul," though neither do they deny this.

(*b*) That while the Holy Scriptures give no ground for hope that the agony of the lost will ever cease, they do not plainly and categorically *assert* its endless continuance.

The Committee finds that this teaching falls short of and contravenes the doctrines universally held and taught in our Church.

In regard to the whole case the Committee, in view of the dread solemnity and admitted mystery of the subject, and the necessity of allowing some freedom of opinion upon it, and out of regard to the fidelity of Dr. Beet to our general system of doctrine, recommends that the Conference take no further action in the matter, on condition that Dr. Beet will not teach in our pulpits the doctrine of his book.

The Conference adopted this report and recommendations, but deleted the word " universally " from the sentence, " contravenes the doctrines universally held and taught in our Church," and added the further conditions :

(a) That Dr. Beet will publish nothing further on the subject without obtaining the consent of the Conference.

(b) That he will not teach these doctrines in the classroom.

My father's leading motives were in keeping with the imperial character of his strategy. He feared to displace a professor of such repute as Dr. Beet, and particularly on a question which involved the doctrine of eternal punishment. By his wide reading and observation he was aware of what ordinary men and women were thinking on such matters, particularly young men and young women ; and he feared the shock to liberal thought the world over, if it came to be taken up by the press, as it undoubtedly would have been, that Wesleyan Methodism had rejected a theological tutor because he disbelieved in eternal punishment. That the outside world would enter into or understand the ins and outs of the case was not to be expected. An issue of that kind he felt would be harmful to Methodism and the whole Church. Those various classes alienated from the Churches over whom he yearned would be increasingly estranged. Not only did he feel that Methodism would suffer in her prestige, but also internally.

In the minds of many of her members, this question of eternal punishment was brooded over, whether with or without equipment, and the effect of such a pronouncement must be, he felt, creative of discord, and, what was worse, of

disastrous effects to the whole world of religious thinking which
is affected by such pronouncements. Wesleyan Methodism,
much as some might wish it, could not live unto itself, but
unto that community of the religious-minded which cannot
escape the effect of such decisions. Inevitably, the avoidance
of such a settlement must make narrow unimaginative thought
the narrower, and deepen the cleavage with that which was in
insurrection against it. His thoughts seemed specially to have
hovered around those, who, young in life and thought, are
peculiarly impressionable to those events and pronouncements
which shock the first ideal of things, often irretrievably. Some
bias for or against anything, while the mind and feeling are in
their pliant stage, will influence and determine the course of
a whole life. His idea that those in responsible positions were
under a special obligation to consider the weak and ill-informed
and innocent, was a characteristic note in his thought on
these matters.

He was less interested in the local details and difficulties
of such a matter than in its effect on the mass of the imperfectly informed, who struggle dimly with ideals and beliefs
more than is supposed. His sympathy with the pains and
struggles of young and insignificant persons was often strikingly manifested. On one occasion he was asked by certain
educationalists to speak concerning high school and public
school education for girls. In the course of his address,
which was highly appreciative of such institutions, he merely
ventured one criticism—that very young, particularly nervous
children, were best not sent there too early. Some lady
who was present almost " devoured him in her rage," he said
afterwards, " rising and saying that I had brought forward
aspersions which were quite unjustifiable." The speaker was
thinking of an educational system ; my father of the children in
the lower first who live in worlds unknown, some of them,
to their elders. As was so often the case, my father and his
opponent were considering different data. He was not looking
at the same things, and it was scarcely to be wondered that
they did not always understand him. Apart from more
general considerations, my father had a personal affection
for Dr. Beet, and a high regard for much that he had
written. With Dr. Beet's peculiar theories concerning the

hereafter he undoubtedly did not agree, but, on the other hand, he appreciated his attack on certain material conceptions of it.

When it was hinted that there was a savour of the illogical in the settlement, he remarked, not without emphasis, that no other branch of Christ's Church would have made so reasonable a compromise on such a matter.   So aware was he of the revolt of the present generation against certain conceptions of one or two previous generations, that he feared excess—a break in the continuity of the most strenuous living.   He felt it unnecessary to join in the protest that was being so efficaciously performed by others.   The scientific propagandists— the litterateurs, current opinion and conversation, the very air— were all militating against certain appurtenances of tradition —and so much so, he feared at times, as to endanger the continuity of what was vital in them.   While so much was still in ferment, responsible Churchmen must wait before committing themselves to expressions of truth which needed carefully considering and from more than one aspect.

A criticism made by an opponent of some of his opinions was as follows : that in youth and early maturity his watchword had been "the people," but that in later years he listened not so much for their voice as for the voice of God, which came to transcend the claims and aspirations of Democracy.   Such a criticism, though it is scarcely fair, and the bias is evident, is certainly suggestive.   It is scarcely fair, because there is no person who lives at all deeply, who does not fall back more and more upon God, and who does not suffer disappointment of some kind both in parties and causes and persons.   The same criticism could be equally applied to those who held opinions, and had watchwords that were the opposite of my father's.   At the same time it does throw light on the difficulties and mental processes of a democratic leader, while it contains a criticism of that half-divine character, which in earlier days he attributed to great popular aspirations and movements.   Some never could understand his enthusiasm for great meetings and his belief in them, though, as far as that goes, they did not understand his enthusiasm and belief about anything.   Part of his insistence lay in the fact that he lived at a time when the *vox populi* sadly needed listening to in his own communion, and as far as that goes in the life of all communions. His own vehemence and absorption in the particular conception of the hour made him appear one-sided at times, though this, as the history of his life shows, was the last thing that could be said about him.

While, undoubtedly, he saw increasingly a pathetic dependence of the multitude on its leaders, as he had not formerly, and while he came to resist even the intense religious conviction of a section of it, he yet never lost his belief and sympathy in the dictates of its heart, in the reality of its best aspirations. His Imperialism, indeed, was the crowning evidence of his unbounded belief in the British Democracy. " In theatres," he would say, "when the actors give vent to noble or unselfish sentiments, it is always the gallery that applauds; and political speakers, when they do the same, are accused of playing to the gallery." "Such a phrase," he would say, "is to the eternal honour of those who can only afford to sit in sixpenny and shilling seats." Thus, to the end, he discerned beneath all the struggle and evil and ignorance, something pure and fresh, as of a child striving to articulate, and whose speech and phrasing has not yet been formed. The criticism that he did ultimately come to make was probably that of Renan, when he says that the people are indeed idealist, and that it is an idealism which blinds, because it leads them to lay such insistence on solitary issues and to overlook others.

A thought which was present as he observed the agitation of the general mind seems to have been as follows :—If the critics of the heathen conception of the hereafter had contented themselves with purely destructive criticisms, instead of making assumptions concerning a future state for which they had no shadow of proof, the case would have been a good deal simpler. All kinds of prophets, he found, had their own particular explanation—attractive or the reverse—which certainly could not claim the serious notice of any theologian, and which lacked the dignity and faith of the best agnostics. A young lay preacher preached Universalism, with various additions of a spiritualistic tendency, which he contended, at the leaders meeting, he was free to enunciate from the different platforms of the West London Mission. My father listened attentively, reasoned with him, and found himself obliged to forbid his preaching further, since he would not consent to keep silent respecting his individual views.   Whereupon the lay preacher told him what he thought, and by the vigour of his denunciation impressed him not a little.   Afterwards my father fell to meditating, as he often did, on the undeniable eloquence and good sense of certain of his critics.   " He regards me as second only to the Pope in iniquity," he said, " and the stifler of thought and freedom.   He spoke up very well, poor fellow, too."   A colleague who had been present passed a criticism on what he thought a lack of courtesy and respect on the part of the lay preacher.   "Oh, do you think so?" my father asked quietly, still meditating.   "The man thinks he is doing God's service, no doubt.   He's a very good preacher too, and clever and amiable when there's no tyrant like myself about. But" (with an access of vigour) "the whole thing is preposterous and impossible.   What else could I have done in my position?   How can I authorise a man to preach to simple uneducated people, not only doctrines which have never been accepted by our Church, like Universalism, but particular suppositions of his own and other unauthorised persons, such as communion with departed spirits, which might have a most injurious effect on our congregations? The whole thing is unthinkable and absurd.   I said to him, 'These suppositions are really not necessary.   Think them if you like, but while there is still so much uncertainty respecting these matters, do not bring them into the pulpit, where there are so many more vital issues to be talked about.' However, he could not be moved, and he has gone home raging against me, poor fellow, I do not doubt!"

My father shared Browning's dislike of spiritualism.   The Christian Scientists and the other sects who had sprung up without preserving the main traditions of the Christian faith— belief in our Lord as a Saviour from sin, and in His resurrection after death, were always spoken of as ephemeral. Such having no depth of earth must wither and die, and beyond the fact that they were indications of the trend of the general mind, he had no special interest in them.

The efforts to make a religion of natural science similarly passed him by.   They gave no hope to man, and did not satisfy the demands of his spirit as Christ Jesus had done

once and for ever. Religion was not hostile to science in
his eyes, because it was a part of the subject of science.   The
birth of our Saviour into the world, and what men had thought
and felt concerning Him, was as much a historic fact, a
natural phenomenon, as any of those natural occurrences
which were reported by men of science.   The wind fanning
his cheek, the rain and the sunshine and the dew, were not
nearer and greater realities to him than the Saviour on whom
he fed in his heart by faith, and whom, on his own confession,
he felt nearer to him than the objects and persons in his
vicinity.   Discoveries, events, doubtings, he wanted to see
through His eyes, not through his own, and to merge his
thoughts in His.

Yet the sacrifice was never complete — frailties he felt
intervened.   So in these matters of doctrine he wanted
Christ's thought to find expression in him.   What was
material, heathen, a denial of the love of God, he felt to
be unspeakably more hateful to Christ than to himself.   On
the other hand, he believed that the race had not been allowed
to be born and to die in certain conceptions of a future state
without some great purpose—some great lesson that was
intended to be taught it.   Christ had deliberately used
terrible language with respect to those who sinned against the
light, who knowingly chose good instead of evil.   The Western
mind had interpreted Oriental allegory in its usual literal
prosaic manner, but such an admission did not dissipate the
tragedy and terror of the vision which the utterances denoted.
To resist the Divine will, to refuse to be maimed in life—
bodily, mentally, and spiritually—so as to perform it, meant
to the soul torture unspeakable, begun here and now, he felt,
if men had the eyes to see.   He could never agree with the
Psalmist that the wicked " flourish like the green bay tree "—
they only appear to.   Yet for all his strength of feeling, and
his insistence on what was vital in tradition, he insisted a few
days before he died that the traditional views concerning
the hereafter needed restatement, and that in their older form
they had ceased to have meaning to the present generation.
What had been slain in the inmost recesses of the best
Christian minds, those most in touch with the evils and
great facts of life, could not be used with advantage by

any religious system. If they did make use of it, he exclaimed, it would be merely using a corpse.

His personal attitude towards Christian doctrine, about which there is some difference of opinion, is perhaps best illustrated by the following:—

A companion said to him: "If it became impossible for the Western mind to conceive of the virgin birth of Christ, would it make any difference to your faith?"

"None," he replied.

"Some though," his companion continued, "seem to be in a great agitation about it, thinking that if this and similar beliefs are taken away from them, that there is little, if anything, left them. Can you understand their state of mind?"

"No," he replied, "I cannot understand it."

"Does it not seem strange that they should feel in this way?"

"Very," he replied, and laughed. He was cutting a new route across Hampstead Heath and attentively observing the points of the compass, and the thought of the human soul vexing itself over such non-essential matters appeared to him almost ludicrous. As he strode on in front with a step that became increasingly elastic, his silence denoted meditation, which communicated itself as meditation can. One thing was certain, he would never touch the doctrine in question with his little finger, and when others did so he would watch them with not a little apprehension. Conceptions that had played a great part in the life of the Church and humanity, he did not care, any more than others, to see lightly cast aside.

Such conversations would sink into his mind, while he brooded over the expediency of what had been said and proposed. The roots of his belief lay far deeper than that which any particular expression of Christian thought could disturb, yet as he conceived it his business to preach Christ to his age, he thought it best to address the jury (to quote his favourite simile) in terms that it could understand. The almost mystic order of portions of his thinking made him lend a readier ear to certain interpretations of events and occurrences than others of his mental calibre. He did not share or, indeed, sympathise with what has come to be the

39

Western opposition to tenets and conceptions of a faith which is of Oriental origin, and he resented the habitual sceptical attitude which was characteristic of many minds of his day. Persons who had had faith-cures or vivid spiritual experiences of some kind, or, in particular, startling answers to prayer, were listened to by him with attention and sympathy. Nor would he allow persons who were present to express incredulity. " How do you know? God may have had a special purpose in connection with this brother."

There was in him something ready to believe, and a child-like disposition to listen and marvel. He could not but think God and the world wonderful, and what God's creatures had to say wonderful also. Observers were sometimes reminded of Whitman's exclamations on the amazing " spirituality of things." Once he suddenly missed my mother, who was walking by his side, and on finding her said, " Do you know, I thought a miracle had taken place, and that you had suddenly been taken from me." Though said humorously, it was half serious. His faith did not depend on recorded miracles, and was independent of them, but he was not averse to their occurrence as some appear to be. Christ's love was a miracle, and after that everything was possible. Those who love greatly, expect miracles. Those who do not love do not expect them. The love of God in Christ was always performing miracles around him, transforming people's lives, so he was ready for what appeared to moderns to be the transcending of natural laws. At the same time he always gave the impression of a sound mind in a sound body, sounder, when one comes to think of it, than those who, in their atrophy, have lost what is natural to the normal human being.

The present controversy concerning documentary evidence he seemed to regard as a passing gust of wind in which nothing vital would be blown away. " When I was a boy," he would say, " the historian Herodotus was regarded by the learned as a garrulous old gossip, whose words had no historical weight. Now he is one of the text-books at the University of Oxford." He struck one as conscious of the progress of the battle, particularly of its shiftings, and in no way perturbed by them. Such had been and would be again, and it was certainly not the business of those who were not expert to raise their voice in the matter. Arguments concerning the evidence of Christianity, documentary or otherwise, between members of his profession and professed agnostics, were always deplored by him, particularly when the zeal of the former outran both their learning and their discretion. Such questions were for experts amid the leisure and absence of haste and passion that should characterise these investigations. These were productive of good, in that they cleared the mind, cleansed it of superstition, and established faster the truths that were vital. To some, at times, he appeared to underestimate the documentary question; but this disregard was a seeming rather than an actual one. He was so aware of scientific criticism generally, as to lay stress on what he thought to be vital in the Christian Church and faith.[1] He knew the negative tone and temper that the scientific propagandists must produce in the general mind, as well as the reaction that must follow towards affirmation of some kind, since humanity had never been able to live without faith. That also which he seemed to fear with regard to certain ecclesiastical opponents—those who leant strongly towards some of the practices and beliefs of Rome—was that they were clinging to non-essentials which must inevitably be shattered in the light of the modern scientific spirit.

The doubts and divergencies of those who had not, he thought, yielded themselves and their life to a Divine discipline, fell on unheeding ears. Arguments with these on such matters were valueless in his eyes, and he did not enter into such arguments. On the other hand, with those who were willing to enter into that discipline which was the Christian life, he evinced a partiality that would strike certain onlookers as incongruous. For, with all his appreciation of definite and correct thinking in certain matters, his maximum attention was paid to the less bound in thought and the sinners generally. Very correctly thinking persons he very seldom paid any heed to. It was the rebellious, the lawless, who appeared to be his delight, and to attempt to marshal them was his peculiar bliss. Active minds, rebels against the conventions, found in him, in many ways, a sympathiser and friend. The persons who satisfied

---

[1] He was greatly influenced by Dr. Dale, and would often say when commenting on the evangelical acceptation of Christianity " You should read Dale. It's all there."

those conditions which he imposed on the lawless, passed by him unheeded.

There is danger, indeed, of undue stress being laid on my father's dogmatic proclivities which, while they were a strong instinct, were not all of him. His personality was ever strangely varied and blended, an undue insistence on one feature of it leading to a misleading presentation. Part of his great feeling, as already indicated, for traditional usage and belief, whether in Church or doctrine, was that it involved a form of discipline, bodily and mental, without which the highest spiritual life was not possible. The orderly in thought and habit he felt might attain to sainthood. Thus he clung to the links of old time, especially to certain of the Puritan tradition—the observance of Sunday, of regular worship and prayer-meeting!

It was not this or that particular infringement of Sunday observance to which he objected, but the passing away of all those restrictions which made of one day, however imperfectly, a day set apart for religious observances, and for meditation on spiritual and abiding things. No one more than himself resented a keeping of Sunday that should be dismal or chilling to the young. Yet, on the other hand, he resented the doing away of a day that implanted the associations and habits which his own youth had brought him. He used to say that it would be a sad day for England if the Continental observance of Sunday came to be the vogue, and that the Puritan, with all its limitations and excesses, was the better.

At the same time he felt the matter to be a difficult one, for he notes in the Journal that many saints even spent much of their Sunday in unprofitable ways, and that it was not possible to lay down hard and fast rules. Right up to the closing years of his life he was ready to attend a six o'clock prayer-meeting (as during the united Free Church Mission in 1900), and wondered, I do not doubt, that others were not equally eager to buy up special opportunities of realising the perpetual presence of Christ in His Church. Indeed it was the uniqueness of his position as the focus of many forces that enabled him to defend Dr. Beet in Methodism, and to succeed in his defence. One who was present said, almost in a whisper, in the writer's hearing, " Only he could have done it, nobody else."

Many contemporaries, including Methodists, thought him

conservative in later life, using that term in its general sense, as the main tendency of a man's thought and action.[1] His own family, indeed, and one or two intimates had often warned him concerning it, knowing, as the outside world did not, certain inherent instincts of his nature. " Only the grace of God," my mother would say laughingly, " enables you to be a Liberal, otherwise you would be a fearful reactionary." Particularly also did some of his Liberal friends fear the effect of the Presidency, that official position which, as a rule, will make men suspicious of new ideas. Supposing that this were so, it would have been in the " strictest nature even," for men over fifty cannot be expected to contribute to a community that element which should be given by younger men. Those who are directly responsible for the conduct and the maintenance of the affairs of a great Church, are bound to feel their momentum, and to have the conserving instinct in the ascendant.

Some, indeed, as Dr. Pope's letter portrays, regretted a life that was cut off in the heyday of its statesmanship, and was thus prevented from displaying to the Methodist people powers and an aspect of itself which they are more inclined to admire and understand, than the gifts of the pioneer. Nevertheless this outward semblance of what to many was an unexpected conservatism, and which was necessitated by the difficulties and responsibilities of an increasingly unique position in Methodism, has been ' exaggerated, for it was contradicted on the side of personal thought and feeling, by an immense modification in more than one respect, and an increasing sympathy, not only with diverse aspects of life as already stated, but with the thought which is their product.

Thus he may be compared from the intimate standpoint to one nearing the summit of a hill, who has fought his way through adversaries, and now on the higher lands sees a wider horizon. Indeed, the singular mellowing and added insight of later years was specially noted by certain opponents as well as by those who, while differing with him in various matters, had watched him with increasing sympathy in the world of affairs. Teachers whose aim he did not formerly appear to discern, became intelligible to him. They were struggling

---

[1] There was a saying in Methodism that after John Wesley no one had contradicted himself more than my father.

to meet a need of the modern mind, and were not merely performing irregular movements as in his more militant days they had sometimes appeared to be doing. He perceived, with the opportunity for reflection that forced inactivity brought him, and as the fruit of experience of former years, that questions which he had once deemed of comparative unimportance, those of definition merely, were vital to many minds of the younger generation.

The fighters for Christianity in the world are bound to define their faith in words, as men will build a wall round a city with the implements which are to hand, yet the essence of the faith is to be found, not in its objective definition, necessarily imperfect, inadequate, and open to attack, but in the deep thought and feeling of the individuals who profess it, and in the great variety of individual apprehension which goes to make up Christendom. He had been so much the man of action, so aware of the world's need and of all that had to be done by those who felt it, that he may well have seemed at times to underestimate the painful struggle of some after clarity of vision. Yet it had been a seeming, rather than a reality, as the experience of certain of the missioners goes to prove.

That sentence of his, "I do not know how it is, but I have no leisure for anything," would be a just explanation of what was sometimes misunderstood in him. Moreover, it was those very persons who under his influence and that of others, had gone forth into the world to battle with great social evils, who were silently arriving at their own less rigid interpretations. The clash with the great realities, the infinite variety of men's lot and circumstance, had the inevitable effect upon their thinking. What he had feared, as already hinted, was the absence of Christian discipline in certain who came forth to do battle with the modern mind, and the presence of that self-assertion, that "trishna," which must impair not only a man's deeds but also his thought. None the less, men did not gather "thorns of grapes or figs of thistles," and to the end, for all his bias and alleged conservatism, he kept a mind that was curiously open, curiously responsive to new ideas. That mystic side to his thought, which had always been present, increased and deepened, and particularly as he came near to death, he struck one as being aware that men may mean the same thing, while they express it differently; not always, but sometimes. A day or two before he passed away he was reading a book by one scarcely in favour with orthodox circles, because he has made an earnest and passionate attempt to make doctrine vital and intelligible to the age. On being asked his impressions, he replied with a smile that was both tender and reflective, as if he divined the aim of the writer, "Oh, the man's a mystic, and he must be read from the mystical point of view," which was a great admission from such an ecclesiastic, such a defender of the faith. The impact of Eastern with Western thought is anticipated in various quarters, as that which shall aid towards the solution of those great problems into which independent minds are born in every age, and he with his keen feeling for "the *Zeitgeist*," his responsiveness to it, and his ardent poetic sense, had already entered the threshold of such an alliance.

As he walked down the Valley of the Shadow, the inner import of what the Church teaches might be described as becoming more and more transparent to him, as the sun at evening will gild and illumine objects, revealing what is within them. With two such divergent strains, that of the ecclesiastical statesman, and an outlook which was increasingly wide, not merely in theological knowledge, but in poetical insight, there was one rôle that he would naturally assume, that of mediator— the rôle in which he appeared in the defence of Dr. Beet. As ever, he would have maintained in affairs not what any instinct dictated, but that which he believed a Divine guidance enjoined. The reflections of his last days, clearly portrayed in his conversation and the books that he read, point to the fact that he was pondering and indeed preparing for this next phase of the Forward Movement. What he desired was an interpretation of Christian doctrine which, though in harmony with what was vital in tradition, should yet respond to the needs of individuals who had at all battled with the social realities of their time, and who had at all reflected concerning them. Thus, in speaking of the doctrine of the Atonement he said, "I wish very much we could find some statement which would reconcile the two schools, the old and the newer exposition." Though trained in the current Latin conceptions of Christian doctrine, he certainly preferred the more ancient Greek school, especially the great Alexandrian Fathers.

In arguments with youth he would often quote St. Paul, but his theology was Johannine rather than Pauline. Increasingly his instinct was to prefer a more elastic and imaginative interpretation of doctrine to that legal interpretation which has so far dominated large sections of Christendom. He understood a generation whose poet has written of God,

"Closer He is than breathing,
  Nearer than hands and feet,"

and which finds repose in the sayings of Christ Himself rather than in any system of salvation which has been deduced from these. Down the tumult of the ages His sayings seem fresh and of yesterday, and it learns from Him above the strife of Church and State that the kingdom of heaven is within men. Yet while my father increasingly understood the outlook and perplexities of a new generation, he perceived that the old legal interpretations of doctrine were the vessels of spiritual truth to many minds, and this made him tender towards them. A precious wine, he felt, needed carefully removing from an old to a new vessel, which must be full ready for its reception, and roomy and durable enough to contain and preserve every drop of the old. Thus he would have welcomed the thought and enthusiasm of youth while he respected the conservatism of age. His last and greatest service to the Church that he loved might have lain in interpreting the one to the other.

"LANDSEER, ST. MICHAEL'S ROAD, BOURNEMOUTH, WEST,
"*February* 8, 1902.

"DEAR SISTER ELIZABETH,—I greatly value your good and kind wishes, and those which you convey on behalf of the Sisters in Katherine House. Nothing could have been a greater pleasure to my wife and me, during all the years of the West London Mission, than the loyal and most kindly co-operation of the Sisters, in whom we have always had complete confidence, and whom we have always trusted with all our heart. I have had much sorrow and a good deal of physical suffering of late. But these things are passing, and I look forward with much happiness to the prospect of resuming my visits to Katherine House, and receiving the help of the Sisters in the work to which God has called us all—although, alas! Sister Edith will no longer be there. I believe that if we are all faithful to Christ and to one another, the future of the Mission will be far brighter than the past. I count confidently upon the continued prayers of the Sisters that God will fully restore me to health. I increasingly yearn to be at work. May God give us all a deeper and more Christlike life.—Yours very gratefully,

"H. PRICE HUGHES.

"Sister Elizabeth."

"LANDSEER, ST. MICHAEL'S ROAD, WEST BOURNEMOUTH, "*Nov.* 15, 1901.

"MY DEAR LUNN,—I am really getting quite ill with a longing to see you. Am I never to see you again? Katie and I very much want you to spend the next week-end with us here. Come next *Friday*, 22nd, or *Saturday* the 23rd— and you can be in London *early on Monday morning*. We have a small extra bedroom. We think you could get your body into the bed. Thus it is and will be empty and useless next week unless you come. I have so many things to say to you, it is useless to begin until I can talk rather than write. Please give our love to Mrs. Lunn, and tell her it is necessary for your soul's welfare and for mine that she should spare you for two days. Business takes you away for weeks. Two days are not much for the sake of friendship and the progress of mankind—especially mine. I must read that book you sent me before next Friday, so as to save you from the trouble of saying it all.—Yours affectionately,

"H. PRICE HUGHES.

"Dr. H. S. Lunn."

CHAPTER XXII

"Then said he, I am going to my Father's; and though with great difficulty I have got hither, yet now I do not repent me of all the troubles I have been at to arrive where I am. My sword I give to him that shall succeed me in my pilgrimage, and my courage and skill to him that can get it. My marks and scars I carry with me, to be a witness for me that I have fought His battles, Who now will be my Rewarder. When the day that he must go hence was come, many accompanied him to the river-side, into which as he went down he said, 'Death, where is thy sting?' And as he went down deeper he said, 'Grave, where is thy victory?'

"So he passed over, and all the trumpets sounded for him on the other side."

The Pilgrim's Progress.
(The passing of Mr. Valiant-for-truth over the Calm river.)

IN May, before Conference, my parents went to Adelboden, Switzerland, my father being particularly anxious to see the flowers of the neighbourhood, which are very beautiful during that month. Thus botanical books as well as the German grammar were conspicuous items of their outfit. Two or three articles shortly appeared in the Journal on Adelboden and its flowers. After six weeks they returned to London in order to view the King's Coronation procession from the window of the *Methodist Times* office.[1] Those windows cause reflection and one remembrance particularly. About the time of Queen Victoria's Diamond Jubilee he summoned the servants into his study with a somewhat grave demeanour. They feared he had something to complain of, so waited with some apprehension. "I have been thinking," he began, "that you would take pleasure in viewing the Jubilee procession from the

---

[1] The procession was expected to take place in June, though on account of the King's illness it was postponed till the autumn. The Queen's funeral he witnessed the previous year, which he afterwards described, like much that he saw, in the pages of the Journal.

windows of my office, so I have told them to reserve one for your use."

In August, after Conference, he went for three weeks to Grindelwald, and there experienced those bursts of vitality and exultation in life and things which were so marked a feature of these later months. He overflowed with anecdote and conversation of all kinds, and on all subjects. In expeditions his vitality would sometimes be such that elder ladies among his acquaintance who intended to walk a few yards with him and were therefore only thinly shod, found themselves going the whole way, because he insisted that they should do so. He quoted, declaimed, and cajoled, so that they arrived at their destination without experiencing any exhaustion. On his return he recounted the feat of these ladies to others of his acquaintance, so that he might incite them to do likewise. His observation was as keen as ever. At *table d'hôte* he noticed certain individuals, and wondered as to their profession and calling. In a low voice he said to his daughter, " I am distressed about that little girl sitting at the end of the table. Her companions have gone away, and she is very lonely without them. I have been noticing her for some time. She is French, and that lady next to her is her governess or chaperone, who is looking after her. Ask her to tea with us." When she came he strove to put himself *en rapport* with her, and to induce her to talk. With a toss of her head she informed him she was " Royaliste," and she evinced a great contempt for Jews and the French Republic. Then he began speaking to her about certain great Frenchmen, so as to elicit her opinions, which amused while they appealed to him. Did she play tennis ? Then she must try a game of tennis with them the following afternoon.

Even more striking was his meeting with a lady and her daughter on whom he created the profoundest impression. They sat next to him at *table d'hôte*, and they walked out and had picnics together for the two or three days that they were thrown in each other's society. He talked, as usual, of all manner of things — his travels, books, persons, etc., and then his daughter overheard him describing the work of the Sisters, which he so loved to do. As he did so his exultation was manifest. Then — somewhat to her surprise, for he did not talk on directly religious things when he met strangers—she heard him mention Christ's name and pass swiftly on to something else. The impression was deepened.

As usual, he had gauged the quality of his listeners. Later, she found one of them reading a book containing selections from Wesley's *Journals*, which he had lent her. With the exception of this incident, his conversation, which bubbled with humour and glanced on all manner of topics, could not be described as partaking of a religious quality—religious, that is to say, in the general acceptation of the term. After he had passed away, one of them wrote that that meeting with him had helped her to believe in the goodness of humanity. The other, whom a member of the family met some months afterwards, said, "Oh, nothing can make you imagine what those two or three days have been to us. You have lived in that environment; we have not. Life must always be different to us now."

One who was trying to tell what my father had been to him, said, "You cannot know the chief things he did. The people who could tell you of them will not; they are too modest. The families whom he stayed with when he was holding meetings and services all over the country are the people whom you should talk to." Sometimes, for instance, when he was reading from the Testament at prayer time, a great silence would fall on all present—the youthful members in particular fastening their eyes on him as if swayed by each word.

After he had gone, the family life was different—something quickening, elevating, had entered into their midst. The albums in which he was asked to write his name in households belonging to a variety of religious denominations, bore characteristic mementoes of him. In one he writes : " Nudi nudum Christum sequi." In a country house in Wales where he was visiting for a day or two, not for religious meetings but for purposes of rest and change during these latter months, he wrote, " Thou, O Christ, art all I want, and those whom Thou hast given me "—an addition to his usual expression.

During all these weeks at Grindelwald he was full of anxiety to return home and continue his work in London. " I am sick," he would say, " of doing nothing." Nothing pleased him more than to be assured of his improved looks and health. "Do you really think I am better?" he would exclaim. "Oh, you really think so?" Often he appeared haunted by inner misgivings concerning a physical strength that he must have known to be failing him. As he was leaving, he said, with that quick nervous look of his, "I don't suppose I shall ever come here again."

London depressed him. Instead of welcoming the sight of it, he delighted to get away. It was arranged that my parents were to spend Friday till Monday at 8 Taviton Street, where Sister Lily and two other Sisters were residing, and the rest of the week at their new house in Haslemere. There was some delay in getting into it, and he chafed under it. His health was not satisfactory, and everything, despite the year's rest, seemed as uncertain as ever. He asked members of his family to go out with him in the middle of the morning (something unheard of!), and they left what they were doing and went. Picnics were arranged for him, seeing that London so depressed him—a youthful party going to Richmond Park one Saturday, where he listened to everything they had to say. His absolute rest and serenity at times was very marked. He felt no care or anxiety of any kind, and when told of them he did not appear to seriously consider them. At the same time the Mission was commencing its winter "campaign," as he was wont to express it, and his presence and inspiration were much desired by everybody. The missioners had arranged a reception service, but that very day he succumbed to influenza. My mother's continued fears and anxiety all through these eighteen months were greater than any one imagined. All the future, she said, seemed dark to her, and, try to pierce it as she would, she afterwards confessed she could not see further than the month of November, over which lay an impenetrable mist. My father, who was in good spirits, despite the influenza, which was seemingly slight, often laughed at her for her depression and fearfulness. The house was now quite ready, and in a few days he was able to go down to it with a secretary and one of his daughters.

The fortnight previous to doing so he had been attending a special mission held by Gipsy Smith, the Free Church missioner, at St. James's Hall, with keen pleasure and appreciation. It was always a favourite method of his to inaugurate a new "campaign" or session with a mission or convention of some kind. Walking with a companion down Shaftesbury Avenue at this time he dilated and glowed over special times and seasons like any High Anglican. "Don't you find it helpful—a necessity?" he inquired; "I do, these times and seasons of self-examination and spiritual rejuvenation, and encouragement." To the answer that everyday life and experience afforded opportunities of spiritual rejuvenation, and that the special occasion seemed artificial compared with those in the course of nature and experience, he gave a half-grudging assent, which a coifed nun who was walking the other side of the road helped to intensify. Without her it is not certain that he would have given it. "Yes, there is truth in what you say. The everyday life of healthy normal manhood and womanhood should be regarded as the highest form of worship, and has its own sacredness. To cast it aside like that poor woman over there in the belief that she is serving God the better by assuming an artificial code opposed to natural instinct, is one of the deadliest delusions that ever entered the Church."

Whatever his zeal for reformed Catholic Orders and various ecclesiastical conceptions, the sight of a man or woman under lifelong vows of celibacy and abstention from the world's affairs, or the sight of a priest assuming more than he thought our Lord would have him, was enough to turn him over, and induce the strongest expressions of opposition to ecclesiasticism in all its forms. "Oh, Jenny Geddes, Jenny Geddes," he has been heard to exclaim, "I salute your memory. She was a godly woman. When that monster Laud insisted on a bishop preaching to the Scotch, and they did not want him, she stood up in the aisle and flung her stool at his head. She —blessed be God—was not going to stand any ecclesiastical tantrums and nonsense." Yet when the nun had gone by he returned to the former strain—a declaration that for him there was something in times and seasons and special occasions which were helpful if not essential to a full spiritual life.

The memories of Haslemere, where my father spent about fourteen days, interspersed over a period of six weeks, was one of those times fraught with spiritual import which the pen of a biographer hesitates to depict, because it is homely and intimate; yet in that homeliness and intimacy must lie the keynote of that music which the reader should hear. Familiar, transparent, he was to the end, and growing in mildness. Nothing is more glued to memory than the persistence of that meekness, which had always underlain the outer fires and vehemence. To one unaccustomed to its displays it would have been alarming. On one of these days he had sunk into a state of depression, which the occasion did not enjoin, and which was in most part due to increasing physical exhaustion. As he lay speechless on the couch, a member of his family bethought herself of arousing him in those vigorous terms which he in days past had been in the habit of addressing to prostrate and despondent saints. As the delivery proceeded he listened with a mildness and attention that deepened into a state of mind in which admiration and gratitude were indelibly blended. At the close he drew himself up to a sitting posture—" Thank you," he said, " I will try and pull myself together."

As my mother noted in his later days, he was for ever listening, not enunciating, and this more than anything else denoted the change in him. As it had once been his instinct to proclaim that which he believed to be right, it became his instinct increasingly in later years to listen, particularly when he was with very young or aged people. The close proximity, not of the squalid streets and of the great city,—" that roar of advancing time," as he had quoted from Lowell in former days, —but of the lanes and wide expanses of rural Surrey, over which autumn hung like some luminous veil, shrouding a thousand tints of leaf and sky, gave to those last days that harmony which only the close proximity of such scenes can bring.

There is something about days spent in the open air, or in the midst of natural scenes, which suggests something infinitely pure and untrammelled. Over all was a certain unearthliness, unreality almost, and that underlying sadness, which is so felt by some in autumn. No care there was, no duty almost, for he seemed to have transcended the region of either. In the middle of the morning he would be wanting to go for a walk, and his secretary had a delightful time of it. He would rejoice to lie down in the evening on the study sofa and be read to, or to read aloud himself. " Oh, it is delightful ! " he would exclaim. " I can rest here." That tense quietness which strangely affects those accustomed to cities, seemed inexpressibly soothing to him. The exhaustion which so easily overtook him, resulted, it was supposed, from the recent attack of influenza. None the less his frailty was manifest, and those about him began to feel that his activities, in public life at any rate, would have to be very much curtailed.

No suspicion of what was imminent crossed their minds, nor did they ever doubt that he had yet many years amongst them. He had become part of the daily life of many who were not akin to him in the flesh, and the same conception of him as eternally active—eternally in their midst—was felt equally by all. Despite his year of illness he still retained the chairmanship of the Second London Synod, and it is needless to say took the most eager interest in it. As chairman he had inaugurated a policy of reform and extension which he was most anxious to ensure and to aid, and the more so because he had come to regard his position as a kind of trust to his sympathisers. His house had been a gift of some of the laity on the Synod—and in addition to the eagerness that he would in any case have felt, was a natural desire to do all that he could to show himself worthy of the kindness and confidence of his followers. In accordance with the general policy over which he and Dr. Pope had talked so intimately of binding together scattered country stations, a " Mission," with new chapels and general extensions, had been established in Surrey and North Hants, with the Rev. W. Sellers in charge.

A speech of my father's on one of these inaugurations was characteristic. An Anglican was in the chair, and sitting around him were various Nonconformist and Methodist ministers of the town in which he was speaking. He seemed overflowing with ideas and kindliness to all men, and spoke at a considerable rate and with the usual ease. At one point he turned round to the chairman, who was a Magistrate, with the following remark :—" If ever, sir, in your duties on the bench you come across a narrow-minded or bigoted Methodist, send him to gaol. Gaol, I assure you, sir, is the only fit place for one who so little understands the principles and character of

John Wesley and that branch of the universal Church of Christ in which God permitted him to play so leading a rôle."

These and similar remarks were listened to with some astonishment by the good people seated in the chapel. Yet his belief in the federation of active denominations as the principle of union in the Christian Church, was attested by a remark like the following when commenting on the programme of extension already denoted :—" I believe that all this activity in the different branches of the Church is an excellent thing. The emulation excited—when within reasonable and Christian bounds—is distinctly helpful." This was also part of his theme at the meeting referred to, *e.g.* that the Congregationalists must not mind new Wesleyan Methodist chapels. There was room for all, and the activity of one must inevitably aid the activity of another. But the final solution was given in his last cycle ride, the day previous to his return to town. He and the young Congregationalist minister from Haslemere, who accompanied him, were lost first in books, and then in ecclesiastical affairs. As they toiled up Hindhead, my father questioned him as to what he had read, and told him what more to read. As they sped down he became very excited and animated, and continually on the breeze floated the following refrain : " The days are coming when Congregationalists, Baptists, and Methodists will worship and preach in each other's chapels, and join hands on every possible occasion. The time of separate sectarian life is at an end. In the days to come Methodists, Baptists, and Congregationalists will . . . Congregationalists, Baptists, and Methodists . . . Baptists, Methodists, and Congregationalists . . ." The three terms shifted their respective positions, but always broke out every other minute with added zest and animation. Yet the cycling was slower than in old days. The refrain came to resemble the repetition of one who repeats what he feels to be his life-message, and the meaning of which he brings home by reiteration. To memory it chimes like the note of a bell. As they neared home he called out excitedly, " Do you know that we are passing George Eliot's house? George Eliot! Think of it!"

The reference to the woman novelist, whom he would never praise in the family hearing, recalls a dispute of those

40

latter days in which he was arbitrator. It was on one of those quiet evenings, which seemed so unreal in their quietness, that a contention arose concerning the well-worn topic of woman's capacities. He listened to either side with interest, balanced, judged, praised a good point, most mildly indicated a weak one, saying often, "On either side there is much sense. I am struck by both your points of view." Only when one of the debaters denied to the sex any creative capacity in the world of mind and art did he approach vehemence. "If you do that," he said, raising himself, "you give the whole thing away. That loss is so serious. If woman is merely to sympathise with the great conceptions of man, not originate them, we cannot prove her equality with him. You touch the key of the whole position."

He said of a member of the little household who was causing great trouble by her wilfulness, "Poor thing, poor thing, she has had great trouble. Be gentle, be pitiful to her." When she refused to attend family prayer he made no comments. Christians probably had given her a false idea of Christ—besides she was in God's hands. A Jewess who was staying in the house for a few days was carefully included in his thought when reading and praying. The Scripture reading chosen was from one of the prophets of her race—the prayer such as any devout Jew might have ardently joined in.

In former days he was felt to have been incessantly striving against mortal limitations. He expected more of himself and of others than was often possible—not in work done, but in qualities of character which, like most else in Nature, are subject to the laws of evolution, and to which time is an essential. He saw that it must be so, yet he strove against it, ever, as he would have expressed it, in a "glorious hurry." Patience was not easy for him to learn in any department, and nothing was more marked in these last years than the acquisition of a virtue which many would previously have deemed impossible to him.

So on a Saturday afternoon he would go up to Hampstead Heath, and all the way on the top of the omnibus he would be talking of endeavours here and movements there, of all that had yet to be done, and then, somehow, when he got on the Heath, the kingdom of God was at hand, and all strife and efforts nearing their crowning and completion. He would walk faster and faster, partly because he had in spirit already begun to taste of the fruit of his endeavours, and partly—for humanity was always mingled with his saintship—because he wanted to have tea at the dairy. The two became bound together, inseparably associated with each other; and when he did drink his first cup of tea, it was as if to the health of the kingdom. "Oh, why is not God in more of a hurry!" he used to exclaim. "I want these things to happen, peace and justice to be established, and the voice of complaining to be heard no longer in our streets. I cannot help wishing God were in more of a hurry. I am so full of impatience for the days that are coming." But gradually in this latter stage there stole over him the great acquiescence. Straining, looking upward, throbbing, he ever was, but with a difference.[1]

At a tea-shop in Holborn a companion said to him, "There seems to be a reaction, does there not, against some of the great ideals of the latter part of the last century? Things seem different. A speech of Mr. Morley's has been making me think of this."

"Yes," he answered, in a deliberate and abstracted manner. "How do you account for it?" continued his questioner.

"Everything is in confusion owing to the advent of the idea of evolution, and we are still in the chaos. I have just been reading Mr. Kidd's article in the *Encyclopædia Britannica.*" His look, distant, wistful, even more than his words, betrayed the keenest comprehension of that strife which he had felt as a young man, and the results of which had left such impress on the pages and policy of his Journal.

"We are still in the midst of it," he indicated; and while his vision seemed piercing its complexities, lighting not on one of them, but meditatively sweeping many, there was not one indication of regret for former days, and still less of dismay. Then after the reverie, for it was almost that, he repeated the old refrain which he had underlined many years ago in *In Memoriam,*—there is no need for distress,—

"... All will be well."

---

[1] The great artists, it will be remembered, conceive of Patience as a towering, winged figure glowing with beauty and vitality, but bound to a wheel, or shorn in some manner, and submitting to the process. Only the impatient are patient.

His reference undoubtedly was to the world of thought, its strife and clash, and it was the more striking, as it was an answer to a question the implication of which was practical rather than speculative.

Not the least striking trait at this time was an undoubtedly increased estimate of the value of educative work. Opponents in the Missionary controversy had noted a deficiency in this respect, and it was a fair criticism. He was a man of action to the finger-tips, with the instincts of such, and his manner of referring to the scholastic profession sometimes seemed to lack appreciation and insight, unless, indeed, he were speaking of an individual member of it, when his generalities underwent modification and revolution.

In these closing days his great desire was to serve foreign missions. Indeed, it was about this time that he said, as he wiped his forehead after an effort of some sort, for the slightest fatigued him, " I should like to devote my last years to the service of foreign missions, if God grant me life, to stir up our people to a great enthusiasm in their cause." Ever since the ill-fated Missionary controversy, he had been wishing to atone for the misunderstandings to which it had given rise. On the personal side he wished to exonerate, not so much his own motives, but those of a loved friend. Yet the *raison d'être* was far deeper than a personal one ; it was that old impatience, of which not even his latter days could cure him. He was not satisfied with foreign missions any more than he was with home missions, and especially was he dissatisfied at the lack of interest that he detected in the Church for the former. The missionary cause and income, so far as Methodism was concerned, had suffered since the controversy of 1890. Of this he was painfully aware, and he wished, if he could, to make some reparation. In 1890 he had been a member of the Foreign Missionary Committee, but the strained relationship which the controversy induced made it impossible for him to continue to sit on it. Thus it was not until the year of Presidency that he was again able to take a direct part in foreign missionary affairs. As chairman *ex officio* of the Foreign Missionary Committee, he suggested that there should be some kind of direct personal canvass throughout the country, and that by some novel method interest should be aroused, and the missionary income trebled. The Committee rejected the suggestion at the time, but about a year after his death they adopted it. At his last Conference, also, he made a missionary speech, and in various ways showed sympathy with the more liberal and ardent spirits.

Such were his hopes for activity in the outer world, but his plans were of a studious nature. At last he was to read, to write, to enjoy the possession that he had envied in others. Indeed, this was the essential part of the bliss he had so confidently foreseen on the tops of omnibuses. "You," he said to one of his daughters, "shall read the German philosophers with me—properly study them I mean from the beginning; and you," indicating his other daughter, "shall play to me in the interval, moving and exquisite strains. How delightful it will be!" He was near clapping his hands. More than once he referred to the campaign in German philosophy to ears that strove to be credulous. So many designs and plans he had made of that which he would do, that even the opportunities of Haslemere could not prevent such a project from assuming mirage-like proportions.

Besides, there was a deeper passion in his mind—that of the ecclesiastic. Observation and reflection had led him to the conclusion that Christian Churchmen must ultimately converge towards Roman Catholicism or Methodism properly interpreted, *i.e.* he saw in these the ecclesiastical organisations which were most consistent and also most suited to the needs of humanity. Other branches among the English-speaking nations must inevitably converge towards one or the other. The idea came to him with increasing force that all the special advantages offered by Romanism to weak and tempted humanity, could be offered by Methodism, without any of the objections which are insuperable to thoughtful Protestants. His experience in London, and particularly his experience of the work of the Sisterhood, convinced him of the weakness and the special needs of masses of humanity that would not occur to Protestants who had not been brought into face-to-face contact with them.

Certain forms of Protestantism were felt by him to be the religion of the strong, not of the weak and erring. The system which John Wesley, under God, had inaugurated, was formed, he thought, to meet the needs of the British multitude, to enter into its life and respond to its needs, just as the Roman system claimed to do. The Roman Catholic friars and the early Wesleyans had alone made an indelible impress on the masses of the people. " The Reformation," he would say, " was essentially an upper and middle class movement, and did not affect the people." " Till Wesley came they were left without any abiding religious influence." He knew the early Quakers to be an exception to this, but as a religious system their influence was nil. It was difficult to conceive how a system which so dispensed with forms could ever have the adherence save that of the few. The Salvation Army again, whose separation from Methodism he always deplored, and the zeal of whose officers he greatly admired, was still less likely to form a permanent organisation. Moreover, he was heard to say, " They do not even make proper provision for the sacraments specially ordained by our Lord, and that is fatal "; and again, " The devotion of their officers is wonderful, but they lack men of signal capacity."

Thus the Methodist ecclesiastical system, "properly interpreted," seemed to him the alternative to Romanism, possessed as she is of the same compactness, the same interpenetration of the ordinary life, the same recognition of the needs of humanity, but suited to the self-respect and good sense of the English people. To show how this was so, he intended to write a book. Preparatory to doing this, he was to make a study of the great Roman Catholic apologists, and, in particular, one of the great German apologists. " I shall then," he said, " in the first place, give what appears to me the just interpretation of the doctrines to which they cling, as well as the absence of any necessity for those practices which they regard as essential." In such a book, for instance, he would have contended that the doctrine of the Mass was the materialisation of a great truth—*e.g.* the perpetual presence of our Lord in His Church, and that the partaking of the bread and wine into the physical system was the specially ordained symbol of that mystic participation in His life, which was the secret of Christianity. By such an interpretation the Methodist Christian did not defy science or sense, while he recognised to the full the time-honoured and sacred character of this supreme rite.

Moreover, he would have gone further (as shown in an earlier chapter) and maintained that Holy Communion being specially ordained by our Lord, did, when duly partaken of, offer a special blessing to the communicant. He would have stated this both cautiously and courteously, mindful of the excellent Christians who had been brought up, in the reaction against Rome, to underestimate, according to his thinking, the sacrament, and to accord it a purely memorial character. If Christian men attained a high devotion and spiritual character without partaking of it as often as High Anglicans did, that was an argument against laying undue stress on any particular method of its observance. Good fruit must spring from a sound tree.

Nothing is more interesting than his attitude towards Holy Communion and the development of his ideas respecting it. Indeed, so various were the instincts in himself, and the chain of thought and feeling that led to the stress that he increasingly came to lay on its observance, that it is scarcely easy to gather them into a luminous whole, and to show in what he disagreed with many Nonconformists, and where again he agreed with them. As he looked out on the Church at large and in all lands, he felt there must be something to give rise to that supreme feeling and reverence for the Eucharist which dominated large, if unprogressive, portions of Christendom.

He realised, as some contemporaries perhaps did not, the historic position of the typical Christian feast, and what it meant in the lives of countless thousands. At one of the Grindelwald Conferences, he read a paper on the Holy Communion which greatly surprised certain Anglican clergymen present. They could never have believed it, they exclaimed, and expressed delight at what they regarded the intense spirituality of the address. Luther, as he said in his Grindelwald speeches, was a believer in consubstantiation, and as great a sacramentarian as any one could desire. The so-called Zwinglian view that the Holy Sacrament is a purely commemorative rite, which is the view of many, though not all Nonconformists, was not held by my father, as he clearly stated in his article on the Catechism. Christ Jesus, many hold, is not more present to believers partaking of the bread and wine, than to believers in any other solemn rite of the Church. This view was to him inadequate and at variance both with the general tradition of Christendom and his own feelings on the matter.

The exposition of the sacrament that was most pleasing to him was that of Hooker. "What is needed for us Nonconformists," he would continually say in the latter part of his life, "is a proper definition and understanding of the Holy Catholic Church and her sacraments." So strong, indeed, were his sacramentarian instincts, that they were felt by those who were by no means intimate with him, and more than one remarked on them to his family and friends. One said, "If it hadn't been for his evangelistic powers and that memorable turning-point at Snargate Street, Dover, he would have left Methodism long ago, and become a High Anglican." The speaker had no authority for such a statement save one of feeling, but it is none the less suggestive, for it shows the great effect on his own thought that his evangelistic powers appeared to have produced, and that when he begged other men to look at the "facts" he had first looked at them himself.

The view that best represents the opposite pole to his, appeared in a review of a book that has lately been written respecting the observance and the right celebration of the Holy Eucharist. The reviewer states that a large portion of the Protestant world is ceasing to be "Christian" altogether, because they neglect what he considers the correct observance of this rite.

Both the "facts" and my father's wide charity and understanding of divergent points of view, would have rendered any too decisive or one-sided statements of the nature of Holy Communion distasteful and opposed to that innate instinct which ever aimed at uniting, not segregating groups of Christians. An increasing feeling for the place and function of Holy Communion in the Christian life led him to prefer more frequent participation than is usual in most Nonconformist Churches, but this could not blind him to the fact that members of the Church of Scotland, for instance, in their high regard for the solemnity of the rite and the necessary preparation for it, communicate only four times in the year. These and kindred interpretations on the part of fellow-Christians would have prevented him from ever formulating hard-and-fast rules. His business, he felt, in all departments of Christian thinking was not to consult his own particular tastes or school of training, but humanity and the " facts." The " facts " were the interpreters of tradition, and he viewed tradition in the light that they shed on it.

At Grindelwald he expounded his particular views of the sacrament to Dr. Berry, who was intensely stirred and interested. The restatement in more positive terms of the Nonconformist position must be accorded, perhaps, in the first instance, to Dr. Berry, though his views were modified, strengthened, and developed by intercourse with my father. But it was my father who was the sacramentarian, and who recognised in a way that was almost unique among men of his own thinking, the peculiar significance and import of Holy Communion. In their addresses throughout England and Wales, the true nature of the sacraments, as well as of the Catholic Church, were proclaimed and emphasised.

His care that the elements should be duly and reverently administered were thought by some to be excessive. On the way to St. James's Hall he said to a friend, a Methodist minister, " As you are leaving at the end of the first service, you might walk home with my son." " I expected," was the reply, " to assist you in the Communion Service. Do you not want me ? " " No, certainly not," was the answer, in tones of genuine horror, " not in that attire. Do you think I would be assisted by any one who was not in clerical dress ? " His companion then remarked that some other ministers would not have been so chary, to which my father replied, and with characteristic force, that certain ministers did not know what was ecclesiastically fitting. None the less, the feeling that this remark implied was in accordance with the general feeling of the Wesleyan ministry, and all that my father deprecated was that there should be any exception to it.

Once during the administration of Holy Communion, at the Sunday morning service at St. James's Hall, there was an insufficiency of wine, on account of the number of communicants. In certain portions of the Church Catholic this might have caused some perturbation. My father said, with reverent solemnity : " Owing to an error of foresight, we are not sufficiently provided with the elements to administer to all the members of the Church now present, but let us rejoice in the fact that to God's grace there is no possible limit—we can never come to the end of that—and that He will pour it abundantly upon all, if we do truly and earnestly lift up our hearts to Him and are in peace and charity with all mankind."

A layman remarked upon the impression produced in the Second London Synod when my father revived the ancient preliminary of administering the sacrament. Though this was customary in Wesley's day, it had fallen into neglect for many years. Indeed, the first great impression that he produced on Conference, was a speech that he delivered, as a young man, which was supposed to possess sacramentarian tendencies, but which were scarcely as decided in form as those which he came to hold later. As President, he called the attention of Conference to the neglect of the Lord's Table by " thousands of our people."

"Some of the most distinguished and saintly Methodists had realised how great a Saviour Christ was to them, when they were receiving the memorials of His death and passion. He bore testimony to the fact that he realised with great vividness, when they took the Lord's Supper together on Monday morning, what he owed to Christ when He shed His blood for him. He was fully persuaded that if that blessed sacramental service were more frequently held, and if ministers would take pains to explain it, not so much theologically or metaphysically, as experimentally, they would prove, as he had proved, that of all the services of the Church, that was the most helpful in urging members to give themselves fully to God. They were fond of gatherings to promote the spiritual life, such as that at Southport. Some of these were liable to cause certain emotions and doctrinal excesses, but there was no gathering more helpful than the Lord's Supper. It should not be forgotten that after receiving the bread and wine, they joined in a prayer of renewed consecration." — Report of a speech of my father's, *Methodist Times*, 4th August 1898.[1]

It has been implied that earlier in his life the Puritan prayer - meeting seemed to supply the need which frequent communion supplies to other Christians.

Again, when our Lord said to St. Peter, " Blessed art thou, Simon Barjona : for flesh and blood hath not revealed it unto thee, but My Father which is in heaven. And I say unto thee,

---

[1] My father always laid great stress on the consecration prayer which follows the administration of the Communion. When persons left the building before this prayer, he was distressed, and would remark that "they had evidently misunderstood the nature of the service in which they had been engaged." At the Synod he would deliver a brief instruction at the close of the sacramental service.

That thou art Peter, and upon this rock I will build My Church;
and the gates of hell shall not prevail against it," and thus
perplexed and rent the ages, he would have explained with
the same care and delicacy the Methodist interpretation of the
same, that the saint addressed was only one billionth part of
the rock our Lord was thinking of, the rock being the heart
of the believer that loved and believed in Him, for not until the
saint had confessed his love for Him did He thus proclaim him
a member of His Church on earth.   He would have laid stress
upon much else of a like character, and shown—to quote a
favourite expression—"that at the root of Roman error lay
great truth, and what was required was to brush off and remove
the accretions which hid the truth from view."   With regard to
the practice, say, of confession, he often said that undoubtedly
experience proved that there was a great longing in the human
heart at times to pour out confession of sin, weakness, and
spiritual need, to some trusted and experienced spiritual
adviser; but to make such a practice compulsory, and to limit
it to a priesthood, who had arrogated to themselves the powers
of absolution which were Christ's alone, was absolutely un-
scriptural and had led to centuries of abuse.   Yet this
legitimate human need was a fact, and when facts were
brought before his notice he did not ignore them.   London,
in particular, had shown him the need of "spiritual directors,"
and in Methodism, he believed, the need was met by the really
efficient, discreet, well-instructed class leader.

   I thought of my father's contention when I heard a
Methodist lady, who had for many years conducted a class
of girls, remark that she had often consulted the advice given
by a certain monk (Brother Laurence) to spiritual directors.
Such a book as my father planned in his mind, written amid
the quiet leisure of Haslemere, in which he so delighted, and
as the fruit of a singularly full and varied experience, would
have been intensely interesting.   Light in particular would
have been shed on the "scriptural" exposition of the Catholic
Church, on the federation of its parts, including Methodism, of
his belief in the episcopal system, and the *via media* that
he adopted in his interpretation of the ministerial office and
its privileges.   Wise and humane remarks he would have
had to make concerning Holy Baptism in accordance with a

gospel of love and sense, and it is probable he would have contended for an impressive and dignified ordinance in Methodism, corresponding to Anglican confirmation, and consisting among other things of definite instruction respecting the Catholic Church, scripturally and comprehensively defined.

In particular, he would have made clear his thought for Methodism, and quite an astonishing number of people on reading it might have found themselves Methodists, just as they used to do in the Mission when they listened to him and worked with him. The interest of the book to the intelligent would have lain not only in a generous and practical interpretation of the Methodist system, and in the love of and belief in Methodism therein revealed, but in its revelation of the author's wider ecclesiastical thought.

Particular systems he seemed to regard as finely wrought instruments for which there must be a player—someone who shall master its intricacies and bring forth that music which it was made to produce, and which human beings are waiting to hear. Of the qualities and possibilities of that instrument on which he played he was an enthusiast. Yet what booted particular methods or time-honoured observances, he felt, in Methodism or anywhere else, unless Christ Jesus kindled the players. That was a point of view to which he continually returned, and as continually asserted.

Yet he was far from neglecting precedent, as stated, and in a book on Methodism he would have sought for his precedent like any High Churchman.

His serenity and contentment did not stifle certain human wishes, one of which he mentioned to a companion. "There is one club I have often wished I could belong to — the Athenæum. I should very much like to belong to it."

"Why don't you apply?" was the rejoinder.

"Oh, it's not possible — not possible," he answered hurriedly, leaping upon the suggestion, "impossible." And again, "I could not venture, and I don't suppose they want a fellow like me. But it would be delightful, and I could get into conversation with some of their members and hear what they have to say. I am sure it would be a great advantage, and I might meet men of literary and scientific repute to whom

I could listen and who would converse with me. I have often thought it is the only club I should care to join—and now that I expect to have more leisure I could really benefit by it."

Most of his last wishes seem to have clustered around the site for the Methodist Church House at Westminster. To the last when he was up in town he would go for an evening airing on the Victoria omnibus so that he might point out the site to a companion. As they neared it on their way back from Victoria, he would become restless, and there was an invariable preliminary. At the top of Ashley Gardens a slight wave of the hand would indicate the Roman Catholic cathedral, then undergoing completion. " You see it ?—cooped away in a back street." The left hand was seen to be quivering with eagerness. " There—our great building will be. Oh! but you cannot see it. It's no good saying you can, because you cannot. Stand up as I am doing (for he had risen). Ah, farther than that, far farther than your eye is at present reaching."

" Not all that ! "

" Yes, all that. I don't suppose you realise it even now. There is not such another site in London."

A preacher in the Principality, in a sermon two or three Sundays after his death, enumerated what he considered his special virtues, and said, as many did: " I disagreed with him often, and while I respected his courage, his zeal, his lofty motives, I was obliged at times to think him mistaken—but what of that ? " In certain things about him he hinted there must always be disagreement; " but there is one matter," he concluded, " on which there can be no manner of doubt. What the architecture of our great building will be at Westminster I do not know—indeed I know nothing whatever concerning the arrangements of those who have this matter in hand. Whether it will be "— (here he let loose his imagination and showed visible signs of a Celtic peroration)—" but this I am assured, that over it and upon it and round about it, three words should be written—Hugh Price Hughes—because he built it." So had his indomitable purpose and zeal in the collection of the Imperial tribute graven itself even on the minds of those who were most inclined to coolly criticise him.

But his last "possession," of which it may be recollected his life was a series, may be described as follows, and it was revealed to the writer as he picked his way down a muddy lane leading to his house in Haslemere. "I have been reading," he began, "a very interesting book on theology, by one of the widest minded and most gifted of our ministry, entitled *The Fatherhood of God*.[1] A new and wider school of thought is coming to the fore, whose attitude and feeling the book indicates. The author considers that the doctrine of the Fatherhood of God in the Trinity has been overlooked, and not sufficiently presented to the Christian mind and imagination. We have been so absorbed in our natural adoration and gratitude to the Eternal Son as to forget that wider aspect of divinity which embraces mankind. It is singularly suggestive, and I am reading the book with care, a copy of which has been sent me to review." The leader which he had intended to write he did not live to pen, but the book was the keynote of the thought of his last days and hours.

Alongside with this theological reading the writer remembers his reading aloud Browning's "Flight of the Duchess" on one of these evenings—the last time he ever read the poet. As usual, he flung off physical weariness for a space, and entered with indescribable zest and elation into a story so framed to evoke his sympathies. The cramping of the ardent spirit of the Duchess within the narrow confines of the castle and its conventions, were indescribably communicated, and then with the advent of the gipsy, release and rapture. The expression of his face and the tender inflexions of the voice as he read the gipsy's words, while the young Duchess lies at her feet, her face upturned, drinking in the wonder and the glory, were never to be forgotten. Perhaps only one about to burst fleshly bonds could have read those words as he did, for he had never read them quite like that before—especially those last lines:

"When the twilight helps to fuse
    The first fresh with the faded hues,
    And the outline of the whole,
    As round eve's shades their framework roll,
    Grandly fronts for once thy soul.

---

[1] *The Fatherhood of God*, by the Rev. Scott Lidgett.

> And then as, 'mid the dark, a gleam
> Of yet another morning breaks,
> And like the hand which ends a dream,
> Death, with the might of his sunbeam,
> Touches the flesh and the soul awakes,
> Then . . . .
>   Ay, then indeed something would happen
> But what? For here her voice changed like a bird's;
> There grew more of the music and less of the words."

The night of that last cycle ride (Thursday, 13th November) left him singularly exhausted. The extreme frailty of his looks at times struck even those who were slowest to believe what others were secretly fearing. A short walk, a day or two previous to this, with a young cousin who had been describing incidents of the South African War, left him in the same curiously overwrought condition. Those who watched him felt that he would not be able to do very much in London, and that he would gradually have to retire more and more into Haslemere and books. Yet of the nearness of the end there was not a suspicion. To people who lived with him, his death seemed something very far away—not anything near or probable. My mother says that he had always had a certain dread of old age. Letters written to aged people revealed a very keen sympathy with those whose descent into the Valley of the Shadow is long and at times wearisome. But this he was to be spared.

As he lay on the study sofa that Thursday evening, a feeling came over the daughter who was with him that there was nothing more she could do for him. He was too tired either to read or be read to. Mr. Stopford Brooke's *Essays on Browning* had been read by him with an effort that was not usual in so congenial a task. There seemed nothing that he cared to read. Mrs. Humphry Ward's novel *Marcella*, which he had been induced to take up as something lighter than his other books, was also finished some days since. "I want to rest," he said once or twice. "Oh, I want to rest."

"You liked those notes of A. B. C. in the *Methodist Times* this morning, did you not?" his companion inquired.

"Oh, immensely."

"Shall I read them?"

"Yes, if you don't mind. They are most witty, don't you think? Most witty!"

The writer in these notes endeavours amid the criticism of melancholy and well-regulated persons to describe how he comes by his optimism, and, as with the Venetian merchant of Shakespeare's play, he can no more define how he caught it and came by it than the prince can show the origin of his melancholy. He rises betimes, does this and that and the other, and is, despite every reason to the contrary, distinctly cheerful and optimistic. At many of this writer's sallies and pungent phrases he laughed repeatedly and with unrestrained delight, certain words being repeated to him two or three times, so that he might the more fully enjoy them. Then again came the strange undefined feeling that it was impossible to do any more for him. He wanted to rest, but appeared to be too exhausted and tired to do so. For this reason he was not allowed to carry his bag to the station the next morning, and as he watched his daughter and the secretary bearing it before him, he protested for the hundredth time, adding half-humorously, half-petulantly, "I do not like to see women struggling under my burdens. I still belong to the age of chivalry, and have not altogether left it behind." It was the only time he was ever heard to refer, even in jest, to participation in a chivalrous age; for, like most who are living in it, he was unconscious that he was doing so.

He did not take pleasure, as he had once done, in returning to town. Nothing was more indicative of this change than his remark to a member of the household. Something had happened in the great world of London of municipal interest, which was eagerly reported to him on his return. His eye, that would have gleamed a response in former years, was unseeing, absorbed. "I cannot tell you," he said, "how exquisite the country was this morning and how lovely the trees were with their autumn foliage—all the colours of the rainbow, and such sunshine and blue sky everywhere. The fields looked so green, and the birds were singing as I walked down the lane. It quite broke my heart to leave them." It was very strange to hear him talking like that on a return to London.

On his arrival in town that Friday morning (14th November) he drove straight to Katherine House, in order to conduct the admission service of two probationers entering the Sisterhood. Mr. Pearse, who was acquainted with one of them, came specially from the North in order to be present, an occurrence that was remarked upon afterwards, for in the ordinary course he would not have come from such a distance to assist in the service. He had withdrawn from active participation in the Mission, so that he might be more at liberty to answer the many calls upon his gifts and energies. It was well known in the Mission that in whatever part of the world Mr. Pearse might be, he took its interests about with him. He pleaded its cause and begged money for it at the antipodes, just as when he was at home. Thus when my father announced Mr. Pearse's withdrawal for some years from the Sunday morning platform at St. James's, it was felt to be an absence on leave, and in no way a separation. The meeting between the two at Katherine House, to quote the expression of the Sisters, was like that of two brothers, so delighted was each to see the other. Mr. Pearse expressed pleased surprise at my father's appearance, and said he had never seen him looking better.

My father's discourse, which was always a feature of that particular service, was taken from the thirteenth chapter of his favourite evangelist—the Feet-washing. As he spoke as one who had deeply entered into its mystical import, to whom it was something more than imagery, the words were felt to be spoken with a peculiar solemnity. It was as much a charge to the little community of Sisters as to the two who had just been admitted into their number. The religious nature of their vocation—that of service instituted in Christ's name to the weaker brethren, to that flesh which strove and starved and went astray—was brought home afresh to the various minds present. Yet there was not need of any specially alert understanding to enter into the full import of his words. They had that simplicity and sincerity of thought which speaks to faculties other than the purely mental. After he had administered the sacrament to his colleague, they together administered the elements to the company, my mother and every Sister being present.

41

That last communion could scarcely have been partaken of more fittingly. Among those who received it from his hands were some who had gone with him, without resources, into the West of London fifteen years before, relying for the success of their venture on faith and prayer. Both with his friends and his family all parting was spared. Neither he nor they knew that meetings were taking place for the last time. In the afternoon the usual executive committee took place, when the few most conversant with the affairs of the Mission met and discussed the expenditure and current business. In the evening he conducted the devotional meeting.[1]

The next morning he and my mother were again present at Katherine House to arrange the various festivities for the coming Christmas, as at that time each class and guild and association has a special festival, just as they do in summer. It was a benediction on that joyous aspect of Christianity, on which he had always insisted. After luncheon he went up with my mother to Hampstead, having tea at the usual dairy, and talking much of those matters which should go to the establishment of Christ's kingdom. As they came down Haverstock Hill in the omnibus my mother began talking to him of Rudyard Kipling's "Just So" stories, and he laughed again and again at the "satiable curiosity" of the elephant's child, and the reward that its relatives in this world thought fit to accord it "immediately and directly." The evening was reposeful, for he was on the verge of a great possession, the possession that springs from vision. The next morning, as he sat writing at his desk, he begged my mother, who was going out to service, to pray specially for him. He had, he said, a

[1] Sister Lily, who was present, has thus described it: "I remember Mr. Hughes reading 'Paul an apostle of Christ Jesus through the will of God,' and then declaring that every Christian should claim his calling, however humble, 'through the will of God'—a minister, a crossing-sweeper, 'through,' etc. Then he dwelt on the fact that we men are 'not pitchforked into this world haphazard' to do as we liked, but God had a programme for every life. For St. Paul it was the life of an apostle. Had we ever tried to discover the programme for our life? Were we fulfilling it? 'To the saints and faithful brethren (in) Christ, which are at Colosse,' said Mr. Hughes; 'put a ring round that word *in*, for it all hinges upon that, to be IN *Christ* is to be a saint. True saintliness is union with Christ, literally to be *in* Christ Jesus. 'Grace to you and peace from God our Father.' *Grace* is love in exercise. The love of God which brings strength and beauty fills the whole being. *Peace* which follows grace, peace *with* God, peace from God. In Him we shall fulfil His programme, and this greeting shall be realised in our life."

vision which he wished to communicate to his congregation that evening, adding, " I feel the strain of preparation more than I used to." He sighed as he spoke, as if wearied with long struggle.

In the middle of the day he lunched with my mother at Mr. Bunting's to meet M. Paul Sabatier. In the conversation, which was carried on in French, he took scarcely any part, being either absorbed or exhausted. Silence, while the French tongue and St. Francis were the order of the day, could have had no other explanation. A young relative came to tea before going to St. James's Hall to hear him preach, and it was decided that she should go down in good time, so that he might take her to the top gallery (as he liked to take visitors), and show her what he considered the sights of the place.

He walked to the hall as usual, and on arriving at Piccadilly, was stirred to deep emotion at the sight of the crowds that were thronging the way. His emotion was shown by exclamation to Sister Lily, who was accompanying him, when compassion, agony, hope, seemed to struggle in the brief utterances that burst from his lips as flames will leap up from the altar when the sacrifice is nearing completion. Humanity was in travail, and knew not that which pertained unto its peace.

But from the sermon that fell from his lips that evening, the hope was undying and quenchless. No one could describe what he said exactly in that sermon, and what its effect was. All the vigour of his youth was in it—pacing to and fro as when he had delivered his discourses on the minor prophets, and in that sense it was the sermon of a young man. In another, it was the sermon of one at the prime of his powers, being remarkable for clarity of thought and variety of illustration. Yet some note there was in it which could not be defined— the old restraint and dumbness intensified, something seen which could not be communicated. The great mellowing of his character had found expression in the tone of his later sermons, which, while deeply appealing to the spiritually minded in his congregation, did not result in so many visible " conversions." He seemed distressed, but he need not have been. The art of preaching must lie in occasionally transcending the understanding of hearers. Yet this last sermon, for all its full and mellowed note, had the old vigour, the old force. Men and women came out to the inquiry room, as usual, to seek for the peace that passeth understanding. The members of the Mission—the missioners, the Sisters, who had noted his altered appearance, his frail looks on recent occasions—were struck by his life and gladness and vigour. " He is back again," they said afterwards the one to the other. " 'Tis his old self."

Later, as they thought about it, they saw that the words had been those of a dying man, so that they said again one to the other, " Now we understand why his sermon was so remarkable." It would be more correct to say they were the last words of a dying man, for, as will be shown, what he thought and said then was, so far as anybody can know, the last thought in his mind, because of what will presently be told. After he had gone, the notes for the sermon, neatly written on a sheet of notepaper in the usual manner, were found in his desk and preserved as a last memento. They are subjoined, and will speak for themselves.

No one knoweth the Son, save the Father; neither
doth any know the Father save the Son; & he to
whomsoever the Son willeth to reveal him.

8, TAVITON STREET,
GORDON SQUARE. W. C.
S. Matt. XI. 27

1. Declared & thought one of the greatest utterances
   ever of it.
   The Fatherhood of God the great revelation
   of xtianity.
   The unique & supreme achievement of Xt:.
   to teach us to say "Our Father &. all in heaven."

2. The deepest of the deep things of God.
   but often rebuked by the intelligence
   of such a congregation as this.
   not skilled theologians.
   but the prayer of Jesus v. 25
   These things spiritually discerned.
   a deep instinct in the human heart
   responds.
   God help me & you!

3. We have to try to understand the text.
   the meaning of the Fatherhood of God.
   the last & crowning revelation.
   The deep theologian met a shepherd on
   the hillside mountain said. "Do you know
   the Father?" bewildered. years past. They
   met again. "Yes. I do now."
   To "Know" the Father. the ultimate knowledge

4 a wise saying "Every nation tend to
become what they believe God to be"
a test question: What is their conception
of God?

5. What does the Jew mean?
marvellous.   hill country
a little nation on a ~~mountain top~~
small as Wales.
survived all their mighty contemporaries.
Beaconsfield "preceded Parliamentary
government ~~and will~~ & will survive ~~and last beyond it~~ it"
the explanation – higher conception of God.

6. First Abraham – a _Personal_ God
"went forth, not knowing whither he went"
not blind force but a "personal
Friend.   "the Friend of God"

7. Secondly Moses.
Jehovah = the Unchangeable one
"God of A. & Isaac & Jacob"

"not fearing the wrath of Pharaoh"
e.g. the negroes in the Washington
prayer meeting: is God dead?
God will remember His promise.
~~&~~ "uniformity of nature"

8 . The prophets = the authors of prayers ::"
God is come a Sovereign .

None treat a just & gracious Sovereign .
the fountain of justice
An unquenchable thirst for justice .
They never quite lost heart .
ah! they still wait for the Messiah!
= Justice, Deliverance, Prosperity

9 . That Messiah has come .
& he has brought more than they ever
dreamed .   taught them to call God
"Father".
the final prophecy - the Parable of the
Prodigal Son = the Loving Father .
well called - "the Gospel within the Gospel.
Like Hamlet - He is you, me, everyman.

10 . The Revelation too great for the Jews -
—. & for the Xtians !
It passed into the background .
for 18 centuries - the idea of God - not as
Father - but as Sovereign
Hence brutal wars - revocation of
Edict of Nantes - Black Bartholomews
Day - The hideous history of the Church
Hence narrowness, bigotry, intolerance Now.
Hence our more than ½ empty churches .

Hence bitter hatred of the manhood of Europe
All these ∴ never understood the Fatherhood
of God.

11. Fatherhood. The greatest fact in the
universe.
All nature the gradual evolution of
Fatherhood.
* From the fire-mist to Christ.
Sir Robert Ball just completes the pedigree!
The Xt explains everything.

12. He explains God.
The tri-unity means not loveless solitude
but an eternity of mutual love.

13. the inevitable, invincible yearning of the
love of God to overflow — to create
myriads of creatures to enjoy & recip=
=rocate that love   sons.
NB not "create"- but to father myriad of creatures
The eternal outgoing of divine love!
                                        Consummated in the Xt
14. He explains Man.
He Himself the ideal man:
The Son of the Divine Father.
As He is, we ought to be.
We are sons of God. Let us realise this IN Xt
      noblesse oblige   the s. of adam the s. of God.
15. You see that prodigal Son, amid the swine
He is miserable " in my Father's House bread
enough & to spare: I will arise & go to my Father,
      (END OF TEXT) "to reveal His Son in me "

The writer may be permitted to explain to lay readers that each sentence epitomises to the preacher's mind the thought which it underlies, and that the sentence is a sign-post rather than an explanation; and second, that the thoughts crowding into his mind as he delivered that pæan of all his thought and all his endeavours, must have been far more remarkable than anything he said or could put into words. The nature of these thoughts, from the recollections of those who heard the sermon, will now be told.

There are certain supreme moments when the past is re-created, and when all the events and faces appear before a human being, and it is not too much to conjecture that such a moment was given to him that Sunday evening. All the previous acts and revelations of his life were recalled and seen in a light that transcended while it explained them. The light brought such joy that it reinvested him with youth, as observers noted. It will also be seen that he feared to begin, as if conscious that it was so much the outcome of his own life, and what that life enabled him to see, that the congregation could not be expected to share his thought and feeling; but he comforts himself with the reflection that the highest truths are spiritually discerned, and that what responds to them is not the wisdom of the subtlest and most highly trained thinkers, but the deep instinct of the human heart. He seems conscious, indeed, of an audience far wider than that which he is addressing, the width of reflection and outlook suggesting a mind which has in imagination outstepped certain limits of time and place. He therefore reminds the "giants" of Christ's prayer where He thanks the Father that He has revealed His deepest secrets to babes and sucklings who cannot reason aright. Thinking of the theologians in the narrow sense of the term—those who preserve the Church's tradition and, like the scribes of old, will not depart one tittle from that which they have received, he cites the story of the shepherd who in the midst of his solitary musings and the tender care of his flock, asks the theologian whether he knows the Father, startling him by so unexpected a question. Years after, the theologian meets the shepherd again, and with face and look that can well be imagined, for he must have grown old in the process, he answers, "Yes, I know the Father now." Perhaps these two reminders, particularly the last, were to himself as much as anybody else, for it has been shown how his great idea of the discipline involved in highest living made him conservative with regard to ways of thinking and very obsequious to the theologians.

Thus he had to clear his path by distinctly stating that he was about to appeal to the deepest instinct and aspiration of man's heart, and that these only would understand him. In Christ Jesus he had had from his youth up many visions, as already shown, but never one that was as clear to his mind and heart as this one, which was a revelation of the Fatherhood of God vaster, clearer than he had yet conceived it.

But no one divined that it was *Nunc Dimittis*. He begins by briefly reviewing the idea of God as conceived by the typical religious men of history, quoting a wise saying to show that the idea of God is both a test of the character of individuals and nations and the ideal which underlies their endeavours. In his survey he confines himself to the Jewish race, because their religious characters, he considers, have had a higher conception of God than any other people, because they have conceived Him not only as supreme in might but as endowed with the highest moral attributes known to man, and therefore best fitted to supply types of the various conceptions of God current in the race. These conceptions he enumerates.

First, there is that view which regards Him not as a blind force but as a Friend, of which Abraham was typical, who went forth from Ur of the Chaldees not knowing whither he went, but conscious that God would befriend him and make clear the way before him. This would seem to be the typical conception of the distinctly religious mind the world over.

Next, he gives that view typified by Moses—Jehovah, the God who ever is, and is uniform, unchangeable in His aspect towards mankind. This belief in His unchangeableness underlay the life of Moses, making him regardless of the wrath of the potentate from whom he would deliver his people. It was that aspect also which urged the old negress to jump to her feet in the prayer-meeting and to cry " Is God dead ? "

The conception so far has lain entirely in the dealing of the supreme power with mankind—in those high moral attributes which the Jewish race did not hesitate to apply to God, regarding Him as their unchangeable Friend. But here in (7) there is a hint of the more modern conception of Him as a supreme force working in Nature through unchangeable laws, so that that name which the old Jews did not dare to frame with the lip because of its sacred character, is comparable in its supreme unchangeable aspect with that creative force working in phenomena through ascertainable laws, which is the supreme power known to modern scientists. This aspect, which is evidently only hinted at here, is taken up later in (11). In (8) come the prophets, the authors of progress, with their conception of God as a sovereign—a conception which modifies, expands, and mellows with the ages. Thus He is not only just and athirst for justice in the world, but gracious, delivering the captives and rejoicing in the prosperity of His people. In this section he clearly had in mind not only the great Jewish representatives of the prophet, and their impassioned utterance, but men of all ages and all climes who had thought and acted and designed in advance of their fellows, living and dying so that the reign of Messiah might be established upon the earth. Bruno, Savonarola, Galileo, Mazzini—all into whose souls the iron had entered, who suffered with the suffering and desired good things for their fellow-creatures, and larger and truer thought—came under his gaze, so that for all their divergence of circumstance and speech, they seemed to speak the same tongue, to think the same thought. He cannot help going specially out to them, and we note the exclamation in which hope and pathos mingle, " They never quite lost heart. Ah ! they still wait for Messiah."

In (9) there is clearly a complete change of the point of view. Messiah, the ideal, has come. He has not come yet to the prophets, who are still, *qua* prophet, waiting for Him, unsatisfied and thirsting, but He has come to the human heart in the person of Jesus Christ to those who will receive Him. To the heart of the race He brings more than even the most daring of the prophets had ever dreamed for it. His great revelation to it is the Fatherhood of God as typified in the parable of the loving Father, who, while His son—humanity— is yet afar off, goes forth to meet him in the way. For it is clear from the notes that he gives the parable a vaster interpretation than is often given it, a universal and not a particular application. The race, as seen in spiritual vision by our Lord, suggests a son, who, taking that portion of goods which he considers to belong to him (here exhibiting what in Buddhism is called "Trishna" and in Christianity "sin"), seeks to devour his living with harlots and to satisfy his soul with the husks on which the swine would feed.

When humanity comes to itself and sets about returning, the Father comes forth to meet it while it is already on the way, His love visibly struggling with it amid the most imperfect conditions, even when it is farthest from perfection. For this son travelling to the house of his Father is, he says, "you, me, every man" (see 9). Just as the intellectual vision of Shakespeare is said to have conceived humanity in the person of Hamlet, so the spiritual vision of our Lord conceived human beings as a son journeying to the house of a Father whom the Father goeth forth to meet on the way. He meets him, as the notes of the sermon have already indicated, in a variety of ways—as a friend, as unchangeable power, as a just and righteous sovereign—but most intimately in the person of Jesus Christ, who alone reveals Him as the loving Father to whose house men and women, when they arise from the husks of the temporal, are returning. Then suddenly after the climax of revelation, of vision, which in its appeal to the imaginative faculty could be better expressed by one of the arts than by words, comes a sudden breaking off—a plunging into the sadness and gloom which can seize the most hopeful human mind.

He is facing what men call reality, which is not vision. That which the audience, of which he is conscious, are crying out at him he divines too well. As he sat preparing in his study, pen in hand, gazing out at the trees which he loved to look upon, now rent and dismantled by November winds, with here and there some yellow shrivelled leaf hanging loosely to the bough, he hears the cry, "By the Jews you say cometh salvation ; and the belief that God is our Father, whence cometh it ? Have the men who call themselves by His name shown the Father unto us ? and in vain we search the earth and the firmament for any sign of that which you confidently tell."

The response to this in music would be an *adagio* movement after the opening *allegro*, introduced by those deep tragic chords with which a composer will suddenly change his theme and seem for a time to alter the whole character of the composition. " Neither Jew nor Christian has understood it," is the burden of the tragic response ; " it has passed into the background for eighteen centuries." The Father still goeth forth to meet the race, but they cannot see Him yet—He is a sovereign merely ; and he goes on to enumerate the results of this incomplete conception—" brutal wars, revocation of the Edict of Nantes, Black Bartholomew's Day—the hideous history of the Church." Hence narrowness, bigotry, intolerance. Hence more than half-empty churches, hatred of manhood, of Europe, because the revelation of the Fatherhood had not yet come home to Christian men. In Christ Jesus—seems to be his thought, though it is not stated—He has whispered many things as men could bear it and as they were able to understand Him, but the world has yet to understand the parable of the loving Father and to enter into the heart and thought of Christ as He uttered it. It will be seen that he is prophet enough himself to sympathise with them, though the accusation is one-sided. But he chooses to base the triumph that he is anticipating on the darkest aspect of the problem, which can be found, he proceeds to point out, in the consciousness of a higher order of Christian, in his thought and outlook. The cry of Abba Father is heard from within, and the kingdom which has yet to be established has its roots in the heart of a man and a woman. The answer is remarkable because it is concerned with what Scripture would call " the thoughts of the heart." These thoughts are to be brought into captivity to that which Christ has revealed, into line with the parable of the loving Father.

In the first place, Nature is to be viewed as the gradual evolution of Fatherhood. To the present phase of the human mind he is aware that this is the most daring, the least understandable of his assertions. Into the music there seems to steal that note of audacity which was characteristic of his chivalry, that defiance and *élan* which went out against great odds. When in Bournemouth the preceding spring, he had attended a popular lecture by Sir Robert Ball describing the formation of the nebulæ or fire mists from which the stellar systems are formed, and at the moment the lecture forms an

illustration.[1]   It was an instance of how everything he saw
and heard sank into his mind, to be made use of when the
occasion required.   Thus the Christian mind of to-day could
say after the lecturer's explanation : " The result and consummation of the stages which you depict is Christ Jesus, for, to
the mind and heart feeding on Him, possessed by Him, there
is nothing fairer and a more integral portion of truth than the
sublime interpretation which He alone has given and shall give
the universe—nothing which so haunts our thoughts as the
music to which He has set it.   His voice within our heart is
more real to us than anything else in the universe.   The rest
is the unsubstantial fabric of a dream.   In Him alone is
reality."

These must have been his thoughts as he tried to depict
the attitude of the Christian mind towards Nature with a
contemporary illustration.   Such an attitude, he would contend, was strictly consistent and as logical as that of any
other mind.   Every man, if he thinks at all, must form,
consciously or unconsciously, he felt, some system of thought,
some one overmastering conception in which the rest is seen
and viewed, and with the Christian worthy the name that
conception was Christ Jesus viewed from the whole Catholic
Church (not from one only of its denominations), and in the
history of civilisation since His coming.   Such a one was as
consistent as any other systematic thinker, more so than some,
because he spoke from experience.   Still he was fully aware of
the great difficulty experienced by the modern mind in giving
adherence to the sublimest of Christ's teachings, a consciousness which makes him more insistent on defying the general
thought.

In (12) and (13) he contends that the consciousness of the
new order of Christian must look upon theology—dominated
by this thought.   The " Fatherhood " must underlie all the
expressions of that thought, irradiating it, so that, instead of
being a metaphysical abstraction, cold and puzzling to many
minds, it may glow and vibrate with the sublimest doctrine
of Christianity, which must colour and explain all theological
teaching.   As an instance he takes the doctrine of the Trinity,

---

[1] The same thought was also suggested by the book he had been reading—*The
Fatherhood of God*—whose perusal led to the main points of this sermon.

which to many minds is a cold metaphysical definition and nothing more. It has lost import, he thinks, because it is not viewed in the light of the Divine Fatherhood. "Apply," he says, "this conception of Fatherhood to the definition of the theologian, and it will illuminate like sunlight, as some previously incrusted stone will gleam and reflect the rays of the sun." Deity, thus viewed, reveals not a loveless solitude, but an eternity of mutual love and (13) the motive and impulse of creation—to Father—not create—myriads of sons who shall enjoy that love and reciprocate it. The idea that the keynote of the Trinity was reciprocity—interchange of blessed love—often haunted him.

Some years before this sermon I can remember his referring to a chapter of Dr. Fairbairn on this subject, and undoubtedly in later years Dante's *Paradiso* haunted his imagination. It was his extreme sensitiveness to symbol which put him *en rapport* with an artist like Mr. Shields, and which made him such a student of the Johannine writings. Thus attacks on Christianity passed him unruffled. The eye which had not pierced the heart of the forms and ceremonies and beliefs dealt with etceteras—temporalities. Jesus Christ the same yesterday, to-day, and for ever, was the vision that he saw as St. John did, and his imagery like that of the blessed apostle was of the warm, glowing, Oriental character which passed into the artists and poets of later time.

In (14) he declares that the Christian consciousness must not only behold Nature and theology in the light of this revelation, but humanity. It was this portion of the spoken sermon that impressed his listeners, continually ringing in their ears, as some said, after he had gone. Each of the headings in (14) have their interest as coming from his lips that evening, and amid such thoughts; but it was the declaration, "We are sons of God," which impressed listeners. "You are all," he said slowly, "sons of God. I cannot expect you to see it as I see it now, but you are all sons of God. In no other manner can your origin be accounted for." The light in his eye as he said these words was that of rapture, yet fraught with solemnity. Thus saying, he answered all his critics, because he had the vision himself, and not one of them could take it from him. It was not an opinion, or a surmise, or a belief, or a revelation, or a hallucination, but something which he saw, and which every moment of his life in the flesh had enabled him to see. In the earlier portion of his sermon he allowed himself sympathy with certain of his critics, but now he leaves them behind him. Having such a vision, he was consumed by its reality. He did not attempt to communicate it, because he saw that it was not his to communicate. Sweeping the creation that was visible to him, he beheld God and the sons of God. In that vision, all that he had laboured and suffered and thought was given back to him a thousand-fold, as were his hopes and aspirations deepened and vivified. It had never done for anybody what it did for himself. It came back to him in that supreme reality—vision. Was it hinted that the vision was to be communicated? Yes, it was, and to all who were listening to him, and in that came the reality. It had already been communicated, and would be again.

From that solemn and serene height to which he had attained, he beckoned his listeners to follow. 'Tis the husks on which men feed, he felt, that envelop them in darkness and make vision impossible. He pleaded with them for the last time. Surely they will return, 'tis such foolishness, such madness to linger. They will say, " I will arise and go to my Father." His heart leapt up as he saw certain making the sign. " They will return. See here and there they rise proving their submission. They must. Yet another! ' Thanks be to God who giveth us the victory in Christ Jesus our Lord.' Ah, no more, my God! no more. ' Thy will be done.'"

Thus ended *Nunc Dimittis*, but all that went to the framing of it few could divine. They alone guessed the completion of that submission, how he was straitened till God's purpose was accomplished in him. To feel his spirit in any matter was to respond to a great freeing and inspiring force, but to feel it intimately was to behold not without bewilderment a force submitting itself to law in every portion of its being. The new he showed was more under restraint than the old. No river hurrying to the ocean was more bound and yoked to irresistible law than the desire of his spirit to Christ. If some passion of the mind seemed likely to intervene between him and Christ, he did not crush what was

God's, but submitted it to God in Christ. Men, he noted, would surrender everything save metaphysic, for that they said was theirs. He said it was not theirs. To his thinking, God was love, and a love that continuously conditioned itself, in order to find finite expression, a truth which the Church has preserved in the mystery of the Incarnation.

Thus when young ministers said to him, "We are in perplexity, we cannot go on," he said, "There is no cause for dismay, but feed upon Christ in your heart and go on studying and thinking. At this moment Christ is nearer and more real to me than you are." Such conversations would have a peculiar benignity, for he greatly coveted the metaphysicians for Christ. He would never have told them to stop thinking and studying, because then they could not lay on His altar what was not theirs to lay. "Some of your thought," he would imply, "it may be His will that you should give forth to the world, and the rest, part of that life that you hide with Him. He will tell you when to speak and when to be silent"; and so kindling he would continue. Some spoke of him with indulgence. "A righteous man," they said, "but he isn't aware of certain speculative issues as we are. Yet these limits render him the more effective." Thus saying, they unknowingly paid him honour and gave God the glory. But every river floweth at last to the sea, and at the bar is heard the wash of fuller tide —the rising and falling of winds that blow from an infinite main. Christ, who imposes, releases, giving back that which was hidden with Him. The eye sees and the ear hears, and to God worship is given, for men see that the sacrifice of life is complete, lively and living. Neither body nor mind is mutilated, but each is fair and whole, and the fire from on high devoureth every portion. Of other sacrifices there are many, but none quite moveth to worship as this one. Thus doth *Nunc Dimittis* speak to some. What it taught did not contradict any discipline he had put upon himself and others, but only fulfilled it, because through the submission came the vision and the reality.

At supper that evening there was merriment, the two or three friends who were present congratulating him on his restoration to full health and vigour. The next morning he was down betimes conducting prayer as usual, and afterwards

42

seeing visitors and representatives from the Press in his study. These were struck by his weariness and the intense sympathy of his allusions to the poor of London. At lunch he was full of conversation and laughter, the weariness noted by his interviewers not being apparent to those who sat at table with him for the last time. The " Just So " stories of Rudyard Kipling again afforded fuel to his mirth, which was infectious. " Really, Mr. Hughes," exclaimed one who was present, " you don't seem to have a moment to yourself. It's engagements and interviews all day long. How you must look forward to resting in heaven." My father shook his head. " I hope I shall have far more service there than here. This does not satisfy me."

When the meal was over he asked his youngest son to walk with him to Sion College on the Victoria Embankment, where Mr. Bunting was to read a paper of Mons. Sabatier on " St. Francis and the Twentieth Century." As they walked he listened with delight to an account of a contest that had just taken place in the classroom where his son had been studying. Certain seats were wrested from the party who had to their thinking a paramount claim to them, with the result that a keen contest had ensued, in which the rightful owners established their claim in the usual manner. Not a detail escaped him. The strife and its vicissitudes raged before him, calling forth questioning and exclamation and much glee. At the door of Sion College they parted. During the lecture which ensued he was observed to be very attentive, taking notes as he sat on the platform. When it was over he shook hands with Mr. Bunting and Mrs. Josephine Butler, who happened to be present, and started homewards.

At the door some one showed him a handkerchief and said, " Is this yours, sir ? " With a courtesy and care that haunted the questioner because it was so marked, he answered, " No, sir, thank you, it is not mine." His intention was to go home, where a meal was awaiting him, and then preach at the St. John's Wood Wesleyan chapel in the evening. As he stepped forth into the way, it was hidden from him that even as he walked Death should come and meet him, but tenderly as a friend. He to whom the unseen and the

invisible had been the visible and the tangible — the light
of light, very God of very God, went forth to meet the unseen
as if to take a walk. Wrapped and consumed in vision, why
should he heed the footfall which mortality has trembled to
hear?

Crossing Ludgate Circus he turned into St. Bride's,
choosing by instinct those quieter thoroughfares which he
preferred. Coming into High Holborn the roar of the traffic
greeted his ear, which in days past had warned him of advancing time and nerved him to greet its advance. The gradual
incline from the Embankment may have tired him, and it is
probable that he walked slowly amid a crowd which hurried
the more in that its day's work was over. So also was his.
No one saw or noted him after leaving the College save a
Sister of the Mission, who had been present and who joined
him. The clocks of the great houses of business had struck
five, and their hands were nearing the half-hour. Behind
the grey towers and chimneys the sun had set in a fiery
red ball, for the day had been bright and serene and by no
means typical of November.

He questioned the Sister about her work and herself,
and in particular about Monsieur Sabatier, with whom she
had just been talking.[1] "What did Sabatier think of my
sermon yesterday evening?" he asked. "What did he think
of it?"

The question revealed his thought, which was of that
kingdom that the Father should reveal unto the myriad sons
whom He had created in His image to share in His joy.

Already the thoughts of the heart were wedded to those
of the mind, and in their chorus there was nothing but what
was primal and what satisfied.

The voice of the Sister sounded strangely. "Mr. Hughes,
you are very ill! What is the matter?" His umbrella had
fallen twice, and the second time he had been unable to pick
it up. After he had been supported into a cab, the Sister
again asked, "What can I do? What is the matter?" For
what seemed a second he struggled to speak, and then fell
back unconscious.

[1] Monsieur Sabatier had been present at the St. James's Hall service the previous
evening.

Thus my mother found him, and thus he was borne to the sofa in his study.   He had been seized with an attack of apoplexy, and breathed his last a few minutes before seven o'clock, in the presence of his wife, his brother-in-law, and two of his children.

" One who never turned his back but marched breast forward,
        Never doubted clouds would break,
    Never dreamed though right were worsted, wrong would triumph,
        Held we fall to rise, are baffled to fight better,
                Sleep to wake.

    No, at noonday in the bustle of man's work-time
        Greet the unseen with a cheer !
    Bid him forward, breast and back as either should be,
        'Strive and thrive !' cry 'Speed,—fight on, fare ever
                There as here !' "

CHAPTER XXIII

AFTER THE PASSING

> " These are such harvests as all master-spirits
> Reap, haply not on earth, but reap no less
> Because the sheaves are bound by hands not theirs ;
> These are the bloodless daggers wherewithal
> They stab fallen tyrants, this their high revenge ;
> For their best part of life on earth is when
> Long after death, prisoned and pent no more,
> Their thoughts, their wild dreams even, have become
> Part of the necessary air men breathe :
> When, like the moon, herself behind a cloud,
> They shed down light before us on life's sea,
> That cheers us to steer onward still in hope.
> Earth with her twining memories ivies o'er
> Their holy sepulchres ; the chainless sea,
> In tempest or wide calm, repeats their thoughts ;
> The lightning and the thunder, all free things,
> Have legends of them for the ears of men.
> All other glories are as falling stars,
> But universal Nature watches theirs :
> Such strength is won by love of humankind."
>
> *Prometheus,* LOWELL.

So still and peaceful the face lay, as if wrought in marble, that the lilies strewn around seemed alone able to bear and tell its tale. The age, when it was told, could not be credited, for the years had rolled back, revealing rather the outset than the end of a life. Only the lilies could remain unshaken. None went away to despair, but rather to hope.[1] " I believe now," one whispered, " in a hereafter. I found it so difficult before." Another straight from the bedside of a dying relative, confessed also to a great assurance, " I know now that all will be

---

[1] A few relatives and friends and many members of the Mission came to look for the last time.

well, and that God is Love." Such remarks were not exceptional, but typical of what was felt and experienced. As the news spread itself over the English-speaking world and in places where English is not spoken, for all news is the world's to-day, men and women prayed, but many could not even pray at once. They felt as if something vital had been torn from them, and that henceforward they must go maimed. That was not to be so, but it was what they felt at the time.

The feeling was the more astonishing in many cases, as it would not previously have been anticipated. Good men disagreed with him, criticised him, and saw his defects, but no sooner did they hear that he had gone than the disagreement and the criticism and the defects vanished like the dew. Then they saw the sacrifice, and how the fire had consumed every part. Death focused. His lineaments stood out plain and spake for him, and to behold them was to be pierced. The grey, chill morning after he had gone revealed strange sights. Some screamed, others sobbed, and many in the reflections which seized them were unable to pursue their ordinary avocations. "I sat down to think," was a typical confession ; or, "As soon as the news came I went home. I could not stay where I was."

The lot of some did not give the breathing space that they desired. One woman dragging her way, for she was old, to the wash-house where she did her daily work, was smitten by the news on a placard. And when she got inside, she afterwards described it. "They said to me, ' Go upstairs, for the work is waiting,' and I thought to myself that they might have said it another time, not then, but another time."

Many on hearing it confessed to experiencing a displacement in the objects around them—they alone remaining transfixed while their environment was in chaos. The stations where they stood went round, and the printed matter in their hands or the faces that they saw became meaningless. Men who had not met or spoken to him for years met each other in the train, and said one to the other, "How chill it is this morning," and then as if in explanation, "and Hugh Price Hughes is gone." Outside the house the policeman saluted as he passed, and the postman asked "Is it true?"

The letters and telegrams and, later, the addresses of condolence and sympathy which came pouring in from all parts, showed that the loss had gone home to some in every class and calling, and particularly to the Church of Christ as he had defined it. But the sorrow for his loss was by far the most inconsolable in back kitchens and parlours. Those who did not write or make known what they felt and experienced were often the truest mourners. It was typical of Fidus Achates that he did not write. He could not, for a great darkness was upon him, and when he came out of it he hesitated to add his word to all the others. Often the darkness was the more poignant because at one time or another, particularly in recent years, he had parted company with him and, as he thought, bade him farewell. But this was not so. For days he cared not to eat or drink, and neither wife nor child brought comfort, because while sorrowing at his sorrow, they could not enter into or comprehend it. In one instance, a day or two after the event, there was a lifting of the shadows and light came. He rose and went about his business as usual. " I saw what a fool I was, and that there was no need for so much ado. Of course Mr. Hughes was not dead. How could he be? He was living." Thus he left the husks of his own grief and returned to the Father. In keen business men he touched the springs of poetry, and that was a marvel. Their letters testified to it. Said one : " May I by the infinite mercy of God be one day admitted to where he is and renew our fellowship there." Said another : " He helped us business men to live the inner life of love."

The poor could not cease giving to him, bringing flowers to the grave of his body. " I like to stand there for some minutes," said one woman ; " it helps me to bear my life."

Nor indeed could the men who dug the grave of his body escape him and his. " Why is there so much fuss ? " they asked ; " he is not a bishop." And one of his, answered, " No, but greater than a bishop. He told me of Christ, and what He can do for me—that was what he told me. Also I have a sermon of his at home which I must bring and read to you." So she brought it and read it to them. Then when she had finished reading, she said, " Let us pray, for we are by his grave." And they, answering, said, " We cannot pray, mum, it is not in our knees somehow." The woman, answering, said, " Stand long enough by the grave and your knees will begin to give way as you stand." And it came to pass as she had said, and their knees gave way and they prayed.

Wesley's chapel in City Road was crowded many hours before the service when they bore his coffin into it. Men unknown to him and his watched it with wistfulness as it passed them in the street, as if something that made for higher life were being taken from them.

Within everybody was standing, and there was a great wave of triumph and hope and sympathy for others which buoyed up all who were present, so that it did not seem a funeral service at all.[1] " A prince among men was given to us," said the President, " and God has taken him to Himself. Nobody," he said, " did more for catholicity than Mr. Hughes. . . . His heart went out to Christians of all denominations. For us, the Methodist people, he did especially two things— he recalled our early fervour and enthusiasm for the souls of men, and he brought us into touch with contemporary life and with the great movements of the time."

The true funeral service took place around the grave before the arrival of the funeral party, and was attended by several hundreds of people and in particular by Fidus Achates. He came from a great distance, often on foot, so as to save a fare which he could not afford. His aunts were there and his sisters and cousins, lining the way as the coffin was borne to the grave, and the service was altogether theirs. Most meet it was that they should form its guard of honour, and nobody else was as entitled to form one as they were. Long before the procession arrived they were singing hymns, and so densely packed that relatives who had been unable to attend the service in the chapel had to remain on the outskirts of the crowd with the rest. A member of the lay order who was present, a Welshman, got up after a while and in a loud voice and with the sing-song of the Principality said something as follows :—" Brethren, there is one thing that Hugh Price Hughes would wish us to do above everything, and that is to give ourselves to Christ. If we have not done so already, let

[1] The gathering was very representative and typical of that various life to which he had always appealed.

us do it now, and afresh and utterly as he taught us to do, so that we be worthy to stand beside his grave. Now, my brethren, that we can live a worthy life in our own strength— such a life as he did—we cannot believe, but we can in Christ if we will yield ourselves to His promptings in our heart. Let this day, friends, be a turning-point and the beginning of something better." And many listening said, " Amen," either to themselves or aloud, and wept afresh. The women, it was noted, were the more contained, but certain of the men could not restrain their sobbing, so that it was painful to see and to hear them.

Mark Guy Pearse committed the coffin to the grave, which bore upon it a solitary wreath, no other being permitted to bear it company. Attached to it was the following inscription :—" To Hugh from Katie. I have fought the good fight, I have finished the course, I have kept the faith," and on the other side the names of his children, with a quotation from Browning's " Grammarian's Funeral "—

" He's for the morning."

Leading literary journals had the intention of making fitting allusions, but were too ignorant of the religious tradition to which he belonged to give him the justice that springs from understanding. The religious Press was unanimous in kindly notices, but the tribute was to what he had wrought rather than to what he was. Strangely enough, what might be termed the avowedly secular journals seemed to understand him the best. Papers which made no special pretension either to religion or culture, but which were representative of those highways of the common life over which he had yearned, seemed to behold something of what he was, and to possess the necessary perspective to do so.

Indeed, the universal comment went to show that no person or institution is really wroth with a man for speaking his mind, if he does so in sincerity and selflessness, and without malice. There is respect if there is not understanding. This he divined himself, for amid the chorus of condolence and praise which that grave evoked, the following incident came to the mind of some. It was not so long before he died that my mother expressed impatience at a fresh attack upon him in the columns of the Press and other quarters. " I am really tired of it," she said ; "when will they let you alone? It goes on unceasingly—first one thing and then another." " Never mind, Katie," he answered, " if I were to die to-morrow they would all speak kindly of me. I am sure they would." At such moments his voice would take upon itself something of that tender caressing inflection which distinguishes the speech of dwellers in the Towy Valley. When he was moved in any way it always did that, so that a listener from the Principality could have easily detected the familiar note. The early religious painters, with their keen perception for qualities of the spirit, would have crowned him with a light of some kind to signify his love for man, how it glowed from him so that nothing could quench it. It was not the Press alone that confirmed his prophecy, but everybody whom one knew or of whom one heard. Some caused surprise by observing that they had long nourished a great admiration for him, and continually were heard the following remarks :—" It is universal, and everybody says the same thing, nothing but good of him—nothing " ; or " You should have heard my husband after he had read the paper yesterday. I have seldom known him so enthusiastic " ; or " Mary was so full of your father this morning. She has been reading out aloud about him in the kitchen, and says there never was a man so greatly beloved."

The manner of life that he would have chosen would have been one to win the understanding and appreciation of the cultivated few, but it was not the manner of life that he did choose. The few, as a rule, did not understand or even approve him. Some did, and markedly so—particularly those who were brought into any direct contact with him ; but the line of life that he had chosen brought him for the most part into the notice and horizon of humble persons. To them he was a friend—and a familiar one—while to the others he was a force indeed which made for righteousness in the community, but of whose nature they were entirely ignorant.

To kindle the life of the finely touched few, to ripen in it thought and hope, and to receive in return that sympathetic homage which only the few can give, is to a certain order of unworldly mind a species of natural instinct. Perhaps there is only one thing greater, and that is a passion to kindle the grey mass of average life—which is not finely touched—which was his passion. He helped it by faith—the substance of things hoped for, the evidence of things not seen, and that is why it was grateful unto him.

The secret of his life and character was that through faith he continually did and advocated that which was opposed to natural instinct and predilection, so that while it perplexed men concerning him, it had a singular power over them. In the tempest they heard his voice if they did not behold his face. As he embarked on the seas that faith enjoined, he brought her message to men, for his valuables were not on land-locked waters, but floating on the deeps that stretch to God.

So his true life, in a sense, would be the life that he never permitted himself to live. The one or two who knew him scarcely recognised the eulogies and comments of those who said they did. Other men forgot that he died daily, as he himself forgot, in the glory of the life that death brought him. None the less he died not that day when the breath left his body—but every day of his life. He fought parties to which instinctively he belonged, and was often attracted by those to whom he was supposed to be most at variance. Such a life was bound to contain contradictory aspects, so that at crises in the history of the Church and the nation he betrayed sympathies and took courses that contemporaries did not anticipate. He was not only consumed with enthusiasm for God and for man, so that others warmed themselves by its fires, but he possessed the rare gift of seeing what was good in opposing traditions and forces. While possessing the full quota of human prejudice, for he was a human saint, he did not suffer it to blind him to that which was good and that which was evil. He was better understood after death than in life. His career, while it touched men and things at a great variety of points, was necessarily solitary. A biographer could well have epitomised it by the two following sentences:—" The common people heard him gladly," or, to give a modern rendering of Scripture, "Unprivileged people heard him gladly." Then what he increasingly felt in later life, " Nobody understood his silences." But he was wiser than any biographer, and in a single sentence revealed the secret of a life which had found sustainment neither in the praise of good men, nor in the understanding of the wise: " Thou, O Christ, art all I want."

INDEX

Printed by
MORRISON & GIBB LIMITED
Edinburgh